2

Microprocessor
Instruction Sets
and
Software Principles

Microprocessor Instruction Sets and Software Principles

DAVID L. HEISERMAN

Research and Development Consultant

Prentice-Hall, Inc., Englewood Cliffs, NJ 07632

Library of Congress Cataloging in Publication Data

Heiserman, David L.
   Microprocessor instruction sets and software
principles.

   Includes index.
   1. Microprocessors—Programming.   I. Title.
QA76.6.H45   001.64′2   82-590
ISBN 0-13-581090-6   AACR2

Editorial/production supervision by Anne Simpson
Interior design by Daniela Lodes
Manufacturing buyer: Gordon Osbourne

Prentice-Hall International, Inc., *London*
Prentice-Hall of Australia Pty. Limited, *Sydney*
Prentice-Hall Canada Inc., *Toronto*
Prentice-Hall of India Private Limited, *New Delhi*
Prentice-Hall of Japan, Inc., *Tokyo*
Prentice-Hall of Southeast Asia Pte. Ltd., *Singapore*
Whitehall Books Limited, *Wellington, New Zealand*

Contents

Chapter 7 Operate Immediate Instructions 101

Chapter 15   Data Shift and Rotate Instructions   292

Appendices 386

Preface

No one can expect to work successfully with a microprocessor system without being fully acquainted with its instruction set and operating principles. A hardware engineer, for example, cannot expect to make intelligent decisions regarding the layout of the memory and I/O ports, a microprogrammer cannot hope to design the simplest software routines, and a technician cannot be expected to test, debug, and modify any part of the system.

Manufacturers of the various microprocessors have responded to the obvious need for describing their own programming principles and instruction sets. Indeed, through the first years of microprocessor technology, the manufacturers' own data books were the most popular references for teaching and learning the fundamentals of microprocessor programming.

But the maturing of microprocessor technology is making it inappropriate to define a well-prepared microprocessor engineer, programmer, or technician as one who has a thorough understanding of one manufacturer's system. It is becoming increasingly necessary to deal with diverse instruction sets and dissimilar programming operations. The rapid pace of new developments and, indeed, practical necessity are justifying the idea that it is time to cut across lines of traditional, one-manufacturer biases and adapt to new and different instruction sets and programming principles.

In an attempt to provide the broadest possible view of microprocessor programming techniques, this book deals with the instruction sets and fundamental programming procedures for four different devices: the Zilog Z-80, Intel 8080A/8085, MOS Technology 6502, and the Motorola 6800. These devices have been selected because they exemplify the similarities and differences one encounters when transferring some previous knowledge of one microprocessor system to another.

The reader, however, must not regard this book as a mere compilation of instructions sets for four different microprocessors. It is not simply four basic handbooks in a single volume. Rather, it is a tightly integrated presentation of microprocessor programming principles; and much would be lost in an attempt to treat the book as a source of information about a given microprocessor device.

The chapters are grouped according to categories of standard microprocessor instructions and operations: load immediate instructions, register transfer instructions, direct and indirect addressing operations, stack operations, arithmetic and logic functions, and so on. The individual chapters are generally organized in such a way that they present the most general principles first. Then one microprocessor is chosen as a model for demonstrating applications of those principles. Finally, the discussions show how these principles can be implemented with the three other types of microprocessor devices.

Relevant portions of the microprocessors' instruction sets are shown as needed in the text. Complete listings of all four instruction sets appear in the appendices as well.

Numerous examples throughout each chapter show specific applications of the principles being discussed. Those examples often demonstrate other important programming principles, such as the development of flowcharts and the organization of memory maps, and they encourage the reader to compare listings for several different microprocessors that are called upon to do the same overall task.

Where appropriate, exercises appear at the conclusion of sections within the chapters. The answers to most questions are included at the end of the book.

David L. Heiserman

Microprocessor
Instruction Sets
and
Software Principles

1

A First Look at Microprocessor Programming

If, by some fanciful quirk of space and time, scientists in the 1940s or 1950s had come across one of our modern microprocessor devices, they most likely would have considered it a most remarkable piece of technology from some vastly superior civilization. Microprocessors are to vacuum tubes and transistors as spacecraft are to horse-drawn carts.

Aside, perhaps, from the development of atomic energy, no other single development in recent history can parallel the long-range impact of microprocessors. And certainly no other technological development has touched the lives of so many individuals in such a short period of time.

Indeed, there is something very special about microprocessors, and getting into the business at this early stage of development offers endless opportunities for building lifelong, rewarding, and satisfying careers.

As remarkable as microprocessors are, however, they are simply tools—tools for doing jobs once deemed too complicated, impractical, or even impossible. But having the tool available is just part of the picture; it is equally important to know how to use that tool effectively. Learning to use microprocessors effectively is the main purpose of this book.

1-1 THE TWO PARTS OF THE MICROPROCESSOR TOOL

There are two distinctly different, but inseparable, parts to this powerful microprocessor tool: the hardware and the instruction set. The *hardware* side of the matter is concerned with the physical components and their interconnecting electrical circuitry. The *instruction set* is the multitude of binary codes that tell the microprocessor what it is supposed to do at any given moment.

Using a microprocessor effectively is a matter of utilizing one's knowledge of both the hardware and instruction set. From the most general point of view, the goal is to transform a mental impression of a task or process to be performed into reality, using the hardware and instruction set to do the job.

Although this book emphasizes the nature of microprocessor instruction sets, showing how the instructions can be organized into working sequences called *programs*, you will soon discover that it is virtually impossible to write such programs without having some understanding of the hardware side of the matter.

This particular text offers just enough material concerning the hardware to make the instruction sets and their use in developing programs a meaningful task. Armed with a knowledge of microprocessor instructions and programming techniques, that sort of understanding can be combined with a good knowledge of basic digital electronics to become an effective and well-rounded microprocessor technician or engineer.

1-2 THE MICROPROCESSOR PROGRAMMING PROCESS

A microprocessor program is a sequence of binary-coded instructions that tell the microprocessor hardware exactly what it is supposed to do and exactly when it is supposed to do it. That might seem rather trivial on the surface, but in reality, a lot of thinking, work, and creativity goes into preparing a working program.

Experienced microprocessor engineers and technicians usually develop a programming style that is as peculiar to themselves as is their fingerprints. But even so, there is a general sequence of program-development procedures that characterize every successful attempt to make a microprocessor perform in the desired fashion:

1. Develop a clear picture of the task to be performed, beginning with an overall definition of the job and gradually evolving a step-by-step procedure in fairly minute detail. The result of this first step generally takes the form of a *flowchart*—a special schematic representation of the task and its steps.

2. Given the hardware system available, transform the details of the operation into a *source-code program*—a semi-English, shorthand representation of the microprocessor's instructions.

3. *Assemble*, or translate, the source-code program into an *object-code program*—a sequence of binary codes that are not necessarily meaningful to the programmer, but altogether meaningful to the microprocessor hardware system.

4. Enter the object-code program into the system's *program memory*—a section of the system hardware that is made up of integrated-circuit (IC) memory devices that can "remember" the coded instructions and data in their intended sequence.

5. *Execute* the program. Let it pick up the coded instructions from the program memory and carry out those orders accordingly. Look for unexpected turns of

events that signal possible problems with the original program design or human errors introduced somewhere along the way.

6. *Debug* the program as necessary. Locate problems in the basic program design or errors in writing or entering the program. Then correct the matter.

7. *Document* the entire scheme. Develop an error-free listing of both the source-code and object-code versions of the program. If circumstances dictate, also prepare a flowchart and verbal description of what the system does and how to use it. Often, a complete electrical schematic diagram of the hardware system is part of the formal documentation.

This book deals mainly with the first three steps in this programming procedure, but you will find occasional references and hints concerning the remaining steps.

The following example illustrates the general programming process. It introduces some conventions and additional terminology along the way. Although you are not expected to understand the details of the program listings offered at this point in your study, it is important to note how human ideas are gradually transformed into a microprocessor-oriented format.

Defining the Task and Developing a Flowchart

Suppose that you have at hand a microprocessor system that is equipped with some electrical hardware that includes a normally open pushbutton switch and a lamp. The task is to write a program that turns on the lamp whenever the pushbutton is depressed, keeps the lamp turned on for about 3 seconds, and then automatically turns off the lamp.

To be sure, this rather simple task could be performed equally well, and at a lower cost, by using some standard IC devices—devices nowhere approaching the complexity of a microprocessor system. The example, however, clearly illustrates an application of the general microprocessor programming procedure.

The sequence of events involved in this task is already defined rather clearly: wait for the pushbutton to be depressed, turn on the light, do a time delay, and turn off the light. As you might imagine, though, not all tasks set before a programmer are so simple, and there has to be some mechanism for illustrating the task in a clear, easy-to-follow fashion. That is the role of a flowchart.

Figure 1-1 is a flowchart for the switch and lamp example. It begins by fetching the switch status, as indicated by the operation labeled FETCH SWITCH STATUS. In a manner of speaking, this operation calls for having the microprocessor system query the switch, finding out whether it is open or closed.

The next figure in the flowchart is a diamond-shaped figure; one representing a *conditional* operation. It represents an IF . . . THEN sort of logical condition. If the switch is *not* closed (see the arrow leaving the conditional that is labeled N), the system *loops* back to look at the switch status again. If the switch is NOT closed, THEN check the status again.

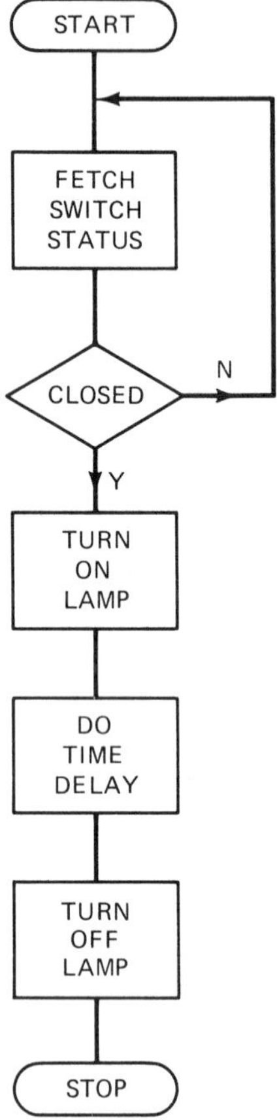

Figure 1-1   Flowchart for the switch-and-light control program.

On the other hand, if the switch *is* closed, the conditional operation is *satisfied* (see the arrow labeled Y) and operations go to the next step down the line. IF the switch IS closed, THEN do the next operation.

The next operation in this case is labeled TURN ON THE LAMP. Upon encountering that operation in the program, the microprocessor does whatever is necessary to turn on the lamp.

Then the system should DO TIME DELAY. That is the point in the program where the system is to mark time until a certain amount of time elapses—3 second is specified for this particular example.

After doing the time delay, the flowchart calls for turning off the light. At that point, the microprocessor must be instructed to carry out operations that ultimately turn off the light.

The program finally comes to a conclusion at the STOP symbol.

A flowchart need not express every detail of the final program, but it must at least indicate the overall flow of events in a clear and unambiguous manner. During the process of writing very long and complicated programs, a flowchart is often the programmer's only contact with reality—the only guide to what is to be done from one moment to the next.

Run through the flowchart several times, making certain that you understand the flow of events and, more importantly, making sure that you can read and interpret such a chart.

Figure 1-2 summarizes the flowchart symbols that appear most often in microprocessor technology. As in the case of electrical schematic symbols, you can expect to find occasional variations of these flowchart symbols, and even some additional ones. In such cases, however, the meaning ought to be at least implied by the context in which they are used.

Flowcharts, incidentally, should be drawn in such a way that the main progress of the operations flows from top to bottom; and secondarily, from left to right. Arrows may be used to point the direction of the flow of operations in situations where confusion might arise.

In the past, it was considered poor practice to show flowchart lines crossing one another. The charts had to be carefully planned so that no such crossing occurred. But with the growing complexity of microprocessor programming, some publications are allowing lines to be crossed on the charts. In such a case, one of the crossing lines is broken, as indicated on the diagram here.

Developing a flowchart such as the one in Fig. 1-1 is the first major step in the programming process. The next step is to define the ways available for accessing the I/O devices—the switch and lamp in this case.

These two external devices will have certain *addresses* assigned to them. The addresses, represented by hexadecimal-coded binary numbers, specify *where* the microprocessor can expect to find them; and those addresses are

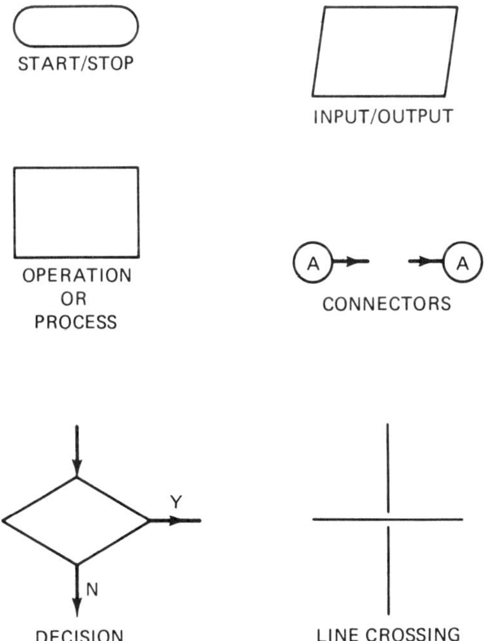

Figure 1-2 Commonly used flowchart symbols.

strictly determined by the system hardware—the physical and electrical arrangement of the circuitry.

The fact that the addresses for the switch and lamp are determined by the nature of their electrical connections to the microprocessor is a reminder that microprocessor programming requires a knowledge of the hardware system at hand.

Suppose, for the sake of this illustration, that the switch is located at address 7000H (7000 hexadecimal). That means that any microprocessor operations concerning the switch circuit will have to include some sort of reference to address location 7000H.

Further suppose that the lamp circuit is located at address 7001H (7001 hexadecimal). Operations concerning the lamp thus refer to that particular address.

There is nothing especially relevant about 7000H and 7001H; they are used here merely for illustrative purposes. Depending on the nature of the system's I/O hardware, the addresses can be any two hexadecimal-coded binary numbers out of thousands of possibilities.

Addresses for microprocessor operations are expressed as either 8-bit or 16-bit numbers, usually translated into a hexadecimal format for easier handling by human programmers and system operators.

So the addresses specify *where* the lamp and switch circuits are located. The next specification concerns *what* is to be received from or sent to those addresses; there is a need to define the status of the I/O devices.

Again, the hardware configuration dictates the way the microprocessor is to interpret the status of the switch (open or closed) and the lamp (turn it on or turn it off). Those parameters are specified as *data*.

A microprocessor address specifies *where* something is to take place, and the data specify *what* is going on there.

Microprocessor data are specified in terms of 8-bit or 16-bit binary numbers, generally translated into a hexadecimal format at the programming level. All the microprocessor devices and systems described in this book feature 8-bit data, but the microprocessor industry is also making available some larger, 16-bit data formats.

Returning to the specific programming example at hand, suppose that data 00H (zero hexadecimal) at address 7000H means that the pushbutton switch is closed. Data greater than 00H at the same address indicate that the switch contact is open. The data *read* from the switch address, 7000H, can thus be any number from 01H to FFH when the switch is open.

As far as the lamp is concerned, we have already established the fact that it is accessed by addressing location 7001H. The data sent to that address by the microprocessor system determine whether the lamp will be turned on or turned off.

Perhaps the lamp hardware is set up in such a way that sending data 00H to the lamp turns it off, and sending data having any value greater than 00H turns it on.

The I/O specifications for the current example are summarized in

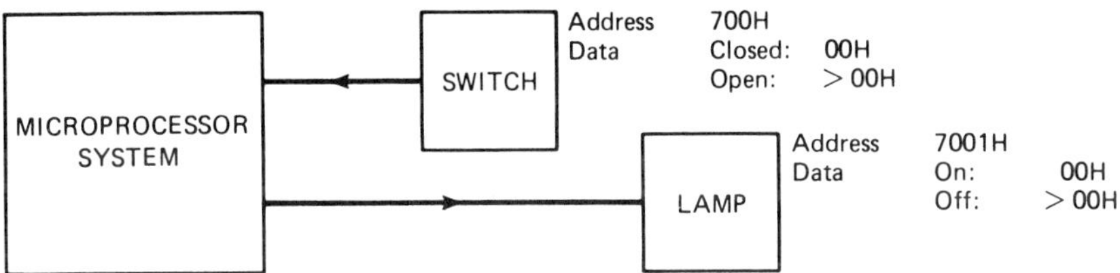

Figure 1-3   Hardware block diagram for the switch-and-light control.

Fig. 1-3. Bear in mind that these specifications are chosen rather arbitrarily for the sake of illustration. In an actual microprocessor system, the parameters will be altogether dictated by the nature of the I/O hardware. Indeed, it is virtually impossible to write a microprocessor program without having knowledge of the hardware configuration, or at least the relevant address locations and data requirements.

The operation is now adequately defined; first, in terms of what operations must be done (the flowchart in Fig. 1-1), and second, in terms of how the input and output devices are accessed (addresses) and treated (data). The programmer has fairly free reign when it comes to designing the flowchart, but he or she is bound to the hardware configuration when it comes to establishing the addresses and data specifications for the I/O devices.

Developing the Source-Code Program

The source-code program is a semi-English, shorthand expression of the microprocessor operations. The source-code expressions, called mnemonics (pronounced as nee-MON-iks), represent the most basic microprocessor operations. Every microprocessor device has a list of mnemonics associated with it—a list generated by the original manufacturer.

Unfortunately, every major manufacturer of microprocessor devices uses mnemonics that most often differ from those used by other manufacturers. Much of the burden of learning to write microprocessor programs is learning to use the mnemonics of the particular device at hand. Operations can be similar, and even identical in many cases; but the mnemonics can be quite different.

In any event, the programmer is obliged to develop a source-code program, using the mnemonics for the particular microprocessor being used; and equally important, using the flowchart and I/O specifications as a guide for selecting and arranging the operations.

Listing 1-1 is the source-code program for the current example—the switch and lamp system. The mnemonics in this case conform to standards established for the Z-80 microprocessor device. Such a listing for other types of microprocessors would have a similar appearance, but the mnemonic expressions would be different.

It is not the purpose of this illustration to define the meaning of any of the mnemonics in the source-code listing, but rather to provide an example of what such a listing looks like. The Z-80 mnemonics in this case are shown in the middle column: LD A,(7000H); CP 0; JR NZ,CHEK; and so on.

A source-code listing represents the actual microprocessor operations that are necessary for carrying out the intended task. The listing is generally divided into three *fields*. The first field, or column, is the *label field*. The label field in Listing 1-1 includes expressions invented by the programmer: CHEK, SETC, and DECC in this example. The *labels* indicate special points of reference in the source-code listing.

The second field is the *instruction field*. This is the one made up of mnemonics specified by the manufacturer of the particular microprocessor device. Note, however, that the instruction field does include programmer-invented labels that are specified in the label field.

The third field in the listing is called the *comment field*. Comments are included merely for the sake of indicating and clarifying what is going on at each step along the way. Comments are optional in any case. The Z-80 convention calls for preceding comments with a semicolon—some other microprocessor source-code listings do not.

The real "meat" of the source-code listing is the instruction field. Those mnemonics, including the addresses and data for the I/O devices, represent the actual microprocessor operations. Labels and comments merely help the programmer set up the program and document it in terms that should be intelligible to anyone else familiar with the particular microprocessor being used.

A source program is written for the benefit of the human programmer and anyone else who might want to analyze its function. Such a listing is wholly unintelligible to a microprocessor device—a device that operates strictly in terms of 8-bit and 16-bit binary numbers. The next step in the programming process is to translate the mnemonics into their binary-oriented, hexadecimal expressions.

Assembling the Object-Code Program

As mentioned earlier in this discussion, the original manufacturer of a microprocessor device must devise and publish a list of mnemonics for the operations the device can perform. Associated with each of the mnemonics is a hexadecimal number. A complete chart of microprocessor instructions, listed as mnemonics, and their associated hexadecimal codes, is called an *instruction set*. Appendices C to F include the complete instruction sets for the Z-80, 8080A/8085, 6502 and 6800 microprocessors.

After writing a source-code version of the program, the next step is to translate the mnemonics into *machine-language* hexadecimal codes, using the appropriate instruction set as a guide. The result is an object-code listing of the program.

The process of translating source codes into object codes is known as

```
CHEK     LD A,(7000H)      ;FETCH SWITCH STATUS
         CP 0              ;IS IT CLOSED?
         JR NZ,CHEK        ;IF NOT, FETCH AGAIN
         LD A,0FH          ;ELSE GET A=0F
         LD (7001),A       ;TURN ON LAMP
         LD B,0FFH         ;START TIME DELAY
SETC     LD C,0FFH         ;SET LSB OF TIME
DECC     DEC C             ;COUNT DOWN LSB
         JR NZ,DECC        ;IF NOT ZERO, COUNT AGAIN
         DEC B             ;ELSE COUNT DOWN MSB
         JR NZ,SETC        ;AND COUNT DOWN LSB CYCLE
         XOR A             ;SET A=0
         LD (7001H),A      ;TURN OFF LAMP
```

an *assembly* process. A source-code listing is said to be assembled into its object-code listing.

The first source-code instruction in Listing 1-1, for example, assembled into the 3-byte (1 byte represents 8 bits) object code: 3A 00 70. The second instruction assembles as a 2-byte object code, FE 00.

Assembling an object-code listing is pretty much a lookup sort of operation: Given the mnemonics in a source-code listing, assembling it to its object-code version is a simple matter of looking up the corresponding hexadecimal codes in the processor's instruction set.

If you happen to have access to a computer system of the proper sort, you can set it up to do the assembly operation for you. Generally, the idea is to type in the source-code listing at a standard keyboard, and then instruct the computer to assemble the object-code listing for you. Without such a system, you are obliged to hand assemble the program. That, incidentally, will be the assumption through most of this book (although many of the sample listings will have been done on a computer in order to reduce the possibility of typing errors).

Listing 1-2 represents the complete program documentation for the example being featured throughout this section. The original source-code listing is included for the sake of anyone wishing to analyze the program, but the listing is extended to include two object-code fields.

The first field on the left is the *program address field*. These four-place hexadecimal numbers represent the 16-bit address locations for each of the machine codes. In this particular case, the program will be loaded into the system's program memory, beginning at hexadecimal address 4A00.

The second field is the *program data field*. The program data field consists of the object codes that represent the instructions and data originally specified as mnemonics.

The first instruction in the listing is LD A,(7000H)—that is the source-code version of it. Its corresponding object-code version is 3A 00 70, and that appears on the same line, but in the program data field.

```
4A00 3A 00 70    CHEK   LD A,(7000H)    ;FETCH SWITCH STATUS
4A03 FE 00              CP 0            ;IS IT CLOSED?
4A05 20 F9              JR NZ,CHEK      ;IF NOT, FETCH AGAIN
4A07 3E 0F              LD A,0FH        ;ELSE SET A=0F
4A09 32 01 70           LD (7001),A     ;TURN ON LAMP
4A0C 06 FF              LD B,0FFH       ;START TIME DELAY
4A0E 0E FF       SETC   LD C,0FFH       ;SET LSB OF TIME
4A10 0D          DECC   DEC C           ;COUNT DOWN LSB
4A11 20 FD              JR NZ,DECC      ;IF NOT ZERO, COUNT AGAIN
4A13 15                 DEC B           ;ELSE COUNT DOWN MSB
4A14 20 F8              JR NZ,SETC      ;AND COUNT DOWN LSB CYCLE
4A16 AF                 XOR A           ;SET A=0
4A17 32 01 70           LD (7001H),A    ;TURN OFF LAMP
```

Now that particular instruction uses 3 bytes of program memory: 4A00, 4A01, and 4A02. Note those are successive address locations. The 3-byte instruction begins at address 4A00, and that address is specified in the address field of the listing.

The second instruction, CP 0, assembles into the 2-byte code FE 00. It begins where the previous instruction left off. Note in the address field that it begins at program address 4A03. Since it is a 2-byte instruction, it also uses 4A04. The latter fact is implied by the fact that the third assembled instruction begins at program address 4A05.

The assembly operation and assignment of program addresses proceeds in that fashion to the end. The last instruction in the listing—LD (7001H),A—assembles into the 3-byte code 32 01 70; and it begins at program address 4A17. It actually occupies three successive address locations, however: 4A17, 4A18, and 4A19.

Taken all together, then, the assembled program will reside in program memory, beginning at address 4A00 and running through successive addresses to 4A19.

The programmer has no choices when it comes to assembling the object codes for each of the mnemonics in the source-code listing. Those codes are dictated by the manufacturer of the microprocessor device being used.

The programmer, however, does have some options concerning the beginning address of the object-code listing. The only hardware requirement is that usable memory exist in the selected program memory space. (If the hardware engineer has not installed memory at locations 4A00 through 4A19, it would be pointless to attempt to put a program there.)

Assuming that the programmer is familiar with the mnemonics, the purpose of writing the source-code version of the program is to work with human perception. A microprocessor, however, cannot directly "understand" the mnemonics, so the whole source-code listing must be assembled into its object-code version—a version that is far less understandable in human terms, but more compatible with the nature of an electronic device.

Entering the Program into the System

The next logical step in the programming process is to get the program into
the microprocessor system, *loading* it into the specified program memory
addresses.

The exact nature of the program-loading operation depends on the configuration of the microprocessor system that is available. On the most primitive level, microprocessors cannot "understand" hexadecimal codes any
better than the source-code mnemonics. Under the most primitive conditions,
then, the hexadecimal-oriented object codes and addresses have to be further
translated into their 8- and 16-bit counterparts, and entered into program
memory by means of an array of "1" and "0" toggle switches.

Fortunately, most microprocessor programmers have access to a slightly
more sophisticated *program development system*. That is a bare-bones microprocessor system that includes a hexadecimal keypad—a set of keys arranged
and labeled with the 16 standard hexadecimal characters. In such cases the
object-code listing can be loaded from that keypad, using the hexadecimal
codes directly. It is up to the internal workings of the development system
to translate the hexadecimal codes into their binary counterparts for the microprocessor itself.

It will be assumed throughout this book that the programmer will be
entering the programs via the hexadecimal keypad on a program development system. Thus the object-code listings and addresses are specified in a
hexadecimal format. (A few earlier development systems used an octal format, but that notion is giving way to the hexadecimal format and will not
be used anywhere in the illustrations in this text.)

Executing, Debugging, and Documenting the Program

With the program loaded into the microprocessor system, it is time to give it
a try. The moment of truth arrives, and the unforgiving nature of microprocessor systems often becomes quite apparent. The slightest error anywhere in
the preceding programming process can give rise to disastrous results when
the program is actually executed. The whole program can "blow up," running away with itself and creating all sorts of crazy effects.

Programmers learn to expect such things, and later discussions in this
book deal with ways to avoid, or at least minimize, the effects of programming errors.

When the initial execution of the program turns up a problem, it is time
to go all the way back to the flowchart or source-code listing, running through
the operations to find the error and correct it. In computer jargon, that sort
of troubleshooting operation is called *debugging* a program.

Once the program is tested, debugged, and doublechecked, it should be
running as originally intended. In the case of the specific programming example featured in this chapter, the system should do nothing until the push-

button is depressed. At that moment, the light should go on, and remain on for about 3 seconds. Then the light should turn itself off. When the program does exactly that, the next and final step is to document the work.

The documentation might consist of little more than source and object listings (corrected versions, of course). Usually, it is necessary to include the flowchart as well.

Electrical schematics are in order if there is something unusual about the system's hardware configuration. And if the system is to be used by others, the programmer might be obliged to prepare a written description of the operating procedures and theory of operation.

1-3 AN OVERALL PERSPECTIVE ON THIS BOOK

The foregoing material presents an overall view of the microprocessor programming process, introducing some conventions and special nomenclature along the way. The real essence of the matter and, indeed, the essence of this book, can be summarized as follows: Given a well-defined task to be performed, transform it into a working reality by applying the available tools—the microprocessor's hardware configuration and its particular instruction set.

The mechanism for carrying out this transformation is the programming process; and that is a process calling for an understanding of the available tools and a "feeling" for composing programs.

Writing a program for a microprocessor system is really an evolutionary process. It begins with an altogether human concept of what must be done, evolves into a somewhat more abstract source-code listing, and ends up as a machine-oriented object-code listing. The farther one goes into the programming process, the more machine-like and less human-like the matter becomes.

The climax of the whole affair comes about when the program is finally executed. At that point, matters return to more human terms: Does the program work right, or doesn't it?

The programming process is thus a fine blend of human intellect and creativity, and machine behavior. Writing a program is not unlike composing a tune or writing a short story. If the process were entirely an objective one, it would be possible to write programs that would write programs. The human element is always present in the programming process, especially during the earlier phases of the task. And the more complex a programming task becomes, the more likely it is to reflect the intellectual personality of the programmer.

Exercises for Chapter 1

Define the following terms and expressions:

1. Microprocessor hardware
2. Program
3. Flowchart
4. Source-code program

5. Assemble a program
7. Program memory
9. Debug a program
11. Conditional operation
13. Data
15. Instruction field
17. Instruction set
19. Program address field
21. Loading a program

6. Object-code program
8. Execute a program
10. Document a program
12. Address
14. Label field
16. Comment field
18. Machine language
20. Program data field

2

More About Hardware and Program Instructions

The discussions in Chapter 1 make numerous references to the fact that the successful preparation of a microprocessor program demands an understanding of both the system's hardware and instruction set. The fact is more clearly established in this chapter.

2-1 A GENERAL VIEW OF THE HARDWARE SYSTEM

Strictly speaking, a microprocessor is an IC device that is capable of carrying out a multitude of logical, arithmetic, and control operations. But in spite of its inherent computing power, a microprocessor IC is helpless when it stands alone; the device must be used in conjunction with some appropriate supporting hardware.

At the very least, the microprocessor must be connected to some input/output (I/O) devices—devices that serve as avenues for getting information into and out of the microprocessor device itself. Then, too, there is a need for some supporting memory devices that keep track of the programmed instructions and often serve as temporary dumping places for information to be used at a later time.

There is a great deal of flexibility with regard to specifying and engineering the supporting hardware for a microprocessor device, but that is a subject beyond the scope of this text. The process of programming the microprocessor—the main topic of this book—generally assumes that an appropriate hardware configuration already exists, and it is the programmer's responsibility to understand the details of the hardware to the extent necessary for writing programs that make effective use of the supporting hardware.

Although there are a virtually infinite number of possible configurations for the supporting hardware, the operating characteristics of the microprocessor device itself remain inalterable. As far as the supporting hardware system is concerned, a programmer can generally regard it as a collection of "black boxes." All one needs to know is what must be done to the input terminals of those boxes to achieve a desired effect at their output terminals.

Figure 2-1 illustrates a working microprocessor system in a very general, black-box fashion. In one way or another, every hardware scheme can be fit into this general plan.

First, there is a *microprocessor* IC device. For the moment, it is considered just another black box, but it will be necessary to take a closer look later at its insides.

Every microprocessor must be connected to some sort of *clock*, or timing circuit. Some microprocessors have the main clock circuitry built into them, whereas others require a set of external IC devices to do the timing job. At the very least, the clock circuit is made up of a quartz crystal or a set of passive timing components.

The purpose of the clock circuit is to pace and synchronize all the microprocessor's activities and, in some instances, the workings of the I/O devices as well. Operating frequencies for the clock circuit are most often in the range 2 to 5 MHz, although 10-MHz versions are becoming available these days.

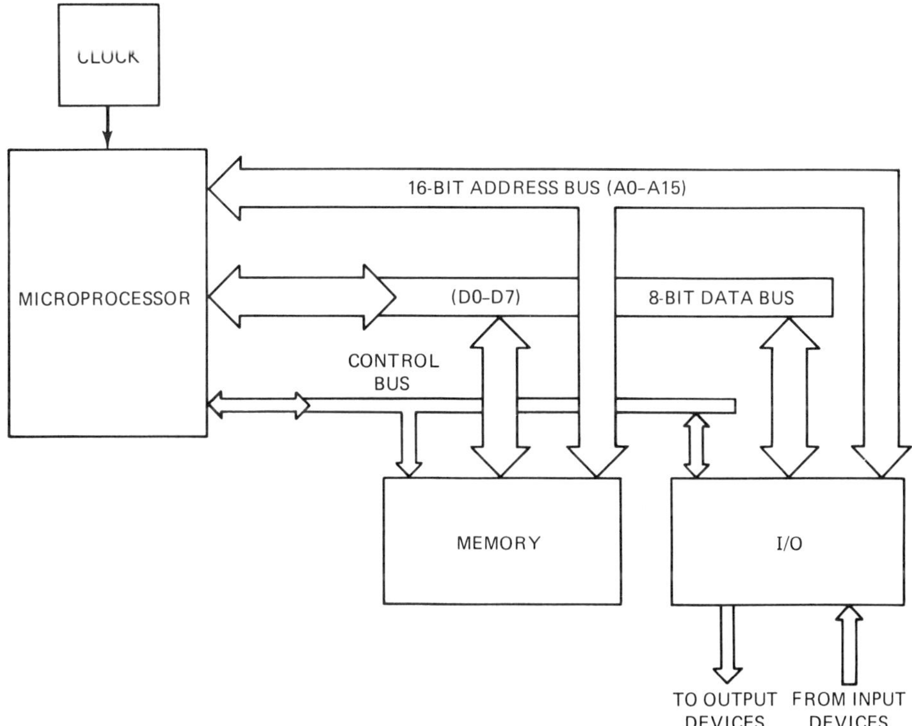

Figure 2-1 General "black box" view of a complete microprocessor hardware system.

Another indispensable part of the hardware configuration is some *memory* circuitry. Memory circuits can serve many different functions and take on several different forms; but the most essential function is to serve as a repository for the program instructions. A microprocessor is useless without program instructions, and the memory is the place where those instructions are stored.

Finally, there is a need for some *I/O* circuits—mechanisms for getting information into the microprocessor and outputting the results of its operations. I/O circuits often have to condition the information flowing into and out of the system. In that respect, the input circuits condition the incoming information to make it compatible with the specifications for the microprocessor's input terminals. Similarly, the output circuits condition outgoing information to make it compatible with the specifications for any external output devices to be controlled.

A programmer might or might not have anything to do with the process of specifying and wiring up the hardware elements of the microprocessor system. In either case, though, the programmer must have some knowledge of the hardware specifications on at least the black-box level.

Exercises for Section 2-1

1. What is the role of an electronic *clock* mechanism in a microprocessor system?
2. What is the most essential role of the *memory* mechanism in a microprocessor system?
3. Classify the following devices as *input* or *output* devices.
    (a) An LED (light-emitting diode)
    (b) A pushbutton switch
    (c) A computer keyboard
    (d) A motor
    (e) An A/D (analog-to-digital) converter
    (f) A D/A (digital-to-analog) converter
        [*Hint for items (e) and (f):* A microprocessor system is a digital system.]
    (g) A computer CRT (cathode-ray tube) display
    (h) A character (typewriter-like) printer

2-2 A GENERAL VIEW OF THE SYSTEM BUS CONFIGURATION

As illustrated in Fig. 2-1, there are three major lines of communication between the microprocessor device and the memory and I/O devices that support it. They are the address bus, data bus, and control bus.

A *bus*, generally speaking, is a group of wires and electrical terminals that perform a common task. The *address bus* thus handles system addressing operations, the *data bus* handles data flowing between the microprocessor and its support devices, and the *control bus* keeps everything straightened out.

At the microprocessor device, the address bus takes the form of 16 pin connections, each providing 1 bit of addressing. By convention, these address points are labeled A0 through A15, with A0 being the least-significant bit. With 16 bits of addressing available, the microprocessor is capable of generating 2^{16}, or 65,536, distinctly different addresses. Using hexadecimal notation, the address bus can generate addresses in the range of 0000 through FFFF. A given microprocessor system rarely uses all possible address locations, however.

With regard to the memory devices, the purpose of the address bus is to select one particular memory location, either to place a byte of data into that location or to pull a byte from it to be used within the microprocessor device.

The address bus serves a similar purpose in instances where it is necessary to set up a line of communication between the microprocessor device and *one* of the I/O devices. The pattern of 1's and 0's on the address bus can be used to select an input device that is to provide data for the microprocessor, or that address bus can specify an output device that is to receive a byte of data from the microprocessor.

The address bus thus services both the memory and I/O elements of the overall system, serving the same purpose in both instances: selecting one element out of a vast array of possibilities.

Whereas the address bus selects a memory location or I/O device, the data bus carries the information between the selected element and the microprocessor. The data bus is *bidirectional*; that is data can flow in either direction through it. Data can flow from a selected memory or I/O element and to the microprocessor, or from the microprocessor and to an element selected by the address bus.

The data bus consists of eight lines, each carrying a 1-or-0 bit of data. Some microprocessors feature a 16-bit data bus scheme, but the examples cited throughout this book feature the more common 8-bit data bus configuration.

The data bus connections are conventionally labeled D0 through D7, with D0 being the least significant bit. The range of data codes, expressed as hexadecimal numbers, is thus from 00 to FF.

It is more difficult to describe the control bus in general terms, because its details can vary from one system design to another. The overall purpose, however, is to keep straight the flow of data among the microprocessor, memory devices, and I/O elements.

Whenever it is necessary to pick up a byte of data previously stored in the memory, for example, a signal on the control bus is responsible for making certain that the data comes out of the memory and goes into the microprocessor, as opposed to making the data flow in the opposite direction—from the microprocessor and into the memory. The same general idea applies to control bus operations for the I/O system.

In a manner of speaking, the control bus serves the function of a traffic controller. The address bus dictates *where* in memory a byte of data is located or which I/O device is to participate in the ongoing action. The data bus carries the information thus involved. And the main task of the control bus, in this case, is to make sure that the data flow in the appropriate direction and are present on the data bus at the appropriate time.

Exercises for Section 2-2

1. What is meant by a *bus*?
2. What is a *bidirectional bus*?
3. The address bus is carrying the binary number 7F (hexadecimal). What is the binary value of the LSB (least-significant bit)? the MSB (most significant bit)? (*Hint*: First convert the hexadecimal number 7F to a 16-bit binary form.)
4. Which bus determines *where* a relevant byte of data is located?
5. Which bus carries a data byte to be manipulated by the microprocessor system?
6. Which bus is primarily responsible for determing the direction of flow of information on the data bus?

2-3 BUS ACTIVITY DURING THE EXECUTION OF A PROGRAM INSTRUCTION

The general view of the microprocessor's hardware presented thus far in this chapter is adequate for introducing some of the activity involved in executing some classes of program instructions. The purpose of the following examples is to illustrate the coordination of bus operations and, at the same time, begin building a bridge between the system hardware and the program tailored for it.

Every microprocessor device features a class of instructions that move a byte of data from the memory and into a register in the microprocessor device. Upon executing such an instruction, the sequence of events follows this general pattern:

1. Place the address location of the byte to be moved onto the address bus.
2. Generate a control bus signal that
   a. Moves the data from the memory to the data bus.
   b. Moves the data from the data bus into a register within the microprocessor.

At the conclusion of the operations, a byte (8 bits) of data previously stored in the memory is resident in the microprocessor device.

There is also a class of program instructions that move a byte of data from the microprocessor to a specified address location in the memory. The sequence of events involved in this sort of instruction is:

1. Place the address location of the data's destination in memory onto the address bus.
2. Generate a control bus signal that
   a. Moves the data byte from the microprocessor onto the data bus.
   b. Moves the data from the bus to the specified address location in memory.

These two classes of instructions are often used in conjunction with one another. At one point during the execution of a program, a data byte is moved from the memory. Then at a later time, it is retrieved by moving it from that same address in memory to the microprocessor. As you might imagine, it is the programmer's responsibility to keep track of the memory address.

The same general notion applies to communications between the microprocessor and I/O devices. Storing a byte of data and retrieving it later is not the purpose of I/O communications, however. Rather, the idea is to send a byte of data to a specified output device so that it will behave in some appropriate fashion. As far as input operations are concerned, the idea is to "look at what an input device is doing, place the data byte it is generating at the moment onto the data bus, and move it into the microprocessor.

Instructions that send data to an output device generally set up the following sequence of bus activity:

1. Place the address location of the output device onto the address bus.
2. Generate a control bus signal that
   a. Moves a byte of data onto the data bus.
   b. Loads the data to the output device.

How the output device responds to those data depends, of course, on the nature of the device and its input specifications. The programmer must be fully aware of those specifications in order to set up the appropriate instruction.

Instructions for picking up a byte of data from an input device follows this general pattern:

1. Place the address location of the input device onto the address bus.
2. Generate a control bus signal that
   a. Moves a byte of data from the input device onto the data bus.
   b. Moves the byte from the data bus into the microprocessor device.

The programmer must know the exact address location of the I/O devices being used. Furthermore, the programmer must know the significance of the data being passed—how a certain byte of data will affect an output device and how the microprocessor should interpret a byte of data from the input device.

The microprocessor is always at the center of bus activity, and every bus-related action has both an address and a byte of data associated with it. That should be apparent from the foregoing examples.

Looking at the same situations from a slightly different viewpoint, suppose that the microprocessor's instruction set includes these instructions:

LD A,*addr*   Load the microprocessor with a byte of data from address *addr*.

ST *addr*,A   Store a byte of data from the microprocessor to an element located at address *addr*.

Before either of these instructions can be used, the programmer must supply the addresses, and that is the part of the programming task that calls

for some knowledge of how the hardware is set up. Suppose that a portion
of the hard-ware is set up this way:

        Address 7C00   memory
              42C0   memory
              F100   input device*
              F200   output device*

The four addresses represent 16-bit numbers in a hexadecimal format,
and they provide the *addr* portion of the instructions.

So in order to pick up a byte of data from memory address 7C00 and
place it into the microprocessor, the appropriate instruction would be LD A,
7C00. To move a byte of data from the microprocessor to memory location
42C0 would be a matter of executing the instruction ST 42C0,A.

Getting a byte of data from the input device and moving it to the microprocessor can be accomplished by doing a LDA,F100. That is, indeed, the
same instruction used for reading a byte of data from a memory location;
but in this case, the address refers to an input device instead.

Finally, it is possible to move a byte of data from the microprocessor to
the output device by doing ST F200,A.

As long as the programmer knows all the appropriate addresses, those
two simple instructions are capable of doing a lot of useful work. It is important to bear in mind, however, that a sequence of bus activity always accompa-
nies the execution of such instructions.

When the microprocessor encounters such an instruction, it first decodes
it to determine its meaning, and then automatically sets up the proper sequence of address and control bus operations. When finding an instruction
such as LD A,7C00, for example, the processor:

1. Places address 7C00 onto the address bus.
2. Generates a control bus signal that
    a. Moves the data byte from address 7C00 to the data bus.
    b. Moves the data from the bus into the microprocessor.

All of that activity is implied by the basic instruction, and the programmer
need not give it constant attention. The programmer's task is to select the
instruction and supply the address. The microprocessor's internal workings
take care of all the behind-the-scene activity that is necessary for carrying
out the instructions.

Of course the available instructions can be combined to create more

---

*Many programming standards require a numeral zero preceding an address that
begins with an alphabetical character, A through F. Addresses can thus have five characters in them. Address F100, for example, can be specified as 0F100, and address F200
can be designated 0F200. Through this book, some addresses will include that fifth lead-
ing-zero character, and others will not. It is a matter of adapting to the standard required
by the programming system being used.

complex and useful sequences of operations. Using the same instructions and addresses cited for the previous examples, suppose that you want to do the following:

1. Pick up a byte of data from the input device at address F100.
2. Load that data byte into memory location 7C00.
3. Pick up a byte of data from memory location 42C0.
4. Load that data byte from memory to the output device at F200.

The appropriate instruction sequence looks like this:

```
LD  A,F100
ST  7C00,A
LD  A,42C0
ST  F200,A
```

The instruction *fetches* a byte of data from the input device and places it into the microprocessor. The second instruction then saves that same byte by moving it from the microprocessor to memory location 7C00.

The third instruction fetches a byte of data from memory location 42C0 and places it into the microprocessor; and the last instruction moves the data from the microprocessor to the output device.

And all through the execution of that short program, the addresses are appearing on the address bus, the data are running to and fro along the data bus, and the control bus is keeping everything straightened out. All of that is under the control of the microprocessor.

As a final example, suppose that you want to move a byte of data from the input device and send it out to the output device. A direct connection between the input and output devices is not possible without the help of some special external hardware (a topic reserved for a later discussion). The microprocessor is at the center of all ongoing activity, so the matter of passing a byte of data from an input device to an output device must include the microprocessor.

The appropriate program looks like this:

```
LD  A,F100
ST  F200,A
```

The first instruction fetches the data byte from the input device and places it into the microprocessor. The second instruction then moves that same byte from the microprocessor to the output device.

No matter how simple or complex the program might be, the microprocessor interprets each instruction, in sequence and one at a time, automatically generating the appropriate combinations of bus activities to get the job done.

The foregoing examples treat the memory, input, and output elements in a very specific fashion, citing a specific address location in each case. The microprocessor, however, is treated in a very general way. It was sufficient, in those examples, to simply state that a byte of data is moved into or out of the microprocessor. In actual practice, the microprocessor situation is somewhat more involved.

Microprocessors have within their basic structure more than one place that can accept a byte from the data bus or deliver a byte to it. Those "places" are properly called *registers*.

Figure 2-2 shows a microprocessor that includes two registers labeled A and B. They are, in fact, 8-bit memory elements; and either one is capable of communicating with the external data bus at any given moment. So when an instruction calls for loading a byte of data into the microprocessor, it is necessary to specify which of the two registers is to receive those data. Similarly, the matter of moving a byte of data out of the microprocessor and onto the data bus has to include some notion of which register is to supply the byte.

The simple instruction set cited in earlier examples can thus be expanded to cover process involving two internal data registers:

LD A,*addr*	Load register A in the microprocessor with a byte of data from address *addr*.
LD B,*addr*	Load register B in the microprocessor with a byte of data from address *addr*.
ST *addr*,A	Store a byte of data from register A in the microprocessor to address *addr*.
ST *addr*,B	Store a byte of data from register B in the microprocessor to address *addr*.
T A,B	Transfer the byte in register B to register A.
T B,A	Transfer the byte in register A to register B.

The first four instructions represent all possible combinations of two-register operations that involve external memory and I/O devices. The two load operations fill either the A or B register with data from the external data bus, and the two store operations place the content of either register A or B onto the bus. In both cases, the associated addresses determine the *source* or *destination* of the data.

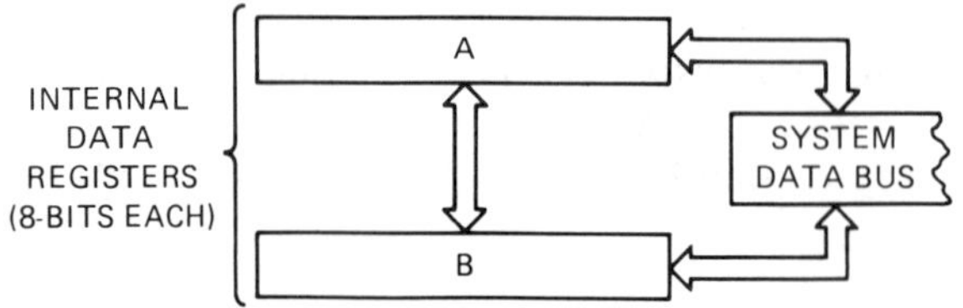

Figure 2-2 Two data registers within a microprocessor IC device.

The last two instructions are new to the present discussion. They are *register transfer* instructions that copy the content of one register into the other. The external devices and buses are not involved in such operations.

An instruction such as T A,B copies the content of the B register into A; and immediately after executing such an instruction, the same data byte exists in both registers—the content of the source register (the one supplying the data) is not changed.

Increasing the number of data registers within the microprocessor greatly expands the number of possible program instructions and, of course, the flexibility of the system. And just as a programmer must be acquainted with the addressing format for external memory and I/O devices, he or she must also be fully aware of the register configuration within the microprocessor. The addresses for the external devices can vary a great deal from one working system to another because the system engineer determines them by the hardware design. The microprocessor's internal register configuration, however, is fixed by the manufacturer of the device, and nearly all the instructions refer to a register.

The following program example is based on this set of external addresses:

Address 4A00 through 4AFF	memory
Address F001	input device
Address F002	output device

The task at hand is to do this:

1. Fetch a byte from the input device and load it to register A in the microprocessor.
2. Fetch a byte from memory address 4A00 and load it into register B.
3. Save the content of register A in memory location 4A01.
4. Load the content of register B to the output device.
5. Transfer the byte in register B to register A.

Admittedly, this sequence of operations is not really very exciting in terms of the overall task it performs; it is simply intended to illustrate the need for knowing both the external hardware and internal register configurations.

Here is the program for carrying out the job:

```
LD  A,F001     FETCH A BYTE FROM THE INPUT DEVICE TO REGISTER A

LD  B,4A00     FETCH A BYTE FROM MEMORY 4A00 TO REGISTER B

ST  4A01,A     SAVE REGISTER A IN MEMORY 4A01

ST  F002,B     LOAD THE CONTENT OF B TO THE OUTPUT DEVICE

T A,B          TRANSFER B TO A
```

As defined in Chapter 1, this is a *source-code* rendition of the program. It shows the mnemonics for the instructions to be performed and a relevant comment in each case.

In order to follow the sequence of events, you must be acquainted with the literal meaning of the mnemonics, the microprocessor's internal register organization, and the meaning of the addresses that refer to external memory and I/O devices. Without this information at hand, the program is largely meaningless; although the comments might help understand matters on a general level.

If it seems difficult to follow a previously written source-code program without knowing about the system's external hardware and internal registers, try writing a program without that knowledge—it is virtually impossible.

Exercises for Section 2-4

1. How many binary bits are included in a byte?
2. How many bytes are required for completely specifying an address?
3. As far as the microprocessor systems featured in this book are concerned, how many bytes are required for a complete data specification?
4. What is a source register? a destination register?

3

Program Memory
and Program Instructions

Discussions in Chapter 2 describe the memory in a microprocessor system as an external device that can serve as a repository for data. Data can be moved from the microprocessor, onto the data bus, and then into the memory—into the memory at an address location specified on the system's address bus. Similarly, data can be pulled from a specific address in memory, placed onto the data bus, and finally inserted into a register within the microprocessor device.

In examples such as these, the overall purpose of the memory is to serve as a place where 8-bit (1-byte) data can be stored at one moment, and then retrieved at a later time. The exact location of the data byte in memory is determined by the 16-bit (2-byte) address specified for it.

Although data and addresses flow around the buses as 8- and 16-bit binary numbers, programmers rarely have to regard them in that awkward format. Rather, programmers most often work and think in terms of the hexadecimal counterparts of those 8- and 16-bit binary numbers.

From a programmer's point of view, then, data take the form of two-character hexadecimal numbers (from 00 through FF), and the addresses take the form of four-character hexadecimal numbers (from 0000 through FFFF).

The main purpose of this chapter is to show how microprocessor programs are assembled into their corresponding hexadecimal codes, deposited into the system's memory, and retrieved as data when the system executes those programs.

3-1 MEMORY SIZE AND LOCATION

The memory system can be viewed as a collection of 1-byte data registers that are named according to their 2-byte addresses. So most of the memory, if not all of it, is composed of a fairly large number of successive data "registers" and corresponding address designations.

Figure 3-1 illustrates a small section of a memory. The addresses are shown from 4000 (hexadecimal) to 4004 (hexadecimal). Each address location contains a single byte of data that is also shown in a hexadecimal format. Neither the range of addresses nor the bytes of data contained therein is really important to this particular example. The important features, as far as this discussion is concerned, are:

1. The use of successive address locations
2. The 2-byte format for the addresses
3. The 1-byte format for the data

The portion of memory illustrated here contains just 5 bytes of data. It can be regarded as a 5-byte section of a much larger memory scheme. Of course, a working microprocessor system has to include more than 5 bytes of memory.

A given system, for example, might have some memory located at locations 0000 through 4FFF (hexadecimal). In that case, there are 5000 (hexadecimal) or 20,480 (decimal) successive memory locations, each capable of holding a *single* byte of data. Such a system can deal with up to 20,480 bytes of data information. In computer jargon, this would be known as a 20K-byte, or simply 20K, memory.

NOTE: The number of bytes available in a memory is equal to the highest memory address minus the lowest memory address—plus 1. Expressed in the form of an equation:

$$B_T = M_H - M_L + 1$$

where B_T = number of bytes in the memory
M_H = highest available address location
M_L = lowest available address location

If the equation is worked out using hexadecimal notation for the addresses, the bit total will be expressed in hexadecimal notation as well. That being the case, it is helpful to convert the result into a more meaningful decimal format. Of course, the memory addresses can be converted to a decimal format before working the equation; and in that case, the bit total will come out in decimal.

Having a 16-bit address format implies 2^{16}, or 65,536 possible address locations from 0000H through FFFFH. (The H suffix denotes a hexadecimal numbering format.) A microprocessor system rarely uses all possible address locations; rather, the hardware engineer will supply memory devices that work within a specified address range. As you might suspect, the programmer must be fully aware of what the addressing range is.

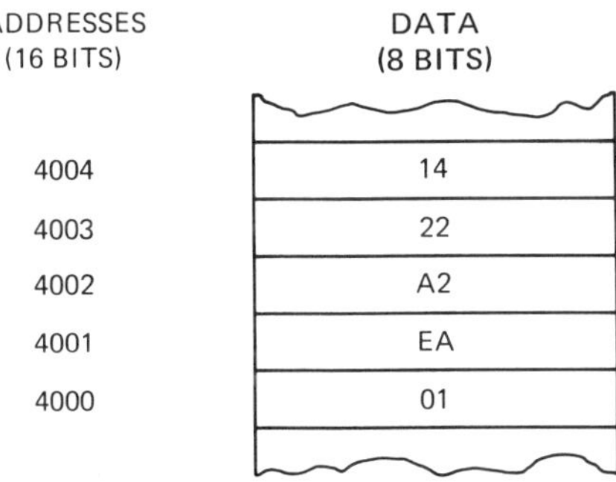

Figure 3-1 A small section of memory. The addresses in this example run from 4000 through 4004 (hexadecimal). Each location contains one byte of data that can be accessed from those addresses.

Suppose that a given microprocessor system has some memory located at addresses 0000H through 03FFH. That figures out to 1024 (decimal) address locations, and that many places where single bytes of data can be stored. The programmer can count on using up to 1024 (decimal) places in memory for storing data, and everything will work out nicely as long as he or she restricts the choices of address locations to the range of 0000H through 03FFH. If no memory elements are connected in the remaining address, 0400H through FFFFH, it would be pointless to attempt writing or reading data at those addresses.

Some microprocessor configurations call for locating the usable memory at the upper end of the available memory addressing locations. The hardware engineer, for instance, might hook up memory devices between C00H and 0FFFH. That still figures out to 1024 (decimal) bytes of memory, but now the addressing range is vastly different from the previous example.

Generally speaking, the hardware engineer is free to install memory devices anywhere within the range of addresses 0000H through FFFFH. Sections of memory can even be separated by gaps of unused addresses. In any case, the programmer must be fully aware of where the usable memory exists. There is little point in writing programs that attempt to use address locations where no memory device exists.

3-2 PROGRAM MEMORY

Thus far, the memory portion of a microprocessor system has been portrayed simply as a place where data can be stored at one moment and then retrieved at a later time. The meaning of the data stored in the memory, however, has not been important to the foregoing discussions. Now that all changes.

A microprocessor system, no matter how elaborate its hardware scheme might be, is useless without some programming that tells it what to do and when to do it. That program information is stored in the system's memory in a special place designated as the *program memory* space.

To be sure, some memory can be used for storing data generated during the execution of a program, but there must be some program memory locations that remain unchanged during the execution of the program contained therein.

During the execution of a program, the microprocessor consults the program memory to see what it is supposed to do next. It fetches the program information, one byte at a time, decodes it, and translates it into an appropriate action. Unless the programmer chooses otherwise, the programming information deposited into the program memory remains intact, no matter how often it is read by the microprocessor. That particular feature allows the system to execute the same program, or sections of a program, an indefinitely large number of times.

The program memory can be located across any range of addresses that point to usable hardware memory devices. It is the programmer's responsibility to specify exactly where the program memory resides and make certain that none of the program instructions call for depositing new data into any of the program-memory addresses. Accidentally depositing such data into the program memory changes the program itself during its execution; and that generally destroys the program, creating a condition computer buffs like to call a "blowup."

3-3 PROGRAM INSTRUCTIONS FOR PROGRAM MEMORY

Every program instruction included in the instruction set for a microprocessor device has at least one 1-byte binary code designated for it. A mnemonic instruction such as TAB might literally mean: Transfer the content of the microprocessor's B register to its A register. Consulting the instruction set for the microprocessor device at hand, the programming will find that the instruction TAB has associated with it a 1-byte code—2A (hexadecimal), for example.

The programmer thinks in terms of the instruction's literal meaning and writes the source-code program in terms of its mnemonic. Before the instruction can be entered into the system's program memory, however, it must be converted into its 1-byte binary format—0010 1010 in this instance. That instruction byte will ultimately end up as a byte of data that fully occupies a specified address in the program memory.

A good many microprocessor instructions, though, call for using more than one byte of information. Some instructions use 2, 3, or 4 bytes. How is it possible to write multibyte program instructions into a program memory that is composed of 1-byte "registers?"

The answer is that *multibyte instructions are stored in the program memory in successive address locations.*

Suppose that a certain microprocessor instruction is made up of four separate bytes: 2A 00 4C 1F. If the first byte is placed into address location 7C00H, the full instruction occupies a portion of the program memory as follows:

```
7C00   2A
7C01   00
7C02   4C
7C03   1F
```

When the microprocessor is called upon to execute that 4-byte instruction at a later time, it fetches the bytes, one at a time, beginning from address 7C00H. When the entire group of 4 bytes is fully decoded by the internal workings of the microprocessor device, they are put into the sort of action they specify.

How does a microprocessor know whether an instruction calls for taking in 1, 2, 3, or 4 bytes before decoding them? It knows by the nature of the first byte in the instruction. In the previous example, the first byte is a 2A. Upon seeing an instruction beginning with 2A, the microprocessor knows that it is to pick up the next three bytes from program memory before decoding the instruction and translating it into the sort of action it specifies.

A different first byte might tell the microprocessor it is to pick up 3, 2, 1, or none of the bytes that follow that follow that first one.

A finished program written by the programmer consits of any number of discrete instructions. The first byte of the first instruction in the program is entered at a designated address in the program memory space. Generally speaking, the bytes for all successive instructions are entered into successively higher program memory address locations. The more instructions a program contains, the more program memory it occupies.

When the system is told to execute the program, it begins reading the instructions, one byte at a time, decoding the byte and, if necessary, reading more bytes to put together a complete instruction. The system then carries out the instruction and looks to the next byte in program memory to determine what is to be done next.

3-4 THE ROLE OF THE PROGRAM COUNTER

Every microprocessor device described in this book contains a 16-bit (2-byte *program counter*. It is the program counter that keeps track of the addressing for the program-reading process.

When a program is to be executed, one of the first steps is to set the program counter so that it *points to* the address of the first byte of the first instruction. Thereafter, the microprocessor's internal workings take care of making the program counter point to the next byte of information in the program memory.

Suppose that a short program is stored in program memory space as follows:

```
4F00   12
4F01   4C 31
4F03   BF 2A
```

Now, that is a three-instruction program. The first instruction code is 12, and it resides at address 4F00 in the program memory. The second instruction is a 2-byte instruction: 4C 31. The first of the two bytes is located at address 4F01, and the second byte is at 4F02. (Although not specifically shown, the address of the second byte resides at address 4F02 by implication.) The third instruction, BF 2A, is located at addresses 4F03 and, by implication, 4F04.

When writing programs in this object-code form, the addresses indicate the address of the first byte of each instruction. Each line in the listing thus specifies a complete instruction, making it far easier for anyone studying the program to separate, in this case, the 1-byte instruction from the 2-byte instructions. If the program were written as it is actually loaded into program memory, it would look like this:

```
4F00   12
4F01   4C
4F02   31
4F03   BF
4F04   2A
```

Written that way, it is difficult for a human observer to tell where one instruction begins and another ends. But with the help of the program counter, the microprocessor, itself, keeps things straight.

To run the program, the program counter is first set to 4F00—then it is left on its own. The microprocessor picks up the data at 4F00 and notes that they comprise a 1-byte instruction. In response to that knowledge, the microprocessor executes the instruction that 12H happens to designate.

Then the program counter automatically increments to the next address location: 4F01. The byte contained in that address, 4C, is transferred to the microprocessor, where it is found to be just the first of a 2-byte instruction. That being the case, the microprocessor defers further action until the program counter is incremented to the next address, 4F02. Thus addressed, the byte at that location, 31, is sent to the microprocessor. The instruction is then complete, and the microprocessor takes the designated action.

Then the program counter is incremented to the next address location: 4F03. The data byte contained therein is sent to the microprocessor for decoding, and the program counter—already incremented to 4F04—points to the next byte in the instruction.

In short, the program counter sets up the address locations for all the programming information. With the exception of a few special program instructions, the program counter works entirely under the control of some mechanisms within the microprocessor device. The programmer, for the most part, need not be concerned with program-counter activity—in a sense, it pretty much takes care of itself, doing all the addressing that is necessary for reading the bytes stored as program information in the program memory.

Incidentally, after the microprocessor receives all the bytes that comprise a complete program instruction, the program counter is already pointing to the next address in the program memory.

Discussions in Section 2-3 described data, address, and control bus activity involved in passing data between the microprocessor and external devices, including a memory device. At that time, there were no specific references to program memory.

Executing the instructions loaded into program memory call for the same kind of bus activity that is associated with any process calling for transferring a byte of data from the memory device to a register within the microprocessor device. Rather than placing the byte into one of the internal working registers, such as register A or B, program-reading operations put the byte from program memory into a special *instruction register.*

A typical instruction-reading cycle runs something like this:

1. Place the content of the program counter onto the system's address bus.
2. Generate a control bus signal that
   a. Moves a byte from program memory onto the data bus.
   b. Moves the byte from the data bus to the instruction register within the microprocessor.
3. Increment the program counter to the next-higher address location.

The first step in the cycle is responsible for addressing the external memory at the place holding the next instruction byte. The second step reads that byte and inserts it into the microprocessor's internal instruction register. Finally, the third step sets up the program counter for addressing the next location in the program memory.

If it turns out that the first byte of an instruction indicates that there are more bytes required for completing a multibyte instruction, the system continues cycling—picking up a byte and incrementing the program counter —until the proper number of instruction bytes is in the instruction register. Then, and only then, is the microprocessor ready to carry out a programmed instruction.

Regardless of how many bytes the microprocessor has to fetch in order to get a complete instruction into its instruction register, the program counter is always left pointing to the first byte of the next instruction in the program.

A microprocessor must know what the programmer wants it to do before it can do it, and that is the purpose of the program-reading cycle just described.

Generally speaking, the program counter works its way through the program memory one address at a time. Whether it increments through one, two, three, or four successive address locations depends on the nature of the program instruction it is picking up at the time.

The program-reading cycle is executed automatically for each instruction the programmer enters into the program memory. The programmer need not be concerned with the matter of telling the microprocessor how and when to pick up an instruction—that programming is permanently fixed within the microprocessor device itself.

3-6 MEMORIES AND MEMORY MAPS

The programmer loads the instruction codes into a section of external memory we have been calling the program memory. Executing the program is a matter of telling the microprocessor to run through that program memory, picking up the instructions, decoding them, and putting them into action.

As pointed out in some earlier examples, there are a number of instructions that call for loading data into memory or fetching it from memory and putting it into a working register within the microprocessor device. Such operations are part of the programming prepared by the programmer, and none of them should alter data residing in the program memory.

It is thus important to know the address range devoted to program memory and the address range that can be used as part of the operating program—and the two should never meet.

Sections of external memory that are set aside for saving and fetching information generated during the course of running a program are most often called *data memory*. Roughly speaking, then, the memory in a microprocessor system can be divided into program memory and data memory.

Quite often, the layouts of data memory and program memory become rather complicated, and keeping things straight is a matter of consulting or preparing a piece of documentation called a *memory map*.

As the name implies, a memory map is a guide to the layout of a system's external memory. Such a map spells out, in great detail, the addresses that are devoted to memory operations specified in the program instructions. Figure 3-2 illustrates one particular memory map.

In that example, the program memory is located in addresses 0000H through 3FFFH. The programmer must load his or her program within that range of addresses.

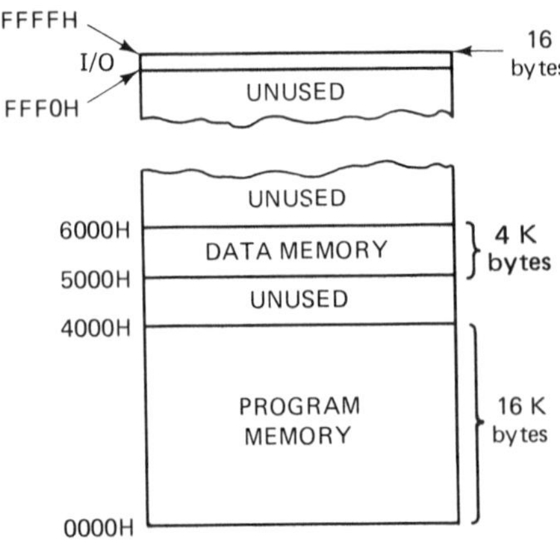

Figure 3-2 A typical system memory map.

Addresses 4000H through 4FFFH are specified as "unused." That generally means there are no memory devices installed at those locations. Any data loaded into that range of addresses will be lost, and any data fetched from there will be meaningless.

Addresses 5000H through 5FFFH are set aside for data memory, and the implication is that the programmer is free to use addresses within that range for program operations that call for saving and fetching data that are vital to the execution of the program at hand.

The space from 6000H through EFFFH is also specified as "unused." Finally, the topmost 16 bytes of memory are devoted to I/O addresses. No memory exists at those locations. Rather, the space is devoted to input and output devices that can be accessed as described in Chapter 1.

The programmer thus has about 16K of memory available for loading his or her programs—addresses 0000H through 3FFFH. There is about 4K of memory available for the data memory, and 16 bytes available for I/O devices.

Note that the program and data memories are separated by some unused memory space—space where no memory hardware exists. That is good engineering practice on the part of the hardware engineer because it eliminates the possibility of having some of the programming or data "crash" into one another, thus creating an undesirable disturbance in the operation of the program. Separating the program and data memory sections in this fashion is not always done, nor is it always possible to do it. Indeed, a memory map is a vital tool for any programming process.

Incidentally, the memory map shown in Fig. 3-2 is an arbitrary one. The program memory can, for example, be located at the upper end of the available memory address locations. With some reservations, it is possible to say that the hardware engineer is free to draw up the memory map any way he or she chooses.

Most microprocessor systems end up being devoted to doing one particular class of operations. The programmer writes a program for a particular task and debugs it. After that, there might be no need to alter large segments of the program again.

Portions of a program that will never change through the lifetime of the system can be built into a special kind of memory device called a *ROM* (*read-only memory*). Once fixed into a ROM, the programming cannot be altered by even the most devastating sort of program errors that might crop up at some later time.

What is more, programming that resides in ROM is not destroyed when electrical power is cut off. ROM programming is always available to the system, and getting to it is a simple matter of setting the program counter to an address that marks the beginning of a ROM-based program routine.

By contrast, a *RAM* (*random-access memory*) device does not retain its programming when electrical power is removed. Any data stored in a RAM will be lost whenever the electrical power is interrupted.

That is not to say, however, that a ROM is better than a RAM under all circumstances. Quite the contrary. A RAM has the advantage of being changeable. It has a feature of programming flexibility that is impossible with a ROM.

What about the data memory space? That has to be a RAM-oriented system. The programmer must be able to execute instructions that alter the data contained in memory during the operation of the program. So there can be no question about the matter of using RAM devices in the data memory portion of the system's memory map.

Then, too, a good many microprocessor applications call for at least a small amount of changeable programming. The main programming might be permanently fixed into some ROM devices, but a bit of RAM in the program memory space is necessary for holding the alterable parts of the programming.

Thus the "program memory" portion of the memory map in Fig. 3-2 might be revised to show address locations devoted to fixed ROM programming and addresses available to the programmer as RAM space.

Exercises for Chapter 3

1. Define the following terms.
   (a) Memory address
   (b) Memory data
   (c) Program memory
   (d) Multibyte instruction
   (e) Program counter
   (f) Increment (as *increment* an address)
   (g) Instruction register
   (h) Memory map
   (i) ROM
   (j) RAM
2. How is a ROM essentially different from a RAM?
3. How many data or program bytes can be stored between hexadecimal addresses C000 and CF20? Express your answer in a decimal format.
4. A system memory map shows that some available RAM begins at hexadecimal address 4100. If you must store 2300 (decimal) bytes of data beginning at that address (4100 hexadecimal), what is the highest address (in hexadecimal) you will use with those data?

4

Load Immediate Instructions

Getting a well-defined byte of data into a specified register in the micro-processor is one of the most elementary, yet vital, programming operations. It is, for instance, virtually impossible to get a meaningful program under way without first setting up some initial values in some registers—there has to be a clearly specified starting point for any sort of microprocessor opera-tion. *Load immediate* operations satisfy that need.

The basic idea of a load immediate operation is to load a byte of data *from the program memory* to a specified register within the microprocessor device. Suppose that you want to write a short program that causes the A register in the microprocessor to count backward from 09H to 00H. The first step would be to set the data in the A register to an initial value of 09H; and that is done by means of a load immediate instruction. The 09H is loaded to the register directly from the program.

Figure 4-1 illustrates the function of an 8-bit load immediate program instruction. In that particular case, the instruction occupies two successive address locations in the program memory, *addr* and *addr+1*. The first byte in the instruction—the one residing at *addr*—is the instruction's *operator code*, or *opcode*. The opcode serves two purposes:

1. It informs the microprocessor that a load immediate instruction is at hand.

2. It specifies which register within the microprocessor is to be loaded with the data at *addr+1*.

The second byte in the instruction—the content of *addr+1* in the program memory—is the data byte that is to be loaded into the specified register.

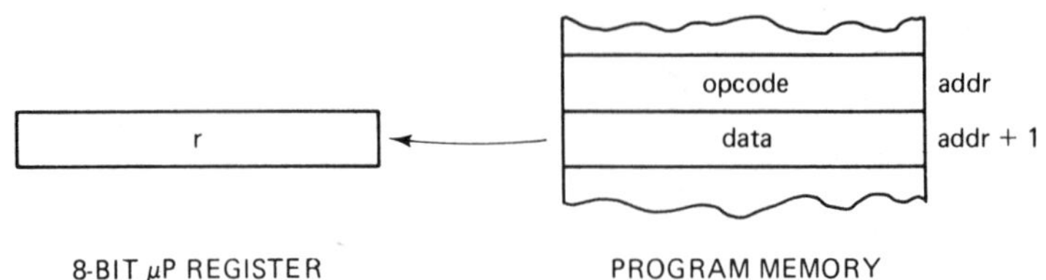

Figure 4-1   Schematic representation of a typical 8-bit load immediate operation.

An 8-bit load immediate instruction is often represented in this symbolic fashion:

$$r \leftarrow data$$

The implication of the notation is that a byte of data is loaded, or copied, directly to some register, r, from the program.

All microprocessors feature at least one, and usually many more, load immediate instructions. A typical mnemonic, source-code form of the instruction looks like this:

```
LD  A,2AH
```

Literally, that says: Load immediate to register A a hexadecimal value of 2A.

The object-code version of that same instruction might take this form:

```
3E  2A
```

The first byte in that 2-byte program instruction, 3E, is the opcode. It informs the processor that a load immediate to register A is at hand. The second byte, 2A, is the value to be loaded.

If it so happens that the instruction begins at address 4C00H in the program memory, the opcode will reside at address 4C00H and the data will be at 4C01H. The instruction looks like this in the program memory:

```
4C00 3E
4C01 2A
```

Upon completing the execution of the instruction, you can be sure that the A register in the microprocessor contains the value 2A. The 2A, incidentally, remains in the program memory at address 4C01H. Load immediate instructions do not alter the program memory in any way; in a manner of speaking, a load immediate instruction copies data from the program memory to a register within the microprocessor device.

A complete program listing for the foregoing example would take this form:

```
4C00 3E 2A    LD  A,2AH    ;INITIALIZE REGISTER A TO 2A
```

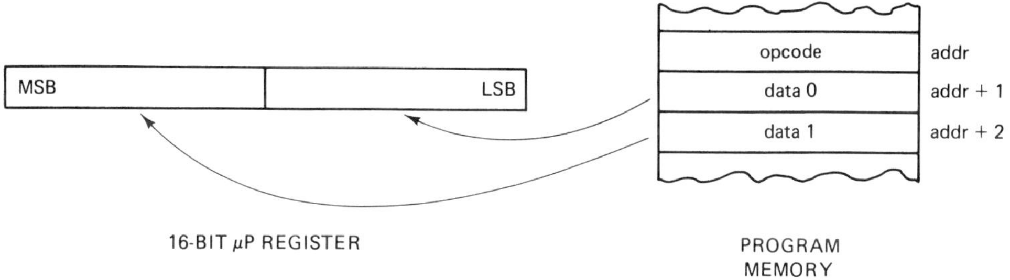

Figure 4-2 Schematic representation of a typical 16-bit load immediate operation.

All microprocessors have at least one 8-bit register, and most have at least one 16-bit register as well. That 16-bit register can be loaded in an immediate fashion, too. It takes twice as many bytes to fill a sixteen bit register, so it figures that the instruction for doing the job will contain at least one more data byte than the 8-bit load immediate instructions do.

A 16-bit load immediate instruction is illustrated in Fig. 4-2. The first byte of the instruction, residing at *addr* in the program memory, is the instruction's opcode. It informs the microprocessor that a 16-bit load immediate operation is at hand, and it specifies which internal 16-bit register is to receive the data.

Since this instruction loads a double-sized register, the data to be loaded have to occupy two successive 8-bit address locations in the program memory: *addr+1* and *addr+2*.

Upon executing this instruction, the data at *addr+1* are loaded directly to the lower-order byte in the microprocessor's 16-bit register. Then the data at *addr+2* are loaded to the higher-order byte in that same register. At the conclusion of the operation, the sequence of two data bytes in the program memory fill the 16-bit microprocessor register.

As far as this sort of 16-bit load immediate instruction is concerned, the second byte in the instruction (the one at *addr+1* in the program memory) is loaded to the LSB of the 16-bit register, and the third byte (at *addr+2*) goes into the MSB position of the register. The only exception to this general load immediate format is found in the instruction set for Motorola's 6800 microprocessor. In that particular case, the second byte in the instruction is data for the MSB position in the 16-bit register, and the third byte goes into the LSB location.

A typical 16-bit load immediate instruction takes this source-code form:

```
LD  SP,413FH
```

The literal meaning is: Load immediate to the 16-bit SP register the 16-bit value 413F.

The object-code version of that instruction might look like this:

```
31  3F  41
```

The first byte in the instruction, 31, is the opcode. The two remaining bytes make up the data to be loaded—LSB followed by MSB.

If the instruction happens to begin at address 4A00H in the program memory, the bytes are assigned this way:

```
4A00  31
4A01  3F
4A02  41
```

Upon executing the instruction, the 3F will go to the LSB portion of the SP register and the 41 will go to the MSB portion. The overall effect is that the microprocessor's internal, 16-bit SP register is loaded with the number 413F (hexadecimal).

The hallmark of a load immediate instruction, whether it loads an 8-bit or a 16-bit register, is the immediate transfer of data from the program memory to the specified register within the microprocessor device. No other class of instructions does that sort of loading job in that particular way.

4-1 LOAD IMMEDIATE INSTRUCTIONS FOR THE Z-80

The Z-80 microprocessor device contains a relatively large number of both 8-bit and 16-bit registers, and most of them can be loaded in an immediate fashion from the program memory.

8-Bit Load Immediate Instructions

Figure 4-3 shows the working registers within the Z-80 microprocessor device. The shaded registers are *not* included in 8-bit load immediate operations, so our immediate concern is with registers labeled A, B, C, D, E, H, and L.

The Z-80 instruction set includes 8-bit load immediate instructions for all seven of those registers. The source and object codes for those instructions are summarized in Table 4-1.

To see how the scheme works, suppose you are writing a source-code program that will load immediate a value of 2DH into register A. The source

TABLE 4-1 Z-80 INSTRUCTION SET FOR 8-BIT LOAD IMMEDIATE OPERATIONS

Source code	Object code	Symbolic notation
LD A,*data*	3E *byte*	
LD B,*data*	06 *byte*	
LD C,*data*	0E *byte*	$r \leftarrow data$
LD D,*data*	16 *byte*	
LD E,*data*	1E *byte*	*data* is loaded into register *r*
LD H,*data*	26 *byte*	
LD L,*data*	2E *byte*	

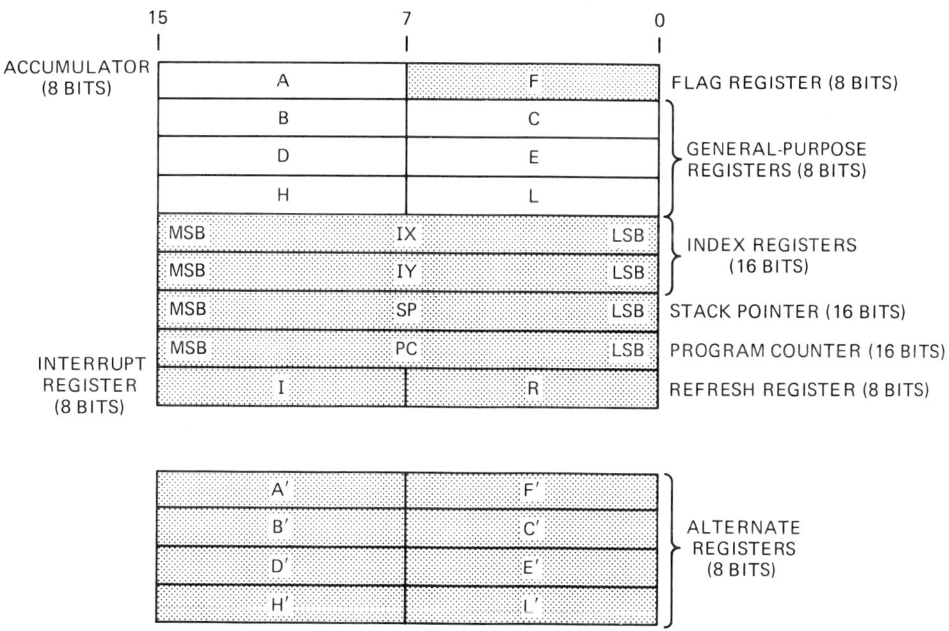

Figure 4-3 Z-80 registers for doing 8-bit load immediate operations. Shaded registers are not involved.

statement in that case is LD A,2DH. The opcode is LD A, and the *operand* (the *data* byte to be loaded) is 2D. (Recall that the H suffix denotes a number in a hexadecimal format.) So the source instruction LD A,2DH implies that the hexadecimal value 2D is to be loaded directly from the program memory into register A.

According to Table 4-1, the corresponding object-code listing is 3E 2D, where 3E is the machine-code operator for the instruction and 2D is the *byte* to be loaded.

But if the value 2DH is supposed to be loaded into the H register, instead of the A register, the source listing is: LD H,2DH. The corresponding object-code designation is 26 2D. Upon executing that instruction, the system will place the value 2D into the Z-80's 8-bit H register.

EXAMPLE 4-1

Write and assemble a program, using only 8-bit load immediate instructions, to do the following:

00H to A, 01H to B, 02H to C, 03H to D, 04H to E, 05H to H, and 06H to L

Begin the program at address 0C00H.
The result is shown in Program 4-1.

Before seeing how this program was put together, note in the comment for the first instruction that register A is called the *accumulator*. All micro-

```
0C00  3E 00   LD A,00H      ;ZERO THE ACCUMULATOR
0C02  06 01   LD B,01H      ;SET B TO 1
0C04  0E 02   LD C,02H      ;SET C TO 2
0C06  16 03   LD D,03H      ;SET D TO 3
0C08  1E 04   LD E,04H      ;SET E TO 4
0C0A  26 05   LD H,05H      ;SET H TO 5
0C0C  2E 06   LD L,06H      ;SET L TO 6
```

processors described in this book have a register that is designated the A register, and it is considered to be the system's accumulator—a register that is uniquely involved in just about all logical and mathematical operations.

The first step in putting together this program is to write out the appropriate sequence of source-code mnemonics and comments. Notice that the mnemonics match those shown for the Z-80 microprocessor in Table 4-1. It is always important to follow the *syntax*—the mnemonic expressions, register designations, separation of operators and operands with a comma, the use of the H suffix to designate hexadecimal notation, and a semicolon preceding a comment—for a given microprocessor device. It is the syntax of the source-code listings that separate a listing for one particular microprocessor device from those offered by other manufacturers.

After preparing the source-code listing, consult the instruction set to determine the opcodes, following each of them with the appropriate *data*.

Finally, assign the sequence of program memory addresses. The example cited the fact that the program should begin at address 0C00H. That was done in Program 4-1; and then successively higher addresses were assigned to all the program bytes that followed the first one.

16-Bit Load Immediate Instructions

Figure 4-4 shows the Z-80 registers that can be directly involved in 16-bit load immediate operations. The system includes three 16-bit registers: IX, IY, and SP. But six 8-bit registers are included as well: B, C, D, E, H, and L.

It should make sense that the three 16-bit registers would be included in the 16-bit load immediate instructions, but how do the little 8-bit registers get involved?

It turns out that the six 8-bit registers can be viewed as *register pairs*. Registers B and C, for example, can be treated as a single 16-bit register. In such a case, they are designated as the BC register pair.

Similarly, the D and E registers can be treated as a 16-bit DE register, and the H and L registers can be treated as a single, 16-bit HL register pair.

So, in effect, the Z-80 can be said to have six 16-bit registers: BC, DE, HL, IX, IY, and SP.

Treating two 8-bit registers as a 16-bit register pair is the programmer's option. It does not have to be done that way. When using the register pair format, however, the programmer has no options when it comes to pairing them. The B register is always paired with the C register, the D register is

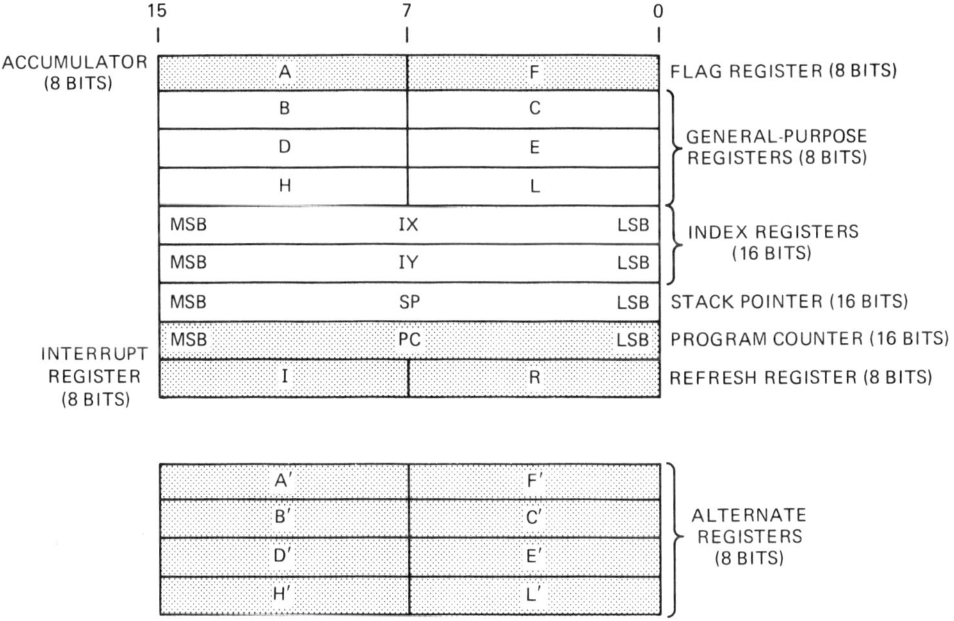

Figure 4-4 Z-80 register configurations for doing 16-bit load immediate operations. Shaded registers are not involved.

always paired with the E register, and the H register is always paired with the L register. It is not possible, for example, to pair the B and E registers.

The Z-80's load immediate instructions for 16-bit registers are summarized in Table 4-2. There are six of them—one for each of the standard register pairs and the three 16-bit registers.

First notice that the operand for the source-code representations must include two data bytes. The program memory is made up of 8-bit locations,

TABLE 4-2 Z-80 INSTRUCTIONS FOR 16-BIT LOAD IMMEDIATE OPERATIONS

Source code	Object code
LD BC, *data data*	01 *byte byte*
LD DE, *data data*	11 *byte byte*
LD HL, *data data*	21 *byte byte*
LD IX, *data data*	DD 21 *byte byte*
LD IY, *data data*	FD 21 *byte byte*
LD SP, *data data*	31 *byte byte*

Note: The first byte following the opcode is loaded into the lower-order register (C, E, L) or the lower-order byte position of register IX, IY, or SP. The last byte in the instruction is loaded into the higher-order (B, D, H) or the higher-order byte position of IX, IY, or SP.

and the matter of loading a register pair or a 16-bit register calls for loading two successive bytes from the program memory.

The data byte immediately following the opcode goes into the lower-order portion of the 16-bit register or register pair, while the final byte in the instruction is loaded to the higher-order portion. (As far as the register-pair operations are concerned, the B, D, and H registers are considered the high-order registers, and the C, E, and L registers are considered their lower-order counterparts).

Suppose that the task is to load 160FH into the BC register pair. The idea is to place a 16 into the B register and 0F into the C register. Of course, the task could be carried out by doing two 8-bit load immediate instructions from Table 4-1:

```
LD  B,16H
LD  C,0FH
```

But such a sequence of instructions would call for using four program bytes: two opcodes and two data bytes. The 16-byte load immediate version of the job would look like this:

```
LD  BC, 160FH
```

According to the instruction set, that is a 3-byte program instruction—one opcode (LD BC) followed by 2 bytes of data (160F). Using the 16-bit load immediate operation does a task with one fewer instruction byte in the program memory.

The object-code version of that 16-bit, register-pair load immediate operation is

```
01 0F 16
```

The first byte in the instruction is the opcode. It tells the microprocessor that a load immediate to register pair BC is in order. The byte following the opcode goes to the lower-order register (the C register), and the last byte goes to the higher-order register (the B register).

It generally confuses beginners when they note that a 2-byte hexadecimal number such as 160F is loaded to a 16-bit register format via an object-code instruction that reverses the order of the two bytes—0F first, followed by 16. But one gets used to the idea with some experience. An explanation of why the bytes are reversed in the object-code version of the instruction would merely muddle the discussion at this point. For the time being, at least, let us simply take it for granted that is the way things have to be.

If that particular 3-byte instruction begins at address 5400H in the program memory, its arrangement in the memory looks like this:

```
5400 01
5401 0F
5402 16
```

And a complete program listing for the operation looks something like this:

```
5400 01 0F 16    LD BC,160FH    ;LOAD THE BC PAIR WITH 160FH
```

The fact that the second and third bytes of the instruction reside in program memory addresses 5401H and 5402H is taken for granted. Any program instruction following that one would begin at address 5403H. That, too, is implied by the source-code portion of the listing.

The SP register is loaded in a similar fashion. It is a 3-byte instruction, where the first byte is the opcode, the second is the data to be loaded into the LSB portion of the SP register, and the third byte is the data to be loaded into the MSB portion of the register.

To load the 16-bit SP register with the number 7FFFH, for instance, the corresponding object code listing would be

```
31 FF 7F
```

Note the reversal of the higher- and lower-order data bytes in the object-code version.

Doing load immediate instructions involving the 16-bit IX and IY registers are unique inasmuch as they use 2-byte opcodes. The opcode for loading the IX register, for instance, is DD 21, and the opcode for doing a LD IY instruction is FD 21.

Loading either the IX or IY registers thus calls for a 4-byte instruction in the program memory: two opcode bytes, a data byte to be loaded to the LSB portion of the register, and a data byte to be loaded to the MSB portion.

An instruction such as

```
LD IX, 3C10H
```

literally means: Load the 16-bit IX register, in an immediate fashion, with the hexadecimal number 3C10. The corresponding object code is

```
DD 21 10 3C
```

DD 21 is the peculiar 2-byte opcode, 10 is the byte to be loaded to the LSB portion of IX, and 3C is the byte to be loaded to the MSB part of that register.

Assuming that the instruction is to be loaded into the program memory, beginning at address 1000H, the complete listing looks like this:

```
1000 DD 21 10 3C    LD IX, 3C10H    ;LOAD THE IX REGISTER WITH 3C10H
```

EXAMPLE 4-2

Write and assemble a program that uses only 16-bit load immediate instructions to carry out the following operations. Begin the program at memory address 7C00H.

1. Load 0001H to the BC register pair.

2. Load 0203H to the DE register pair.

3. Load 0405H to the HL register pair.

4. Load 0607H to the SP register.

5. Load 0809H to the IX register.

6. Load 0A0BH to the IY register.

The result is shown in Program 4-2.

PROGRAM 4-2   Z-80 LISTING FOR EXAMPLE 4-2

```
7C00  01  01 00     LD BC,0001H    ;0001H TO THE BC REGISTER PAIR
7C03  11  03 02     LD DE,0203H    ;0203H TO THE DE REGISTER PAIR
7C06  21  05 04     LD HL,0405H    ;0405H TO THE HL REGISTER PAIR
7C09  31  07 06     LD SP,0607H    ;0607H TO THE SP REGISTER
7C0C  DD  21 09 08  LD IX,0809H    ;0809H TO THE IX REGISTER
7C10  FD  21 0B 0A  LD IY,0A0BH    ;0A0BH TO THE IY REGISTER
```

EXAMPLE 4-3

Write and assemble a program that uses 8-bit load immediate instructions to load the
B, C, D, E, H, and L registers, and 16-bit load immediate instructions to load the IX,
IY, and SP registers as follows. Begin the program at memory address 7C00H.

```
B=00H      C=01H       D=02H       E=03H       H=04H
L=05H      SP=0607H    IX=0809H    IY=0A0BH
```

The result is shown in Program 4-3.

PROGRAM 4-3   Z-80 LISTING FOR EXAMPLE 4-3

```
7C00  06  00      LD B,00H       ;00H TO THE B REGISTER
7C02  0E  01      LD C,01H       ;01H TO THE C REGISTER
7C04  16  02      LD D,02H       ;02H TO THE D REGISTER
7C06  1E  03      LD E,03H       ;03H TO THE E REGISTER
7C08  26  04      LD H,04H       ;04H TO THE H REGISTER
7C0A  2E  05      LD L,05H       ;05H TO THE L REGISTER
7C0C  31  07 06   LD SP,0607H    ;0607H TO THE SP REGISTER
7C0F  DD  21 09 08 LD IX,0809H   ;0809H TO THE IX REGISTER
7C13  FD  21 0B 0A LD IY,0A0BH   ;0A0BH TO THE IY REGISTER
```

Compare the content of the registers involved in Examples 4-2 and
4-3. You should discover that the same overall task is performed in both
instances—the register contents are the same after executing Programs 4-2
and 4-3.

Exercises for Section 4-1

1. Name the Z-80 registers that can be loaded by means of 8-bit load immediate instructions.

2. Which 8-bit registers in the Z-80 can be paired to be loaded as 16-bit registers?

3. Which registers in the Z-80 can be loaded *only* by means of 16-bit load immediate instructions?

4. Which *one* 8-bit register can be loaded with an 8-bit load immediate instruction, but cannot be affected by any of the 16-bit load immediate instructions?

5. Specify a sequence of two 8-byte instructions and then a single 16-byte instruction that will set D=2A and E=1F.

6. Use only 8-bit load immediate instructions to write and assemble a program that loads some registers as follows:

A=1FH   B=2EH   C=3DH   D=4CH   E=5BH   H=6AH   L=79H

Begin the program at address 1000H.

7. Use only 16-bit load immediate instructions to load the B, C, D, E, H, and L registers as specified in problem 6.

8. Why are the SP, IX, and IY registers excluded from the 8-bit load immediate instructions?

9. Why is the accumulator (A register) excluded from the set of 16-bit load immediate instructions?

4-2 LOAD IMMEDIATE INSTRUCTIONS FOR THE 8080A/8085

In many respects, Intel's 8080A/8085 and Zilog's Z-80 microprocessors are very much alike. What you learn about the Z-80 instruction set can be applied to the 8080A/8085 device.

8-Bit Load Immediate Instructions

Figure 4-5 shows the 8-bit registers that can take part in load immediate instructions for the 8080A/8085 microprocessor. It can be helpful to note that the seven registers have the same letter designations as those used for the Z-80 device.

Table 4-3 shows the corresponding load immediate instructions—one for loading each of the seven 8-bit registers from the program memory.

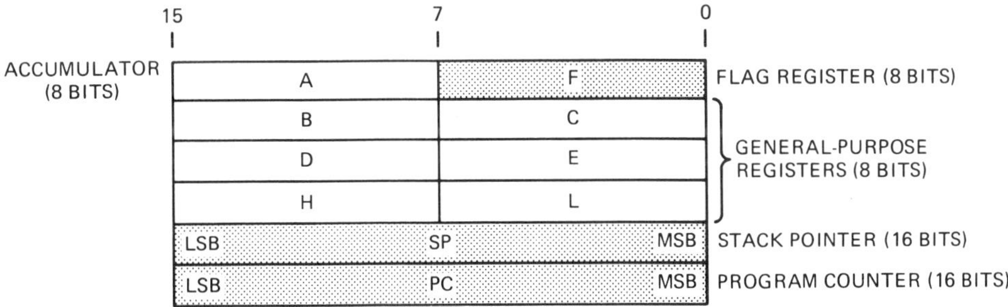

Figure 4-5 8080A/8085 registers for doing 8-bit load immediate operations. Shaded registers are not involved.

TABLE 4-3 8080A/8085 INSTRUCTION SET FOR 8-BIT LOAD IMMEDIATE OPERATIONS

Source code	Object code	Symbolic notation
MVI A,*data*	3E *byte*	
MVI B,*data*	06 *byte*	
MVI C,*data*	0E *byte*	$r \leftarrow data$
MVI D,*data*	16 *byte*	*data* is loaded into register *r*
MVI E,*data*	1E *byte*	
MVI H,*data*	26 *byte*	
MVI L,*data*	2E *byte*	

As far as the source-code mnemonics are concerned, the 8080A/8085 scheme uses MVI, followed by a register designation, a comma, and the 8-bit data to be loaded from program memory to the register. For example, MVI D,30H literally means: Move immediate (or load) to register D the value 30 hexadecimal.

The object codes are all 2-byte codes—an opcode followed by a hexadecimal representation of the 8-bit data to be loaded. It cannot pass without noticing that the opcodes are identical to those designated for the corresponding Z-80 load immediate operations.

So if you have thoroughly studied the 8-bit load immediate instructions for the Z-80 in Section 4-1, you will have no difficulty understanding the 8080A/8085 versions. Only the mnemonics for the source-code operators are different.

EXAMPLE 4-4

Write and assemble an 8080A/8085 program, using only 8-bit load immediate instructions, to do the following:

00H to A, 01H to B, 02H to C, 03H to D, 04H to E, 05H to H and 06H to L

Begin the program at address 0C00H.
The result is shown in Program 4-4. Compare that listing with the Z-80 version of the same programming task in Program 4-1.

16-Bit Load Immediate Instructions

Figure 4-6 illustrates the 8080A/8085 registers involved in its family of 16-bit load immediate instructions. The only true 16-bit register involved is the

PROGRAM 4-4 8080A/8085 LISTING FOR EXAMPLE 4-4

```
0C00  3E  00    MVI  A,00H      ;00H TO THE ACCUMULATOR
0C02  06  01    MVI  B,01H      ;01H TO REGISTER  B
0C04  0E  02    MVI  C,02H      ;02H TO REGISTER  C
0C06  16  03    MVI  D,03H      ;03H TO REGISTER  D
0C08  1E  04    MVI  E,04H      ;04H TO REGISTER  E
0C0A  26  05    MVI  H,05H      ;05H TO REGISTER  H
0C0C  2E  06    MVI  L,06H      ;06H TO REGISTER  L
```

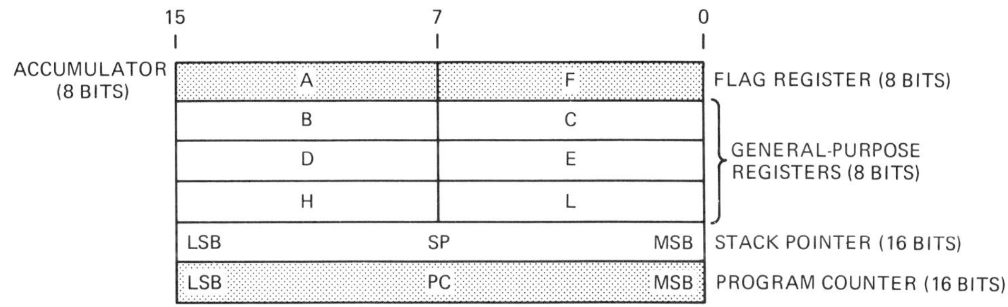

Figure 4-6 8080A/8085 register configurations for doing 16-bit load immediate operations. Shaded registers are not involved.

stack pointer (SP) register. The remaining registers are really 8-bit register pairs: B and C, D and E, H and L.

The 8-bit registers can be loaded separately by the 8-bit load immediate instructions, or they can be loaded two at a time by means of the appropriate 16-bit load immediate versions.

The only significant difference between this 16-bit load immediate scheme and that used with the Z-80 system is the fact that this one does not include operations for the IX and IY registers—the 8080A/8085 does not have such registers available.

The 16-bit load immediate instruction set is summarized in Table 4-4.

The source-code mnemonic for 16-bit load immediate instructions is LXI, followed by a register designation and the two bytes to be loaded into it. The object-code format uses 3 bytes of program memory. The first byte is the operand, designating the register pair, and the 2 bytes of data to be loaded to the register or register pair.

TABLE 4-4 8080A/8085 INSTRUCTION SET FOR 16-BIT LOAD IMMEDIATE OPERATIONS

Source code	Object code
LXI B, *data data*	01 *byte byte*
LXI D, *data data*	11 *byte byte*
LXI H, *data data*	21 *byte byte*
LXI SP, *data data*	31 *byte byte*

Note: The designations for registers B, D, and H actually imply register-pair loading operations: BC pair, DE pair, and HL pair. The first byte following the opcode is loaded into the lower order of the register [pairs (C, E, L) or the lower-order byte position of register] SP. The last byte is loaded into the higher order of the register pairs (B, D, H) or the higher-order byte position of register SP.

When necessary to load the 16-bit SP register, the source code listing might look like this:

LXI SP,4FFFH

That means: Load immediate the SP register with hexadecimal 4FFF.

The object-code version of that same instruction is

31 FF 4F

The first byte in the instruction, 31, is the opcode from the instruction set. The second byte is the data to be loaded to the LSB portion of the SP register, and the third byte is the data to be loaded into the MSB portion. Like the Z-80 scheme, this one uses an apparent reversal of the two bytes to be loaded—LSB followed by MSB.

An instruction for loading the BC register pair by means of a 16-bit load immediate instruction looks like this:

LXI B,4A12H   01 12 4A

Although the mnemonic in the source-code expression designates only the B register, the fact that the C register is involved is implied. Literally, LXI B, 4A12H means: Load immediate the BC register pair with the hexadecimal number 4A12. Similarly, an LXI D implies a load immediate to the DE register pair, and LXI H implies a load immediate to the HL register pair.

The operations are identical to those of the Z-80; only the syntax of the source-code listings are different.

EXAMPLE 4-5

Write and assemble a program that uses only 16-bit load immediate instructions to carry out the following operations with an 8080A/8085 microprocessor. Begin the program at memory address 7C00H.

1. Load 0001H to the BC register pair.
2. Load 0203H to the DE register pair.
3. Load 0405H to the HL register pair.
4. Load 0607H to the SP register.

See the result in Program 4-5. Compare the listing with the Z-80 version of a similar program in Program 4-2. Explain the differences.

PROGRAM 4-5   8080A/8085 LISTING FOR EXAMPLE 4-5

```
7C00 01 01 00    LXI B, 0001H    ;0001H TO THE BC REGISTER PAIR
7C03 11 03 02    LXI D, 0203H    ;0203H TO THE DE REGISTER PAIR
7C06 21 05 04    LXI H, 0405H    ;0405H TO THE HL REGISTER PAIR
7C08 31 07 06    LXI SP,0607H    ;0607H TO THE SP REGISTER
```

Exercises for Section 4-2

1. Name the 8080A/8085 registers that can be loaded by means of 8-bit load immediate instructions.
2. Which 8-bit registers in the 8080A/8085 can be paired to be loaded as 16-bit registers?
3. Name the 8080A/8085 register that can be loaded *only* by means of an 8-bit load immediate instruction.
4. Name the 8080A/8085 register that can be loaded only by means of a 16-bit load immediate instruction.
5. Use only 8-bit load immediate instructions to write and assemble an 8080A/8085 program that loads some registers as follows:

    A=1FH   B=2EH   C=3DH   D=4CH   E=5BH   H=6AH   L=79H

    Begin the program at address 1000H.
6. Use only 16-bit load immediate instructions to load the 8080A/8085 registers as follows:

    B=2EH   C=3DH   D=4CH   E=5BH   H=6AH   L=79H

    Begin the program at address 1000H, and compare your results with the listing generated in problem 5.
7. Draw up a table showing Z-80 and 8080A/8085 load immediate instructions that perform identical tasks.
8. Why are there no 16-bit load immediate instructions for loading the A register?

4-3 LOAD IMMEDIATE INSTRUCTIONS FOR THE 6502

The instruction set for MOS Technology's 6502 microprocessor is a rather simple one. The simplicity results from two special features of the 6502 device: It has only three 8-bit registers that are open to load immediate operations, and it has no 16-bit registers that can be loaded in that fashion. Figure 4-7 thus completely illustrates the 6502 registers involved in the load immediate instructions.

The corresponding load immediate instruction set is shown in Table 4-5.

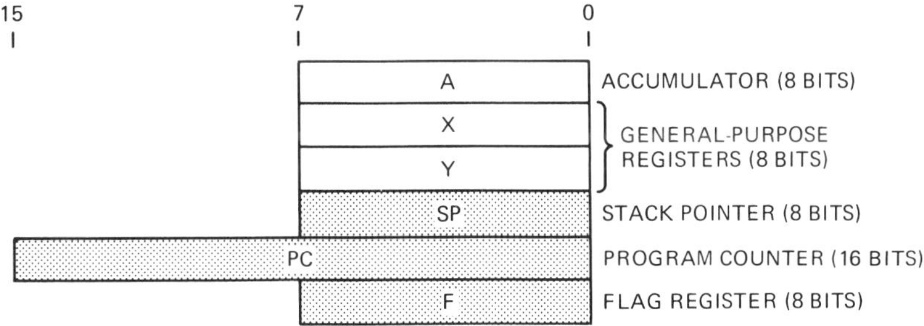

Figure 4-7   6502 registers for doing 8-bit load immediate operations. Shaded registers are not involved.

TABLE 4-5 6502 INSTRUCTION SET
FOR LOAD IMMEDIATE OPERATIONS

Source code	Object code
LDA #*data*	A9 *byte*
LDX #*data*	A2 *byte*
LDY #*data*	A0 *byte*

The general idea is to load one of the three working registers—A, X, or Y—with a byte of data from the program memory. Such an operation requires a 2-byte object code—an opcode followed by the byte to be loaded. The opcode specifies the register to receive the data byte.

The syntax for 6502 load immediate operations is quite different from either the Z-80 or 8080A/8085 devices. The operators in this case are LDA, LDX, and LDY, implying load operations to registers A, X, and Y, respectively.

As far as the load immediate operations are concerned, the operand in the source-code mnemonic must be preceded with a pound-sign symbol (#). This particular symbol distinguishes a load immediate operation from other families of register-loading operations that use the same LDA-LDX-LDY operators.

Another difference in the 6502 syntax is that hexadecimal numbers are marked by preceding them with a dollar-sign ($), as opposed to an H suffix used in the syntax for Z-80 and 8080A/8085 devices.

Thus

LDA #$2A

literally means: Load immediate to register A the hexadecimal value 2A. Omitting the dollar-sign symbol implies that the data is in a decimal format. LDA #42, in other words, loads register A with the same bit format as LDA #$2A does.

EXAMPLE 4-6

Write and assemble a 6502 program that uses load immediate operations to do the following:

$00 to A, $01 to X, and $02 to Y

Begin the program at address $FFF0. See the results in Program 4-6.

Exercises for Section 4-3

1. Why are there no 16-bit load immediate operations for the 6502 microprocessor?
2. Write and assemble a 6502 program that uses load immediate instructions to load the registers as follows:

A=$1F   X=$2E   Y=$3D

Begin the program at address $1000.

```
FFF0 A0 00   LDA #$00     $00 TO THE A REGISTER
FFF2 A9 01   LDX #$01     $01 TO THE X REGISTER
FFF4 A0 02   LDY #$02     $02 TO THE Y REGISTER
```

3. As far as the source-code syntax is concerned, what distinguishes a load immediate operation from other instructions using the same operators?

4. As far as the 6502 syntax is concerned, how are source-code hexadecimal numbers distinguished from decimal numbers?

5. How do the X and Y registers in the 6502 microprocessor differ from the IX and IY registers in the Z-80?

4-4 LOAD IMMEDIATE INSTRUCTIONS FOR THE 6800

Just as there are many similarities between the load immediate instructions and operations for the Z-80 and 8080A/8085 devices, there are some similarities of the same sort between the 6502 and Motorola's 6800 microprocessors. In any case, the whole idea behind a load immediate instruction is to load a register with data specified in the program memory.

8-Bit Load Immediate Instructions

As indicated in Fig. 4-8, the 6800 has two 8-bit registers that can be loaded in an immediate fashion: accumulators A and B. Although 6800 users tend to call these registers *accumulator A* and *accumulator B*, we will refer to accumulator B as simply the *B register*. That nomenclature will provide a thread of consistency through the discussions.

Since there are only two 8-bit registers available for load immediate instructions, it figures that there are only two such instructions in the 6800's instruction set. They are specified in Table 4-6.

The object codes are quite different from those used with the 6502 device, but there are some striking similarities as far as the source-code syntax is concerned.

LDAA and LDAB are the source-code operators for doing a load imme-

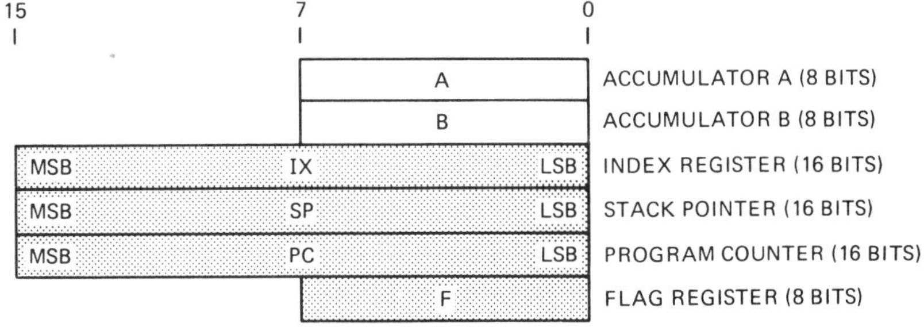

Figure 4-8   6800 registers for doing 8-bit load immediate operations. Shaded registers are not involved.

TABLE 4-6 6800 INSTRUCTION SET
FOR 8-BIT LOAD IMMEDIATE
OPERATIONS

Source code	Object code
LDAA #*data*	86 *byte*
LDAB #*data*	C6 *byte*

diate to registers A and B, respectively. A pound-sign symbol precedes the data designation, signaling a load immediate operation (as opposed to some other types of loading operations that also carry the LDAA and LDAB operators). Then, too, hexadecimal numbers are marked with a dollar-sign symbol preceding them.

Thus

```
LDAA  #$2A
LDAB  #$10
```

means: Load the A register in an immediate fashion with hexadecimal 2A, and load immediate the B register with hexadecimal 10.

A complete program listing for that particular sequence of load immediate operations would look like this:

```
0C00 86 2A   LDAA #$2A    $2A TO ACCUMULATOR A
0C02 C6 10   LDAB L$10    $10 TO REGISTER B
```

That example assumes that the program listing begins at address $0C00. The arrangement of bytes in the program memory would follow this pattern:

```
0C00  86
0C01  2A
0C02  C6
0C03  10
```

The next instruction would thus begin at address $0C04.

16-Bit Load Immediate Instructions

Figure 4-9 shows that the 6800 microprocessor has two 16-bit registers, and Table 4-7 illustrates the fact that they can be loaded only by 16-bit instructions.

Two 16-bit registers; two 16-bit load immediate instructions—that figures. An instruction such as LDX #$2345 literally means: Load immediate the 16-bit IX register with the hexadecimal number 2345. LDS #$4A2B means: Load immediate the SP register with hexadecimal 4A2B.

If you have been following the discussions in this chapter with due care, you should find nothing strikingly different, or at least unusual, about these

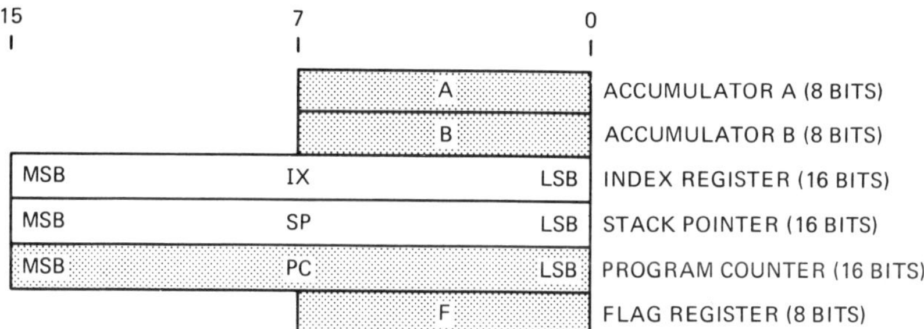

Figure 4-9   6800 registers for doing 16-bit load immediate operations. Shaded registers are not involved.

TABLE 4-7 6800 INSTRUCTION SET FOR 16-BIT LOAD IMMEDIATE OPERATIONS

Source code	Object code
LDX *data data*	CE *byte byte*
LDS *data data*	8E *byte byte*

Note: The byte following the opcode goes into the MSB position of the register, while the third byte goes to the LSB position. This is contrary to the typical 16-bit loading operation illustrated in Fig. 4-2.

16-bit instruction formats. But there is a big and vital difference as far as the object-code format is concerned.

Unlike all other microprocessors described in this chapter, *the 16-bit load immediate object codes are written such that the byte following the opcode goes to the MSB position in the register, and the final byte goes to the LSB position.* By contrast, the other microprocessors load the LSB position first.

The object-code listing for LDX #$2345 is thus CE 23 45, *not* CE 45 23. Suppose that the programming situation is this:

1.   Load immediate to the IX register $4A00.
2.   Load immediate to the SP register $0FFF.

If the program address begins at $7000, the assembled listing takes this general form:

```
7000 CE 4A 00   LDX #$4A00   $4A00 TO THE IX REGISTER
7003 8E 0F FF   LDS #$0FFF   $0FFF TO THE SP REGISTER
```

As far as the program memory is concerned, these instructions would appear in this order:

```
7000  CE
7001  4A
7002  00
7003  8E
7004  0F
7005  FF
```

Exercises for Section 4-4

1. Name the 6800 registers that can be loaded by means of 8-bit load immediate instructions.
2. Name the 6800 registers that can be loaded by means of 16-bit load immediate instructions.
3. Write a 6800 program that loads the registers as follows:

   A=$01   B-$2F   IX=$1F2E   SP=$FF00

   Begin the program at address $1000.
4. Describe the most significant difference between the 16-bit load immediate operations for the 6800 and those for the Z-80 and 8080A/8085.

5

Register Transfer Instructions

Most microprocessor programming instructions concern the matter of moving data from one place in the system to another. In the case of load immediate instructions (Chapter 4), the data are moved from their place in the program memory to a designated register within the microprocessor device.

The register transfer instructions featured in this chapter also move data from one place to another. But in this case, the data are simply moved from one register to another within the microprocessor.

Figure 5-1 illustrates a typical register transfer operation. A byte of data resides in register A at the outset. Perhaps it was loaded there at an earlier time by means of a load immediate instruction. Upon executing the proper sort of register transfer instruction, the data originally appearing in register A are transferred to register B. *At the conclusion of the operation, the same byte of data appears in both registers.* In a manner of speaking, a register transfer operation copies data from one register to another.

The register supplying the data is called the *source register*, and the one receiving the transferred data is called the *destination register*. Register transfer operations are thus represented as a source-to-destination register operations. The symbolic form of a register transfer instruction generally takes this form:

$$r_d \leftarrow r_s$$

where r_d is the destination register and r_s is the source register.

The data are always copied from the source register to the destination register. The original content of the source register then appears in both of them, and *the original content of the destination register is lost.*

Microprocessors generally include register transfer instructions for every

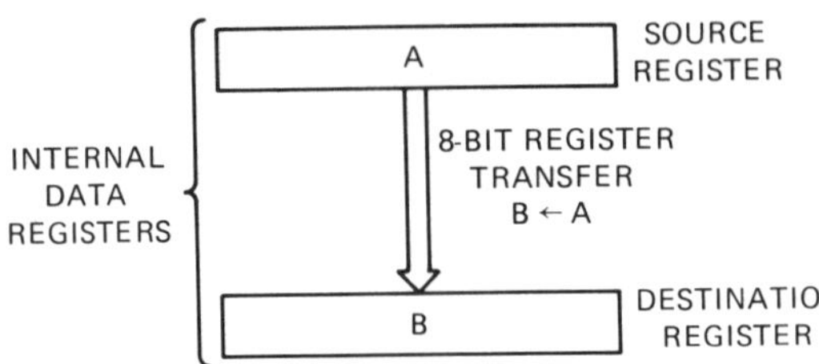

Figure 5-1 Schematic representation of an 8-bit register transfer operation.

8-bit register, and the program instructions are most often simple, 1-byte instructions. The 1-byte instruction designates:

1. That a register transfer instruction is at hand
2. The source register
3. The destination register

The register transfer instruction includes nothing concerning the exact nature of the data to be transferred. The source register must be loaded with some well-defined data prior to doing a register transfer. Otherwise, the programmer has no idea at all concerning the nature of the data being transferred.

Using Z-80 mnemonics, a typical program sequence involving a register transfer instructions looks like this:

```
LD  A,02H
LD  B,A
```

The first instruction in that particular sequence does a load immediate to register A. A well-defined byte of data, 02 hexadecimal, is loaded to register A from the program memory.

The second instruction is a register transfer instruction that calls for transferring the byte from register A to register B. At the conclusion of the two operations, the 02H byte appears in both of those registers.

In principle, at least, microprocessor instruction sets could also include register transfer operations for 16-bit registers. The idea would be to transfer 2 bytes of data from one 16-bit register (or an 8-bit register pair) to another register of the same size. In practice, however, there are very few 16-bit register transfer instructions.

But there is a distinctly different kind of register transfer instruction that most often applies to 16-bit registers—register exchange instructions.

A *register exchange* instruction literally swaps the contents of two registers. The data originally appearing in the two registers are not lost—merely exchange. Figure 5-2 illustrates a case where the content of an HL register pair is exchanged with that of a DE register pair. What originally appeared in the HL pair is transferred to the DE pair, and vice versa.

The fact that none of the original data are lost distinguishes a register exchange instruction from a simple register transfer instruction.

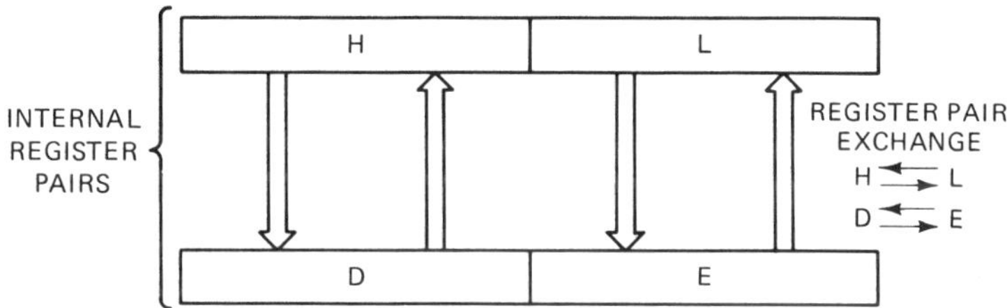

Figure 5-2   Schematic representation of a register-pair exchange operation.

The commonly accepted symbolic notation for a register exchange operation shows the arrow pointing in two directions:

$$r_1 \leftrightharpoons r_2$$

Neither can be considered the source or destination register. Both registers play a dual role in this sense.

5-1 Z-80 REGISTER TRANSFERS AND EXCHANGES

The Z-80 microprocessor, having more internal working registers than any other described in this book, features the largest number of register transfer and exchange instructions.

8-Bit Register Transfer Instructions

Figure 5-3 shows the Z-80's registers that can be directly involved in its 8-bit register transfer instructions. The registers include all seven primary, 8-bit working registers as well as two special-purpose registers, I and R.

The I and R registers are included here merely for the sake of completeness; a discussion of their purpose in the system appears in a later chapter.

Table 5-1 lists the source and object codes for the register transfer instructions. The table is a rather extensive one, for the simple reason that there are a lot of different combinations of source and destination registers.

If a system had only two registers, say registers A and B, there would be just two register transfer instructions: one for transferring the content of A to B, and a second for transferring the content of register B to A. But the Z-80 has seven main working registers, and that figures out to a lot of possible source-to-destination combinations.

Note from the listing in Table 5-1 that all the mnemonics begin with LD. That implies a loading operation of some sort; and, indeed, a register transfer operation falls into that general category.

The first letter following the LD operator is the destination register, and the letter following the comma is the source register. A mnemonic such as LD A,C thus means: Load the current content of register C into register A. Or, alternatively, transfer the content of register C to register A. An ex-

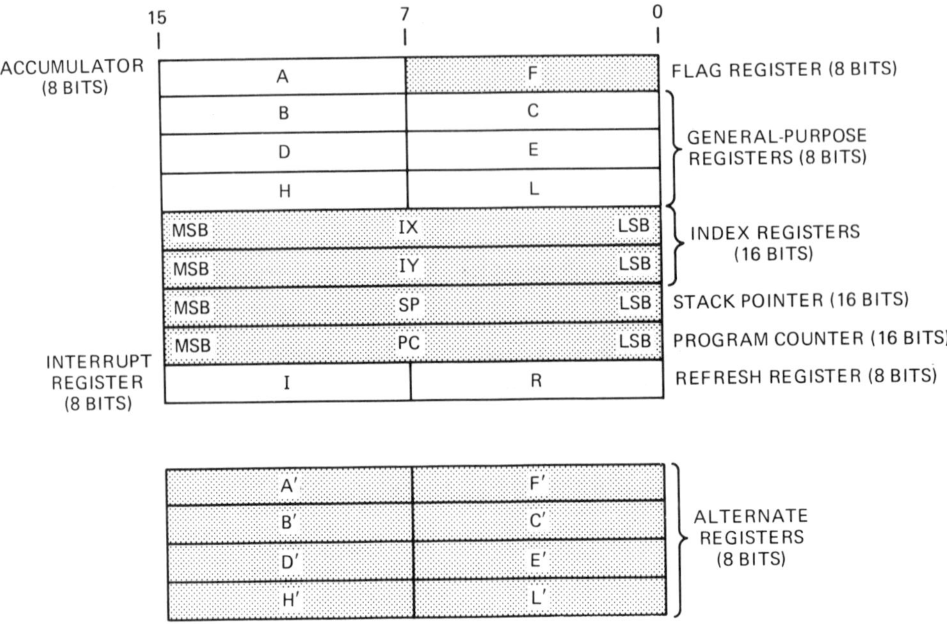

Figure 5-3 Z-80 registers for 8-bit register transfer instructions. Shaded registers are not involved.

pression such as LD C,A, on the other hand, means: Load the content of register A to register C.

Looking over the listing, you will find expressions such as LD A,A and LD B,B. Those are "transfer-to-self" instructions. LD A,A literally means: Load the content of register A to itself. The data do not go anywhere, and one must wonder about the practical value of an instruction that essentially does nothing. It seems that the only reason for including such instructions is to make the register transfer family of operations logically complete. As described later, however, there are some practical applications for them.

TABLE 5-1 Z-80 INSTRUCTION SET FOR 8-BIT REGISTER TRANSFER INSTRUCTIONS

Source code	Object code	Symbolic notation
LD A,A	7F	
LD A,B	78	
LD A,C	79	$A \leftarrow r$
LD A,D	7A	(load the content of register r to register A)
LD A,E	7B	
LD A,H	7C	
LD A,L	7D	
LD B,A	47	
LD B,B	40	
LD B,C	41	

Source code	Object code	Symbolic notation
LD B,D	42	$B \leftarrow r$
LD B,E	43	(load the content of register r to register B)
LD B,H	44	
LD B,L	45	
LD C,A	4F	
LD C,B	48	
LD C,C	49	$C \leftarrow r$
LD C,D	4A	(load the content of register r to register C)
LD C,E	4B	
LD C,H	4C	
LD C,L	4D	
LD D,A	57	
LD D,B	50	
LD D,C	51	$D \leftarrow r$
LD D,D	52	(load the content of register r to register D)
LD D,E	53	
LD D,H	54	
LD D,L	55	
LD E,A	5F	
LD E,B	58	
LD E,C	59	$E \leftarrow r$
LD E,D	5A	(load the content of register r to register E)
LD E,E	5B	
LD E,H	5C	
LD E,L	5D	
LD H,A	67	
LD H,B	60	
LD H,C	61	$H \leftarrow r$
LD H,D	62	(load the content of register r to register H)
LD H,E	63	
LD H,H	64	
LD H,L	65	
LD L,A	6F	
LD L,B	68	
LD L,C	69	$L \leftarrow r$
LD L,D	6A	(load the content of register r to register L)
LD L,E	6B	
LD L,H	6C	
LD L,L	6D	

Specials

Source code	Object code	Symbolic notation
LD A,I	ED 57	$A \leftarrow I$
LD I,A	ED 47	$I \leftarrow A$
LD A,R	ED 5F	$A \leftarrow R$
LD R,A	ED 4F	$R \leftarrow A$

Aside from the special transfer instructions involving registers I and R, all Z-80 register transfers are programmed as 1-byte instructions. Each requires just 1 byte of program memory. As far as programming efficiency is concerned, they are very efficient instructions.

To get a preliminary idea about how the Z-80 register transfer instructions work, suppose you want to write a program that uses a load immediate instruction to place a hexadecimal 21 into the A register, and then use a transfer instruction to move that same byte to register B. The source-code version of the program would look like this:

```
LD A,21H      ;21H TO THE A REGISTER
LD B,A        ;TRANSFER A TO B
```

If the program is to begin at address 7000H, the assembled, object-code version of the program will take on this appearance:

```
7000 3E 21
7002 47
```

And the complete listing looks like this:

```
7000 3E 21   LD A,21H     ;21H TO THE A REGISTER
7002 47      LD B,A       ;TRANSFER A TO B
```

When this short program is executed, the data byte (21H) is loaded from the program memory to register A via the load immediate instruction. Then that same byte is effectively copied into register B by the register transfer instruction. The overall result is that 21 (hexadecimal) appears in *both* registers A and B.

How does the result of that example compare with this one?

```
7000 06 21   LD B,21H     ;21H TO REGISTER B
7002 78      LD A,B       ;TRANSFER B TO A
```

The end result is the same in both cases: a 21 (hexadecimal) ends up in both register A and B.

EXAMPLE 5-1

Write and assemble a program that uses a single 8-bit load immediate operation and a series of 8-bit register transfer instructions to load all seven working registers with zeros. Begin the program at address 4C00H.

The result is shown in Program 5-1. Actually, that listing is just one of many possible listings for doing the same overall task. You should be able to work out several different listings that accomplish the same task. .

The next example emphasizes the point that the data content of the destination register is always lost during a register transfer operation. The

```
4C00 3E 00   LD A,00H      ;LOAD IMMEDIATE 00 TO A
4C02 47      LD B,A        ;TRANSFER 00 FROM A TO B
4C03 48      LD C,B        ;TRANSFER 00 FROM B TO C
4C04 51      LD D,C        ;TRANSFER 00 FROM C TO D
4C05 5A      LD E,D        ;TRANSFER 00 FROM D TO E
4C06 63      LD H,E        ;TRANSFER 00 FROM E TO H
4C07 6C      LD L,H        ;TRANSFER 00 FROM H TO L
```

example calls for exchanging the contents of two registers without losing the original data in either of them. Doing that sort of procedure calls for using a third register as a temporary data storage place.

EXAMPLE 5-2

Write and assemble a program that exchanges the content of registers A and B. Use register C as a temporary storage place as necessary, and begin the program at address 1000H.

The result is shown in Program 5-2. It begins by saving the original content of register A in C, and then transferring the content of the B register to register A. At that point in the program, the exchange is one-half done: the original content of register B is in A. The final instruction fetches the original A-register data, transferring it to register B. The exchange is thus complete. Register C still holds the original content of register A, but that is of no consequence here.

16-Bit Register Transfers and Exchanges

Figure 5-4 shows the Z-80 registers that can be included in 16-bit register transfers and exchange operations. Judging from the large number of registers involved in these operations, it would seem that there would be a large number of instructions for carrying them out. But it turns out that the instruction set covers very few of the 16-bit transfer/exchange possibilities. See Table 5-2.

The first three instructions in Table 5-2 are the Z-80's 16-bit register transfers:

```
LD SP,HL
LD SP,IX
LD SP,IY
```

Notice that all three of them load the SP register and that the sources are limited to the HL register pair and the IX and IY registers. No other Z-80 registers are directly involved in such transfers. Those instructions literally

PROGRAM 5-2 Z-80 LISTING FOR EXAMPLE 5-2

```
1000 4F   LD C,A   ;SAVE A IN C
1001 78   LD A,B   ;TRANSFER B TO A
1002 41   LD B,C   ;ORIGINAL A TO B
```

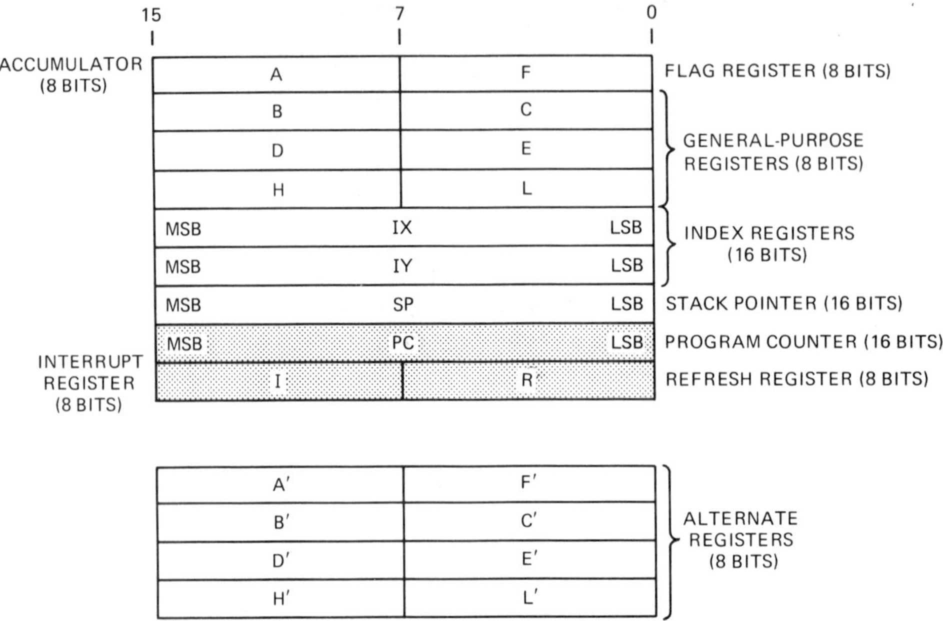

Figure 5-4 Z-80 register configurations for 16-bit register transfer and exchange instructions. Shaded registers are not involved.

mean: Load the stack pointer (SP register) with the content of the designated 16-bit register, or 8-bit register pair. Upon executing the instruction, the SP register takes on the same 16-bit number that is present in the source register.

In the case of a transfer from the HL register pair to the SP register (LD SP,HL), the content of the H register goes to the MSB position in the SP register, and the content of the L register goes to the LSB position.

The remaining instructions in Table 5-2 are register exchange instructions. Most of them involve the alternate registers: A', B', C', D', E', F', H', and L'. In fact, the 16-bit exchange instructions provide the only avenue for communicating with the alternate registers in the Z-80 microprocessor device.

TABLE 5-2 Z-80 INSTRUCTION SET FOR 16-BIT REGISTER TRANSFER AND EXCHANGE INSTRUCTIONS

Source code	Object code	Symbolic notation
LD SP,HL	F9	SP←HL
LD SP,IX	DD F9	SP←IX
LD SP,IY	FD F9	SP←IY
EX AF,AF'	08	AF⇌AF'
EX DE,HL	E8	DE⇌HL
EXX	D9	BC⇌BC' DE⇌DE' HL⇌HL'

There are no load immediate instructions for the alternate registers, for instance. The only way to do an effective load immediate to them is by loading their primary counterparts first, and then doing an exchange operation. If, for example, you want to load hexadecimal 2A to register B', it is necessary to load that value to the nonprimed B register (LD B,2AH), and then do an EXX instruction.

As shown in the instruction set, the EXX instruction exchanges the BC, DE, and HL register pairs with their primed, or alternate, versions. There are no provisions for exchanging just one of the registers or even just one of the register pairs—it is a matter of taking all three register-pair exchanges, or none at all.

The exchange instruction EX AF,AF' is the only available mechanism for working with the A' register, and one of very few instructions that deal directly with the F (flag) register. We have not yet discussed the purpose of the flag register, but it is sufficient to realize that it is possible to exchange its 8-bit content with its F' counterpart. This exchange instruction works with both the A and F registers, and one cannot be exchanged with the alternate counterpart without exchanging the other as well.

Perhaps the most commonly used exchange instruction, however, is one that exchanges the content of the DE register pair with the HL register pair (EX DE,HL). Upon executing this instruction, the content of the DE register pair appears in the HL pair, and vice versa. Example 5-3 illustrates the effectiveness of this register exchange instruction.

EXAMPLE 5-3

Write and assemble a program that uses only 8-bit register transfer instructions to perform the tasks accomplished by the EX DE,HL instruction. Begin the program at address 7000H.

The result is shown in Program 5-3. The first three instructions in the program effectively exchange the contents of the H and D registers, using the C register as a temporary storage place. Then the last three instructions exchange the contents of the L and E registers, again using the C register as a temporary storage register. The end result is that the content of the HL register pair is exchanged with that of the DE register pair.

By contrast, the same job could be done this way:

```
7000 E8   EX DE,HL      ;EXCHANGE DE,HL
```

PROGRAM 5-3   Z-80 LISTING FOR EXAMPLE 5-3

```
7000 4C   LD C,H      ;SAVE H IN C
7001 62   LD H,D      ;LOAD D TO H
7002 51   LD D,C      ;LOAD C TO D
                      ;THE H-D EXCHANGE IS DONE
7003 4D   LD C,L      ;SAVE L IN C
7004 6B   LD L,E      ;LOAD E TO L
7005 59   LD E,C      ;LOAD C TO E
                      ;THE L-E EXCHANGE IS DONE
```

1. List the Z-80 source and object codes for carrying out the following operations.
   (a) Load the content of register C to register A.
   (b) Load the content of register A to register C.
   (c) Load the content of register L to register H.
   (d) Load the content of register E to itself.

2. Verbally describe and write the object codes for the following source-code instructions.
   (a) LD E,L   (b) LD C,A   (c) LD A,C   (d) LD A,A   (e) LD SP,HL

3. Write and assemble a program that uses just *one* load immediate instruction and the fewest possible number of register transfers to fill the seven operating registers with hexadecimal FF. Begin the program addressing at 0A00H.

4. Write and assemble a Z-80 program that uses the fewest number of 8-bit and 16-bit load immediate instructions to fill all seven working registers with hexadecimal FF. Use *no* register transfer or exchange instructions, and begin the program at address 0A00H. How does the programming efficiency, in terms of program memory bytes, compare with the same overall task in problem 3?

5. Write and assemble a program that does the following:

   1. Load immediate 21H to A.
   2. Load immediate 34FFH to the BC register pair.
   3. Exchange the contents of the A and B registers without destroying the content of another register being used in the program.
   4. Load the content of C to D.

   Begin the listing at address 0A00H.

6. *Disassemble* (write the source-code program from its object-code listing) the following program. Specify the content of all seven operating registers at the conclusion of the program. (Where the content of a register cannot be determined, list its content as "undefined.")

```
0A00 01  00  3C
0A03 61
0A04 68
0A05 3E  FF
0A07 5F
```

5-2 8080A/8085 REGISTER TRANSFERS AND EXCHANGES

Given the fact that the 8080A/8085 microprocessor has fewer 16-bit registers and no alternate registers, its instruction set for register transfer and exchange operations is very similar to that of the Z-80. In fact, a complete understanding of such operations for the Z-80 is more than adequate for understanding the corresponding instructions for the 8080A/8085.

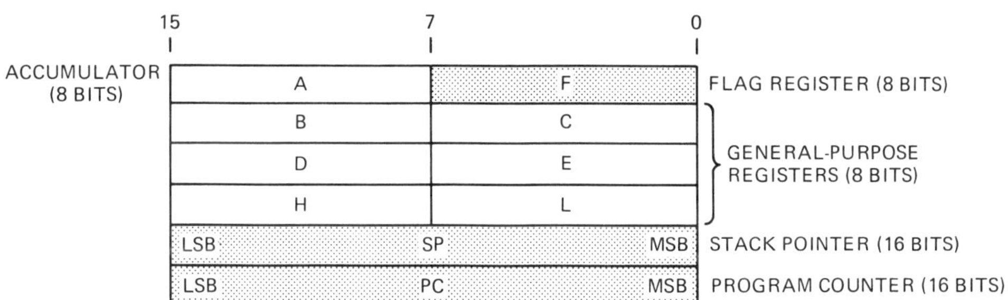

Figure 5-5   8080A/8085 registers for 8-bit register transfer instructions. Shaded registers are not involved.

8-Bit Register Transfer Instructions

Figure 5-5 shows the 8080A/8085 registers that can be involved in 8-bit register transfer operations, and Table 5-3 lists the instructions.

The similarities between this instruction set and the Z-80 version in Table 5-1 are striking. Aside from the fact that the 8080A/8085 does not have I and R registers that are accessible from the program instructions, the only difference is the mnemonics. Even the object codes are the same.

Consider the process of loading the content of register B to register A. This transfer instruction reads LD A, B for the Z-80 system, and MOV A, B for the 8080A/8085. The object codes are identical—78 hexadecimal. There is a clear, one-for-one correspondence between the 8-bit register transfer instructions for these two devices.

EXAMPLE 5-4

Write and assemble an 8080A/8085 program that uses a single 8-bit load immediate instruction and a series of 8-bit register transfer instructions to load all seven working registers with zeros. Begin the program at address 4C00H.

The result is shown in Program 5-4. Compare it with an identical task written for the Z-80 microprocessor in Program 5-1.

As in the case of the Z-80 instruction set, the 8080A/8085 system has no instructions for carrying out 8-bit register exchanges. That sort of operation has to be carried out by applying an appropriate sequence of 8-bit register transfer instructions. Look at Example 5-5.

EXAMPLE 5-5

Write and assemble an 8080A/8085 program that effectively exchanges the content of registers A and B. Use register C as a temporary storage place as necessary, and begin the program at address 1000H.

The result is shown as Program 5-5. Compare it with the same task as prescribed for the Z-80 in Program 5-2.

TABLE 5-3 8080A/8085 INSTRUCTION SET FOR 8-BIT REGISTER TRANSFER INSTRUCTIONS

Source code	Object code	Symbolic notation
MOV A,A	7F	
MOV A,B	78	
MOV A,C	79	
MOV A,D	7A	$A \leftarrow r$
MOV A,E	7B	(load the content of register r to register A)
MOV A,H	7C	
MOV A,L	7D	
MOV B,A	47	
MOV B,B	40	
MOV B,C	41	
MOV B,D	42	$B \leftarrow r$
MOV B,E	43	(load the content of register r to register B)
MOV B,H	44	
MOV B,L	45	
MOV C,A	4F	
MOV C,B	48	
MOV C,C	49	
MOV C,D	4A	$C \leftarrow r$
MOV C,E	4B	(load the content of register r to register C)
MOV C,H	4C	
MOV C,L	4D	
MOV D,A	57	
MOV D,B	50	
MOV D,C	51	
MOV D,D	52	$D \leftarrow r$
MOV D,E	53	(load the content of register r to register D)
MOV D,H	54	
MOV D,L	55	
MOV E,A	5F	
MOV E,B	58	
MOV E,C	59	
MOV E,D	5A	$E \leftarrow r$
MOV E,E	5B	(load the content of register r to register E)
MOV E,H	5C	
MOV E,L	5D	
MOV H,A	67	
MOV H,B	60	
MOV H,C	61	
MOV H,D	62	$H \leftarrow r$
MOV H,E	63	(load the content of register r to register H)
MOV H,H	64	
MOV H,L	65	
MOV L,A	6F	
MOV L,B	68	
MOV L,C	69	

Source code	Object code	Symbolic notation
MOV L,D	6A	$L \leftarrow r$
MOV L,E	6B	(load the content of register *r* to register L)
MOV L,H	6C	
MOV L,L	6D	

PROGRAM 5-4 8080A/8085 LISTING FOR EXAMPLE 5-4

```
4C00 3E 00   MVI A,00H  ;LOAD IMMEDIATE 00 TO A
4C02 47      MOV B,A    ;TRANSFER 00 FROM A TO B
4C03 48      MOV C,B    ;TRANSFER 00 FROM B TO C
4C04 51      MOV D,C    ;TRANSFER 00 FROM C TO D
4C05 5A      MOV E,D    ;TRANSFER 00 FROM D TO E
4C06 63      MOV H,E    ;TRANSFER 00 FROM E TO H
4C07 6C      MOV L,H    ;TRANSFER 00 FROM H TO L
```

PROGRAM 5-5 8080A/8085 LISTING FOR EXAMPLE 5-5

```
1000 4F   MOV C,A  ;SAVE A IN C
1001 78   MOV A,B  ;TRANSFER B TO A
1002 41   MOV B,C  ;ORIGINAL A TO B
```

If you are feeling that this presentation of 8-bit register transfer instructions is too brief, you should review the discussions of the same instructions for the Z-80 device in Section 5-1.

16-Bit Register Transfers and Exchanges

Figure 5-6 shows the 8080A/8085 registers that can be involved in 16-bit register transfer and exchange instructions. Table 5-4 summarizes the corresponding instruction codes.

Indeed, that is a very small set of instructions. There is just one 16-bit

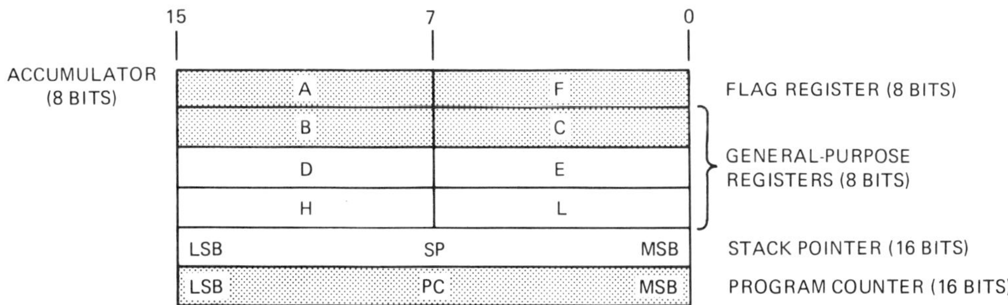

Figure 5-6 8080A/8085 register configurations for 16-bit register transfer and exchange instructions. Shaded registers are not involved.

Source code	Object code	Symbolic notation
SPHL	F9	SP ← HL
XCHG	EB	DE ⇌ HL

register transfer instruction, SPHL; and there is just one 16-bit register exchange, XCHG. Both involve the HL register pair.

As far as the 16-bit register transfer is concerned, the content of the HL register pair is loaded, or copied, into the SP register. The content of the H register goes to the MSB position in SP, and the content of the L register goes to the LSB position. After executing this instruction, the original content of the HL pair appears in both 16-bit registers.

The lone 16-bit exchange instruction, XCHG, swaps the contents of the DE and HL register pairs.

Exercises for Section 5-2

1. List the 8080A/8085 source and object codes for carrying out the following operations:
   (a) Load the content of register E to register H.
   (b) Load the content of register B to itself.
   (c) Load the content of register C to register D.
   (d) Load the content of the HL register pair to SP.
2. Verbally describe and write the object codes for the following source-code instructions:
   (a) MOV H,L   (b) MOV E,A   (c) MOV A,E   (d) XCHG
3. Write and assemble an 8080A/8085 program that uses only 8-bit register exchange instructions to perform the task of the XCHG instruction. Begin at address 4A00H.
4. Disassemble the following object-code program, using 8080A/8085 mnemonics. Specify the content of all seven 8-bit working registers after the program has been executed. (Where the content of a register cannot be determined, list its content as "undefined.") Compare the results with that of problem 6 in the Exercises for Section 5-1.

```
7000 01 00 3C
7003 61
7004 68
7005 3E FF
7007 5F
```

5-3 6502 REGISTER TRANSFER INSTRUCTIONS AND EXCHANGE OPERATIONS

Figure 5-7 and Table 5-5 completely summarize the 8-bit register transfer instructions available to the 6502 programmer. The general principles of reg-

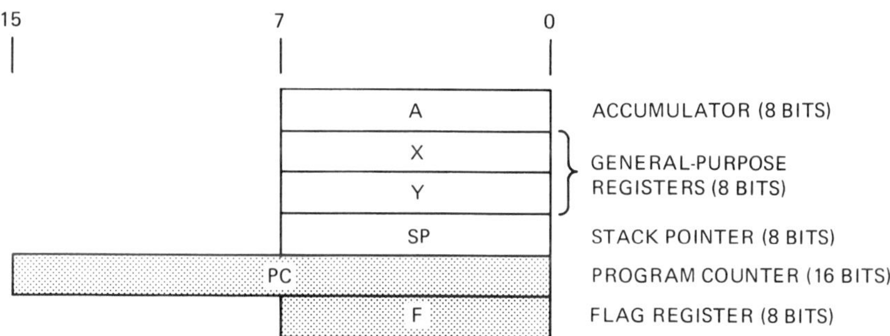

Figure 5-7 6502 registers for register transfer instructions. Shaded registers are not involved.

TABLE 5-5 6502 INSTRUCTION SET FOR 8-BIT REGISTER TRANSFER INSTRUCTIONS

Source code	Object code	Symbolic notation
TXA	8A	A ← X
TYA	98	A ← Y
TAX	AA	X ← A
TAY	A8	Y ← A
TSX	BA	X ← SP
TXS	9A	SP ← X

ister transfer are essentially the same as those described for the Z-80 and 8080A/8085 systems. In this case, however, there are fewer registers involved, and it turns out that all possible transfer combinations are not allowed.

Also, the 6502 registers available for transfer operations are all 8-bit registers, so there are no 16-bit register transfer instructions anywhere in the entire 6502 instruction set. Add the fact that there are no register exchange instructions, and the whole business comes out looking simpler than any of the transfer/exchange schemes described so far in this chapter.

Register Transfer Instructions

Registers A, X, and Y can be copied into one another, provided that the A register is involved. TAX, for example, loads the content of register A into register X, while TXA calls for loading register X into A. The same sort of transfers can take place between the A and Y registers. But there are no instructions for directly transferring the content of register X to Y, or Y to X.

To transfer the content of the X register to the Y register, a sequence of transfers is necessary:

```
8A   TXA   LOAD X TO A
A8   TAY   LOAD A TO Y
```

That sequence of operations effectively transfers the content of the X register to the Y register, using A as a go-between. See if you can work out a similar sequence of transfer instructions to load the content of the Y register to the X register.

A similar situation exists with register transfers to and from the 8-bit SP register. Register X provides the only direct means of communicating with the SP register. So if it is necessary to load the SP register with the content of the Y register, the following sort of sequence is necessary:

```
98   TYA     LOAD Y TO A
AA   TAX     LOAD A TO X
9A   TXS     LOAD X TO SP
```

To be sure, it takes three instructions to make the Y-to-SP transfer, but it can be done. And that illustrates an important point concerning the 6502 microprocessor and its rather limited instruction set. While the 6502 is a relatively "small" microprocessor, in the context of the number of working registers and instructions available for working with them, it can be made to perform as a larger system—conceding the need for using a set of instructions in place of just one or two.

EXAMPLE 6-6

Write and assemble a 6502 program that uses just one load immediate and a series of register transfer instructions to load the A, X, Y, and SP registers with zeros. Begin the program at $2000.

The result is shown in Program 5-6. The first step loads the A register with $00 in an immediate fashion. The next two steps transfer the $00 to registers X and Y, and the final step transfers the $00 from X to SP.

Register Exchange Operations

The 6502 instruction set includes no instructions for exchanging the contents of any two registers. In keeping with the general notion that anything that can be done with a Z-80 or 8080A/8085 can be done with the 6502, one might think it possible to put together a sequence of register transfers to come up with the equivalent of a register exchange operation. Attempting such an operation with the instruction set described thus far, however, is an exercise in futility.

The matter of doing register exchanges calls for using some instructions that have not been introduced yet—using a byte in memory as the temporary storage place for one of the bytes to be exchanged.

PROGRAM 5-6   6502 LISTING FOR EXAMPLE 5-6

```
2000 A9 00   LDA #$00   LOAD IMMEDIATE $00 TO A
2002 AA      TAX        LOAD $00 FROM A TO X
2003 A8      TAY        LOAD $00 FROM A TO Y
2004 9A      TXS        LOAD $00 FROM X TO SP
```

Exercises for Section 5-3

1. Show the source code, or combination of more than one source code, for performing the following register exchange operations for the 6502.

   (a) $A \leftarrow X$ (b) $X \leftarrow A$ (c) $A \leftarrow Y$ (d) $Y \leftarrow A$
   (e) $X \leftarrow Y$ (f) $Y \leftarrow X$ (g) $A \leftarrow SP$ (h) $SP \leftarrow A$
   (i) $X \leftarrow SP$ (j) $SP \leftarrow X$ (k) $Y \leftarrow SP$ (l) $SP \leftarrow Y$

2. Show the source code, or combination of more than one source code, for performing the following load immediate operations.

   (a) $A \leftarrow data$ (b) $X \leftarrow data$ (c) $Y \leftarrow data$ (d) $SP \leftarrow data$

3. Write and assemble a program that uses a single load immediate instruction and a minimum number of register transfer instructions to insert \$FF into the A, X, Y, and SP registers. Begin at address \$0C00.

4. Disassemble the following program and list the content of the A, X, Y, and SP registers after the program has been executed:

```
0C00  A2 00
0C02  9A
0C03  A0 0C
0C05  98
```

5-4 6800 REGISTER TRANSFER INSTRUCTIONS

Figure 5-8 shows the 6800 registers involved in its 8-bit register transfer set. The instruction set itself is shown in Table 5-6.

An unusual feature of this instruction set is that the flag (F) register is involved. No other microprocessor described in this book has direct, register transfer instructions that include the flag register.

Other than the involvement of the F register, the 6800's 8-bit register transfer instructions match up to what one might expect from a system having just two 8-bit working registers, A and B, and a flag register. TAB, for example, transfers the content of the A register to the B register, thus leaving the original content of the A register in both of them. TBA, on the other

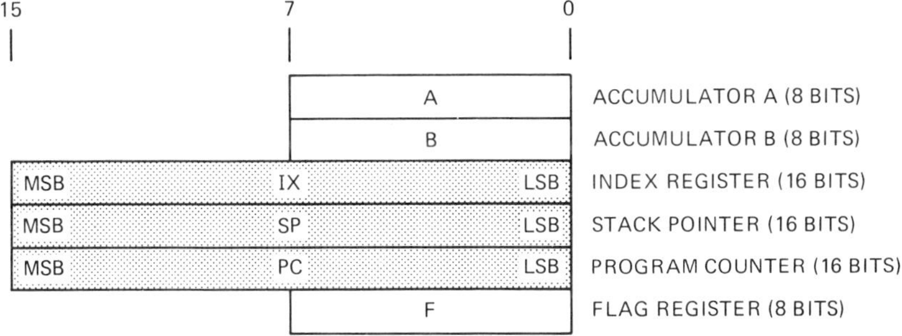

Figure 5-8   6800 registers for 8-bit register transfer instructions. Shaded registers are not involved.

TABLE 5-6 6800 INSTRUCTION SET FOR 8-BIT
REGISTER TRANSFER INSTRUCTIONS

Source code	Object code	Symbolic notation
TAB	16	B ← A
TBA	17	A ← B
TAP	06	F ← A
TPA	07	A ← F

hand, transfers the content of the B register to the A register, leaving the
original content of B in both of them.

Transfers to and from the F register work only with the A register. So if
it is ever necessary to transfer the content of the F register to the B register,
the programmer has to use a sequence such as this:

```
07  TPA     LOAD F TO A
16  TAB     LOAD A TO B
```

At the conclusion of that two-instruction program, the content of the F register appears in the A and B registers as well.

EXAMPLE 5-7

Write and assemble a 6800 program that uses a single load immediate instruction
and a sequence of register transfer instructions to fill all the 8-bit registers with $00.
Begin the program at address $CA00.

The result appears in Program 5-7.

Figure 5-9 and Table 5-7 completely represent the 16-bit register transfer instructions available to the 6800 programmer. There are only two 16-bit

PROGRAM 5-7 6800 LISTING FOR EXAMPLE 5-7

```
CA00 86 00  LDAA #$00   $00 TO ACCUMULATOR A
CA02 16     TAB         $00 TO ACCUMULATOR B
CA03 06     TAP         $00 TO F
```

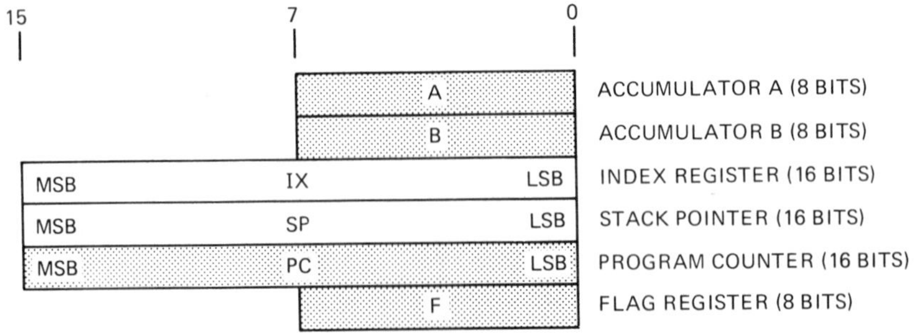

15   7   0

                              A   ACCUMULATOR A (8 BITS)
                              B   ACCUMULATOR B (8 BITS)
MSB   IX   LSB INDEX REGISTER (16 BITS)
MSB   SP   LSB STACK POINTER (16 BITS)
MSB   PC   LSB PROGRAM COUNTER (16 BITS)
                              F   FLAG REGISTER (8 BITS)

Figure 5-9 6800 registers for 16-bit register transfer instructions.

TABLE 5-7 6800 INSTRUCTION SET FOR 16-BIT
REGISTER TRANSFER INSTRUCTIONS

Source code	Object code	Symbolic notation
TSX	30	IX ← SP
TXS	35	SP ← IX

working registers, so the transfer instruction set is limited to two appropriate transfers—from SP to IX, and from IX to SP.

There are no register exchange instructions. But as in the case of the 6802 device, register exchanges are entirely possible when the programmer has access to external memory registers. That notion is introduced in Chapter 6.

Exercises for Section 5-4

1. Show the source- and object-code listings for performing the following operations with the 6800 microprocessor. (*Note:* Some require more than one instruction.)

   (a) A ← B   (b) B ← A   (c) A ← F   (d) F ← A
   (e) B ← F   (f) F ← B   (g) IX ← SP   (h) SP ← IX

3. Write and assemble a 6800 program that uses only *two* load immediate instructions and a series of register transfer instructions to fill the registers as follows:

   A=$FF   B=$FF   F=$FF   IX=$FFFF   SP=$FFFF

Begin the program at address $0A00.

6

Direct Memory Addressing

The discussions in Chapter 5 illustrate the fact that every microprocessor device has a well defined number of working registers. Some have a relatively large number of 8-bit and 16-bit working registers (Z-80 and 8080A/8085), whereas others have relatively few (6502 and 6800).

No matter how many working registers a given microprocessor might have, it seems that there are never enough of them for doing anything but the simplest kinds of programs. It would be nice if it were possible to expand the number of available registers at will, having the ability to use as many working registers as needed for a given task.

The fact of the matter is that the number of working registers can, indeed, be expanded a great deal beyond the array available within the microprocessor device. Such an expansion, when it is necessary, takes place in some external memory. It takes place where some useful RAM exists, but is not devoted to program memory.

For all practical purposes, there is an unlimited number of working registers available for shifting data around within a microprocessor system. The only problem is keeping track of them; but that is easily solved through the mechanism of memory addressing.

By coupling a microprocessor instruction with a memory address, it is possible to treat the data residing in that location as though they were residing within one of the internal working registers. Portions of external memory that are devoted to data-handling operations of this sort are called *data memory* locations. As described in an earlier discussion, there must never be any overlap between *data memory* and *program memory*; avoiding such an overlap is the responsibility of the programmer.

One way to associate a byte of data with a chosen memory address is by coupling that data with the exact address. Suppose, for example, that it is necessary to transfer the content of the A register to memory address location 4000H. The general idea is to let address 4000H serve as an auxiliary working register—an extension of the registers available within the microprocessor device itself.

Using a Z-80 mnemonics, such an instruction takes this form:

LD (4000H), A

Literally, that means: Load to address location 4000 (hexadecimal) the content of the A register. That is a form of register transfer. The 8-bit data from register A is transferred to the 8-bit memory location at address 4000H.

Working the transfer the other way around—from memory to the microprocessor—the instruction looks like this:

LD A, (4000H)

And that one means: Load to the A register the content of address 4000 (hexadecimal). The 8 bits of data at memory address 4000H is transferred to the A register.

Instructions that use external memory locations as working registers and cite those addresses specifically are called *direct address* instructions. Alternative techniques for citing address locations are described in subsequent chapters.

This chapter deals specifically with data transfers and exchanges, using direct memory addressing. It is important to bear in mind that some microprocessors have internal registers with both 8-bit and 16-bit capacities, but that the external memory is made up exclusively of 8-bit "registers." This tends to complicate matters somewhat when attempting to transfer the content of a 16-bit working register to 8-bit memory locations, but it can be done.

**Transferring 8-Bit Data via Direct
Memory Addressing**

Figure 6-1 blocks out the main elements of a microprocessor system that are directly involved in transferring 8-bit data between an internal register and an external memory location. There is an 8-bit microprocessor register and an 8-bit data memory location. The transfer is to take place between these two places in the system.

The third vital element in the scheme is the instruction that resides

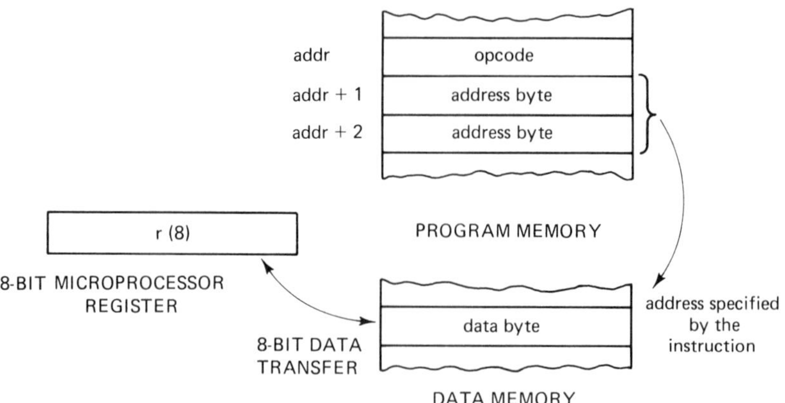

Figure 6-1   8-bit memory/register transfers with direct addressing.

somewhere in program memory. In this example, it is a 3-byte instruction. The first byte is the opcode, and the two remaining bytes cite the address of the external memory "register." For our immediate purposes, the instruction occupies the program memory at locations *addr*, *addr+1*, and *addr+2*. The instruction, in other words, occupies three successive address locations in the program memory.

The opcode in the instruction specifies four things:

1.   That a data transfer between an internal register and an external memory location is at hand
2.   Which internal register is to be involved in the transfer
3.   The direction of the transfer (from the microprocessor to the memory, or vice versa)
4.   That the operation is to use direct memory addressing

Item 4 implies that the exact memory address follows in the next two address locations in program memory. In fact, the microprocessor cannot execute the instruction until it has decoded the opcode and, subsequently, picked up the two address bytes—two bytes that are necessary for completely specifying a 16-bit memory location.

The opcode byte in the program memory tells *what* is to be done, while the second and third bytes in the instruction specify where the external memory "register" is located.

A complete listing for such an operation, using Z-80 mnemonics and syntax, looks like this:

```
0A00 3A 00 40  LD A,(4000H)   ;TRANSFER THE CONTENT OF
                              ;ADDRESS 4000H TO REGISTER A
```

The program listing begins at address 0A00 and runs through 0A02. Those are locations in program memory. The opcode in this instance is 3A (hexadecimal), and the sequence 00 40 indicate an address in data memory—LSB followed by MSB.

If a transfer is to take place from register A to address 4000H in external memory, the complete listing looks like this:

```
0A00 32 00 40   LD (4000H),A    ;TRANSFER THE CONTENT OF
                                ;REGISTER A TO ADDRESS 4000H
```

The opcode in this case is 32 (hexadecimal) instead of 3A. That switches around the direction of transfer, making the A register the source register and address 4000H the destination register.

The parentheses enclosing the memory address in these examples means "content of . . . ." An instruction such as LD A, (4000H) does *not* mean: Load 4000H to register A. First, that would imply a load immediate operation, and second, it would be an impossible task since 4000H is 1 16-bit number and register A is an 8-bit register. No, the expression means: Load the "content of" address location 4000H to the A register. It loads the 8-bit "content of" a memory address location to the 8-bit A register.

Not all microprocessor instruction sets call for this particular use of parentheses, and the "content of . . ." notion is implied.

Quite often, a transfer of data from an internal register to an address in external memory is called a *store operation*. A transfer in the opposite direction, from an address in external memory to an internal register, is called a *load operation*. The Z-80 mnemonics used in the foregoing examples do not express this difference—both are shown as LD instructions. But some of the other microprocessors discussed in this book clearly distinguish mnemonics for load and store operations.

**Transferring 16-Bit Data via
Direct Memory Addressing**

The matter of transferring 16-bit data between an internal register and an external memory location is a rather straightforward extension of the 8-bit transfers described in the previous discussion. The only problem is that the external memory locations are all 8-bit locations; but that is easily solved by using two successive address locations—one for each byte to be transferred.

Figure 6-2 illustrates the scheme for making direct-addressed, 16-bit transfers. The essential elements of the scheme include a 16-bit microprocessor register, or 8-bit register pair, and two successive address locations in the data memory space. The final element is the instruction in data memory.

When transferring 16-bit data from the microprocessor to data memory, the general idea is to store the lower byte of the big register into one data memory address location, and the higher-order byte of that register into the next-higher data memory address location. In this illustration, the first data byte goes to address n and the second goes to address $n+1$.

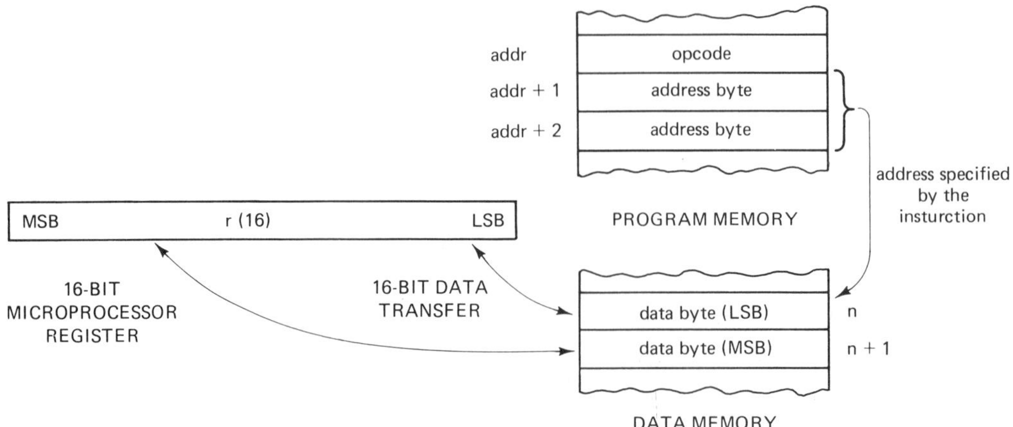

Figure 6-2   16-bit memory/register transfers with direct addressing.

And when transferring 16 bits from data memory to a 16-bit register, or register pair, within the microprocessor, the idea is to load the content of address n to the LSB portion of the big register, and the content of address $n+1$ to the MSB portion of that same register.

So while we are dealing with a 16-bit microprocessor register and 8-bit data memory locations, they are made compatible by using two successive data memory locations.

Notice that the instruction in the program memory has the same format that is used for simpler 8-bit transfers between the microprocessor and data memory. The first byte is the opcode, and it specifies all the information regarding which 16-bit register is to be involved, the direction of transfer, and that a direct addressing mode is being used.

The second and third bytes in the instruction, occupying *addr+1* and *addr+2*, specify the address of the *first byte* to be transferred. The address clearly specified in the instruction, in other words, points to the data memory address of the first data byte—the one shown here at address n. It is then taken for granted that the second byte to be transferred exists at the next-higher address location in the data memory—at address $n+1$.

Here is an example of a 16-bit register/memory transfer, using Z-80 mnemonics and syntax:

```
LD  HL,(4000H)
```

That means: Load to the HL register pair the content of data memory addresses 4000H *and* 4001H. The content of address 4000H goes to the 8-bit L register, and the content of address 4001H goes to the 8-bit H register. In effect, the instruction implements a 16-bit data transfer from data memory to the HL register pair within the microprocessor.

There is no need to specify both memory addresses involved in the transfer—just the first one. The microprocessor's internal workings automatically take care of picking up the second address location.

The following instruction transfers 16 bits in the opposite direction. The data memory is the destination and the internal HL register pair is the source:

```
LD (4000H),HL
```

Here the content of the 8-bit L register is transferred to address location 4000H, and then the content of the higher-order H register is transferred to location 4001H. Again, there is no need to specify both addresses in the data memory; just the first one—the lower-numbered one that is to receive the least-significant byte of data.

A complete listing for a 16-bit data transfer with direct memory addressing looks like this:

```
0A00 2A 00 40   LD HL,(4000H)   ;LOAD THE HL REGISTER PAIR
                                ;WITH TWO BYTES OF DATA, BE-
                                ;GINNING AT ADDRESS 4000H
```

That one loads the content of data memory address 4000H to the L register and the content of address 4001H to the H register. The opcode in this case is 2A (hexadecimal), and the first data memory address is specified in the object code with the LSB ahead of the MSB. (The 6800 microprocessor reverses this format.)

The complementary version of that instruction looks like this:

```
0A00 22 00 40   LD (4000H),HL   ;STORE THE CONTENT OF THE HL
                                ;REGISTER PAIR, BEGINNING
                                ;AT ADDRESS 4000H
```

The object-code instruction begins with the opcode, 22H, followed by the address in data memory to receive the first byte of the 2-byte data to be stored. The microprocessor takes care of addressing location 4001H for the second byte of data.

6-2 Z-80 TRANSFER INSTRUCTIONS

Figure 6-3 shows the Z-80 registers that can be loaded from data memory, or whose contents can be saved in data memory, using direct memory addressing instructions. It turns out that the A register is the only one that can use an 8-bit transfer instruction of this type. The remaining registers or register pairs call for using 16-bit transfer instructions.

8-Bit Transfer Instructions and Operations

Table 6-1 shows the two Z-80 instructions for doing register/memory transfers of the 8-bit type—transfers using direct memory addressing. In the first case, the content of the A register is saved at some specified location in data

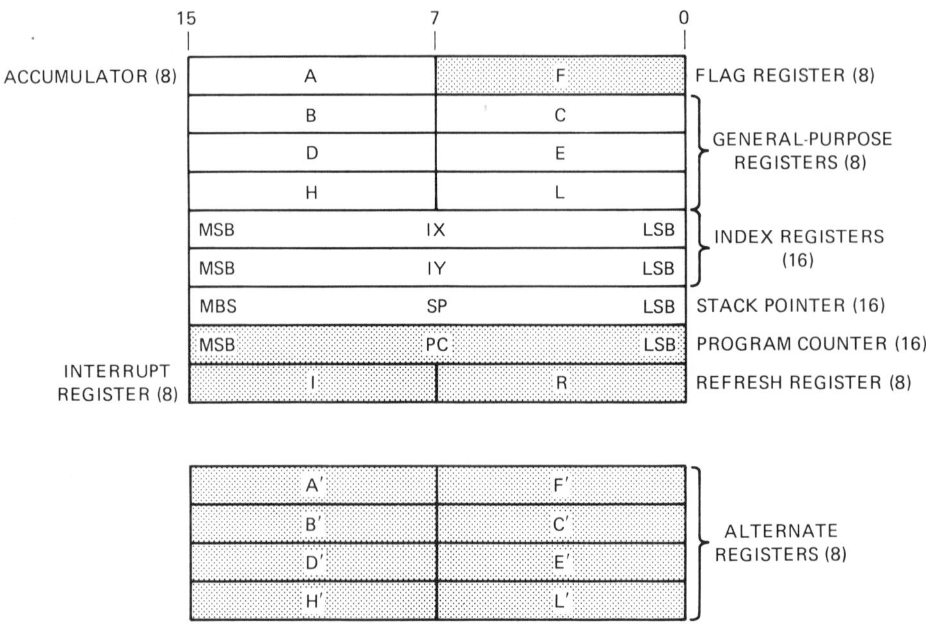

Figure 6-3 Z-80 registers included in memory/register transfer instructions that use direct memory addressing. Shaded registers are not involved. The A register is the only one involved in 8-bit transfers, and it is excluded from 16-bit transfers.

memory. In the second case, the content of some data memory address is loaded to the A register.

In those instructions, (*addr*) refers to the 8-bit data at address *addr*. Thus a source code instruction such as

LD (500FH),A

means: Load to address 500F, hexadecimal, the 8-bit content of register A. Using a slightly different nomenclature, the instruction can be interpreted as: Save the content of the A register at address 500FH in data memory. In either case, the idea is to transfer the 8-bit content of register A to the

TABLE 6-1 Z-80 INSTRUCTIONS FOR 8-BIT TRANSFERS WITH DIRECT MEMORY ADDRESSING

Source code	Object code	Symbolic Notation
LD (*addr*),A	32 *byte byte*	(*addr*)←A
LD A,(*addr*)	3A *byte byte*	A←(*addr*)

directly addressed memory location. At the conclusion of the operation, the original content of register A appears in data memory, at address 500F, as well. In a manner of speaking, the programmer has defined address 500FH as an extension of the Z-80's family of working registers.

Working the operation the other way around,

```
LD  A,(500FH)
```

means: Load register A with the 8-bit content of data memory location 500F, hexadecimal. After that instruction has been executed, the original content of memory address 500F appears in the A register as well.

Both of the instructions use 3-byte object codes. The first byte in the instruction is the opcode, and the two remaining bytes specify the memory address involved in the transfer. *The byte following the opcode is the LSB of the address, and the final byte is the MSB of that same address.* Complete program listings for the two instructions can look like this:

```
32 OF 50   LD (500FH),A   ;SAVE A IN MEMORY AT 500FH

3A OF 50   LD A,(500FH)   ;LOAD A WITH THE CONTENT OF
                          ;MEMORY LOCATION 500FH
```

Although there are just two 8-bit transfer instructions that use direct memory addressing, they have some powerful applications. The instructions cited in Table 6-1 can be used for:

1. Temporarily saving the content of the A register, freeing it for other operations, and then retrieving the original content
2. Simulating a load immediate instruction to a register in data memory
3. Transferring data between the A register and any 8-bit, memory-mapped input or output device

The remainder of the present discussion illustrates these applications.

The Z-80 microprocessor features an unusually large number of internal working registers. But it seems that no matter how many registers are available, there is often a need for more of them. The register/memory transfer instructions, using direct memory addressing, provide a means for effectively extending the number of available working registers.

EXAMPLE 6-1

Write and assemble a Z-80 program that:

1. Saves the content of the A register in data memory location 5C00H
2. Transfers the content of register B to A
3. Sets the content of register A to zero

4. Transfers the zero from register A to B

5. Retrieves the original content of register A from data memory

Begin the program at address 1000H.

The point of the example is to show how it is possible to save the content of the A register somewhere in data memory, thus freeing it for other operations that destroy the original content of that register. When that operation is done, the example shows that the original content of the A register can be restored.

The result is shown in Program 6-1.

PROGRAM 6-1   Z-80 LISTING FOR EXAMPLE 6-1

```
1000 32 00 5C   LD (5C00H),A   ;SAVE A AT 5C00H
1003 78         LD A,B         ;LOAD B TO A
1004 3E 00      LD A,00H       ;SET A TO ZERO
1006 47         LD B,A         ;LOAD THE ZERO TO B
1007 3A 00 5C   LD A,(5C00H)   ;RESTORE ORIGINAL CONTENT OF A
```

Although designated addresses in data memory can be regarded as extensions of the microprocessor's working registers, the Z-80 instruction set includes no instructions for doing load immediate operations to data memory. If, indeed, some external memory locations are to be treated as extra working registers, there ought to be some means for initializing them—for doing load immediates to them from the program memory.

Any data memory location can, in effect, be loaded in an immediate fashion via the LD (*addr*),A, provided that the A register is first loaded. Consider this:

```
LD A,7FH    ;LOAD IMMEDIATE 7FH TO A
LD (6B12H)  ;TRANSFER A TO ADDRESS 6B12H
```

Executing these two instructions ultimately places 7F, hexadecimal, into data memory location 6B12. The data originate in the program memory, giving the overall impression that a load immediate to a "register" in data memory is taking place.

The next example illustrates a somewhat more involved "load immediate" operation to data memory. The basic idea is to initialize the values contained in a set of data memory locations.

EXAMPLE 6-2

Write and assemble a Z-80 program that uses load immediate instructions and direct memory addressing to initialize some data memory locations as follows:

```
5C00H=2DH, 5C01H=1AH, 5C02H=33H, 5DE0H=14H
```

Begin the program at address 7000H.

The resulting listing appears in Program 6-2. In each phase of the job, the data to be loaded are first loaded to the A register from the load immediate program instruction. Then the data are stored from register A to the designated address in data memory.

```
7000 3E 2D      LD A,2DH        ;2DH IMMEDIATE TO REGISTER A
7002 32 00 5C   LD (5C00H),A    ;LOAD A DIRECT TO 5C00H
7005 3E 1A      LD A,1AH        ;1AH IMMEDIATE TO REGISTER A
7007 32 01 5C   LD (5C01H),A    ;LOAD A DIRECT TO 5C01H
700A 3E 33      LD A,33H        ;33H IMMEDIATE TO REGISTER A
700C 32 02 5C   LD (5C02H),A    ;LOAD A DIRECT TO 5C02H
700F 3E 14      LD A,14H        ;14H IMMEDIATE TO REGISTER A
7011 32 EO 5D   LD (5DE0H),A    ;LOAD A DIRECT TO 5DE0H
```

The data stored in directly addressed memory locations can be retrieved at any time by doing a LD A,(*addr*) and substituting the designated memory locations at *addr*.

As described in earlier chapters, it is possible to substitute input and output devices for memory locations. An output device, such as a lamp or motor, can be interfaced and addressed as though it were a memory location. By the same token, and input device such as a switch can be interfaced with the system at some prescribed "memory" address.

Substituting input and output devices at addresses normally reserved for actual memory devices is called memory-mapping I/O devices. As long as the programmer knows which input and output devices are connected to well-specified address locations, the notion offers a very flexible means for communicating with the world outside the microprocessor system.

Suppose that a lamp is connected to address 7FFFH; further suppose that the lamp is turned on whenever a data value of 01H is directed to it. That being the case, turning on the lamp is a relatively simple matter of doing this:

```
LD A,01H        ;LOAD IMMEDIATE 01H TO A
LD (7FFFH),A    ;STORE THE 01H TO ADDRESS 7FFFH
```

The first instruction sets up the data required for turning on the lamp, and the second instruction outputs those data to the lamp's address.

If it happens that the lamp in that example is turned off whenever it is fed 00H for data, the following sequence of instructions will turn it off:

```
LD A,00H        ;LOAD IMMEDIATE 00H TO A
LD (7FFFH),A    ;STORE THE 00H TO ADDRESS 7FFFH
```

In both those examples, a load immediate operation sets up the desired data byte to be delivered to the lamp. The lamp circuit, being located at address 7FFFH, receives those data the moment the second instruction is executed.

The same general idea applies to input devices. Suppose that a toggle switch is located at address 7FFEH. Things are worked out so that the data from that address are 01H if the switch is open, and 00H is the switch is closed. Finding out what the switch status might be is a matter of doing this:

```
LD A,(7FFEH)    ;LOAD A WITH THE CONTENT OF 7FFEH
```

```
7C00 78          LD  A,B         ;LOAD  B TO A
7C01 32 00 4E    LD  (4E00H),A   ;LOAD ORIGINAL B TO 4E00H
7C04 79          LD  A,C         ;LOAD  C TO A
7C05 32 01 4E    LD  (4E01H),A   ;LOAD ORIGINAL C TO 4E01H
7C08 7A          LD  A,D         ;LOAD  D TO A
7C09 32 F0 4F    LD  (4FF0H),A   ;LOAD ORIGINAL D TO 4FF0H
7C0C 7B          LD  A,E         ;LOAD  E TO A
7C0D 32 F1 4F    LD  (4FF1H),A   ;LOAD ORIGINAL E TO 4FF1H
```

If the data thus transferred to register A are equal to 01H, the switch is apparently open; but if the operation turns up a 00H in register A, the switch must be closed.

All 8-bit register/memory transfers that use direct memory addressing include references to the A register. If any other 8-bit register is to take part in such a transfer, the data must pass through register A in the process. The next example illustrates this particular point.

EXAMPLE 6-3

Write and assemble a Z-80 program that uses 8-bit, direct memory addressing to make the specified transfers:

Register B to 4E00H

Register C to 4E01H

Register D to 4FF0H

Register E to 4FF1H

Begin the program at address 7C00H.

The result is shown in Program 6-3. Note that the data must be passed to the A register before they can be transferred to data memory.

16-Bit Transfer Instructions and Operations

Table 6-2 summarizes the Z-80 instructions for transferring 16-bit data between 16-bit registers, or 8-bit register pairs, and data memory. Bear in mind that the address specified in the instruction codes points to the first of two successive address locations in data memory.

Consider, first, the source-code instruction

```
LD (addr), HL
```

The literal meaning is: Store the content of the HL register pair in data memory, beginning at address *addr*. As indicated by the corresponding symbolic notation, the content of the L register goes to *addr*, while the content of the H register goes to *addr+1*.

The complementary instruction is

```
LD HL,(addr)
```

That one loads the HL register pair with 2 bytes of data from data memory. The byte from *addr* is loaded to the L register, and the byte from *addr+1* goes to the H register.

See if you can interpret the following examples before reading the explanations.

```
7000 21 FF 40   LD HL,40FFH      ;LOAD IMMEDIATE 40FFH TO HL
7003 22 00 3C   LD (3C00H),HL    ;STORE HL TO ADDRESS 3C00H
```

The first instruction does a 16-bit load immediate to the HL pair. In this case, 40FF (hexadecimal) is loaded, with the FF byte going to the L register and the 40 byte going to the H register. That step merely puts some well-defined data into the HL register pair.

The second instruction stores those bytes in data memory, beginning at address 3C00H. The content of the L register is stored at 3C00H, and the microprocessor takes care of the matter of loading the content of the H register to the next-higher data memory location, 3C01H.

So when that two-instruction program has been executed, data FF end up in data memory address 3C00H, and data 40 end up at 3C01H. The next example fetches the two bytes of data back into the HL pair:

```
7006 2A 00 3C   LD HL,(3C00H)    ;LOAD THE HL PAIR FROM MEMORY
```

Upon executing this instruction, the byte resident in address 3C00H of the data memory is loaded to the L register; and the content of address 3C001H is loaded to the H register. It is a 2-byte register-loading operation that begins loading from the designated address in data memory.

These 16-bit register/memory transfers, using direct memory addressing, serve the same general purpose as their 8-bit counterpart. The only difference, in principle, is that 2-byte, rather than 1-byte, data are transferred.

There is, however, one important practical difference that a programmer must bear in mind. Every 16-bit transfer automatically involves two successive data memory address locations; and that brings up the possibility of making a careless error. Here is an example of that error:

```
LD HL,0102H     ;LOAD IMMEDIATE 0102H TO HL PAIR
LD (4000H),HL   ;LOAD HL TO 4000H
LD HL,0304H     ;LOAD IMMEDIATE 0304H TO HL PAIR
LD (4001H),HL   ;LOAD HL TO 4001H
```

Apparently, the programmer wants to simulate a load immediate operation to some places in data memory. The general approach to the situation is a sound one: First do a load immediate of the 16-bit data to the HL register pair, and then transfer the data to a designated place in data memory. But doing two of these 16-bit "load immediate" operations to successive address locations is causing some trouble. Here is what the arrangement of data will look like in the data memory:

                                4000   02
                                4001   04
                                4002   03

The programmer is attempting to save two 2-byte numbers, 0102 and 0304,
in successive address locations. But the 01 has gotten lost. What happened?

The programmer neglected to take into account the fact that a 16-bit
transfer-to-memory operations takes up two successive address locations. In
that error example, the beginning of the second storing operation writes over
the second part of the first operation. A corrected version of the program
looks like this:

```
LD HL,0102H      ;LOAD IMMEDIATE 0102H TO HL PAIR
LD (4000H),HL    ;LOAD HL TO 4000H
LD HL,0304H      ;LOAD IMMEDIATE 0304H TO HL PAIR
LD (4002H),HL    :LOAD HL TO 4002H
```

Now the arrangement of saved data in the data memory takes this form:

                                4000   02
                                4001   01
                                4002   04
                                4003   03

Whenever the programmer wants to retrieve the 0102H data at some
later time, the appropriate instruction is

```
LD HL,(4000H)   ;FETCH 2 BYTES FROM 4000H TO HL PAIR
```

As a result, the content of 4000H (02H) will end up in register L and the
content of 4001H will be loaded to register H. The overall result is that the
HL register pair will be loaded with 0102 from the data memory. Similarly,
the instruction LD HL,(4002H) will return the previously saved 0304H to
the HL register pair.

*Remember that a single, 16-bit register-to-memory transfer uses two
successive address locations in data memory.*

The remaining instructions in Table 6-2 work the same way as the ones
referring to the HL register pair. The only difference of special note is that
they are all 4-byte program instructions. The opcode uses the first two bytes,
and the two remaining bytes are used for specifying the data memory
address—LSB followed by MSB.

EXAMPLE 6-4

Write and assemble a Z-80 program that uses 16-bit register-to-memory transfer instructions to do the following:

1.   Save the content of the BC register pair at 4000H.

2.   Save the content of the DE register pair at 4002H.

TABLE 6-2 Z-80 INSTRUCTIONS FOR 16-BIT TRANSFERS WITH DIRECT MEMORY ADDRESSING

Source code	Object code	Symbolic notation
LD (*addr*),BC	ED 43 *byte byte*	(*addr*)←C (*addr+1*)←B
LD BC,(*addr*)	ED 4B *byte byte*	C←(*addr*) B←(*addr+1*)
LD (*addr*),DE	ED 53 *byte byte*	(*addr*)←E (*addr+1*)←D
LD DE,(*addr*)	ED 5B *byte byte*	E←(*addr*) D←(addr+1)
LD (*addr*),HL	22 *byte byte*	(*addr*)←L (*addr+1*)←H
LD HL,(*addr*)	2A *byte byte*	L←(*addr*) H←(*addr+1*)
LD (*addr*),IX	DD 22 *byte byte*	(*addr*)←IXL (*addr+1*)←IXH
LD IX,(*addr*)	DD 2A *byte byte*	IXL←(*addr*) IXH←(*addr+1*)
LD (*addr*),IY	FD 22 *byte byte*	(*addr*)←IYL (*addr+1*)←IYH
LD IY,(*addr*)	FD 2A *byte byte*	IYL←(*addr*) IYH←(*addr+1*)
LD (*addr*),SP	ED 73 *byte byte*	(*addr*)←SPL (*addr+1*)←SPH
LD SP,(*addr*)	ED 7B *byte byte*	SPL←(*addr*) SPH←(*addr+1*)

3. Save the content of the HL register pair at 4004H.
4. Save the content of the IX register pair at 4006H.
5. Save the content of the IY register pair at 4008H.
6. Save the content of the SP register at 400AH.
7. Save the content of the B′C′ register pair at 400CH.
8. Save the content of the D′E′ register pair at 400EH.
9. Save the content of the H′L′ register pair at 4010H.

Begin the programming at address 4C00H.

This particular task is perhaps more tedious than complicated. See one possible approach to the job in Program 6-4.

One of the less tedious and more meaningful applications of these 16-bit register/memory transfers is that of exchanging the content of 16-bit registers or register pairs. Recall that the Z-80 instruction set has just one double-register exchange instruction for the primary registers: EX DE,HL. That one exchanges the contents of the DE and HL register pairs.

```
4C00  ED 43 00 40      LD (4000H),BC    ;BC TO 4000H
4C04  ED 53 02 40      LD (4002H),DE    ;DE TO 4002H
4C08  22 04 40         LD (4004H),HL    ;HL TO 4004H
4C0B  DD 22 06 40      LD (4006H),IX    ;IX  TO 4006H
4C0F  FD 22 08 40      LD (4008H),IY    ;IY  TO 4008H
4C13  ED 73 0A 40      LD (400AH),SP    ;SP  TO 400AH
4C17  D9               EXX              ;GET ALTERNATE REGISTERS
4C18  ED 43 0C 40      LD (400CH),BC    ;B'C' TO 400CH
4C1C  ED 53 0E 40      LD (400EH),DE    ;D'E' TO 400EH
4C20  22 10 40         LD (4010H),HL    ;H'L' TO 4010H
```

But what if you want to exchange, say, the content of the BC and DE register pairs? or the IX and HL registers? The former can be carried out using 8-bit register transfers as described in Chapter 5, but most other exchanges with 16-bit registers cannot be handled that way. As you might suspect, the 16-bit register/memory transfer operations come to the rescue. See the next example.

EXAMPLE 6-5

Write and assemble a Z-80 program that uses 16-bit register/memory transfer instructions to:

1.   Exchange the contents of the BC and DE register pairs.
2.   Exchange the contents of the HL register pair with that of the IX register.

Begin the program listing at 7000H.
See the program in Program 6-5.

Program 6-5 illustrates the fact that a memory location that is loaded from one register pair does not necessarily have to be loaded back to that same register or register pair. In the first half of Program 6-5, for example, address 4000H is first loaded from the BC register pair; but a few instructions later, the content of 4000H is loaded back to the DE register pair. That is how the data exchange takes place in this particular exercise.

PROGRAM 6-5   Z-80 LISTING FOR EXAMPLE 6-5

```
7000  ED 43 00 40      LD (4000H),BC    ;STORE BC TO 4000H
7004  ED 53 02 40      LD (4002H),DE    ;STORE DE TO 4002H
7008  ED 48 02 40      LD BC,(4002H)    ;LOAD ORIGINAL DE TO BC
700C  ED 5B 00 40      LD DE,(4000H)    ;LOAD ORIGINAL BC TO DE
                                        ;BC/DE EXCHANGE IS DONE
7010  22 00 40         LD (4000H),HL    ;STORE HL TO 4000H
7013  DD 22 02 04      LD (4002H),IX    ;STORE IX TO 4002H
7017  DD 2A 00 40      LD IX,(4000H)    ;LOAD ORIGINAL HL TO IX
701B  2A 02 40         LD HL,(4002H)    ;LOAD ORIGINAL IX TO HL
                                        ;HL/IX EXCHANGE IS DONE
```

Exercises for Section 6-2

1. Write the object-code listings for the following source-code instructions.
   (a) LD A,(1234H)   (b) LD (0401H),A   (c) LD HL,(1625H)
   (d) LD (255AH),HL   (e) LD SP,(00FFH)   (f) LD (F000H),SP
2. Disassemble the following object-code listings to their source-code forms.
   (a) 32 FF 00   (b) 3A 12 34   (c) 2A 00 9A
   (d) ED 7B 11 7F   (e) ED 4B 01 23
3. Describe the essential difference between these two instructions:

   ```
   LD  BC,2000H     and     LD  BC,(2000H)
   ```

4. Assume the system has just executed this program:

   ```
   LD  BC,2000H
   LD  HL,3AFFH
   LD  (4000H),HL
   LD  (4002H),BC
   LD  IX,(4000H)
   LD  IY,(4002H)
   LD  DE,(4001H)
   ```

   Cite the data content of the following registers and data memory locations.
   (a) B register   (b) C register   (c) D register
   (d) E register   (e) H register   (f) L register
   (g) Address 4000H   (h) Address 4001H   (i) Address 4002H
   (j) Address 4003H   (k) IX register   (l) IY register
5. Assemble the program listed in problem 4, beginning at program address 7000H.
6. Write and assemble a program that exchanges the contents of the IX and IY registers. Use 16-bit register/memory transfers with direct memory addressing. Begin the program at address 4C00H, and use data memory addresses 1000H through 1003H as required.

6-3 8080A/8085 TRANSFER INSTRUCTIONS

Table 6-3 and Figure 6-4 completely summarize the register/memory transfer instructions that use direct memory addressing for the 8080A/8085 device. Certainly, the instruction set is much smaller than the one for comparable operations with the Z-80, but they are quite adequate.

Note that there are just two instructions of the 8-bit variety. They are identical to those used with the Z-80 in principle, and the only significant difference is the source-code mnemonics. Whereas the Z-80 stores the content of the A register to an address with LD *(addr)*,A, the 8080A/8085 scheme calls for a STA *addr*. Where the Z-80 loads the A register from a designated address with LD A,*(addr)*, the 8080A/8085 mnemonics demands a LDA *addr*. The object codes are identical.

As far as the 16-bit versions of the direct-addressed, register/memory

TABLE 6-3 8080A/8085 INSTRUCTIONS FOR TRANSFERS WITH DIRECT MEMORY ADDRESSING

Source code	Object code	Symbolic notation
8-Bit Instructions		
STA *addr*	32 *byte byte*	(*addr*)←A
LDA *addr*	3A *byte byte*	A←(*addr*)
16-Bit Instructions		
SHLD *addr*	22 *byte byte*	(*addr*)←L (*addr+1*)←H
LHLD *addr*	2A *byte byte*	L←(*addr*) H←(*addr+1*)

transfer are concerned, the 8080A/8085 works only with the HL register pair. SHLD *addr*, for instance, stores the content of the HL pair at *addr*. Actually, the content of the L register is stored at *addr* and the content of the H register is stored at *addr+1*. Except for the source-code mnemonic, the operation is identical to the Z-80's LD (*addr*),HL instruction.

Similarly, LHLD *addr* for the 8080A/8085 is identical to the Z-80's LD HL,(*addr*) instruction. Upon executing it, the content of *addr* is loaded to the L register, and the content of *addr+1* is loaded to the H register.

In short, if you have mastered the direct-addressed, register/memory transfers for the Z-80 as presented in Section 6-2, you should have no trouble understanding the smaller instruction set for the same operations with an 8080A/8085 system.

Assuming that you have, indeed, mastered the Z-80 discussions in Section 6-2, there is little need to dwell on exercises that merely demonstrate the workings of these register/memory transfer instructions. Instead, it will be more instructive to show how it is possible to make up for the smaller instruction set available with the 8080A/8085.

A case in point concerns the matter of transferring 16-bit data between

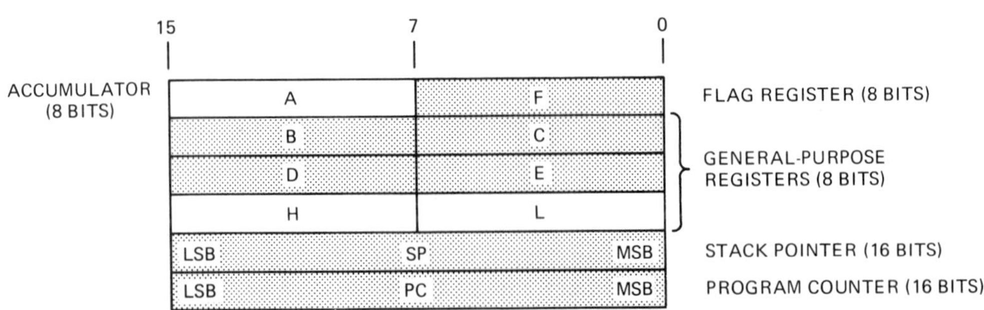

Figure 6-4 8080A/8085 registers included in memory/register transfer instructions that use direct memory addressing. Shaded registers are not involved.

the data memory and registers other than the HL pair. Suppose, for example, that you want to transfer the content of the BC register pair to data memory address 4000H. The Z-80 has an instruction for doing that—for storing the content of the L register to 4000H and the content of the H register to 4001H. How can this be done with the 8080A/8085?

Since the only 16-bit route to data memory is through the HL register pair, it figures that the content of the BC pair must first be transferred to the HL pair. Then the SHLD *addr* instruction can take care of storing the 16-bit data to data memory. Thus

```
MOV H,B      ;TRANSFER B TO H
MOV L,C      ;TRANSFER C TO L
SHLD 4000H   ;STORE HL AT ADDRESS 4000H
```

That sequence of instructions does the job of the Z-80's LD (4000H),BC instruction. This example requires a couple of additional instructions, but the task can be done. A similar approach allows you to transfer the contents of any register pair to data memory. Just get things into the HL pair first, then do the SHLD *addr* operation to store it.

Of course that approach destroys the original contents of the HL pair, and you might not want that to happen. The HL pair might be holding some valuable information that must not be lost. If that is the case, simply store the content of the HL pair somewhere else in data memory *before* executing the routine just cited. Then restore the original content of the HL pair by fetching the data with an LHLD *addr* instruction. Applying that idea to the previous example, the program looks like this:

```
SHLD 4002H   ;SAVE ORIGINAL HL AT ADDRESS 4002H
MOV H,B      ;TRANSFER B TO H
MOV L,C      ;TRANSFER C TO L
SHLD 4000H   ;SAVE ORIGINAL BC AT ADDRESS 4000H
LHLD 4002H   ;FETCH ORIGINAL HL FROM ADDRESS 4002H
```

Now the transfer is carried out without losing the original content of the HL register pair.

Unfortunately, the 8080A/8085 instructions presented thus far do not permit a 16-bit transfer from the SP register to a directly addressed location in data memory. It is possible, however, to load the SP register from data memory:

```
LHLD 7000H   ;LOAD THE HL PAIR WITH 16-BITS FROM
             ;7000H AND 7001H
SPHL         ;TRANSFER HL TO SP
```

The overall effect is that the LSB portion of the SP register is loaded with the content of data memory address 7000H, and the MSB portion is loaded from address 7001H.

PROGRAM 6-6   8080A/8085 LISTING FOR EXAMPLE 6-6

```
4C00 22 04 40    SHLD 4004H    ;HL TO ADDRESS 4004H
4C03 60          MOV H,B       ;TRANSFER B TO H
4C04 69          MOV L,C       ;TRANSFER C TO L
4C05 22 00 40    SHLD 4000H    ;ORIGINAL BC TO ADDRESS 4000H
4C08 EB          XCHG          ;DE TO HL
4C09 22 02 40    SHLD 4002H    ;ORIGINAL DE TO ADDRESS 4002H
```

EXAMPLE 6-6

Write and assemble an 8080A/8085 program that uses 16-bit register/memory transfers and direct memory addressing to accomplish the following:

1.   Save the content of the BC register pair at 4000H.

2.   Save the content of the DE register pair at 4002H.

3.   Save the content of the HL register pair at 4004H.

Begin the program at address 4C00H.

See one programming approach in Program 6-6. Compare it with a similar Z-80 task in Program 6-4.

Register-pair exchanges are possible, using the general technique suggested for the Z-80. The general idea is to save the content of the two register pairs as separate data memory addresses, then reload them by exchanging the memory addresses. The next example illustrates how this can be done with the 8080A/8085's limited instruction set.

EXAMPLE 6-7

Write and assemble a program that uses 16-bit register/memory transfers and direct memory addressing to exchange the contents of the BC and DE register pairs. Use data memory locations 4000H through 4003H, and begin the program at 7000H. Assume that the original content of the HL pair is not important.

See the result in Program 6-7.

PROGRAM 6-7   8080A/8085 LISTING FOR EXAMPLE 6-7

```
7000 60          MOV H,B       ;TRANSFER B TO H
7001 69          MOV L,C       ;TRANSFER C TO L
                               ;ORIGINAL BC NOW IN HL
7002 22 00 40    SHLD 4000H    ;ORIGINAL BC TO 4000H
7005 EB          XCHG          ;ORIGINAL DE TO HL
7006 22 02 40    SHLD 4002H    ;ORIGINAL DE TO 4002H
7009 2A 00 40    LHLD 4000H    ;ORIGINAL BC TO HL
700C EB          XCHG          ;ORIGINAL BC NOW IN DE
700D 2A 02 40    LHLD 4002H    ;ORIGINAL DE TO HL
7010 44          MOV B,H       ;ORIGINAL D TO B
7011 4D          MOV C,L       ;ORIGINAL E TO C
                               ;ORIGINAL DE NOW IN BC
```

1. Describe the essential difference between these two instructions: LXI H,4000H and LHLD 4000H.

2. Write 8080A/8085 source-code programs for doing the tasks described as Z-80 instructions.

    (a) LD A,(3C00H)   (b) LD (421FH),A   (c) LD BC,(3C00H)
    (d) LD (4100H),BC   (e) LD DE,(3C00H)   (f) LD (4100H),DE
    (g) LD HL,(3C00H)   (h) LD (4100H),HL   (i) LD SP,(3C00H)

3. Assume that the system has just executed this program:

```
MVI  A,20H
LXI  D,2000H
LXI  H,3AFFH
SHLD  4000H
XCHG
SHLD  4001H
STA  4003H
LHLD  4000H
XCHG
LHLD  4002H
```

    Cite the data content of the following registers and data memory locations.

    (a) Register A   (b) Register D   (c) Register E
    (d) Register H   (e) Register L   (f) Address 4000H
    (g) Address 4001H   (h) Address 4002H   (i) Address 4003H

4. Assemble the program listed in problem 3, beginning at program address 7000H.

6-4 6502 REGISTER/MEMORY TRANSFERS WITH DIRECT ADDRESSING

Moving into a study of register/memory data transfers with direct memory addressing for the 6502 and 6800 microprocessors introduces a new topic: *zero-page addressing*.

Zero-Page Addressing

Here are two different 6502 instructions that store the content of the A register into data memory address 002F, hexadecimal:

```
STA $2F     and     STA $002F
```

The difference might appear to be a purely notational one at first—the operand $2F seems to be nothing more than $002F with the leading zeros removed. In the 6502 and 6800 instruction sets, however, the differences are quite important; so important, in fact, that the two instructions carry entirely different object codes.

As far as the 6502 system is concerned, the object code for STA $2F is

85 2F. The 85 is the opcode, and the 2F is the 1-byte address. STA $2F is a 2-byte instruction that will store the content of the A register at data memory location $2F.

The instruction STA $002F, however, carries the object code 8D 2F 00, where 8D is the opcode, 2F is the LSB of the address, and 00 is its MSB. That is a 3-byte instruction that does the same job as the 2-byte version.

So when it comes to storing the content of the A register into some directly addressed memory location, the programmer has two options:

1. Storing the data at a point specified at a 1-byte address
2. Storing the data at a point specified by a 2-byte address

When using the 1-byte addressing, the data can be stored anywhere in memory between $00 and $FF. That figures out to be a block of 256 memory bytes at the very lowest end of the system's memory space. That lowest possible block of memory is called the *zero page*. (A *page* of memory is considered a block of 256 bytes.) One-byte addresses referring to the zero page are called *zero-page addresses*.

By contrast, a 2-byte address can be anywhere in the 65K range of $0000 through $FFFF. That covers the entire addressing range for a 16-bit addressing scheme and, incidentally, includes the zero page as well. To keep matters straight, using 2-byte addresses is called *absolute addressing*.

The advantage of single-byte, zero-page addressing is that it uses one less byte of program memory—the address is specified as one byte instead of two. This is especially meaningful for the 6502 and 6800 microprocessor systems because those two happen to have so few internal working registers compared to the Z-80 and 8080A/8085 devices. Having fewer registers, most register-related operations have to be shifted to data memory locations, thus making it necessary to do a relatively large number of register/memory transfers. And while saving just one byte of program space for an address-related instruction does not seem like much of a savings in program memory space, it adds up quite rapidly when working out even a moderately complicated program sequence.

The only drawback inherent in the zero-page addressing mode is that there are just 256 data memory locations available for it. A good many programming tasks call for more than one page of data memory. For that reason, the 2-byte, absolute addressing mode is available as well.

Direct Addressing for Register/Memory Transfers

Figure 6-5 shows the 6502 registers that can be involved in register/memory transfers that use direct memory addressing. The corresponding instruction set is summarized in Table 6-4.

There are store and load instructions for each of the three 8-bit working registers. Normally, that would figure out to just six instructions; but the zero-page and absolute addressing options doubles that number.

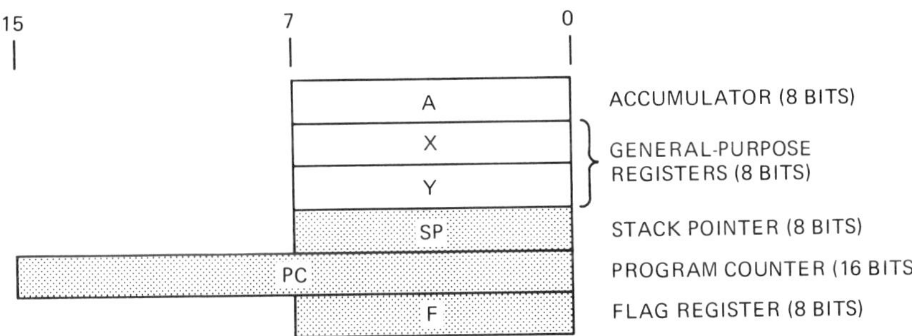

Figure 6-5 6502 registers included in memory/register transfer instructions. Shaded registers are not involved.

TABLE 6-4 6502 INSTRUCTIONS FOR TRANSFERS WITH DIRECT MEMORY ADDRESSING

Source code	Object code	Symbolic notation
LDA *addr*0	A5 *byte*	$A \leftarrow (addr0)$
STA *addr*0	85 *byte*	$(addr0) \leftarrow A$
LDA *addr*	AD *byte byte*	$A \leftarrow (addr)$
STA *addr*	8D *byte byte*	$(addr) \leftarrow A$
LDX *addr*0	A6 *byte*	$X \leftarrow (addr0)$
STX *addr*0	86 *byte*	$(addr0) \leftarrow X$
LDX *addr*	AE *byte byte*	$X \leftarrow (addr)$
STX *addr*	8E *byte byte*	$(addr) \leftarrow X$
LDY *addr*0	A4 *byte*	$Y \leftarrow (addr0)$
STY *addr*0	84 *byte*	$(addr0) \leftarrow Y$
LDY *addr*	AC *byte byte*	$Y \leftarrow (addr)$
STY *addr*	8C *byte byte*	$(addr) \leftarrow Y$

*Note: addr*0 represents a zero-page, 1-byte memory address; *addr* represents an absolute, 2-byte memory address.

For example, you will find two different LDA instructions. In both instances, they load the A register from data memory. LDA *addr0*, however, loads the A register from an address in zero-page memory (somewhere between \$00 and \$FF). LDA *addr*, however, loads the A register from an address anywhere in the system's available memory space (anywhere between \$0000 and \$FFFF). The same general idea applies to the STA instructions—store the content of the A register at zero-page address *addr0* or absolute address *addr*.

EXAMPLE 6-8

Write and assemble a 6502 program that exchanges the contents of the X and Y registers without involving the A register. Use zero-page memory locations \$20 and \$21 as required. Begin the listing at 7000.

See the result, or at least one possible result, in Program 6-8. The first two instructions store the contents of the X and Y registers at zero-page memory locations

PROGRAM 6-8 6502 LISTING FOR EXAMPLE 6-8

```
7000 86 20    STX $20    STORE X REGISTER AT $20
7002 84 21    STY $21    STORE Y REGISTER AT $21
7004 A6 21    LDX $21    LOAD X FROM ADDRESS $21
7006 A4 20    LDY $20    LOAD Y FROM ADDRESS $20
```

PROGRAM 6-9 6502 LISTING FOR EXAMPLE 6-9

```
7000 A9 2A       LDA #$2A    LOAD IMMEDIATE $2A TO A
7002 8D 00 45    STA $4500   STORE A TO $4500
7005 A9 FF       LDA #$FF    LOAD IMMEDIATE $FF TO A
7007 8D 01 45    STA $4501   STORE A TO $4501
700A A9 4E       LDA #$4E    LOAD IMMEDIATE $4E TO A
700C 85 2E       STA $2E     STORE A TO ZERO PAGE $2E
```

$20 and $21, respectively. The third instruction then loads register X from address $21, and the final instruction completes the exchange by loading the Y register with the content of address $20.

And as an example of 6502 absolute addressing, consider this example:

EXAMPLE 6-9

Using the A register and some load immediate instructions, initialize some data memory locations this way:

($4500)=$2A, ($4501)=$FF, ($2E)=$4E

The complete listing is shown in Program 6-9. Notice that absolute, direct memory addressing requires 3 bytes of program memory, whereas the zero-page instruction requires just 2 bytes. The moral of the story is to use zero-page memory as often as possible to keep the programs as short as possible.

Exercises for Section 6-4

1. Write the object-code listings for the following source-code instructions, using zero-page addressing wherever possible.
   (a) LDA $4C00   (b) STA $4C   (c) STX $002A   (d) STY $3300   (e) LDY $2A

2. Write and assemble a 6502 program that exchanges the contents of the A and Y registers without affecting the content of the X register. Use zero-page memory locations $CD and $CE as required, and begin the program at $7000.

3. Cite the highest and lowest possible zero-page memory addresses; the highest and lowest possible absolute memory addresses.

4. Assume that the following program has just been completely executed on a 6502 system:

```
LDA #$4A
LDX #$FF
LDY #$3E
STA $25
```

```
STX  $26
STY  $4FFF
LDA  $26
LDY  $25
```

Then cite the content of the following registers and address locations.

(a) Register A   (b) Register X   (c) Register Y
(b) Address $0025   (e) Address $0026   (f) Address $4FFF

5. Assemble the program in problem 4, using zero-page addressing wherever possible. Begin the listing at program address $2000.

6-5 6800 REGISTER/MEMORY TRANSFERS USING DIRECT MEMORY ADDRESSING

Once you have become familiar with the notion of zero-page addressing in the context of the 6502 system, there are no new principles to be found when dealing with similar operations for the 6800 microprocessor device.

Figure 6-6 illustrates the 6800 registers that can be involved in register/memory transfers, and Table 6-5 summarizes the 8-bit transfers that are possible. The 16-bit versions of these operations are listed later in Table 6-6.

8-Bit Transfers

The 8-bit register/memory transfers for the 6800 device involve only the A and B registers. There is a load and store operation for each of them, but the number of available instructions is doubled by the option of using zero-page or absolute memory addressing.

LDAA $50, for example, implies a loading operation to accumulator A from zero-page address $50. The very same operation can be carried out using absolute memory addressing, however: LDAA $0050. Given the choice of using zero-page or absolute addressing, most programmers will opt for the former because it uses one less byte of program memory. Consider the complete listings for these two instructions.

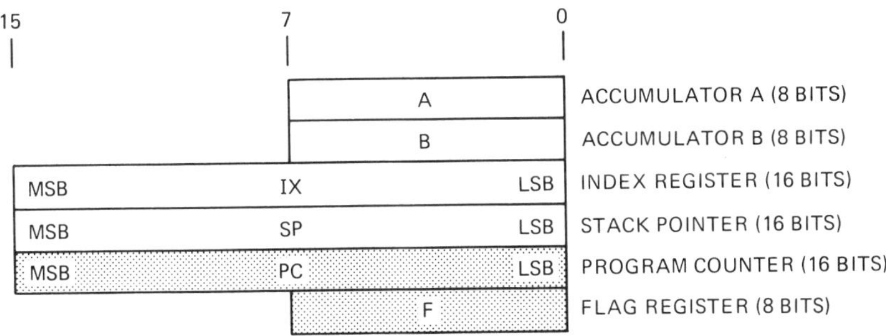

Figure 6-6 6800 registers included in memory/register transfer instructions. Shaded registers are not involved. Registers A and B are included in 8-bit transfers; registers IX and SP are included in 16-bit transfers.

Source code	Object code	Symbolic notation
LDAA *addr*0	96 *byte*	$A \leftarrow (addr0)$
STAA *addr*0	97 *byte*	$(addr0) \leftarrow A$
LDAA *addr*	B6 *byte byte*	$A \leftarrow (addr)$
STAA *addr*	B7 *byte byte*	$(addr) \leftarrow A$
LDAB *addr*0	D6 *byte*	$B \leftarrow (addr0)$
STAB *addr*0	D7 *byte*	$(addr0) \leftarrow B$
LDAB *addr*	F6 *byte byte*	$B \leftarrow (addr)$
STAB *addr*	F7 *byte byte*	$(addr) \leftarrow B$

*Note: addr*0 represents a zero-page, 1-byte memory
address; *addr* represents an absolute, 2-byte memory
address.

```
96  50    LDAA $50    LOAD ACCUMULATOR A FROM ZERO-
                      PAGE ADDRESS $50
```

and

```
B6  00  50    LDAA $0050    LOAD ACCUMULATOR A FROM AB-
                           SOLUTE MEMORY ADDRESS $0050
```

The first object-code byte in both instances is the opcode: 96 for zero-page addressing, and B6 for absolute memory addressing. In the zero-page version, the second byte is the 1-byte, zero-page memory address, 50. The second example requires two address bytes—MSB of the address, followed by the LSB. (Remember that the 6800 is unique in that the MSB of a 2-byte address always precedes the LSB.)

16-Bit Transfers

The 6800's 16-bit register/memory transfers are summarized in Table 6-6. When storing the contents of the IX or SP registers, bear in mind that their data will occupy two successive data memory address locations. Further bear in mind that the 6800 features a turned-around sequence for 2-byte addresses and data.

Thus an instruction such as

```
STS $3C00
```

literally means: Store the content of the SP register at address $3C00. The MSB portion of the SP register will be stored at the designated address, $3C00, and the LSB portion of the data will automatically go to address $3C01.

The object-code listing for that particular instruction is

```
BF  3C  00
```

Source code	Object code	Symbolic notation
LDS *addr0*	9E *byte*	SPH←(*addr0*) SPL←(*addr0+1*)
STS *addr0*	9F *byte*	(*addr0*)←SPH (*addr0+1*)←SPH
LDS *addr*	BE *byte byte*	SPH←(*addr*) SPL←(*addr+1*)
STS *addr*	BF *byte byte*	(*addr*)←SPH (*addr+1*)←SPL
LDX *addr0*	DE *byte*	IXH←(*addr0*) IXL←(*addr0+1*)
STX *addr0*	DF *byte*	(*addr0*)←IXH (*addr0+1*)←IXL
LDX *addr*	FE *byte byte*	IXH←(*addr*) IXL←(*addr+1*)
STX *addr*	FF *byte byte*	(*addr*)←IXH (*addr+1*)←IXL

Note: addr0 represents a zero-page, 1-byte memory
address; *addr* represents an absolute, 2-byte memory
address.

Zero-page addressing is available, even for the 16-bit register transfers.
So an instruction such as STS $4C will store the MSB of the SP register at
$4C in zero-page memory, and the LSB of that register will go to $4D.

EXAMPLE 6-10

Write and assemble a 6800 program that exchanges the contents of the SP and IX
registers. Use zero-page memory locations $00 through $03 as required. Begin the
program at $7000.

See the result in Program 6-10. The first instruction stores the MSB of the SP
register at data memory location $00 and the LSB of that same register at $01. The
second instruction transfers the 16-bit content of the IX register to zero-page
memory locations $02 and $03, with the MSB of the IX register going to $02.

The two final instructions simply reload the registers from zero-page addresses used by their opposite number in the first two instructions. The overall
result is an exchange of the SP and IX registers, using just 8 bytes of program
memory and 4 bytes of zero-page data memory.

PROGRAM 6-10 6800 LISTING FOR EXAMPLE 6-10

```
7000 9F 00   STS $00   STORE THE SP REGISTER AT $00
7002 DF 02   STX $02   STORE THE IX REGISTER AT $02
7004 DE 00   LDX $00   LOAD THE IX REGISTER FROM $00
7006 9E 02   LDS $02   LOAD THE SP REGISTER FROM $02
```

Write the object code listings for the following source code instructions, using zero-page addressing wherever possible.

1. LDAA $4C00
2. STAB $4C
3. STS $002A
4. STX $3300
5. LDAB $2A

7

Operate Immediate Instructions

Discussions in the preceding chapters might leave the impression that a microprocessor can do little more that pass data around from one place to another. But that is hardly the case. The fact of the matter is that some of the more computer-like instructions, such as doing some logic and arithmetic operations, are virtually useless without being able to move the data around within the system.

This chapter introduces a family of logic and arithmetic instructions. Specifically, it is about *operate immediate* instructions—logic and arithmetic instructions that receive one of the two terms from the instruction itself.

Generally speaking, microprocessors are capable of carrying out eight types of logic and arithmetic functions. Some microprocessors offer a few more and some offer a few less. But the following introduction to the subject covers the ground fairly well. The exceptions will be described in connection with the specific microprocessor devices later in the chapter.

Here are the eight fundamental logic and arithmetic functions:

1. Logically AND two bytes of data.
2. Logically OR two bytes of data.
3. Logically EXCLUSIVE-OR two bytes of data.
4. COMPARE the numerical values of two bytes of data.
5. ADD two bytes of data.
6. ADD WITH CARRY two bytes of data.
7. SUBTRACT two bytes of data.
8. SUBTRACT WITH BORROW two bytes of data.

There is at least one important feature that is common to all eight of the functions—they all work with two bytes of data at a time. A microprocessor, for example, cannot work with three or more bytes of data at one time. Of course, it is possible to do things such as sum three bytes, but not simultaneously. Such an operation calls for summing two of the bytes, and then summing the result with the third byte.

Notice that there are no instructions for other kinds of arithmetic operations, such as multiplication, division, extracting square roots, and the like. Such operations can be performed, but only as a sequence of the basic add and subtract instructions.

It would seem that the eight general logic and arithmetic instructions are inadequate for meeting the demands of modern computing technology. But they are entirely adequate in the hands of a knowledgeable programmer, and one day you might be making a good living transforming those eight simple functions into useful and sophisticated computer operations.

7-1 A GENERAL VIEW OF THE OPERATE IMMEDIATE INSTRUCTIONS

The eight basic logic and arithmetic functions all involve two bytes of data. That fact is emphasized in the list of instructions in the opening paragraphs of this chapter. The *immediate* versions of these instructions assume that one of the two bytes is already residing in the microprocessor's accumulator. The second byte is introduced into the system by the instruction itself. Alternative, nonimmediate versions of these same functions are described in a later chapter.

Logical AND Function

Table 7-1 summarizes the essential features of the AND logic function. The *truth table* shows that ANDing any two binary bits results in a logic 1 only if the two original bits are logic 1s. Otherwise, the AND function turns up a logic 0.

The *Boolean expression* is more commonly used in the context of hardware-oriented digital electronics; the corresponding *symbolic notation* is used more often in computer programming. Thus the expression $A \wedge B$ literally means: AND together the binary values of bytes A and B.

The examples in Table 7-1 show how the AND function applies to sets of 8-bit binary values—the format most often used in microprocessor technology. ANDing such bytes is a matter of ANDing the corresponding place values.

Using the truth table as a guide, AND together the least-significant bits of the two bytes. Then AND the next-higher bits, one bit position at a time, until the job is done.

Aside from performing outright AND operations on some data, the AND instruction is also useful for setting any bit, or combination of more

Boolean expression: C=A·B   or   C=AB

Symbolic notation: A∧B

Truth table:

A	B	C
0	0	0
0	1	0
1	0	0
1	1	1

8-Bit AND examples:

(1)	00001111	(2)	11011001
	01010101		10110101
	00000101		10010001

than one bit, to logic 0. Being able to selectively set bits to logic zero is a powerful programming tool for microprocessor control applications.

The task of selectively zeroing some bits and leaving others unchanged is called *bit isolation*. The bits that are left unchanged to zero are said to be isolated from the others.

Recall that the bits in an 8-bit data register are numbered from 0 through 7, beginning with the least-signifcant bit. Then suppose that it is necessary to isolate the four lower-order bits, bits 0 through 3. That amounts to setting the four higher-order bits to zero, but leaving the four lower-order bits unchanged. The job can be done by ANDing the byte with 0F hexadecimal.

Suppose that the byte to be manipulated in this fashion is 2A hexadecimal. Isolating its four lower-order bits is a matter of ANDing it with 0F hexadecimal. Here is the operation as shown in a binary form:

```
00101010     byte to be manipulated, 2AH
00001111     masking byte, 0FH
00001010     AND result
```

In that example, the four higher-order bits of the original number are *masked*—changed to zero, regardless of their original values. The four lower-order bits are thus isolated—left unchanged by the AND operation.

This matter of isolating selected bits is a matter of ANDing the byte with a binary number that has 1s in the bit positions to be isolated and 0s in the bit positions to be masked off.

By way of another example, suppose that it is necessary to isolate bits 2, 5, and 6 in a byte of data. No matter what the value of that byte might be, isolating those three bits is a matter of ANDing it with 01100100—a binary number having 1s at bit positions 2, 5, and 6. In the context of a hexadecimal-oriented program, doing the job is a matter of ANDing the original byte with 64H.

The main features of the logical OR function are summarized in Table 7-2. According to the truth table, the OR function turns up a logic-1 result whenever any or all of the original bits is a logic 1. A zero shows up in the result only when both of the original bits are zero.

The Boolean version of the OR function uses a plus sign as an operator. But since that sign is identical to the common sum, or add, operator, programmers prefer the upside-down carat symbol.

The two examples illustrate how the OR function is applied to 8-bit data. The corresponding bit positions are simply ORed on a one-for-one basis.

Just as the AND function can be used for selectively setting bit positions to logic 0, the OR function can selectively set bit positions to logic 1. The latter fact is based on the principle that any bit value that is ORed with a logic 1 will take on a value of logic 1.

Suppose that a byte such as A2 hexadecimal is resident in the microprocessor's accumulator, or A register. Doing an OR immediate instruction with hexadecimal 0F guarantees that the four lower-order bits in the original byte of data are set to logic 1. The four higher-order bytes—those ORed with zeros—are left unchanged.

10100010	original data byte, A2H
00001111	OR immediate bytes, 0FH
10101111	ORed result

Sometimes it is necessary to set just one bit in the data to logic 1. If that happens to be bit 7, an OR immediate with 80H will do the job. Bit 7 will, indeed, be set to logic 1, while the remaining bits will be left unchanged by the operation.

TABLE 7-2 SUMMARY OF LOGICAL **OR** FUNCTIONS

Boolean expression: C=A+B

Symbolic notation: A∨B

Truth table:

A	B	C
0	0	0
0	1	1
1	0	1
1	1	1

8-Bit **OR** examples:

(1)	00001111	(2)	11011001
	01010101		10110101
	01011111		11111101

Logical EXCLUSIVE-OR Function

The EXCLUSIVE-OR function, summarized in Table 7-3, works very much like the simple OR function. The primary difference is that the EXCLUSIVE-OR version *excludes* the case where both original bit values are logic 1. In short, an EXCLUSIVE-OR function turns up a logic-1 result whenever the original bit values are different from one another.

As far as computer programmers are concerned, the EXCLUSIVE-OR operation is an upside-down carat with an arc drawn near its top.

In order to appreciate a powerful application of the EXCLUSIVE-OR function, it is important to note the following characteristic: EXCLUSIVE-ORing any binary bit with a logic 0 leaves the original bit unchanged, but EXCLUSIVE-ORing it with a logic 1 complements it—switches its value from 0 to 1, or vice versa.

That leads to the notion of selectively complementing the bits in a byte of data. If, for example, it is necessary to complement bit 0 in a data byte, the job can be done by EXCLUSIVE-ORing that byte with 01 hexadecimal. Suppose that original byte is 2AH. Doing an EXCLUSIVE-OR immediate instruction with 01H, the binary version of the operation looks like this:

00101010	original data byte, 2AH
00000001	EXCLUSIVE-OR immediate byte, 01H
00101011	resulting byte

Bit for bit, the resulting byte is identical to the original one, but with one exception: The bit-0 position has been complemented—switched from 0 to 1 in this case.

An entire data byte can be complemented by doing an EXCLUSIVE-OR immediate with FFH. Thus

TABLE 7-3 SUMMARY OF LOGICAL **EXCLUSIVE-OR** FUNCTIONS

Boolean expression: $C = A \oplus B$

Symbolic notation: $A \triangledown B$

Truth table:

A	B	C
0	0	0
0	1	1
1	0	1
1	1	0

8-Bit **EXCLUSIVE-OR** examples:

(1)	00001111	(2)	11011001
	01010101		10110101
	01011010		01101100

$$
\begin{array}{ll}
00101010 & \text{original data byte, 2AH} \\
\underline{11111111} & \text{EXCLUSIVE-OR immediate byte, FFH} \\
11010101 & \text{resulting byte}
\end{array}
$$

Indeed, the original byte has been fully complemented.

ADD Function

Summation functions of any kind are virtually meaningless without reference to carry operations. When summing just two binary bits, for example, the carry operation figures in at two places—before the summation begins, and after the summation is done.

The truth table in Table 7-4 illustrates this dual role of the carry bits. C_{in} is the value of the bit that figures into the operation *before* the summation begins. This is a carry bit that is passed from a previous summation operation. In instances where there have been no previous summation operations, the value of C_{in} automatically assumes a zero value.

C_{out} is the value of the carry bit that results from a summation operation. Sometimes the C_{out} bit is ignored, but at other times, it can be more important than the sum itself.

In general terms, a summation operation takes this form:

$$C_{in}+A+B=\text{Sum}, C_{out}$$

TABLE 7-4   SUMMARY OF **ADD** FUNCTIONS, INCLUDING **ADD WITH CARRY**

Symbolic notation: A+B

Truth table:

C_{in}	A	B	Sum	C_{out}
0	0	0	0	0
0	0	1	1	0
0	1	0	1	0
0	1	1	0	1
1	0	0	1	0
1	0	1	0	1
1	1	0	0	1
1	1	1	1	1

8-Bit **ADD** examples:

$$
\begin{array}{ll}
(1) & \begin{array}{l} 00001111 \\ \underline{01010101} \\ 01100100 \end{array} \quad C_{out} \text{ of the MSB position is zero} \\
& Cs=0
\end{array}
$$

$$
\begin{array}{ll}
(2) & \begin{array}{l} 11011001 \\ \underline{10110101} \\ 10001110 \end{array} \quad C_{out} \text{ of the MSB position is 1} \\
& Cs=1
\end{array}
$$

Carry status from the previous operation is ignored.

The carry-in bit, plus the A bit, plus the B bit equals both a Sum bit and a C_{out} bit.

Thus far, the discussion has dealt with the matter of summing two binary bits, taking into account any carry-in and carry-out values. The same general notion applies to the process of summing two multibit numbers, including 8-bit binary numbers of the sort used in most microprocessor systems.

In effect, the microprocessor works the addition truth table for each bit position, beginning with the least-significant bit position and proceeding, one bit at a time, through the most-significant bit position. The C_{in} and C_{out} bits figure into each of these simple summation steps, with the C_{out} of one bit position becoming the C_{in} bit for the next.

When summing two multibit numbers, two carry values take on special importance—the carry-in bit to the least-signficant bit position, and the carry-out bit from the most-significant bit position. Where does the original carry-in bit come from, and where does the final carry-out bit go? The answer to that question leads to the notion of the microprocessor's *carry status*.

The system's carry status prior to a summation operation reflects the value of the carry-in bit to the least-significant bit position. As the summation comes to a conclusion, however, the system's carry status reflects the value of the carry-out bit from the most-significant bit position.

So the system's carry status is a single bit that, at one moment, indicates a carry-in bit value, but at another moment, the carry-out bit value. If, just prior to doing a summation operation, the carry status has a value of 1, the implication is that a carry-in value of 1 is in order. If, at the conclusion of the summation operation, the carry status is a 0, the implication is that the operation turned up a carry-out value of 0.

The system's carry status is held as a bit in the flag, or F, register. Every microprocessor has an F register, and every microprocessor's F register includes a carry-status bit. Although manufacturers of the various microprocessor tend to name the carry-status bit differently, the convention through this book is to label it Cs. Thus any future reference to a Cs bit is a reference to the value of the carry status of the system.

In the examples in Table 7-4, the first one results in a carry-out of logic 0 from the most-significant bit position. Cs thus takes on a value of 0. The second example happens to have a carry-out of logic 1, so the Cs is set to logic 1.

It so happens that the carry status prior to doing the summation is not relevant to the simple ADD function featured in this section. It is ignored— it plays no part in the summation operation. The carry status prior to doing the summation is quite important, however, when doing an ADD WITH CARRY function; but that is a topic reserved for the next section.

Before leaving the present discussion, it is important to address the matter of adding two binary numbers having a sum that is greater than decimal 255. An 8-bit number can take on any integer value between 0 and 255 decimal. In a hexadecimal context, the range is from 0 to FFH. But what happens when one attempts to add two numbers such as 200 and 100? The result,

300 decimal, cannot be fit into an 8-bit binary format—it is too large. It requires a 9-bit binary number.

But there is nothing built into the microprocessor to prevent one from attempting to sum numbers having a result that is larger than an 8-bit register can handle. Whenever such a thing happens, the numbers in the register simply *wrap around* past the highest possible number (255 decimal) and begin all over from zero.

Suppose that the decimal number 254 is residing in the accumulator when you attempt to add a decimal 3 to it. The "correct answer" is, of course, 257; but that number cannot be represented with just 8 binary bits. So the accumulator wraps around through zero and starts all over. In response to the 254 + 3 situation, the result will be 1, decimal.

Looking at the same situation from a different angle, suppose that a decimal 254 is in the accumulator and you *increment* that value by 1. If you increment three times in succession, that is the same thing as adding 3 to the original number. The increment sequence looks like this:

    254   the starting point
    255   increment 1 count
      0   increment—wraparound occurs
      1   increment 1 more

Using a hexadecimal format, the same sequence looks like this:

    FE
    FF
    00   wraparound occurs here
    01

In binary, the sequence looks like this:

    11111110
    11111111
    00000000
    00000001

Wraparounds can thus occur anytime a program is using ADD functions. Fortunately, there is a built-in mechanism for detecting the occurrence of a wraparound condition. The Cs flag signals it.

That carry status flag, you recall, responds to a carry-out condition from the most-significant bit position. When doing ADD functions, the only time a carry-out of that sort occurs is when a wraparound takes place. The Cs flag is thus an effective wraparound detector. It is set to logic 1 when wraparound occurs; otherwise, it is set to logic 0.

ADD WITH CARRY Function

The ADD WITH CARRY function is an extension of the simple ADD function just described. The only difference is that the carry version takes into account the carry status of the system prior to doing the summation. It simply adds the carry status bit to the sum of the two original numbers. If the Cs bit happens to be a zero, the result is no different from that found by doing a simple ADD function. But if the Cs bit happens to be a logic 1 when the summation begins, the result is affected—it is one number larger than a simple ADD function would turn up. Here is the general symbolic form of the ADD WITH CARRY function:

$$A+B+Cs$$

After the summation with carry is done, the Cs bit is again affected. It is set to logic 1 if a carry-out occurs from the most-significant bit position (a wraparound takes place), and it is set to zero if no such carry-out occurs.

The ADD WITH CARRY function is used when summing numbers that are too large to fit into an 8-bit register. It is too early in the discussion to describe this sort of multibyte, or *double-precision*, addition in any detail, so it is sufficient to say that the carry status from one byte of summation serves as the carry-in bit for the next byte of addition.

SUBTRACT Function

There is always a potential for some confusion regarding the terminology used for microprocessor subtraction operations. Most of us are accustomed to the notion of borrowing place values when attempting to subtract one digit from another that has a smaller value. The "borrowing" mechanism commonly used by human beings is not the same one used by microprocessors. Microprocessors use a carry mechanism that is, in principle, identical to the carry operations for summation operations.

This fact is driven home when you notice that all the microprocessor devices described in this book use the same flag bit—the Cs carry status bit—for both addition and subtraction functions. When doing subtraction operations, the carry status is a reflection of the "borrow" that is to take place.

Note the truth table in Table 7-5. It is used in exactly the same way as the summation truth table in Table 7-4; only the pattern of 1's and 0's in the "Diff" and "C_{out}" columns are different.

In this case, the C_{out} bit indicates whether or not a borrow was necessary to subtract the two bits. A value of 1 indicates that a borrow was necessary; a 0 indicates that it was not. Whether or not a borrow was necessary, the correct solution already exists as Diff; and if a borrow was necessary to get that solution, the system compensates by subtracting 1 from the next-higher bit subtraction operation.

C_{in} signals whether or not the previous operation called for doing a borrow.

The system thus carries out the subtraction operation, beginning from the least-significant bit position and proceeding, one bit at a time, through the most-significant bit position. The C_{out} from one bit manipulation is thus considered the C_{in} bit for the next one. See the two examples in Table 7-5.

As in the case of summation operations, two carries (or "borrows") are

Symbolic notation: A–B

Truth table:

C_{in}	A	B	Diff	C_{out}
0	0	0	0	0
0	0	1	1	1
0	1	0	1	0
0	1	1	0	0
1	0	0	1	1
1	0	1	0	1
1	1	0	0	0
1	1	1	1	1

8-Bit SUBTRACT examples:

(1)   00001111 C_{out} of the MSB position is zero
       01010101
       10111010
    Cs=1

(2)   11011001 C_{out} of the MSB position is 1
       10110101
       00100100
    Cs=0

Carry status (Cs) from the previous operation is ignored.

of special significance: the C_{in} to the least-significant bit position and the C_{out} from the most-significant bit position. The carry status flag, Cs, holds those values.

Prior to doing a subtraction operation, the Cs flag holds the C_{in} bit. When the operation is completed, that same flag indicates the C_{out} bit from the most-significant bit position.

The simple SUBTRACT function ignores the carry status at the beginning of the operation. It assumes that the C_{in} to the least-significant bit position is 0. The function takes the general form

$$\text{A–B Diff, Cs}$$

Byte B is subtracted from byte A, resulting in the difference between the two and a setting of the Cs flag to 1 or 0.

It is quite possible to cause a wraparound condition when doing subtraction operations. In this case, a wraparound occurs whenever the correct solution is a number less than zero.

Suppose that you are attempting to subtract 3 from 1. The correct answer is – 2, but we have not discussed the matter of representing negative numbers. Subtracting decimal 3 from decimal 1 will turn up a decimal 254— a number created by backing up the register through zero and into the higher range of 8-bit numbers. Doing the same sort of job by *decrementing* the register three times in succession, the decimal format looks like this:

1	the original number
0	decrement by 1
255	decrement by 1—wraparound occurs
254	decrement by 1

When doing subtraction operations, a carry-out (or "borrow") occurs from the most-significant bit position only when the wraparound occurs. Thus the Cs flag bit is a good indicator of that situation.

SUBTRACT WITH BORROW Function

This function is identical to the simple SUBTRACT function, except that the "borrow" version takes into account the system's carry status prior to doing the actual subtraction operation. The general symbolic notation is

$$A - B - Cs$$

If the carry status is zero at the outset, the result of the SUBTRACT WITH BORROW will be identical to that found by doing a simple SUBTRACT function. On the other hand, if the carry status is 1, the result will be 1 less than that found by doing a simple SUBTRACT.

COMPARE Function

The COMPARE function merely compares the numerical values, setting or resetting some flag bits according to the relative magnitudes of those two numbers. This function actually performs a simple SUBTRACT operation, but does not generate the "answer."

When doing a COMPARE immediate, for instance, it is assumed that one of the two numbers to be compared is in the accumulator. The other number is introduced as the second byte in the object-code instruction. The system, in effect, *subtracts the number introduced by the instruction from the one in the accumulator*. The operation does not affect the value in the accumulator, but sets some flag bits.

The general symbolic form is

$$A - data$$

where *data* is the number introduced from the instruction.

As far as the affected flags are concerned, the Cs flag will be set to 1 if *data* happens to be larger than the content of the A register. Otherwise, the Cs bit is set to logic 0.

But the Cs flag cannot specify whether A is larger or equal to *data*. Another flag has to be introduced.

All microprocessors have a *zero flag* bit in the F register. This Z flag indicates whether or not the result of an operation is zero. It is set to logic 1 when, indeed, the result is zero, and it is reset to 0 when the result is some value other than zero.

If A is greater than *data*	Z=0, Cs=0
If A is equal to *data*	Z=1, Cs=0
If A is less than *data*	Z=0, Cs=1

It is thus possible to compare two 8-bit numerical values and determine their relative values by noting the status of the Z and Cs flag bits in the F register.

Exercises for Section 7-1

Use the following combinations of 8-bit binary numbers for answering the questions in this set of exercises.

(a) 00001011	(b) 10010010	(c) 11110001	(d) 01111110
00000111	01111101	11110000	10000000

1. Logically AND the numbers.
2. Logically OR the numbers.
3. EXCLUSIVE-OR the numbers.
4. Perform a simple ADD function, showing the Cs bit at the conclusion of each.
5. Perform an ADD WITH CARRY function, assuming that the Cs bit is 0 prior to the operation. Indicate the carry status at the conclusion of each.
6. Repeat problem 5, assuming that the initial carry status is 1.
7. Perform the simple SUBTRACT function, showing the carry status at the conclusion of each.
8. Perform a SUBTRACT WITH BORROW function, assuming that the Cs bit is 0 prior to the operation. Indicate the carry status at the conclusion of each problem.
9. Repeat problem 8, assuming that the initial carry status is 1.

7-2 Z-80 OPERATE IMMEDIATE INSTRUCTIONS

Table 7-6 summarizes the Z-80 instructions for performing the eight arithmetic and logic functions in an immediate fashion. They are all 2-byte instruc-

TABLE 7-6 Z-80 OPERATE IMMEDIATE INSTRUCTIONS

Source code	Object code	Symbolic notation
AND *data*	E6 *byte*	A←A∧*data*
OR *data*	F6 *byte*	A←A∨*data*
XOR *data*	EE *byte*	A←A⩒*data*
CP *data*	FE *byte*	A–*data* (only flags affected)
ADD A,*data*	C6 *byte*	A←A+*data*
ADC A,*data*	CE *byte*	A←A+*data*+Cs
SUB *data*	D6 *byte*	A←A–*data*
SBC A,*data*	DE *byte*	A←A–*data*–Cs

tions, with the first byte being the opcode and the second the *data* to be introduced from the program.

The mnemonics in the source codes fairly well reflect the nature of the function:

AND *data*	logical AND immediate function
OR *data*	logical OR immediate function
XOR *data*	logical EXCLUSIVE-OR immediate function
CP *data*	COMPARE immediate function
ADD A,*data*	ADD immediate function
ADC A,*data*	ADD WITH CARRY immediate function
SUB *data*	SUBTRACT immediate function
SBC A,*data*	SUBTRACT WITH CARRY (or "borrow") function

The mnemonics and symbolic notations both show or imply that the accumulator—the A register—is the central point for all of these operate immediate instructions. The data currently residing in the accumulator participate in all the operations and, with the notable exception of the COMPARE function, the "answer" appears in the accumulator when the operation is completed.

AND *data*, for example, logically ANDs the current content of the A register with the *data* introduced by the instruction—the data carried by the second byte in the object code. The result of the AND operation then appears in the A register, and the original data in A is lost.

As far as the COMPARE operation is concerned, the *data* introduced by the instruction is, in effect, subtracted from the current content of the A register. But in that case, no "answer" is generated; only the Z and Cs flags in the flag register are affected. The original content of the accumulator is saved—it remains intact.

And as far as the SUBTRACT and SUBTRACT WITH CARRY functions are concerned, the current content of the accumulator is always the minuend, and the *data* introduced by the instruction is always subtracted from that value. The "answer" then appears in the accumulator.

The Z flag is affected by all eight operations. If the result happens to be zero, the Z flag in the F register is set to logic 1. Otherwise, it is reset to 0. In essence, the Z flag answers this question: Is the result of the operation zero? If the answer is "yes," the Z flag is set to 1; otherwise, it is set to 0.

The carry status flag, Cs, is always reset to 0 by the three logic functions AND, OR, and EXCLUSIVE-OR. But it plays a vital role in the COMPARE and arithmetic functions.

In the case of the COMPARE and arithmetic functions, the Cs flag is set to logic 1 if a wraparound condition occurs or, in other words, there is a carry of 1 from the most-significant bit position. Otherwise, the Cs flag is reset to 0.

Suppose that you must logically AND two bytes of data, say, 2AH and 12H. Assuming that the 2AH is already residing in the accumulator, the proper instruction listing is

E6 12   AND 12H

In the object-code listing, E6 is the AND immediate opcode, and 12 is the hexadecimal number to be ANDed with the content of the accumulator.

At the conclusion of that instruction (still assuming that 2AH was originally residing in the accumulator), the accumulator will contain 02H. The Z-flag status will be 0, because the result is a nonzero number; and the Cs status flag will show a 0, because that is always the case for the three logic functions.

Now suppose that the content of the accumulator is 2AH, and you wish to ADD 12H to it. The instruction looks like this:

C6 12   ADD 12H

The C6 is the opcode for ADD immediate, and the 12 is the number to be summed with the content of the accumulator.

Running this instruction turns up a 3C hexadecimal in the accumulator. The Z flag is set to 0 because that is a nonzero result, and the Cs flag is set to 0 because no wraparound, or carry-out of the most-significant bit position, occurs.

Now, try comparing the number 12H with the content of the accumulator. Again, assume that the accumulator holds the number 2A. The instruction is

FE 12   CP 12H

The FE is the opcode for COMPARE immediate, and the 12 is the number to be compared with the content of the accumulator.

The COMPARE operation does not affect the content of the accumulator, so the accumulator will still contain the 2A at the conclusion of the instruction. The Z and Cs flags are affected, however. In this instance the number originally residing in the accumulator, 2AH, is greater than the number introduced by the instruction, 12A. Thus the Z flag is reset to 0 because the effective subtraction turns up a nonzero result—the two numbers are *not equal*. The Cs flag is also reset to 0 because the minuend, the number in the accumulator, is larger than the number being compared from the instruction.

But suppose that the numbers are reversed: The accumulator contains a 12H, and 2AH is introduced by the instruction.

FE 2A   CP 2AH

The accumulator is not affected by the result of the operation, but the flags are. As before, the Z flag is reset to zero because the two numbers are not equal—there is a nonzero difference between them. But the Cs flag is set to logic 1. Why? Because the subtrahend—the number introduced by the instruction—is larger than the number residing in the accumulator. A wraparound thus occurs, and that is responsible for setting Cs to logic 1.

Finally, suppose that you COMPARE two numbers of equal magnitude. Perhaps 2AH is resident in the accumulator and you do:

FE 2A CP 2AH

In that case, the Z flag is set to logic 1 because the difference between the two numbers is zero. The Cs flag, however, is reset to 0 because no wraparound occurs.

When doing ADD A,*data* or SUB *data*, the status of the Cs flag is ignored at the outset. There is to be no carry-in from the previous operation. The two numbers are simply summed or subtracted. The result appears in the accumulator, the Z flag is set to 1 only if the result is zero, and the Cs flag is set to 1 only if a wraparound, or carry from the most-significant bit position, occurs.

When doing ADC A,*data* or SBC A,*data*, however, the carry status prior to executing the instruction is quite important. If the Cs flag is 0 at the outset, the functions work exactly like their simple, noncarry counterparts. But if the Cs flag is 1 at the start of the operation, it plays a vital role in determining the result in the accumulator. Doing an ADC A,*data* when the Cs flag is set to 1, the result includes that extra 1: accumulator+*data*+1. Doing a SBC A,*data* when the Cs flag is set to 1, the 1 is subtracted from the overall result: accumulator−*data*−1.

Suppose, for example, that you wish to subtract 21H from the accumulator, taking into account the current carry status. Further suppose that the current content of the accumulator is 2A. The instruction looks like this:

DE 21 SBC A,21H

Literally, that means: Subtract 21H and the carry status bit from the current content of the accumulator. If the carry status happens to be zero at the outset, the results are

A=09H

Z=0

Cs=0

The accumulator contains the result of the subtraction, where Cs is originally at 0. Thus 2AH−21H−0=09H. The Z and Cs flags are both zero at the conclusion of the operation because 09H is a nonzero number and no carry occurred from the most-significant bit position.

But the answer is quite different if the Cs flag is at logic 1 at the outset. The instruction is identical, but the result is different:

A=08H

Z=0

Cs=0

The accumulator now contains the result of the subtraction, where Cs was originally at logic 1. Thus 2AH−21H−1=08H. The Z flag is cleared to 0 because 08H is a nonzero result. The Cs flag, originally at logic 1, is now reset to 0 because no carry-out from the most-significant bit position occurred during the operation.

A programmer must be cautious about using the ADC and SBC instructions, especially when preceding instructions happen to set the Cs flag to logic 1. If there is any doubt about the status of the carry flag prior to doing one of these carry-sensitive operations, the Cs flag can be intentionally set to zero or 1.

Note: The Z-80 instruction set includes two instructions that directly affect the status of the Cs flag in the F register:

```
                          37   SCF
```

and

```
                          3F   CCF
```

Both are simple, 1-byte instructions. The first one sets the carry flag to 1. CCF, however, complements the carry flag.

There are no instructions for directly clearing the Cs bit to zero. It can be done, though, by applying the two status instructions just described:

```
          37   SCF   ;SET CARRY FLAG TO 1
          3F   CCF   ;COMPLEMENT CS
```

Further routines for affecting the Cs flag in an indirect fashion are described later.

EXAMPLE 7-1

Write and assemble a Z-80 program that performs the following operations. Begin the program at address 7000H.

1. Isolate bit 0 from the B register, and load the result to address 4C00H.
2. Isolate bits 4, 5, and 6 from the C register, and load the result to address 4C01H.
3. Isolate bits 4, 5, 6, and 7 from the H register, and save the result in the H register.

The listing in Program 7-1 shows the finished program. The procedures clearly illustrate the fact that the AND operation can be carried out only in the A register. Such

```
7000 78          LD A,B        ;FETCH B REGISTER
7001 E6 01       AND 01H       ;ISOLATE BIT 0
7003 32 00 4C    LD (4C00H),A  ;LOAD RESULT TO 4C00H
7006 79          LD A,C        ;FETCH C REGISTER
7007 E6 70       AND 70H       ;ISOLATE BITS 4, 5 AND 6
7009 32 01 4C    LD (4C01H),A  ;LOAD RESULT TO 4C01H
700C 7C          LD A,H        ;FETCH H REGISTER
700D E6 F0       AND F0H       ;ISOLATE BITS 4, 5, 6 AND 7
700F 67          LD H,A        ;SAVE RESULT IN H
```

operations to be performed on data residing in other registers call for moving those data to the A register first.

EXAMPLE 7-2

Write and assemble a Z-80 program that performs the following operations. Begin the program at address 7000H.

1.   Isolate the four lower-order bits of the H register.
2.   Set bits 1 and 2 to logic 1.
3.   Complement bits 0 and 3.
4.   Save the result in the L register.

The appropriate listing is shown in Program 7-2. The example uses an AND function to isolate some bits, an OR function to set some of the bits to logic 1, and an EXCLUSIVE-OR function to complement a couple of selected bits.

EXAMPLE 7-3

Write and assemble a Z-80 program that performs this decimal-type operation: 16-4+2. Begin the program at 7000H.

See the result in Program 7-3. The first instruction does a load immediate of 16 decimal (10H) to the accumulator. The second instruction subtracts 4 decimal (04H) from the content of the accumulator, and the final instruction adds 2 to the result. At the conclusion of the program, the "answer"—14 decimal, or 0EH—will reside in the accumulator.


```
7000 7C       LD A,H     ;FETCH THE H REGISTER
7001 E6 0F     AND 0FH    ;ISOLATE BITS 0, 1, 2, AND 3
7003 F6 06     OR 06H     ;SET BITS 1 AND 2
7005 EE 09     XOR 09H    ;COMPLEMENT BITS 0 AND 3
7007 6F       MOV L,A    ;SAVE RESULT IN L
```



```
7000 3E 10  LD A,16D   ;LOAD IMMEDIATE 16D TO A
7002 D6 04  SUB 4D     ;SUBTRACT IMMEDIATE 4 DECIMAL
7004 C6 02  ADD A,2D   ;ADD IMMEDIATE 2 DECIMAL
```

NOTE: A D suffix in the source-code listing indicates that the number is written in a decimal format. The object-code listing, however, must specify the number in a hexadecimal format.

The matter of applying the ADC and SBC instructions is left to a later discussion of *double-precision arithmetic*—arithmetic using numbers larger than a single, 8-bit register can handle. That is the purpose of those instructions, anyway.

Exercises for Section 7-2

1. Using operate immediate instructions wherever possible, show the object and source codes for each of the following operations.
   (a) Isolate bits 0 and 7 in the accumulator.
   (b) Isolate the four higher-order bits in the accumulator.
   (c) Isolate bits 3 and 4 in the accumulator.
   (d) Set bits 0 and 7 in the accumulator to logic 1.
   (e) Set the four higher-order bits in the accumulator to logic 1.
   (f) Set bits 3 and 4 in the accumulator to logic 1.
   (g) Set the Cs bit in the F register to logic 1.
   (h) Set bits 0 and 1 in the accumulator to logic 0.
   (i) Complement bits 0 and 7 in the accumulator.
   (j) Complement the four lower-order bits in the accumulator.
   (k) Complement bits 3 and 4 in the accumulator.
   (l) Complement the Cs bit in the F register.

2. In each of the following cases, assume that data 0AH is resident in the A register prior to executing the indicated instruction. Show the content of the A register and the status of the Z and Cs flags after the instruction has been executed.
   (a) CP 05H   (b) CP 0AH   (c) CP 0FH
   (d) ADD A,05H   (e) ADD A,0AH   (f) ADD A,0FH
   (g) SUB 05H   (h) SUB 0AH   (i) SUB 0FH

3. Determine the content of the A register and the status of the Z and Cs flags after completing the execution of the following program:

```
LD   A,27H
ADD  A,11H
XOR    FFH
SUB    11H
AND    0FH
OR     80H
```

4. Assemble the program in problem 3, beginning at address 4C00H.

5. Write and assemble a Z-80 program that performs the following decimal-oriented arithmetic sequence. Begin the address at 1000H.

$$100 - 20 + 5 + 50$$

7-3 8080A/8085 OPERATE IMMEDIATE INSTRUCTIONS

With the notable exception of the mnemonics for the source-code instructions, the eight fundamental arithmetic and logic functions are identical for the Z-80 and 8080A/8085 systems. Compare Tables 7-6 and 7-7.

Source code	Object code	Symbolic notation
ANI *data*	E6 *byte*	$A \leftarrow A \wedge data$
ORI *data*	F6 *byte*	$A \leftarrow A \vee data$
XRI *data*	EE *byte*	$A \leftarrow A \triangledown data$
CPI *data*	FE *byte*	A-*data* (only flags affected)
ADI *data*	C6 *byte*	$A \leftarrow A + data$
ACI *data*	CE *byte*	$A \leftarrow A + data + Cs$
SUI *data*	D6 *byte*	$A \leftarrow A - data$
SBI *data*	DE *byte*	$A \leftarrow A - data - Cs$

The mnemonics in Table 7-7 correspond to the general descriptions of the operations as follows:

ANI *data*	logical AND immediate function
ORI *data*	logical OR immediate function
XRI *data*	logical EXCLUSIVE-OR immediate function
CPI *data*	COMPARE immediate function
ADI *data*	ADD function
ACI *data*	ADD WITH CARRY function
SUI *data*	SUBTRACT function
SBI *data*	SUBTRACT WITH BORROW (or "carry") function

These are all 2-byte instructions, with the opcode preceding the data byte to be introduced. All operations refer to the content of the A register. With the exception of the COMPARE operation, the result of the operation is found in the A register, or accumulator.

In all eight cases, the zero-status flag bit, Z, is set to a logic 1 whenever the result is zero. Otherwise it is reset to logic 0.

The carry-status flag bit, Cs, is always set to zero at the conclusion of one of the logic operations ANI, ORI and XRI. At the conclusion of any of the arithmetic operations, however, the Cs bit is set to 1 or 0 as follows:

Cs is set to logic 1 if the arithmetic operation results in a wraparound condition, or in other words, there is a carry-out of 1 from the most-significant bit position.

Cs is reset to logic 0 if no wraparound occurs, or if there is a carry-out of 0 from the most-significant bit position.

The foregoing discussion of accumulator activity and the status of the Z and Cs flags is really a review of the same topic presented earlier for the Z-80 device. This clearly illustrates some of the strong similarities between the Z-80 and 8080A/8085 microprocessor systems.

NOTE: Two additional instructions directly affect the carry status flag bit:

37	STC	sets the Cs flag to logic 1
3F	CMC	complements the Cs flag bit

Both are functionally identical to the Z-80's SCF and CCF instructions.

```
7000  78         MOV  A,B      ;FETCH B REGISTER
7001  E6 01      ANI  01H      ;ISOLATE BIT 0
7003  32 00 4C   STA  4C00H    ;LOAD RESULT TO 4C00H
7006  79         MOV  A,C      ;FETCH C REGISTER
7007  E6 70      ANI  70H      ;ISOLATE BITS 4, 5 AND 6
7009  32 01 4C   STA  4C01H    ;LOAD RESULT TO 4C01H
700C  7C         MOV  A,H      ;FETCH H REGISTER
700D  E6 F0      ANI  F0H      ;ISOLATE BITS 4, 5, 6 AND 7
700F  67         MOV  H,A      ;SAVE RESULT IN H
```

EXAMPLE 7-4

Write and assemble an 8080A/8085 program that performs the following operations. Begin the program at address 7000H.

1. Isolate bit 0 from the B register, and load the result to address 4C00H.
2. Isolate bits 4, 5, and 6 from the C register, and load the result to address 4C01H.
3. Isolate bits 4, 5, 6, and 7 from the H register, and save the result in the H register.

See the listing in Program 7-4. Compare it with the same task as written for the Z-80 in Program 7-1.

By way of a special exercise, see if you can rewrite Programs 7-2 and 7-3 to conform with the 8080A/8085 syntax.

7-4 6502 OPERATE IMMEDIATE INSTRUCTIONS

Table 7-8 summarizes the eight basic operate immediate instructions for the 6502 system. Recall that a pound-sign symbol (#) preceding the *data* portion of the source code specifies an immediate operation.

Although there are eight operate immediate instructions, two of them are different from any found in the instruction sets for the Z-80 and 8080A/8085. Specifically, they are COMPARE immediate operations for the X and

TABLE 7-8 6502 OPERATE IMMEDIATE INSTRUCTIONS

Source code	Object code	Symbolic notation
AND #*data*	29 *byte*	$A \leftarrow A \wedge data$
ORA #*data*	09 *byte*	$A \leftarrow A \vee data$
EOR #*data*	49 *byte*	$A \leftarrow A \triangledown data$
CMP #*data*	C9 *byte*	A-*data* (only flags affected)
CPX #*data*	E0 *byte*	X-*data* (only flags affected)
CPY #*data*	C0 *byte*	Y-*data* (only flags affected)
ADC #*data*	69 *byte*	$A \leftarrow A + data + Cs$
SBC #*data*	E9 *byte*	$A \leftarrow A - data - \overline{Cs}$

Y registers. The two systems previously described can do COMPARE operations only in the A register.

As far as the 6502 instruction set is concerned:

CMP #*data* means COMPARE the content of the A register with *data*.

CPX #*data* means COMPARE the content of the X register with *data*.

CPY #*data* means COMPARE the content of the Y register with *data*.

Two kinds of instructions are absent from the 6502 system: the simple ADD and SUBTRACT functions. The 6502 uses only ADD WITH CARRY and SUBTRACT WITH BORROW.

The remaining instructions can be related to the general expressions already described in this chapter:

AND #*data*   logical AND immediate function

ORA #*data*   logical OR immediate function

EOR #*data*   logical EXCLUSIVE-OR immediate function

All of the object codes are 2-byte instructions, with the second byte being the *data* to be introduced. And with the exception of the CPX and CPY instructions, they all assume that the A register participates in the operation.

The Logic Instructions

In principle, the three logic instructions for the 6502 work exactly like their counterparts for the Z-80 and 8080A/8085 systems. The only difference that might be worthy of any note is that the carry-status flag, Cs, is unaffected by the 6502's logic immediate operations—it is left unchanged from its status prior to doing the operations. The Cs flag in the Z 80 and 8080A/8085 systems is always reset to 0 after a logic immediate operation.

The zero-status flag bit, Z, is set to logic 1 only if the result is zero. Otherwise, it is set to logic 0. That conforms to the Z-80 and 8080A/8085 procedures.

EXAMPLE 7-5

Write and assemble a 6502 program that performs the following sequence of operations. Begin the program at address $7000.

1.   Isolate bit 0 from the X register, and load the results to address $4C00.
2.   Isolate bits 4, 5, and 6 from the Y register, and load the result to address $4C01.
3.   Isolate bits 4, 5, 6, and 7 from zero-page memory location $20, and save the result in zero-page memory location $20.

See the resulting listing in Program 7-5. Compare it with programs for similar tasks in Programs 7-1 and 7-4.

```
7000 8A           TXA              FETCH X REGISTER
7001 29 01        AND #$01         ISOLATE BIT 0
7003 8D 00 4C     STA $4C00        LOAD RESULT TO $4C00
7006 98           TYA              FETCH Y REGISTER
7007 29 70        AND #$70         ISOLATE BITS 4, 5 AND 6
7009 8D 01 4C     STA $4C01        LOAD RESULT TO $4C01
700C A5 20        LDA $20          FETCH CONTENT OF $20
700E 29 F0        AND #$F0         ISOLATE BITS 4, 5, 6 AND 7
7010 85 20        STA $20          LOAD RESULT TO $20
```

PROGRAM 7-6 COMPLETE LISTING FOR EXAMPLE 7-6

```
7000 8A           TXA              FETCH THE X REGISTER
7001 29 0F        AND #$0F         ISOLATE BITS 0, 1, 2 AND 3
7003 09 06        ORA #$06         SET BITS 1 AND 2
7005 49 09        EOR #$09         COMPLEMENT BITS 0 AND 3
7007 A8           TAY              SAVE RESULT IN Y
```

EXAMPLE 7-6

Write and assemble a 6502 program that performs the following sequence of operations. Begin the program at $7000.

1. Isolate the four lower-order bits from the X register.

2. Set bits 1 and 2 to logic 1.

3. Complement bits 0 and 3.

4. Save the result in the Y register.

This example illustrates an application of all three logic functions—AND function to isolate selected bits, OR function to set selected bits to logic 1, and the EXCLUSIVE-OR function to complement selected bits. See the listing in Program 7-6, and compare it with a similar task for the Z-80 system in Program 7-2.

COMPARE Operations

The 6502's three COMPARE functions are much like those of the other types of microprocessor devices. The operation is essentially a simple subtraction operation, with the *data* introduced by the instruction being subtracted from that residing in the specified register. The data originally in the register remain unchanged through the operation, and only some status flags are affected in an appropriate fashion.

Since it is a simple subtract function, the carry status just prior to doing the operation is ignored. If the two numbers compare (their difference in value is zero), the Z flag in the F register is set to logic 1. If the numbers have different values, the Z flag is reset to 0.

It might appear that the only difference, in principle, between the COMPARE functions for the 6502 and the other devices is the fact that the 6502 can do compare immediate operations in registers A, X, and Y, whereas the

Z-80 and 8080A/8085 devices allow compare functions only in the A register.

But there is a significant difference in the way the carry-status flag responds to the COMPARE function. At the conclusion of the COMPARE operation, and any other subtraction function for that matter, *the 6502 system inverts the Cs flag bit.*

Whenever any 6502 subtraction operation, including a COMPARE, takes place, the Cs flag is set to logic 0 when a wraparound condition occurs. In other words, the Cs flag is set to 0 whenever a subtraction operation results in a carry-out of 1 from the most-significant bit position. Otherwise, the Cs flag is set to logic 1.

Suppose that the A register contains the number $0A just prior to doing a compare immediate operation. If that number is compared with $01 (by doing a CMP #$01 instruction), $0A will remain in the A register because compare functions to not affect its content, the Z flag will be reset to 0 because the two numbers are not equal, and *the Cs flag will be set to 1.* That Cs flag status is the complement of that found by doing a simple compare immediate with the other microprocessor systems.

When comparing two numbers of equal magnitude, the content of the register is left unchanged as usual, the Z flag is set to logic 1 because the numbers are equal (zero difference in their magnitudes), and the Cs flag is set to 1 because there is no carry-out from the most-significant bit position.

Finally, if the *data* value introduced by the compare immediate instruction is greater than the value in the specified 6502 register, the Z flag will be set to 0 because there is some nonzero difference between them, and the Cs flag will be reset to 0 because there is a carry-out of 1 from the most-significant bit position.

In summary:

> If the content of register A, X, or Y is *greater than* the *data* from the compare immediate instruction, Z=0 and Cs=1.

> If the content of register A, X, or Y is *equal* to the *data* from the compare immediate instruction, Z=1 and Cs=1.

> If the content of register A, X, or Y is *less than* the *data* from the compare immediate instruction, Z=0 and Cs=0.

Indeed, the Cs flag responds differently from similar operations for the other microprocessors, but the scheme is nevertheless quite adequate for determing the relative magnitudes of two numbers: one in a register and one from the compare immediate instruction itself.

The ADD WITH CARRY and SUBTRACT WITH BORROW Functions

The 6502 does not have specific instructions for doing simple ADD and simple SUBTRACT operations. The effect of the simple arithmetic functions can be simulated, however, by first making certain the Cs flag has an appropriate status prior to doing the operation.

If, for example, you want to do a simple ADD function, simply make sure that the Cs flag is set to zero, and then specify an ADC instruction. That is an ADD WITH CARRY instruction; but with the Cs flag previously cleared to 0, the carry status has no effect on the summation operation.

And for simple SUBTRACT functions, the Cs flag ought to be set to logic 1 just prior to doing an SBC instruction. That is, indeed, a SUBTRACT WITH BORROW instruction; but since a Cs value of 1 indicates a borrow of 0 from the least-significant bit position (a feature peculiar to the 6502), the Cs status has no effect on the result.

So, even though the 6502 has no simple ADD and simple SUBTRACT instructions, the appropriate effect can be achieved by properly presetting the Cs status flag—setting it so that it has no effect on the result. Then do the ADD WITH CARRY or SUBTRACT WITH BORROW instruction as desired.

But how does one go about presetting the Cs flag bit to 0 or 1? See the following note.

NOTE: The 6502 instruction set includes two 1-byte instructions that directly affect the carry status flag bit, Cs:

38   SEC   sets the Cs flag to logic 1

18   CLC   resets the Cs flag to logic 0

When it is necessary to do a simple ADD function and one cannot be sure about the status of the Cs bit, a sequence of two instructions is advisable:

```
CLC         CLEAR THE CARRY FLAG
ADD #data   ADD A NUMBER TO THE A REGISTER
```

In that example, *data* from the second instruction is added in an immediate fashion to the content of the A register, or accumulator, and the result is left in the A register. The carry status prior to the add immediate instruction has no bearing on the result because it was cleared to zero by the CLC instruction prior to doing the add operation.

Doing a simple SUBTRACT function is a matter of preceding an SBC instruction with an SEC instruction. In other words, the Cs status should be set to logic 1, thereby causing it to have no effect on the subtraction operation.

```
SEC         SET THE CARRY FLAG TO 1
SBC #data   SUBTRACT A NUMBER FROM THE A REGISTER
```

EXAMPLE 7-7

Write and assemble a 6502 program that performs this decimal-formatted operation: 16-4+2. Begin the program at $7000.

See the listing in Program 7-7. Justify the use of the SEC and CLC instructions.

```
7000 A9 10    LDA #16    LOAD IMMEDIATE 16 TO A
7002 38       SEC        SET CARRY STATUS TO 1
7003 E9 04    SBC #04    SUBTRACT 4
7005 18       CLC        CLEAR CARRY STATUS TO 0
7006 69 02    ADC #02    ADD 2
```

Note: Data in the source-code mnemonics are assumed to be in a decimal format unless preceded by a dollar sign. In this case, all three numbers are introduced in a decimal format. The object code listing, however, must show hexadecimal data, whether the source code data are in decimal or hexadecimal format.

Exercises for Section 7-4

1. Using operate immediate instructions wherever possible, show the object and source codes for the following operations.
   (a) Isolate bits 0 and 7 in the accumulator.
   (b) Isolate the four higher-order bits in the accumulator.
   (c) Isolate bits 3 and 4 in the accumulator.
   (d) Set bit 0 in the accumulator to 0.
   (e) Set bits 3 and 4 in the accumulator to logic 1.
   (f) Set the carry status bit in the F register to 0.
   (g) Set the carry status bit in the F register to 1.
   (h) Complement bits 0 and 7 in the accumulator.

2. In each of the following cases, assume that data $0A is resident in the A register prior to executing the indicated instructions. Show the content of the A register and the status of the Z and Cs flags after the instructions have been executed.

   (a) CMP #$05   (b) CMP #$0A   (c) CMP #$0F
   (d) CLC   (e) CLC   (f) CLC
       ADC #$05   ADC #$0A   ADC #$0F
   (g) SEC   (h) SEC   (i) SEC
       SBC #$05   SBC #$0A   SBC #$0F

3. Determine the content of the A register and the status of the Z and Cs flags after completing execution of the following program:

```
LDA #$27
CLC
ADC #$11
EOR #$FF
SEC
SBC #$11
AND #$0F
ORA #$80
```

4. Assemble the program in problem 3, beginning at address $1C00.

7-5 6800 OPERATE IMMEDIATE INSTRUCTIONS

One of the unique features of the 6800 microprocessor is the possibility of using two separate accumulators, accumulator A and accumulator B. The Z-80, 8080A/8085, and 6502 have just one accumulator—the A register.

The practical significance of having two accumulators is that arithmetic and logic operations can be carried out in either or both of them. Thus the 6800's operate immediate instruction set has 16 instructions. Those 16 include the eight basic logic/arithmetic functions for two registers. See Table 7-9.

Here is how the instructions line up with the operate immediate instructions described throughout this chapter:

In principle, the operate immediate instructions for the 6800 are identical to those for the Z-80 and 8080A/8085 devices. For instance, they are all 2-byte instructions, with the *data* to be introduced following the opcode.

The zero flag status, Z, is affected by all the operations, going to logic 1 only when the result of the operation is zero. Otherwise, the Z flag bit is set to logic 0.

The carry status flag, Cs, is not affected by the six logic operations. (That follows the 6502 convention. Recall that the Cs flag is cleared to zero when running logic operations on the Z-80 and 8080A/8085 systems.) But for all the arithmetic operations, the Cs bit is set to 1 whenever there is a carry-out of 1 from the most-significant bit position or, in other words, a wraparound condition occurs. Otherwise, the Cs bit is cleared to zero.

When it comes to the SUBTRACT WITH CARRY functions, Cs is set to 1 when that carry-out of 1 occurs. That lines up with the carry/borrow convention for the Z-80 and 8080A/8085 devices. The matter of complementing the carry bit after doing a SUBTRACT WITH CARRY function is strictly a 6502 convention.

With the exception of the COMPARE operations, the result of the function is left in the designated accumulator. The content of the designated register is left unchanged after a COMPARE operation—only the flags are affected.

TABLE 7-9 6800 OPERATE IMMEDIATE INSTRUCTIONS

Source code	Object code	Symbolic notation
ANDA #data	84 byte	A←A∧data
ANDB #data	C4 byte	B←B∧data
ORAA #data	8A byte	A←A∨data
ORAB #data	CA byte	B←B∨data
EORA #data	88 byte	A←A∀data
EORB #data	C8 byte	B←B∀data
CMPA #data	81 byte	A−data (only flags affected)
CMPB #data	C1 byte	B−data (only flags affected)
ADDA #data	8B byte	A←A+data
ADDB #data	CB byte	B←B+data
ADCA #data	89 byte	A←A+data+Cs
ADCB #data	C9 byte	B←B+data+Cs
SUBA #data	80 byte	A←A−data
SUBB #data	C0 byte	B←B−data
SBCA #data	82 byte	A←A−data−Cs
SBCB #data	C2 byte	B←B−data−Cs

PROGRAM 7-8 COMPLETE LISTING FOR EXAMPLE 7-8

```
7000  84 01       ANDA  #$01     ISOLATE BIT 0 IN A
7002  B7 4C 00    STAA  $4C00    SAVE IN $4C00
7005  C4 70       ANDB  #$70     ISOLATE BITS 4, 5, AND 6 IN B
7007  F7 4C 01    STAB  $4C01    SAVE IN $4C01
700A  96 20       LDAA  $20      FETCH CONTENT OF $20 TO A
700C  84 F0       ANDA  #$F0     ISOLATE BITS 4, 5, 6 AND 7 IN A
700E  97 20       STAA  $20      SAVE RESULT IN $20
```

EXAMPLE 7-8

Write and assemble a 6800 program that carries out the following sequence of operations. Begin the program at $7000.

1. Isolate bit 0 in the A register, and load the result to address $4C00.
2. Isolate bits 4, 5, and 6 in the B register, and load the results to address $4C01.
3. Isolate bits 4, 5, 6, and 7 from zero-page memory location $20. Use the A accumulator, and load the result to zero-page memory location $20.

See the listing in Program 7-8, and compare it with a similar task as shown in Programs 7-1, 7-4, and 7-5.

EXAMPLE 7-9

Write and assemble a 6800 program that performs the following sequence of operations. Begin the listing at address $7000.

1. Isolate the four lower-order bits in the A register.
2. Set bits 1 and 2 in the A register to logic 1.
3. Complement bits 0 and 3 in the A register.
4. Load the result to the B register.

See the listing in Program 7-9, and compare it with similar programming jobs in Programs 7-2 and 7-6.

Special Carry-Status Instructions

Like most other microprocessors, including all of them described in this book, the 6800 instruction set has some 1-byte instructions that directly influence the carry-flag status.

PROGRAM 7-9 LISTING FOR EXAMPLE 7-9

```
7000  84 0F    ANDA  #$0F    ISOLATE BITS 0, 1, 2 AND 3 IN A
7002  8A 06    ORAA  #$06    SETS BITS 1 AND 2 IN A TO 1
7004  81 09    CMPA  #$09    COMPLEMENT BITS 0 AND 3 IN A
7006  17       TAB           TRANSFER A TO B
```

        0D   SEC   sets the Cs bit to logic 1
        0C   CLC   clears the Cs bit to logic 0

Since the 6800 (unlike the 6502) has simple ADD and SUBTRACT instructions available, the carry setting and clearing operations are not as critical for most arithmetic operations.

Exercises for Section 7-5

1. Using operate immediate instructions wherever possible, show the object and source codes for doing each of the following operations.
   (a) Isolate bits 0 and 7 in the A accumulator.
   (b) Isolate the four higher-order bits in the B accumulator.
   (c) Clear bits 3 and 4 in the A accumulator to 0.
   (d) Clear the Cs flag bit to 0.
   (e) Set bits 0 and 7 in the A accumulator to logic 1.
   (f) Set the four higher-order bits in the B accumulator to logic 1.
   (g) Set the Cs bit in the flag register to logic 1.
   (h) Complement bits 0 and 1 in the A accumulator.
   (i) Complement the four lower-order bits in the B accumulator.

2. In each of the following cases, assume that data $0A is resident in the A accumulator prior to executing the indicated instructions. Show the content of the A accumulator and the status of the Z and Cs flags after each instruction has been executed.

   (a) CMPA #$05   (b) CMPA #$0A   (c) CMPA #$0F
   (d) ADDA #$05   (e) ADDA #$0A   (f) ADDA #$0F
   (g) SUBA #$05   (h) SUBA #$0A   (i) SUBA #$0F

3. Determine the content of the B accumulator and the status of the Z and Cs flags after completing execution of the following program:

```
LDAB  #$27
ADDB  #$11
EORB  #$FF
SUBB  #$11
ANDB  #$0F
ORAB  #$80
```

4. Assemble the program in problem 3, beginning at address $1C00.

ANDA #data	logic AND immediate in the A accumulator
ANDB #data	logic AND immediate in the B accumulator
ORAA #data	logic OR immediate in the A accumulator
ORAB #data	logic OR immediate in the B accumulator
EORA #data	logic EXCLUSIVE-OR immediate in the A accumulator
EORB #data	logic EXCLUSIVE-OR immediate in the B accumulator
CMPA #data	COMPARE immediate in the A accumulator
CMPB #data	COMPARE immediate in the B accumulator
ADDA #data	ADD immediate in the A accumulator

ADDB *#data*   ADD immediate in the B accumulator
ADCA *#data*   ADD WITH CARRY in the A accumulator
ADCB *#data*   ADD WITH CARRY in the B accumulator
SUBA *#data*   SUBTRACT immediate in the A accumulator
SUBB *#data*   SUBTRACT immediate in the B accumulator
SBCA *#data*   SUBTRACT WITH CARRY (or "borrow") in the A accumulator
SBCB *#data*   SUBTRACT WITH CARRY (or "borrow") in the B accumulator

8

Operate Register Instructions

Chapter 7 introduced eight basic logic and arithmetic functions that are common to most microprocessor systems. Those functions are: Logic AND, logic OR, logic EXCLUSIVE-OR, ADD, ADD WITH CARRY, SUBTRACT, SUBTRACT WITH CARRY (or "borrow"), and COMPARE.

Those functions were introduced in the context of register immediate operations, however. In that case it is assumed that one of the two bytes to participate in the operation is already resident in the system's accumulator, and the second byte is introduced by the immediate instruction itself. That is the hallmark of any immediate instruction—introducing a byte or two of data from the program instruction.

This chapter features the same eight logic and arithmetic functions, but in a different context. Here it is assumed that both bytes of data to be manipulated are already resident in the microprocessor device. The program instruction, usually a simple 1-byte instruction, specifies the operation to be performed on the data.

None of the operate immediate instructions deal with double-register, or 16-bit register, arithmetic. That is possible with the *operate register* instructions featured in this chapter. What is more, there is now the possibility of doing simple *increment* and *decrement* instructions—instructions that call for increasing by one or decreasing by one the value in a specified register or register pair.

8-1 AN OVERVIEW OF THE OPERATE REGISTER INSTRUCTIONS

The following discussion is a very general one. The purpose is to convey an overall impression of the sorts of operations that can be performed within the microprocessor's internal registers. There are some significant variations among the various types of microprocessors, and those are clearly spelled out in later sections of this chapter.

AND the Contents of Two Registers

The register AND instruction logically ANDs the content of the accumulator with that of some other specified register. The result is placed into the accumulator at the conclusion of the operation. The A register is assumed to be the accumulator, so a Z-80 instruction such as

```
AND B
```

logically ANDs the current content of the A register with that of the B register. The result is saved in the A register.

The original content of the B register is preserved, but the original data in the A register are lost, being replaced by the result of the AND function.

The carry status flag, Cs, is usually considered irrelevant through any logic operation, but the Z flag is affected according to the result. If the result is a zero in the accumulator, the Z flag is set to logic 1. A nonzero result clears the Z flag to 0.

The Z-80 and 8080A/8085 microprocessors have a relatively large number of 8-bit working registers, so it follows that their instruction sets have a number of register-AND-instructions—one for each of those registers. There is even a do-nothing instruction, AND A. That one ANDs the content of the A register with itself, and that never changes anything.

The accumulator must always be part of an operate register instruction. So when it is necessary to AND the content of the B and C registers, for instance, the content of one of those registers must first be transferred to the A register. The following program sequence, using Z-80 mnemonics, effectively ANDs the contents of the B and C registers:

```
LD  A,B   ;FETCH B TO A
AND C   ;AND WITH C
```

At the conclusion of that sequence, the two original bytes of data still reside in their respective registers. The result, however, appears in the A register.

OR the Contents of Two Registers

ORing the contents of two internal registers is a process that is virtually identical to the one just described for ANDing them. One of the two bytes must be in the accumulator, and the instruction specifies the register location of the second byte.

At the conclusion of the register-OR operation, the result appears in the accumulator, and the Z flag is set or cleared according to the result—set to 1 if the result is zero, or cleared to zero if the result is a nonzero number. The Cs flag is usually ignored.

The Z-80 instruction

OR B

logically ORs the content of the B register with that of the A register, and the result is placed into the A register.

The OR version of a do-nothing instruction is OR A. That one ORs the content of the A register with itself; and ORing any number with itself yields no change in its value.

EXCLUSIVE-OR the Contents of Two Registers

There are no special surprises regarding the register version of the EXCLU-SIVE-OR function. The content of the accumulator is EXCLUSIVE-ORd with that of the register specified in the instruction, and the result is placed into the accumulator, or A register.

XOR B, for example, is the Z-80's version of a register EXCLUSIVE-OR instruction. The current content of the B register is EXCLUSIVE-ORd with the current content of the accumulator, and the result appears in the accumulator.

The Z and Cs flag bits follow the format already described for the AND and OR functions.

The matter of EXCLUSIVE-ORing a byte of data with itself has special significance, especially for the Z-80, 8080A/8085, and 6502 microprocessor devices. Those devices have no instructions for directly clearing the accumulator to zero. (You will find later that the 6800 does.) The accumulator in the three devices just cited can be cleared to zero by doing an EXCLUSIVE-OR instruction on the accumulator.

Using Z-80 mnemonics,

XOR A

quite effectively zeros the accumulator, because *any value EXCLUSIVE-ORed with itself yields a zero result.*

COMPARE the Contents of Two Registers

The register-COMPARE instruction allows the content of a specified 8-bit register to be compared with that residing in the accumulator. In effect, this is a subtraction operation, and *the value in the specified register is always subtracted from the value in the accumulator.*

As in the case of any COMPARE operation, the original content of the accumulator is left unchanged, and only the flags are affected according to the relative magnitudes of the data.

Using Z-80 mnemonics, the instruction *CP B* literally means: Compare the binary values of the data in register B with that in the accumulator, register A. The value of B is, in effect, subtracted from that in the accumulator. The flags are affected as follows:

If A is greater than B   Z=0,   Cs=0

If A is equal to B   Z=1,   Cs=0

If A is less than B   Z=0,   Cs=1

Comparing the value of the A register with itself—doing a CP A—might seem to be another one of those do-nothing instructions. But that is not necessarily the case for the Z-80 and 8080A/8085 microprocessors. Recall that the instruction sets for those two devices do not have simple, 1-byte instructions for setting the Cs flag to 0—an operation sometimes necessary prior to doing a SUBTRACT WITH CARRY instruction. There is no need for such an instruction, because the compare-with-self instruction does just that; it guarantees that the Cs flag bit is cleared to 0.

ADD the Contents of Two Registers

The register version of the ADD function allows the programmer to sum the content of a designated register with the content of the accumulator. The result is placed into the accumulator at the conclusion of the operation, and the Z and Cs flags are affected according to the result. The Z flag is set to 1 only if the "answer" in the accumulator is zero; otherwise, it is cleared to 0. And the Cs flag bit is set to logic 1 only if a wraparound condition results—the sum of the two numbers is greater than decimal 255.

Since any number added to itself effectively doubles the value of that number, instructions calling for adding the content of the accumulator to itself forms an important link in multiplication operations.

An ADD WITH CARRY instruction is also available in the operate register group of instructions. It works much like the corresponding immediate version, taking into account the carry status prior to doing the addition operation.

SUBTRACT the Contents of Two Registers

Finally, the instruction sets have to include some subtraction operations between a designated register and the content of the accumulator. In such cases, the content of the designated register is subtracted from the content of the accumulator, and the result is found in the accumulator. Using Z-80 mnemonics,

SUB B

literally means: Subtract the content of the B register from the A register, and save the results in the A register. That particular instruction ignores any carry, or borrow, status from the previous arithmetic operation.

Subtracting the content of the accumulator from itself, doing a SUB A, always turns up a zero result, setting the Z flag to 1 and the Cs flag to 0. But it is not a desirable procedure for clearing the Cs flag (as the COMPARE with self instruction is). Unlike the CP A instruction, SUB A affects the value in the accumulator—it sets it to zero. The CP A instruction, on the other hand, clears the Cs flag bit, but leaves the number in the accumulator unchanged.

A SUBTRACT WITH CARRY (or "borrow") instruction is available in a register-register format. That instruction subtracts the content of the designated register from that of the accumulator, taking into account the carry status prior to doing the operation and placing the result in the accumulator.

INCREMENT and DECREMENT the Content
of a Register

Counting operations form the basis for many different kinds of programming routines, so the instruction sets include INCREMENT and DECREMENT instructions aimed at some of the working registers.

Using Z-80 mnemonics, INC B means: Increment the value of the B register. In other words, it instructs the system to increase the number in the B register by a count of 1.

An instruction such as DEC B means: Decrement the value of the B register, decreasing its value by a count of 1.

The 8-bit register INCREMENT and DECREMENT instructions affect the Z and Cs flags. Whenever a register is decremented to zero, for example, the Z flag is set to logic 1 immediately following the operation. And when either instruction causes a wraparound condition to occur, the Cs flag is set to logic 1.

16-Bit Operate Register Instructions

Most of the arithmetic and INCREMENT/DECREMENT instructions can apply specifically to 8-bit register pairs and 16-bit registers. A Z-80 instruction such as ADD HL,BC means: ADD the content of the HL register pair to that of the BC register pair, and place the result into the HL pair. That is a case of 16-bit addition. A similar sort of instruction allows you to subtract the content of the BC register pair from that of the HL pair, placing the result into the HL pair.

INC HL is an example of an instruction that increments the content of the HL register pair, while DEC BC decrements the content of the BC pair.

All the microprocessors described in this book, with the exception of the 6502 (which has no 16-bit working registers or register pairs), have some 16-bit operate register instructions. Their features are described in connection with the specific devices in the remainder of this chapter.

Table 8-1 summarizes the Z-80's operate register instructions, and Fig. 8-1 shows the registers that can participate directly in those instructions.

They are all 1-byte instructions that involve the accumulator, or A register, and the register designated by the instruction itself. The mnemonics are interpreted as follows:

AND r Logically AND the content of register r with the content of the accumulator, and place the result into the accumulator.

OR r Logically OR the content of register r with the content of the accumulator, and place the result into the accumulator.

XOR r Logically EXCLUSIVE-OR the content of register r with the content of the accumulator, and place the result into the accumulator.

Those three logic operations leave the CS flag bit cleared to zero. The carry status is actually irrelevant during a logic function. The Z flag is affected, however; it is set to logic 1 only if the result in the accumulator is all 0s. Otherwise, Z is cleared to 0.

TABLE 8-1   Z-80 8-BIT OPERATE REGISTER INSTRUCTIONS

Source code	Object code	Symbolic notation
AND A	A7	
AND B	A0	
AND C	A1	
AND D	A2	$A \leftarrow A \wedge r$
AND E	A3	(logic AND functions)
AND H	A4	
AND L	A5	
OR A	B7	
OR B	B0	
OR C	B1	
OR D	B2	$A \leftarrow A \wedge r$
OR E	B3	(logic OR functions)
OR H	B4	
OR L	B5	
XOR A	AF	
XOR B	A8	
XOR C	A9	
XOR D	AA	$A \leftarrow A \triangledown r$
XOR E	AB	(logic EXCLUSIVE-OR functions)
XOR H	AC	
XOR L	AD	
CP A	BF	
CP B	B8	
CP C	B9	A-r (only flags affected)
CP D	BA	(COMPARE functions)

Source code	Object code	Symbolic notation
CP E	BB	
CP H	BC	
CP L	BD	
ADD A,A	87	
ADD A,B	80	
ADD A,C	81	$A \leftarrow A + r$
ADD A,D	82	(ADD functions)
ADD A,E	83	
ADD A,H	84	
ADD A,L	85	
ADC A,A	8F	
ADC A,B	88	
ADC A,C	89	$A \leftarrow A + r + Cs$
ADC A,D	8A	(ADD WITH CARRY functions)
ADC A,E	8B	
ADC A,H	8C	
ADC A,L	8D	
SUB A	97	
SUB B	90	
SUB C	91	$A \leftarrow A - r$
SUB D	92	(SUBTRACT functions)
SUB E	93	
SUB H	94	
SUB L	95	
SBC A,A	9F	
SBC A,B	98	
SBC A,C	99	$A \leftarrow A - r - Cs$
SBC A,D	9A	[SUBTRACT WITH BORROW (or "carry") functions]
SBC A,E	9B	
SBC A,H	9C	
SBC A,L	9D	
INC A	3C	
INC B	04	
INC C	0C	$r \leftarrow r + 1$
INC D	14	(INCREMENT instructions)
INC E	1C	
INC H	24	
INC L	2C	
DEC A	3D	
DEC B	05	
DEC C	0D	$r \leftarrow r - 1$
DEC D	15	(DECREMENT instructions)
DEC E	1D	
DEC H	25	
DEC L	2D	

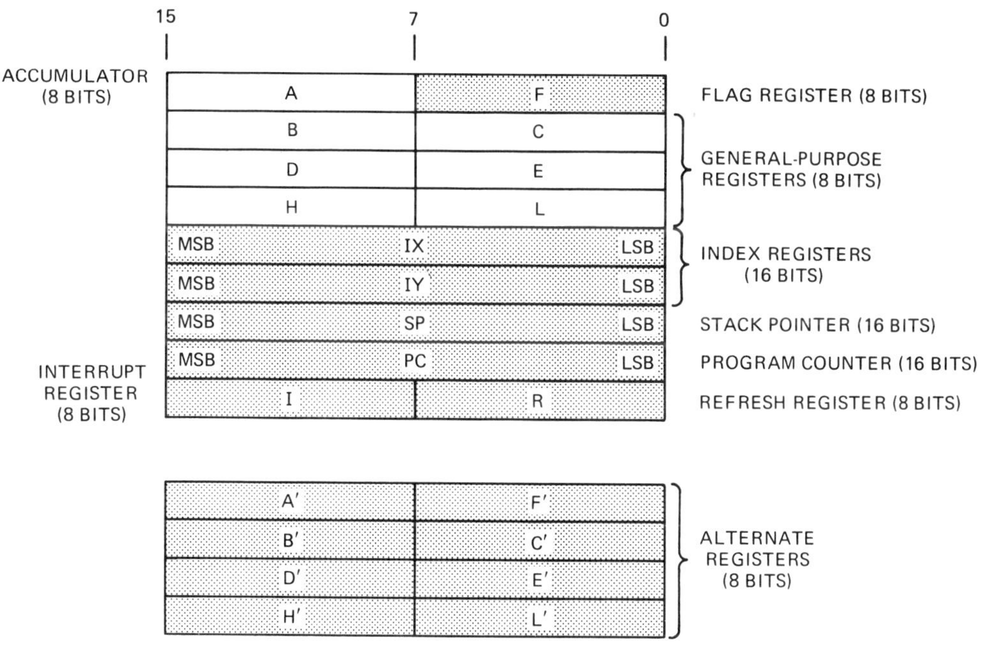

Figure 8-1 Z-80 registers involved in 8-bit operate register instructions. Shaded registers are not involved.

CP *r*	COMPARE the value in register *r* with the content of the accumulator. The data in both registers are left unchanged, but the Z and Cs flag bits are affected according to the relative magnitudes of the two numbers. In effect, the content of register *r* is always subtracted from the content of the accumulator.
ADD A,*r*	Do a simple ADD on the data in register *r* and the content of the accumulator. The result is placed into the accumulator, and the Z and Cs flags are affected according to the result of the operation.
ADC A,*r*	Do an ADD WITH CARRY operation on the values contained in register *r* and the accumulator. The result appears in the accumulator, and the Z and Cs flags are affected accordingly.
SUB r	Do a simple SUBTRACT operation, subtracting the value in register *r* from that of the accumulator. The result shows up in the accumulator, and the status flags are affected according to the result.
SBC A,*r*	Do a SUBTRACT WITH BORROW (or "carry"), subtracting the content of the *r* register from the accumulator. The answer is deposited into the accumulator, and the Z and Cs flags follow the result.
INC *r*	INCREMENT the data in register *r* by 1. The result remains in register *r*, and with the exception of the INC A instruction, the data in the accumulator are unaffected. The Z and Cs flags are affected, however, according to the result.

DEC *r* DECREMENT the data in register *r* by 1. The result remains in register *r*, and the Z and Cs flags are affected in the appropriate fashion.

A nontrivial application of these instructions is determining whether or not the data in two different registers have the same value. There are a couple of ways to approach the situation, as illustrated here.

Suppose that the idea is to compare the values in registers D and E. Here is one approach:

```
7A   LD A,D   ;FETCH D TO A
BB   CP E     ;COMPARE WITH E
```

The first instruction transfers the content of register D to A, where it can be compared with the content of register E in the second instruction. The data in registers D and E are left unchanged, and the Z flag will be set to logic 1 only if the two numbers are identical. The Cs flag is set to logic 1 if it happens that the value in register E is greater than that in D.

A second approach to the same situation:

```
7A   LD A,D   ;FETCH D TO A
AB   XOR E    ;EXCLUSIVE-OR WITH E
```

The first instruction transfers the content of the D register to the accumulator, and the second instruction does an EXCLUSIVE-OR between the content of the accumulator and the E register. Recall that doing that sort of logic operation on identical data turns up zero as a result. In this case, all 0s in the accumulator indicates that the contents of the D and E registers is identical. The data originally in registers D and E remain intact—only the content of the A register and the Z flag are affected. This particular technique does not affect the Cs flag bit, so there is no information regarding the relative magnitudes of the two original numbers.

More examples of Z-80, 8-bit operate register instructions appear in the exercises at the end of this section.

16-Bit Operations

Table 8-2 shows the 16-bit versions of the operate register instructions for the Z-80 system, and Fig. 8-2 shows the register pairs and 16-bit register that can be involved.

These instructions can be summed up as follows:

ADD HL,r_{16} Do a simple, 16-bit ADD operation between the content of the HL register pair and register(s) r_{16}. In a manner of speaking, the HL register pair is the 16-bit "accumulator." The result of the ADD operation is placed into the HL register pair, and its original data are lost. The data in r_{16}, however, are preserved. *The Z flag is not affected by this operation*, but the Cs flag bit is affected.

TABLE 8-2 Z-80 16-BIT OPERATE REGISTER INSTRUCTIONS

Source code	Object code	Symbolic notation
ADD HL,BC	09	
ADD HL,DE	19	$HL \leftarrow HL + r_{16}$
ADD HL,HL	29	(ADD to HL a register pair or SP register [a])
ADD HL,SP	39	
ADD IX,BC	DD 09	
ADD IX,DE	DD 19	$IX \leftarrow IX + r_{16}$
ADD IX,IX	DD 29	(ADD to IX register a register pair or SP register [a])
ADD IX,SP	DD 39	
ADD IY,BC	FD 09	
ADD IY,DE	FD 19	$IY \leftarrow IY + r_{16}$
ADD IY,IY	FD 29	(ADD to IX register a register pair or SP register [a])
ADD IY,SP	FD 39	
ADC HL,BC	ED 4A	
ADC HL,DE	ED 5A	$HL \leftarrow HL + r_{16} + Cs$
ADC HL,HL	ED 6A	(ADD WITH CARRY to HL a register or register pair)
ADC HL,SP	ED 7A	
SBC HL,BC	ED 42	
SBC HL,DE	ED 52	$HL \leftarrow HL - r_{16} - Cs$
SBC HL,HL	ED 62	(SUBTRACT WITH BORROW from HL a register or register pair)
SBC HL,SP	ED 72	
INC BC	03	
INC DE	13	
INC HL	23	$r_{16} \leftarrow r_{16} + 1$
INC IX	DD 23	(INCREMENT 16-bit register or register pair [a])
INC IY	FD 23	
INC SP	33	
DEC BC	0B	
DEC DE	1B	
DEC HL	2B	$r_{16} \leftarrow r_{16} - 1$
DEC IX	DD 2B	(DECREMENT 16-bit register or register pair [a])
DEC IY	FD 2B	
DEC SP	3B	

[a]The Z flag is unaffected by the instruction.

The Cs flag is set to logic 1 only if a carry-out of 1 occurs from the most-significant bit position in the H register or, in other words, a 16-bit wraparound effect occurs.

ADD IX,r_{16} — This operation is virtually identical to ADD HL,r_{16}, except that the 16-bit IX register serves as the "accumulator."

ADD IY,r_{16} — The 16-bit IY register is the "accumulator" for this instruction. Otherwise, it is identical to the other two 16-bit ADD instructions.

ADC HL,r_{16} — Do a 16-bit ADD WITH CARRY operation between the content

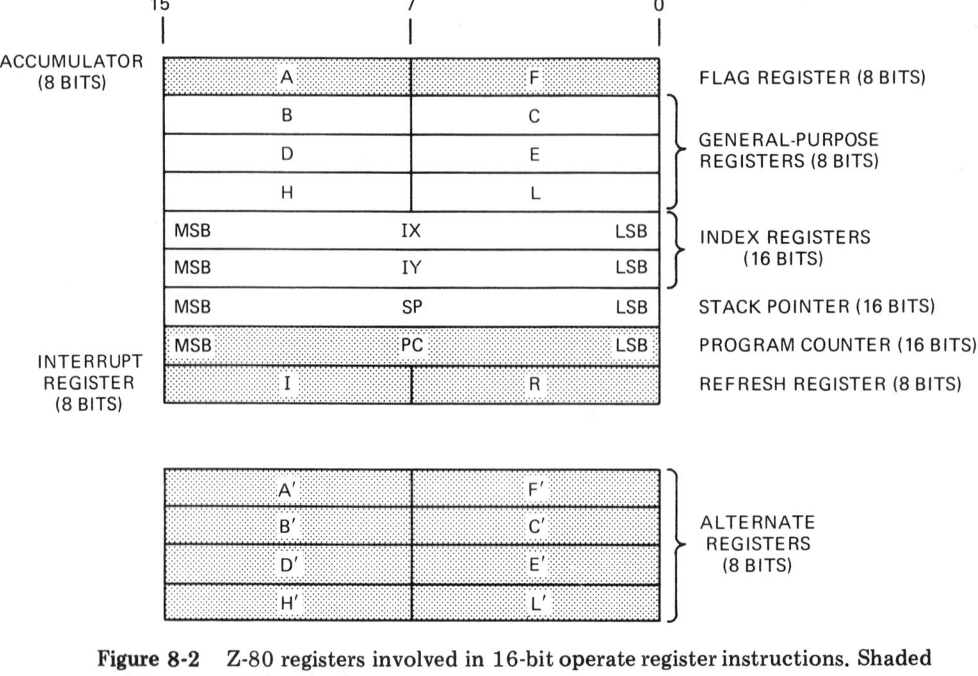

Figure 8-2 Z-80 registers involved in 16-bit operate register instructions. Shaded registers are not involved.

of the HL register pair and register(s) r_{16}. The carry status prior to doing this operation is taken into account. That is one significant difference between this instruction and the simple, 16-bit ADD version of it. Another important difference is that *the Z flag bit is affected*, going to logic 1 if the result in the HL pair is 16 zeros. The Cs flag bit is affected according to the value of the bit carried out from the most significant bit position of the HL-pair "accumulator."

SBC HL,r_{16} Do a 16-bit SUBTRACT WITH BORROW, with the HL register pair acting as the accumulator. Both the Z and Cs are affected in the appropriate fashion.

INC r_{16} INCREMENT by 1 the content of the designated register(s), r_{16}. *No flags are affected by this instruction.*

DEC r_{16} DECREMENT by 1 the content of the designated register(s), r_{16}. Again, *no flags are affected*.

These double-register operations can deal with 16-bit, 2-byte numbers ranging from decimal zero through decimal 65,535. Obviously, they are used when it is necessary to work with numbers that are too large to fit into the usual 8-bit format—from decimal 0 through decimal 255.

The fact that many of these particular operations do not affect the zero flag can be a nuisance, however. Suppose you are writing a program that is supposed to decrement the HL register pair to zero. That is a matter of applying the DEC HL instruction over and over again. But how can the system detect the moment the HL pair has reached zero so that some other critical operation can take place?

There is a fairly simple procedure for compensating for the lack of zero detection in most of these double-register instructions. The general idea is to transfer the byte from one of the registers to the accumulator, and then do an OR operation involving the other register. If, indeed, the register pair is filled with zeros, that particular OR operation will set the Z flag bit to logic 1. Here is a specific example:

```
DEC  BC
LD   A,C
OR   B
```

The first instruction decrements the content of the BC register pair. The two remaining instructions are intended to see whether or not the BC pair has been decremented to zero. First, the content of the C register is transferred to the A register, then it is logically ORd with the content of the B register. If the BC pair has been decremented to zero, the sequence—specifically, the OR instruction—sets the Z flag to logic 1. Otherwise, the Z flag is cleared to 0.

If the register in question is one of the 16-bit registers SP, IX, or IY, the zero-detection procedure requires two additional steps:

```
DEC  IX
LD   4200H,IX
LD   HL,4200H
LD   A,L
OR   H
```

The first instruction decrements the content of the IX register, and the remaining ones test for a zero result. Steps 2 and 3 effectively transfer the content of the IX register to the HL register pair, using a couple of uncommitted bytes in data memory as a common transfer point. The problem, then, is to determine whether or not the content of the HL pair is zero; and that is done as described in the preceding example. The Z flag will be set to logic 1 if, indeed, the DEC IX instruction has decremented that register to zero. Otherwise, the Z flag is cleared to zero.

The same general procedures apply to other 16-bit register and register-pair operations that do not have an inherent Z-flag setting feature.

Exercises for Section 8-2

1. Describe the literal meaning of the following Z-80 instructions.

(a) AND B	(b) AND *byte*	(c) OR C
(d) OR *byte*	(e) XOR L	(f) XOR *byte*
(g) CP B	(h) CP *byte*	(i) ADD A,B
(j) ADD A,*byte*	(k) ADC A,B	(l) SUB H
(m) SBC A,L	(n) INC A	(o) INC HL
(p) DEC A	(q) DEC SP	

2. Write the object codes for the instructions in problem 1. Use 1AH wherever an operate immediate data byte is required.

3. In each of the following cases, assume that the A register contains 05H and the B register contains 01H at the outset. Cite the contents of the A and B registers, and show the status of the Z and Cs flags at the conclusion of each operation.

(a) AND B   (b) OR B   (c) XOR B
(d) CP B   (e) ADD A,B   (f) SUB B

8-3 8080A/8085 OPERATE REGISTER INSTRUCTIONS

The 8-bit operate register instructions for the 8080A/8085 are virtually identical to those already described for the Z-80 system. Compare Tables 8-3 and 8-1. Only the source-code mnemonics are slightly different; the object codes are exactly the same. See Fig. 8-3 for the registers involved in the 8080A/8085 operate register instructions.

Since the Z-80 version of these instructions have already been described in Section 8-2, there is little to be gained by dwelling on the 8080A/8085 versions here.

TABLE 8-3   8080A/8085 8-BIT OPERATE REGISTER INSTRUCTIONS

Source code	Object code	Symbolic notation
ANA A	A7	
ANA B	A0	
ANA C	A1	
ANA D	A2	$A \leftarrow A \wedge r$
ANA E	A3	(logic AND functions)
ANA H	A4	
ANA L	A5	
ORA A	87	
ORA B	B0	
ORA C	B1	
ORA D	B2	$A \leftarrow A \vee r$
ORA E	B3	(logic OR functions)
ORA H	B4	
ORA L	B5	
XRA A	AF	
XRA B	A8	
XRA C	A9	
XRA D	AA	$A \leftarrow A \triangledown r$
XRA E	AB	(logic EXCLUSIVE-OR functions)
XRA H	AC	
XRA L	AD	
CMP A	BF	
CMP B	B8	
CMP C	B9	$A - r$ (only flags affected)
CMP D	BA	(COMPARE functions)

TABLE 8-3 (*Continued*)

Source code	Object code	Symbolic notation
CMP E	BB	
CMP H	BC	
CMP L	BD	
ADD A	87	
ADD B	80	
ADD C	81	$A \leftarrow A + r$
ADD D	82	(ADD functions)
ADD E	83	
ADD H	84	
ADD L	85	
ADC A	8F	
ADC B	88	
ADC C	89	$A \leftarrow A + r + C_s$
ADC D	8A	(ADD WITH CARRY functions)
ADC E	8B	
ADC H	8C	
ADC L	8D	
SUB A	97	
SUB B	90	
SUB C	91	$A \leftarrow A - r$
SUB D	92	(SUBTRACT functions)
SUB E	93	
SUB H	94	
SUB L	95	
SBB A	9F	
SBB B	98	
SBB C	99	$A \leftarrow A - r - C_s$
SBB D	9A	[SUBTRACT WITH BORROW (or "carry") functions]
SBB E	9B	
SBB H	9C	
SBB L	9D	
INR A	3C	
INR B	04	
INR C	0C	$r \leftarrow r + 1$
INR D	14	(INCREMENT instructions)
INR E	1C	
INR H	24	
INR L	2C	
DCR A	3D	
DCR B	05	
DCR C	0D	$r \leftarrow r - 1$
DCR D	15	(DECREMENT instructions)
DCR E	1D	
DCR H	25	
DCR L	2D	

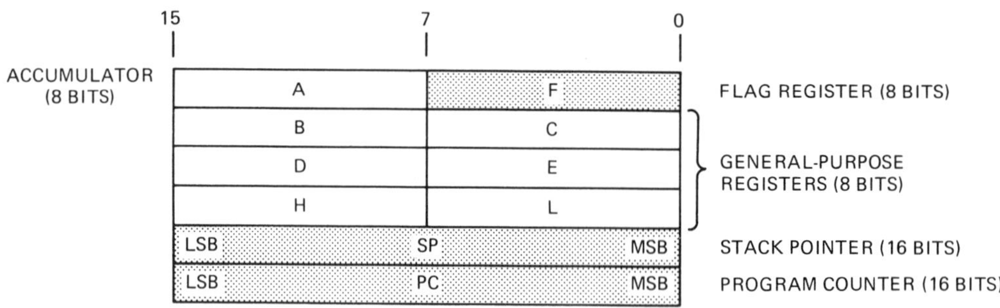

Figure 8-3 8080A/8085 registers involved in 8-bit operate register instructions. Shaded registers are not involved.

16-Bit Operations

The 16-bit operate register instruction set is considerably smaller for the 8080A/8085 system. See Table 8-4. Only the simple ADD, INCREMENT, and DECREMENT operations are available. Figure 8-4 shows the registers involved.

The DAD, or "double add," instructions all use the HL register pair as the "accumulator" for the simple ADD operation. DAD B, for example, adds the content of the BC register pair with that of the HL pair, and places the result into the HL pair. The Cs status is affected by the value carried out from the most-significant bit position in the H register, but the Z flag is not affected at all.

Having only instructions for doing a simple ADD on register pairs and the SP register, one must wonder how it is possible to do some of the other 16-bit arithmetic operations featured in the Z-80's instruction set. In most

TABLE 8-4 8080A/8085 16-BIT OPERATE REGISTER INSTRUCTIONS

Source code	Object code	Symbolic notation
DAD B	09	
DAD D	19	$HL \leftarrow HL + r_{16}$
DAD H	29	(ADD to HL a register pair or the SP register)
DAD SP	39	
INX B	03	
INX D	13	$r_{16} \leftarrow r_{16} + 1$
INX H	23	(INCREMENT register pair or the SP register)
INX SP	33	
DCX B	0B	
DCX D	1B	$r_{16} \leftarrow r_{16} - 1$
DCX H	2B	(DECREMENT register pair or the SP register)
DCX SP	3B	

Note: None of these instructions affect the Z flag.

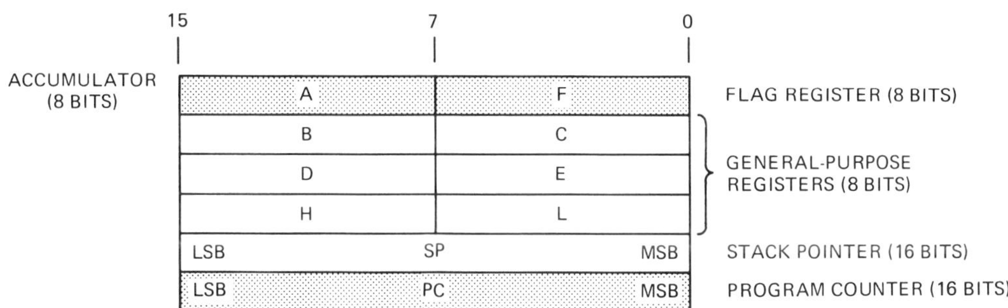

Figure 8-4 8080A/8085 registers involved in 16-bit operate register instructions. Shaded registers are not involved.

instances, the solution to the situation is to break up the job into a series of 8-bit register operations.

EXAMPLE 8-1

Write and assemble an 8080A/8085 program that does the job of the Z-80's ADC HL,BC instruction. Begin the program at address 4A00H.

See the result in Program 8-1. The first three instructions do an ADD WITH CARRY operation on the lower-order bytes of the HL and BC register pairs, saving the result in the L register. The next three instructions do an ADD WITH CARRY on the higher-order bytes, saving the result in the H register. At that point, the double-register ADD WITH CARRY is done, and the result is in the HL register pair. All that remains is to affect the Z flag according to the result. That is accomplished by the final instruction.

At the conclusion of Program 8-1, the sum of the HL and BC register pairs is in the HL registers. The Z flag is set to 1 only if the result is zero; otherwise, it is cleared to zero. Unfortunately, the carry status is valid just before the ORA L instruction is executed. Since logic operations for the 8080A/8085 always set the Cs bit to 0, any carry from this operation is lost. There is an effective way to deal with the matter, but that must await a later discussion.

It is possible to mimic the Z-80's SBC HL,BC instructions by substituting the SBB L and SBB H instructions for ADC L and ADC H, respectively, in Program 8-1.

PROGRAM 8-1 LISTING FOR EXAMPLE 8-1

```
4A00 79    MOV A,C    ;TRANSFER LSB OF BC TO A
4A01 8D    ADC L      ;ADD WITH CARRY TO LSB OF HL
4A02 6F    MOV L,A    ;TRANSFER RESULT TO L
4A03 78    MOV A,B    ;TRANSFER MSB OF BC TO A
4A04 8C    ADC H      ;ADD WITH CARRY TO MSB OF HL
4A05 67    MOV H,A    ;TRANSFER RESULT TO H
                      ;SUM NOW IN HL PAIR
4A06 B5    ORA L      ;CHECK FOR ZERO RESULT
```

Exercises for Section 8-3

1. Assume that the following operations have just been performed. In each case, determine the content of the A and B registers, and the status of the Cs and Z flags.

(a) MVI A,2AH
    MVI B,01H
    ANA B

(b) MVI A,2AH
    MVI B,01H
    ORA B

(c) MVI A,2AH
    MVI B,01H
    XRA B

(d) MVI A,2AH
    ANA A

(e) MVI A,2AH
    OR A

(f) MVI A,2AH
    XRA A

(g) MVI A,2AH
    MVI B,01H
    CMP B

(h) MVI A,2AH
    MVI B,2AH
    CMP B

(i) MVI A,2AH
    MVI B,2CH
    CMP B

(j) MVI A,2AH
    CMP A

(k) MVI A,2AH
    MVI B,01H
    ADD B

(l) MVI A,2AH
    MVI B,01H
    CMP A
    ADC B

(m) MVI A,2AH
    MVI B,01H
    STC
    ADC B

(n) MVI A,2AH
    MVI B,01H
    SUB B

(o) MVI A,2AH
    MVI B,2AH
    SUB B

(p) MVI A,2AH
    MVI B,2CH
    SUB B

(q) MVI A,2AH
    MVI B,01H
    STC
    SBB B

(r) MVI A,2AH
    MVI B,2AH
    STC
    SBB B

(s) MVI A,2AH
    MVI B,2CH
    STC
    SBB

(t) MVI A,2AH
    INR A

(u) MVI A,2AH
    DCR A

8-4 6502 OPERATE REGISTER INSTRUCTIONS

A mere glance at Table 8-5 shows that there must be something quite different about the way the 6502 handles arithmetic and logic operations within its registers. There are, in fact, just four instructions that work like the operate register instructions for the Z-80 and 8080A/8085 devices. And those four instructions do nothing more than increment and decrement the X and Y registers. See Fig. 8-5.

INX and INY increment the value in the X and Y registers, respectively. The DEX and DEY decrement those registers by 1. In both instances, the Z flag is affected by the result, but the Cs flag is not.

TABLE 8-5 6502 OPERATE-REGISTER-ONLY INSTRUCTIONS

Source code	Object code	Symbolic notation	
INX	E8	$X \leftarrow X+1$	(INCREMENT X)
INY	C8	$Y \leftarrow Y+1$	(INCREMENT Y)
DEX	CA	$X \leftarrow X-1$	(DECREMENT X)
DEY	88	$Y \leftarrow Y-1$	(DECREMENT Y)

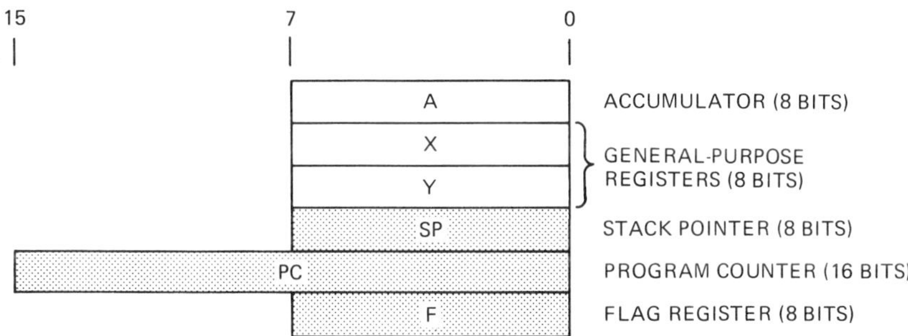

Figure 8-5　6502 registers directly involved in operate register/memory instructions. Shaded registers are not involved.

It is nice that these two 8-bit registers can be incremented and decremented, but one has to wonder about the value of the 6502 as a computing device. Where are those valuable arithmetic and logic operations that involve the accumulator, or A register?

It turns out that the 6502 handles register-type operations in a manner that is quite different from the other two devices already described in this chapter. The key to the 6502's in-house logic and arithmetic operations is an ever-present reference to a byte of data that is saved somewhere in data memory. See Table 8-6.

Now, that is a respectable list of logic and arithmetic instructions.

TABLE 8-6　6502 OPERATE REGISTER/MEMORY INSTRUCTIONS

Source code	Object code	Symbolic notation
AND $addr_0$	25 *byte*	$A \leftarrow A \wedge (addr_0)$
AND *addr*	2D *byte byte*	$A \leftarrow A \wedge (addr)$
ORA $addr_0$	05 *byte*	$A \leftarrow A \vee (addr_0)$
ORA *addr*	0D *byte byte*	$A \leftarrow A \vee (addr)$
EOR $addr_0$	45 *byte*	$A \leftarrow A \triangledown (addr_0)$
EOR *addr*	4D *byte byte*	$A \leftarrow A \triangledown (addr)$
CMP $addr_0$	C5 *byte*	$A - (addr_0)$　(only flags affected)
CMP *addr*	CD *byte byte*	$A - (addr)$　(only flags affected)
CPX $addr_0$	E4 *byte*	$X - (addr_0)$　(only flags affected)
CPX *addr*	EC *byte byte*	$X - (addr)$　(only flags affected)
CPY $addr_0$	C4 *byte*	$Y - (addr_0)$　(only flags affected)
CPY *addr*	CC *byte byte*	$Y - (addr)$　(only flags affected)
ADC $addr_0$	65 *byte*	$A \leftarrow A + (addr_0) + Cs$
ADC *addr*	6D *byte byte*	$A \leftarrow A + (addr) + Cs$
SBC $addr_0$	E5 *byte*	$A \leftarrow A - (addr_0) - \overline{Cs}$
SBC *addr*	ED *byte byte*	$A \leftarrow A - (addr) - \overline{Cs}$
INC $addr_0$	E6 *byte*	$(addr_0) \leftarrow (addr_0) + 1$
INC *addr*	EE *byte byte*	$(addr) \leftarrow (addr) + 1$
DEC $addr_0$	C6 *byte*	$(addr_0) \leftarrow (addr_0) - 1$
DEC *addr*	CE *byte byte*	$(addr) \leftarrow (addr) - 1$

Note: $addr_0$ refers to zero-page memory address; addr refers to absolute memory address; and parentheses imply "content of."

What might appear to be something of a disadvantage at first actually turns out to be a real advantage. The Z-80 and 8080A/8085 devices offer no instructions that perform these operations on directly addressed data.

As far as the source-code instructions are concerned, the operator is immediately followed by an address—an address indicating the location of the byte to participate in the operation.

The address can be either a zero-page address, $addr_0$, or an absolute address, $addr$. Recall that zero-page addresses are specified by a single byte, while absolute addresses are specified as two bytes (LSB of the address, followed by the MSB).

Thus an instruction such as AND $30 means: AND the content of the accumulator with the data byte residing in zero-page address $30, and place the result in the accumulator. The object code for that particular instruction is 25 30—the opcode followed by the 1-byte, zero-page address.

An instruction such as AND $4C00, on the other hand, does the same sort of ANDing operation, and the result is placed into the accumulator. But the data byte to be ANDed with the content of the accumulator comes from absolute address location $4C00. The appropriate object code is 2D 00 4C— a 1-byte opcode, followed by a 2-byte address (LSB first).

The literal meanings of the instructions are summarized this way:

AND $addr_0$ or $addr$	Logically AND the content of the accumulator with the data byte residing at memory location $addr_0$ or $addr$. Place the result into the accumulator, and set the Z flag accordingly (Z=1 if the result is zero). The Cs flag is unaffected.
ORA $addr_0$ or $addr$	Logically OR the content of the accumulator with the data byte currently in memory location $addr_0$ or $addr$. Deposit the result into the accumulator, and set the Z flag according to the result.
EOR $addr_0$ or $addr$	Logically EXCLUSIVE-OR the content of the accumulator with the data byte at zero-page address $addr_0$ or absolute memory address $addr$. Place the result into the A register, adjusting the Z flag according to the result.
CMP $addr_0$ or $addr$	COMPARE the values of the bytes in the accumulator and the designated address location, $addr_0$ or $addr$. In effect, the instruction subtracts the addressed byte from the one in the accumulator. The two original data bytes are left unchanged, but the Z and Cs flags are adjusted to reflect the relative magnitudes of the two numbers.
	If the content of the accumulator is *greater than* the data at the designated address location, Z is cleared to 0 and Cs is set to 1.
	If the content of the accumulator is *equal to* the data at the designated address, Z and Cs are both set to logic 1.
	If the content of the accumulator is *less than* the data at the designated address location, Z and Cs are both cleared to 0.

If it appears that the Cs flag is responding to the CMP instructions in the opposite fashion that one might think it should, recall that the Cs flag in the 6502 is always inverted at the conclusion of a subtraction-type operation. The CMP instructions are subtraction-type operations. See *COMPARE Operations* in Section 7-4 for further clarification of this matter.

CPX $addr_0$ or *addr*	COMPARE the values of the bytes in the X register and the designated address location. The byte residing at the designated address location is effectively subtracted from the byte in the X register. Neither data byte is changed, but the Z and Cs flags are affected according to the relative magnitudes of the two numbers.
CPY $addr_0$ or *addr*	COMPARE the values of the bytes in the Y register and the one at the designated address location. The content of the designated address is effectively subtracted from that in the Y register. Neither byte is changed, but the Z and Cs flags are affected as described for the CMP and CPX instructions.
ADC $addr_0$ or *addr*	ADD WITH CARRY the content of the A register with the content of memory location $addr_0$ or *addr*. Place the result into the A register, and set the Z and Cs flags according to the final result.
SBC $addr_0$ or *addr*	SUBTRACT WITH BORROW the content of the accumulator and the content of memory location $addr_0$ or *addr*. The content of the designated address location is subtracted from the content of the accumulator, and the result is placed into the accumulator. The Z and Cs flags respond as described for the CMP instructions.
INC $addr_0$ or *addr*	INCREMENT by 1 the content of address location $addr_0$ or *addr*. The Z flag is set to logic 1 if the result happens to be zero. Otherwise, it is cleared to 0. The Cs flag is not affected.
DEC $addr_0$ or *addr*	DECREMENT by 1 the content of address location $addr_0$ or *addr*. The Z and Cs flags respond as described for the INC instructions.

Indeed, that is a powerful instruction set. Aside from the fact that the 6502 contains no 16-bit working registers, anything that can be done on the Z-80 or 8080A/8085 systems can be done here. The only difference of special note is that the 6502's versions involve a data memory byte.

Suppose you must do a 6502 operation that works like the Z-80's AND B instruction. As far as the Z-80 system is concerned, the instruction logically ANDs the content of the accumulator with that of register B. The 6502 version must replace the B register with an address location, say, zero-page address $4F. The equivalent of AND B thus becomes AND $4F.

ANDing the content of the 6502's accumulator with itself (something the Z-80 system does with its AND A instruction) is a two-step process. First, transfer the content of the accumulator to some memory address, and then do an AND instruction that references that same memory location. For example:

```
STA  $4F
AND  $4F
```

Table 8-7 shows examples of all the Z-80's 8-bit operate register instructions and 6502 versions for each one of them.

16-Bit Operations

Although the 6502 does not have any 16-bit working registers, it is still possible to perform 16-bit logic and arithmetic operations. The general idea is to devote some bytes of data memory to the operations, using successive address locations to simulate the effect of register pairs.

Suppose that the idea is to add two 16-bit numbers. That can be done in a straightforward fashion with the Z-80's ADD HL,DE and the 8080A/8085's DAD D instructions. The 6502 version is somewhat more involved, requiring more instructions, but it is equally effective.

Assume that the numbers to be summed are $1022 and $4F00. Suppose further they have already been stored in zero-page memory locations $50 through $53. The memory map can look like this:

Address	Data	
$50	$22	LSB of the first number
$51	$10	MSB of the first number
$52	$00	LSB of the second number
$53	$4F	MSB of the second number

In a manner of speaking, address $51 is playing the role of the Z-80's H register, and address $50 is acting as the L register. Similarly, address $53 might be considered a D register and address $52 an E register.

The following source-code listing sums the two 16-bit numbers and places the result into the simulated HL register pair, addresses $50 and $51.

```
LDA  $50     FETCH LSB OF THE FIRST NUMBER
CLC          CLEAR THE CARRY STATUS TO ZERO
ADC  $52     ADD THE LSB'S
STA  $50     SAVE SUM IN $50
LDA  $51     FETCH MSB OF THE FIRST NUMBER
ADC  $53     ADD WITH CARRY THE MSB'S
STA  $51     SAVE SUM IN $51
```

The sum of the two 16-bit numbers thus appears in address locations $50 and $51, with $50 holding the LSB of that answer.

A similar process can be used for subtracting 16-bit numbers as well.

TABLE 8-7 COMPARISON OF SOME Z-80 OPERATE REGISTER INSTRUCTIONS AND THEIR 6502 VERSIONS

Z-80 instruction	6502 version	Literal meaning
AND A	STA $4F	STORE A AT $4F
	AND $4F	AND A WITH ($4F)
AND B	AND $4F	
OR A	STA $4F	STORE A AT $4F
	ORA $4F	OR A WITH ($4F)
OR B	ORA $4F	
XOR A	STA $4F	STORE A AT $4F
	EOR $4F	EXCLUSIVE-OR A WITH ($4F)
XOR B	EOR $4F	
CP A	STA $4F	STORE A AT $4F
	CMP $4F	COMPARE A WITH ($4F)
CP B	CMP $4F	
ADD A,A	STA $4F	STORE A AT $4F
	CLC	CLEAR CARRY TO ZERO
	ADC $4F	ADD A AND ($4F)
ADD A,B	CLC	CLEAR CARRY FLAG
	ADC $4F	ADD A TO ($4F)
ADC A,A	STA $4F	STORE A AT $4F
	ADC $4F	ADD A TO ($4F)
ADC A,B	ADC $4F	
SUB A	STA $4F	STORE A AT $4F
	SEC	SET CARRY FLAG TO 1
	SBC $4F	SUBTRACT A,($4F)
SUB B	SEC	SET CARRY FLAG TO 1
	SBC $4F	SUBTRACT A,($4F)
SBC A,A	STA $4F	STORE A AT $4F
	SBC $4F	SUBTRACT A,($4F)
SBC A,B	SBC $4F	
INC A	STA $4F	STORE A AT $4F
	INC $4F	INCREMENT ($4F)
	LDA $4F	RETURN IT TO A
DEC A	STA $4F	STORE A AT $4F
	DEC $4F	DECREMENT ($4F)
	LDA $4F	RETURN IT TO A

Note: In all of these examples, the Z-80's B register is replaced by zero-page address $4F in the 6502 equivalent operations. Any uncommitted data memory location could be used, however.

```
1F00  A9 34   LDA  #$34    LOAD IMMEDIATE LSB OF MINUEND
1F02  85 70   STA  $70     LSB OF MINUEND TO $70
1F04  A9 12   LDA  #$12    LOAD IMMEDIATE MSB OF MINUEND
1F06  85 71   STA  $71     MSB OF MINUEND TO $71
1F08  A9 23   LDA  #$23    LOAD IMMEDIATE LSB OF SUBTRAHEND
1F0A  85 72   STA  $72     LSB OF SUBTRAHEND TO $72
1F0C  A9 01   LDA  #$01    LOAD IMMEDIATE MSB OF SUBTRAHEND
1F0E  85 73   STA  $73     MSB OF SUBTRAHEND TO $73
1F10  A5 70   LDA  $70     FETCH LSB OF MINUEND
1F12  38      SEC          SET CARRY FLAG (ZERO THE 'BORROW')
1F13  E5 72   SBC  $72     SUBTRACT LSB'S
1F15  85 74   STA  $74     SAVE LSB OF RESULT IN $74
1F17  A5 71   LDA  $71     FETCH MSB OF MINUEND
1F19  E5 73   SBC  $73     SUBTRACT MSB'S
1F1B  85 75   STA  $75     SAVE MSB OF RESULT IN $75
```

EXAMPLE 8-2

Write and assemble a 6502 program that subtracts \$0123 from \$1234. Use the following procedure, and begin the program at address \$1F00:

1. Load the minuend, \$1234, to zero-page memory addresses \$70 and \$71, with \$70 taking the LSB.

2. Load the subtrahend, \$0123, to addresses \$72 and \$73, with the LSB in \$72.

3. Subtract the two numbers, loading the result to addresses \$74 and \$75, with the LSB in \$74.

See the listing in Program 8-2. The result of the operation is \$1111 in zero-page addresses \$74 and \$75.

A discussion in an earlier chapter pointed out that data memory can be viewed as an extension of the microprocessor's internal working registers. The example just cited serves as a convincing confirmation of the idea.

Exercises for Section 8-4

1. Assume that the following operations have just been performed. In each case, determine the content of the A register and the status of the Cs and Z flag bits.

(a) LDA #$01
    STA $7F
    LDA #$2A
    CMP $7F

(b) LDA #$2A
    STA $7F
    CMP $7F

(c) LDA #$2C
    STA $7F
    LDA #$2A
    CMP $7F

(d) LDA #$2A
    STA $7F
    LDA #$2A
    CMP $007F

(e) LDA #$01
    STA $7F
    LDA #$2A
    CLC
    ADC $7F

(f) LDA #$01
    STA $7F00
    LDA #$2A
    CLC
    ADC $7F00

(g) LDA #$01
    STA $7F

(h) LDA #$01
    STA $7F

(i) LDA #$01
    STA $7F

LDA #$2A	LDA #$2A	LDA #$2A
SEC	CLC	SEC
ADC $7F	SBC $7F	SBC $7F

2. Assemble the operations in problem 1, beginning each at address $1F00.

3. Explain why the Cs bit cannot be determined at the conclusion of the following 6502 routine:

```
LDA  L$01
STA  $7F
LDA  L$2A
AND  $7F
```

8-5 6800 OPERATE REGISTER INSTRUCTIONS

The 6800 instruction set has a respectable list of operations that can be performed without reference to any external data memory, but it also has a long list of instructions that can be performed as operate register/memory operations.

Register-Only Instructions

Table 8-8 represents the 6800's instructions that can be performed without referencing any external data memory, and Fig. 8-6 shows the registers involved in these instructions. Note from the following literal descriptions that they are all closely related to arithmetic operations—there are none of the standard logic operations included here.

ABA   ADD the content of 8-bit accumulators A and B, placing the result into the A accumulator. The Z and Cs flags are affected according to the

TABLE 8-8 6800 OPERATE-REGISTER-ONLY INSTRUCTIONS

Source code	Object code	Symbolic notation
ABA	1B	A←A+B
SBA	10	A←A−B
CBA	11	A−B(only flags affected)
CLRA	4F	A←$00
CLRB	5F	B←$00
INCA	4C	A←A+1
INCB	5C	B←B+1
INX	08	IX←IX+1
INS	31	SP←SP+1
DECA	4A	A←A−1
DECB	5A	B←B−1
DEX	09	IX←IX−1
DES	34	SP←SP−1

Note: The INCREMENT and DECREMENT instructions do not affect the Cs flag. The Z flag, however, is affected according to the result: It is set to 1 if the result is zero.

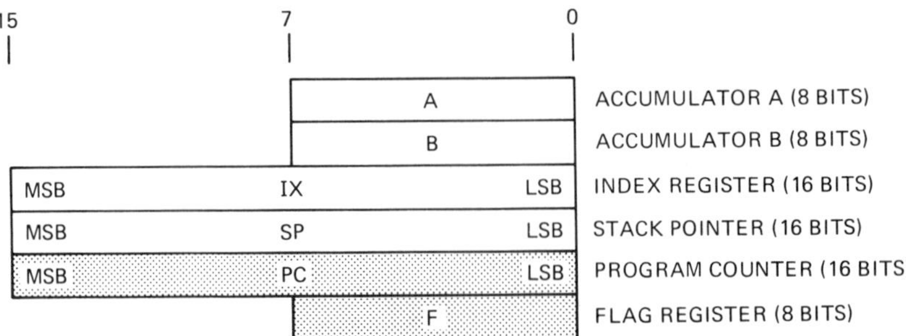

Figure 8-6   6800 registers involved in operate register instructions. Shaded registers are not involved.

result. The Z flag is set to 1 only if the result is zero, and the Cs flag is set only if a wraparound occurs. Otherwise, the Z and Cs flags are cleared to 0.

SBA   SUBTRACT the content of the B accumulator from the content of the A accumulator, and place the result in A. The Z and Cs flags are affected according to the result.

CBA   COMPARE the contents of accumulators A and B. The content of B is, in effect, subtracted from that of A, but the content of neither accumulator is altered—only the flags are affected according to the result.

CLRA   CLEAR the content of the A accumulator to zero. This instruction, and its CLRB companion, are unique to the 6800 system. Doing the same task with the Z-80, for instance, calls for instructions such as LD A,00H or XOR A. The instruction guarantees that the Z flag is set to 1 and the Cs flag is cleared to 0.

CLRB   CLEAR the content of the B accumulator to zero. The Z flag is set to 1 and the Cs flag is cleared to 0.

INCA   INCREMENT the 8-bit A accumulator by 1. The Cs flag is unaffected, but the Z flag is set to 1 whenever the operation results in a wraparound from $FF to $00.

INCB   INCREMENT the B accumulator by 1. The Z flag responds as described for the INCA instruction.

INX   INCREMENT the 16-bit IX register by 1. This is a 16-bit operate-register instruction that sets the Z flag to 1 only when a wraparound from $FFFF to $0000 occurs. The Cs flag is not affected at all.

INS   INCREMENT the content of the 16-bit SP (stack pointer) register by 1. The Z flag is affected as described for the INX instruction.

DECA   DECREMENT the A accumulator by 1. The Z flag is set to 1 only when the operation decrements the content of the A accumulator from $01 to $00. The Cs flag is not affected. The S flag, described in a later chapter, can be used for detecting wraparound from $00 to $FF.

DECB   DECREMENT the content of the B accumulator by 1. The flags are affected as described for DECA.

DECX   DECREMENT the content of the 16-bit IX register by 1. The Z flag is set to 1 only when the instruction decrements the IX register to $0000. The Cs flag is not affected at all.

DECS   DECREMENT the content of the SP register by 1. The flags work as described for DECX.

As described at the beginning of this description of 6800 register-only instructions, there are no instructions for doing logic operations between the internal registers. Also note that the ADD and SUBTRACT instructions, ABA and SBA, are simple ADD and SUBTRACT operations—any carry from a previous operation is ignored.

If this appears to be a useful, but somewhat restrictive, instruction set, just look at the register/memory versions; operations that are quite similar to those featured in the 6502 system.

Register/Memory Instructions

The instructions summarized in Table 8-9 perform logic and arithmetic operations between the designated accumulator and a data memory location

TABLE 8-9 6800 OPERATE REGISTER/MEMORY INSTRUCTIONS

Source code	Object code	Symbolic notation
ANDA $addr_0$	94 *byte*	$A \leftarrow A \wedge (addr_0)$
ANDA *addr*	B4 *byte byte*	$A \leftarrow A \wedge (addr)$
ANDB $addr_0$	C4 *byte*	$B \leftarrow B \wedge (addr_0)$
ANDB *addr*	F4 *byte byte*	$B \leftarrow B \wedge (addr)$
ORAA $addr_0$	9A *byte*	$A \leftarrow A \vee (addr_0)$
ORAA *addr*	BA *byte byte*	$A \leftarrow A \vee (addr)$
ORAB $addr_0$	DA *byte*	$B \leftarrow A \vee (addr_0)$
ORAB *addr*	FA *byte byte*	$B \leftarrow B \vee (addr)$
EORA $addr_0$	98 *byte*	$A \leftarrow A \triangledown (addr_0)$
EORA *addr*	B8 *byte byte*	$A \leftarrow A \triangledown (addr)$
EORB $addr_0$	D8 *byte*	$B \leftarrow B \triangledown (addr_0)$
EORB *addr*	F8 *byte byte*	$B \leftarrow B \triangledown (addr)$
CMPA $addr_0$	91 *byte*	$A - (addr_0)$ (only flags affected)
CMPA *addr*	B1 *byte byte*	$A - (addr)$ (only flags affected)
CMPB $addr_0$	D1 *byte*	$B - (addr_0)$ (only flags affected)
CMPB *addr*	F1 *byte byte*	$B - (addr)$ (only flags affected)
ADCA $addr_0$	99 *byte*	$A \leftarrow A + (addr_0) + Cs$
ADCA *addr*	B9 *byte byte*	$A \leftarrow A + (addr) + Cs$
ADCB $addr_0$	D9 *byte*	$B \leftarrow B + (addr_0) + Cs$
ADCB *addr*	F9 *byte byte*	$B \leftarrow B + (addr) + Cs$
SBCA $addr_0$	92 *byte*	$A \leftarrow A - (addr_0) - Cs$
SBCA *addr*	B2 *byte byte*	$A \leftarrow A - (addr) - Cs$
SBCB $addr_0$	D2 *byte*	$B \leftarrow B - (addr_0) - Cs$
SBCB *addr*	F2 *byte byte*	$B \leftarrow B - (addr) - Cs$
INC *addr*	7C *byte byte*	$(addr) \leftarrow (addr) + 1$
DEC *addr*	7A *byte byte*	$(addr) \leftarrow (addr) - 1$

specifically cited in the instruction itself. Technically speaking, these are *operate with direct memory addressing instructions.* (The distinction will become clear when comparing them with the *indirect memory addressing* operations in Chapter 9.)

ANDA *addr*$_0$ or ANDA *addr*	Logically AND the content of accumulator A with the data byte addressed by zero-page address *addr*$_0$ or absolute address *addr*. Place the result into the A accumulator, and set the Z flag to 1 if the result is zero.
ANDB *addr*$_0$ or ANDA *addr*	Logically AND the content of accumulator B with the data byte from zero-page address *addr*$_0$ or absolute memory address *addr*. Place the result into the B accumulator, and set or clear the Z flag according to the result.
ORAA *addr*$_0$ or ORAA *addr*	Logically OR the content of accumulator A with the data byte contained in address *addr*$_0$ or *addr*. Adjust the Z flag according to the result, and place the result into the A accumulator.
ORAB *addr*$_0$ or ORAB *addr*	Logically OR the content of accumulator B with the data byte from zero page address *addr*$_0$ or absolute address *addr*. Place the result into accumulator B and set the Z flag to 1 only if the result is zero.
EORA *addr*$_0$ or EORA *addr*	Logically EXCLUSIVE-OR the content of accumulator A with the data byte at *addr*$_0$ or *addr*. Place the result into the A accumulator, and set the Z flag to 1 only if the result is zero.
EORB *addr*$_0$ or EORB *addr*	Logically EXCLUSIVE-OR the content of accumulator B with the data byte at *addr*$_0$ or *addr*. Place the result into the B accumulator, and set the Z flag to 1 only if the result is zero.
CMPA *addr*$_0$ or CMPA *addr*	COMPARE the content of the byte at address *addr*$_0$ or *addr* with that of the A accumulator. The addressed byte is effectively subtracted from the content of the A accumulator, but neither data byte is changed—only the flags are affected.
CMPB *addr*$_0$ or CMPB *addr*	COMPARE the content of the addressed byte with that of the B accumulator. The addressed byte, either at zero-page address *addr*$_0$ or *addr*, is effectively subtracted from the content of the B accumulator, but only the flags are affected by the result.
ADCA *addr*$_0$ or ADC *addr*	ADD WITH CARRY the content of the A accumulator and the byte addressed by *addr*$_0$ or *addr*. Place the result into accumulator A, and adjust the Z and Cs flags according to the result.

ADCB *addr*$_0$ or ADC *addr*	ADD WITH CARRY the content of the B accumulator and the byte addressed by *addr*$_0$ or *addr*. Place the result into accumulator B, and adjust the Z and Cs flag bits accordingly.
SBCA *addr*$_0$ or SBCA *addr*	SUBTRACT WITH CARRY (or "borrow") the the data byte address by *addr*$_0$ or *addr* from the content of the A accumulator. Place the result into the A accumulator and adjust the Z and Cs flags according to the result.
SBCB *addr*$_0$ or SBCB *addr*	SUBTRACT WITH CARRY (or "borrow") an addressed data byte, at *addr*$_0$ or *addr*, from the content of accumulator B. Place the result into accumulator B and adjust the Z and Cs flags accordingly.
INC *addr*	INCREMENT by 1 the content of absolute address *addr*. The Z flag is set to 1 only when the byte at *addr* is wrapped around from \$FF to \$00. The Cs flag is not affected by the instruction.
DEC *addr*	DECREMENT by 1 the content of address *addr*. The Z flag is set to 1 only when (*addr*) is decremented from \$01 to \$00. Otherwise, it is cleared to 0. The Cs flag is not affected at all; and a reference to the sign flag, S, is necessary for detecting decrement wraparound from \$00 to \$FF. That S flag bit is described in a later chapter.

Synthesizing Other Important Operations

The 6800's register/memory instructions in Table 8-9 can more than make up for the apparent shortcomings of the register-only instructions. Suppose that you want to logically AND the contents of the A and B accumulators. There is no register-only instruction for doing that job, but it can by synthesized by calling upon some register/memory instructions:

```
STAB  $50
ANDA  $50
```

The first instruction moves the content of the B accumulator to zero-page address \$50. The second one logically ANDs the content of the A accumulator with that of zero-page address \$50—the original content of the B accumulator. The result is found in the A accumulator after the two-instruction sequence has been executed.

Or what if you wanted to COMPARE the contents of accumulators A and B? Simply move the content of one of the accumulators to some data memory address, and then execute the appropriate register/memory COM-PARE instruction. For example:

```
STAB  $25
CMPA  $25
```

That one compares the content of accumulator A with the original content of accumulator B, effectively subtracting B from A. It makes up for the lack of a single instruction that might be listed as CMPAB.

Sixteen-bit arithmetic is handled the same way it is for the 6502.

Exercises for Section 8-5

1. Logic operations for the Z-80 and 8080A/8085 automatically clear the Cs flag bit to zero, regardless of the result of the operation in the accumulator. The same logic instructions for the 6502, on the other hand, leave the Cs bit unaffected. What is the case for the 6800 system?

2. Arithmetic operations, including COMPARE, for the Z-80 and 8080A/8085 systems set the Cs flag bit to 1 whenever the operation produces a wraparound condition. The 6502 does the same thing for addition functions, but inverts the Cs flag bit for subtraction functions. Does the 6800's Cs flag respond as it does for the Z-80 and 8080A/8085 or the 6502?

3. Which register is affected by the 6800's INC and DEC instructions?

9

Indirect Memory Addressing

External memory is just as important to a microprocessor system as the microprocessor device itself. If nothing else, the memory holds the program the system is to execute; and, most often, it serves as a storage place for data as well.

All of the instructions described so far in this book fall into the general categories of *immediate* and *direct memory* instructions. Both, in their own fashion, make a specific reference to a register or a specific address location in data memory.

In the case of the immediate instructions, the instruction provides some of the data to be used in the operation. A load immediate instruction, for example, specifies both a target register and the data byte to be loaded. Then there are the operate immediate instructions—instructions that specify both a logic or arithmetic operation to be performed and one of the pieces of data to participate in the operation.

Instructions for operations using direct memory addressing clearly specify the memory address involved. A load instruction using direct memory addressing includes an opcode and an address. Chapter 8 dealt with logic and arithmetic operations that also use direct memory addressing to refer to a specific address in data memory.

When looking over a program that uses direct memory addressing instructions, there can be no doubt about the memory addresses involved; they appear in the instructions themselves.

That is not the case with indirect memory addressing instructions. Such instructions do not make specific reference to a particular memory location. Rather, the desired memory address is carried by one of the microprocessor's internal registers.

In a manner of speaking, an instruction using indirect memory addressing says this: Look into a specified register, and use its content as a data memory address.

Here is an example of an instruction that uses direct memory addressing:

```
LD  A,4500H
```

That instruction calls for loading register A with a data byte from memory address 4500, hexadecimal.

Then there is another way to do the same job, but using indirect memory addressing:

```
LD  HL,4500H
LD  A,(HL)
```

The first instruction is an ordinary load immediate operation that fills the HL register pair with the 2-byte number 4500H. There is nothing new about that. The second instruction, however, uses indirect memory addressing to load the A register with a data byte from memory—from an address indicated by the content of the HL register pair. In that second instruction, the content of the HL register pair is said to *point to* the memory address. And when the instruction is executed, the data byte from 4500H is loaded to the A register.

It is a bit premature to suggest some compelling reasons for using indirect memory addressing in lieu of its direct memory counterpart. The power of indirect memory addressing will become apparent as discussions in the next few chapters unfold.

9-1 INDIRECT ADDRESSING FOR THE 8080A/8085

The 8080A/8085 microprocessor device features the least sophisticated instructions for indirect memory addressing. Table 9-1 summarizes register/memory transfer instructions that use indirect memory addressing, and Table 9-2 shows the operate instructions that use indirect memory addressing.

With only one exception, the 8080A/8085's indirect memory addressing instructions are simple 1-byte instructions. Looking over the transfer instructions in Table 9-1, you should be able to find three of them that load a data byte to the A register:

```
MOV  A,M
LDAX B
LDAX D
```

In the first case, MOV A,M, the M refers to the content of the HL register pair. That instruction says: Load the A register with a data byte found at a memory address contained in the HL register pair.

LDAX B calls for loading the A register with a data byte addressed by

TABLE 9-1 LOAD REGISTER/MEMORY INDIRECT INSTRUCTIONS FOR THE 8080A/8085

Source code	Object code	Symbolic notation
MOV A,M	7E	A←(HL)
MOV B,M	46	B←(HL)
MOV C,M	4E	C←(HL)
MOV D,M	56	D←(HL)
MOV E,M	5E	E←(HL)
MOV H,M	66	H←(HL)
MOV L,M	6E	L←(HL)
LDAX B	0A	A←(BC)
LDAX D	1A	A←(DE)
MOV M,A	77	(HL)←A
MOV M,B	70	(HL)←B
MOV M,C	71	(HL)←C
MOV M,D	72	(HL)←D
MOV M,E	73	(HL)←E
MOV M,H	74	(HL)←H
MOV M,L	75	(HL)←L
STAX B	02	(BC)←A
STAX D	12	(DE)←A
MVI M,*data*	36 *byte*	(HL)←*data*

the content of the BC register pair; and LDAX D does the same job, but using the content of the DE register pair as the address pointer.

So the A register can be loaded indirectly with a byte of data residing at an address indicated by one of three different register pairs.

By the same token, the content of the A register can be stored to data memory in an indirect fashion:

```
MOV   M,A
STAX  B
STAX  D
```

Those instructions load the data byte from the A register to a data memory address that is specified by the HL, BC, or DE register pairs, respectively.

TABLE 9-2 OPERATE REGISTER/MEMORY INDIRECT INSTRUCTIONS FOR THE 8080A/8085

Source code	Object code	Symbolic notation
ANA M	A6	A←A∧(HL)
ORA M	B6	A←A∨(HL)
XRA M	AE	A←A▽(HL)
CMP M	BE	A−(HL) (only flags affected)
ADD M	86	A←A+(HL)
ADC M	8E	A←A+(HL)+Cs
SUB M	96	A←A−(HL)
SBB M	9E	A←A−(HL)−Cs
INR M	34	(HL)←(HL)+1
DCR M	35	(HL)←(HL)−1

A data byte can be transferred between a data memory address and any of the other 8-bit working registers in a similar fashion. In those cases not involving the A register, however, only the HL register pair can be used as an address pointer.

MOV E,M, for example, calls for loading the E register with a byte addressed by the HL register pair. (Remember that the M implies indirect addressing from the HL pair.) An instruction such as MOV M,D means: Load the content of the D register to an address indicated by the HL register pair.

The lone 2-byte instruction—MVI M,data—is actually a load immediate operation. The *data* byte specified in the instruction is loaded to data memory, and to an address specified by the HL register pair. So if you wish to load 2AH to memory address 4C00H, an appropriate instruction sequence would be

```
LXI  H,4C00H   ;SET HL PAIR TO ADDRESS
MVI  M,2AH     ;MOVE 2AH TO ADDRESS
```

EXAMPLE 9-1

Write and assemble an 8080A/8085 program that uses indirect addressing to clear the content of addresses 4C00H through 4C04H to zero. Begin the program at program memory address 7000H.

See the listing in Program 9-1. The first instruction clears the A register to zero, and the second makes the HL register pair point to the lowest address to be cleared. Subsequent instructions transfer the zero data from the A register to the memory address indicated by the HL pair, then increments the HL pair to point to the next-higher address location. At the conclusion of the program, address locations 4C00H through 4C04H do, indeed, contain zero data bytes.

PROGRAM 9-1   Z-80 PROGRAM LISTING FOR EXAMPLE 9-1

```
7000 AF          XRA  A       ;CLEAR THE ACCUMULATOR TO ZERO
7001 21  00 4C   LXI  H,4C00H  ;POINT TO LOWEST ADDRESS
7004 77          MOV  M,A     ;ZERO CONTENT OF 4C00H
7005 23          INX  H       ;POINT TO NEXT ADDRESS
7006 77          MOV  M,A     ;ZERO CONTENT OF 4C01H
7007 23          INX  H       ;POINT TO NEXT ADDRESS
7008 77          MOV  M,A     ;ZERO CONTENT OF 4C02H
7009 23          INX  H       ;POINT TO NEXT ADDRESS
700A 77          MOV  M,A     ;ZERO CONTENT OF 4C03H
700B 23          INX  H       ;POINT TO NEXT ADDRESS
700C 77          MOV  M,A     ;ZERO CONTENT OF 4C04H
```

EXAMPLE 9-2

Write and assemble an 8080A/8085 program that uses indirect memory addressing to do the following operations. Begin the program at address 7000H.

1. Load the A register from address 3C00H.

2. Load the B register from address 3C01H.

3. Load the C register from address 3C02H.

4. Load the D register from address 3C03H.

5. Load the E register from address 3C04H.

See the listing in Program 9-2.

PROGRAM 9-2 Z-80 PROGRAM LISTING FOR EXAMPLE 9-2

```
7000 21 00 3C   LXI  H,3C00H  ;SET POINTER TO LOWEST ADDR
7003 7E         MOV  A,M      ;(3C00H) TO A
7004 23         INX  H        ;INCREMENT POINTER
7005 46         MOV  B,M      ;(3C01H) TO B
7006 23         INX  H        ;INCREMENT POINTER
7007 4E         MOV  C,M      ;(3C02H) TO C
7008 23         INX  H        ;INCREMENT POINTER
7009 56         MOV  D,M      ;(3C03H) TO D
700A 23         INX  H        ;INCREMENT POINTER
700B 5E         MOV  E,M      ;(3C04H) TO E
```

Why do you suppose that Example 9-2 does not go on to include similar loading operations to the H and L registers?

Table 9-2 cites the 8080A/8085's logic and arithmetic operations that use indirect memory addressing. In all instances, the M in the source code implies a data byte taken from an address location specified by the HL register pair. An instruction such as ORA M thus means: OR the content of the accumulator with a data byte taken from an address specified by the HL register pair, and place the result into the accumulator.

The accumulator, or A register, is the center of all the logic and arithmetic activity. Instructions INR M and DCR M do not involve the accumulator, however. Rather, they increment or decrement the data byte that is addressed by the 2-byte content of the HL register pair.

9-2 INDIRECT ADDRESSING FOR THE Z-80

The instruction set for the Z-80 microprocessor includes indirect address operations that are, to all intents and purposes, identical to those used by the 8080A/8085 system. See Tables 9-3 and 9-4, and then compare them with Tables 9-1 and 9-2, respectively. The principles are identical; only the mnemonics are different.

Indexed Addressing

The Z-80 system carries the matter of indirect memory addressing one step further—it includes instructions for *indexed indirect addressing*. Table 9-5 shows the register/memory transfer instructions that use indexed addressing, and Table 9-6 summarizes the logic and arithmetic instructions that employ that particular addressing mode.

It must be clearly understood from the outset that indexed addressing is a form of indirect addressing by its very nature. So any discussion of indexed addressing is dealing with indirect addressing as well.

TABLE 9-3 LOAD REGISTER/MEMORY INDIRECT
INSTRUCTIONS FOR THE Z-80

Source code	Object code	Symbolic notation
LD A,(HL)	7E	A←(HL)
LD A,(BC)	0A	A←(BC)
LD A,(DE)	1A	A←(DE)
LD B,(HL)	46	B←(HL)
LD C,(HL)	4E	C←(HL)
LD D,(HL)	56	D←(HL)
LD E,(HL)	5E	E←(HL)
LD H,(HL)	66	H←(HL)
LD L,(HL)	6E	L←(HL)
LD (HL),A	77	(HL)←A
LD (BC),A	02	(BC)←A
LD (DE),A	12	(DE)←A
LD (HL),B	70	(HL)←B
LD (HL),C	71	(HL)←C
LD (HL),D	72	(HL)←D
LD (HL),E	73	(HL)←E
LD (HL),H	74	(HL)←H
LD (HL),L	75	(HL)←L
LD (HL),*data*	36 *byte*	(HL)←*data*

As far as the Z-80 system is concerned, the 16-bit IX and IY registers
are considered the index registers. Although they can be used for other purposes, their primary purpose is to serve the needs of indexed indirect memory addressing.

Consider the first indexed instruction in Table 9-5, LD A,(IX+*indx*).
The form of the mnemonic implies that the 2-byte content of the IX index
register is summed with an *indx* term to form an address—an address that
points to a byte in data memory. The mnemonic also implies that the byte
from data memory is loaded to the A register.

But what is that *indx* term? It is a 1-byte *index term*. The instruction

TABLE 9-4 OPERATE REGISTER/MEMORY INDIRECT
INSTRUCTIONS FOR THE Z-80

Source code	Object code	Symbolic notation
AND (HL)	A6	A←A∧(HL)
OR (HL)	B6	A←A∨(HL)
XOR (HL)	AE	A←A▽(HL)
CP (HL)	BE	A−(HL) (only flags affected)
ADD A,(HL)	86	A←A+(HL)
ADC A,(HL)	8E	A←A+(HL)+Cs
SUB (HL)	96	A←A−(HL)
SBC A,(HL)	9E	A←A−(HL)−Cs
INC (HL)	34	(HL)←(HL)+1
DEC (HL)	35	(HL)←(HL)−1

Source code	Object code	Symbolic notation
LD A,(IX+*indx*)	DD 7E *byte*	A←(IX+*indx*)
LD A,(IY+*indx*)	FD 7E *byte*	A←(IY+*indx*)
LD B,(IX+*indx*)	DD 46 *byte*	B←(IX+*indx*)
LD B,(IY+*indx*)	FD 46 *byte*	B←(IY+*indx*)
LD C,(IX+*indx*)	DD 4E *byte*	C←(IX+*indx*)
LD C,(IY+*indx*)	FD 4E *byte*	C←(IY+*indx*)
LD D,(IX+*indx*)	DD 56 *byte*	D←(IX+*indx*)
LD D,(IY+*indx*)	FD 56 *byte*	D←(IY+*indx*)
LD E,(IX+*indx*)	DD 5E *byte*	E←(IX+*indx*)
LD E,(IY+*indx*)	FD 5E *byte*	E←(IY+*indx*)
LD H,(IX+*indx*)	DD 66 *byte*	H←(IX+*indx*)
LD H,(IY+*indx*)	FD 66 *byte*	H←(IY+*indx*)
LD L,(IX+*indx*)	DD 6E *byte*	L←(IX+*indx*)
LD L,(IY+*indx*)	FD 6E *byte*	L←(IY+*indx*)
LD (IX+*indx*),A	DD 77 *byte*	(IX+*indx*)←A
LD (IY+*indx*),A	FD 77 *byte*	(IY+*indx*)←A
LD (IX+*indx*),B	DD 70 *byte*	(IX+*indx*)←B
LD (IY+*indx*),B	FD 70 *byte*	(IY+*indx*)←B
LD (IX+*indx*),C	DD 4E *byte*	(IX+*indx*)←C
LD (IY+*indx*),C	FD 4E *byte*	(IY+*indx*)←C
LD (IX+*indx*),D	DD 56 *byte*	(IX+*indx*)←D
LD (IY+*indx*),D	FD 56 *byte*	(IY+*indx*)←D
LD (IX+*indx*),E	DD 5E *byte*	(IX+*indx*)←E
LD (IY+*indx*),E	FD 5E *byte*	(IY+*indx*)←E
LD (IX+*indx*),H	DD 66 *byte*	(IX+*indx*)←H
LD (IY+*indx*),H	FD 66 *byte*	(IY+*indx*)←H
LD (IX+*indx*),L	DD 6E *byte*	(IX+*indx*)←L
LD (IY+*indx*),L	FD 6E *byte*	(IY+*indx*)←L
LD (IX+*indx*),*data*	DD 36 *byte byte*	(IX+*indx*)←*data*
LD (IY+*indx*),*data*	FD 36 *byte byte*	(IY+*indx*)←*data*

Note: indx is a 1-byte index displacement term that uses signed, 2's-complement notation. The indexed displacement is thus between −128 decimal and 127 decimal.

sums the content of the index register with the index term to make up an *effective address* for indirect addressing applications.

Note that the instruction shows a 3-byte object code. The first two bytes make up the opcode, and the third is the index term—the byte to be summed with the content of the IX or IY register.

Suppose that the IX register happens to contain the number 4C00H. Further suppose that the instruction reads:

LD A,(IX+21H)

The effective address in that case is 4C00H+21H, or 4C21H. Literally speaking, the instruction says: Load the A register from an address location deter-

Source code	Object code	Symbolic notation
AND (IX+*indx*)	DD A6 byte	A←A∧(IX+*indx*)
AND (IY+*indx*)	FD A6 *byte*	A←A∧(IY+*indx*)
OR (IX+*indx*)	DD B6 *byte*	A←A∨(IX+*indx*)
OR (IY+*indx*)	FD B6 *byte*	A←A∨(IY+*indx*)
XOR (IX+*indx*)	DD AE *byte*	A←A▽(IX+*indx*)
XOR (IY+*indx*)	FD AE *byte*	A←A▽(IY+*indx*)
CP (IX+*indx*)	DD BE *byte*	A−(IX+*indx*) (only flags affected)
CP (IY+*indx*)	FD BE *byte*	A−(IY+*indx*) (only flags affected)
ADD (IX+*indx*)	DD 86 *byte*	A←A+(IX+*indx*)
ADD (IY+*indx*)	FD 86 *byte*	A←A+(IY+*indx*)
ADC (IX+*indx*)	DD 8E *byte*	A←A+(IX+*indx*)+Cs
ADC (IY+*indx*)	FD 8E *byte*	A←A+(IY+*indx*)+Cs
SUB (IX+*indx*)	DD 96 *byte*	A←A−(IX+*indx*)
SUB (IY+*indx*)	FD 96 *byte*	A←A−(IY+*indx*)
SBC A,(IX+*indx*)	DD 9E *byte*	A←A−(IX+*indx*)−Cs
SBC A,(IY+*indx*)	FD 9E *byte*	A←A−(IY+*indx*)−Cs
INC (IX+*indx*)	DD 34 *byte*	(IX+*ind*)←(IX+*indx*)+1
INC (IY+*indx*)	FD 34 *byte*	(IY+*ind*)←(IY+*indx*)+1
DEC (IX+*indx*)	DD 35 *byte*	(IX+*ind*)←(IX+*indx*)−1
DEC (IY+*indx*)	FD 35 *byte*	(IY+*ind*)←(IY+*indx*)−1

mined by the sum of the IX register and the index term, or address 4C21H.
The appropriate object code listing is

DD 7E 21

where the combination DD 7E is the 2-byte opcode, and the 21 is the hexadecimal index term. As in the case of ordinary, nonindexed, indirect addressing, it is assumed that the index register has been set to some known 2-byte
value prior to doing the indexed instruction.

Before considering further examples of indexed addressing, two special
points must be made. First, the matter of *summing the content of the 2-byte
index register with the index term does not alter the content of the index
register*. The microprocessor calculates the effective address, but retains it
only long enough to place it onto the address bus and carry out the specified instruction. The effective address value is lost at the conclusion of the
instruction.

The second important point is that the Z-80's indexed instructions use
the signed, 2's-complement convention for the index term. That is, the index
term can take on values having the decimal equivalents of −128 through
+127. Whenever the high-order bit in the index term is a 1, the term is pre-
sumed to be a negative one; and that being the case, the resulting effective
address is less than the address contained in the index register.

In each of the following examples, assume that the IX register contains
4C00H:

LD A,(IX+0AH)   effective address is 4C0AH

LD A,(IX+0H)   effective address is 4C00H

LD A,(IX+F7H)   effective address is 4BF7H

Since the index terms in the first two examples have a zero in their most-significant bit positions, they represent positive indices. The effective address is thus the simple sum of the content of the IX register and the index value.

The third example, however, has an index term that represents a number less than zero—a negative number. *Any index term between 80H and FFH, inclusively, represents a negative index term*, and anyone only vaguely familiar with the hexadecimal versions of 8-bit, signed, 2's-complement numbers might find some difficulty working with negative indices. Perhaps a brief discussion of the topic is in order.

Let the instruction be LD A,(IX+F7H). Assuming that the content of the IX register is known, the problem becomes one of converting the negative index term, F7H, to a form that can be subtracted from the data in the IX register. One approach to the conversion is to subtract the index term from 100H. In this case

$$\begin{array}{r} 100H \\ -\ \ F7H \\ \hline 09H \end{array}$$

The result is the absolute value of the negative index term. All that remains, then, is to subtract that number from the content of the IX register. And if the IX register happens to contain 4C00H:

$$\begin{array}{r} 4C00H \\ -\ \ \ \ 09H \\ \hline 4B07H \end{array}$$

The effective address is thus 4B07H, and the instruction LD A,(IX+F7H) will load the A register with the data byte contained in data memory address 4B07H.

Note: For any Z-80 indexed instruction having an index term between 80H and FFH, inclusively, the effective address can be determined by this equation:

$$EA = R_{16} - (100H - indx)$$

where   EA   is the effective address

          R_{16} is the 2-byte content of the index register

          indx   is the 1-byte index term

All numbers are expressed in the hexadecimal form.

The two instructions at the end of Table 9-5 call for some special attention. They are basically load immediate instructions that load a designated byte of data into an indexed memory location. What makes them special is the fact that they both have 4-byte object codes. The first two bytes are the instructions' opcodes. One of the remaining bytes is the index term and the other is the data byte to be passed to data memory. The question is this: Which of the last two bytes is the index term, and which is the data byte to be loaded to memory?

The answer is simple, but keeping it straight without referring to this discussion or a Z-80 instruction manual is another matter. It turns out that *the third byte in the object-code instruction is the index term*, and *the fourth byte is the load-immediate data byte.*

Suppose, for example, that it is necessary to load a data byte 50H to an effective address represented by (IY+2FH). The source-code instruction is

LD (IY+2FH),50H

and the object-code version is

FD 36 2F 50

Exercises for Section 9-2

1. Write out the literal meaning of the following Z-80 instructions.

(a) LD A,(HL)	(b) LD (BC),A	(c) LD (HL),*data*
(d) AND (HL)	(e) CP (HL)	(f) ADD A,(HL)
(g) DEC (HL)	(h) LD A,(IY+*indx*)	(i) LD (IX+*indx*),B
(j) LD (IX+*indx*),*data*	(k) OR (IY+*indx*)	(l) CP (IX+*indx*)

2. Which Z-80 registers may be used as index registers?

3. What is the range of index-term values in hexadecimal? in decimal?

4. Determine the effective address for the following Z-80 instructions. Assume that the content of the IX register is 3C02H in each case.

(a) LD A,(IX+2AH)	(b) LD (IX+FEH),L	(c) LD H,(IX+7FH)
(d) LD (IX+00H),A	(e) AND (IX+80H)	(f) SBC A,(IX+FFH)

5. Write the object codes for the following Z-80 instructions. Let the *data* be 3E in each case, and let the index term be 15H where necessary.

(a) LD (HL),*data*	(b) LD (IX+*indx*),*data*	(c) LD (IY+*indx*),*data*

9-3 6800 INDIRECT MEMORY ADDRESSING

Recall that the 8080A/8085 system has a respectable family of instructions using indirect addressing, but that none of them use indexed addressing. Then the Z-80 system has a family of indirect addressing modes that are practically identical to the 8080A/8085 system, but also includes instructions for indexed indirect addressing.

Just as the 8080A/8085 has no indexed addressing, the 6800 system described here has nothing but indexed indirect addressing instructions. So in a manner of speaking, the Z-80 has addressing features common to both the 8080A/8085 and the 6800, but those two have virtually nothing in common.

TABLE 9-7 LOAD REGISTER/MEMORY INDEXED INDIRECT INSTRUCTIONS FOR THE 6800

Source code	Object code	Symbolic notation
LDAA *indx*,X	A6 *byte*	$A \leftarrow (IX+indx)$
LDAB *indx*,X	E6 *byte*	$B \leftarrow (IX+indx)$
STAA *indx*,X	A7 *byte*	$(IX+indx) \leftarrow A$
STAB *indx*,X	E7 *byte*	$(IX+indx) \leftarrow B$
LDX *indx*,X	EE *byte*	$IX_H \leftarrow (IX+indx)$ $IX_L \leftarrow (IX+indx+1)$
LDS *indx*,X	AE *byte*	$SP_H \leftarrow (IX+indx)$ $SP_L \leftarrow (IX+indx+1)$
STZ *indx*,X	EF *byte*	$(IX+indx) \leftarrow IX_H$ $(IX+indx+1) \leftarrow IX_L$
STS *indx*,X	AF *byte*	$(IX+indx) \leftarrow SP_H$ $(IX+indx+1) \leftarrow SP_L$
CLR *indx*,X	6F *byte*	$(IX+indx) \leftarrow \$00$

Note: *indx* is a 1-byte index displacement term having nonnegative values between 0 and 255 decimal.

The indexed instruction set for the 6800 is completely summarized in Tables 9-7 and 9-8. Indeed, they all use indexed addressing.

There are two important differences between the 6800's indexed addressing format and that of the Z-80. The first difference is that the index term is always considered a positive number—an 8-bit number that can only advance the effective address. The second difference is the presence of 2-

TABLE 9-8 OPERATE REGISTER/MEMORY INDEXED INDIRECT INSTRUCTIONS FOR THE 6800

Source code	Object code	Symbolic notation
ANDA *indx*,X	A4 *byte*	$A \leftarrow A \wedge (IX+indx)$
ANDB *indx*,X	E4 *byte*	$B \leftarrow B \wedge (IX+indx)$
ORAA *indx*,X	AA *byte*	$A \leftarrow A \vee (IX+indx)$
ORAB *indx*,X	EA *byte*	$B \leftarrow B \vee (IX+indx)$
EORA *indx*,X	A8 *byte*	$A \leftarrow A \triangledown (IX+indx)$
EORB *indx*,X	E8 *byte*	$B \leftarrow B \triangledown (IX+indx)$
CMPA *indx*,X	A1 *byte*	$A - (IX+indx)$ (only flags affected)
CMPB *indx*,X	E1 *byte*	$B - (IX+indx)$ (only flags affected)
CPX *indx*,X	AC *byte*	$IX - (IX+indx, IX+indx+1)$ (only flags affected)
ADDA *indx*,X	AB *byte*	$A \leftarrow A + (IX+indx)$
ADDB *indx*,X	EB *byte*	$B \leftarrow B + (IX+indx)$
ADCA *indx*,X	A9 *byte*	$A \leftarrow A + (IX+indx) + Cs$
ADCB *indx*,X	E9 *byte*	$B \leftarrow B + (IX+indx) + Cs$
SUBA *indx*,X	A0 *byte*	$A \leftarrow A - (IX+indx)$
SUBB *indx*,X	E0 *byte*	$B \leftarrow B - (IX+indx)$
SBCA *indx*,X	A2 *byte*	$A \leftarrow A - (IX+indx) - Cs$
SBCB *indx*,X	E2 *byte*	$B \leftarrow B - (IX+indx) - Cs$
INC *indx*,X	6C *byte*	$(IX+indx) \leftarrow (IX+indx) + 1$
DEC *indx*,X	6A *byte*	$(IX+indx) \leftarrow (IX+indx) - 1$

byte loading operations; operations that transfer two bytes of data between 2-byte registers and successive address locations in data memory.

The fact that the index term is always a positive value greatly simplifies the task of determining effective addresses. The hexadecimal range of values is still 00 through FF, but the decimal equivalents are 0 through 255.

The 6800's lone 16-bit index register, IX, is the basis for the indexed addressing operations—the index term is summed with the content of the IX register to come up with the effective address. But in the 6800 system, the effective address is always equal to or greater than the 2-byte number in the index register.

In each of the following examples, assume that the IX register contains $4C00:

    LDAA $0A,X   effective address is $4C0A

    LDAA $00,X   effective address is $4C00

    LDAA $F7,X   effective address is $4CF7

The index term in the last example is $F7, and the effective address is larger than the content of the IX register. Compare that result with a similar instruction from the Z-80 system: LD A,(IX+F7H). That one yields an effective address of 4BF7H.

The 6800's indexed instructions are all 2-byte instructions. The first byte is the opcode and the second is the index term.

The unique indexed instructions appear in Table 9-7. They are the ones that transfer 16 bits from the IX or SP registers to data memory, or transfer 16 bits from successive locations in data memory to the IX or SP registers.

LDS *indx*,X is one of those instructions. In that case, two bytes of data are loaded to the 16-bit SP register. As the symbolic notations indicate, the content of address (IX+*indx*) goes to the higher-order byte position in the SP register, while the content of the next-higher address, (IX+*indx+1*), goes to the lower-order byte position.

The STS *indx*,X instruction works matters the other way around. The high-order byte from the SP register goes to address IX+*indx*, and the lower-order byte goes to IX+*indx+1*. So if the SP register happens to contain the number $1234, and the index term is set to $08, and the IX register contains $7000, address $7C08 gets the 12 byte from the SP register, and address $7C09 gets the 34 byte.

Two-byte, indexed transfers involving the IX register—LDX *indx*,X and STX *indx*,X—follow the same operating pattern as those involving the SP register.

The following summary of literal translations should offer sufficient clues for figuring out the meaning of the others:

    LDAB *indx*,X   Load the B accumulator with a data byte from an effective address formed by summing the content of the IX register with the *indx* byte.

    CLR *indx*,X   CLEAR to zero the byte found by the effective address IX+*indx*.

ANDA *indx*,X	Logically AND the content of the A accumulator with a memory byte addressed by IX+*indx*. Place the result into the A accumulator.
CPX *indx*,X	COMPARE the 16-bit value in the IX register with the content of two successive 8-bit data locations found at IX+*indx* and IX+*indx+1*. Only the flags are affected by the result.
DEC *indx*,X	DECREMENT by 1 the memory data byte found by summing the content of the IX register and the index term.

Exercises for Section 9-3

1. Which 6800 register serves as the index register?
2. What is the range of index-term values in hexadecimal? in decimal?
3. Determine the effective address for the following 6800 instructions. Assume that the content of the IX register is $3C02 in each case.

   (a) LDAA $2A,X   (b) LDAB $FE,X   (c) STAB $7F,X
   (d) STX $00,X   (e) ANDB $80,X   (f) CMPA $FF,X

4. Let the IX register contain $3400, the SP register contain $0235, and let *indx* be $02.
   (a) Write the source code for loading the content of SP to data memory in an indirect indexed fashion.
   (b) Write the object code for that instruction.
   (c) Cite the relevant data memory addresses and their content after the instruction has been executed.

9-4 INDIRECT ADDRESSING FOR THE 6502

The 6502 has the most unusual and sophisticated set of instructions for indirect memory addressing. After completing your study of this section, you might be inclined to think that is an understatement of the matter.

This system uses four different indirect addressing modes. Those modes must be described individually, and the complete summary of instructions are offered in Tables 9-9 and 9-10 at this point just for reference purposes. You are not expected to understand any of them at this moment.

Zero-Page, Single-Byte Indexing

A survey of Tables 9-9 and 9-10 show a complete set of register/memory transfer and register operations using an index mode written as $addr_0$,X or $addr_0$,Y. From Table 9-9, those instructions include:

```
LDA  addr0,X
STA  addr0,X
LDX  addr0,Y
STX  addr0,Y
LDY  addr0,X
STY  addr0,X
```

TABLE 9-9 LOAD REGISTER/MEMORY INDEXED INDIRECT INSTRUCTIONS FOR THE 6502

Source code	Object code	Notes
LDA $addr_0$,X	B5 $byte$	A←($addr_0$+X)
LDA $addr$,X	BD $byte\ byte$	A←($addr$+X)
LDA $addr$,Y	B9 $byte\ byte$	A←($addr$+Y)
LDA ($addr_0$,X)	A1 $byte$	Pre-indexed
LDA ($addr_0$,X)	B1 $byte$	Post-indexed
STA $addr_0$,X	95 $byte$	($addr_0$+X)←A
STA $addr$,X	9D $byte\ byte$	($addr$+X)←A
STA $addr$,Y	99 $byte\ byte$	($addr$+Y)←A
STA ($addr_0$,X)	81 $byte$	Pre-indexed
STA ($addr_0$),Y	91 $byte$	Post-indexed
LDX $addr_0$,Y	B6 $byte$	X←($addr_0$+Y)
LDX $addr$,Y	BE $byte\ hvte$	X←($addr$+Y)
STX $addr_0$,Y	96 $byte$	($addr_0$+Y)←X
LDY $addr_0$,X	B4 $byte$	Y←($addr_0$+Y)
LDY $addr$,X	BC $byte\ byte$	Y←($addr$+Y)
STY $addr_0$,X	94 $byte$	($addr_0$+X)←Y

Those instructions transfer a single byte of data between an 8-bit register and a location in zero-page data memory. The instruction must include a specification for a zero-page base address, $addr_0$. The effective address is then determined by summing that base address with the content of the 8-bit X or Y register.

Thus an instruction such as LDA $02,X has an effective address found by summing the current content of the X register with $02. That effective address then points to a place in zero-page memory, and the A register is loaded with the byte contained therein. It is impossible to say what that target address in memory will be without knowing the content of the X register, however.

So suppose that the X register is set to $40. Knowing that, the effective address for the instruction LDA $02,X is fixed at $42. The A register is loaded with the byte contained in zero-page address location $42.

Using the nomenclature introduced for the other microprocessor devices described earlier in this chapter, the X or Y register in these instructions make up the index term. That being the case, $addr_0$ is the *base address*. The index term is summed with the base address to form the effective address for the instruction.

It is a fairly simple concept, especially if one avoids the temptation of comparing it with similar operations for the microprocessors described earlier in this chapter. At this point in the discussion, such comparisons can be more confusing than enlightening.

The effective address is reckoned in the same way for the zero-page, single-byte operate instructions in Table 9-10. See if you can recall the meaning of these instructions and extend your understanding to their indexed

TABLE 9-10 OPERATE REGISTER/MEMORY INDEXED INDIRECT INSTRUCTIONS FOR THE 6502

Source code	Object code	Symbolic notation
AND $addr_0$,X	35 *byte*	
AND *addr*,X	3D *byte byte*	
AND *addr*,Y	39 *byte byte*	$A \leftarrow A \wedge M$
AND ($addr_0$,X)	61 *byte*	
AND ($addr_0$),Y	31 *byte*	
ORA $addr_0$,X	15 *byte*	
ORA *addr*,X	1D *byte byte*	
ORA *addr*,Y	19 *byte byte*	$A \leftarrow A \vee M$
ORA ($addr_0$,X)	01 *byte*	
ORA ($addr_0$),Y	11 *byte*	
EOR $addr_0$,X	55 *byte*	
EOR *addr*,X	5D *byte byte*	
EOR *addr*,Y	59 *byte byte*	$A \leftarrow A \triangledown M$
EOR ($addr_0$,X)	41 *byte*	
EOR ($addr_0$),Y	51 *byte*	
CMP $addr_0$,X	D5 *byte*	
CMP *addr*,X	DD *byte byte*	
CMP *addr*,Y	D9 *byte byte*	$A - M$ (only flags affected)
CMP ($addr_0$,X)	C1 *byte*	
CMP ($addr_0$),Y	D1 *byte*	
ADC $addr_0$,X	75 *byte*	
ADC *addr*,X	7D *byte byte*	
ADC *addr*,Y	79 *byte byte*	$A \leftarrow A + M + Cs$
ADC ($addr_0$,X)	61 *byte*	
ADC ($addr_0$),Y	71 *byte*	
SBC $addr_0$,X	F5 *byte*	
SBC *addr*,X	FD *byte byte*	
SBC *addr*,Y	F9 *byte byte*	$A \leftarrow A - M - Cs$
SBC ($addr_0$,X)	E1 *byte*	
SBC ($addr_0$),Y	F1 *byte*	
INC $addr_0$,X	F6 *byte*	$M \leftarrow M + 1$
INC *addr*,X	FE *byte byte*	
DEC $addr_0$,X	D6 *byte*	$M \leftarrow M - 1$
DEC *addr*,X	DE *byte byte*	

Note: M represents the content of the addressed memory byte; $addr_0$ represents 1-byte, zero-page memory address.

mode of addressing:

AND $addr_0$,X	ORA $addr_0$,X	EOR $addr_0$,X
CMP $addr_0$,X	ADC $addr_0$,X	SBC $addr_0$,X
INC $addr_0$,X	DEC $addr_0$,X	

The operators work exactly as described for the 6502 system in Chapters 7 and 8. The only difference here is the addressing mode for the operand.

Absolute Indexed Addressing

You will find a series of instructions in Tables 9-9 and 9-10 that take this general form:

operator *addr*,X

operator *addr*,Y

The *operator* specifies the type of operation to take place—LDA, STA, LDX, STY, AND, EOR, and so on. The *addr* term is the base address, and X or Y term refers to the current content of the 8-bit X or Y register. These instructions work just like the zero-page versions described in the previous discussion. The only real difference is that the base address is a 2-byte address, rather than a single-byte, zero-page address.

The effective address is found by summing the 2-byte base address with the content of the designated X or Y register. Rather than being confined to addresses between \$00 and \$FF, these instructions open the door to the 6502's full range of addressing—from \$0000 through \$FFFF.

Thus an instruction such as

AND \$3C00,X

literally means: Logically AND the content of the A register with a data byte found at an address determined by the sum of \$3C00 (the base address) and the content of the X register. If the X register happens to be holding \$22, the effective address of that data byte is \$3C22.

Pre-Indexed Addressing

Another survey of Tables 9-9 and 9-10 reveals a set of source-code instructions having addressing modes designated as $(addr_0,X)$. They appear to be zero-page indexed addresses; and, indeed, that is part of the picture—the content of the 1-byte X register is summed with a specified zero-page base address, $addr_0$.

Compare these two kinds of instructions:

LDA $addr_0$,X
LDA ($addr_0$,X)

Both point to an address in zero-page memory. If $addr_0$ is set to \$45 and the X register contains \$02, both instructions point to zero-page address \$47.

As far as the first of the two instructions is concerned, it then loads the A register with the data byte contained at the effective address location \$47. And that would be the end of the matter. That is an instruction already described under the heading "Zero-Page, Single-Byte Indexing."

The second instruction, LDA $(addr_0,X)$, carries matters a couple of steps further. Indeed, it points to a zero-page address that is determined by summing the $addr_0$ base address term with the content of the X register. But the data byte contained in that address is not loaded to the A register. Rather, it is saved in an internal address register until the system has a chance to pick up another byte of data from the next-higher address location in zero-page memory: from address $addr_0+X+1$.

The instruction LDA $(addr_0,X)$ thus picks up two bytes of data from zero-page memory: one from $addr_0+X$ and another from $addr_0+X+1$. Together, the two bytes of data from zero-page memory make up a full 2-byte address, and it is the content of that absolute-memory location that is loaded to the A register.

The effective address for an instruction having an operand reading $(addr_0,X)$ is always a 2-byte address formed from data residing in two successive zero-page memory addresses—zero-page addresses located by $addr_0+X$ and $addr_0+X+1$.

Suppose that zero-page address $0E contains data $00, and address $0F contains data $4C. The two successive address locations, $0E and $0F, contain data bytes $00 and $4C, respectively. Now suppose that a program calls for the instruction, LDA ($0A,X) and the X register contains $04.

Summing $0A and the content of the X register makes the system point to zero-page address $0E. The data byte contained therein, $00, is saved in a special address register, and the system automatically increments the on-line address pointer to the next-higher address location, $0F. The byte contained in that location, $4C, is also loaded to the special address register.

Now, that special address register contains two bytes of data: $00 and $4C. They are combined to make up a full, 2-byte address, $4C00. The first byte fetched from zero-page memory is used as the LSB, and the second is used as the MSB. That is the instruction's effective address.

Finally, the data byte contained in absolute memory address, $4C00, is loaded to the A register. And that completes the operation.

The process for determining the effective address for pre-indexed operations can be summarized this way:

1. Find the LSB of the effective address at a zero-page memory address determined by $addr_0+X$.
2. Find the MSB of the effective address at the next-higher zero-page address, at $addr_0+X+1$.

Tables 9-9 and 9-10 show that pre-indexed addressing can be applied to a full range of register/memory transfers, and logic and arithmetic operations.

Post-Indexed Addressing

A final survey of the instruction set in Tables 9-9 and 9-10 show some operations using an addressing mode written as $(addr_0),Y$. In these instances, $addr_0$ points to the first of two successive bytes of data in zero-page memory; and those two bytes make up the LSB and MSB of a 2-byte address in absolute memory space. That is not the effective address, however.

The bytes found at $addr_0$ and $addr_0+1$ are combined to make up a 2-byte number. But then the content of the Y register is summed with it to produce the effective address for the instruction.

This post-indexed addressing mode generates the effective address this way:

1. Fetch the LSB of a 2-byte address from zero-page address $addr_0$.
2. Fetch the MSB of the 2-byte address from zero-page address $addr_0+1$.
3. Determine the effective address by summing the preliminary 2-byte address with the content of the Y register.

An instruction such as LDA ($2A),Y will first fetch data bytes from $2A and $2B. Then the content of the Y register is summed with the resulting 2-byte number to derive the effective address. So if the contents of zero-page addresses $2A and $2B happen to be $00 and $3D, respectively, and the Y register contains $02, the effective address is $3D00+$02, or $3D02. It is the data content of address $3D02 that is ultimately loaded to the A register by this example.

Pre-indexing differs from post-indexing in two ways. First, the pre-indexed operations use the index register for determining the zero-page address locations, while post-indexed operations refer to the index register after the zero-page addressing is done. The second difference is that pre-indexed operations use only the X index register, while post-indexed operations use only the Y register.

In either case, the system comes up with a 2-byte address location, and it is the data contained in that address that participate in the function specied by the instruction.

Summary of 6502 Addressing Modes

Table 9-11 summarizes the 6502's four addressing modes that fall into the general category of indexed addressing.

Zero-page, single-byte addressing picks up a data byte directly from zero-page memory. The base address, $addr_0$, is specified in the instruction, and that 1-byte address is summed with the 1-byte content of the X register to arrive at the effective address.

Absolute indexing fetches a data byte from anywhere in memory. The base address, $addr$, is a 2-byte address specified in the instruction, and the effective address is determined by summing the base address with the content of either the X or Y index register.

Pre-indexed addressing fetches two data bytes from zero-page memory. Those bytes are found by summing the base address, $addr_0$, with the content of the X register, and then fetching them from the resulting zero-page address

TABLE 9-11 SUMMARY OF PROCEDURES FOR DETERMINING
THE EFFECTIVE ADDRESS FOR THE 6502's ADDRESSING MODES

Addressing mode	Source-code operand	Effective address
Zero-page, single-byte	$addr_0$,X	$addr_0$+X
Absolute indexed	$addr$,X	$addr$+X
	$addr$,Y	$addr$+Y
Pre-indexed	($addr_0$,X)	LSB = ($addr_0$+X)
		MSB = ($addr_0$+X+1)
Post-indexed	($addr_0$),Y	LSB = ($addr_0$)+Y
		MSB = ($addr_0$+1)+Y

Note: Parentheses in the "Effective address" column denote "content of."

and the next-higher address. The two bytes found in that indexing operation then form the effective address in absolute, 2-byte memory space.

Post-indexed addressing also fetches two bytes from successive address locations in zero-page memory. The first byte comes from the specified $addr_0$, and the second comes out of the next-higher address location. Together, the two bytes make up a 2-byte address, but then the effective address is formed by summing the content of the Y register to the 2-byte number previously fetched from zero-page memory.

Exercises for Section 9-4

Use the following memory maps for working all the exercises:

Zero-page memory		Absolute memory	
Address	Data	Address	Data
$40	$00	$2A00	$08
$41	$2A	$2A01	$09
$42	$02	$2A02	$0A
$43	$2A	$4F03	$0B
$44	$03	$4F04	$0C
$45	$4F	$4F05	$0D
$46	$06	$6106	$0E
$47	$61	$6107	$0F

1. The content of the X register is $02. Determine the effective address and content of the A register after executing the instruction LDA $43,X.
2. The content of the X register is $02. Determine the effective address and the content of the A register after executing the instruction LDA $4F03,X.
3. The content of the Y register is $00. Determine the effective address and the content of the A register after executing the instruction LDA $2A02,Y.

4. The content of the X register is $04. Determine the effective address and the content of the A register after executing the instruction LDA ($42,X).

5. The content of the Y register is $02. Determine the effective address and the content of the A register after executing the instruction LDA ($44),Y.

9-5 A PERSPECTIVE ON INDIRECT AND INDEXED ADDRESSING

Indirect and indexed addressing is simply an alternative method for accessing a byte of data in the data memory, however roundabout the methods might seem at times. It is a dynamic alternative to direct memory addressing, and it makes possible some vital programming operations that are virtually impossible with register-immediate instructions.

The microprocessor functions that can be performed—transferring data, doing arithmetic and logic operations—are common to direct and indirect addressing. Those operations were discussed at length in Chapters 7 and 8, and nothing about their essential features is changed by using indirect and indexed addressing. In fact, this chapter has treated the fundamental microprocessor functions as an incidental matter compared to the procedures for determining the effective address of the data to be manipulated by them.

Many readers will leave this chapter with at least a vague feeling of having lost a grasp on the meaning of it all. That is to be expected. It is possible to have an excellent understanding of direct and indirect addressing modes, but fail to see the overall purpose of it all.

The problem is one of presenting new information about microprocessors in a fashion that is both consistent and meaningful. Unfortunately, it is sometimes impossible to be both consistent and meaningful at the same time. That is the case here.

The solution has been to trade off a sense of meaning or relevance for consistency. The discussions through this chapter have grown away from "the real world," offering new ideas and topics in a rather abstract fashion. That has been necessary, however, to pave the way for the subjects in the next few chapters. I can promise that the material in the next few chapters will begin pulling together the loose ends from this chapter, giving you a feeling that a lot of seemingly unrelated ideas are finally falling into place. What is perhaps even more important, you will find an ever-increasing number of practical examples and applications.

Through your study of the remainder of this book, you will probably find it necessary to refer back to this chapter. The more often you do that, the clearer the ideas will become.

10

An Introduction to Jump and Branch Instructions

The instructions introduced in this chapter are the first in this book to have some influence on the execution of the program itself. In all previous discussions, the programs simply grind away, executing one instruction at a time, from beginning to end.

But now it will become possible to compose the programs that can, under certain conditions, skip portions of a program. It will be possible to repeat sequences of instructions any number of times before resuming the normal flow of instructions.

Jump, or *branch*, instructions directly affect the content of the microprocessors' 16-bit program counter (PC) register, and that is the key to writing programs that can jump out of an ongoing sequence of program instructions and reenter at another place in the program.

Recall that the purpose of the PC register is to point to the address of the program instruction to be executed next. Although little has been said about the PC register in recent discussions, it has been doing its vital program-reading task in the background.

A jump instruction can, in effect, do a 16-bit load immediate to the PC register. Suppose the system is executing a program that has instructions stored in program memory at locations 2000H, 2001H, 2002H, ... The program counter is incrementing its way through the bytes of the program, feeding instructions to the microprocessor via the data bus. But then suppose that the system comes across a jump instruction—an instruction that says, in essence, jump to program address 20FFH.

Upon executing that particular jump instruction, the ongoing sequence is interrupted; the PC register is set to 20FFH, and program execution resumes as 20FFH, 2100H, 2101H, ... Any programming between the place where the jump instruction occurs and the place where the program jumps is simply skipped.

Here is an example of a short program that uses a jump instruction and Z-80 mnemonics:

Address	Source code	Comment
4C00	LD HL,0000H	;INITIALIZE HL TO ZERO
4C03	INC HL	;INCREMENT HL
4C04	JP 4C03H	;INCREMENT AGAIN

The first instruction clears the HL register pair to zero by doing a load immediate operation. The second instruction increments the data in the HL register pair by 1. The third instruction is the jump instruction. It tells the system to jump to program address 4C03H; and you should note that program address 4C03H is the one calling for incrementing the HL register pair. In a sense, the program is backed up to the INCREMENT step. The increment is done again.

Then the system encounters the same jump instruction; it responds by doing the increment instruction, then the jump, then the increment, then the jump, ... The *looping* process between the increment and jump instructions goes on indefinitely. The overall result is that the content of the HL register pair is incremented over and over again, causing it to count upward indefinitely.

Although the program sequence in this particular example has a rather questionable practical value, it at least suggests one of the most powerful program sequences for practical microprocessor applications—counting operations. All that is needed to make it a truly useful program is some means for breaking out of the counting loop when the number in the HL register pair reaches a specified value. But that notion is left to a later discussion in this chapter.

There are a couple of different ways to classify jump instructions. First, they can be classified as either *unconditional* or *conditional* jumps. Unconditional jump operations cause the program counter to jump to a new address in program memory under any circumstances. That is the case in the example just cited. A conditional jump, on the other hand, causes the jumping effect only under certain conditions—conditions dictated by the status of some flag bits in the microprocessor's F register.

The second way to classify jump instructions is as *absolute* or *relative*. Absolute jump instructions specify the exact target address as part of the instruction. The jump instruction in the preceding example is an absolute jump instruction because it tells the system to jump to a specific address. A relative jump instruction, however, does not specify an exact target address. Rather, it specifies the number of program memory locations to be jumped. The jumping effect is relative to the current program address in that case.

So jump instructions can be classified as unconditional or conditional, and absolute or relative. Actually, the classifications can be combined to come up with four kinds of jump instructions:

Jump unconditional absolute

Jump unconditional relative

Jump conditional absolute

Jump conditional relative

Any jump, or branch, instruction in a microprocessor's instruction set can be fit into one of those four types.

10-1 JUMP INSTRUCTIONS FOR THE 8080A/8085

Table 10-1 shows all the jump instructions for the 8080A/8085 microprocessor. They are all absolute jumps, and only two of them are considered unconditional jumps.

With the exception of the PCHL instruction, these jumps specify the absolute target addresses as two bytes. The first byte in the object code is the operator, and the two remaining bytes spell out the target address, *addr*. Of those two bytes, the first represents the LSB of *addr*, while the final byte represents the MSB of *addr*. Thus the instruction JMP 4C00H would use the object code, C3 00 4C. Literally it means: Jump unconditionally to program address 4C00 hexadecimal.

Unconditional Absolute Jump Instructions

The 8080A/8085 instruction set features just two unconditional jumps, JMP *addr* and PCHL. Note from the table that neither make reference to flag conditions existing the moment they are executed. That, of course, is the hallmark of unconditional jump instructions.

JMP *addr* has already been cited in this discussion. Upon encountering this instruction, *addr* is loaded into the microprocessor's PC register, and program operations are forced to resume from that program address.

TABLE 10-1 JUMP INSTRUCTIONS FOR THE 8080A/8085

Source code	Object code	Flag conditions
JMP *addr*	C3 *byte byte*	None
JZ *addr*	CA *byte byte*	Z=1
JNZ *addr*	C2 *byte byte*	Z=0
JC *addr*	DA *byte byte*	Cs=1
JNC *addr*	D2 *byte byte*	Cs=0
JM *addr*	FA *byte byte*	S=1
JP *addr*	F2 *byte byte*	S=0
JPE *addr*	EA *byte byte*	P=1
JPO *addr*	E2 *byte byte*	P=0
PCHL	E9	None

PCHL is a special, 1-byte instruction that loads the current content of the HL register pair to the PC register. As a result, program operations jump to an address specified by the HL register pair.

Conditional Absolute Jump Instructions

The 8080A/8085 features eight jump instructions that make specific reference to flag bits in the F register. These conditional jump instructions are executed only if their designated flag conditions are met. *Otherwise, the jump instruction is totally ignored.* An unconditional jump instruction, on the other hand, is always executed, making no reference at all to flag bits in the F register.

Before using conditional jump instructions, the programmer must be familiar with the relevant flag conditions and the mechanisms that set and clear them. A great deal of discussion in earlier chapters has already been devoted to the responses of the Z (zero) and Cs (carry status) flags. The S (sign) and P (parity) flags have not yet been discussed; and since they play an important role in four of the conditional jump instructions, it is time to look at them in some detail.*

Figure 10-1 shows the layout of the F register for the 8080A/8085 microprocessor. It shows the Z and Cs bits in the bit-6 and bit-0 positions, respectively.

The sign bit, S, is the one in the bit-7 position of the F register. As suggested in the summary of flag functions in the figure, the S bit takes on the value of the most-significant bit position of the accumulator, following an arithmetic or logic operation.

It serves as a sign bit in the sense that it indicates the sign (positive or negative) of an 8-bit number expressed in a 2's-complement format. By that convention, positive numbers have a sign bit of zero, and the seven remaining bits contain the value of that number. When the sign bit is a logic 1, the number in the lower 7 bits of the accumulator is a negative number in a 2's-complement form.

The S bit is thus set to 1 whenever the result of a logic or arithmetic operation turns up a negative value in the accumulator. The sign bit is cleared to zero whenever such operations yield a positive result in the accumulator.

The literal meanings of the conditional jump instructions can thus be summarized this way:

JZ *addr*   Jump to *addr* if the result is *zero*.

JNZ *addr*   Jump to *addr* if the result is *not zero*.

---

*I have exercised the option of naming the flag bits in a consistent fashion through this book. In many instances, the names are identical to those suggested by the manufacturers. For the sake of making a clear comparison between microprocessors, however, some of the names of flag bits differ from those of the manufacturers'. The functions of those flags are "correct" in all cases, though.

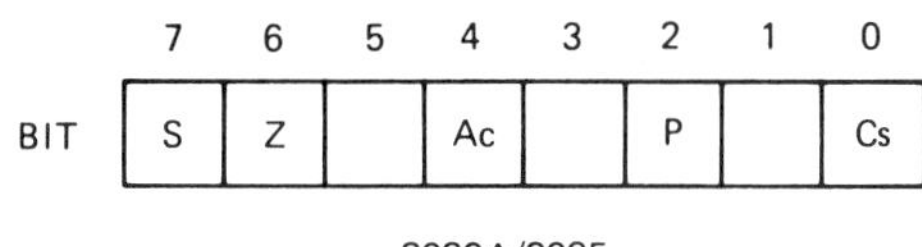

S   The S (sign) bit takes on the value of the most-significant bit of a number resulting from an arithmetic or logic operation. Using 2's-complement notation, 1 represents a negative number, and 0 represents a positive number.

Z   The Z (zero) bit takes on a value of 1 or 0 following an arithmetic or logic operation. It is set to 1 if the result is zero, and it is cleared to 0 if the result is a nonzero number.

Ac The Ac (auxiliary carry) bit is used only for BCD (binary-coded decimal) arithmetic operations, and is not relevant to any jump operations.

P   The P (parity) bit as affected by arithmetic and logic operations. If the result has even parity (an even number of 1's) the P flag bit is set to 1. If the result has odd parity (an odd number of 1's), the P flag is cleared to zero.

Cs The Cs (carry status) flag is cleared to 0 by a logic operation. Following an arithmetic operation, it is set to logic 1 whenever a carry-out of 1 occurs from the most significant bit position of the result. Otherwise, Cs is cleared to 0.

Figure 10-1   The 8080A/8085 flag register.

JC *addr*	Jump to *addr* if a *carry* occurs.
JNC *addr*	Jump to *addr* if *no carry* occurs.
JM *addr*	Jump to *addr* if the result is *negative*.
JP *addr*	Jump to *addr* if the result is *positive*.
JPE *addr*	Jump to *addr* if *even parity* results.
JPO *addr*	Jump to *addr* if *odd parity* results.

If the prevailing flag conditions fail to satisfy the instruction, it is automatically passed over, and the program operations pick up at the next instruction.

The programming power inherent in such conditional jump instructions is at least suggested by the following example.

EXAMPLE 10-1

Write and assemble an 8080A/8085 program that initializes the accumulator to FFH, then decrements that number, one step at a time, until it is counted down to zero. Begin the listing at address 7000H.

See the complete listing and a flowchart in Program 10-1.

The first instruction initializes the accumulator by doing a load immediate of hexadecimal FF to it. The second instruction simply decrements the number in the accumulator by 1. Then the third instruction—jump if not zero—tests the Z flag in the accumulator. If it finds that the accumulator has not yet been decremented all the way to zero, it jumps the program op-

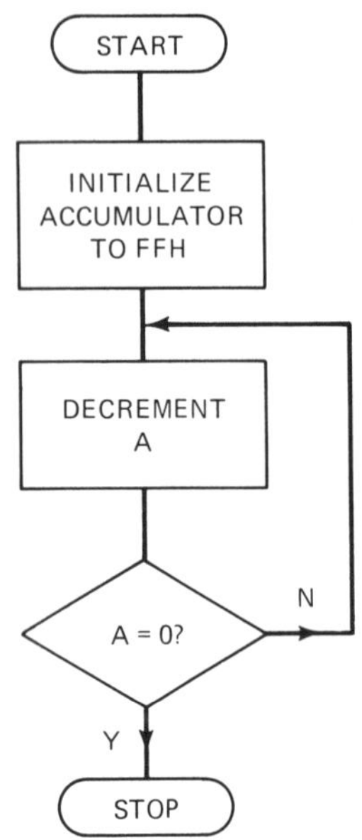

PROGRAM 10-1 PROGRAM LISTING AND FLOWCHART FOR EXAMPLE 10-1

```
7000 3E FF     MVI A,FFH    ;INITIALIZE THE ACCUMULATOR
7002 3D        DCR A        ;DECREMENT THE ACCUMULATOR
7003 C2 02 70  JNZ 7002H    ;IF NOT ZERO, DECREMENT AGAIN
```

eration back up to the address of the decrement instruction. As a result, the content of the accumulator is decremented once again.

The program continues looping in this fashion until the conditional jump instruction finds that the accumulator has finally been counted down to zero—the Z flag bit is set to 1. At that moment, the jump conditional is no longer satisfied, and the program comes to a conclusion.

EXERCISES FOR SECTION 10-1

1. Describe the essential difference between conditional and unconditional jump instructions.
2. Under what conditions will the following 8080A/8085 flag bits be set to logic 1? to logic 0?
   (a) Z   (b) Cs   (c) S   (d) P
3. What flag conditions (1 or 0) are necessary for satisfying the following jump instructions?
   (a) JMP *addr*   (b) JNC *addr*   (c) JZ *addr*
   (b) JP *addr*   (e) JPE *addr*   (f) JM *addr*
4. Explain what the following jump instruction does:

```
4C00 C3 00 4C   JMP 4C00H
```

10-2 JUMP INSTRUCTIONS FOR THE Z-80

Table 10-2 summarizes the Z-80 jump instructions. The list includes those featured in the 8080A/8085, plus a few more unconditional absolute jumps and a small but useful family of relative jumps.

Source code	Object code	Flag conditions
JP *addr*	C3 *byte byte*	None
JP Z,*addr*	CA *byte byte*	Z=1
JP NZ,*addr*	C2 *byte byte*	Z=0
JP C,*addr*	DA *byte byte*	Cs=1
JP NC,*addr*	D2 *byte byte*	Cs=0
JP M,*addr*	FA *byte byte*	S=1
JP P,*addr*	F2 *byte byte*	S=0
JP PE,*addr*	EA *byte byte*	P=1
JP PO,*addr*	E2 *byte byte*	P=0
JP (HL)	E9	None
JP (IX)	DD E9	None
JP (IY)	FD E9	None
JR *disp*	38 *byte*	None
JR Z,*disp*	28 *byte*	Z=1
JR NZ,*disp*	20 *byte*	Z=0
JR C,*disp*	38 *byte*	Cs=1
JR NC,*disp*	30 *byte*	Cs=0

The following list of jump instructions are, in principle, identical to those used by the 8080A/8085 system. Take a moment to compare the mnemonics and literal meanings in the context of discussions in Section 10-1.

JMP *addr*	Jump unconditionally to *addr*.
JP Z,*addr*	Jump to *addr* if result is *zero*.
JP NZ,*addr*	Jump to *addr* if result is *not zero*.
JP M,*addr*	Jump to *addr* if result is *negative* (*minus*).
JP P,*addr*	Jump to *addr* if result is *positive*.
JP PE,*addr*	Jump to *addr* if *even parity* (following a logic operation), or Jump to *addr* if *overflow* occurs (following an arithmetic operation).
JP PO,*addr*	Jump to *addr* if *odd parity* (following a logic operation), or Jump to *addr* if *no overflow* (following an arithmetic operation).
JP (HL)	Jump unconditionally to the address pointed by the HL register pair.

The dual role of the parity jumps is described shortly in the context of the Z-80's P flag bit.

The Z-80 instruction set includes two additional unconditional jump instructions:

JP (IX)	Jump unconditionally to the address pointed by the 16-bit IX register.
JP (IY)	Jump unconditionally to the address pointed by the 16-bit IY register.

Those instructions work just like the JP (HL) instruction, loading the content of the 16-bit register or register pair into the PC register.

The remaining jump instructions in Table 10-2 are relative jumps that are described later in this section.

The Z-80 Flag Register

Figure 10-2 describes the essential feature of the Z-80's flag register.

In many respects, the Z-80's flag bits are like those of the 8080A/8085 system. However, there is an additional bit, N, that is set to logic 1 during any subtraction operation and cleared to 0 by a summation instruction. The N bit is really used only for internal operations, and it is not relevant to any of the conditional jump instructions.

The P flag bit plays two different roles as far as the Z-80 system is concerned. As with the 8080A/8085's version, it serves as a parity indication, but *only after logic operations*. Following a logic operation, the P flag is set to logic 1 if the result has even parity (an even number of 1's in the result), and it is cleared to 0 if the result has odd parity (an odd number of 1's in the result).

That P flag, however, plays an entirely different role following arithmetic operations. Instead of indicating the parity of the result (as is the case for the 8080A/8085), the *P flag signals an overflow condition resulting from an arithmetic operation.*

Overflow is a relevant term only when dealing with signed, 2's-complement numbers. An overflow occurs, for instance, whenever the sum of

	7	6	5	4	3	2	1	0
BIT	S	Z		Ac		P	N	Cs

Z-80 FLAG REGISTER

S   The S (sign bit takes on the value of the most-significant bit of a number resulting from an arithmetic or logic operation. Using 2's-complement notation, 1 represents a negative number, and 0 represents a positive number.

Z   The Z (zero) bit takes on a value of 1 or 0 following an arithmetic or logic operation. It is set to 1 if the result is zero, and cleared to 0 if the result is a nonzero number.

Ac   The Ac (auxiliary carry) bit is used only for BCD arithmetic operations, and does not participate in any jump instructions.

P   The P (parity/overflow) flag is affected by arithmetic and logic operations. Following logic operations, the P flag indicates the parity of the result—1 for even parity and 0 for odd parity. Following arithmetic operations, the P flag shows a logic 1 if overflow has occurred; otherwise, it is cleared to 0.

N   The N (subtract) status flag simply indicates whether or not a subtraction-type operation is taking place. It is set to 1 during such operations, and cleared to 0 by addition operations. Its status is not relevant to any jump instructions.

Cs   The Cs (carry status) flag is cleared to 0 by a logic operation. Following arithmetic operations, it is set to 1 whenever a carry-out of 1 occurs from the most-significant bit position of the result. Otherwise, it is cleared to 0.

Figure 10-2   The Z-80 flag register.

two positive numbers yields a negative result—whenever the most-significant bit position of the result is a logic 1. Similarly, an overflow condition exists when effectively summing two negative numbers, and the result is a positive number—one having a 0 in the most-significant bit position.

Looking at the matter of overflow in a somewhat different light, it occurs whenever the result of an arithmetic operation exceeds the bit capacity of the register, or, in other words, the result turns up an incorrect sign.

In the Z-80 system, the P flag is set to logic 1 when an arithmetic overflow condition occurs, and it is cleared to zero when no such overflow exists.

Overflow is different from wraparound in the sense that a wraparound (sensed by the Cs flag bit) need not occur under the same conditions that an overflow does. Using 8-bit, signed, 2's-complement notation, the range of integer values is -128 through +127, decimal. The sum of two positive numbers, such as 100 and 50, should turn up 150 as a result; but it cannot in the 2's-complement format. The answer, exceeding 127, actually turns up a number considered to be negative in the complement format. It is an "incorrect" answer, and the P flag is set to 1. Wraparound does not occur, however, because there is not a carry-out of 1 from the most-significant bit position; and the Cs bit remains cleared to 0.

Relative Jump Instructions

The Z-80 instruction set includes five relative jump instructions. Recall that the 8080A/8085 system has none. The Z-80's relative jumps are:

JR *disp*

JR Z,*disp*

JR NZ,*disp*

JR C,*disp*

JR NC,*disp*

JR *disp* is an unconditional relative jump instruction, while the remainder are conditional relative jumps. Rather than specifying an absolute, 2-byte target address for the jump operation, these specify a displacement, *disp*, from the current address in program memory. The 1-byte *displacement term* is summed with the current content of the PC register (program counter), jumping program operations a designated number of steps ahead or behind.

The displacement term must be specified as an 8-bit signed number, using 2's-complement notation. A displacement term of 04H, for example, advances the PC register four address locations ahead of its current point. So if the program counter happens to be pointing to an instruction at 4C00H in the program memory, a relative jump instruction having a displacement term of 04H will advance the operations to an instruction at address 4C04H. The instructions between those two points will be passed over.

Using signed, 2's-complement notation, it is possible to back up the program counter, thereby executing instructions having a lower address. The program counter can be backed up four address locations by using a displacement term of FCH (- 4 decimal).

It is thus possible to jump ahead 127 addresses in program memory, or jump back as many as 128 addresses. The actual, or absolute, addresses are not taken into account. They are important for absolute jump operations, but not for these relative jumps.

The main advantage of relative jumps is that the programmer need not know the actual program addresses involved—only the number of addresses to be jumped is important.

So relative jump instructions clearly specify how many addresses are to be jumped. One important question remains: From what point in program memory does the jump begin? at the beginning or end of the jump instruction?

The microprocessor must read both bytes in a relative jump instruction—an opcode followed by a displacement term. And that means that the program counter is left resting at the address just following the relative jump instruction. It is from that point that the relative jump takes place.

If the relative jump instruction happens to occupy program memory addresses 3C01H and 3C02H, the jump takes place relative to address 3C03H. The instruction that might reside at 3C03H is not executed, but it is nevertheless the reference point for a relative jump operation.

EXAMPLE 10-2

Write and assemble a Z-80 program that initializes the accumulator to FFH, then decrements that number, one step at a time, until it is counted down to zero. Use only relative jump instructions, and begin the listing at 7000H.

See the program listing in Program 10-2, and compare its operation with the 8080A/8085 version in Program 10-1.

The first instruction simply initializes the A register to a value of FF, hexadecimal. The second instruction decrements the current content of that register by 1. The third instruction is the conditional, relative jump instruction. That last instruction literally says: If the result is not zero, jump back three instructions from the current address pointed by the PC register (from address 7005H).

After reading the relative jump instruction, the program counter (PC register) will have advanced to the next instruction following the relative jump instruction. In this case, that address is 7005H. But one need not know

PROGRAM 10-2 LISTING FOR EXAMPLE 10-2

```
7000 3A FF   LD A,FFH   ;INITIALIZE THE ACCUMULATOR
7002 3D      DEC A      ;DECREMENT THE ACCUMULATOR
7003 20 FD   JR NZ,FDH  ;IF NOT ZERO, DECREMENT AGAIN
```

the actual, or absolute, address because the jump takes place relative to the current setting of the program counter.

And since FDH is the hexadecimal version of −3 decimal, the jump instruction carries operations back three instructions—from 7005H to 7002H.

Please take a moment to convince yourself that you, as the programmer, need not know any of the program addresses shown in Program 10-2. They are shown only for the purpose of illustrating the way the program counter responds to relative jump instructions. Omit the program addresses, and the program is just as meaningful. That is not at all the case when using absolute jump instructions (see Program 10-1).

The same general idea applies when specifying relative jump instructions that advance the program execution to higher address locations. The jump takes place relative to the address just following the jump instruction.

Whether jumping to lower or higher program address instructions, the displacement term is determined by actually counting the number of program address locations to be skipped over, and then converting it to a hexadecimal format.

Exercises for Section 10-2

1. Describe the dual role of the P flag bit in the Z-80 system.

2. Which of the following arithmetic operations will create an overflow condition? a wraparound condition?

   (a) LD A,10H
       ADD A,20H

   (b) LD A,72H
       ADD A,10H

   (c) LD A,10H
       SUB 11H

   (d) LD A,DEH
       ADD A,10H

   (e) LD A, AFH
       ADD A,FEH

   (f) LD A,10H
       SUB FEH

   (g) LD A,FEH
       SUB 10H

3. Describe the literal meaning of the following instructions.

   (a) JR *disp*   (b) JR NZ,*disp*   (c) JR C,*disp*

4. Specify the absolute program address resulting from doing relative jumps having the following displacement terms. Assume in each case that the microprocessor has just read the jump instruction and is pointing to the next instruction at address 2000H.

   (a) 02H   (b) 10H   (c) FFH   (d) EDH

5. Determine the hexadecimal displacement terms required for doing a relative jump by the number of decimal steps indicated here.

   (a) 5   (b) 25   (c) −1   (d) −25

6. Explain what this instruction does:

```
JR FEH
```

7. Which jump instructions are conditioned by the overflow status following arithmetic operations?

In principle, the jump instructions do not differ significantly from those used by the 8080A/8085 and Z-80 microprocessor systems. The differences that do exist are more along the lines of differences in terminology than anything else.

Table 10-3 summarizes the 6502's jump and branch instructions. The term *branch* is applied to the conditional jumps for the 6502, but as you have seen in earlier discussions, is not used by the 8080A/8085 and Z-80 systems.

The unconditional jump instructions are

JMP *addr*

JMP (*addr*)

Both are 3-byte instructions. The first byte is the opcode, and the two remaining bytes are representations of the target address.

In the JUMP *addr* instruction, *addr* directly specifies the target address. Thus JMP $7291 means: Jump unconditionally to program address $7291. The corresponding object code is 4C 91 72. Note that the LSB of the target address precedes the MSB.

The JMP (*addr*) instruction uses indirect memory addressing. The *addr* enclosed in parentheses does not point directly to the target address. Rather, it points to the first of a 2-byte location in data memory that contains the target address. So doing a JMP ($7291) literally means: Find the target address for the jump instruction at data memory locations $7291 and $7292.

If the content of data memory location $7291 happens to be $00, and location $7292 is $4C, JMP ($7291) actually jumps to the program instruction at $4C00.

The JMP (*addr*) instruction is closely related to the 8080A/8085's PCHL instruction and the Z-80's JMP (HL) instruction. The 6502 version, however, references a pair of bytes stored in external data memory as op-

TABLE 10-3 JUMP AND BRANCH INSTRUCTIONS
FOR THE 6502

Source code	Object code	Flag conditions
JMP *addr*	4C *byte byte*	None
JMP (*addr*)	6C *byte byte*	None
BEQ *disp*	F0 *byte*	Z=1
BNE *disp*	D0 *byte*	Z=0
BCS *disp*	B0 *byte*	Cs=1
BCC *disp*	90 *byte*	Cs=0
BMI *disp*	30 *byte*	S=1
BPL *disp*	10 *byte*	S=0
BVS *disp*	70 *byte*	V=1
BVC *disp*	50 *byte*	V=0

posed to the content of an internal register pair. Can you justify the reason for the difference?

Branch, or Relative Jump, Instructions

The 6502's branch instructions are closely related to the Z-80's relative jump instructions. In each case, the instruction requires a displacement term, *disp*. It is a 1-byte number specified in 2's-complement notation.

Upon reading a branch instruction, the program counter (PC register) points to the address following that branch instruction, and that is the reference point for the displacement.

Displacement terms between $01 and $7F cause the program to skip forward 1 to 127 address locations. Displacement terms between $FF and $80 move the operations back between 1 and 128 address locations.

The literal meaning of the branch terms is quite different from their Z-80 counterparts. The essential functions, however, are practically identical.

BEQ *disp* — Branch if *equal*. This is the same as Z-80's Jr Z,*disp* instruction—jump if *zero*.

BNE *disp* — Branch if *not equal*. The corresponding Z-80 instruction is JR NZ,*disp*—jump if not *zero*.

BCS *disp* — Branch if *carry is set*. The Z-80 counterpart is JR C,*disp*—jump if *carry*.

BCC *disp* — Branch if *carry is cleared*. The Z-80 does the same thing with JR NC,*disp*—jump if *no carry*.

BMI *disp* — Branch if *minus*. The Z-80 has no relative-jump counterpart, but it does have an absolute jump version, JP M,*addr*—jump if *minus*.

BPL *disp* — Branch if *plus* (*positive*). Again, there is no relative jump of that type in the Z-80 instruction set. The JP P,*addr* instruction comes close, though—jump if *positive*.

BVS *disp* — Branch if *overflow is set*. The Z-80 has an absolute jump version that follows an arithmetic operation: JP PE,*addr*—*jump* if parity (*overflow*) is set.

BVC *disp* — Branch if *overflow is cleared*. The Z-80's JP PO,*addr* is an absolute jump version.

The flag register for the 6502 is analyzed in Fig. 10-3. The bits relevant to the branch instructions are the Z, Cs, S, and V (overflow) bits. Comparing the information in that figure with Table 10-3 should put the final touches on your understanding of the branch instructions.

Although there are many functional similarities between the branch instructions for the 6502 and jump instructions for the Z-80, there is a related feature that can be subtle, but powerful. Unlike the Z-80 and 8080A/8085 systems, the 6502's S and Z flags are affected by load instructions.

Doing a LD A,00H on the Z-80, for example, does not affect the Z flag. That instruction does a load immediate of zero to the A register, but the Z flag is unaffected. By contrast, doing the same sort of instruction with

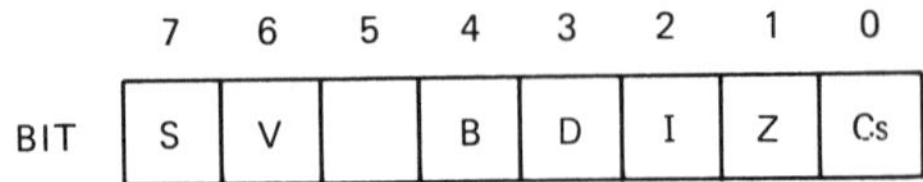

S   The S (sign) flag takes on the value of the most-significant bit of a number resulting from a load, arithmetic, or logic operation. Using 2's-complement notation, S is set to 1 for negative values and cleared to 0 for positive values.

V   The V (overflow) flag is set to logic 1 whenever an arithmetic operation yields an overflow condition. The V flag is cleared to 0 following an arithmetic operation that does not cause an overflow in the result.

B   The B (break) status flag is set to 1 only when the system is executing its BRK instruction. Otherwise, it is cleared to 0. It is not relevant to jump instructions.

D   The D (decimal) status flag is set to 1 when the program specifies the need for doing a BCD arithmetic operation. It is not relevant to jump instructions.

I   The I (interrupt) status flag is set to 1 only when the program calls for setting the interrupt mode. It is cleared to 0 by an interrupt-disabling instruction. It is not relevant to jump instructions.

Z   The Z (zero) bit takes on a value of 1 or 0 following load, arithmetic and logic operations. A zero result sets Z to 1; a nonzero result clears it to 0.

Cs   The Cs (carry status) flag is not affected by load and logic operations, but it responds to the carry condition of a number resulting from arithmetic operations.

Figure 10-3   The 6502 flag register.

the 6502—LDA #\$00—does affect the Z flag; it is set to a logic 1, indicating a zero result.

The Z and S flags in the Z-80 and 8080A/8085 systems are affected only by the result of arithmetic and logic operations. Those same flags in the 6502 are affected by arithmetic, logic, and load instructions.

The practical significance of the Z flag's response to loading operations is that a programmer does not have to test for a zero condition by means of a COMPARE instruction. The BEQ instruction can sense the zero condition directly. Doing the same thing with the Z-80 calls for the sequence:

```
CP 00H
JR Z,disp
```

EXAMPLE 10-3

Write and assemble a 6502 program that initializes the A register to \$FF, then decrements that number, one step at a time, until it is counted down to zero. Begin the listing at address \$7000.

See the listing in Program 10-3, and compare the results with an identical task for other microprocessors in Programs 10-1 and 10-2.

The situation specified in the example calls for making the accumulator decrement from \$FF to \$00. There are, however, no decrementing instructions for the accumulator. The X and Y registers may be decremented, but the accumulator cannot.

```
7000 A9 FF   LDA #$FF   INITIALIZE THE ACCUMULATOR
7002 AA      TAX        TRANSFER TO X REGISTER
7003 CA      DEX        DECREMENT THE X REGISTER
7004 8A      TXA        TRANSFER RESULT TO ACCUMULATOR
7005 D0 FC   BNE $FC    IF NOT ZERO, DECREMENT AGAIN
```

So the listing in Program 10-3 mimics the notion of decrementing the accumulator by actually doing the decrementing in the X register and transferring the result to the accumulator.

The first instruction loads $FF to the accumulator, and the second instruction transfers that number to the X register. The third instruction decrements the content of the X register, and the fourth one transfers the result to the accumulator.

The last instruction tests for $00 in the accumulator. If the number has not yet decremented to that point, the $FC displacement term sends operations back up to the DEX instruction at address 7003.

The content of the X register is thus decremented again, passed to the accumulator, and tested for zero. That loop continues until the conditional instruction finds that the register has finally been decremented to zero. At that time, the conditional instruction is no longer satisfied, and program operations resume from address 7007.

Exercises for Section 10-3

1. Name the status flag that is most relevant to the following 6502 jump instructions.
   (a) BEQ *disp*   (b) BVC *disp*   (c) JMP *addr*
   (d) BCC *disp*   (e) BMI *disp*   (f) BPL *disp*

2. Write and assemble a 6502 program that continuously loops the X register through all integer values between 0 and 59, decimal. Use the flowchart in Fig. 10-4 as a guide, and begin the listing at address $3100.

3. Explain the difference between overflow and wraparound. Which 6502 flag bit is sensitive to overflow? to wraparound?

10-4 JUMP AND BRANCH INSTRUCTIONS FOR THE 6800

In many respects, the jump and branch instructions for the 6800 follow the format just described for the 6502. What is more, the flag bits that are relevant to the jump and branch instructions are identical.

Table 10-4 lists the jump and branch instructions for the 6800 device. Compare it with the instructions for the 6502 in Table 10-3, and you should have no trouble finding the similarities. Indeed, many of the instructions differ only in their opcodes—the mnemonics are often identical.

Also compare the description of the 6800's flag register in Fig. 10-5 with the 6502 version in Fig. 10-3.

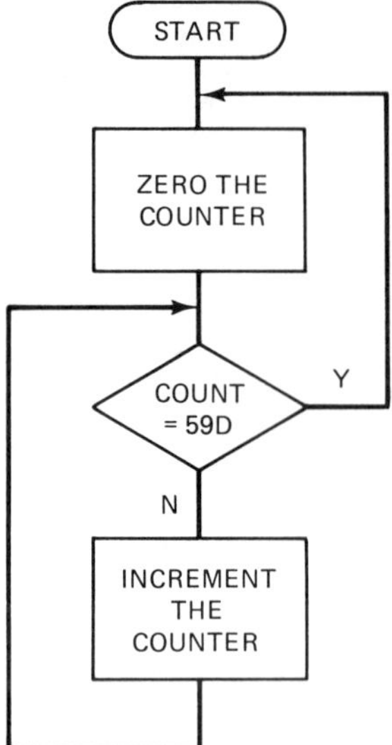

Figure 10-4 Program flowchart for problem 2.

The 6800 instruction set features three unconditional jump instructions:

JMP *addr*
JMP *indx*,X
BRA *disp*

TABLE 10-4 JUMP AND BRANCH INSTRUCTIONS FOR THE 6800

Source code	Object code	Flag conditions
JMP *addr*	7E *byte byte*	None
JMP *indx*,X	6E *byte*	None
BRA *disp*	20 *byte*	None
BNE *disp*	26 *byte*	$Z=0$
BEQ *disp*	27 *byte*	$Z=1$
BCC *disp*	24 *byte*	$Cs=0$
BCS *disp*	25 *byte*	$Cs=1$
BPL *disp*	2A *byte*	$S=0$
BMI *disp*	2B *byte*	$S=1$
BVC *disp*	28 *byte*	$V=0$
BVS *disp*	29 *byte*	$V=1$
BHI *disp*	22 *byte*	$Cs=0$ and $Z=0$
BLS *disp*	23 *byte*	$Cs=1$ or $Z=1$
BGT *disp*	2E *byte*	$Z=0$ and $S=V$
BGE *disp*	2C *byte*	$S=V$
BLE *disp*	2F *byte*	$Z=1$ or $S\neq V$
BLT *disp*	2D *byte*	$S\neq V$

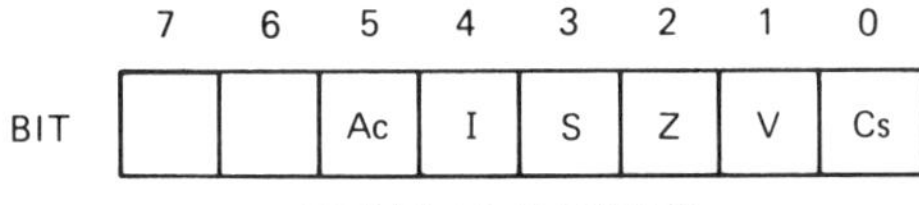

Ac   The Ac (auxiliary carry) bit is used only for BCD arithmetic operations, and it is not relevant to any jump instructions.

I   The I (interrupt) status flag is set to 1 only when the program calls for setting the interrupt mode. It is cleared to 0 by instructions that disable the interrupt mode. It is not relevant to any jump instructions.

S   The S (sign) flag takes on the value of the most-significant bit of a number resulting from a load, arithmetic or logic operation. Using 2's-complement notation, S is set to 1 for negative numbers and cleared to 0 for positive numbers.

Z   The Z (zero) bit takes on a value of 1 or 0 following load, arithmetic and logic operations. A zero result sets Z to 1; a nonzero result clears the flag to 0.

V   The V (overflow) flag is set to 1 whenever an arithmetic operation yields an overflow condition. It is cleared to 0 by arithmetic operations that do not yield an overflow.

Cs   The Cs (carry status) flag is unaffected by load and logic operations, but it responds to the carry condition of a number resulting from an arithmetic operation.

Figure 10-5   The 6800 flag register.

The first one is the only unconditional jump instruction. Upon executing it, the program counter and programming operation immediately go to the specified address, *addr*.

The second of these instructions—JMP *indx*,X—is an indexed jump. No other microprocessor described in this book uses an indexed jump instruction. It is a 2-byte instruction, with the first being the opcode and the second being the index term.

Like indexed addressing for the 6800, the address for the indexed jump instruction is found by summing the current content of the 16-bit IX register with the unsigned, 8-bit index term. The index term, *indx*, *is not specified in a 2's-complement form*, so it allows only forward indexing.

As an example, suppose that the content of the IX register is $3000 when the instruction JMP $FC,X is executed. At that moment, program operations are sent to address $30FC, and resume from there.

The third unconditional jump instruction is a true relative jump. BRA literally means: branch always. Its displacement term, *disp*, is a 1-byte number in 2's-complement form. Functionally, it is identical to the Z-80's JR *disp* instruction.

The following 6800 instructions are functionally identical to those listed for the 6502:

BNE *disp*   Branch relative if *not equal.*

BEQ *disp*   Branch relative if *equal.*

BCC *disp*	Branch relative if *carry is cleared* (no carry).
BCS *disp*	Branch relative if *carry is set* (carry).
BPL *disp*	Branch relative if *plus* (positive).
BMI *disp*	Branch relative if *minus* (negative).
BVC *disp*	Branch relative if *overflow is cleared* (no overflow).
BVS *disp*	Branch relative if *overflow is set* (overflow).

The remaining instructions are unique to the 6800 system:

BHI *disp*	Branch relative if an *unsigned* number in the accumulator is *greater than* a value compared with it.
BLS *disp*	Branch relative if an *unsigned* number in the accumulator is *less than or equal to* a value compared with it.
BGT *disp*	Branch relative if a *signed* number in the accumulator is *greater than* a value compared with it.
BGE *disp*	Branch relative if a *signed* number in the accumulator is *greater than or equal to* a value compared with it.
BLE *disp*	Branch relative if a *signed* number in the accumulator is *less than or equal to* a value compared with it.
BLT *disp*	Branch relative if a *signed* number in the accumulator is *less than a* value compared with it.

These special branch instructions apply only after doing COMPARE or SUBTRACT operations. The first two, BHI *disp* and BLS *disp*, are used when the numbers being compared are unsigned 8-bit numbers. The remainder are used when the numbers are in an 8-bit, signed, 2's-complement form.

Applications of these relative branch instructions are described in Chapter 11.

Exercises for Section 10-4

1. List the flag bits that serve identical purposes for the 6800 and 6502. Briefly describe the function in each case.
2. Assuming that the IX register contains the number $4500, what is the target address for the instruction JMP $2A,X?
3. Assuming that the PC register contains $4000 *after* reading the following instructions, cite the target address.
   (a) BRA $2A   (b) BRA $FE   (c) BCC $80   (d) BVC $7F
4. Write the complete object code for the following 6800 jump instruction: JMP $3A2E. Write the complete object code for the 6502 version of that same instruction.
5. Write and assemble a 6800 program that continuously loops the A accumulator through all integer values between 0 and 59, decimal. Use only relative jump instructions and omit any references to program addresses. Use the flowchart in Fig. 10-4 as a guide to designing the program.

11

Magnitude Comparisons for Conditional Operations

Conditional jump instructions, such as those introduced in Chapter 10, are powerful programming tools. They represent "yes" or "no" choice points in the flow of program operations; most often, the "yes" or "no" response depends on the value of one byte of data relative to another.

For example, a program might fetch a byte of data from some external input device, compare its value with a reference byte, and then take a course of action that depends on the relative magnitudes of the two bytes. Perhaps the tested byte is rejected outright if it is larger than the reference byte, but used for further processing if it is equal to or less than the tested byte.

This common sort of comparison operation is generally made up of a COMPARE instruction, immediately followed by one or more conditional JUMP instructions. The COMPARE instruction sets up some relevant flag conditions in the F register, and the subsequent conditional JUMP instructions use those flag conditions to make the appropriate "yes" or "no" decisions.

Table 11-1 summarizes the most useful magnitude relationships. Value A is the one being tested in each case, and value B is the reference value. C is sometimes used as a second reference value.

The table shows five comparisons between two values. Value A can be greater than B, equal to B, less than B, greater than or equal to B, or less than or equal to B.

Then there are four possible relationships between three values; A, B, and C. The idea here is to test the value of A within a range of values bounded by B and C. In each case here, B marks the lower boundary and C marks the upper boundary.

Value A may be between values B and C, but not equal to either of them. Or A might be less than or equal to C, but still greater than B. Alternatively, A might be greater than or equal to B, but less than C. And finally, A may be bounded by values B and C, and equal to either of them.

The notation in Table 11-1 follows standard algebraic notation for numerical inequalities, and that convention is used quite frequently in the programming business.

When working with comparison operations and relative magnitudes, a programmer must draw a sharp distinction between comparisons of 8-bit unsigned numbers and 8-bit signed, 2's-complement numbers. The relationships expressed in Table 11-1 apply equally well to signed and unsigned binary values, but it turns out that the microprocessor instructions, especially the conditional JUMP instructions, are handled quite differently for signed or unsigned numbers.

When using unsigned 8-bit numbers, the counting range is between 00H and FFH, with FFH being much larger than 00H. The range of values, in decimal notation, is 0 through 255.

The picture is quite different for 8-bit, signed, 2's-complement numbers. Negative numbers are considered less than any positive number, so FFH (-1 decimal) is less than 00H. The critical turnaround point in the 2's-complement counting range is between 7FH (127 decimal) and 80H (-128 decimal). At that particular point 7FH is considered much larger than 80H. Why? Because 7FH is the largest positive number that can fit into an 8-bit, 2's-complement format, and 80H is the most negative number—the smallest possible number.

The matter of making magnitude comparisons is thus quite different for signed or unsigned numbers. That clearly justifies the division of this chapter into two basic sections: magnitude comparisons for unsigned numbers, and magnitude comparisons for signed, 2's-complement numbers.

TABLE 11-1 SUMMARY OF ALL USEFUL MAGNITUDE COMPARISONS BETWEEN VALUES A AND B, AND VALUES A, B, AND C

Algebraic notation	Literal meaning
$A > B$	A GREATER THAN B
$A = B$	A EQUALS B
$A < B$	A LESS THAN B
$A \geq B$	A GREATER THAN OR EQUAL TO B
$A \leq B$	A LESS THAN OR EQUAL TO B
$B < A < C$	A GREATER THAN B, LESS THAN C
$B < A \leq C$	A GREATER THAN B, LESS THAN OR EQUAL TO C
$B \leq A < C$	A GREATER THAN OR EQUAL TO B, LESS THAN C
$B \leq A \leq C$	A GREATER THAN OR EQUAL TO B, LESS THAN OR EQUAL TO C

Note: The terms A, B, and C merely indicate magnitudes of some data, and do not necessarily refer to specific working registers within a microprocessor.

When using an 8-bit, unsigned number format, the range of decimal values is between 0 and 255, inclusively. All values are considered positive, and the range of values in hexadecimal notation is 00H through FFH.

Comparing Two Unsigned Values

Figure 11-1 shows three flowcharts for comparing two unsigned, 8-bit values. In each case, value A is considered the value to be tested, and value B is the reference value—the value that A is being tested against.

The general programming scheme begins by comparing the two values, and then doing one or two conditional operations. Notice that the conditional operations consider the Z flag bit in all cases, and the Cs bit in two cases. A hallmark of unsigned value comparisons is the use of those two particular flag bits.

The flowchart in Fig. 11-1a tests only for equality or inequality between the two values. A is compared with B, and then the conditional JUMP instruction takes appropriate action depending on the status of the Z flag bit. If, indeed, it turns out that the result of the comparison is zero, it means that there is no difference between the two numbers—A−B=0. Thus the two values are equal.

But if the result of the comparison turns up a nonzero result, it means that the values are unequal.

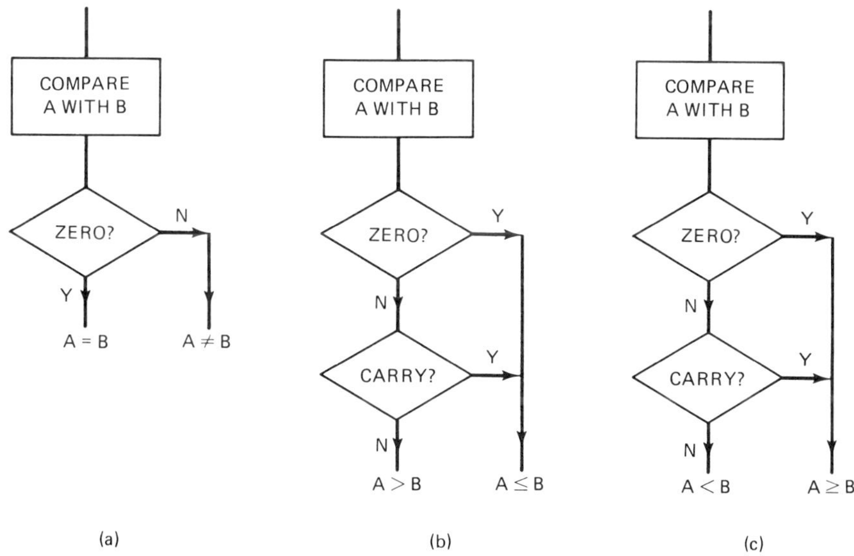

Figure 11-1   Flowcharts for basic 8-bit, unsigned magnitude comparisons between two values.

The instruction sequence for this operation goes something like this:

Load value A to the accumulator
COMPARE IMMEDIATE with value B
JUMP IF ZERO to A=B
Else consider A≠B

The chart in Fig. 11-1b tests for two inequalities: A > B and A ≤ B. The flow of operations begins with a comparison between values A and B. If the result is zero, it means that the two values are equal, and the chart shows a flow to A ≤ B. In that case A=B.

But if the ZERO test fails, it means that A≠B, and a further test is necessary. The second conditional tests the Cs bit. If a carry condition results from the comparison, the CARRY conditional is satisfied, and it is concluded that A < B. The flow of operations thus goes to A ≤ B. But if the CARRY condition is not met, the overall conclusion is that A must be greater than B.

Work your way through that flowchart (Fig. 11-1b) three times. The first time, pick values A and B such that A is less than B. Then do the job again with A equal to B; and finally, with A greater than B. In each case, you should end up at the proper exit point of the flowchart.

The flowchart in Fig. 11-1c tests for two other inequality conditions: A < B or A ≥ B. The flow of operations is practically identical to the previous example. The only difference is the course of action taken from the CARRY conditional.

The general flow of program instructions looks like this:

LOAD value A to the accumulator
COMPARE IMMEDIATE with value B
JUMP IF ZERO to A ≥ B
JUMP IF NO CARRY to A ≥ B
Else conclude that A < B

One of the three flowcharts in Fig. 11-1 will meet the need for making any sort of magnitude comparison between two unsigned, 8-bit values.

EXAMPLE 11-1

A microprocessor system is hardware-wired such that a switch-type input device can be found at address FFF0H and a lamp-type output device is at address FFF1H. The input device, such as a set of switches or a keyboard, generates 1-byte numbers between 00H and FFH. The output lamp is turned on by delivering a 0FH byte to its address location, and it is turned off by sending a 00H byte to it.

Write and assemble program listings for the Z-80, 8080A/8085, 6502, and 6800 that will turn on the lamp whenever the input is exactly 2AH. Otherwise, the lamp should be turned off.

See the program flowchart in Fig. 11-2 and the program listings in Program 11-1.

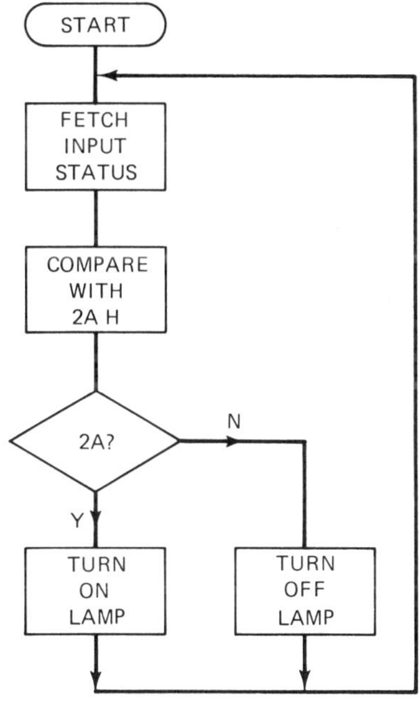

Figure 11-2 Flowchart for the comparison task in Example 11-1.

Referring to the flowchart, the system first fetches the current data byte from the input device. Then it compares the byte with 2AH. If, indeed, the byte is a 2AH, the comparison operation turns up a ZERO result (as in Fig. 10-6a), and the system responds by turning on the lamp. But if the comparison turns up a nonzero result—if the byte from the input device is *not* a 2AH, the system turns off the lamp.

Whether the lamp is turned on or off, operations loop back up to the beginning, where the input status is fetched again. In effect, the lamp is turned on as long as the input device is generating a byte equal to 2AH. Otherwise, the lamp is turned off.

The program listings for all four microprocessor devices use assembly language *labels* to point out critical lines in the programs. The labels in these examples are FETCH, DOIT, and LON. The programmer is free to make up labels at will, as long as they meet a few prescribed standards.

Labels, for example, must begin with an alphabetical character and should not include any special punctuation, including spaces. Generally, labels should contain no more than six characters.

Note how the source listings refer to the label names. In the Z-80 listing, for example, the third instruction calls out the LON label: JR Z,LON. That

Z-80 Version

```
7000  3A F0 FF   FETCH   LD A,(FFF0H)   ;FETCH INPUT STATUS
7003  FE 2A               CP 2AH         ;IS IT 2A?
7005  28 06               JR Z,LON       ;IF SO, TURN ON LIGHT
7007  AF                  XOR A          ;ELSE ZERO THE ACCUMULATOR
7008  32 F1 FF   DOIT     LD (FFF1H),A   ;OUTPUT THE LAMP STATUS
700B  18 F3               JR FETCH       ;AND FETCH INPUT AGAIN
700D  3E 0F      LON      LD A,0FH       ;SET LAMP-ON BYTE
700F  18 F7               JR DOIT        ;AND OUTPUT IT
```

8080A/8085 Version

```
7000  3A F0 FF   FETCH   LDA FFF0H       ;FETCH INPUT STATUS
7003  FE 2A               CPI  2AH        ;IS IT 2A?
7005  CA 0F 70            JZ LON          ;IF SO, TURN ON LIGHT
7008  AF                  XRA A           ;ELSE ZERO THE ACCUMULATOR
7009  32 F1 FF   DOIT     STA FFF1H       ;OUTPUT THE LAMP STATUS
700C  C3 00 70            JMP FETCH       ;AND FETCH INPUT AGAIN
700F  3E 0F      LON      MVI A,0FH       ;SET LAMP-ON BYTE
7011  C3 09 70            JMP  DOIT       ;AND OUTPUT IT
```

6502 Version

```
7000  AD F0 FF   FETCH   LDA $FFF0       FETCH INPUT STATUS
7003  C9 2A               CMP #$2A        IS IT 2A?
7005  F0 08               BEQ LON         IF SO, TURN ON LIGHT
7007  A9 00               LDA #0          ELSE ZERO THE ACCUMULATOR
7009  8D F1 FF   DOIT     STA $FFF1       OUTPUT THE LAMP STATUS
700C  4C 00 70            JMP FETCH       AND FETCH INPUT AGAIN
700F  A9 0F      LON      LDA #$0F        SET LAMP-ON BYTE
7011  4C 09 70            JMP DOIT        AND OUTPUT IT
```

6800 Version

```
7000  B6 FF F0   FETCH   LDAA $FFF0      FETCH INPUT STATUS
7003  81 2A               CMPA #$2A       IS IT 2A?
7005  27 06               BEQ LON         IF SO, TURN ON LIGHT
7007  4F                  CLRA            ELSE ZERO THE ACCUMULATOR
7008  B7 FF F1   DOIT     STAA $FFF1      OUTPUT THE LAMP STATUS
700B  20 F3               BRA FETCH       AND FETCH INPUT AGAIN
700D  86 0F      LON      LDAA #$0F       SET LAMP-ON BYTE
700F  20 F7               BRA DOIT        AND OUTPUT IT
```

means JUMP RELATIVE to the instruction labeled LON. Further down in that same listing is an instruction, JR FETCH. That one means JUMP RELATIVE to the instruction labeled FETCH. Finally, the last instruction reads: JR DOIT. That is taken to mean JUMP RELATIVE to a line labeled DOIT.

Such labels are used only as guides for writing and studying an assembly language program. Labels do not directly affect the object code listings.

The first instruction in all four programs fetches the byte from the input device and places it into the microprocessor's accumulator. The second instruction compares the byte with 2A hexadecimal, and the third instruction does a conditional jump, or branch, operation. If the result of the COMPARE instruction is zero—if the fetched byte is equal to 2A hexadecimal—the conditional jump takes operations down to the line labeled LON; and that line sets the lamp's turn-on code, 0F hexadecimal, into the accumulator. After that, an unconditional jump instruction sends operations to DOIT.

The instruction labeled DOIT stores the current content of the accumulator to the output device at FFF1 hexadecimal. If the accumulator has been set to 0F, the lamp is turned on.

But if the JUMP IF ZERO condition is *not* satisfied (meaning that the fetching operation turned up a byte that does not equal 2A hexadecimal), the accumulator is set to zero, and the DOIT sequence is executed to turn off the lamp.

Whether the lamp is turned off or on by the DOIT instruction, an unconditional jump instruction moves program operations back up to FETCH, thus picking up an input byte once again.

Compare the four listings, noting how they use some of the special features inherent in their own instruction sets. Although the object codes and mnemonics are quite different in most instances, the labels and comments are identical. Any microprocessor can do the overall job that any other one can; only the *how* of the matter differs.

EXAMPLE 11-2

A microprocessor system has an 8-bit input port located at address FFF0H and an 8-bit output port at address FFF1H. The input device, perhaps a small keyboard assembly or an A/D (analog-to-digital) converter, generates binary numbers between 00H and FFH. The output device, however, is to accept data bytes that have values greater than 40H. Data bytes of 40H or lower are rejected.

Write and assemble program listings for the Z-80, 8080A/8085, 6502, and 6800 that meet the specifications and follow the general flowchart in Fig. 11-3a. Begin the listing at program address 7000H in each case.

The important parameters are clearly defined in the statement of this example, and the basic flowchart is shown in Fig. 11-3a. According to that flowchart, the procedure is to fetch the byte of data from the input port, test it to see whether or not the byte is greater than 40H, and then take the appropriate action. If the byte is greater than 40H, it is delivered, unaltered, to the output device. Otherwise, the byte is rejected. In either case, the system loops back up to fetch the next input byte.

Overall, the system feeds the data to the output port continuously as long as the input is generating values greater than 40H.

Although the simpler flowchart in Fig. 11-3a is often adequate for the final documentation of the program, it is usually helpful for the programmer to develop a more detailed version of it. That is the version in Fig. 11-3b.

In that detailed flowchart, the first operation sets some pointers to the addresses of the input and output ports. The idea is to use indirect addressing wherever possible, thus saving a few bytes in the program listing. Then the program fetches the input byte, compares it with 40H, and tests for ZERO and CARRY results. That part of the flowchart follows the general A > B or A ⩽ B scheme in Fig. 11-1b.

The program listings are shown in Program 11-2. As far as the present discussion is concerned, the important instructions are those that compare the input byte with 40 hexadecimal and test the resulting flag bits. Generally,

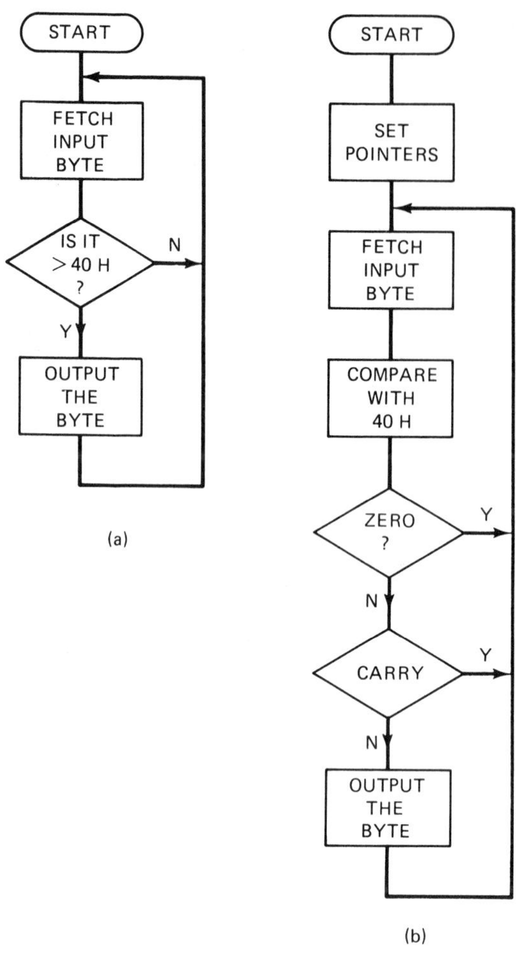

Figure 11-3   A two-step evolution of flowcharts for the task in Example 11-2.

the sequence has this pattern:

FETCH   fetch input byte
            COMPARE with 40 hexadecimal
            if ZERO then FETCH again
            if CARRY then FETCH again

The 6800 version is slightly different and simpler, however, because that system features a special conditional branch statement that does a less-than-or-equal-to decision. That is the BLS *disp* instruction.

The Z-80 and 8080A/8085 versions begin by setting the HL pair to the

Z-80 Version

```
7000  21  F0  FF              LD    HL,FFF0H    ;SET INPUT POINTER
7003  11  F1  FF              LD    DE,FFF1H    ;SET OUTPUT POINTER
7006  7E              FETCH   LD    A,(HL)      ;FETCH INPUT BYTE
7007  FE  40                  CP    40H         ;COMPARE WITH 40H
7009  28  FB                  JR    Z,FETCH     ;IF SAME, FETCH AGAIN
700B  38  F9                  JR    C,FETCH     ;IF LESS, FETCH AGAIN
700D  12                      LD    (DE),A      ;ELSE OUTPUT THE BYTE
700E  18  F6                  JR    FETCH       ;AND FETCH AGAIN
```

8080A/8085 Version

```
7000  21  F0  FF              LXI   H,FFF0H     ;SET INPUT POINTER
7003  11  F1  FF              LXI   D,FFF1H     ;SET OUTPUT POINTER
7006  7E              FETCH   MOV   A,M         ;FETCH INPUT BYTE
7007  FE  40                  CPI   40H         ;COMPARE WITH 40H
7009  CA  06  70              JZ    FETCH       ;IF SAME, FETCH AGAIN
700C  DA  06  70              JC    FETCH       ;IF LESS, FETCH AGAIN
700F  12                      STAX  D           ;ELSE OUTPUT THE BYTE
7010  C3  06  70              JMP   FETCH       ;AND FETCH AGAIN
```

6502 Version

```
7000  AD  F0  FF    FETCH     LDA   $FFF0       FETCH INPUT BYTE
7003  C9  40                  CMP   #$40        COMPARE WITH $40
7005  F0  F9                  BEQ   FETCH       IF SAME, FETCH AGAIN
7007  B0  F7                  BCS   FETCH       IF LESS, FETCH AGAIN
7009  8D  F1  FF              STA   $FFF1       ELSE OUTPUT THE BYTE
700C  4C  00  70              JMP   FETCH       AND FETCH AGAIN
```

6800 Version

```
7000  CE  FF  F0              LDX   $FFF0       SET INDEX POINTER
7003  A6  00        FETCH     LDAA  $00,X       FETCH INPUT BYTE
7005  81  40                  CMPA  #$40        COMPARE WITH $40
7007  23  FA                  BLS   FETCH       IF SAME OR LESS, FETCH AGAIN
7009  A7  01                  STAA  $01,X       ELSE OUTPUT THE BYTE
700B  20  F6                  BRA   FETCH       AND FETCH AGAIN
```

input port address and the DE pair to the output port address. When those addresses are needed later in the program, they can be used in an indirect fashion. Really, there is no savings in byte space in this case, but the technique would certainly pay off if the programs were longer and called on those addresses more than one time.

The 6800 version uses indirect indexed addressing for the input and output ports. The X index register is preset to the address of the input port, $FFF0. Specifying the address of the input port later in the program is then a matter of indexing the content of the X register with $00. Since the output port has the address $FFF1, it can be found by indexing the content of the X register with $01.

The 6502 version does not use indirect addressing for the input and output ports in this case. The process of setting up that particular system for indirect addressing is, in this case, too cumbersome to justify its use.

Study all four program listings carefully. Note that the flow of operations is virtually identical and follow the expanded flowchart in Fig. 11-3b almost step for step.

Table 11-1 cites four magnitude comparisons that allow the value of A to fall within a range of values bounded by B and C. The following discussion demonstrates the fact that testing a value within a range of values is a matter of combining two two-value comparisons into one.

Figure 11-4 shows a two-step analysis of a flowchart for determining whether or not value A is bounded by values B and C, but not equal to either of them.

The flowchart in Fig. 11-4a uses a more direct, and perhaps clearer, approach to the matter. First, values A and B are compared. If it turns out that A is greater than B, the conditional $A > B$ is satisfied, and then value A is compared with C. If A is less than C, one can rightly conclude that $B <$

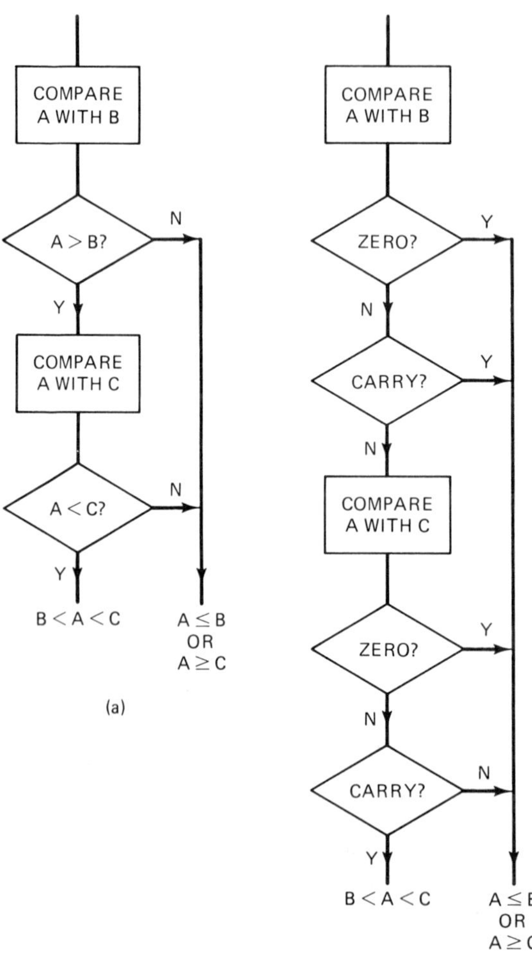

Figure 11-4 Evolution of a detailed flowchart for determining if the unsigned value A is greater than B and less than C.

$A < C$. But if the first conditional is not true, it means that A must be less than or equal to B, and there is no need for testing A against C—the procedure has already eliminated the possibility that $B < A < C$. By a similar kind of reasoning, the overall test fails if the second conditional statement, $A < C$, turns up a "no" response. In that case, A must be greater than or equal to C.

Convince yourself of the validity of the tests in Fig. 11-4a before looking at the expanded version of it in Fig. 11-4b.

Once you have established a general flowchart on the basis of inequality conditional statements, it is possible to generate a more detailed version that makes direct reference to the ZERO and CARRY instructions involved.

In this case, the basic conditional $A > B$ is replaced with its ZERO/CARRY version described earlier in this chapter. Then the $A < C$ conditional is replaced with its ZERO/CARRY counterpart—another situation already

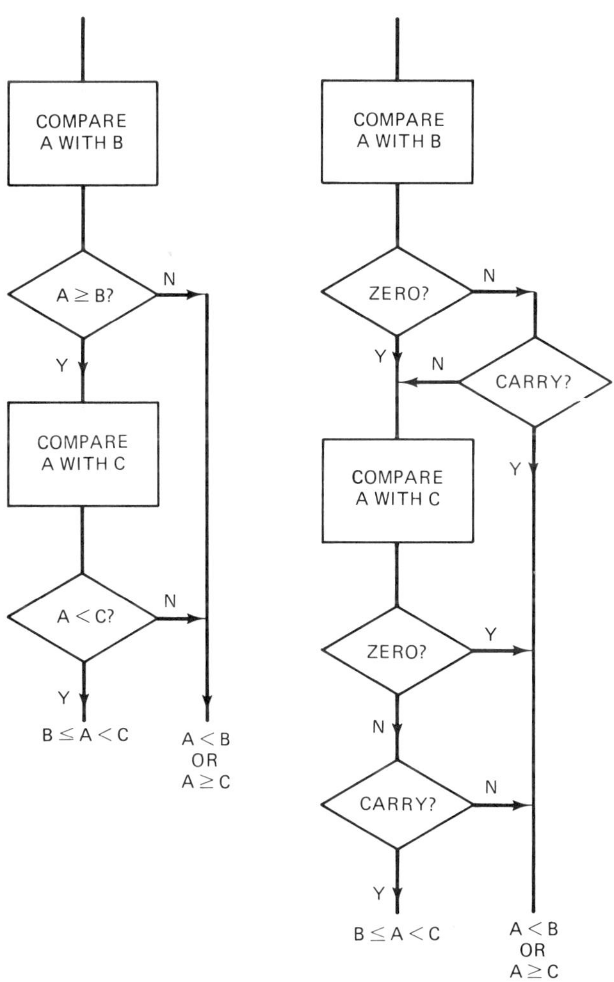

Figure 11-5 Evolution of a flowchart for the unsigned magnitude comparison, $B \leqslant A < C$.

described in this chapter. (The fact that term C replaces the B used in earlier discussions does not change the "truth" of the matter.)

The conversion from the general flowchart to the more detailed one can be considered a matter of flowchart substitution. The more general conditional statements are replaced, directly, with their detailed counterparts. The simpler and more general version might be appropriate for the final documentation of the system, but the detailed version is far more helpful during the task of writing the original program instructions.

Figures 11-5 through 11-7 illustrate a similar analysis of flowchart development. In each case, the comparisons are first drawn up as more direct and meaningful forms—the inequalities are expressed in a straightforward

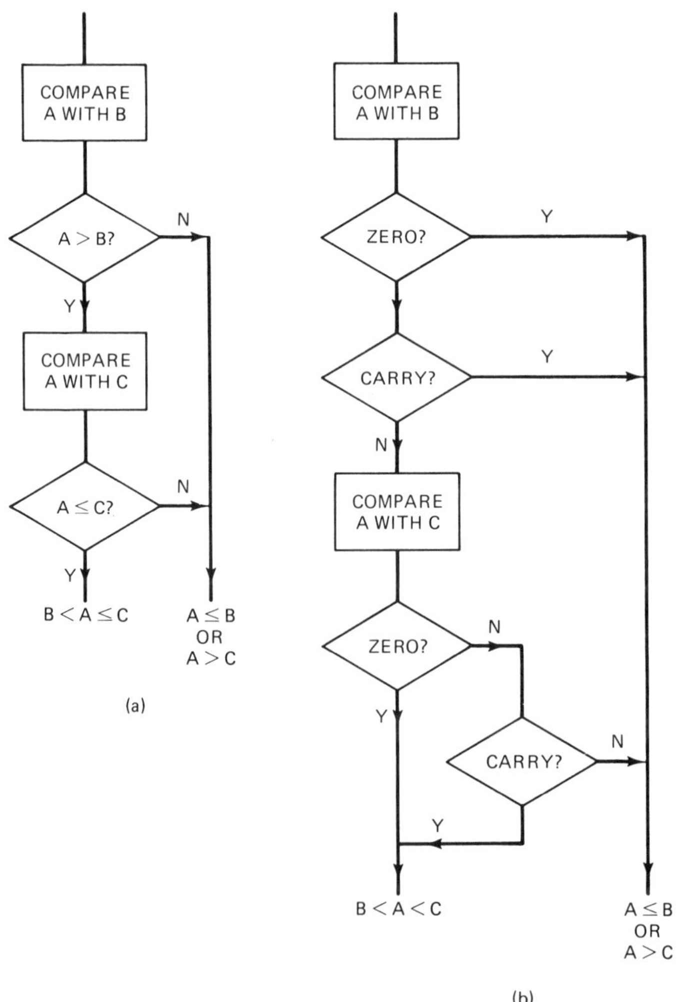

Figure 11-6 Evolution of a flowchart for the unsigned magnitude comparison, B < A ≤ C.

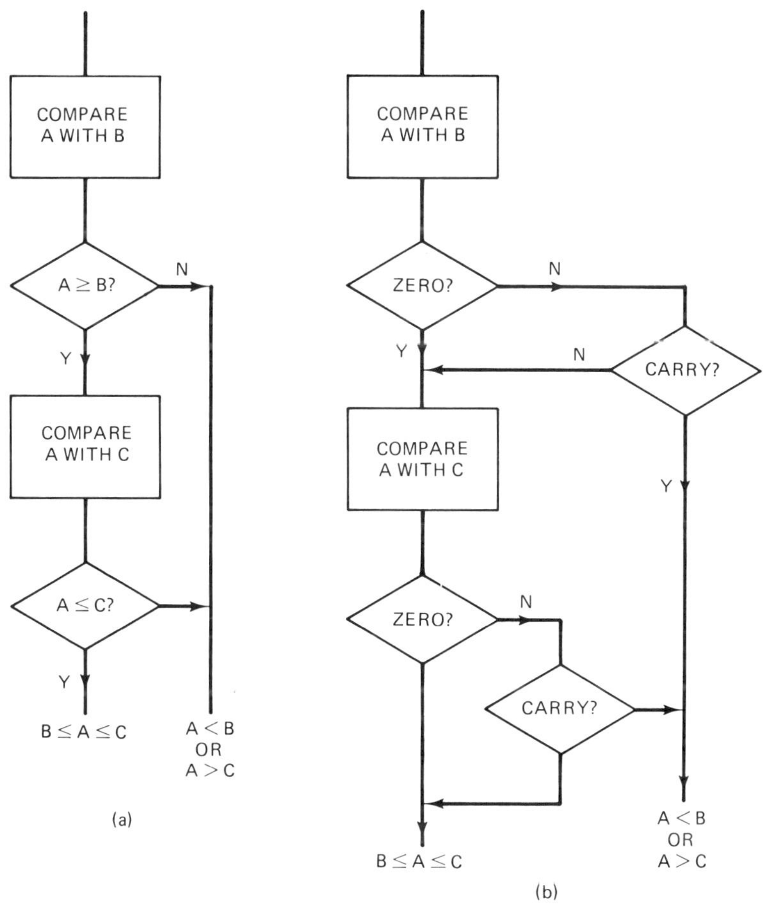

Figure 11-7 Evolution of a flowchart for the unsigned magnitude comparison, $B \leqslant A \leqslant C$.

manner. Then the inequality conditionals are replaced with their ZERO- and CARRY-testing counterparts, all drawn from the basic sequences in Fig. 11-1.

EXAMPLE 11-3

A microprocessor system is hardware-wired (or *hardwired*) with an 8-bit input port at address FFF0 hexadecimal and an 8-bit output device at address FFF1 hexadecimal. The input device is a keyboard that can generate *ASCII code* bytes between 00 and 7F hexadecimal. The output device, however, must accept only those ASCII codes representing numerals 0 through 9 (ASCII codes 30 hexadecimal through 39 hexadecimal).

Write and assemble program listings for the Z-80, 8080A/8085, 6502, and 6800 that do the following.

1.   Fetch a byte from the input keyboard.

2. If no key is depressed (byte is FF hexadecimal), fetch again.

3. Otherwise, check to see whether or not the byte is greater than or equal to 30 hexadecimal (ASCII code for 0 decimal).

4. If not greater than or equal to 30 hexadecimal, fetch a new byte again.

5. Otherwise, check to see whether or not the byte is less than or equal to 39 hexadecimal (ASCII code for 9 decimal).

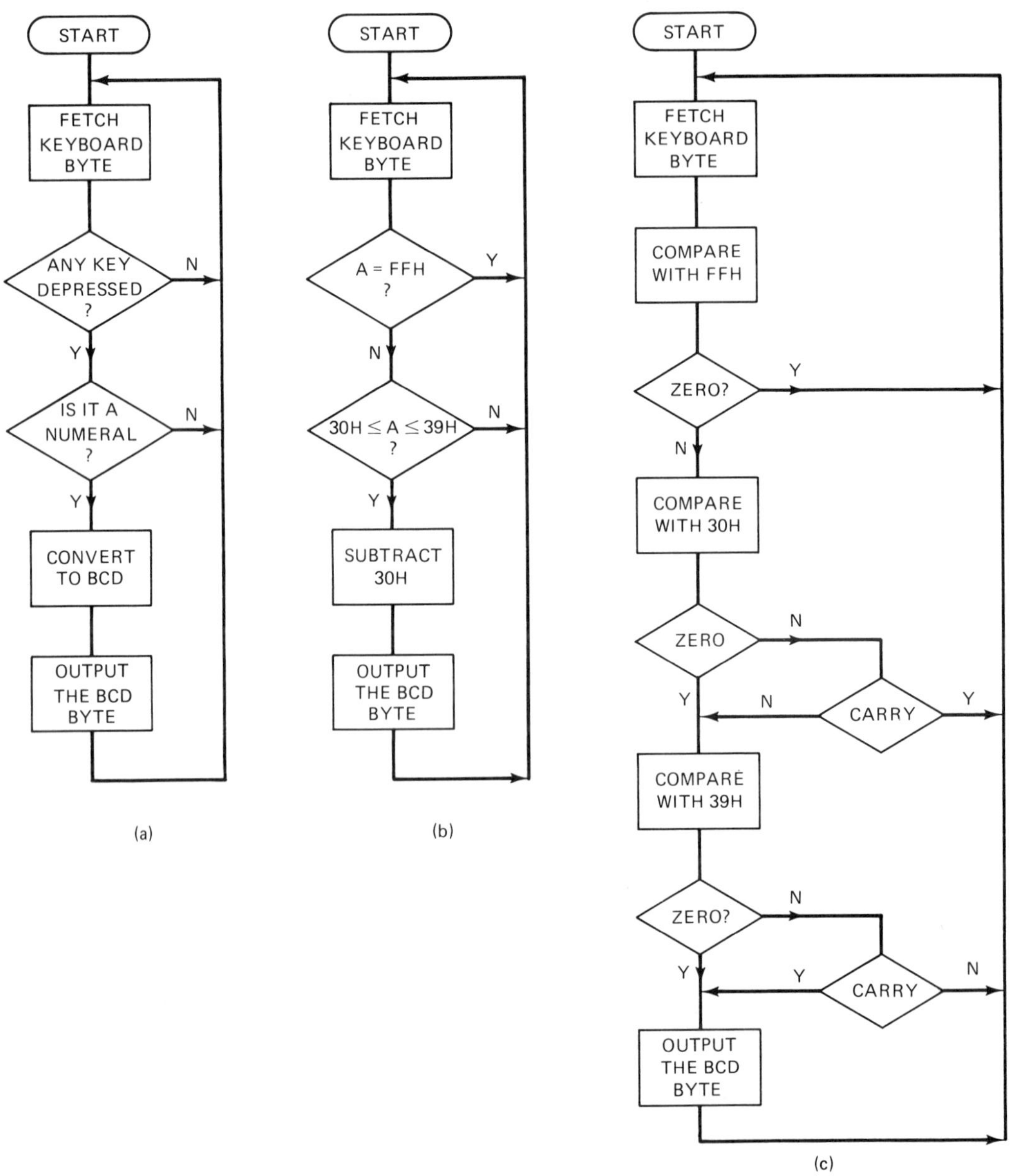

Figure 11-8 Evolution of a flowchart for the task in Example 11-3.

6. If not less than or equal to 39 hexadecimal, fetch a new byte again.

7. Otherwise, convert the byte from ASCII code to BCD (00 hexadecimal through 09 hexadecimal).

8. Output the BCD byte that results.

Begin the listing in each case at program address 4A00 hexadecimal.

Figure 11-8 shows the evolution of a flowchart for the plan just described. The basic idea is to accept any ASCII code byte from the keyboard input, then test it to see whether or not it represents a numeral between 0 and 9, inclusively. According to the ASCII code table, the 0 through 9 keys generates bytes 30H through 39H. And if, indeed, the fetched byte falls within that range, it is converted to a standard BCD form (0 through 9 decimal) and sent to the output device.

Figure 11-8a shows the simplest flowchart for the operation. If no key is depressed (input byte is equal to FFH) or if the byte is not the ASCII version of a numeral between 0 and 9, the system simply loops back to fetch another byte. Otherwise, the byte is converted to a BCD format and sent to the output device—perhaps a CRT display or a printing mechanism.

The second chart expands on the first one, filling in a few more specific details—including the fact that an ASCII code for a numeral is converted to a BCD format by simply subtracting 30 hexadecimal from it.

Figure 11-8c is the programmer's working flowchart for the project. This one contains the level of detail that is necessary for selecting the appropriate COMPARE and conditional JUMP instructions.

Overall, the example is an application of the $B \leqslant A \leqslant C$ magnitude comparison procedure. The required listings are shown in Program 11-3.

Exercises for Section 11-1

1. Cite the smallest and largest hexadecimal values of A that suit the following relative magnitude expressions. Assume that all values are in an 8-bit, unsigned hexadecimal format.

   (a) $12H < A < 2AH$ (b) $10H \leqslant A < 2AH$ (c) $0H < A \leqslant 9H$
   (d) $0H \leqslant A \leqslant 10H$ (e) $EFH < A < FEH$ (f) $DEH < A < DFH$

2. It is often possible to find more than one inequality expression for doing exactly the same magnitude comparison task. Suppose that A is to have 8-bit, unsigned hexadecimal values between, and including, 20H and 30H. Cite the appropriate upper and lower boundary values for doing that job in each of the following cases.

   (a) _____ $< A <$ _____
   (b) _____ $\leqslant A <$ _____
   (c) _____ $< A \leqslant$ _____
   (d) _____ $\leqslant A \leqslant$ _____

3. Evolve a set of flowcharts for the magnitude comparisons cited in problem 2. Use formats such as those suggested in Figs. 11-4 through 11-7.

Z-80 Version

```
4A00 3A F0 FF   FETCH  LD A,(FFF0H)   ;FETCH KEYBOARD BYTE
4A03 FE FF             CP  FFH        ;ANY KEY DEPRESSED?
4A05 28 F9             JR  Z,FETCH    ;IF NOT, FETCH AGAIN
4A07 FE 30             CP  30H        ;IS IT ASCII 30H OR MORE?
4A09 28 02             JR  Z,UBND     ;IF 30H, CHECK UPPER BOUND
4A0B 38 F3             JR  C,FETCH    ;IF LESS, FETCH AGAIN
4A0D FE 39      UBND   CP  39H        ;IS IT ASCII 39H OR LESS?
4A0F 28 02             JR  Z,BCDO     ;IF 39H, OUTPUT THE BYTE
4A11 30 ED             JR  NC,FETCH   ;IF GREATER, FETCH AGAIN
4A13 32 F1 FF   BCDO   LD  (FFF1H),A  ;OUTPUT THE BCD BYTE
4A15 18 E8             JR  FETCH      ;AND FETCH AGAIN
```

8080A/8085 Version

```
4A00 3A F0 FF   FETCH  LDA FFF0H      ;FETCH KEYBOARD BYTE
4A03 FE FF             CPI  FFH       ;ANY KEY DEPRESSED?
4A05 CA 00 4A          JZ FETCH       ;IF NOT, FETCH AGAIN
4A08 FE 30             CPI  30H       ;IS IT ASCII 30H OR MORE?
4A0A CA 10 4A          JZ UBND        ;IF 30H, CHECK UPPER BOUND
4A0D DA 00 4A          JC FETCH       ;IF LESS, FETCH AGAIN
4A10 FE 39      UBND   CPI  39H       ;IS IT ASCII 39H OR LESS?
4A12 CA 18 4A          JZ BCDO        ;IF 39H, OUTPUT THE BYTE
4A15 D2 00 4A          JNC FETCH      ;IF GREATER, FETCH AGAIN
4A18 32 F1 FF   BCDO   STA FFF1H      ;OUTPUT THE BCD BYTE
4A1B C3 00 4A          JMP FETCH      ;AND FETCH AGAIN
```

6502 Versions

```
4A00 AD F0 FF   FETCH  LDA $FFF0      FETCH KEYBOARD BYTE
4A03 C9 FF             CMP #$FF       ANY KEY DEPRESSED?
4A05 F0 F9             BEQ FETCH      IF NOT, FETCH AGAIN
4A07 C9 30             CMP #$30       IS IT ASCII $30 OR MORE?
4A09 F0 02             BEQ UBND       IF $30, CHECK UPPER BOUND
4A0B B0 F3             BCS FETCH      IF LESS, FETCH AGAIN
4A0D C9 39      UBND   CMP #$39       IS IT ASCII $39 OR LESS?
4A0F F0 02             BEQ BDCO       IF $39, OUTPUT THE BYTE
4A11 90 ED             BCC FETCH      IF GREATER, FETCH AGAIN
4A13 8D F1 FF   BCDO   STA $FFF1      OUTPUT THE BCD BYTE
4A16 4C 00 4A          JMP FETCH      AND FETCH AGAIN
```

6800 Version

```
4A00 B6 FF F0   FETCH  LDAA $FFF0     FETCH KEYBOARD BYTE
4A03 81 FF             CMPA #$FF      ANY KEY DEPRESSED?
4A05 27 F9             BEQ FETCH      IF NOT, FETCH AGAIN
4A07 81 30             CMPA #$30      IS IT ASCII $30 OR MORE?
4A09 27 02             BEQ UBND       IF $30, CHECK UPPER BOUND
4A0B 25 F3             BCS FETCH      IF LESS, FETCH AGAIN
4A0D 81 39      UBND   CMPA #$39      IS IT ASCII $39 OR LESS?
4A0F 22 EF             BHI FETCH      IF MORE THAN $39, FETCH AGAIN
4A01 B7 FF F1          STAA $FFF1     ELSE OUTPUT THE BCD BYTE
4A04 20 EA             BRA FETCH      AND FETCH AGAIN
```

11-2 COMPARING 8-BIT SIGNED VALUES

Like 8-bit unsigned numbers, 8-bit signed numbers are represented by hexadecimal characters 00H through FFH. The relative magnitudes of the numbers within that range of characters can be vastly different, however.

The smallest 8-bit signed number is 80H (−128 decimal), and the largest is F7H (+127 decimal). That is quite different from the more common 8-bit unsigned-number format, where 00H (0 decimal) is the smallest number and FFH (255 decimal) is the largest.

Eight-bit signed numbers fall into the same set of magnitude comparisons of the algebraic form shown in Fig. 11-1. A signed number can be equal to another signed number, less than it, greater than or equal to it, and so on. But the implementation of the comparisons is a matter quite different from that used for programming comparisons of unsigned numbers.

For example, unsigned numbers can be compared and their relative magnitudes determined by the ZERO and CARRY statuses that result. The ZERO status is often used when comparing magnitudes of signed values, but the SIGN and OVERFLOW conditions are equally important.

The technique for doing magnitude comparisons on signed numbers varies from one microprocessor device to another. In fact, the four devices featured in this book use a different procedure in each case (although there are some similarities between the Z-80 and 6502 methods).

Signed Magnitude Comparisons for the 6800

The instruction set for the 6800 device includes some conditional jump instructions that are tailormade for doing signed-value comparisons:

BGT   BRANCH IF GREATER
If satisfied, the value of the byte in the accumulator is greater than the compared byte.
If *not* satisfied, the value of the byte in the accumulator is either equal to or less than the compared byte.
To satisfy the conditional, the Z flag must be cleared to zero (unequal values) and, at the same time, the S (sign) and V (overflow) flags must have the same value—both 1 or both 0.

BGE   BRANCH IF GREATER OR EQUAL
If satisfied, the 2's-complement value of the byte in the accumulator is greater than or equal to the compared byte.
If *not* satisfied, the byte in the accumulator must be less than the compared byte.
To satisfy the conditional, the S and V flags must have the same value.

BLE   BRANCH IF LESS OR EQUAL
If satisfied, it means that the 2's-complement value of the byte in the accumulator is less than or equal to the compared byte. Otherwise, the byte in the accumulator has to be greater than the compared byte.
In a sense, BLE and BGT are redundant instructions.

BLT   BRANCH IF LESS THAN
If this conditional is satisfied, it means that the 2's-complement byte in the accumulator is less than the compared byte. Otherwise, the byte in the accumulator is greater than or equal to the compared byte.
BLT and BGE are redundant instructions.

Those four conditional branch instructions apply only to the matter of comparing 8-bit, signed, 2's-complement numbers. The other 6800 inequality branch instructions, BCC and BCS, do not apply; but the equality instructions, BNE and BEQ, do.

Figure 11-9 illustrates an application of an equality operation with 8-bit signed numbers. The program in this case calls for testing an input byte against −10 decimal ($F6 hexadecimal). If, indeed, the two numbers have the same value, the equality condition is satisfied and the system outputs the fetched byte. If the condition of equality is not satisfied, the system simply loops back up the FETCH operation to pick up another byte from the input.

The program makes a point of the fact that the 6800's BNE and BEQ conditional jump instructions apply to signed, as well as unsigned, magnitude comparison operations.

The flowchart in Fig. 11-10 tests the input byte to see whether or not it

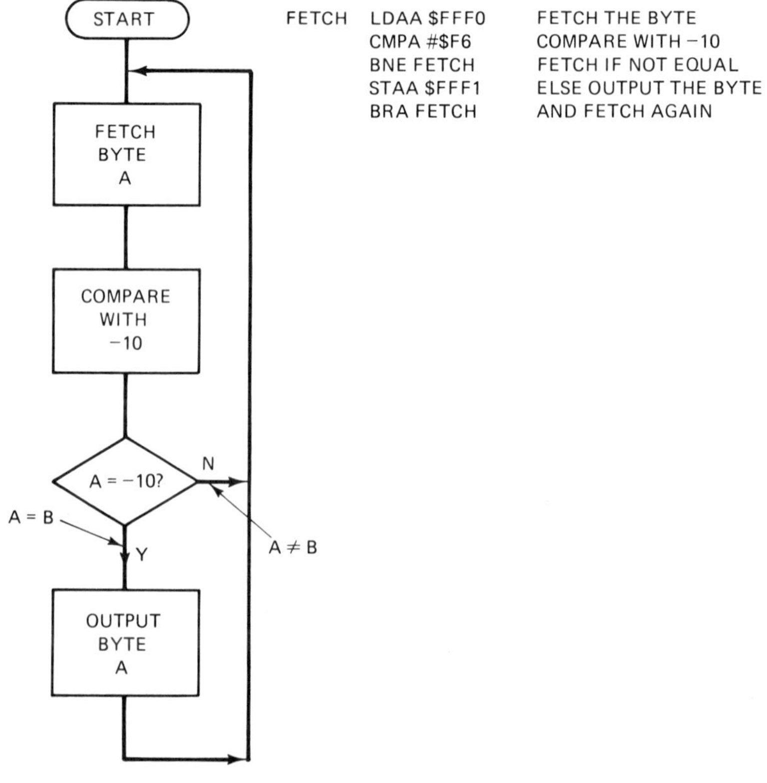

Figure 11-9   Application of an equality operation for the 6800 microprocessor.

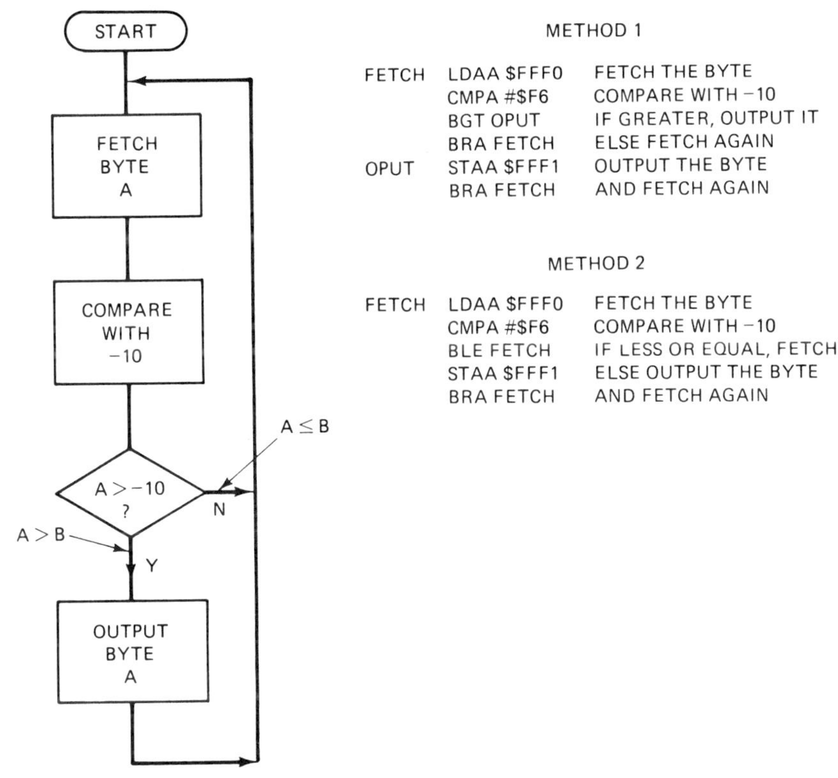

Figure 11-10 Application of an equality operation, $A > -10$, for the 6800 microprocessor.

is larger than -10 decimal. If so, the byte is set to the output port; otherwise, it is not.

There are, however, two approaches to writing a program for that particular comparison operation. *Method 1* follows the flowchart exactly, executing the conditional step, $A -10$, with a BGT—branch if greater than. Like the flowchart, the program says: Branch to the output step if A is greater than -10; otherwise, fetch another byte.

Method 2 achieves the same overall result, but in a somewhat simpler programming fashion. Instead of looking for the situation where A is greater than -10, it senses the same situation where A is less than or equal to -10. It uses the BLE conditional branch instruction and, in effect, says: If A is less than or equal to -10, fetch another byte; otherwise, return directly to FETCH.

Compare the two methods carefully, and convince yourself that the operations are the same. In both cases, byte A is sent to the output only if it is a signed value between −9 and +127 decimal.

The flowchart in Fig. 11-11 can be treated in a similar way. *Method 1* in that example uses the BGE—branch if greater than or equal to—conditional instruction. That is exactly what the conditional operation in the flowchart calls for.

Method 2 does the same job, but reverses the conditional statement. Instead of looking directly for the case where A is greater than or equal to −10, it looks for the case where A is simply less than −10. No matter which method is used in the programming, the scheme still sends byte A to the output port only if it has a value between −10 and +127, inclusively.

The programming examples in Figs. 11-10 and 11-11 point to the fact that conditional statements appearing on initial flowcharts are not cast in concrete, so to speak. A general flowchart ought to express the most direct and clear expression for conditional jumps, but the program itself should employ the most effective and efficient method for implementing the conditional operation.

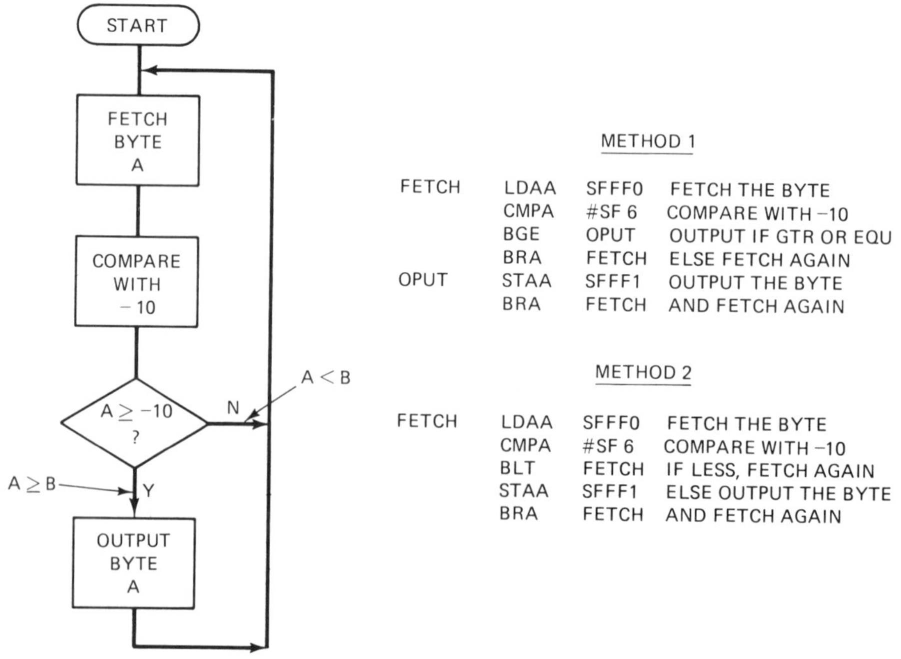

Figure 11-11 Application of an equality operation, $A \geq -10$, for the 6800 microprocessor.

Figure 11-12 combines two 6800 conditional branch operations to perform a comparison of the general form B ≤ A ≤ C. In that example, the lower boundary is set at -10 decimal, and the upper boundary is +10 decimal.

The notations in the conditional operations in the flowchart directly reflect the nature of the comparison, but the program itself uses the simpler,

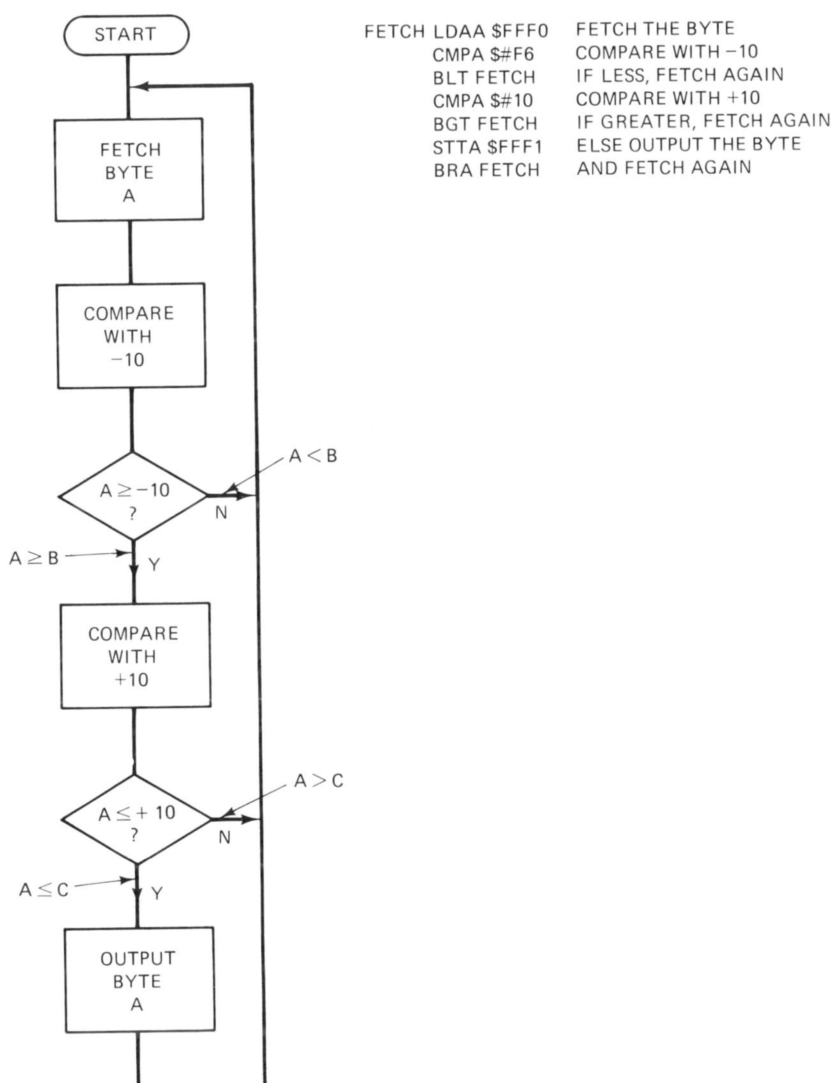

Input: Address $FFF0; data in an 8-bit, 2's-complement form

Output: Address $FFF1

Output the byte only if it is greater than or equal to -10, and less than or equal to +10 (-10 through +10)

Figure 11-12 Application of an equality operation, -10 ≤ A ≤ + 10, for the 6800 microprocessor.

if somewhat less direct, branch statements for implementing the comparisons. Study both the flowchart and program, making sure you understand that byte A is sent to the output only when it has a value between −10 and +10, inclusively.

Signed Magnitude Comparisons for the Z-80 and 6502

Instruction sets for the Z-80 and 6502 do not have conditional jump instructions that are tailormade for working with 8-bit signed numbers. The matter of designing programs for doing conditional operations of this sort is thus going to be somewhat more difficult than it is for the 6800 device—the one that does have special, signed-number instruction.

The function of the signed-number conditional operations for the Z-80 and 6502 rests with the nature of the zero, sign, and overflow bits in their flag registers. The conditions are summarized in Table 11-2.

In each case, value A is the one being tested against value B. The general procedure, then, is to get value A into the accumulator, COMPARE it with B, and then take appropriate JUMP action that is conditioned by the relevant flag conditions—flag conditions cited in the table.

Figure 11-13 shows how the six basic signed magnitude comparisons can be implemented.

The chart in Fig. 11-13a, for example, illustrates the rather simple task of determining whether or not value A is equal to B. If, after making the comparison, a ZERO condition exists, it figures that the two values are identical. Otherwise, they are not.

The flowchart in Fig. 11-13b also tests for two relative magnitude conditions: $A > B$ and $A \leq B$. In this case, the ZERO, SIGN, and OVERFLOW statuses are relevant. According to Table 11-2, $A > B$ only if the status bits show that the difference is NOT ZERO, and that the SIGN and OVERFLOW bits are the same (both 1 or both 0).

After doing the COMPARE operation, the first step is to test the re-

TABLE 11-2 SIGNED MAGNITUDE COMPARISONS
AND THEIR RELEVANT FLAG CONDITIONS FOR
THE Z-80 AND 6502 MICROPROCESSORS

Relative magnitude	Conditions
$A > B$	Sign equals Overflow AND difference is NOT Zero
$A \geq B$	Sign equals Overflow
$A < B$	Sign does not equal Overflow
$A \leq B$	Sign does not equal Overflow OR difference is Zero
$A = B$	Difference is Zero
$A \neq B$	Difference is NOT Zero

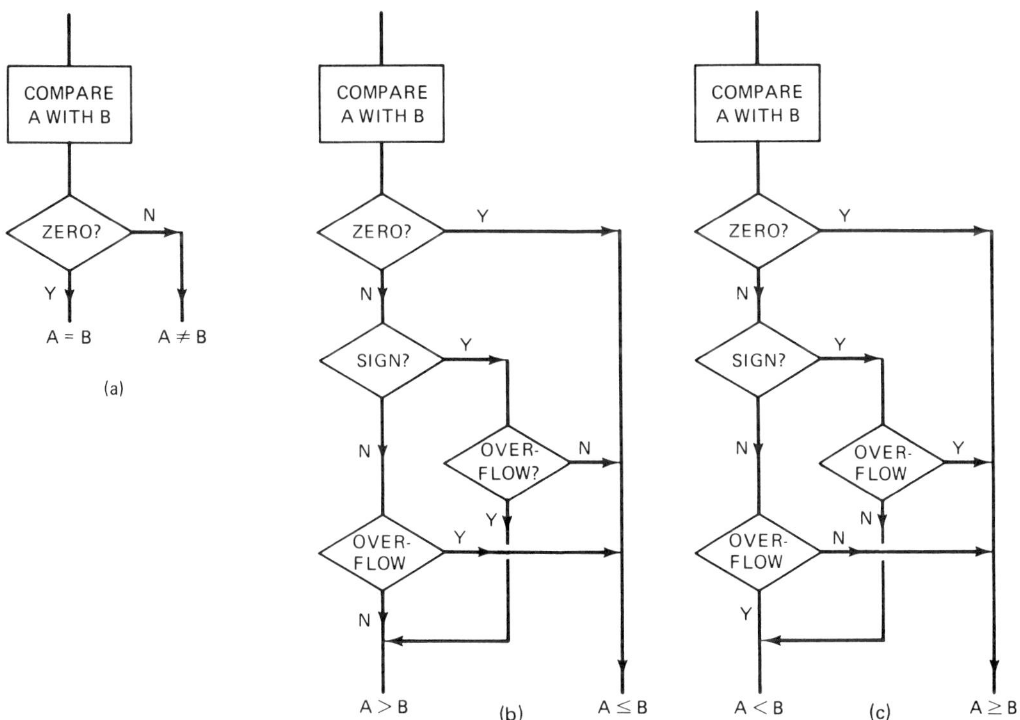

Figure 11-13   Flowcharts for 2's-complement magnitude comparisons for the Z-80 and 6502 microprocessors.

sulting ZERO condition. If a ZERO condition exists, A cannot possibly be greater than B, so the flowchart exits at the point labeled A ≤ B. But if the ZERO conditional operation is NOT satisfied, the next step is to check the SIGN status; and no matter what the result of that check might be, the program tests the OVERFLOW status. The "yes" and "no" paths from those two OVERFLOW tests, however, are quite different. Notice, in particular, how the routine ends up at *A > B when the SIGN and subsequent OVER-FLOW tests have the same "yes" or "no" result.* That is the simplest procedure for testing for the equality of the microprocessor's SIGN and OVERFLOW status bits.

Also note from Fig. 11-13b that the flowchart exits at A ≤ B whenever one of the "yes" or "no" paths from the SIGN conditional leads to an OVERFLOW test that turns up the opposite "yes" or "no" result. That is how the scheme finds the situation where the SIGN and OVERFLOW bits are different (either SIGN is 1 and OVERFLOW is 0, or SIGN is 0 and OVERFLOW is 1). That, according to Table 11-2, is the criterion for A < B.

Figure 11-13c illustrates a comparison that determines whether A < B or A ≥ B. In this case, *A < B when the SIGN and subsequent OVERFLOW tests have the opposite "yes" or "no" result.*

These operations test the relative magnitudes of signed 8-bit numbers that are represented in a 2's-complement form. Compare the basic flowcharts with their counterparts for unsigned 8-bit values in Fig. 11-1.

Figures 11-14 through 11-17 show the evolution of flowcharts for determining whether or not value A falls within the boundaries of two other values, B and C. The general procedure is identical to the one used in Section 11-1 for generating similar flowcharts that test unsigned numbers. Thus the details of these four illustrations are left for you to sort out.

EXAMPLE 11-4

A microprocessor system is hardwired with an 8-bit input port at address FFF0 and an output at address FFF1. The program accepts all 8-bit, 2's-complement numbers from the input, but delivers that byte to the output only if the byte has a value equal to or greater than ⌐10 (decimal). See the basic flowchart in Fig. 11-18a.

Write and assemble Z-80 and 6502 programs for carrying out the task. Begin the programming at 4000 hexadecimal. Note the evolution of the flowchart from a basic form that directly indicates the magnitude comparison to take place to the less direct, but more useful, version that shows the relevant flag conditions. The suggested program listings are shown in **Program 11-4.**

EXAMPLE 11-5

Alter the programming circumstances cited in Example 11-4 so that the system will output values in the range −10 through +10 (decimal).

See the evolution of the working flowchart in Fig. 11-19 and the suggested program listings in Program 11-5.

Signed Magnitude Comparisons for the 8080A/8085

The fact that the 8080A/8085 microprocessor does not have an overflow flag makes it relatively unsuitable for doing 8-bit, 2's-complement magnitude comparisons. The job can be done, however, using the techniques cited here. (Intel, incidentally, has remedied this awkward situation with the newer 8-bit microprocessor, the 8088.)

Eight-bit signed magnitude comparisons with the 8080A/8085 system begin in the usual fashion—getting value A into the accumulator and comparing it with value B. What happens after that, however, depends on the resulting carry status.

If the resulting carry status is a 1:
    A < B if the two values have the *same sign.*
    A > B if the two values have the *opposite sign.*

If the resulting carry status is a 0:
    A ≥ B if the two values have the *same sign.*
    A < B is the two values have the *opposite sign.*

Every signed magnitude comparison must deal with both the carry and sign flags, and, in some instances, the zero flag as well.

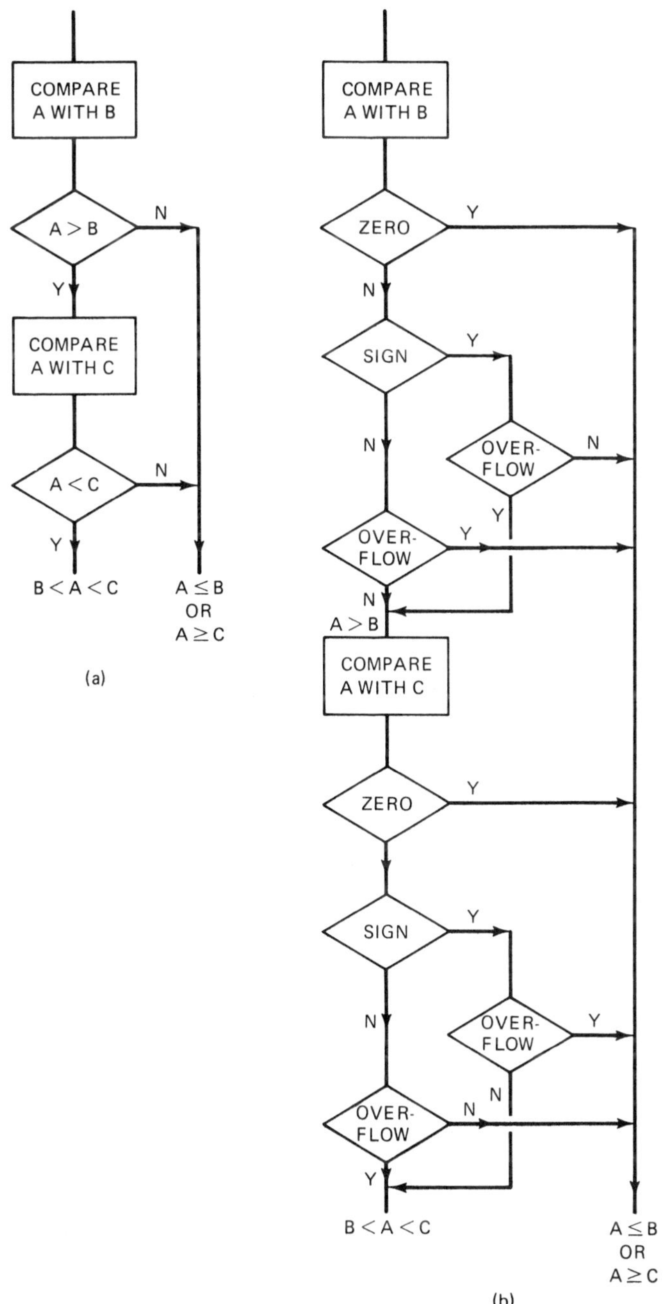

Figure 11-14 Evolution of a flowchart for the 2's-complement magnitude comparison, B < A < C, for the Z-80 and 6502.

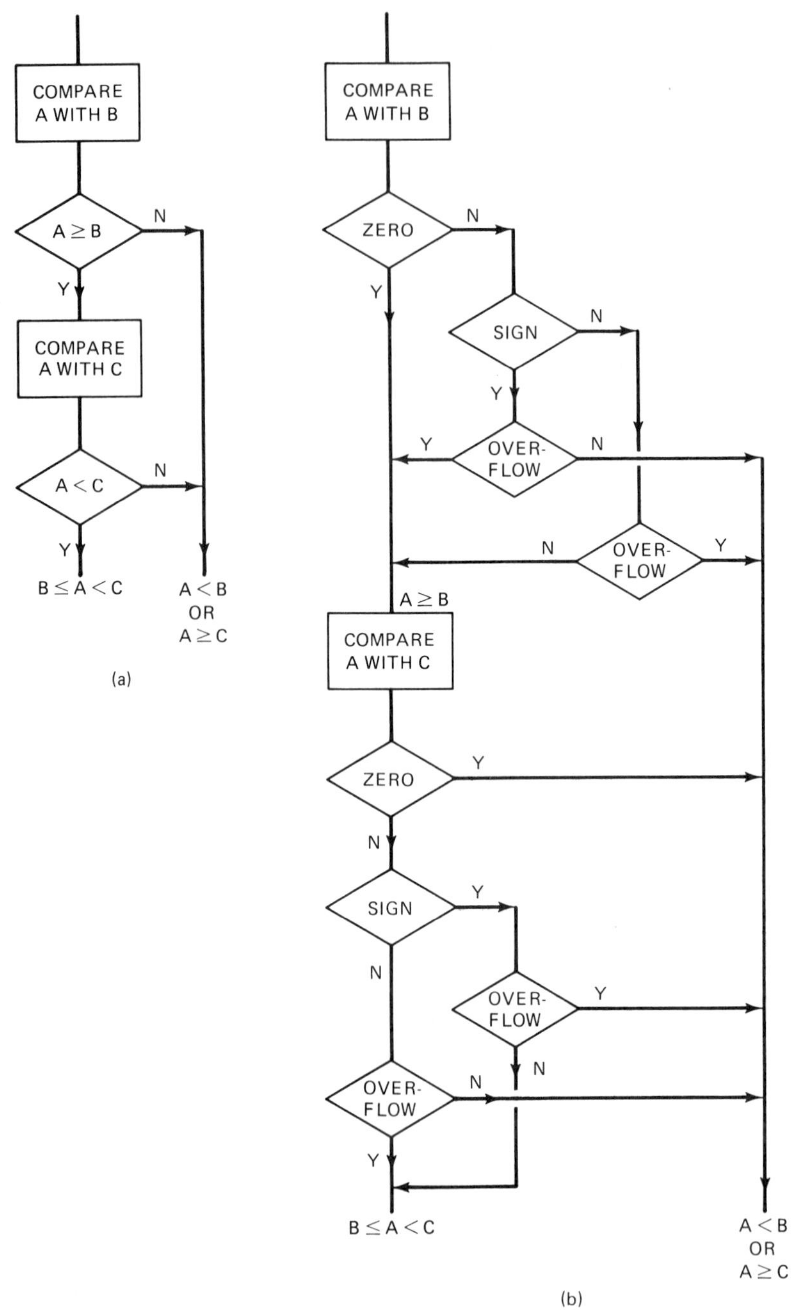

Figure 11-15 Flowcharts for the 2's-complement magnitude comparison, $B \leqslant A < C$, for the Z-80 and 6502.

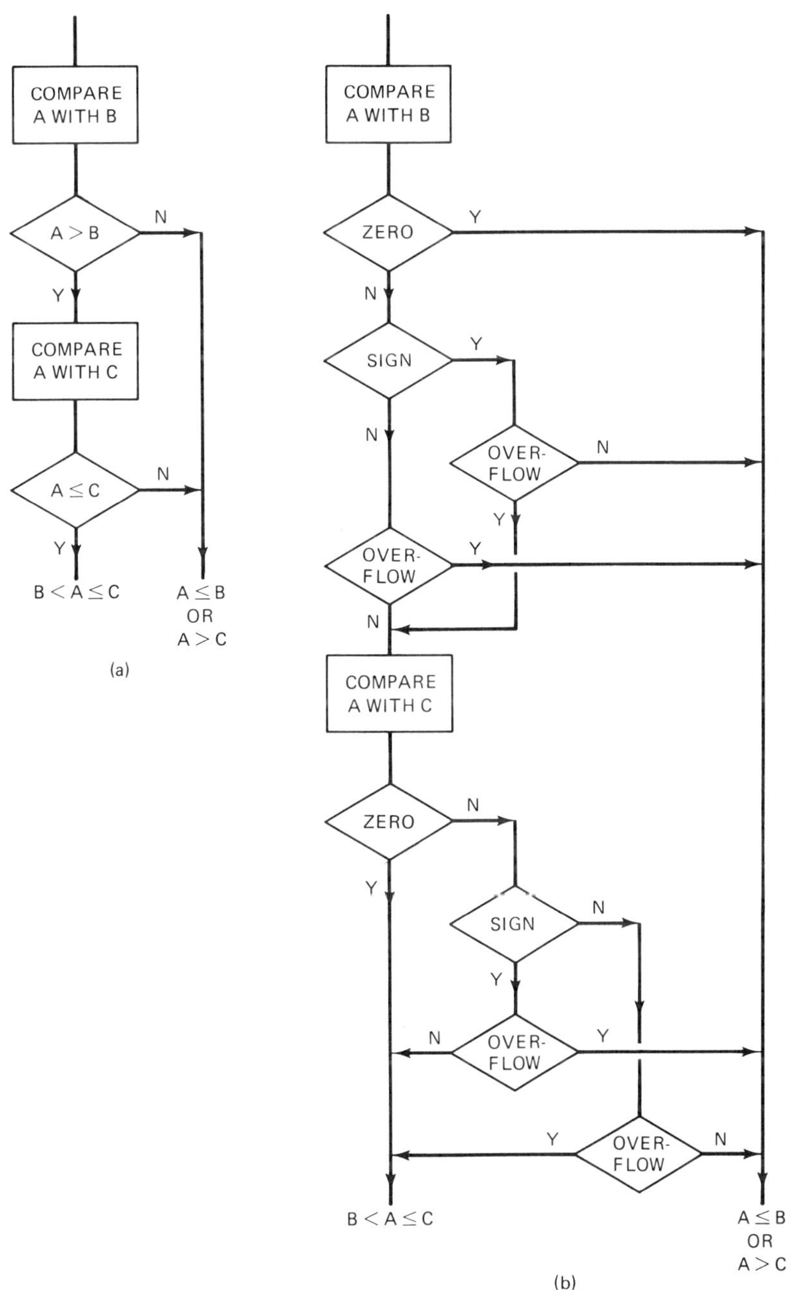

Figure 11-16 Flowcharts for the 2's-complement magnitude comparison, $B < A \leqslant C$, for the Z-80 and 6502.

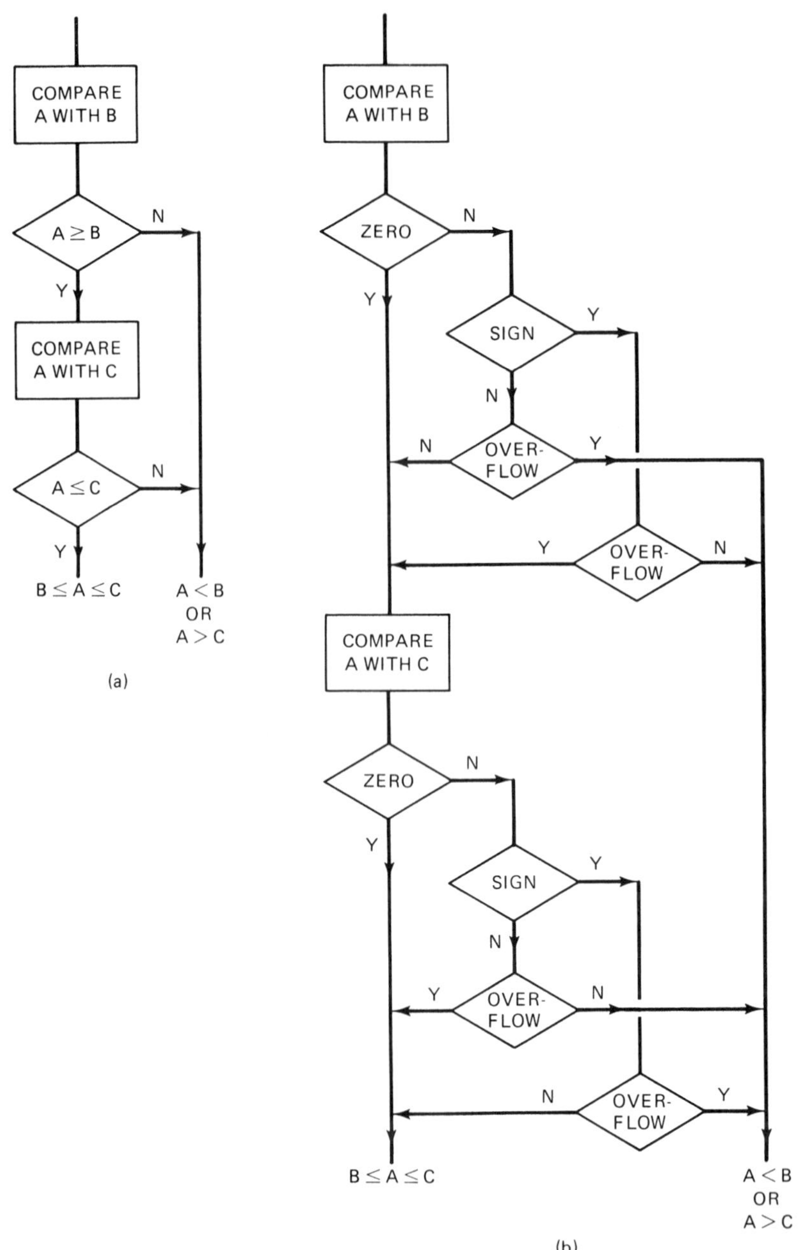

Figure 11-17 Flowcharts for the 2's-complement magnitude comparison, B ≤ A ≤ C, for the Z-80 and 6502.

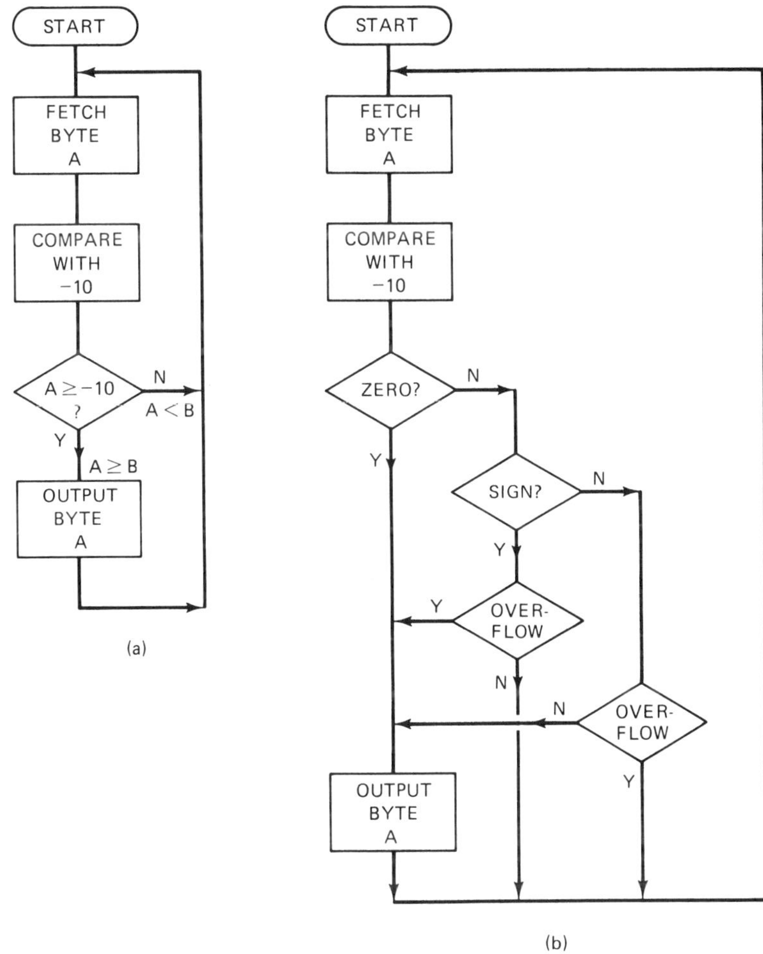

Figure 11-18   Flowcharts for the 2's-complement magnitude comparison task in Example 11-4.

Figure 11-20 is a basic flowchart for these comparison operations. The first block calls for comparing the values of A and B (assuming that value A is in the accumulator at the time). If the result is a carry of 1, the chart shows an EXCLUSIVE-OR operation between values A and B. What is the purpose of the EXCLUSIVE-OR? The purpose is to determine the relative values of the sign bits in the two values.

If A and B have the same sign bit, the EXCLUSIVE-OR operation will turn up a 0 in the sign flag position. If the values have opposite signs, the S bit in the flag register will be set to logic 1. Thus the answer to the SAME SIGN conditional is a "yes" if the S flag in the F register is zero; the answer is "no" if the S flag bit is set to 1.

PROGRAM 11-4 PROGRAM LISTINGS FOR THE TASK IN EXAMPLE 11-4

Z-80 Version

```
4000  3A F0 FF   FETCH   LD  A,(FFF0H)   ;FETCH THE BYTE
4003  FE F6              CP  F6H         ;COMPARE WITH –10
4005  28 0B              JR  Z,OPUT      ;IF SAME, DO OUTPUT
4007  F2 0F 40           JP  P,NEXT1     ;IF SIGN, DO NEXT1
400A  E2 12 40           JP  PO,OPUT     ;IF NOT O'FLOW, OUTPUT IT
400D  18 F1              JR  FETCH       ;ELSE FETCH ANOTHER BYTE
400F  E2 00 40   NEXT1   JP  PO,FETCH    ;IF NOT O'FLOW, FETCH AGAIN
4012  32 F1 FF   OPUT    LD  (FFF1H),A   ;OUTPUT THE BYTE
4015  18 E9              JR  FETCH       ;AND FETCH ANOTHER ONE
```

6502 Version

```
4000  AD F0 FF   FETCH   LDA $FFF0       FETCH THE BYTE
4003  C9 F6              CMP #$F6        COMPARE WITH –10
4005  F0 09              BEQ OPUT        IF SAME, DO OUTPUT
4007  10 02              BPL NEXT1       IF SIGN, DO NEXT1
4009  50 05              BVC OPUT        IF NOT O'FLOW, OUTPUT IT
400B  4C 00 40           JMP FETCH       ELSE FETCH ANOTHER BYTE
400E  50 F0      NEXT1   BVC FETCH       IF NOT O'FLOW, FETCH AGAIN
4010  8D F1 FF   OPUT    STA $FFF1       OUTPUT THE BYTE
4013  4C 00 40           JMP FETCH       AND FETCH ANOTHER ONE
```

PROGRAM 11-5 PROGRAM LISTINGS FOR THE TASK IN EXAMPLE 11-5

Z-80 Version

```
4000  3A F0 FF   FETCH   LD  A,(FFF0H)   ;FETCH THE BYTE
4003  FE F6              CP  F6H         ;COMPARE WITH –10
4005  28 0B              JR  Z,UBND      ;IF SAME, TEST UPPER BOUND
5007  FA 0F 40           JP  M,NEXT1     ;IF NOT SIGN, DO NEXT1
400A  E2 00 40           JP  PO,FETCH    ;IF NOT O'FLOW, FETCH AGAIN
400D  18 03              JR  UBND        ;ELSE TEST UPPER BOUND
400F  EA 00 40   NEXT1   JP  PE,FETCH    ;IF O'FLOW, FETCH AGAIN
4012  FE 10      UBND    CP  10H         ;COMPARE WITH 10
4014  28 0B              JR  Z,OPUT      ;IF SAME, OUTPUT THE BYTE
4016  FA 1E 40           JP  M,NEXT2     ;IF NOT SIGN, DO NEXT2
4019  EA 00 40           JP  PE,FETCH    ;IF O'FLOW, FETCH AGAIN
401C  18 03              JR  OPUT        ;ELSE OUTPUT THE BYTE
401E  E2 00 40   NEXT2   JP  PO,FETCH    ;IF NOT O'FLOW, FETCH AGAIN
4021  32 F1 FF   OPUT    LD  (FFF1H),A   ;OUTPUT THE BYTE
4024  18 DA              JR  FETCH       ;AND FETCH AGAIN
```

6502 Version

```
4000  AD F0 FF   FETCH   LDA $FFF0       FETCH THE BYTE
4003  C9 F6              CMP #$F6        COMPARE WITH –10
4005  F0 09              BEQ UBND        IF SAME, TEST UPPER BOUND
4007  30 02              BMI NEXT1       IF NOT SIGN, DO NEXT1
4009  50 F5              BVC FETCH       IF NOT O'FLOW, FETCH AGAIN
400B  4C 10 40           JMP UBND        ELSE TEST UPPER BOUND
400E  70 F0      NEXT1   BVS FETCH       IF O'FLOW, FETCH AGAIN
4010  C9 10      UBND    CMP #$10        COMPARE WITH 10
4012  F0 09              BEQ OPUT        IF SAME, OUTPUT THE BYTE
4014  30 05              BMI NEXT2       IF NOT SIGN, DO NEXT2
4016  70 E8              BVS FETCH       IF O'FLOW, FETCH AGAIN
4018  4C 10 40           JMP OPUT        ELSE OUTPUT THE BYTE
401B  50 E3      NEXT2   BVC FETCH       IF NOT O'FLOW, FETCH AGAIN
401D  8D F1 FF   OPUT    STA $FFF1       OUTPUT THE BYTE
4020  4C 00 40           JMP FETCH       AND FETCH AGAIN
```

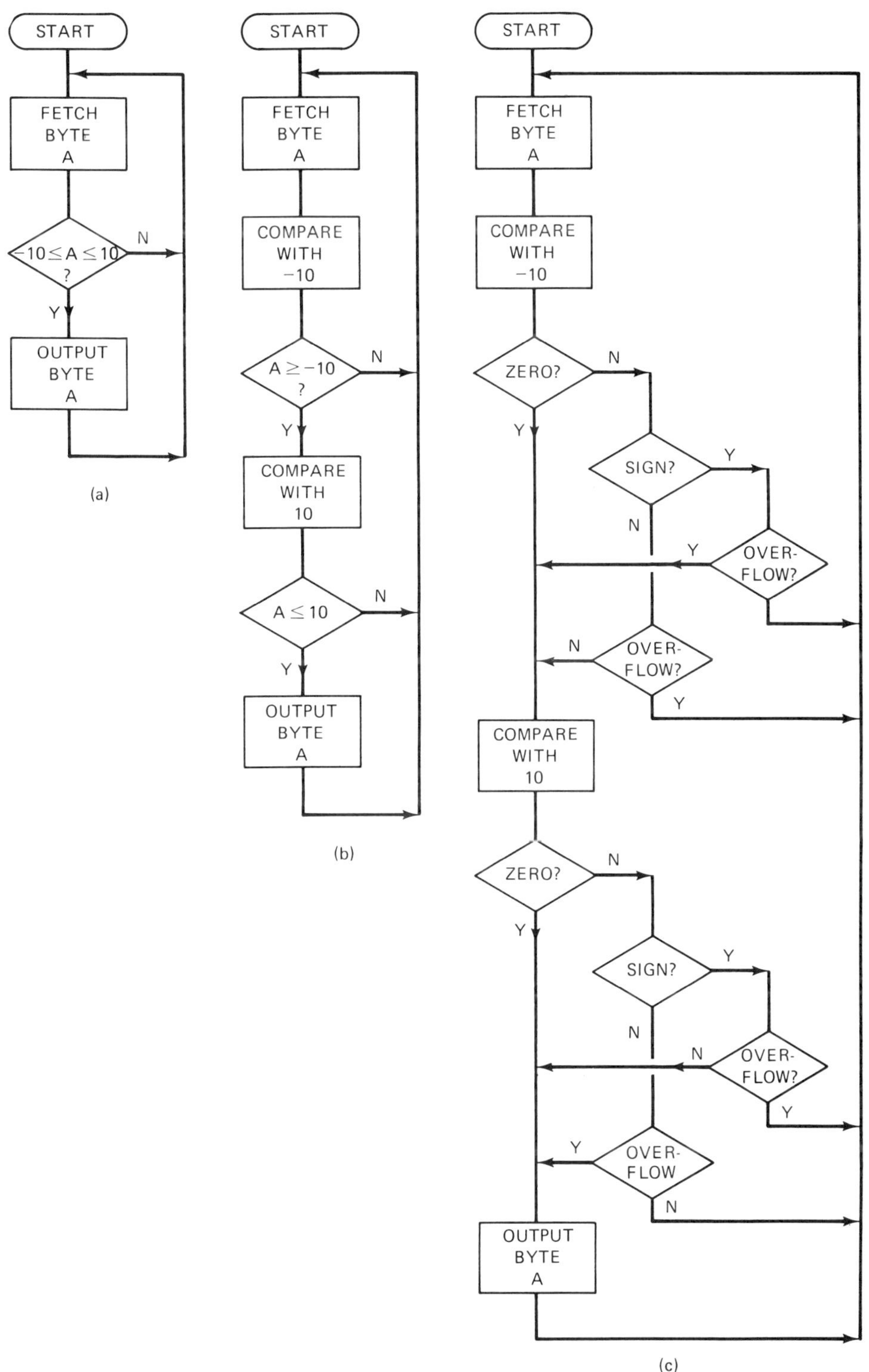

Figure 11-19 Evolution of a detailed flowchart for the magnitude comparison task in Example 11-5.

The real question, then, is whether or not the EXCLUSIVE-OR operations turns up a positive sign bit. If the result is "positive," the two values must have the same sign. Otherwise, the signs must be different.

The same general idea applies to the branch that is executed whenever the compare operations shows no carry.

One practical difficulty with the scheme in Fig. 11-20 is that the value of number A is lost during the EXCLUSIVE-OR operation. It is not affected by the initial compare operation, but a copy of it should be saved in another register or somewhere in external memory before doing the EXCLUSIVE-OR.

The following example illustrates an application of these ideas.

EXAMPLE 11-6

Write an 8080A/8085 program for the following task:

1. Fetch an 8-bit, 2's-complement value from an input port addressed by F000H.
2. Compare the value with decimal -10.
3. If the value is greater than or equal to -10 (decimal), output it to address F001H.
4. Jump back to step 1.

Begin the listing at program address 7000H.

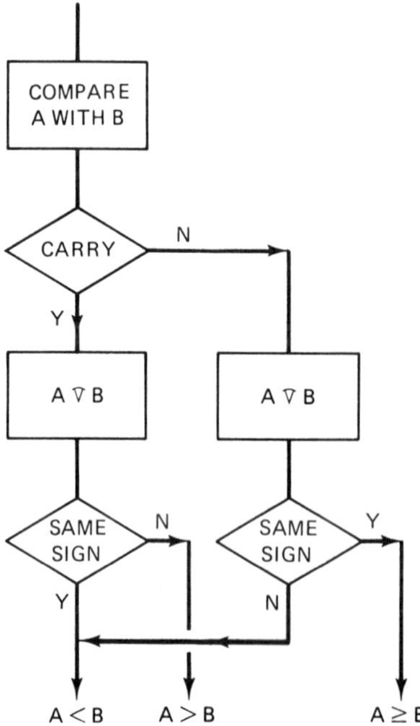

Figure 11-20 Basic flowcharts for 2's-complement magnitude comparisons for the 8080A/8085 system.

PROGRAM 11-6 8080A/8085 LISTING FOR THE SIGNED MAGNITUDE
COMPARISON TASK IN EXAMPLE 11-6

```
7000 3A 00 F0   FETCH    LDA  0F000H    ;FETCH THE BYTE
7003 FE F6               CPI  0F6H      ;COMPARE WITH -10
7005 DA 00 70            JC   FETCH     ;IF CARRY, FETCH AGAIN
7008 47                  MOV  B,A       ;SAVE BYTE IN B
7009 EE F6               XRI  0F6H      ;EX-OR WITH -10
700B FA 00 70            JM   FETCH     ;IF NOT SAME SIGN, FETCH AGAIN
700E 78                  MOV  B,A       ;ELSE GET ORIGINAL BYTE
700F 32 01 F0            STA  0F001H    ;OUTPUT THE BYTE
7012 C3 00 70            JMP  FETCH     ;AND FETCH AGAIN
```

The listing in Program 11-6 begins by fetching the byte from address
F000H and comparing it with decimal -10. If a carry of 1 results, the program jumps back immediately to fetch another byte—the value is not greater
than or equal to -10.

But if there is no carry, the value is saved in the B register (MOV B,A),
and it is EXCLUSIVE-ORd with -10. Now, if the signs are the same, the sign
bit in the F register will be a 0—a condition that will satisfy a JP (jump if
positive) instruction. The program, however, takes the alternative approach,
doing a jump if minus (S flag is 1, or NOT positive). Thus JM FETCH returns operations directly to FETCH if the SAME SIGN test fails. Otherwise,
the original value of the byte is brought to the accumulator from the B
register and sent to the output. The final instructions loops the program
back to the beginning.

Exercises for Section 11-2

1. What is the most negative value possible with an 8-bit, 2's-complement format? the
   most positive value?

2. Which 6800 branch instructions apply only to comparisons for unsigned 8-bit values?
   only 2's-complement values? to both unsigned- and signed-value comparisons?

3. Explain the role of the S flag bit in 8080A/8085 2's-complement number comparisons.

12

The Stack Pointer and Stack Operations

Every microprocessor has a stack pointer (SP) register built into it. The 6502, for instance, has an 8-bit SP register, while the Z-80, 8080A/8085, and 6800 have 16-bit SP registers.

The stack pointer has been mentioned a number of times in previous discussions, but its purpose has not yet been fully defined. This chapter deals exclusively with the SP register: what it does and what it is used for.

The SP and PC registers are similar in the sense that they both point to an address somewhere in external memory space. Whereas the PC register points to the address of the next program instruction to be read and executed, the SP register points to a place in data memory where a byte of data can be fetched or stored. It is possible to say that *the SP register is to data memory as the PC register is to program memory*.

A *stack* is defined as a portion of data memory that is set aside for storing and retrieving bytes of data in a sequential fashion. The operation of the stack pointer and its stack memory conjures up a mental impression of stacking items—bytes of data—on top of one another. Once the stack pointer has been set to a particular address in data memory, the internal workings of the microprocessor take care of the task of incrementing and decrementing the stack pointer as data are fetched or stored into that stack memory.

To get at least a preliminary appreciation of what the stack pointer can do, consider a series of data-stacking operations that are carried out without any reference to the SP register. The example in this case loads the content of the Z-80's B, C, D, and E registers into successively lower address locations in data memory. With the HL register pair serving as a stack pointer, the task might be handled this way:

```
LD HL,4000H   ;SET HL POINTER TO 4000H
DEC HL        ;DECREMENT HL
LD (HL),B     ;B TO ADDRESS 3FFFH
DEC HL        ;DECREMENT HL
LD (HL),C     ;C TO ADDRESS 3FFEH
DEC HL        ;DECREMENT HL
LD (HL),D     ;D TO ADDRESS 3FFDH
DEC HL        ;DECREMENT HL
LD (HL),E     ;E TO ADDRESS 3FFCH
```

The first instruction initializes the address pointer, the HL register pair, to 4000H, and the second instruction decrements that pointer to 3FFFH. So when the byte from register B is stored into the "stack," it goes to address location 3FFFH. Then the pointer is decremented and the next byte goes to address 3FFEH. This process continues—decrement the pointer and store the byte—until all four bytes are stored. At the conclusion of the sequence, the HL pointer is left pointing to the address of the last-stored byte, address 3FFCH.

In a sense, the contents of the four registers are stacked one below the other. Thus saved in the "stack," the content of those registers is preserved for later use, and the registers are free to be used for other purposes. At a later time, the registers can be restored by loading the "stack" back to them.

Assuming that the HL pair is still pointing to the last-stored byte in the preceding example, the contents of the registers can be restored by doing an "unstacking" operation of this sort:

```
LD E,(HL)   ;CONTENT OF ADDRESS 3FFCH TO E
INC HL      ;INCREMENT HL
LD D,(HL)   ;CONTENT OF ADDRESS 3FFDH TO D
INC HL      ;INCREMENT HL
LD C,(HL)   ;CONTENT OF ADDRESS 3FFEH TO C
INC HL      ;INCREMENT HI
LD B,(HL)   ;CONTENT OF ADDRESS 3FFFH TO B
INC HL      ;INCREMENT HL
```

The content of the four registers, originally pushed onto the stack, is thus restored, and the HL pointer is left pointing to the original starting address, 4000H.

What purpose is served by this combination of stacking and unstacking operations? For one, it preserves the contents of the working registers so they can be put to other uses; and when the original contents are to be recovered, they are all readily available—in a well-defined sequence—in the stack memory space.

Such an operation is so useful that all microprocessors have special instructions dedicated to that type of task. The following sequences of operations use stack operations to carry out the register-saving routines just described:

```
LD SP,4000H   ;SET THE STACK POINTER TO 4000H
PUSH BC       ;BC REGISTER PAIR TO STACK
PUSH DE       ;DE REGISTER PAIR TO STACK
```

At the conclusion of that sequence, the contents of the B, C, D, and E registers are saved on the stack, and the SP register is left pointing to address 3FFCH—the location of the last-saved register byte.

The stack can be unloaded to the registers this way:

```
POP DE   ;LOAD DE REGISTER PAIR FROM STACK
POP BC   ;LOAD BC REGISTER PAIR FROM STACK
```

The registers are restored to their original contents, and the stack pointer is left pointing to its original address, 4000H.

Some special features of the stack can be cited at this point in the discussion.

First, the stack pointer has to be initialized just one time, and usually very early in the program sequence—certainly before it is used. The SP register is dedicated solely to stack operations, and there is no need to keep track of its contents once it is initialized.

Second, the stack always "grows downward." Once initialized, the stack pointer always loads new data into successively lower address locations. If the stack is initialized at 8000H, for instance, the first byte placed into the stack will go to address 7FFFH, the second byte will go to 7FFEH, and so on. In theory at least, the size of the stack is limited only by the amount of RAM space available (the 6502 is an exception to that general notion, however).

Third, the stack takes care of its own addressing; it monitors its own decrementing when data are being placed onto the stack and takes care of its own incrementing when data are being popped off the stack. Once initialized, the programmer need not be concerned with the exact content of the stack pointer. It is important, however, to set aside sufficient memory space for the stack. If the stack is allowed to grow far enough, there is a chance it will begin loading data into portions of memory that have been set aside for other applications—other kinds of data and even the program itself. Such a "crash" between the downward-growing stack and other important elements in the memory can be disastrous to a program.

Finally, data are removed from the stack in a sequence that is opposite from the way they were loaded originally. Stack operations, in other words, are characterized by a *first-in-last-out* register operation.

12.1 STACK INSTRUCTIONS FOR THE Z-80

Table 12-1 shows the most-used stack instructions for the Z-80 microprocessor. Figure 12-1 illustrates the 16-bit registers and 8-bit register pairs that can be involved in stack operations.

LD SP,addr is a 16-bit load immediate instruction that is most often used for initializing the stack pointer. The first byte following the opcode is the LSB of the desired stack address, and the remaining byte is the MSB. So if you want to initialize the stack at 4000H, an appropriate listing would be

```
31 00 40  LD SP,4000H  ;INITIALIZE THE STACK AT 4000H
```

Source code	Object code	Notes
LD SP,*addr*	31 *byte byte*	SP←*addr*
PUSH AF	F5	
PUSH BC	C5	
PUSH DE	D5	Store register pair or a 16-bit register to the stack
PUSH HL	E5	
PUSH IX	DD E5	
PUSH IY	FD E5	
POP AF	F1	
POP BC	C1	
POP DE	D1	Load register pair or a 16-bit register from the stack
POP HL	E1	
POP IX	DD E1	
POP IY	FD E1	

The first byte of data placed onto the stack would thus go to address 3FFFH—always one address lower than the address currently contained in the stack pointer.

The PUSH instructions place the contents of some 16-bit registers or 8-bit registers pairs onto the stack, with the MSB going in first. If the SP register happens to be at 4000H when you do a PUSH HL instruction, the content of the H register will go to address 3FFFH and the content of the L reg-

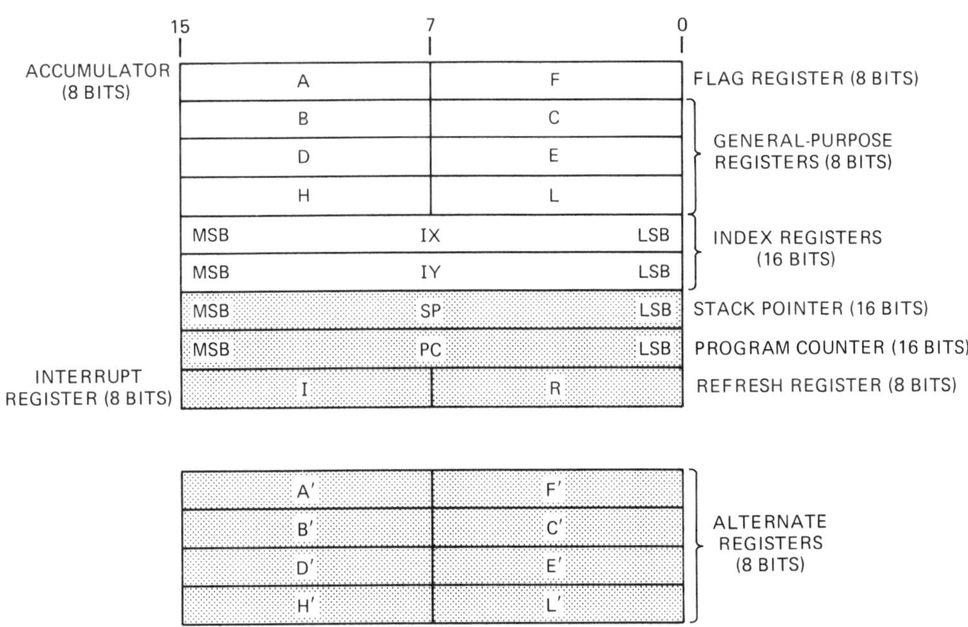

Figure 12-1 Z-80 registers directly involved in stack operations. Shaded registers are not involved.

ister will go to address 3FFEH—and that will be the content of the SP register until the next stack instruction comes along.

Note that all PUSH instructions involve 16 bits. There are no instructions for placing a single byte of data onto the stack. So if you want to save the content of the accumulator on the stack, the F register has to go along with it. That is accomplished with the PUSH AF instruction.

The POP instructions remove two bytes of data from the stack and place them into the designated 16-bit registers or 8-bit register pairs. Bearing in mind that the stack always works on a first-in-last-out basis, it figures that the POP instructions unstack the LSB first, followed immediately by the MSB.

EXAMPLE 12-1

Write and assemble a Z-80 program that does the following:

1. Initialize the stack pointer at 3C00H.
2. Load the content of all primary registers to the stack.
3. Load the content of all alternate registers to the stack.
4. Unload the entire stack to restore all registers to their original content.

Begin the listing at program address 2F00H.
See the suggested listing in Program 12-1.

The first instruction sets the stack pointer for the whole operation. Then six consecutive PUSH instructions load the contents of all the primary

PROGRAM 12-1   Z-80 LISTING FOR EXAMPLE 12-1

```
2F00  31 00 3C   LD SP,3C00H   ;SET THE STACK POINTER TO 3C00H
2F03  F5          PUSH AF       ;AF REGISTERS TO STACK
2F04  C5          PUSH BC       ;BC REGISTERS TO STACK
2F05  D5          PUSH DE       ;DE REGISTERS TO STACK
2F06  E5          PUSH HL       ;HL REGISTERS TO STACK
2F07  DD E5       PUSH IX       ;IX REGISTER TO STACK
2F09  FD E5       PUSH IY       ;IY REGISTER TO STACK
2F0B  08          EX AF,AF'     ;A'F' REGISTERS TO A AND F
2F0C  D9          EXX           ;MORE ALTERNATE REGISTERS
2F0D  F5          PUSH AF       ;A'F' REGISTERS TO STACK
2F0E  C5          PUSH BC       ;B'C' REGISTERS TO STACK
2F0F  D5          PUSH DE       ;D'E' REGISTERS TO STACK
2F10  E5          PUSH HL       ;H'L' REGISTERS TO STACK
2F11  E1          POP HL        ;LOAD HL REGISTERS FROM STACK
2F12  D1          POP DE        ;LOAD DE REGISTERS FROM STACK
2F13  C1          POP BC        ;LOAD BC REGISTERS FROM STACK
2F14  F1          POP AF        ;LOAD AF REGISTERS FROM STACK
2F15  08          EX AF,AF'     ;RESTORE ORIGINAL A'F'
2F16  D9          EXX           ;RESTORE OTHER ALTERNATE REGISTERS
2F17  FD E1       POP IY        ;RESTORE IY FROM STACK
2F19  DD E1       POP IX        ;RESTORE IX FROM STACK
2F1B  E1          POP HL        ;RESTORE HL REGISTERS FROM STACK
2F1C  D1          POP DE        ;RESTORE DE REGISTERS FROM STACK
2F1D  C1          POP BC        ;RESTORE BC REGISTERS FROM STACK
2F1E  F1          POP AF        ;RESTORE AF REGISTERS FROM STACK
```

working registers to the stack. In this case the AF register pair goes in first, and the content of the 16-bit IY register goes onto the stack last.

There are no instructions for directly transferring the contents of the alternate registers to the stack. So it is necessary to do a couple of register exchange operations—operations aimed at getting the contents of the alternate registers into the primary, where the information can be transferred to the stack.

After doing that, the program calls for four consecutive PUSH instructions that effectively move the contents of the alternate registers onto the stack. That completes the first part of the task.

The second half of the task begins with a sequence of four POP instructions. The information is popped off the stack beginning with loads to the HL register pair and ending with a load from the stack to the AF register pair. Note that the data are pulled from the stack in the opposite order from that in which they were pushed onto it originally.

The data that are transferred from the stack via those first four POP instructions really represent information from the alternate register pairs. So if things are to be restored to their original conditions, that information has to be exchanged to the alternate registers.

Finally, a sequence of six more POP instructions restores the original data in the primary registers. Again, the data are pulled off the stack in the opposite sequence from that in which they were placed onto the stack. First-in-last-out or last-in-first-out; it makes no difference how you regard the matter. The idea is to unstack the data and put them into their original places in the registers.

Program 12-1 is really just a demonstration program. It actually does nothing of any real use. Justifying the whole affair would call for using the primary registers for some other operations between the PUSH and POP phases of the job. Even then, there would be no need to PUSH the contents of the primary registers onto the stack because it would all be saved in the alternate registers area—all but the content of the IX and IY registers, anyway.

The next example illustrates a *real* application for the stack operations described thus far.

EXAMPLE 12-2

A Z-80 system is hardwired so that there is an 8-bit output port at address F000H. Write and assemble a program that outputs the content of the F register to that port. Initialize the stack pointer at FFFFH and begin the program at address 4C0D. See the results in Program 12-2.

PROGRAM 12-2 Z-80 LISTING FOR EXAMPLE 12-2

```
4C0D 31 FF FF  LD SP,FFFFH  ;SET STACK TO FFFFH
4C10 F5        PUSH AF      ;LOAD AF REGISTER PAIR TO STACK
4C11 C5        POP BC       ;ORIGINAL AF TO BC FROM STACK
4C12 79        LD A,C       ;ORIGINAL F TO A
4C13 32 00 F0  LD (F000H)   ;OUTPUT ORIGINAL F TO F000H
```

Notice first that the contents of the A and F registers are loaded to the stack, but then that same data are loaded from the stack to the BC register pair. There is no reason why the data load to the stack has to be unloaded to the originating register pair. In this case, loading the stack from the AF registers and then unloading the stack to the BC pair achieves a particular purpose—the content of the F register is put into a position where it can be directly manipulated. The POP instruction gets the original content of the F register into the C register; then a register transfer operation—LD A,C—gets it into the A register. (In effect, the F register has been transferred to the A register via a set of simple stack operations.) The final instruction finished the specified task by sending those data to the output port.

That is truly useful sequence of operations because there are no instructions for directly transferring the content of the F register to any place in memory or to an output port.

In fact, a number of difficult register exchange operations become quite simple through the stack operations. Suppose, for example, that you want to exchange the contents of the IX and IY registers. Once the stack pointer has been initialized, such an exchange can take place this way:

```
PUSH  IX
PUSH  IY
POP   IX
POP   IY
```

Study the sequence of instructions carefully, making certain that you understand how the resulting exchange between the two 16-bit registers is taking place.

Table 12-2 lists some other Z-80 stack instructions. They are described here in literal terms, but particular applications of them are left to later examples.

TABLE 12-2 OTHER STACK INSTRUCTIONS FOR THE Z-80

Source code	Object code	Notes
LD SP,(addr)	ED 7B byte byte	
LD SP,HL	F9	
LD SP,IX	DD F9	Transfer to or from the SP register
LD SP,IY	FD F9	
LD (addr),SP	ED 73 byte byte	
EX (SP),HL	E3	Exchange current *content of the*
EX (SP),IX	DD E3	*stack* with the register pair or 16-
EX (SP),IY	FD E3	bit register
ADD HL,SP	39	HL←HL+SP
ADD IX,SP	DD 39	IX←IX+SP
ADD IY,SP	FD 39	IY←IY+SP
ADC HL,SP	ED 7A	HL←HL+SP+Cs
SBC HL,SP	ED 72	HL←HL−SP−Cs
INC SP	33	SP←SP+1
DEC SP	3B	SP←SP −1

LD SP,(*addr*)	Indirectly load the stack pointer with data beginning at *addr*. This is an alternative technique for initializing or resetting the stack pointer. It is the stack pointer itself that is affected, not its contents.
LD SP,HL	Transfer the content of the HL pair to the stack pointer. This also resets the stack pointer. Convince yourself that this instruction is quite different from PUSH HL.
LD SP,IX	Set the stack pointer to the address contained in the IX register. This is something quite different from PUSH IX.
LD SP,IY	Set the stack pointer to the address contained in the IY register.
LD (*addr*),SP	Load the current address in the stack pointer to data memory location *addr*. This is simply the complement of the LD SP,(*addr*) instruction.
EX (SP),HL	Exchange the current content of the stack (not the content of the stack pointer itself) with the content of the HL register pair. In this case, it is the data in the stack that are exchanged. An equivalent set of instructions could take this form:

```
POP DE
PUSH HL
EX DE,HL
```

EX (SP),IX	The current top of stack is exchanged with the content of the IX register. This is similar in principle to EX (SP),HL.
EX (SP),IY	The current top of stack is exchanged with the content of the IY register.
ADD HL,SP	The 16-bit content of the SP register itself is summed with the current content of the HL register pair, and the result is placed into the HL pair. The SP register is not affected, nor is the content of the stack.
ADD IX,SP	The content of the SP register is summed with that of the IX register, and the result is placed into the IX register. The stack and SP register are not affected.
ADD IY,SP	The content of the SP register is summed with that of the IY register, and the result is placed into the IY register. The stack and stack pointer are not affected.
ADC HL,SP	This is the same as ADD HL,SP, but takes into account the status of the carry flag.
SBC HL,SP	SUBTRACT WITH BORROW the content of the SP register from that of the HL register, and place the result into the HL register pair.
INC SP	Increment the stack pointer. This instruction affects the SP register, but not the content of the stack.
DEC SP	Decrement the current address in the SP register.

The stack-oriented instructions in Table 12-2 must be used with great care. There is a good chance that an offhand application of them can completly ruin an otherwise good set of stack operations.

Exercises for Section 12-1

1. A particular program initializes the SP register with the instruction LD SP,3000H. If the first PUSH operation following that initilization step is PUSH BC, cite the stack addresses for the B and C registers.

2. At one point in a program, the following series of PUSH operations are executed in order to save the content of the registers involved:

```
PUSH  AF
PUSH  IX
PUSH  BC
```

What series of POP operations are required at a later time to restore those registers to their original content?

12-2 STACK INSTRUCTIONS FOR THE 8080A/8085

Table 12-3 lists all the stack instructions for the 8080A/8085 microprocessor, and Fig. 12-2 shows the internal registers that can be directly involved in those instructions.

In principle, the function of these instructions is so similar to that of the Z-80 stack instructions that there is little need to dwell on their details. Perhaps a brief description of each and a few specific examples are in order, however.

LXI SP,*addr* This is a 16-bit load immediate instruction that is most often used for setting the stack pointer early in the program. Its Z-80 counterpart is LD SP,*addr*.

SPHL This is a 16-bit register transfer instruction that loads the content of the HL register pair to the stack pointer. It is the stack pointer itself that is altered, not the content of the stack.

TABLE 12-3 STACK INSTRUCTIONS FOR THE 8080A/8085

Source code	Object code	Notes
LXI SP,*addr*	31 *byte byte*	SP←*addr*
SPHL	F9	SP←HL
XTHL	E3	(SP)⇌HL
PUSH PSW	F5	
PUSH B	C5	Store register pair to the stack
PUSH D	D5	
PUSH H	E5	
POP PSW	F1	
POP B	C1	Load register pair from the stack
POP D	D1	
POP H	E1	

Note: PSW denotes the A and F register pair.

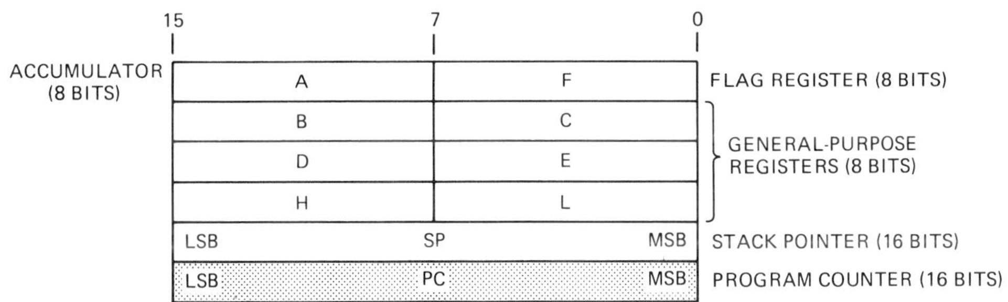

Figure 12-2 8080A/8085 registers directly involved in stack operations. Shaded registers are not involved.

XTHL	This is a 16-bit exchange operation that swaps the content of the HL register pair with the last two bytes of data loaded onto the stack. Here the content of the stack is altered, but the content of the stack pointer register is left unchanged.
PUSH *rp*	These instructions load two bytes of data from a register pair *rp* onto the stack. The function of these instructions are identical to the Z-80's PUSH instructions; the mnemonics call for some definition, however:

PSW	A and F registers (processor status word)
B	B and C registers
D	D and E registers
H	H and L registers

POP *rp*	These instructions unload two bytes from the top of the stack and place them into register pair *rp*. The function is identical to the POP instructions for the Z-80 system.

EXAMPLE 12-3

Write and assemble an 8080A/8085 program that does the following:

1. Initialize the stack pointer at 3C00H.
2. Save the content of the working registers in the stack.
3. Retrieve the original content of all working registers from the stack.

Begin the program listing at address 2F00H.

See the results in Program 12-3, and compare them with a similar operation for the Z-80 in Program 12-1.

First-in-last-out: that is the key to saving registers on the stack and restoring them at a later time. The programmer need not be constantly aware of the actual stack addressing, but he or she must keep track of the order in which the data are placed onto the stack.

One of the important applications of the stack instructions is to gain direct access to the F register. The idea is to get the content of the F register

```
2F00  31 00 3C   LXI SP,3C00H   ;INITIALIZE STACK AT 3C00H
2F03  F5         PUSH PSW       ;A AND F REGISTERS TO STACK
2F04  C5         PUSH B         ;B AND C REGISTERS TO STACK
2F05  D5         PUSH D         ;D AND E REGISTERS TO STACK
2F06  E5         PUSH H         ;H AND L REGISTERS TO STACK
2F07  E1         POP H          ;RESTORE HL FROM STACK
2F08  D1         POP D          ;RESTORE DE FROM STACK
2F09  C1         POP B          ;RESTORE BC FROM STACK
2F0A  F1         POP PSW        ;RESTORE A AND F FROM STACK
```

into a position where it can be dealt with directly and, perhaps, sent to an output port via the data bus. Try this sequence of instructions:

```
POP PSW   ;REGISTERS A AND F TO STACK
PUSH B    ;ORIGINAL A TO B, ORIGINAL F TO C
MOV A,C   ;ORIGINAL F CONTENTS TO REGISTER A
```

At the conclusion of that series of instructions, the original content of the F register is in the A register. From there, its bits can be tested, manipulated, and even sent to an output port for direct observation. The sequence assumes, of course, that the stack pointer has been set to some well-defined place in RAM.

Exercises for Section 12-2

1. Make up a chart showing the source and object codes for stack instructions that are common to both the Z-80 and 8080A/8085 microprocessors. Cite a literal definition for each of them.
2. Write and assemble an 8080A/8085 program that effectively exchanges the contents of the BC and DE register pairs. Use stack operations where possible, initialize the SP register at 4000H, and begin the listing at address 2000H.

12-3 STACK INSTRUCTIONS FOR THE 6502

The preceding discussions of stack operations for the Z-80 and 8080A/8085 systems assumes that the stack can be initialized anywhere in the systems' full range of memory addresses—anywhere between 0000H and FFFFH. That, indeed, is the case for those two devices; but not for the 6502.

In principle, the stack operations work the same way, but the fact that the 6502 has a smaller 8-bit SP register limits the range of stack locations. As far as the 6502 is concerned, the stack must be set somewhere in page-1 memory, between $0100 and $01FF.

As shown in Fig. 12-3, the SP register is an 8-bit register; but what is not shown is the fact that it is actually a 9-bit register that has its most-significant bit permanently set to logic 1. Any 8-bit number that a programmer might load into the SP register thus specifies an address in the range of $01SS, where *SS* is the byte the programmer enters into that register.

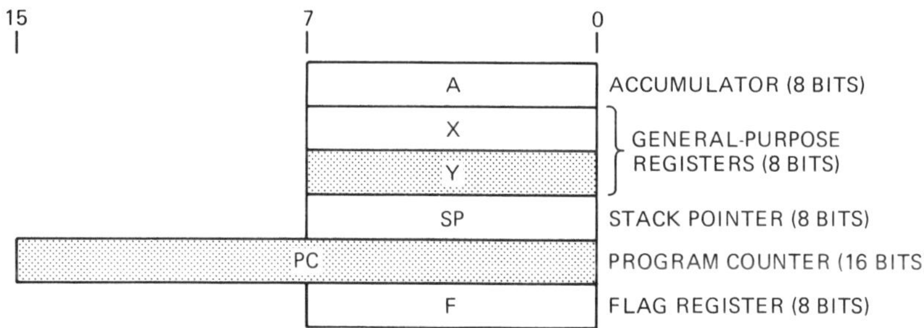

Figure 12-3 6502 registers directly involved in stack operations. Shaded registers are not involved.

Of course, this notion of limiting the stack addresses to page-1 memory limits the size of the stack to 256 bytes. In actual practice, however, that turns out to be plenty of room. Only the most lengthy and complex programs come close to using that much stack space.

Note: As far as the 6502 device is concerned:

1. Memory addresses \$0000 through \$00FF must be used for zero-page memory operations.
2. Memory addresses \$0100 through \$01FF must be used for the stack.

A programmer thus has some restrictions with regard to setting up the memory map for a 6502 system.

The stack operations for the 6502 differ from the others in another important respect: All stack operations are 8-bit operations. Whereas the Z-80 and 8080A/8085 both transfer 16-bit data to or from the stack, the 6502, with its lack of 16-bit working registers, transfers only 8-bit data between the stack and working registers. See the instructions in Table 12-4.

TABLE 12-4   STACK INSTRUCTIONS FOR THE 6502

Source code	Object code	Notes
TXS	9A	SP←X
TSX	BA	X←SP
PHA	48	Push A to stack
PHP	08	Push F to stack
PLA	68	Pop to A from stack
PLP	28	Pop to F from stack

TXS	Transfer the content of the X register to the stack pointer.
TSX	Transfer the content of the stack register to the X register.
PHA	Push the content of the A register onto the stack.
PHP	Push the content of the F register onto the stack.
PLA	Pop the data from the top of the stack into the A register.
PLP	Pop the data from the top of the stack into the F register.

Conspicuous by its absence is an instruction for doing a load immediate to the stack pointer. Such an operation is commonly used in other systems to initialize the stack before it can be used in the program. Initializing the stack pointer for the 6502 is a two-step process:

```
LDX  #F0   LOAD IMMEDIATE $F0 TO X
TXS        INITIALIZE STACK AT $F0
```

The stack is thus initialized via the X register—a load immediate to the X register, followed by a transfer of those data to the SP register.

In the example, the stack is effectively initialized at page-1 address $01F0, and the first byte of data that is pushed onto the stack will actually go to address $01EF. In that respect the 6502 is like the other devices; every new byte of data pushed onto the stack goes into an address location that is equal to SP-1.

When it comes to popping bytes of data from the stack, the first-in-last-out principle holds for the 6502. The following example first loads the contents of the A and F registers to the stack, and then restores them to their original register locations:

```
PHA   REGISTER A TO STACK
PHP   REGISTER F TO STACK
PLP   REGISTER F LOADED FROM STACK
PLA   REGISTER A LOADED FROM STACK
```

But what if you want to save the content of the Y register on the stack? See the following example.

EXAMPLE 12-4

Write and assemble a 6502 program that does the following:

1.   Initialize the stack at page-1 address $20.
2.   Save the contents of the A, X, Y, and F registers on the stack.
3.   Restore the original contents of the A, X, Y, and F registers from the stack.

Begin the listing at address $4000.
See the suggested listing in Program 12-4.

```
4000  A2 20   LDX  #$20    LOAD $20 TO X
4002  9A      TXS          SET STACK TO $20
4003  48      PHA          SAVE A ON THE STACK
4004  8A      TXA          MOVE X TO A
4005  48      PHA          SAVE ORIGINAL X ON THE STACK
4006  98      TYA          MOVE Y TO A
4007  48      PHA          SAVE ORIGINAL Y ON THE STACK
4008  08      PHP          SAVE F ON THE STACK
4009  28      PLP          ORIGINAL F TO F FROM THE STACK
400A  68      PLA          ORIGINAL Y TO A FROM THE STACK
400B  A8      TAY          ORIGINAL Y FROM A TO Y
400C  68      PLA          ORIGINAL X TO A FROM THE STACK
400D  AA      TAX          ORIGINAL X FROM A TO X
400E  68      PLA          ORIGINAL A FROM STACK TO A
```

Exercises for Section 12-3

1. What is the allowable range of initial stack pointer addresses for the Z-80? 8080A/8085? 6502?

2. Write and assemble a 6502 program that does the following:

   a. Initialize the stack pointer to page-1 memory address $4F.

   b. Use a series of stack instructions to get the content of the F register to the A register.

   c. Output the original content of the F register to an output port at address $2000.

Begin the listing at address $7000.

12-4 STACK INSTRUCTIONS FOR THE 6800

Stack instructions for the 6800 blend features of the Z-80 and 6502. Like the Z-80 and 8080A/8085 system, for instance, the 6800 uses a 16-bit stack, and that means that the programmer is free to set the stack anywhere in the system's usable memory range—between $0000 and $FFFF.

But like the 6502 system, only 8-bit data are transferred between the stack and working registers.

See the relevant registers in Fig. 12-4 and the complete stack instruction listing in Table 12-5.

The LDS group of stack instructions load the SP register with a 2-byte number—the desired initial stack address. Of the four LDS instructions, LDS #addr is probably the most-used one; it does a load immediate to the stack pointer register, and is equivalent to the Z-80's LD SP,*addr* and the 8080A/8085's LXI SP, *addr*.

The remaining LDS instructions pull the stack address from two successive data memory locations that are addressed in an indirect fashion.

The three STS instructions are used for saving the current content of the SP register, and all three use indirect addressing.

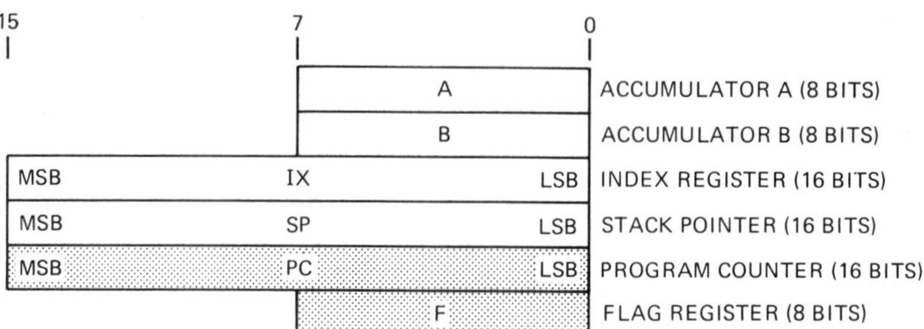

Figure 12-4 6800 registers directly involved in stack operations. Shaded registers are not involved.

TABLE 12-5 STACK INSTRUCTIONS FOR THE 6800

Source code	Object code	Notes
LDS #*addr*	8E *byte byte*	Load immediate
LDS *addr*$_0$	9E *byte*	Zero-page indirect
LDS *addr*	BE *byte byte*	Absolute indirect
LDS *disp*,X	AE *byte*	Indexed indirect
STS *addr*$_0$	9F *byte*	Zero-page indirect
STS *addr*	BF *byte byte*	Absolute indirect
STS *disp*,X	AF *byte*	Indexed indirect
TXS	30	SP←X
TSX	35	X←SP
DES	34	SP←SP−1
INS	31	SP←SP+1
PSHA	36	A to top of stack
PSHB	37	B to top of stack
PULA	32	Load A from top of stack
PULB	33	Load B from top of stack

TXS and TSX transfer 16-bit data between the SP and IX registers, while DES and INS decrement and increment the content of the SP register.

PSHA and PSHB are the 6800's PUSH instructions. They push the content of the A and B registers onto the top of the stack. PSHA is equivalent to the 6502's PHA instruction—one that pushes the 8-bit content of the A register onto the stack. PSHB does the same sort of job, but it is the content of the B register that is saved on the stack.

PULA and PULB effectively "pull" a byte of data from the top of the stack and place it into the A or B register. They are the 6800's version of POP instructions.

The following listing initializes the SP register at $4200, pushes the contents of the A and B accumulators onto the stack, and then retrieves the data, placing them into their original registers:

```
7000 8E 42 00   LDS #$4200   SET STACK TO $4200
7003 36         PSHA         A TO STACK
7004 37         PSHB         B TO STACK
7005 33         PULB         LOAD B FROM STACK
7006 32         PULA         LOAD A FROM STACK
```

Exercises for Section 12-4

1. Of the four microprocessor devices described in this chapter, which two use strictly 8-bit stack operations? 16-bit stack operations?

2. Write and assemble a 6800 program that uses stack operations to exchange the contents of the A and B accumulators. Begin the listing at address $3C00 and initialize the stack at $4000.

13

Subroutines, CALL and RETURN Instructions

Generally speaking, a program *routine* is a sequence of instructions that carry out at least one well-defined task. Most of the examples and exercises in the preceding chapters have been relatively simple program routines.

A *subroutine* can be defined in the same way, but it deserves a different name because it is a separate programming entity that is used only when it is called on by another program routine.

A program that uses subroutines has a *mainline* routine. The mainline routine controls the overall flow of events, calling on subroutines whenever they are needed.

Suppose, for example, that a microprocessor system is hardwired with 8-bit data inputs at hexadecimal addresses 4000, 4001, 4002, and 4003. There is a single output port at hexadecimal address F000. The task is to *poll* those inputs one at a time, testing them to see whether or not the data are 80 hexadecimal or greater. The polling operation runs continuously until it finds a port generating a data byte greater than hexadecimal 80. At that time, the system outputs hexadecimal FF to the output port, and then resumes the polling operation.

The instruction sequence could take this form:

```
START    POINT TO INPUT PORT 4000H
         LOAD DATA FROM 4000H TO THE ACCUMULATOR
         COMPARE WITH 80H
         IF NOT EQUAL OR GREATER, THEN JUMP TO NEXT1
         ELSE OUTPUT FFH TO PORT F000H
NEXT1    POINT TO INPUT PORT 4001H
         LOAD DATA FROM 4001H TO THE ACCUMULATOR
         COMPARE WITH 80H
         IF NOT EQUAL OR  GREATER, THEN JUMP TO NEXT2
         ELSE OUTPUT FFH TO PORT F000H
```

```
NEXT2   POINT TO INPUT PORT 4002H
        LOAD DATA FROM 4002H TO THE ACCUMULATOR
        COMPARE WITH 80H
        IF NOT EQUAL OR GREATER, THEN JUMP TO NEXT3
        ELSE OUTPUT FFH TO PORT 4002H
NEXT3   POINT TO INPUT PORT 4003H
        LOAD DATA FROM 4003H TO THE ACCUMULATOR
        COMPARE WITH 80H
        IF NOT EQUAL OR GREATER, THEN JUMP TO START
        ELSE OUTPUT FFH TO PORT 4003H
        JUMP TO START
```

That is a monotonous routine, to say the least; but it will do the polling task set before it.

The program is easily divided into four separate phases; and the only difference between them is the input port address. It is that sort of situation that leads quite nicely to the use of at least one subroutine:

```
POLL    SET THE STACK POINTER
START   POINT TO INPUT PORT 4000H
        CALL DOIT
        POINT TO INPUT PORT 4001H
        CALL DOIT
        POINT TO INPUT PORT 4002H
        CALL DOIT
        POINT TO INPUT PORT 4003H
        CALL DOIT
        JUMP TO START
DOIT    LOAD DATA FROM INPUT PORT TO THE ACCUMULATOR
        COMPARE WITH 80H
        IF NOT EQUAL OR GREATER, THEN RETURN
        ELSE OUTPUT FFH TO PORT F000H
        RETURN
```

That version will carry out exactly the same task. In this case, the mainline routine includes all the instructions from label POLL down to, but not including, DOIT. DOIT is the program's subroutine.

So the program begins by setting the stack pointer to some well-defined address in memory. There is more to be said about that operation later in this discussion. Actual program operations begin at label START.

The first polling step is to indicate that input port 4000H is the one to be tested. Immediately after that, there is an instruction CALL DOIT. That CALL instruction causes program operations to break out of the mainline routine and jump down to the sequence of operations labeled DOIT.

Now, DOIT fetches the data from the indicated input port address, compares them with 80H, and then takes some action that depends on whether or not the data fetched from the current input port are greater than or equal to 80H. If the data happen to be less than 80H, the instruction specifies a RETURN operation. What does RETURN mean?

A RETURN instruction appears only in a subroutine, and it tells the system to return to the routine that called the subroutine in the first place. To where do operations return? They return to the instruction immediately following the CALL instruction responsible for executing the subroutine operations.

So if the data fetched from the current input port are less than 80H, the system breaks away from the subroutine and returns to the mainline routine. In the present case, operations return to the point in the mainline that specifies POINT TO INPUT PORT 4001H.

Let us go through that calling sequence again, beginning with the mainline instruction labeled START. That instruction points to input port address 4000H, and the next one calls the DOIT subroutine.

As described before, DOIT fetches the data byte from the current input port address and compares it with 80H. This time, however, assume that the byte is, indeed, greater than or equal to 80H. In that case, the system executes the OUTPUT FFH TO PORT F000H routine, and then does an unconditional RETURN. RETURN to where? RETURN to the instruction immediately following the original CALL instruction—to POINT TO INPUT PORT 4001H.

Subroutine DOIT is CALLed four different times in the mainline sequence. Each time the DOIT is executed, program operations return to the instruction immediately following the CALL instruction that called it.

The example illustrates one of the most compelling reasons for using a subroutine: A series of instructions that are to be repeated a number of times through the course of a program sequence can be written just one time as a subroutine. The mainline program can then call that subroutine whenever the sequence is required.

So a subroutine is initiated by a CALL instruction, and the subroutine must be concluded with a RETURN instruction. The CALL instruction gets the subroutine running, and the RETURN instruction concludes the subroutine operations and returns matters to the mainline.

But how does the microprocessor system know where it is to return at the conclusion of a subroutine operation? The foregoing discussion simply states that operations return to the instruction immediately following the CALL instruction that initiated the subroutine sequence in the first place. But how does the microprocessor know where that instruction is?

Whenever the microprocessor encounters a CALL instruction during the course of executing a program, two important events take place automatically. First, the address of the next instruction, currently residing in the program counter register, is transferred to the system's stack. Immediately after reading the CALL instruction, the program counter is pointing to the next instruction—that is the address loaded to the stack. Second, the starting address of the CALLed subroutine is loaded directly into the program counter; and that is how the system knows where it is to begin running the subroutine instructions.

Now the system is executing the subroutine instructions. Eventually, it comes across a RETURN instruction. At that moment, the top two bytes on the stack are loaded into the program counter. What are those two bytes? Recall that the CALL instruction loads the address of the next instruction onto the stack. Thus those two bytes loaded into the program counter represent the address of the instruction immediately following the original CALL instruction. That is how the system knows where it is to RETURN. That is why the last example begins with an instruction that sets the stack pointer.

Although a program might not use any outright stack operations of the kind described in Chapter 12, the system will use the stack if that program happens to contain any CALL instructions. If the stack is not properly initialized prior to doing a CALL instruction, there is a good chance that the RETURN address will be loaded into some unknown part of memory where it will write over valuable program data or instructions.

Summarizing the most important features of the discussion to this point:

1. A CALL instruction
    a. Saves the address of the next instruction on the stack
    b. Loads the called subroutine's starting address into the PC register
    c. Initiates execution of the subroutine it CALLs

2. A RETURN instruction
    a. Loads the return address saved on the stack into the PC register
    b. Causes execution of the mainline routine to resume at the instruction immediately following the CALL instruction

A program can employ any number of subroutines. Those subroutines can be written anywhere in program memory, and they can be butted up against their calling routines or separated by any amount of unused memory locations. The subroutines need not be written into program memory in any particular sequence, but the programmer must keep track of their starting addresses. With regard to that last point, CALL instructions all take the general form CALL addr, where *addr* is the starting address of the subroutine to be executed.

RETURN instructions residing in the subroutines do not have addresses directly associated with them. The RETURN address is saved on the stack, and the programmer does not have to worry about it at all. The matter of saving the RETURN address is handled in an automatic fashion by the microprocessor itself. Just be sure that the stack pointer is properly initialized so that those automatically saved RETURN addresses are not lost or do not interfere with the normal course of programming events.

It is possible, and often quite desirable to *nest* subroutines—write subroutines that call other subroutines. Each time a subroutine CALLs another subroutine, the stack grows by two more bytes, keeping track of the sequence of RETURN addresses necessary for moving, in reverse order, out of the nested subroutine operations. No matter how "deep" subroutines are nested, the stack keeps track of the return path. All the programmer must do is make certain that each CALL instruction has a RETURN associated with it.

Table 13-1 lists the CALL and RETURN instructions for the Z-80 system. Although it might appear to be a rather imposing list of instructions at first glance, a close inspection shows that they are all simple variations of the same ideas.

There are two unconditional subroutine instructions: CALL *addr* and RET. CALL addr calls a subroutine that begins at program memory address *addr* and, of course, saves the RETURN address on the stack. RET is the unconditional RETURN instruction that must be used in the subroutine to return operations back to the calling routine.

The remaining CALL instructions in the list are conditional CALLs. The subroutine beginning at address *addr* is CALLed only if the designated flag conditions are satisfied. Instructions such as CALL Z,2234H will call a subroutine that starts at program address 2234H only if the result of the previous operation is zero. Otherwise, that CALL instruction is ignored.

The conditional RETURN instructions work the same way, RETurning to the calling routine only if the designated results of some operations are satisfied.

TABLE 13-1 SUBROUTINE CALL AND RETURN INSTRUCTIONS
FOR THE Z-80

Source code	Object code	Notes
CALL *addr*	CD *byte byte*	CALL unconditionally
CALL Z,*addr*	CC *byte byte*	CALL IF ZERO
CALL NZ,*addr*	C4 *byte byte*	CALL IF NOT ZERO
CALL C,*addr*	DC *byte byte*	CALL IF CARRY
CALL NC,*addr*	D4 *byte byte*	CALL IF NO CARRY
CALL P,*addr*	F4 *byte byte*	CALL IF POSITIVE
CALL M,*addr*	FC *byte byte*	CALL IF NEGATIVE
CALL PE,*addr*	EC *byte byte*	CALL IF EVEN PARITY or OVERFLOW
CALL PO,*addr*	E4 *byte byte*	CALL IF ODD PARITY or NO OVERFLOW
RET	C9	RETURN unconditionally
RET Z	C8	RETURN IF ZERO
RET NZ	C0	RETURN IF NOT ZERO
RET C	D8	RETURN IF CARRY
RET NC	D0	RETURN IF NO CARRY
RET P	F0	RETURN IF POSITIVE
RET M	F8	RETURN IF NEGATIVE
RET PE	E8	RETURN IF EVEN PARITY or OVERFLOW
RET PO	E0	RETURN IF ODD PARITY or NO OVERFLOW

Write and assemble a Z-80 program that uses a subroutine to do the following task:

1. Make the accumulator count decimal integer values from 0 through 9, sending each count to an output port at address 4000H.

2. Do the same counting and outputting operations for output addresses 4020H, 4040H, and 4080H.

3. Return to step 1.

Begin the mainline program at program address 7000H, and initialize the stack at F000H.

See the suggested listing in Program 13-1.

The mainline program begins at address 7000H by initializing the stack pointer to F000H. Although the routine does not use any overt stack operations, remember that the CALL instructions do use the stack for saving their respective RETURN addresses.

The primary task of the mainline program, in this particular instance, is to set up the output port addresses and keep the overall flow of events in the proper order. CALL DOIT follows each of the four port-addressing instructions, and the mainline concludes with JR START—jump relative to the instruction labeled START. The mainline routine thus loops indefinitely. It is necessary to initialize the stack just at the outset, so that instruction is not included in the loop.

The sequence of instructions beginning with DOIT represent the program's only subroutine. It first clears the accumulator to zero, outputs that byte to the address indicated by the HL register pair (an address that is always set by the mainline prior to calling DOIT), and then the subroutine increments the byte in the accumulator.

A COMPARE instruction tests the current byte in the accumulator,

PROGRAM 13-1 Z-80 LISTING FOR EXAMPLE 13-1

```
7000 31 00 F0           LD SP,F000H   ;SET THE STACK POINTER
7003 21 00 40   START   LD HL,4000H   ;POINT TO PORT 4000H
7006 CD 20 70           CALL DOIT     ;DO COUNTING ROUTINE
7009 21 20 40           LD HL,4020H   ;POINT TO PORT 4020H
700C CD 20 70           CALL DOIT     ;DO COUNTING ROUTINE
700F 21 40 40           LD HL,4040H   ;POINT TO PORT 4040H
7012 CD 20 70           CALL DOIT     ;DO COUNTING ROUTINE
7015 21 80 40           LD HL,4080H   ;POINT TO PORT 4080H
7018 CD 20 70           CALL DOIT     ;DO COUNTING ROUTINE
701B 18 E6              JR  START     ;AND START ALL OVER

7020 AF         DOIT    XOR A         ;ZERO THE ACCUMULATOR
7021 77         SEND    LD (HL),A     ;OUTPUT THE COUNT
7022 3C                 INC  A        ;INCREMENT THE COUNT
7023 FE 0A              CP  0AH       ;IS IT 10?
7025 20 FA              JR  NZ,SEND   ;IF NOT, SEND AGAIN
7027 C9                 RET           ;ELSE RETURN TO MAINLINE
```

determining whether or not it is equal to decimal 10. (Actually, the COMPARE instruction merely sets the relevant flag bits, and the subsequent relative jump instruction determines the proper course of action.)

If the accumulator has not yet reached the count of decimal 10, the subroutine operation loops back up to SEND, and the new byte is sent out to the output port.

When the byte in the accumulator finally reaches a value of decimal 10, the JR NZ,SEND instruction is no longer satisfied, and operations default to the final instruction in the subroutine: RET. That instruction returns operations to the mainline program—to the instruction immediately following the one that CALLed the subroutine in the first place.

Incidentally, the stack never contains more than a single RETURN address in this case. The RETURN address is placed onto the top of the stack as one of the mainline CALL instructions is executed. The corresponding RETURN instruction unstacks that address, however, leaving the stack pointer in its initial position.

The next example illustrates an application of some conditional RETURN instructions and nested subroutines. It also shows how time delays can be created by setting a register or register pair to some value, and then decrementing that value until it is equal to zero.

EXAMPLE 13-2

Write and assemble a Z-80 program that does the following:

1. Point to an output port at address 4000H.
2. Send BCD numbers 0 through 9 to the port in succession, inserting a time delay of approximately 3 seconds between each count.
3. Repeat step 2 for output ports at addresses 4020H, 4040H, and 4080H.
4. Return to step 1 to repeat the sequence indefinitely.

See the three flowcharts in Fig. 13-1. The flowchart for the mainline program, Fig. 13-1a, sets up the output port addresses and CALLs a routine designated COUNT WITH DELAY. The counting routine appears in the flowchart in Fig. 13-1b; aside from generating BCD numbers 0 through 9 and outputting them to the specified port address, it calls a TIME DELAY subroutine. The time delay is executed by the flowchart in Fig. 13-1c, counting down the content of a register pair to generate the time delay.

Begin the listing at program address 7000H, and set the stack pointer at F000H.

Referring to the suggested listing in Program 13-2, the mainline program begins with the instruction labeled MAIN. The BCD counting routine starts at instruction OPUT, and the time delay subroutine begins with the instruction labeled TDLY. The two subroutines, OPUT and TDLY, begin at program addresses 701DH and 7028H, respectively.

For the most part, the mainline program is identical to the one generated for a similar task in Example 13-1 (see the listing in Program 13-1). In this case, however, it calls the subroutine located at address 701DH instead

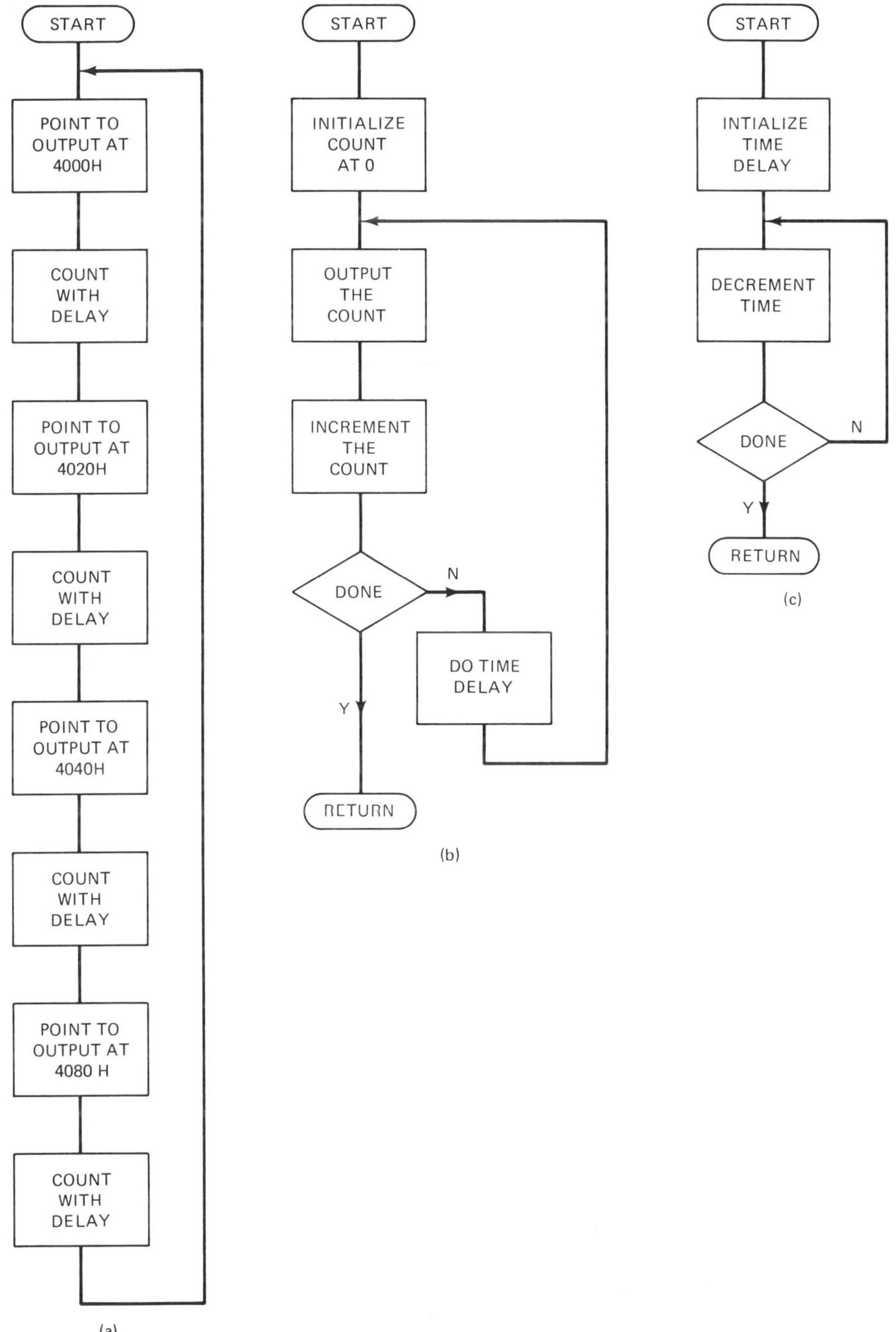

Figure 13-1 Flowcharts for the Z-80 program in Example 13-2. (a) Mainline routine. (b) Counting subroutine. (c) Time delay subroutine.

```
7000 31 00 FO  MAIN    LD SP,F000H    ;INITIALIZE THE STACK
7003 21 00 40  START   LD HL,4000H    ;POINT TO OUTPUT 4000H
7006 CD 1D 70          CALL OPUT      ;CALL OUTPUT ROUTINE
7009 21 20 40          LD HL,4020H    ;POINT TO OUTPUT 4020H
700C CD 1D 70          CALL OPUT      ;CALL OUTPUT ROUTINE
700F 21 40 40          LD HL,4040H    ;POINT TO OUTPUT 4040H
7012 CD 1D 70          CALL OPUT      ;CALL OUTPUT ROUTINE
7015 21 80 40          LD HL,4080H    ;POINT TO OUTPUT 4080H
7018 CD 1D 70          CALL OPUT      ;CALL OUTPUT ROUTINE
701B 18 E6            JR START       ;AND START ALL OVER
                      ;BEGINNING OF COUNT WITH DELAY SUBROUTINE
701D AF        OPUT    XOR A          ;ZERO THE ACCUMULATOR
701E 77        SEND    LD(HL),A       ;OUTPUT THE COUNT
701F 3C                INC A          ;INCREMENT THE COUNT
7020 FE 0A             CP 0AH         ;IS IT 10?
7022 C8                RET Z          ;IF SO, RETURN TO MAINLINE
7023 CD 28 70          CALL TDLY      ;ELSE CALL TIME DELAY ROUTINE
7026 18 F6             JR SEND        ;AND SEND AGAIN
                      ;BEGINNING OF TIME DELAY SUBROUTINE
7028 01 FF FF  TDLY    LD BC,0FFFFH   ;INITIALIZE DELAY AT FFFFH
702B 79        CPR     LD A,C         ;LSB OF TIME TO A
702C B0                OR B           ;OR WITH MSB OF TIME
702D C8                RET Z          ;IF ZERO, RETURN TO OPUT
702E 0B                DEC BC         ;ELSE DECREMENT TIME
702F 18 FA             JR CPR         ;AND CHECK AGAIN
```

of 7020H. This particular listing leaves no unused program memory locations between the end of the mainline and the beginning of the subroutine that follows it.

The OPUT subroutine is much like the DOIT subroutine in Example 13-1, but here it calls the time delay subroutine with a CALL TDLY.

The time delay subroutine, beginning at program address 7028H, does its job by decrementing the BC register pair from FFFFH down to zero. (Note that the source listing shows 0FFFFH instead of FFFFH. The leading zero is sometimes required when specifying hexadecimal numbers that begin with alphabetical characters: A, B, C, D, E, or F. The leading zero, when used in the source listing, never appears in the object-code version, though.)

If the Z-80's master clock oscillator is running at about 2 MHz, it will take some time on the order of 2 seconds to count down the BC register pair from FFFFH to zero. Other clock frequencies will cause a different amount of time delay. If the clock is running at 4 MHz, for example, the same counting routine will yield a delay on the order of 1 second; getting back up to a 2-second delay in that case is a matter of counting down two register pairs instead of just 1.

Since the Z-80's DEC BC instruction does not affect the Z flag bit, it is necessary to check the registers individually for the 0000H condition. That is done with the LD A,C and OR B sequence. If, indeed, the BC count has reached zero, that sequence of operations will set the Z flag bit; otherwise, the Z flag will remain cleared.

The RET Z instruction in the time delay subroutine returns operations to the OPUT subroutine whenever the BC count reaches zero.

The RET Z instruction in the OPUT subroutine, at address 7022H, returns operations to the mainline routine when the BCD counting operation is done.

The mainline routine thus CALLs the OPUT subroutine, and the OPUT subroutine, in turn, calls the TDLY subroutine when it is needed. That is an example of nested subroutines—they are nested "two deep" in this case.

Exercises for Section 13-1

1. What sort of instruction in a routine is responsible for breaking away from that routine and going to a subroutine?
2. What sort of instruction is necessary for breaking out of a subroutine and going back to the routine that called it in the first place?
3. Why is it necessary to set the stack pointer before doing any operations related to subroutines?
4. How does a microprocessor know where to return from the end of a subroutine operation?
5. How does a microprocessor know where it is supposed to go when a subroutine is called?

13-2 CALL AND RETURN INSTRUCTIONS FOR THE 8080A/8085

The CALL and RETURN instructions for the 8080A/8085 are virtually identical to those for the Z-80 system. Compare Tables 13-1 and 13-2. The only

TABLE 13-2 SUBROUTINE CALL AND RETURN INSTRUCTIONS FOR THE 8080A/8085

Source code	Object code	Notes
CALL *addr*	CD *byte byte*	CALL unconditionally
CZ *addr*	CC *byte byte*	CALL IF ZERO
CNZ *addr*	C4 *byte byte*	CALL IF NOT ZERO
CC *addr*	DC *byte byte*	CALL IF CARRY
CNC *addr*	D4 *byte byte*	CALL IF NO CARRY
CP *addr*	F4 *byte byte*	CALL IF POSITIVE
CM *addr*	FC *byte byte*	CALL IF NEGATIVE
CPE *addr*	EC *byte byte*	CALL IF EVEN PARITY
CPO *addr*	E4 *byte byte*	CALL IF ODD PARITY
RET	C9	RETURN unconditionally
RZ	C8	RETURN IF ZERO
RNZ	C0	RETURN IF NOT ZERO
RC	D8	RETURN IF CARRY
RNC	D0	RETURN IF NO CARRY
RP	F0	RETURN IF POSITIVE
RM	F8	RETURN IF NEGATIVE
RPE	E8	RETURN IF EVEN PARITY
RPO	E0	RETURN IF ODD PARITY

differences worthy of any special note are the source-code mnemonics. The operating characteristics and object codes are identical.

EXAMPLE 13-3

Rewrite and assemble the program for the task in Example 13-1 to conform to 8080A/8085 methods and nomenclature. See the result in Program 13-3.

See if you can account for all the differences between Programs 13-1 and 13-3. Note that none of the differences has anything to do with the CALL and RETURN instructions.

PROGRAM 13-3 8080A/8085 LISTING FOR EXAMPLE 13-3

```
7000 31 00 F0           LXI  SP,F000H   ;SET THE STACK POINTER
7003 21 00 40   START   LXI  H,4000H    ;POINT TO PORT 4000H
7006 CD 20 70           CALL DOIT       ;DO COUNTING ROUTINE
7009 21 20 40           LXI  H,4020H    ;POINT TO PORT 4020H
700C CD 20 70           CALL DOIT       ;DO COUNTING ROUTINE
700F 21 40 40           LXI  H,4040H    ;POINT TO PORT 4040H
7012 CD 20 70           CALL DOIT       ;DO COUNTING ROUTINE
7015 21 80 40           LXI  H,4080H    ;POINT TO PORT 4080H
7018 CD 20 70           CALL DOIT       ;DO COUNTING ROUTINE
701B C3 03 70           JMP  START      ;AND START ALL OVER

7020 AF         DOIT    XRA  A          ;ZERO THE ACCUMULATOR
7021 77         SEND    MOV  M,A        ;OUTPUT THE COUNT
7022 3C                 INR  A          ;INCREMENT THE COUNT
7023 FE 0A              CPI  0AH        ;IS IT 10?
7025 C2 21 70           JNZ  SEND       ;IF NOT, SEND AGAIN
7028 C9                 RET             ;ELSE RETURN TO MAINLINE
```

Exercise for Section 13-2

1. Rewrite the program for Example 13-2 to conform to 8080A/8085 procedures and nomenclature.

13-3 CALL AND RETURN INSTRUCTIONS FOR THE 6502

As shown in Table 13-3, the 6502 has the shortest possible listing of instructions for CALL and RETURN operations. What is missing is any form of conditional instructions. As demonstrated in this section, however, anything that can be done with a larger instruction set can be done with this very small one.

TABLE 13-3 SUBROUTINE CALL AND RETURN INSTRUCTIONS FOR THE 6502

Source code	Object code	Notes
JSR *addr*	20 *byte byte*	CALL unconditionally
RTS	60	RETURN unconditionally

The 6502's JSR addr instruction would be called a CALL instruction in the worlds of the Z-80 and 8080A/8085. Literally it means: *J*ump to address *addr* and *S*ave the *R*eturn address (on the stack). That nomenclature is perhaps more descriptive of what happens than *CALL* is.

RTS is an unconditional RETURN instruction, and it literally means: *R*e*T*urn from *S*ubroutine.

Table 13-4 shows how it is possible to get around the fact that the 6502

TABLE 13-4 6502 EQUIVALENT INSTRUCTIONS FOR THE Z-80's CONDITIONAL CALL AND RETURN INSTRUCTIONS

Z-80 instruction	6502 equivalent	Literal meaning
CALL Z,*addr*	BNE *disp* JSR *addr*	BRANCH IF NOT ZERO ELSE CALL SUBROUTINE
CALL NZ,*addr*	BEQ *disp* JSR *addr*	BRANCH IF ZERO ELSE CALL SUBROUTINE
CALL C,*addr*	BCC *disp* JSR *addr*	BRANCH IF CARRY IS CLEAR ELSE CALL SUBROUTINE
CALL NC,*addr*	BCS *disp* JSR *addr*	BRANCH IF CARRY IS SET ELSE CALL SUBROUTINE
CALL P,*addr*	BMI *disp* JSR *addr*	BRANCH IF NEGATIVE ELSE CALL SUBROUTINE
CALL M,*addr*	BPL *disp* JSR *addr*	BRANCH IF POSITIVE ELSE CALL SUBROUTINE
CALL PE,*addr*	BVC *disp* JSR *addr*	BRANCH IF NO OVERFLOW ELSE CALL SUBROUTINE
CALL PO,*addr*	BVS *disp* JSR *addr*	BRANCH IF OVERFLOW ELSE CALL SUBROUTINE
RET Z	BNE *disp* RTS	BRANCH IF NOT ZERO ELSE RETURN
RET NZ	BEQ *disp* RTS	BRANCH IF ZERO ELSE RETURN
RET C	BCC *disp* RTS	BRANCH IF CARRY IS CLEAR ELSE RETURN
RET NC	BCS *disp* RTS	BRANCH IF CARRY IS SET ELSE RETURN
RET P	BMI *disp* RTS	BRANCH IF NEGATIVE ELSE RETURN
RET M	BPL *disp* RTS	BRANCH IF POSITIVE ELSE RETURN
RET PE	BVC *disp* RTS	BRANCH IF NO OVERFLOW ELSE RETURN
RET PO	BVS *disp* RTS	BRANCH IF OVERFLOW ELSE RETURN

has no conditional CALL or RETURN instructions. Using the Z-80's conditional CALLs and RETURNs as models, the table shows how each can be implemented with the 6502. The general idea is to precede the unconditional JSR or RTS instruction with a conditional branch instruction of the type opposite that shown for the Z-80.

Suppose that a programming situation calls for going to a subroutine only if the result of a previous operation is zero. Using the Z-80 system, the appropriate instruction would be *CALL Z,addr*, where *addr* is the starting address, or *entry point*, of the subroutine. Doing the same thing with the 6502 means avoiding the JSR instruction if the result of the previous operation is *not zero*; that is the purpose of the BNE disp instruction: It does not allow the subroutine to be called as long as the result of the previous operation is not zero. But if the result *is* zero, the BNE instruction is ignored, and the system executes the unconditional JSR. In short, the 6502 goes to the subroutine only if the result of the previous operation is zero; and that situation mimics the action of the Z-80's CALL Z instruction.

Study the table carefully, convincing yourself that each of the two-instruction sequences for the 6502 do, indeed, mimic the action of their Z-80 counterparts.

EXAMPLE 13-4

Write and assemble a 6502 version of the program described in Example 13-2. Begin the program at the same program address, but initialize the stack pointer at $F0.

See the suggested listing in Program 13-4, and compare it with the Z-80 version in Program 13-2.

The mainline routine begins at label MAIN, the outputting subroutine begins at label OPUT, and the time delay subroutine begins at TDLY. More than anything else, the differences between this listing and the Z-80 version are brought about by the fact that the 6502 has fewer working registers. Then, too, it is important to deal with the fact that the 6502 has no 16-bit working registers.

So the mainline program begins by initializing the stack at page-1 address $F0. Then the instruction sequence beginning at START sets the LSB of the output address into the Y register and calls the OPUT subroutine. The philosophy in this case is the same one used for the Z-80 version of the task.

The OPUT subroutine begins by setting the X register to zero, and then the instruction at SEND outputs the content of the X register to an address determined by $4000 plus the current content of the Y register. If the Y register happens to be set to $40 at the moment, the content of the X register goes to output port $4040.

After outputting the number from the X register, the routine increments the value in the X register and compares it with the hexadecimal version of decimal 10. The next two instructions then mimic the action of the Z-80's RET Z instruction. If, indeed, the X register has been incremented to 10, operations return to the mainline routine. Otherwise, the sequence of operations beginning at NEXT are executed.

The NEXT operations are responsible for saving the current content of the X and Y registers on the stack. This is absolutely necessary because the same two registers are needed for doing the 16-bit, countdown time delay operation under subroutine TDLY.

After the current contents of the X and Y registers are saved on the stack, JSR TDLY calls the time delay subroutine.

TDLY initializes the X and Y registers to $FF, decrements the Y register until it reaches zero, and then decrements the X register by one count. If, at that moment, the X register has not been decremented to zero, the system loops back up to SLSB, where the Y register is reset to $FF and counted down to zero again.

The looping operation under TDLY continues until both registers have been counted down to zero. At that moment, the RTS instruction carries the operation back to the OPUT instruction at address $702C.

That instruction begins a sequence of operations that restore the original contents of the X and Y registers from the stack. Those values, you should recall, represent the current number to be sent to the output and the index portion of the output port address.

The overall behavior of this program is identical to its Z-80 counterpart in Example 3-2. The 6502 can implement the program, however, only by using some indexed addressing for the output port and saving the current contents of the X and Y registers before using them in the time delay sequence.

Exercises for Section 13-3

1. Referring to Example 13-4 and Program 13-4:
   (a) Explain why it is necessary to specify a 1-byte initial stack address.
   (b) Explain why it is necessary to use two instructions for initializing the stack pointer. What are the instructions?
   (c) Explain why the program does not use the A register for generating the count to be sent to the output ports.
   (d) Draw up a detailed flowchart for the time delay subroutine.
2. Rewrite and assemble the program in Example 13-1 to conform to the 6502 system. Initialize the stack pointer at $FF.

13-4 CALL AND RETURN INSTRUCTIONS
FOR THE 6800

The small family of call and return instructions for the 6800 system is, in principle, quite similar to that of the 6502 system (Table 13-5). They have the same JSR *addr* and RTS instructions, but the 6800 has two additional subroutine-calling instructions:

JSR *indx*,X   Jump and save the return address (on the stack) to a program address found by summing the current content of the IX register with a 2's-complement index term, *indx*. This instruction is thus

```
7000  A2 F0        MAIN     LDX  #$F0
7002  9A                    TXS              SET STACK TO $F0
7003  A0 00        START    LDY  #$00        SET OUTPUT POINTER INDEX TO $00
7005  20 1A 70              JSR  OPUT        CALL OUTPUT ROUTINE
7008  A0 20                 LDY  #$20        SET OUTPUT POINTER INDEX TO $20
700A  20 1A 70              JSR  OPUT        CALL OUTPUT ROUTINE
700D  A0 40                 LDY  #$40        SET OUTPUT POINTER INDEX TO $40
700F  20 1A 70              JSR  OPUT        CALL OUTPUT ROUTINE
7012  A0 80                 LDY  #$80        SET OUTPUT POINTER INDEX TO $80
7014  20 1A 70              JSR  OPUT        CALL OUTPUT ROUTINE
7017  4C 03 70              JMP  START       AND START ALL OVER
701A  A2 00        OPUT     LDX  #$00        ZERO BCD COUNTER
701C  96 00 40     SEND     STX  $4000,Y     OUTPUT THE BCD COUNT
701F  E8                    INX              INCREMENT THE COUNT
7020  E0 0A                 CPX  #$0A        IS IT 10?
7022  D0 01                 BNE  NEXT        IF NOT, JUMP TO NEXT
7024  60                    RTS              IF SO, RETURN TO MAINLINE
7025  8A           NEXT     TXA              TRANSFER BCD COUNT TO A
7026  48                    PHA              SAVE IT ON THE STACK
7027  98                    TYA              TRANSFER POINTER INDEX TO A
7028  48                    PHA              SAVE IT ON THE STACK
7029  20 33 70              JSR  TDLY        AND DO TIME DELAY SUBROUTINE
702C  68                    PLA              FETCH POINTER INDEX FROM STACK
702D  A8                    TAY              TRANSFER IT TO Y
702E  68                    PLA              FETCH BCD COUNT FROM STACK
702F  AA                    TAX              TRANSFER IT TO X
7030  4C 1C 70              JMP  SEND        AND SEND AGAIN
7033  A2 FF        TDLY     LDX  #$FF        SET MSB OF TIME DELAY
7035  A0 FF        SLSB     LDY  #$FF        SET LSB OF TIME DELAY
7037  88           DECY     DEY              DECREMENT LSB OF TIME DELAY
7038  D0 FD                 BNE  DECY        IF NOT ZERO, DEC. LSB AGAIN
703A  CA                    DEX              ELSE DECREMENT MSB OF TIME DELAY
703B  D0 F8                 BNE  SLSB        IF NOT ZERO, START LSB COUNT AGAIN
703D  60                    RTS              ELSE RETURN TO OPUT SUBROUTINE
```

capable of calling subroutines having entry points 128 address locations below or 127 locations above the current program address.

BSR *disp*	Branch and save the return address (on the stack) to a program address found by summing the current program address with an unsigned, 8-bit displacement term, *disp*. This instruction can call subroutines having entry points up to 255 address locations above the current one.

Suppose that a mainline program requires some sort of subroutine-calling instruction at program address $4A00. Further, the subroutine to

TABLE 13-5   6800 CALL AND RETURN INSTRUCTIONS

Source code	Object code	Notes
JSR *addr*	BD *byte byte*	All are unconditional CALL instructions
JSR *indx*,X	AD *byte*	
BSR *disp*	8D *byte*	
RTS	39	RETURN unconditionally

be called is at program address $4A7F. There are three ways to get to that subroutine:

```
4A00 BD 4A 7F   JSR  $4A7F
```

or

```
4A00 CE 4A 00   LDX  #$4A00
4A03 AD 7F      JSR  $4A,X
```

or

```
4A00 8D 7D      BSR  $7D
```

EXAMPLE 13-5

Write and assemble a 6800 program that does the following:

1. Initialize the stack pointer at $7000.
2. Send values 0 through 9 to output port $F000, inserting a double-register time delay between each count.
3. Repeat the count/delay cycle indefinitely.

Use the BSR instruction where appropriate, and begin the listing at program address $1000.

The first two steps are responsible for initializing the stack pointer at address $7000 (see Program 13-5). The instruction at label DOIT clears accumulator A to zero. That accumulator will be used for generating the numbers to be sent to the output port. The instruction at OPUT sends the current count to the output port. After that, the program calls the time delay routine at address $1011.

When the time delay is done, program operations resume from the instruction at $100A. That instruction increments the 0 through 9 counter, and the remaining instructions in the mainline program are responsible for recycling the counter when its count exceeds 9.

PROGRAM 13-5 6800 LISTING FOR EXAMPLE 13-5

```
1000 CE 70 00         LDX  #$7000
1003 35               TXS              SET STACK TO $7000
1004 4F          DOIT  CLRA            ZERO THE ACCUMULATOR
1005 B7 F0 00    OPUT  STAA $F000      OUTPUT THE COUNT TO $F000
1008 BD 07             BSR  TDLY       CALL TIME DELAY ROUTINE
100A 4C               INCA             INCREMENT THE COUNT
100B 81 0A            CMPA #$0A        COUNTER ABOVE 9?
100D 27 F5            BEQ  DOIT        IF SO, START COUNT ALL OVER
100F 20 F4            BRA  OPUT        ELSE OUTPUT THE COUNT
1011 CE FF FF    TDLY  LDX  #$FFFF     INITIALIZE TIME DELAY
1014 09          CNT   DEX             COUNTDOWN THE TIMER
1015 26 FD            BNE  CNT         IF NOT DONE, COUNTDOWN AGAIN
1017 39               RTS              ELSE RETURN TO MAINLINE
```

14

Bit Testing, Setting, and Resetting Operations

It is possible, and often quite necessary, to compose routines that work with individual bits within a data byte. Sometimes it is necessary to test the 1-or-0 status of a certain bit, or selected group of bits, within a data byte, and then take a course of action based on the results. Other times, it is necessary to set selected bits to a logic-1 state or clear them to zero.

This matter of testing, setting, and resetting selected bits within a given data byte has been mentioned to some extent in Chapter 7. At that time, the operations were used merely as examples of applications of certain logic operations. This chapter takes up the subject in a more detailed way.

14-1 BIT OPERATIONS FOR THE 8080A/8085

The 8080A/8085 instruction set has no special instructions for individual bit manipulations; the bit testing, setting, and resetting operations must be synthesized from the available logic operations. Knowing how to carry out the operations on this fundamental level will make it easier to understand and appreciate some of the special bit-manipulation instructions available for some of the other microprocessor devices.

Bit Testing Operations

A data byte is made up of 8 binary bits, and by convention, those bits are labeled B0 through B7, with B0 being the least-significant bit.

With the 8080A/8085 system, it is possible to test the 1-or-0 status of any one of the 8 bits residing in the 8-bit working registers. The general idea

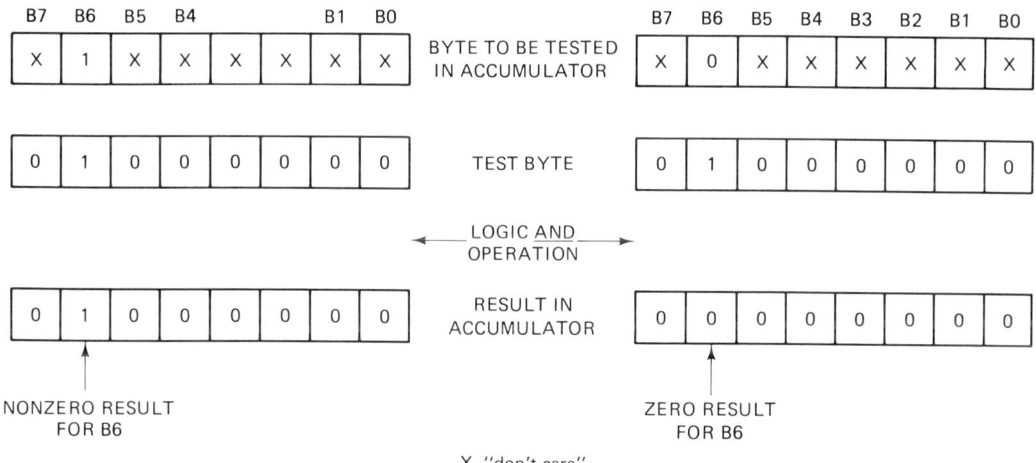

Figure 14-1 Testing the 1-or-0 status of B6 in the accumulator. The test byte is logically ANDed with the content of the accumulator, and the B6 position of the result indicates the original status of that bit.

is to load a byte of data to the accumulator and then do an AND immediate operation with a test byte that has 1's only in those bit positions to be tested. So if you want to isolate bit 6 (B6) in the accumulator, it can be isolated from the other 7 bits by ANDing it with hexadecimal 40—a byte having a 1 in the B6 position. As a result, the B6 bit in the accumulator will retain its original 1-or-0 status, and the other 7 bits will be ANDed to zero. See Fig. 14-1.

Now, an AND operation affects the flags according to the result; and in this case, the Z flag is the most relevant one. If B6 in the original data byte happens to be a logic 1, the ANDing with 40H leaves a single logic 1 residing in the B6 position in the accumulator. The Z flag will respond to a nonzero result, and subsequent conditional instructions such as JNZ and CNZ will be satisfied.

On the other hand, if B6 in the original data byte is a logic 0, ANDing with 40H will leave all zeros in the accumulator, and the Z flag will respond to a zero result. Subsequent conditionals such as JZ and CZ will be satisfied.

That is the essence of a bit testing operation. The tricky part, as far as the programmer is concerned, is to come up with the appropriate testing byte—the one having 1's in the bit positions to be tested.

EXAMPLE 14-1

Write and assemble an 8080A/8085 routine that does the following:

1. Fetch a data byte from an input port at address F000H.
2. Test B4 of that byte.
3. If B4 of the byte is a zero, loop back to step 1 to fetch the byte again.

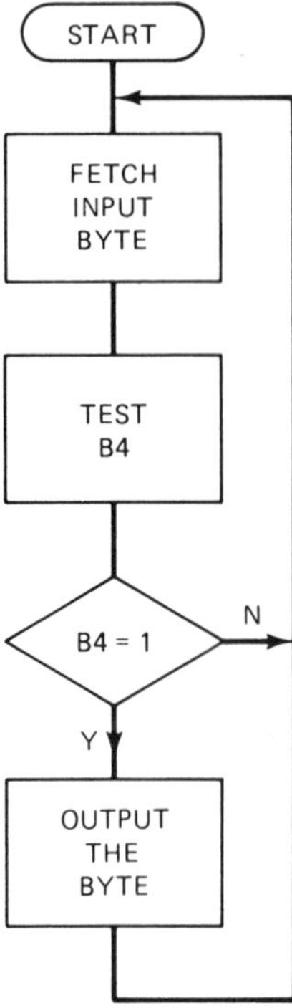

Figure 14-2 Flowchart for Example 14-1.

4. If B4 of the fetched byte is a logic 1, output the fetched byte to an output port at address F001H.

5. Return to step 1.

See the flowchart in Fig. 14-2. Begin the program listing at address 7000H.

The suggested program listing in Program 14-1 follows the flowchart fairly closely. Study the comments in the listing carefully; they ought to amount to an adequate explanation of how the program works.

But why is the fetched data byte saved in the B register by the second instruction, and then later retrieved from the B register in the instruction MOV A,B? In this particular example, the fetched data byte must be saved somewhere in the system through the bit testing operation. Why? Because the bit testing operation, ANI 10H, sets all but the tested bit to logic 0, and

PROGRAM 14-1   8080A/8085 LISTING FOR EXAMPLE 14-1

```
7000 3A 00 F0   FETCH   LDA  F000H  ;FETCH THE INPUT BYTE
7003 47                 MOV  B,A    ;SAVE THE BYTE IN B
7004 E6 10              ANI  10H    ;TEST (ISOLATE) B4
7006 CA 00 70           JZ FETCH    ;IF B4=0, FETCH AGAIN
7009 78                 MOV  A,B    ;GET ORIGINAL BYTE FROM B
700A 32 01 F0           STA  F001H  ;OUTPUT THE BYTE
700D C3 00 70           JMP  FETCH  ;AND FETCH AGAIN
```

that certainly destroys any information carried by the nontested bits in the original data byte.

The 8080A/8085's bit testing routine destroys any information that might be carried by the nontested bits. For that reason, the tested byte must be saved for future operations and retrieved when it is needed.

It is possible to test more than one bit at a time by selecting a test byte that has more than a single logic 1 in it. Such a scheme, however, works properly only if one is testing for an all-zero condition—a condition where all the tested bytes are to be logic zeros.

A better all-around technique for testing the 1-or-0 status of more than one bit is to test them separately, one at a time.

EXAMPLE 14-2

Write and assemble an 8080A/8085 routine that does the following:

1. Fetch a data byte from input port F000H.
2. Test bits B2 and B7.
3. If either or both bits are logic 0, fetch the data byte again.
4. If both bytes are logic 1, output the original data byte to output port F001H and fetch again.

See the flowchart in Fig. 14-3. Begin the program listing at address 7000H.

The flowchart and the suggested listing in Program 14-2 show how the two relevant bits are tested. Indeed, the fetched byte is sent to the output port only if both bits are logic 1. Note how the original data byte is saved in the B register, then moved to the accumulator whenever it is needed. If this were not done, the original data byte would be lost after the first bit testing operation.

Bit Setting Operations

A bit is said to be *set* whenever an operation guarantees that it will be a logic 1 at the conclusion of that operation, no matter what the original status of the bit might be. Assuming that a relevant byte of data is residing in the accumulator, the simplest way to set a selected bit is to do an OR immediate instruction with another byte that has a logic 1 only in the selected bit position. Figure 14-4 shows how B6 in a data byte can be set to logic 1 by ORing it with a set byte, 40H.

In that particular example, the set byte sets B6 in the original data. It makes no difference what B6 might have been; it ends up as a logic 1. The 7 other bits in the original data are left unchanged by the whole operation.

It is quite easy to set more than one selected byte at the same time. Just pick a set byte that has 1's in the bit positions to be set.

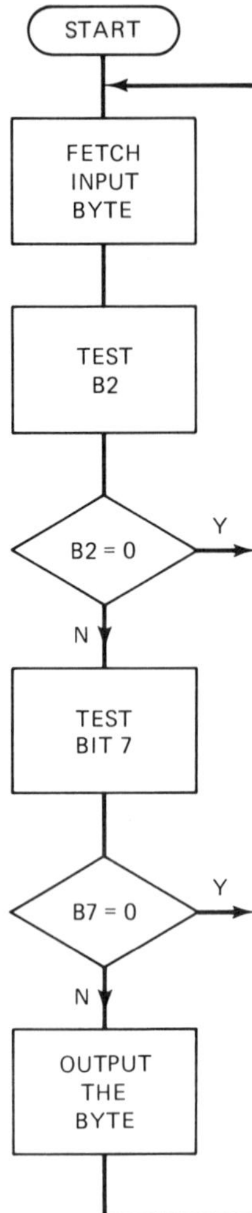

Figure 14-3 Flowchart for Example 14-2.

PROGRAM 14-2 8080A/8085 LISTING FOR EXAMPLE 14-2

```
7000  3A 00 F0   FETCH   LDA  F000H   ;FETCH THE INPUT BYTE
7003  47                 MOV  B,A     ;SAVE THE BYTE IN B
7004  E6 04              ANI  04H     ;TEST (ISOLATE) B2
7006  CA 00 70           JZ   FETCH   ;IF B2=0,FETCH AGAIN
7009  78                 MOV  A,B     ;GET ORIGINAL BYTE FROM B
700A  E6 80              ANI  80H     ;TEST (ISOLATE) B7
700C  CA 00 70           JZ   FETCH   ;IF B7=0,FETCH AGAIN
700F  78                 MOV  A,B     ;GET ORIGINAL BYTE FROM B
7010  32 01 F0           STA  F001H   ;OUTPUT THE BYTE
7013  C3 70              JMP  FETCH   ;AND FETCH AGAIN
```

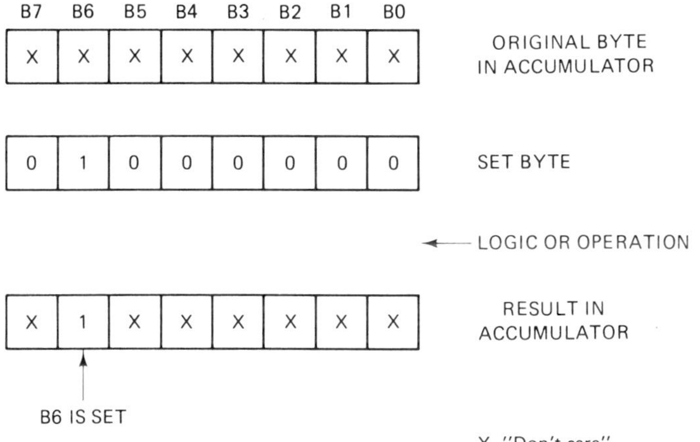

Figure 14-4 Setting a selected bit (B6 in this case) within the accumulator. The set byte is logically ORed with the byte in the accumulator, and the selected bit is set to 1 as a result. The other 7 bits are left unchanged.

EXAMPLE 14-3

Write and assemble an 8080A/8085 routine that does the following:

1. Fetch a data byte from an input device located at address F000H.
2. Test B7 of that data byte.
3. If B7 = 0, then output the byte, unchanged, to a device located at address F001H and return to step 1.
4. If B7 = 1, then set bits B0 and B1 in the original byte to logic 1.
5. Output the altered data to address F001H and return to step 1 to begin the whole procedure over again.

Begin the program listing at address 7000H.

See the flowchart and suggested listing in Fig. 14-5 and Program 14-3, respectively.

The first four instructions fetch the data byte, save a copy of it in register B, test B7, and then do a conditional jump operation. If it turns out that B7 is a one, the routine executes instructions MOV A,B and ORI 03H—those get a copy of the original data byte into the accumulator and set bits B0 and B1 to logic 1. After that, the OPUT sequence sends the resulting data byte to the output address and returns operations to the beginning.

But if the bit testing sequence turns up a logic 0 in the B7 position, the JZ NOSET instruction is satisfied, and operations jump down to NOSET. The instructions at that point get a copy of the original data byte from register B, and then jump to the OPUT sequence—the same sequence used for outputting the data byte that is altered by the set routine.

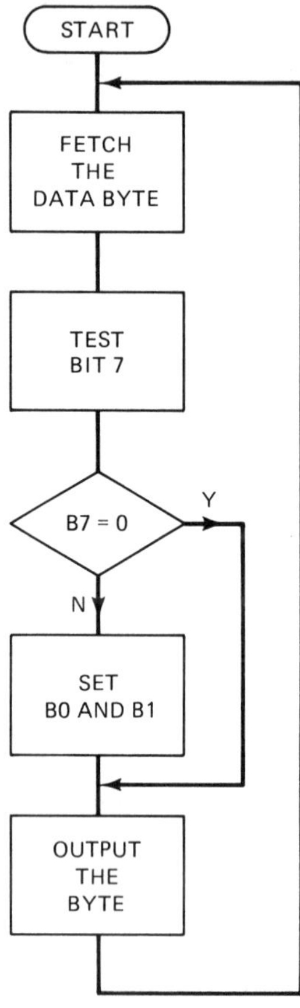

Figure 14-5 Flowchart for Example 14-3.

PROGRAM 14-3   8080A/8085 LISTING FOR EXAMPLE 14-3

```
7000  3A 00 F0  FETCH  LDA   F000H   ;FETCH THE INPUT BYTE
7003  47               MOV   B,A     ;SAVE THE BYTE IN B
7004  E6 80            ANI   80H     ;TEST (ISOLATE) B7
7006  CA 12 70         JZ    NOSET   ;IF ZERO, DO NOSET
7009  78               MOV   A,B     ;ELSE GET THE ORIGINAL BYTE
700A  F6 03            ORI   03H     ;SET BITS B0 AND B1
700C  32 01 F0  OPUT   STA   F001H   ;OUTPUT THE BYTE
700F  C3 00 70         JMP   FETCH   ;AND FETCH AGAIN
7012  78        NOSET  MOV   A,B     ;GET THE ORIGINAL BYTE
7013  C3 0C 70         JMP   OPUT    ;AND OUTPUT IT UNCHANGED
```

Bit Resetting Operations

A bit is said to be *reset, or cleared,* whenever an operation forces it to logic 0, regardless of its previous status. Selected bits residing in the accumulator can be reset by ANDing the byte with a reset byte having 0's in the bit positions that are to be reset.

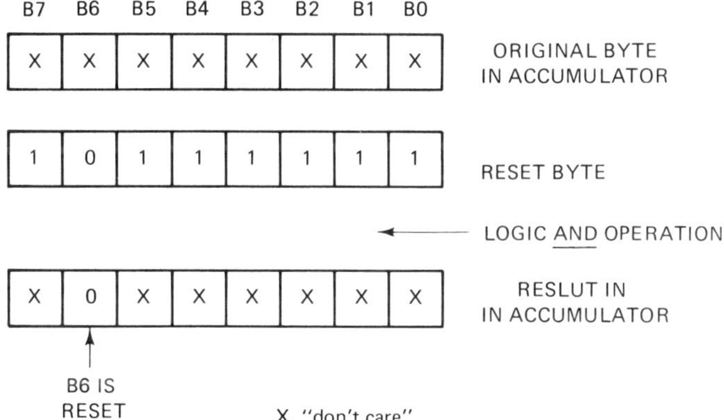

Figure 14-6 Resetting a selected bit (B6 in this case) within the accumulator. The reset byte is logically ANDed with the byte in the accumulator, and the selected bit is reset to 0 as a result. The other 7 bits are left unchanged.

The illustration in Fig. 14-6 shows an instance where B6 in the original data byte is reset to 0 by ANDing it with BF hexadecimal.

EXAMPLE 14-4

Write and assemble an 8080A/8085 routine that does the following:

1. Fetch an input byte from a device located at address F000H.
2. Test bits B6 and B7.
3. If B6 is set and B7 is reset, continue from step 4; otherwise, go back to step 1.
4. Reset bits B0 and B1 in the original data byte.
5. Output the altered byte to address F001H and return to step 1.

Begin the listing at address 7000H.

See the flowchart and listing in Fig. 14-7 and Program 14-4, respectively.

PROGRAM 14-4 8080A/8085 LISTING FOR EXAMPLE 14-4

```
7000  3A 00 70   FETCH   LDA  F000H  ;FETCH THE INPUT BYTE
7003  47                 MOV  B,A    ;SAVE IN B
7004  E6 40              ANI  40H    ;TEST B6
7006  CA 00 70           JZ   FETCH  ;IF ZERO,FETCH AGAIN
7009  78                 MOV  A,B    ;GET ORIGINAL BYTE FROM B
700A  E6 80              ANI  80H    ;TEST B7
700C  C2 00 70           JNZ  FETCH  ;IF SET,FETCH AGAIN
700F  78                 MOV  A,B    ;GET ORIGINAL BYTE FROM B
7010  E6 FC              ANI  0FCH   ;RESET B0,B1
7012  32 01 F0           STA  F001H  ;OUTPUT ALTERED DATA BYTE
7015  C3 00 70           JMP  FETCH  ;AND START ALL OVER
```

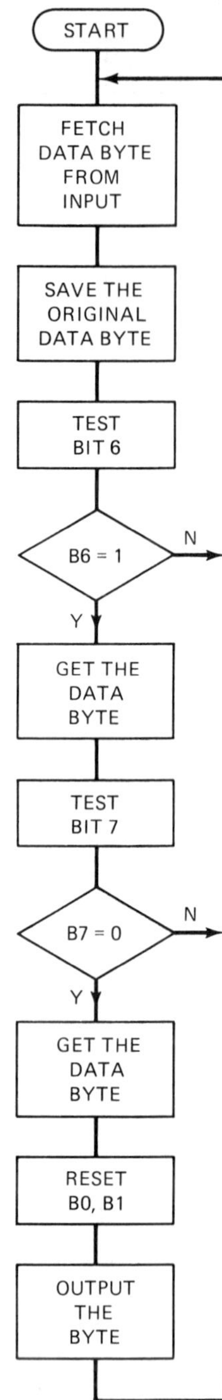

Figure 14-7 Flowchart for Example 14-4.

Exercises for Section 14-1

1. What is meant by a *bit test*? *bit set*? *bit reset*?

2. Why is it often necessary to save a data byte in some register just prior to doing a bit test routine with the 8080A/8085 system?

3. Specify the hexadecimal value of a test byte needed for testing the following bits in a data byte.
   (a) BO   (b) B1   (c) B2   (d) B3
   (e) B4   (f) B5   (g) B6   (h) B7

4. Specify the hexadecimal value of a set byte required for setting the following bits in a data byte.
   (a) B0   (b) B1 and B2   (c) B3   (d) B3 and B4
   (e) B7   (f) B6 and B7   (g) B0, B1, B3, and B7

5. Specify the hexadecimal value of a reset byte required for resetting the following bits in a data byte.
   (a) B1   (b) B1 and B3   (c) B4, B5, and B6
   (d) B0 and B7   (e) B0, B1, B2, and B3

6. Using the same general approaches suggested in the examples from this section, draw a flowchart, and write and assemble an 8080A/8085 program that does the following:

   a. Fetch a data byte from input F000H.
   b. Test bits B3 and B7.
   c. If B3 is set and B7 is reset, go to step 6.
   d. If B3 is set and B7 is set, go to step 8.
   e. Return to step 1.
   f. Set bits B0 and B1, reset bits B3 and B4.
   g. Output the altered byte of F001H and return to step 1.
   h. Reset bits B0 and B1, set bits B5 and B6.
   i. Output the altered byte to F001H and return to step 1.

   Begin the listing at address 7000H.

14-2 BIT OPERATIONS FOR THE 6502

As far as the 6502 is concerned, the bit testing and resetting operations are, in principle, identical to those of the 8080A/8085 system. The bit testing procedures can be somewhat simpler, however, because the 6502's instruction set includes two special bit testing instructions.

Bit Testing Instructions and Operations

Any data byte that can be loaded into the 6502's accumulator can be bit-tested as described for the 8080A/8085 system. The general procedure is to load the data byte to be tested into the accumulator, then do an AND immediate with a test byte having a logic 1 at the desired bit testing position. The Z flag will respond to either the zero or nonzero result, effectively signaling whether the tested bit is a 0 or a 1. But as in the case of the 8080A/8085 scheme, the byte loaded to the accumulator is, for all practical purposes, destroyed.

EXAMPLE 14-5

Rewrite and assemble a 6502 version of the programming task described for the 8080A/8085 in Example 14-1.

Use the flowchart in Fig. 14-2 as a guide, and begin the program listing at $7000.

The first instruction loads the input byte to the accumulator, and the second saves that byte in the X register (see Program 14-5). The version remaining in the accumulator is then bit-tested, and if the result is zero, operations branch back up to FETCH. But if the bit test turns up a logic 1 in the B4 position, the branch instruction is not satisfied, and the original data byte, now residing in the X register, is transferred to the output address.

The ability to do a transfer from some register, other than the accumulator, to a directly addressed memory location makes this routine a bit simpler that its 8080A/8085 version (where direct-addressed transfer can take place only through the accumulator).

When it comes to bit testing a data byte in external memory, the 6502 offers a couple of special instructions. See Table 14-1. The 2-byte version, BIT $addr_0$, does a bit test on a byte residing in zero-page memory at address $addr_0$. The 3-byte version does the same sort of bit test, but at any 16-bit address location, *addr*.

To use either of these BIT instructions, the test byte must be residing in the accumulator. So if you want to test B4 of a byte at memory address

PROGRAM 14-5 6502 LISTING FOR EXAMPLE 14-5

```
7000  AD 00 F0   FETCH   LDA  $F000    FETCH INPUT BYTE
7003  AA                 TAX           SAVE IN X
7004  29 10              AND  #$10     TEST BIT 4
7006  F0 F8              BEQ  FETCH    IF BIT 4 IS RESET,FETCH AGAIN
7008  8E 01 F0           STX  $F001    ELSE OUTPUT THE BYTE
700B  4C 00 70           JMP  FETCH    AND FETCH AGAIN
```

TABLE 14-1 BIT TESTING INSTRUCTIONS FOR THE 6502

Source code	Object code	Notes
BIT $addr_0$	24 *byte*	Zero-page memory
BIT *addr*	2C *byte byte*	Absolute memory

Note: The Z flag is affected according to the result of the bit test. The S flag is set equal to B7 of the byte being tested, and the V flag is set equal to B6 of the byte being tested.

$F000, the appropriate sequence of operations might look like this:

```
LDA  L$10
BIT  $F000
```

The first instruction gets the test bit into the accumulator, and the second instruction carries out the bit test. The Z flag is affected according to the result of the test, but *the content of neither the accumulator nor the tested byte is changed*. Whereas the AND-immediate bit testing technique always upsets the accumulator, these BIT instructions do not.

EXAMPLE 14-6

Rewrite the program for Example 14-5, using the BIT **addr** instruction to test B4 at the input port.

The first instruction sets up the system for doing a test on a bit 4 (see Program 14-6). That test byte, $10, is loaded to the accumulator. The second instruction tests B4 in byte byte of data at input address $F000. No data are being transferred at this point in the program, and the data in the accumulator and at address $F00 remain unaffected by the procedure.

PROGRAM 14-6 6502 LISTING FOR EXAMPLE 14-6

```
7000  A9  10       START   LDA  #$10    TEST BYTE TO ACCUMULATOR
7002  2C  00  F0   TEST    BIT  $F000   TEST THE INPUT BYTE
7005  F0  FB               BEQ  TEST    IF B4 IS RESET, TEST AGAIN
7007  AD  00  F0            LDA  $F000   INPUT BYTE TO ACCUMULATOR
700A  8D  01  F0            STA  $F001   OUTPUT THE BYTE
700D  4C  00  70            JMP  START   AND DO IT ALL OVER AGAIN
```

The branch instruction continues looping the operations back to TEST as long as B4 of address $F000 remains at zero. The moment that bit changes to a logic 1 for any reason, the branch instruction is no longer satisfied, and the system executes the last three instructions. Those instructions effectively transfer the current input byte from $F000 to the output address, $F001. Finally, the whole program jumps back up to the beginning.

Whether a programmer uses the 6502's BIT instructions or uses the ANDing technique similar to the one used by the 8080A/8085 system is a matter of judgment and programming style.

Testing more than one bit in a data byte is a matter of applying the bit testing routine one time for each test.

EXAMPLE 14-7

Using the flowchart in Fig. 14-3 as a guide, rewrite the task in Example 14-2 to conform to 6502 standards. Use the BIT instruction where possible.

See the listing in Program 14-7. The first instruction sets up the system for testing B2, and the second instruction tests that bit at input address

```
7000  A9 04       START  LDA  #$04    SETUP B2 TEST
7002  2C 00 F0     TEST   BIT  $F000   TEST B2 OF INPUT BYTE
7005  F0 FB               BEQ  TEST    IF ZERO, TEST AGAIN
7007  A9 80               LDA  #$80    ELSE SETUP B7 TEST
7009  2C 00 F0             BIT  $F000   TEST B7 OF INPUT BYTE
700C  F0 F2               BEQ  START   IF ZERO, START ALL OVER
700E  AD 00 F0             LDA  $F000   ELSE FETCH INPUT BYTE
7011  8D 01 F0             STA  $F001   OUTPUT THE BYTE
7014  4C 00 70             JMP  START   AND START ALL OVER AGAIN
```

$F000. If that bit happens to be a zero, the conditional branch instruction (the third instruction) loops operations back to TEST. But when B2 at address $F000 is set, the program enters the testing sequence:

```
LDA  #$80
BIT  $F000
BEQ  START
```

That sequence tests B7 at the input address. As long as that bit is a zero, the program loops all the way back to start.

The only way the program gets out of those two testing loops is by finding 1's at both the B2 and B7 positions of the data byte at $F000. Whenever that happens, the program enters the final instruction sequence:

```
LDA  $F000
STA  $F001
JMP  START
```

The first of the three loads the input byte to the accumulator, and the second instruction loads that byte out to the output address, $F001. The final instruction loops the whole works back to the beginning of the program.

Bit Setting and Resetting Operations

The instruction set for the 6502 offers no special instructions for selectively setting and resetting bits in a data byte. The procedures for doing that sort of task are thus essentially the same as those used for the 8080A/8085 system.

So an instruction such as ORA #$03 sets B0 and B1 of any data byte residing in the accumulator. Doing an AND #$FC resets B0 and B1 in the accumulator.

Exercises for Section 14-2

1. Prepare a flowchart for the following source code listing, then assemble it, beginning at program address $1000. Include comments in your listing.

```
START   LDA  #$08
TEST    BIT  $F0
        BNE  TEST
        LDA  #$80
        BIT  $F0
        BEQ  F1OUT
        LDA  $F0
        STA  $4000
        JMP  START
F1OUT   LDA  $F0
        STA  $F1
        JMP  START
```

2. Referring to the listing in Problem 1, which of the following bytes at address $F0 will pass the first bit test and allow the remaining instructions to be run?

   (a) $F0   (b) $FF   (c) $08   (d) $11   (e) $F7

3. Referring to the listing in Problem 1, which of the following bytes will be transferred to address $4000? to address $F1?

   (a) $80   (b) $71   (c) $47   (d) $77   (e) $11

14-3 BIT OPERATIONS FOR THE 6800

The bit operations for the 6800 device are quite similar to those of the 6502. The 6800, for instance, has some special bit testing instructions, but none for bit setting and resetting.

Bit Testing Instructions

Table 14-2 summarizes the special bit testing instructions for the 6800 microprocessor device. The list is a bit more extensive than the 6502 version, but the general principles of application are basically the same.

The 6800, however, allows bit tests on bytes residing in the accumulator. BITA #data, for instance, can test any selected bit in accumulator A. The bit to be tested is designated as a logic 1 in *data*—the test byte is specified in an immediate fashion.

Doing an instruction as BITA #$01 thus tests bit 0 of the byte cur-

TABLE 14-2 BIT TESTING INSTRUCTIONS FOR THE 6800

Source code	Object code	Addressing mode
BITA #*data*	85 *byte*	Immediate
BITA *addr*$_0$	95 *byte*	Zero-page
BITA *addr*	B5 *byte byte*	Absolute
BITA *indx*,X	A5 *byte*	Indexed
BITB #*data*	C5 *byte*	Immediate
BITB *addr*$_0$	D5 *byte*	Zero-page
BITB *addr*	F5 *byte byte*	Absolute
BITB *indx*,X	E5 *byte*	Indexed

rently residing in the A accumulator. If that bit is a zero, the Z flag responds as to an operation that yields a zero result. If the bit is a 1, the Z flag sets up a situation analogous to an operation that produces a nonzero result.

BITB *#data* works the same way, but references the data byte in the B accumulator.

In either case, the data byte in the accumulator is left unchanged by the bit testing operation. That is in marked contrast to the idea of bit testing with an AND immediate instruction.

Instructions BITA $addr_0$ and BITA *addr* test a bit within a byte at zero-page address $addr_0$ or absolute address *addr*. They are, in principle, identical to the 6502's BIT $addr_0$ and BIT *addr* instructions. That means that the test byte—the one containing a logic 1 only in the bit position to be tested—must be loaded to accumulator A before the instruction can be executed. The following sequence of instructions tests B1 at address $4000:

```
LDAA #$02
BITA $4000
```

BITB $addr_0$ and BITB *addr* work the same way. The test byte, however, must be loaded to the B accumulator before the instruction is applied. This sequence of instructions does exactly the same test as the example just cited:

```
LDAB #$02
BITB $4000
```

As you might imagine, it is inappropriate to load the test byte into one accumulator and then do a bit instruction referencing the other accumulator.

The 6800 also allows bit tests on data bytes at indexed address locations. In such instances, the address of the byte to be tested is found by summing the index term (8-bit, unsigned format) with the current content of the IX register. So if the IX register happens to contain $4000, BITA $FE,X will test the byte located at address $40FE; and it will use the best byte in the A accumulator.

EXAMPLE 14-8

Rewrite and program in Example 14-1 to conform to 6800 standards. Use the BITA *#data* instruction where possible.

Clearly, the ability to test a bit in the accumulator without altering its content can simplify many kinds of bit testing routines. See the listing in Program 14-8.

PROGRAM 14-8 6800 LISTING FOR EXAMPLE 14-8

```
7000 B6 F0 00   FETCH   LDAA $F000   FETCH THE INPUT BYTE
7003 85 10              BITA #$10    TEST B4
7005 27 F9              BEQ FETCH    IF ZERO, FETCH AGAIN
7007 B7 F0 01           STAA $F001   ELSE OUTPUT THE BYTE
700A 20 F4              BRA FETCH    AND START ALL OVER
```

The first instruction loads the byte to be tested to accumulator A, and the second instruction tests bit 4 in that byte. If that bit is a 1, the conditional branch instruction is not satisfied, and the data byte, already residing in accumulator A, is simply loaded from there to the output address, $F001. Compare the listing with the 6502 version in Program 14-5.

EXAMPLE 14-9

Write and assemble a 6800 program that does the following:

1. Fetch a byte from zero-page address $F0.
2. Test bits 3 and 7.
3. If B3 is set and B7 is reset, then jump back to step 1.
4. Else output the data byte to zero-page address $F1 and go back to step 1.

Use BITB #*data* instructions where possible, and begin the listing at address $3C00.
See the flowchart and a suggested program listing in Fig. 14-8 and Program 14-9, respectively.

Bit Setting and Resetting Operations

The procedures for setting and resetting selected bits in the accumulators are, in principle, identical to those used by the other microprocessors described thus far in this chapter.

The following examples fetch a data byte from zero-page address $2A, set bits 6 and 7, and then output the result to absolute memory address $4010:

```
LDAA  $2A
ORAA  #$C0
STAA  $4010

LDAB  $2A
ORAB  #$C0
STAB  $4010
```

The only difference between those two sequences of instructions is that the first one uses the A accumulator, whereas the second uses the B accumulator.

The next two examples work with the same input and output addresses, but reset bits 6 and 7:

```
LDAA  $2A
ANDA  #$3F
STAA  $4010

LDAB  $2A
ANDB  #$3F
STAB  $4010
```

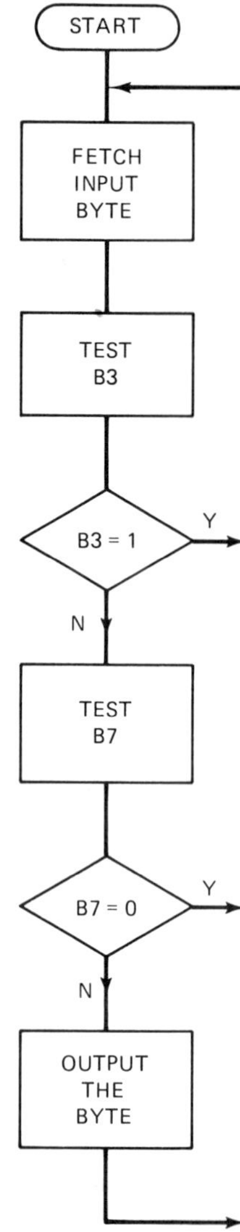

Figure 14-8 Flowchart for Example 14-9.

PROGRAM 14-9 6800 LISTING FOR EXAMPLE 14-9

```
3C00  D6 FA  START  LDAB  $F0     FETCH INPUT BYTE TO B
3C02  C5 08          BITB  #$08    TEST B3
3C04  26 FA          BNE   START   IF SET, START OVER
3C06  C5 80          BITB  #$80    TEST B7
3C08  27 F6          BEQ   START   IF RESET, START OVER
3C0A  D7 F1          STAB  $F1     ELSE OUTPUT THE BYTE
3C0C  20 F2          BRA   START   AND START ALL OVER
```

Exercises for Section 14-3

1. Specify which bit is tested by each of the following 6800 instruction sequences.

(a) LDAA $20	(b) LDAA $40	(c) LDAA $20	(d) LDX #$2040
BITA #$40	LDAB $20	BITA $40	LDAB #$10
	BITA #$80		BITB $80,X

2. Write and assemble a 6800 program that does the following:

   1. Fetch a data byte from zero-page address $F0.
   2. Test bits 0 and 1.
   3. If B0 is reset, jump back to step A.
   4. If B1 is set, jump to step F.
   5. If B1 is reset: set B7, reset B6, output the result to address $10, and return to step A.
   6. Set B7, set B6, reset B5, output the result to address $10, and return to step A.

   Start the program at address $7000, and use the BITA #*data* instruction where possible.

14-4 BIT INSTRUCTIONS FOR THE Z-80

The Z-80 differs from the three previously described systems; and the differences are quite significant. Unlike the other systems, the Z-80 instruction set includes special instructions for bit testing, bit setting, and bit resetting operations.

The operations can be carried out according to the principles described for the 8080A/8085; but once you have seen the special instructions for the Z-80, you will realize there is little need to resort to such roundabout techniques.

Bit Testing Instructions

Table 14-3 represents a rather extensive set of Z-80 instructions for testing a single bit within a data byte. In all instances, the byte containing the bit to be tested is left unchanged by the operation, and the status of the Z flag reflects the result of the test.

Most of the bit testing instructions have this general form:

$$\text{BIT } bit,r$$

where *bit* is the bit number to be tested (0 through 7), and *r* designates an 8-bit register within the Z-80 device.

An instruction such as BIT 0,A thus means: Test B0 of the byte currently residing in the A register. Instruction BIT 5,C, on the other hand, can be interpreted as: Test B5 of the data byte in register C.

In all cases, the Z flag responds in such a way that it signals the 1-or-0

TABLE 14-3 BIT TESTING INSTRUCTIONS FOR THE Z-80

Source code	Object code
BIT 0,A	CB 47
BIT 0,B	CB 40
BIT 0,C	CB 41
BIT 0,D	CB 42
BIT 0,E	CB 43
BIT 0,H	CB 44
BIT 0,L	CB 45
BIT 0,(HL)	CB 46
BIT 0,(IX+*indx*)	DD CB *byte* 46
BIT 0,(IY+*indx*)	FD CB *byte* 46
BIT 1,A	CB 4F
BIT 1,B	CB 48
BIT 1,C	CB 49
BIT 1,D	CB 4A
BIT 1,E	CB 4B
BIT 1,H	CB 4C
BIT 1,L	CB 4D
BIT 1,(HL)	CB 4E
BIT 1,(IX+*indx*)	DD CB *byte* 4E
BIT 1,(IY+*indx*)	FD CB *byte* 4E
BIT 2,A	CB 57
BIT 2,B	CB 50
BIT 2,C	CB 51
BIT 2,D	CB 52
BIT 2,E	CB 53
BIT 2,H	CB 54
BIT 2,L	CB 55
BIT 2,(HL)	CB 56
BIT 2,(IX+*indx*)	DD CB *byte* 56
BIT 2,(IY+*indx*)	FD CB *byte* 56
BIT 3,A	CB 5F
BIT 3,B	CB 58
BIT 3,C	CB 59
BIT 3,D	CB 5A
BIT 3,E	CB 5B
BIT 3,H	CB 5C
BIT 3,L	CB 5D
BIT 3,(HL)	CB 5E
BIT 3,(IX+*indx*)	DD CB *byte* 5E
BIT 3,(IY+*indx*)	FD CB *byte* 5E
BIT 4,A	CB 67
BIT 4,B	CB 60
BIT 4,C	CB 61
BIT 4,D	CB 62
BIT 4,E	CB 63
BIT 4,H	CB 64

Source code	Object code
BIT 4,L	CB 65
BIT 4,(HL)	CB 66
BIT 4,(IX+*indx*)	DD CB *byte* 6E
BIT 4,(IY+*indx*)	FD CB *byte* 6E
BIT 5,A	CB 6F
BIT 5,B	CB 68
BIT 5,C	CB 69
BIT 5,D	CB 6A
BIT 5,E	CB 6B
BIT 5,H	CB 6C
BIT 5,L	CB 6D
BIT 5,(HL)	CB 6E
BIT 5,(IX+*indx*)	DD CB *byte* 6E
BIT 5,(IY+*indx*)	FD CB *byte* 6E
BIT 6,A	CB 77
BIT 6,B	CB 70
BIT 6,C	CB 71
BIT 6,D	CB 72
BIT 6,E	CB 73
BIT 6,H	CB 74
BIT 6,L	CB 75
BIT 6,(HL)	CB 76
BIT 6,(IX+*indx*)	DD CB *byte* 76
BIT 6,(IY+*indx*)	FD CB *byte* 76
BIT 7,A	CB 7F
BIT 7,B	CB 78
BIT 7,C	CB 79
BIT 7,D	CB 7A
BIT 7,E	CB 7B
BIT 7,H	CB 7C
BIT 7,L	CB 7D
BIT 7,(HL)	CB 7E
BIT 7,(IX+*indx*)	DD CB *byte* 7E
BIT 7,(IY+*indx*)	FD CB *byte* 7E

status of the tested bit. If the test happens to show a logic 1 in the tested bit position, the Z flag reflects a nonzero result, and conditional operations such as JP NZ, JR NZ, and CALL NZ will be satisfied. But if the tested bit has a logic-0 level, the Z flag indicates a zero result, and conditionals such as JP NZ, JR NZ, and CALL NZ will be satisfied.

The following source-code routine fetches a byte from address F000H to the A register, and then tests the status of bit 6. If it is a zero, the program loops back to fetch another byte from the same address location. But if the tested bit is a logic 1, the program loads the fetched byte to an output port at address F001H.

```
FETCH   LD A,(F000H)   ;FETCH THE INPUT BYTE
        BIT 6,A        ;TEST B6
        JR Z,FETCH     ;IF ZERO, FETCH AGAIN
        LD (F001H),A   ;ELSE OUTPUT THE BYTE
        JR FETCH       ;AND FETCH AGAIN
```

The fact that the content of the A register is unaffected by the bit test simplifies many types of bit testing routines.

There are also instructions for testing bits residing in locations outside the microprocessor itself. Table 14-3 shows some instructions of the form

$$BIT \ bit,(HL)$$

where *bit* is the individual bit number (0 through 7) to be tested, and (HL) indicates an address in external memory pointed to by the HL register pair. So an instruction such as BIT 5,(HL) will test the 1-or-0 status of bit 5 in a data byte residing at the address indicated by the content of the HL registers. Specifically, if HL happens to be set at 4000H, the instruction tests bit 5 at memory address 4000H.

The advantage inherent in the BIT *bit*,(HL) instructions is that a bit in memory can be tested without having to load it into an internal working register. Technically speaking, the instruction does a bit test using indirect memory addressing.

The remaining instructions test a designated bit in external memory, but they used indexed indirect addressing. Those are the instructions having this form:

$$BIT \ bit,(IX+indx)$$
$$BIT \ bit,(IY+indx)$$

They are 4-byte instructions, and the third byte is the index term—a 2's-complement number that is summed with the current content of the IX or IY register to form an effective address.

Thus, the source-code instruction

$$BIT \ 1,(IX+20H)$$

tests bit 1 at a memory address determined by summing the current content of the IX register with 20H. If IX happens to be set at 4000H, the instruction tests the 1-or-0 status of bit 1 at address 4020H, and sets the Z flag accordingly. The appropriate object code for this particular instruction is

```
DD CB 20 4E
```

Putting it all together, the Z-80's bit testing instructions allow the programmer to test any bit residing in an internal 8-bit register or external data memory. What's more, the byte containing the bit to be tested is not altered by the testing instruction.

Exercises at the conclusion of this section ask you to find ways to test selected bits within the Z-80's alternate registers and 16-bit registers.

It is possible to test more than one bit within a designated data byte, but only by doing a succession of bit testing instructions. So if you must test bits 2 and 7, you must write a bit-2 test followed by a bit-7 test.

EXAMPLE 14-10

Write and assemble a Z-80 program that does the following:

1. Test bits 2 and 7 at address 3C00H.
2. If both bits are set: load the tested byte to register A and jump back to step 1.
3. Otherwise, jump back to step 1.

Begin the listing at program address 7000H. See the flowchart in Fig. 14-9 and the suggested program listing in Program 14-10.

The first instruction sets the HL register pair to the input address, 3C00H. Thereafter, any references to the input address can be handled by addressing it in an indirect fashion; by means of an (HL) expression.

The layout of the flowchart and, subsequently, the program itself suggests a logical AND function on two tested bits: The input byte is loaded to the accumulator only if bits 2 AND 7 are equal to logic 1.

Bit Setting Instructions

Unlike the other microprocessors described here, the Z-80 instruction set includes special instructions that set a selected bit to logic 1. See Table 14-4.

These instructions have the same general form as the bit testing instructions. Most have the general form

SET bit,r

where *bit* is the bit to be set (0 through 7), and *r* is an internal 8-bit register designation—a designation for the register holding the byte to be manipulated. When, for example, it is necessary to set bit 4 in the L register, it can be done with the simple instruction Bit 4,C.

It is also possible to set a bit somewhere in external memory, using indirect memory addressing. These instructions have this form:

BIT bit,(HL)

where *bit* is the bit to be set and (HL) implies an address location indicated by the current content of the HL register pair. The following sequence will set bit 7 in a byte residing at memory location 4FFFH:

```
LD  HL,4FFFH
BIT 7,(HL)
```

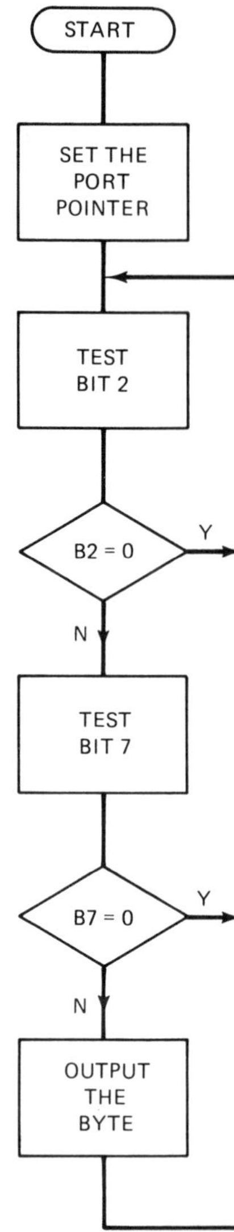

Figure 14-9 Flowchart for Example 14-10.

PROGRAM 14-10 Z-80 LISTING FOR EXAMPLE 14-10

```
7000  21 00 3C   START   LD HL,3C00H    ;SET PORT POINTER
7003  CB 56      TEST    BIT 2,(HL)     ;TEST BIT 2
7005  28 FC              JR Z,TEST      ;IF ZERO, TEST AGAIN
7007  CB 7E              BIT 7,(HL)     ;ELSE TEST BIT 7
7009  28 F8              JR Z,TEST      ;IF ZERO, TEST AGAIN
700B  7E                 LD A,(HL)      ;ELSE INPUT TO A
700C  18 F5              JR TEST        ;AND TEST AGAIN
```

Source code	Object code
SET 0,A	CB C7
SET 0,B	CB C0
SET 0,C	CB C1
SET 0,D	CB C2
SET 0,E	CB C3
SET 0,H	CB C4
SET 0,L	CB C5
SET 0,(HL)	CB C6
SET 0,(IX+*indx*)	DD CB *byte* C6
SET 0,(IY+*indx*)	FD CB *byte* C6
SET 1,A	CB CF
SET 1,B	CB C8
SET 1,C	CB C9
SET 1,D	CB CA
SET 1,E	CB CB
SET 1,H	CB CC
SET 1,L	CB CD
SET 1,(HL)	CB CE
SET 1,(IX+*indx*)	DD CB *byte* CE
SET 1,(IY+*indx*)	FD CB *byte* CE
SET 2,A	CB D7
SET 2,B	CB D0
SET 2,C	CB D1
SET 2,D	CB D2
SET 2,E	CB D3
SET 2,H	CB D4
SET 2,L	CB D5
SET 2,(HL)	CB D6
SET 2,(IX+*indx*)	DD CB *byte* D6
SET 2,(IY+*indx*)	FD CB *byte* D6
SET 3,A	CB DF
SET 3,B	CB D8
SET 3,C	CB D9
SET 3,D	CB DA
SET 3,E	CB DB
SET 3,H	CB DC
SET 3,L	CB DD
SET 3,(HL)	CB DE
SET 3,(IX+*indx*)	DD CB *byte* DE
SET 3,(IY+*indx*)	FD CB *byte* DE
SET 4,A	CB E7
SET 4,B	CB E0
SET 4,C	CB E1
SET 4,D	CB E2
SET 4,E	CB E3
SET 4,H	CB E4
SET 4,L	CB E5

Source code	Object code
SET 4,(HL)	CB E6
SET 4,(IX+*indx*)	DD CB *byte* E6
SET 4,(IY+*indx*)	FD CB *byte* E6
SET 5,A	CB EF
SET 5,B	CB E8
SET 5,C	CB E9
SET 5,D	CB EA
SET 5,E	CB EB
SET 5,H	CB EC
SET 5,L	CB ED
SET 5,(HL)	CB EE
SET 5,(IX+*indx*)	DD CB *byte* EE
SET 5,(IY+*indx*)	FD CB *byte* EE
SET 6,A	CB F7
SET 6,B	CB F0
SET 6,C	CB F1
SET 6,D	CB F2
SET 6,E	CB F3
SET 6,H	CB F4
SET 6,L	CB F5
SET 6,(HL)	CB F6
SET 6,(IX+*indx*)	DD CB *byte* F6
SET 6,(IY+*indx*)	FD CB *byte* F6
SET 7,A	CB FF
SET 7,B	CB F8
SET 7,C	CB F9
SET 7,D	CB FA
SET 7,E	CB FB
SET 7,H	CB FC
SET 7,L	CB FD
SET 7,(HL)	CB FE
SET 7,(IX+*indx*)	DD CB *byte* FE
SET 7,(IY+*indx*)	FD CB *byte* FE

Finally, there are some bit setting instructions that used indexed, indirect addressing. Those are

$$\text{BIT}\ \ bit,(\text{IX}+ind)$$
$$\text{BIT}\ \ bit,(\text{IY}+ind)$$

In those instances, *bit* designates which of the 8 bits is to be set to logic 1. The address of the byte that is affected by the operation is found by summing the current content of the IX or IY register with a 2's-complement index term, *ind*.

Bit Resetting Instructions

The Z-80's instructions for resetting selected bits to zero follow the same general form as the bit testing and setting instructions already described in this section. See Table 14-5.

There can be no room for arguing with the fact that these bit resetting instructions save the programmer some time, effort, and, most important, a concern about making errors in converting binary to hexadecimal numbers.

TABLE 14-5 BIT RESETTING INSTRUCTIONS FOR THE Z-80

Source code	Object code
RES 0,A	CB 87
RES 0,B	CB 80
RES 0,C	CB 81
RES 0,D	CB 82
RES 0,E	CB 83
RES 0,H	CB 84
RES 0,L	CB 85
RES 0,(HL)	CB 86
RES 0,(IX+*indx*)	DD CB *byte* 86
RES 0,(IY+*indx*)	FD CB *byte* 86
RES 1,A	CB 8F
RES 1,B	CB 88
RES 1,C	CB 89
RES 1,D	CB 8A
RES 1,E	CB 8B
RES 1,H	CB 8C
RES 1,L	CB 8D
RES 1,(HL)	CB 8E
RES 1,(IX+*indx*)	DD CB *byte* 8E
RES 1,(IY+*indx*)	FD CB *byte* 8E
RES 2,A	CB 97
RES 2,B	CB 90
RES 2,C	CB 91
RES 2,D	CB 92
RES 2,E	CB 93
RES 2,H	CB 94
RES 2,L	CB 95
RES 2,(HL)	CB 96
RES 2,(IX+*indx*)	DD CB *byte* 96
RES 2,(IY+*indx*)	FD CB *byte* 96
RES 3,A	CB 9F
RES 3,B	CB 98
RES 3,C	CB 99
RES 3,D	CB 9A

Source code	Object code
RES 3,E	CB 9B
RES 3,H	CB 9C
RES 3,L	CB 9D
RES 3,(HL)	CB 9E
RES 3,(IX+*indx*)	DD CB *byte* 9E
RES 3,(IY+*indx*)	FD CB *byte* 9E
RES 4,A	CB A7
RES 4,B	CB A0
RES 4,C	CB A1
RES 4,D	CB A2
RES 4,E	CB A3
RES 4,H	CB A4
RES 4,L	CB A5
RES 4,(HL)	CB A6
RES 4,(IX+*indx*)	DD CB *byte* A6
RES 4,(IY+*indx*)	FD CB *byte* A6
RES 5,A	CB AF
RES 5,B	CB A8
RES 5,C	CB A9
RES 5,D	CB AA
RES 5,E	CB AB
RES 5,H	CB AC
RES 5,L	CB AD
RES 5,(HL)	CB AE
RES 5,(IX+*indx*)	DD CB *byte* AE
RES 5,(IY+*indx*)	FD CB *byte* AE
RES 6,A	CB B7
RES 6,B	CB B0
RES 6,C	CB B1
RES 6,D	CB B2
RES 6,E	CB B3
RES 6,H	CB B4
RES 6,L	CB B5
RES 6,(HL)	CB B6
RES 6,(IX+*indx*)	DD CB *byte* B6
RES 6,(IY+*indx*)	FD CB *byte* B6
RES 7,A	CB BF
RES 7,B	CB B8
RES 7,C	CB B9
RES 7,D	CB BA
RES 7,E	CB BB
RES 7,H	CB BC
RES 7,L	CB BD
RES 7,(HL)	CB BE
RES 7,(IX+*indx*)	DD CB *byte* BE
RES 7,(IY+*indx*)	FD CB *byte* BE

Write and assemble a Z-80 program that does the following:

1. Test bits 3 and 4 of a data byte at address 4C00H.
2. If B3 is set and B4 is reset, go to step 3; otherwise, jump to step 1.
3. Test bit 0 of that same data byte.
4. If B0 is set, jump to step 5; otherwise: set bit 1, reset bit 2, and jump to step 1.
5. Reset bit 1, set bit 2, and jump to step 1.

Use the flowchart in Fig. 14-10 as a guide, and begin the program listing at 4A00H.

The suggested listing in Program 14-11 uses the HL register pair as an address pointer. The content of that register pair points to the data byte at 4C00H. All of the bit test, set, and reset operations can thus take on a simple form of indirect addressing.

PROGRAM 14-11   Z-80 LISTING FOR EXAMPLE 14-11

```
4A00  21 00 4C   START   LD  HL,4C00H    ;SET BYTE POINTER
4A03  CB 4E      TEST    BIT  1,(HL)     ;TEST BIT 1
4A05  28 FC              JR  Z,TEST      ;IF ZERO, TEST AGAIN
4A07  CB 66              BIT  4,(HL)     ;TEST BIT 4
4A09  20 F8              JR  NZ,TEST     ;IF SET, TEST AGAIN
4A0B  CB 46              BIT  0,(HL)     ;TEST BIT 0
4A0D  20 06              JR  NZ,STEP5    ;IF SET, JUMP TO STEP 5
4A0F  CB CE              SET  1,(HL)     ;ELSE SET BIT 1
4A11  CB 96              RES  2,(HL)     ;AND CLEAR BIT 2
4A13  18 EE              JR  TEST        ;TEST AGAIN
4A15  CB 8E      SETP5   RES  1,(HL)     ;RESET BIT 1
4A17  CB D6              SET  2,(HL)     ;SET BIT 2
4A19  18 E8              JR  TEST        ;AND BEGIN TEST AGAIN
```

So the first instruction sets the HL pair to point to the byte at address 4C00H. The next series of BIT and conditional jump instructions carry out all of the required bit testing operations. The program concludes with the appropriate set of bit setting and resetting instructions—sequences of instructions that depend on the status of B0 in the original data byte.

The Z-80's BIT, SET, and RES instructions can point to data bytes in any of the 8-bit working registers. There are no such instructions that point directly to the IX and IY registers. Sometimes it is necessary to do some bit manipulations and tests on the content of those registers, and the matter is handled most easily by transferring the content of one of those 16-bit registers to one of the standard register pairs. How is that done? How about loading the content of one of the 16-bit registers onto the stack, then unloading the stack to a register pair? After doing that, the direct BIT, SET, and RES instructions can be applied.

EXAMPLE 14-12

Write and assemble a Z-80 program that resets bit 12 in the IX register. Begin the listing at program address 7000H, and set the stack at FF00H.

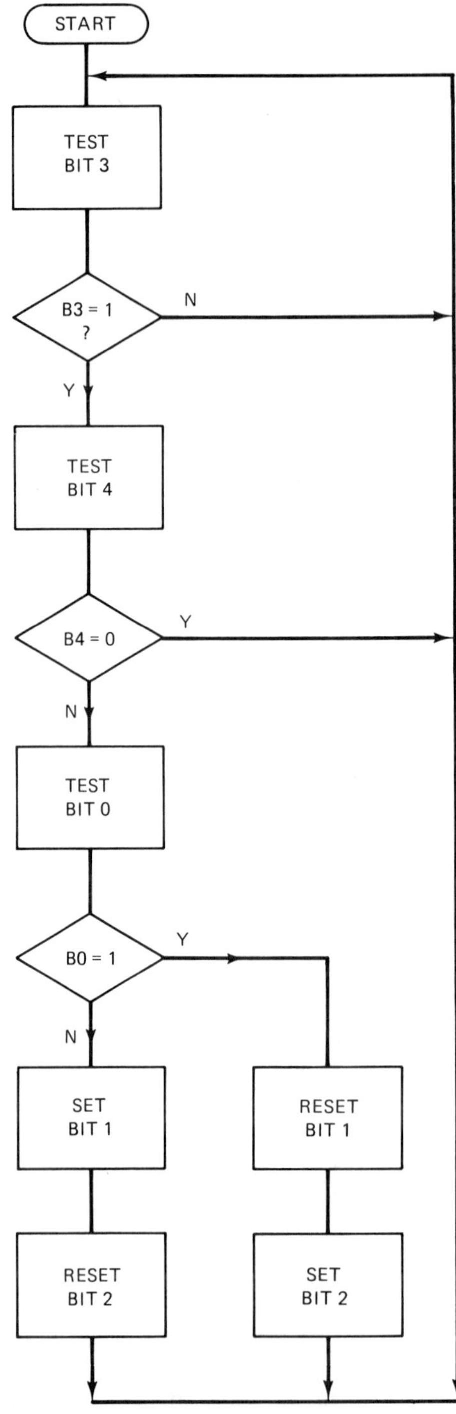

Figure 14-10 Flowchart for Example 14-11.

```
7000 31 00 FF    START  LD SP,FF00H    ;INITIALIZE THE STACK AT FF00H
7003 DD E5              PUSH IX        ;LOAD IX TO STACK
7005 C1                 POP BC         ;ORIGINAL IX TO BC PAIR
7006 CB A0              RES 4,B        ;RESET BIT 12 OF IX
7008 C5                 PUSH BC        ;NEW IX TO STACK
7009 DD E1              POP IX         ;NEW VERSION TO IX REGISTER
```

The first instruction initializes the stack pointer at address FF00H (see Program 14-12). This step is necessary because the simplest procedure for transferring 16-bit data between the IX register and an 8-bit register pair is through the top of the stack.

The second instruction pushes the content of the IX register onto the stack, and the third instruction puts it into the BC register pair. At this point in the routine, the C register holds B0 through B7 of the IX register's data, and register B holds B8 through B15. Thus B12 of the original IX data now resides in the B4 position of the B register.

Instruction RES 4,B resets B4 of register B (B12 of the original IX data) to zero. After that, all that remains is to get the modified 16-bit data back into the IX register. PUSH BC puts that data onto the stack, and POP IX returns it to the IX register.

Similar operations can modify or test any bit in the IX or IY register.

Exercises for Section 14-4

1. Assuming that data 46H resides in the D register at the beginning of each operation, cite the revised content of that register after the following instructions have been executed.

   (a) SET 1,D   (b) SET 4,D   (c) RES 0,D
   (d) RES 7,D   (e) RES 4,D   (f) SET 3,B

2. Assuming that data byte 46H resides in the L register at the beginning of each operation, cite the content of the Z flag bit after the following instructions have been executed.

   (a) BIT 0,L   (b) BIT 7,L   (c) BIT 2,L
   (d) BIT 4,L   (e) BIT 3,L

3. Write and assemble a Z-80 program that does the following:

   1. Test bits B3 and B7 at address F000H.

   2. If B3 is set and B7 is reset, jump to step E.

   3. If B3 is set and B7 is set, jump to step F.

   4. Otherwise jump back to step A.

   5. Set bits B0 and B1, reset bits B3 and B4, output the result to address F001H, and jump back to step A.

   6. Reset bits B0 and B1, set bits B5 and B6, output the result to address F001H, and jump back to step A.

Begin the listing at address 7000H.

15

Data Shift
and Rotate Instructions

The bit setting and resetting operations described in Chapter 14 can alter the status of a selected bit within a given data byte. The mechanisms discussed in this chapter also alter the content of a data byte, but in a significantly different fashion.

15-1 THE FAMILY OF DATA SHIFT AND ROTATE OPERATIONS

Imagine an 8-bit data register filled with some arbitrary combination of 1's and 0's. Then picture yourself punching little round zeros into the left-hand end of the register. Every time you punch in a new zero, all the other bits are shoved one bit location to the right. The bit at the extreme right-hand end drops to the floor, so that the byte always contains no more than 8 bits. If you punch in eight zeros in succession, all the original bits will have fallen out of the end of the register, and it will be filled with your zeros. You can continue punching in more zeros, but the data byte will not seem to change much.

That illustration represents a data *shift* operation. A shift operation moves all the data bits one bit location to the left or right. A *right-shift* operation moves everything one location to the right (in a direction from the most-significant to the least-significant bit), and a *left-shift* operation moves everything one bit location to the left (from the least-significant to the most-significant bit).

But it isn't absolutely necessary to let the bit at one end of the byte fall out of the system. That is allowed to happen sometimes, but often it is necessary to wrap it around to the other end of the register, creating a merry-go-round effect.

An operation that shifts the bits in one particular direction, but feeds the bit coming out of the end back to the beginning, is called a *rotate* operation. A *right-rotate* operation shifts the bits one bit location to the right, and replaces the B7 bit with the one that is shoved out of the opposite end. A *left-rotate* shifts the bits one location to the left, replacing B0 with the bit that comes out of the opposite end. The visual impression might be that of a merry-go-round—the important feature is that no bits are lost in the process.

Data Shift Operations

Figure 15-1 shows the two most common kinds of data shift operations. When doing a left shift, a 0 is punched into the B0 position. The original B0 is shifted to the B1 location, the original B1 goes to B2, and so on down the line. The bit that is forced out of the B7 position goes to the Cs flag bit. The original content of the Cs bit is lost.

Suppose that the original data in a register is 00101101. After doing a single left-shift instruction, the data are changed to 01011010. A zero is punched into the B0 position, and everything else moves one bit location to the left. The zero that was originally in the B7 position can be found in the Cs bit of the flag register.

Now suppose that the data in the register is 00101101 when a right-shift instruction is executed. The result will be 00010110. A zero is punched into the B7 position, the original bits move one location to the right, and the 1 that was originally in the B0 position can be found in Cs.

One of the most compelling applications of data shifts is to convert a data byte into a serial string of 1's and 0's. You might, for instance, want to output the byte one bit at a time. You could do a series of eight left-shift operations, sending the 0-or-1 status of the Cs bit to an output port after each shift. That way, all 8 bits will appear, one at a time and in succession, at the output port.

Another important application of data shift operations concerns multiplying or dividing a number by 2. Suppose that 00000100 is in the register. That is equivalent to decimal 4. Now do a single left shift, and the content of the register is changed to 00001000—decimal 8. If you do another left

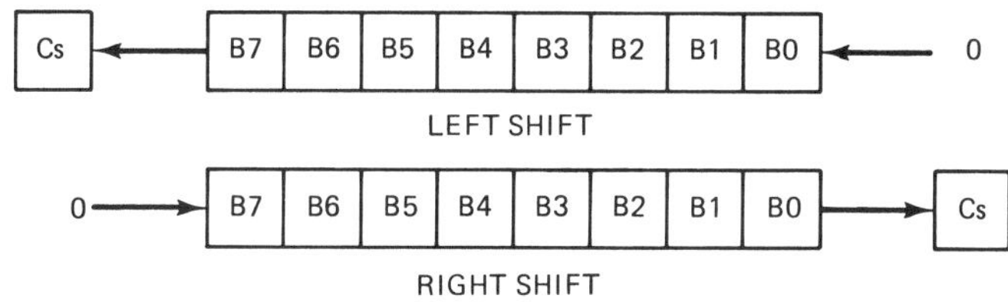

Figure 15-1 Register shift operations.

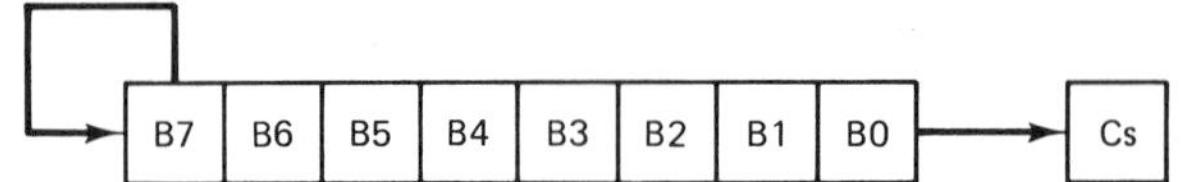

Figure 15-2 The arithmetic right shift operation.

shift, you get 000100000, or decimal 16. *Left shifts effectively multiply a number by 2.*

Now suppose that the register contains the number 00011000, or decimal 24. Doing a single right shift alters the content of that register to 00001100, or decimal 12. Indeed, *the single right-shift operation divided the original number by 2.* Another right shift would bring up 00000110, or decimal 6.

Some microprocessors include a special right-shift instruction that does not necessarily punch a zero into the B7 position every time it is executed. As shown in Fig. 15-2, this arithmetic right shift does not change the 1-or-0 status of the B7 position—it never changes. All the other bits shift one location to the right, however, with the status of the B7 position filling in behind. So if B7 happens to be a 1, this special arithmetic right shift will push a 1 into the B6 position, the original B6 will go to B5, and so on down the line.

A right shift always divides a number by 2, but an arithmetic right shift is used for dividing an 8-bit negative number that is expressed in 2's-complement form. As an example, suppose that the register contains 1111100, or decimal - 4. Doing an arithmetic right shift, the byte changes to 11111110, which is decimal - 2. The absolute value of the original number is divided by 2, and the appropriate sign is maintained.

Simple left shifts will take care of multiplying a number by 2, whether it is in a 2's-complement format or not.

Circular Rotate Operations

The circular rotate operations, illustrated in Fig. 15-3, work very much like their simple shift counterparts. Each bit shifts one location to the left or right, and the Cs flag takes on the status of the bit emerging from the register. But instead of filling in the register with zeros, the circular rotate operations return the emerging bit to the input end, thus setting up the 8-bit merry-go-round effect.

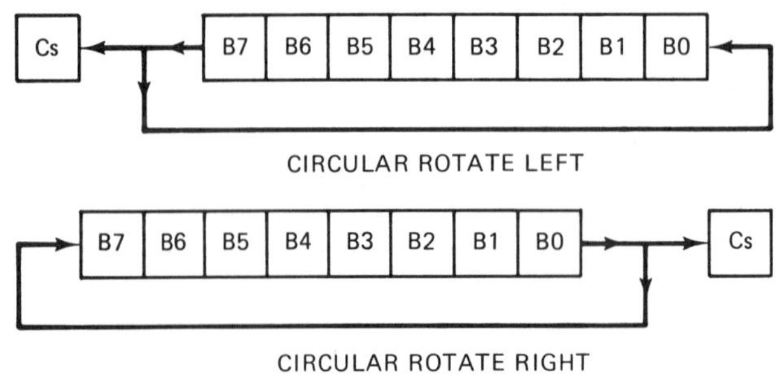

Figure 15-3 Circular rotate operations.

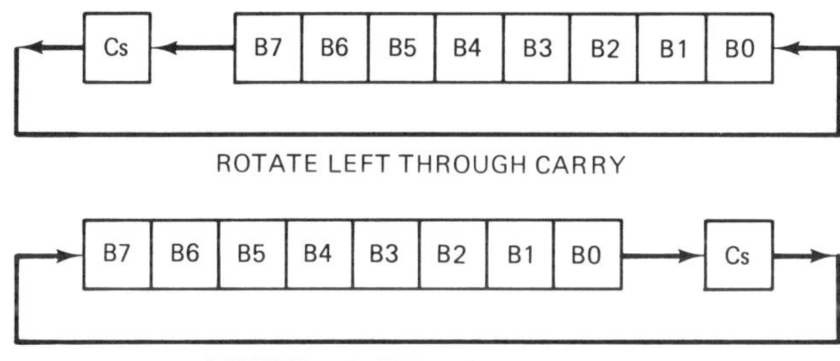

Figure 15-4 Rotate through carry operations.

Suppose that 10110110 is residing in the register when a circular left rotation is executed. The result will be 01101101 in the register, and the Cs bit will be set to logic 1. Everything shifted one bit position to the left, and the 1 emerging from the B7 position went both to the B0 position and the Cs flag bit.

Circular rotates are used mainly for certain classes of control operations. Each bit, for instance, can be directed to the Cs bit in a one-at-a-time sequence. And if the rotate is done eight times in succession, the register ends up having the same bit pattern it had at the beginning. Contrast that with the notion of sending bits to the Cs bit position using simple shift operations—the original byte is lost in the process.

Rotate Through Carry Operations

A second type of rotate operation actually uses the Cs bit in the flag register as a ninth bit. The content of the register actually rotates through the Cs bit. See the diagrams in Fig. 15-4.

As shown in examples later in this chapter, the rotate through carry operations serve many kinds of control applications and can be used for multiplying or dividing multiple-precision (multiregister) numbers by 2.

15-2 SHIFT AND ROTATE INSTRUCTIONS FOR THE Z-80

The Z-80 instruction set includes a full complement of shift and rotate instructions. In all cases the shifted or rotated byte can be residing in one of the main 8-bit working registers, at a memory location that is indirectly addressed by the content of the HL register pair, or at a memory location determined by indexing the IX or IY registers.

Shift Instructions and Operations

Table 15-1 summarizes the Z-80's shift instructions. The SLA instructions shift the designated byte to the left as illustrated in Fig. 15-1. The SRL instructions do a simple, sometimes called a *logical*, shift right as shown in that

TABLE 15-1 SHIFT INSTRUCTIONS FOR THE Z-80

Source code	Object code	Notes
SLA A	CB 27	
SLA B	CB 20	
SLA C	CB 21	
SLA D	CB 22	
SLA E	CB 23	Left shift
SLA H	CB 24	(see Fig. 15-1)
SLA L	CB 25	
SLA (HL)	CB 26	
SLA (IX+*indx*)	DD CB *byte* 26	
SLA (IY+*indx*)	FD CB *byte* 26	
SRA A	CB 2F	
SRA B	CB 28	
SRA C	CB 29	
SRA D	CB 2A	
SRA E	CB 2B	Arithmetic right shift
SRA H	CB 2C	(see Fig. 15-2)
SRA L	CB 2D	
SRA (HL)	CB 2E	
SRA (IX+*indx*)	DD CB *byte* 2E	
SRA (IY+*indx*)	FD CB *byte* 2E	
SRL A	CB 3F	
SRL B	CB 38	
SRL C	CB 39	
SRL D	CB 3A	
SRL E	CB 3B	Right shift
SRL H	CB 3C	(see Fig. 15-1)
SRL L	CB 3D	
SRL (HL)	CB 3E	
SRL (IX+*indx*)	DD CB *byte* 3E	
SRL (IY+*indx*)	FD CB *byte* 3E	

same diagram. In effect, the SLA and SRL instructions are complements of one another.

The SRA instructions do the arithmetic right shift that is shown in Fig. 15-2.

Most of the instructions have the general form

$$oper\ r$$

where *oper* is the shift operator SLA, SRA, or SRL, and *r* is the 8-bit working register containing the byte to be shifted.

One can shift a byte in external memory by means of an instruction of the form

$$oper\ \text{(HL)}$$

where *oper* is the desired shift operator. The byte that is shifted is located at an address pointed by the HL register pair. So if you wish to do a left shift on a byte of data residing at address 3000H, an appropriate instruction sequence would be

```
LD   HL,3000H
SLA  (HL)
```

An alternative form of addressing permits shifting of the bytes in a memory address that is found by summing the content of the IX or IY register with a 2's-complement index term:

$$oper \; (IX+indx)$$

and

$$oper \; (IY+indx)$$

where *oper* is the desired shift operator, and *indx* is the index term.

EXAMPLE 15-1

Write and assemble a Z-80 program that does the following:

1. Fetch a data byte from address F000H.
2. Left shift the bits, one at a time, sending the resulting Cs status to B0 of address F001H.
3. When all bits have been sent out of the system in this fashion, loop back to step 1.

See the flowchart in Fig. 15-5, taking special note of the fact that the B register counts the bits as they are shifted out of the A register (that is how the program knows when the 8-bit shifting operation is done). Begin the listing at address 6100H.

The first step in the program sets the HL register pair to the project's output address, F001H (see Program 15-1). Later references to that address can then be expressed with indirect addressing.

The second instruction fetches the data byte from an input at address F000H, and the third instruction initializes a bit counter at 8. The shifting operation, begun in the next step, must take place eight times in succession; and the purpose of that bit counter (the B register in this example) is to

PROGRAM 15-1   Z-80 LISTING FOR EXAMPLE 15-1

```
6100  21 01 F0    START    LD HL,(F001H)    ;INITIALIZE OUTPUT POINTER
6103  3A 00 F0    FETCH     LD A,(FOOOH)     ;FETCH INPUT BYTE
6106  06 08                LD B,08H          ;INITIALIZE BIT COUNTER
6108  CB 27       SHIFT     SLA A             ;LEFT SHIFT THE BYTE
610A  30 04                JR NC,ZEROUT      ;IF ZERO, DO ZERO OUT
610C  CB C6                SET 0,(HL)        ;SET B0 OF OUTPUT
610E  18 02                JR NEXT           ;AND SETUP NEXT
6110  CB 86       ZEROUT    RES 0,(HL)        ;RESET B0 OF OUTPUT
6112  05          NEXT      DEC B             ;DECREMENT BIT COUNTER
6113  20 F3                JR NZ,SHIFT       ;IF NOT DONE, SHIFT AGAIN
6115  18 EC                JR FETCH          ;ELSE FETCH A NEW BYTE
```

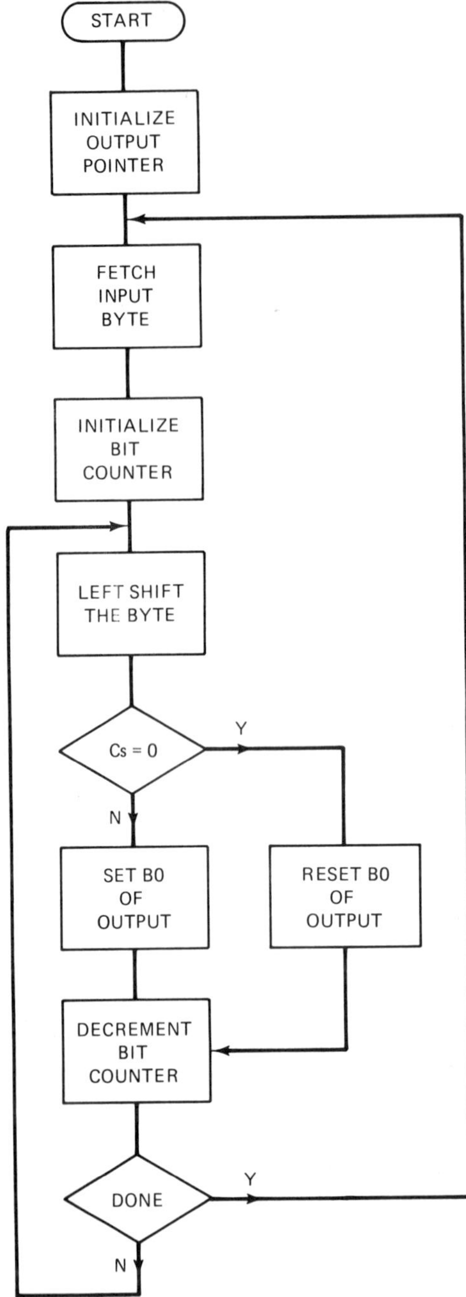

Figure 15-5 Flowchart for the task in Example 15-1.

allow bits to continue shifting to the output until all eight have been treated that way.

Immediately after the left-shift operation is done, the bit from the B7 position appears in the Cs flag position. If Cs is equal to zero, it means that the bit previously in the B7 position of the A register must have been a zero. Otherwise, the Cs bit will be set to 1.

If it turns out that Cs is 0, a BIT instruction resets B0 of the output address to zero. If the Cs bit is a 1, on the other hand, a different BIT instruction sets B0 of the output to logic 1. Bit 0 at address F001H thus takes on the 1-or-0 status of the bit just shifted out of the accumulator.

When that shifting and bit setting sequence is done, the bit counter is decremented by one count. If it has not yet reached zero, as signaled by the zero flag bit, the program loops back to SHIFT and another bit shifting sequence takes place. If the bit counter is decremented to 0, however, it means that the bit shifting job is done; and operations loop back to FETCH to start the whole thing over again.

Such a program can be technically classified as a *parallel-to-serial data converter*. The parallel, 8-bit content of address F000H is converted into a string of serial 1-and-0 bits at the B0 position of address F001H.

Left-shift operations can be used for multiplying a number by 2. Every shift doubles the value residing in the register prior to that shift. Thus it is possible to do multiple left-shift operations and effectively multiply a value by 2, 4, 8, 16, 32, 64, or 128. One must make certain, however, that the final result does not attempt to exceed 255 (decimal) when doing that sort of multiplication with unsigned 8-bit values.

Multiplying a byte by 8 calls for doing three left shifts in succession. The largest original number that can be treated that way is hexadecimal 1F, or decimal 31. The following example goof-proofs the multiply-by-8 operation by testing the initial value, allowing the operation to take place only if it is equal to or less than 1FH.

EXAMPLE 15-2

Write and assemble a Z-80 program that fetches an unsigned 8-bit number from an input port at address F000H. If the byte is less than or equal to 1FH, multiply it by 8 and output the result to a port at address F001H. If the fetched byte is greater than 1FH, ignore it and fetch again. Begin the listing at program address 7000H.

See the result in Program 15-2.

PROGRAM 15-2 Z-80 LISTING FOR EXAMPLE 15-2

```
7000  3A 00 F0   FETCH   LD  A,(F000H)    ;FETCH THE INPUT BYTE
7003  FE 1F               CP  1FH          ;COMPARE WITH MAX VALUE
7005  28 02               JR  Z,MULT       ;IF EQUAL, THEN MULTIPLY
7007  30 F7               JR  NC, FETCH    ;IF GREATER, THEN FETCH AGAIN
7009  CB 27      MULT     SLA  A           ;MULTIPLY BY 2
700B  CB 27               SLA  A           ;DOUBLE AGAIN
700D  CB 27               SLA  A           ;DOUBLE AGAIN
700F  32 01 F0            LD  (F001H),A    ;OUTPUT THE RESULT
7012  18 EC               JR  FETCH        ;AND START ALL OVER
```

The first instruction fetches the byte from input address F000H. It is then compared with the maximum multiply-by-8 value of 1FH; and if the numbers are equal, the program jumps to MULT. If the numbers are not equal and there is no carry, the fetched byte is too large, and operations return to FETCH.

The MULT routine simply does three shift-left operations in sequence, effectively multiplying the fetched value by 8. The result is then output to address F001H, and operations loop back up to FETCH to start the whole operation all over again.

Another way to determine whether or not the result of a multiplication operation fits into an 8-bit format is to compare the final result with the original data byte. If the result is a number that is smaller than the original, it figures that the register has been wrapped around—the result is invalid. But if the result is larger than the original value (and the multiplication has not shifted the data by more than seven times), the result is good. The next example illustrates this checking procedure.

The next example also demonstrates how it is possible to multiply a byte by some number other than a power-of-2 value.

EXAMPLE 15-3

Write and assemble a Z-80 program that does the following:

1. Fetch a data byte from an input port located at address F000H.
2. Multiply the byte by 5. (*Hint:* If the original byte is n, $5n = 2n \times 2n + n$.)
3. If the result is less than the original value, jump back to fetch again.
4. Otherwise, output the result to a port located at address F001H.

See the flowchart in Fig. 15-6, and begin the listing at 7000H. The suggesting listing is shown in Program 15-3.

The first major part of the program fetches the data byte from the input address, doubles its value twice in succession, and then sums the result with the original value. The original value, saved in register B by the second instruction in the program, is thus multiplied by 5. The result is in the ac-

PROGRAM 15-3   Z-80 LISTING FOR EXAMPLE 15-3

```
7000  3A 00 F0   FETCH   LD A,(F000H)    ;FETCH THE INPUT BYTE
7003  47                 LD B,A          ;SAVE A COPY IN B
7004  CB 27              SLA  A          ;MULTIPLY BY 2
7006  CB 27              SLA  A          ;MULTIPLY BY 2 AGAIN
7008  80                 ADD A,B         ;ADD ORIGINAL
7009  B8                 CP  B           ;COMPARE WITH ORIGINAL
700A  28 02              JR Z,OPUT        ;IF EQUAL, THEN OUTPUT IT
700C  30 F2              JR NC,FETCH     ;IF LESS, FETCH A NEW BYTE
700E  32 01 F0   OPUT    LD (F001H),A    ;ELSE OUTPUT THE RESULT
7011  18 ED              JR FETCH        ;AND START ALL OVER
```

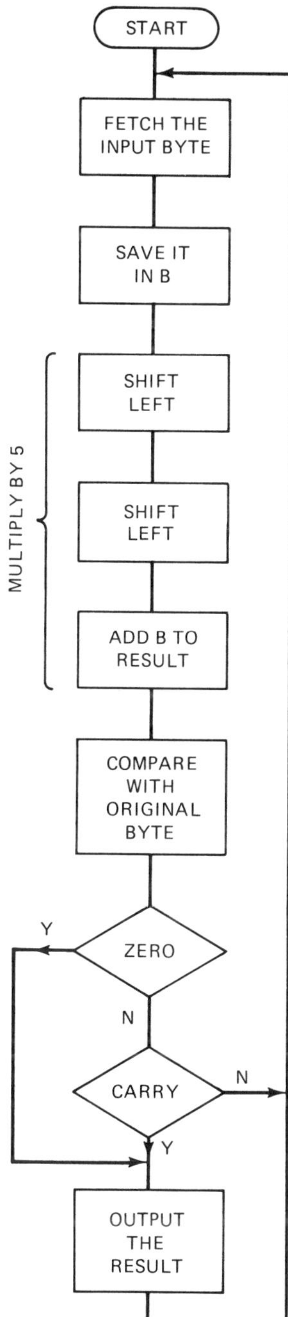

Figure 15-6 Flowchart for the multiply-by-5 task in Example 15-3.

cumulator, or A register, by the time the program reaches the CP B instruction.

The CP B instruction begins a series of steps designed to find out whether or not the result of the multiplication is a value that is too large to fit into an unsigned 8-bit format. If the value in register A is greater than or equal to the original value residing in register B, the conditional jump instructions allow the result to be sent to the output port. Otherwise, the result is considered invalid, and it is not sent to the output—operations return directly back to FETCH.

Circular Rotate Instructions

The Z-80's circular rotate instructions are summarized in Table 15-2. They affect the rotated byte and Cs flag as indicated in Fig. 15-3, and they use the same addressing formats as the shift instructions do.

It should not pass without mentioning that instructions RLCA and RLC A are redundant—they both do a circular left rotate. It is not our business to suggest any reasons why such redundant instructions should exist; but we can point out that the RLCA version is a 1-byte instruction, whereas its RLC A version calls for a 2-byte instruction. Given the choice, most programmers will opt for the simpler, 1-byte version.

A similar redundancy exists for the RRCA and RRC A instructions.

TABLE 15-2 CIRCULAR ROTATE INSTRUCTIONS FOR THE Z-80

Source code	Object code	Notes
RLCA	07	
RLC A	CB 07	
RLC B	CB 00	
RLC C	CB 01	
RLC D	CB 02	
RLC E	CB 03	Rotate left circular (see Fig. 15-3)
RLC H	CB 04	
RLC L	CB 05	
RLC (HL)	CB 06	
RLC (IX+*indx*)	DD CB *byte* 06	
RLC (IY+*indx*)	FD CB *byte* 06	
RRCA	0F	
RRC A	CB 0F	
RRC B	CB 08	
RRC C	CB 09	
RRC D	CB 0A	
RRC E	CB 0B	Rotate right circular (see Fig. 15-3)
RRC H	CB 0C	
RRC L	CB 0D	
RRC (HL)	CB 0E	
RRC (IX+*indx*)	DD CB *byte* 0E	
RRC (IY+*indx*)	FD CB *byte* 0E	

Figure 15-7a shows an 8-bit output circuit that operates from data sent to memory-mapped address F001H. Whenever one of the bits from the data bus is set to a logic 1, its corresponding LED lights. A logic 0 on any of bit connections turns off the corresponding LED. Write and assemble a Z-80 program that lights the LEDs, one at a time, from left to right (from LED 7 to LED 0). The "scanning" should take place continuously, and there must be a time delay of about 2 seconds between each step in the scan. Begin the listing at 4000H and use the flowchart in Fig. 15-7b as a guide.

The idea behind the example is to rotate a single logic-1 bit to the right, inserting a time delay between each rotate operation. The fact that a circular right rotate wraps around the bit from the left end to the right end makes it possible to keep "scanning" effect running continuously. See the suggested listing in Program 15-4.

The program begins by setting the HL register pair to point to the output port at address F001H. The next instruction initializes the whole operation by sending 80 hexadecimal, or 10000000 binary, to the output. That operation thus lights the first LED on the left, LED 7.

The third instruction, at label DOIT, calls a time delay subroutine. That subroutine will be described a bit later; for the time being, it is sufficient to know that TDLY carries out a time delay operation on the order of 2 seconds.

After the time delay has been executed, program operation returns to RRC (HL). That is a circular right rotate; and by indicating the content of the HL register pair, the rotate actually takes place at the byte located at the output port—at address F001H. As a result, the lighted bit moves one LED location to the right.

Instruction JR DOIT concludes the mainline program, sending the whole operation back to DOIT. The time delay is executed again, keeping the lamp lit for about 2 seconds, and then the energizing bit is moved one more step to the right.

After LED 0 has been lit and the time delay is executed, the RRC (HL) instruction simply rotates that energizing bit back to the LED 7 location, and the scanning cycle begins all over again.

PROGRAM 15-4 Z-80 LISTING FOR EXAMPLE 15-4

```
4000  21 01 F0  START  LD  HL,F001H    ;SETUP OUTPUT POINTER
4003  36 80            LD  (HL),80H    ;INITIALIZE THE OUTPUT
4005  CD 0C 40  DOIT   CALL TDLY       ;DO TIME DELAY
4008  CB 0E            RRC (HL)        ;ROTATE RIGHT
400A  18 F9            JR  DOIT        ;AND DO IT AGAIN
400C  01 FF FF  TDLY   LD  BC,0FFFFH   ;INITIALIZE TIME DELAY
400F  0B        CNT    DEC BC          ;DECREMENT TIME COUNT
4010  79               LD  A,C         ;GET LSB OF TIME COUNT
4011  B0               OR  B           ;OR WITH MSB
4012  20 FB            JR  NZ,CNT      ;IF NOT DONE, COUNT MORE
4014  C9               RET             ;ELSE RETURN
```

Note: It is assumed that the stack pointer was initialized at some earlier point in the program.

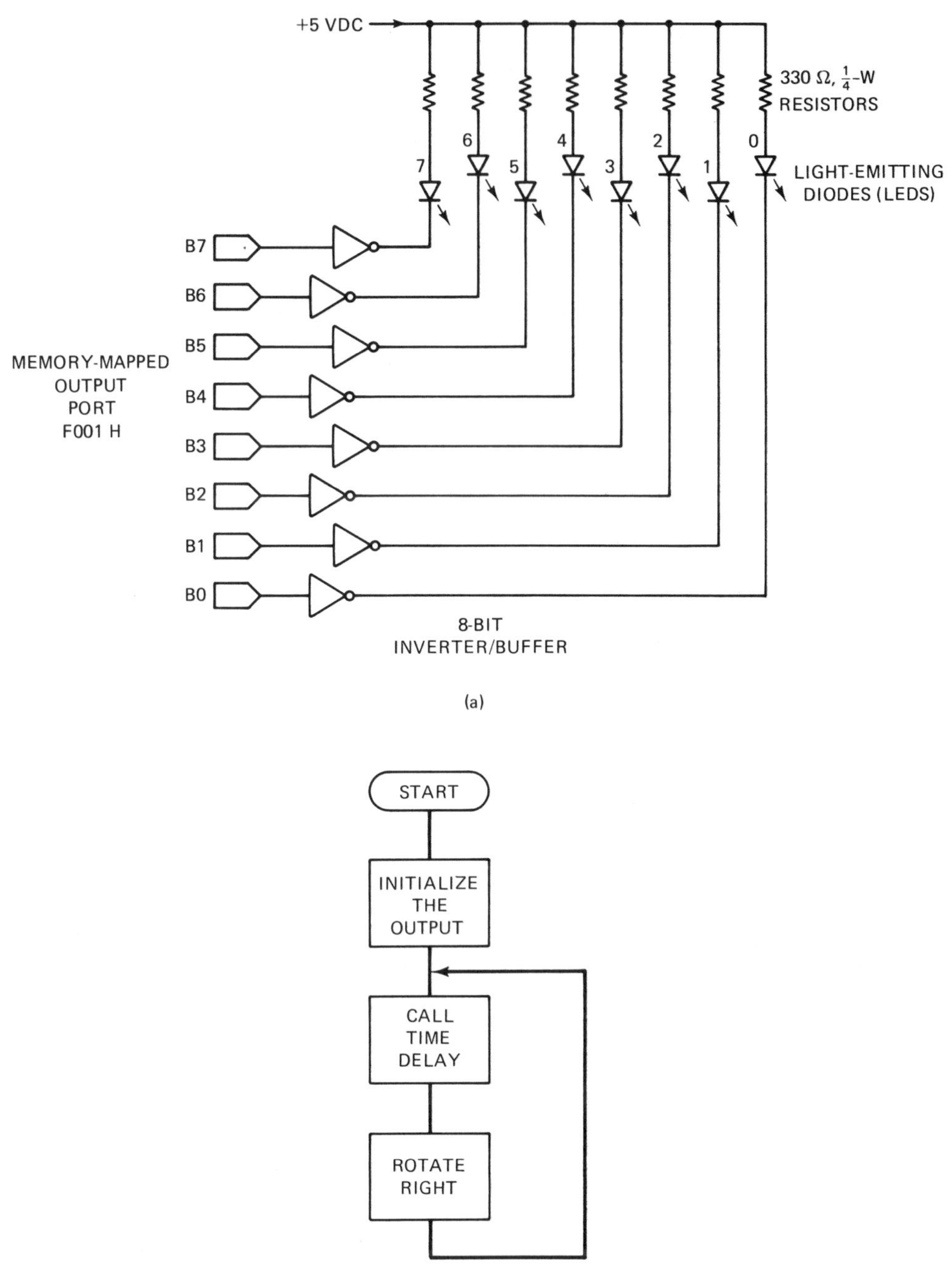

Figure 15-7 Electrical diagram and flowchart for Example 15-4. (a) Diagram of an 8-bit LED output circuit. (b) Flowchart for a routine that shifts the lighted lamp at the output.

The visual impression is that the lighted bit moves from left to right at 2-second intervals. When it reaches LED 0, it rests there for about 2 seconds, then moves back to LED 7 to start another cycle.

The time delay routine, beginning at label TDLY, does its job by counting down the content of the BC register pair to zero. The first instruction is that subroutine initializes the BC register pair at FFFFH. The next step decrements that register pair; and the subsequent operations determine whether or not the BC pair has been counted down to zero. If not, operations jump back to CNT to decrement another count. If, however, the counting has reached zero, the RET instruction returns operations to the mainline program.

EXAMPLE 15-5

Using the circuit in Fig. 15-7a, rewrite Example 15-4 so that the light scans one position at a time to the right, then reverses its direction to scan to the left. Continue the right/left scanning cycles indefinitely. See the flowcharts in Fig. 15-8.

In the context of the circuit shown in Fig. 15-7a, doing circular right rotates make the lighted LED appear to scan from left to right—in a direction from LED 7 to LED 0. A circular left rotate, on the other hand, would

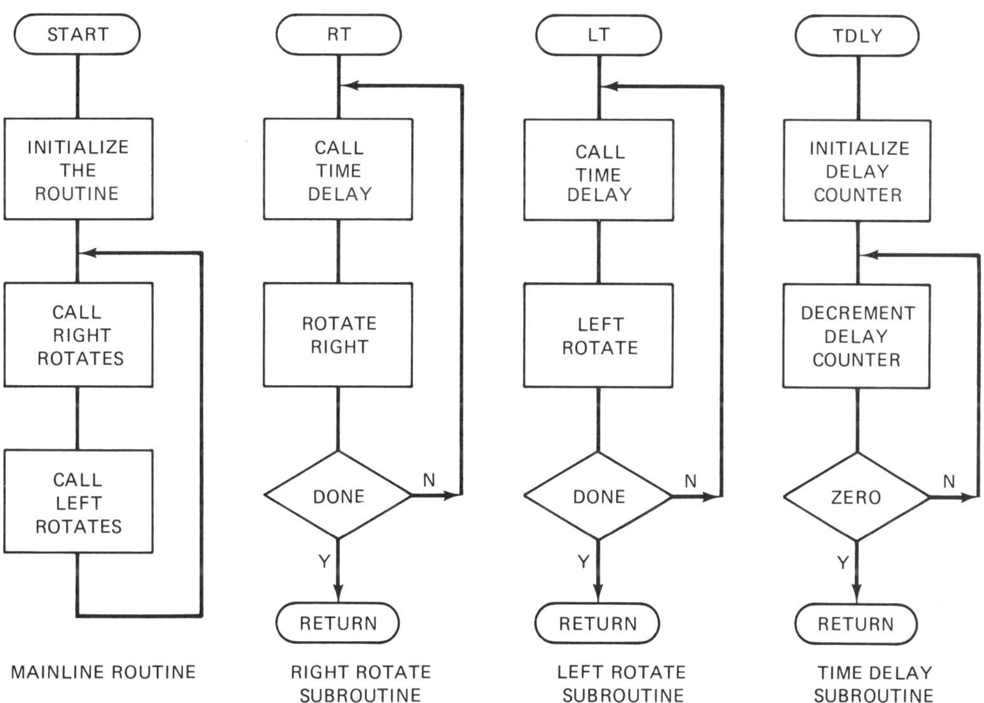

Figure 15-8 Flowcharts for the task in Example 15-5. (a) Mainline routine. (b) Right-rotate subroutine. (c) Left-rotate subroutine. (d) Time delay subroutine.

create a scanning effect of the opposite direction—from LED 0 to LED 7. The essence of the current example is to create the impression of having the lighted lamp scan back and forth in a continuous fashion.

The flowchart for the mainline portion of the program begins by initializing the routine. That amounts to setting up the output address pointer and initializing the operation for starting with a right-rotate routine.

The mainline then calls a subroutine that makes the light-energizing bit move one step at a time to the right. And when that right-scanning cycle is done, the next block on the flowchart shows the mainline calling a similar subroutine that moves the light-energizing bit to the left. When that cycle is completed, the program simply jumps back to execute the right-rotate operations again. See the first block of five instructions in the suggested program listing, Program 15-5.

The mainline part of the program begins by setting the HL register pair to point to the output byte. The second instruction initializes the whole operation by, in effect, lighting LED 7. Then the mainline calls the right-rotate subroutine, RT; and when operations return to the mainline, it calls the left-rotate subroutine, LT. After that, the JR DOIT instruction loops operations back up to the point where the RT subroutine is called again. The mainline program thus runs indefinitely.

The right-rotate subroutine is shown in a flowchart form in Fig. 15-8. The general idea is to call a 2-second time delay, and then do a single circular right rotate. Now, if the lamp-energizing bit has been rotated all the way to the B0 position, the Cs flag bit will also be set to logic 1. Otherwise, it will

PROGRAM 15-5 Z-80 LISTING FOR EXAMPLE 15-5

```
4000   21 01 F0   START   LD HL,F001H      ;SETUP OUTPUT POINTER
4003   36 80              LD (HL),80H      ;INITIALIZE OUTPUT
4005   CD 0D 40   DOIT    CALL RT          ;DO RIGHT ROTATE
4008   CD 15 40           CALL LT          ;DO LEFT ROTATE
400B   18 F8              JR DOIT          ;AND START ALL OVER
                   ;END OF MAINLINE ROUTINE
400D   CD 1D 40   RT      CALL TDLY        ;DO TIME DELAY
4010   CB 0E              RRC (HL)         ;ROTATE RIGHT
4012   30 F9              JR NC,RT         ;IF NOT DONE, DO AGAIN
4014   C9                 RET              ;ELSE RETURN
                   ;END OF RIGHT ROTATE SUBROUTINE
4015   CD 1D 40   LT      CALL TDLY        ;DO TIME DELAY
4018   CB 06              RLC (HL)         ;ROTATE LEFT
401A   30 F9              JR NC,LT         ;IF NOT DONE, DO AGAIN
401C   C9                 RET              ;ELSE RETURN
                   ;END OF LEFT ROTATE SUBROUTINE
401D   01 FF FF   TDLY    LD BC,0FFFFH     ;INITIALIZE TIME DELAY
4020   0B         CNT     DEC BC           ;DECREMENT TIME COUNT
4021   79                 LD A,C           ;GET LSB OF TIME COUNT
4022   B0                 OR B             ;OR WITH MSB
4023   20 FB              JR NZ,CNT        ;IF NOT DONE, DELAY MORE
4025   C9                 RET              ;ELSE RETURN
                   ;END OF TIME DELAY SUBROUTINE
```

Note: It is assumed that the stack pointer was initialized at an earlier point in the program.

be reset to 0. Thus the DONE conditional operation in the flowchart is asking this question: Is the Cs flag bit set to 1? If not, loop back to call another time delay and then shift again. If the Cs bit is set, the right-rotate portion of the cycle must be done, and it is time to return to the mainline program.

The right-rotate instructions appear in the listing under the label RT. The CALL TDLY instruction calls the time delay subroutine. And when operations return to the RT subroutine, the next instruction, RRC (HL), executes a single, circular right rotate at the byte addressed by the HL register pair—the output byte at address F001H. (Recall that the HL register pair was initialized at F001H as the first instruction in the mainline routine.) JR NC,RT senses whether or not the lamp-energizing bit has reached the B0 position. If there is no carry—the bit has not reached the B0 position—the relative jump instruction forces a repeat of the entire RT subroutine. The time delay is executed and the bit is rotated one more position to the right. But when the Cs bit is found to be a logic 1, the right rotation is done, and the RT subroutine calls for returning to the mainline program.

The left-rotate subroutine does the same job as its right-rotating counterpart. The only difference is the direction of rotation. Compare the flowcharts for those two subroutines, and see the listing under label LT.

The time delay subroutine is called from both the LT and RT. It works exactly like the TDLY routine described in connection with Example 15-4. For the sake of presenting some complete documentation, that subroutine's flowchart appears with the others in Fig. 15-8.

Rotate Through Carry Instructions

Table 15-3 shows the Z-80's instructions for doing rotates through the carry, or Cs, bit. They follow the operations diagrammed in Fig. 15-4, and they use the same addressing modes as the other shift and rotate instructions.

There are two sets of redundant instructions: RLA and RL A, and RRA and RR A. Use the simpler, 1-byte versions, RLA and RRA, whenever possible.

Rotate through carry instructions are especially important when attempting to write program routines that shift the data contained in more than one register. Suppose you face a situation where you have to double the value of a 2-byte number. Doubling a 1-byte number is a simple matter of doing a single left-shift operation on the byte. But doing a left shift on a 2-byte, or 16-bit, number is another matter.

Assuming that the double-precision number is already residing in the DE register pair (with the MSB in the D register and the LSB in the E register), a simple pair of instructions is adequate for doubling the value—for doing a 16-bit left-shift operation:

```
SLA E   ;SHIFT LEFT THROUGH LSB
RL  D   ;ROTATE LEFT THROUGH MSB
```

TABLE 15-3 ROTATE THROUGH CARRY INSTRUCTIONS FOR THE Z-80

Source code	Object code			Notes
RLA	17			
RL A	CB	17		
RL B	CB	10		
RL C	CB	11		
RL D	CB	12		
RL E	CB	13		Rotate left through carry (see Fig. 15-4)
RL H	CB	14		
RL L	CB	15		
RL (HL)	CB	16		
RL (IX+*indx*)	DD	CB	*byte* 16	
RL (IY+*indx*)	FD	CB	*byte* 16	
RRA	1F			
RR A	CB	1F		
RR B	CB	18		
RR C	CB	19		
RR D	CB	1A		
RR E	CB	1B		Rotate right through carry (see Fig. 15-4)
RR H	CB	1C		
RR L	CB	1D		
RR (HL)	CB	1E		
RR (IX+*indx*)	DD	CB	*byte* 1E	
RR (IY+*indx*)	FD	CB	*byte* 1E	

The first instruction shifts the data in the E register one bit location to the left; the original B0 is replaced with a zero, and the original B7 goes to the Cs flag bit in the F register. That completes the left shift as far as the LSB portion of the number is concerned.

The second instruction does a rotate left through carry. Since the previous operation placed the original B7 bit from the E register into the Cs bit position, the RL D instruction picks up that bit and places it into the B0 position of the D register. Everything else in the D register is shoved one location to the left, and the double-precision left-shift operation is done. The original B7 from the MSB, incidentally, is left in the Cs bit.

EXAMPLE 15-6

Write and assemble a Z-80 program that does the following:

1. Fetch a double byte from address F000H and F001H to the C and B registers, respectively.

2. Consider the content of the B register the MSB, and do a double-register left-shift operation.

3. Store the result to output addresses FF00H and FF01H, with the latter taking the MSB.

4. Jump back to step 1.

Begin the listing at address 4000H and see the suggested program in Program 15-6.

```
4000  ED 4B 00 F0   FETCH   LD BC,(F000H)   ;FETCH THE BYTES
4004  CB 21                  SLA C           ;SHIFT LSB LEFT
4006  CB 10                  RL B            ;ROTATE MSB LEFT
4008  ED 43 00 FF            LD (FF00H),BC   ;OUTPUT THE RESULTS
400C  18 F2                  JR FETCH        ;AND START ALL OVER
```

The first instruction does a double-byte loading operation to the BC register pair. The content of input address F000H goes to the LSB position (register C), and the content of input address F001H goes to the MSB position (register B).

The next two instructions do the double-register left-shift as described earlier. LD (FF00H), BC does a double-register output to addresses FF00H and FF01H, and the final instruction loops operations back to the beginning.

Double-register right shifts can be accomplished using the same general approach. In this case, a logical right shift is applied to the MSB, followed by a right rotate to the LSB. For instance:

```
SRL D   ;LOGICAL SHIFT RIGHT THROUGH MSB
RR E    ;CIRCULAR ROTATE RIGHT THROUGH LSB
```

EXAMPLE 15-7

Two bytes of data reside in memory locations F000H and F001H, with the LSB being at F000H. Write and assemble a Z-80 program that does a parallel-to-serial data conversion of all 16 bits, outputting the bits to the B0 position at address F002H. Use right shifting and indexed addressing where possible. Begin the program at 4000H.

See the flowchart in Fig. 15-9.

The suggested listing in Program 15-7 begins by setting the IX index register to F000H. Doing that, the LSB of the data being shifted can be accessed by (IX+0) instructions, the MSB of the data can be found at (IX+01H), and the output is at B0 of (IX+02H).

The second instruction initializes the bit counter at 10H, or 16 decimal. That counter will keep track of how many bits are shifted out of the data

PROGRAM 15-7   Z-80 LISTING FOR EXAMPLE 15-7

```
4000  DD 21 00 F0   START   LD IX,F000H     ;SETUP INDEX POINTER
4004  06 10         RUN     LD B,10H        ;INITIALIZE BIT COUNTER
4006  DD CB 01 3E   SHIFT   SRL (IX+01H)    ;SHIFT RIGHT THROUGH MSB
400A  DD CB 00 16           RL (IX+00H)     ;ROTATE RIGHT THROUGH LSB
400E  30 06                 JR NC,OUT1      ;IF NO CARRY, JUMP TO OUT1
4010  DD CB 02 86           RES 0,(IX+02)   ;RESET OUTPUT BIT
4014  18 04                 JR NEXT         ;AND JUMP TO NEXT
4016  DD CB 02 C6   OUT1    SET 0,(IX+02)   ;SET OUTPUT BIT
401A  05            NEXT    DEC B           ;DECREMENT BIT COUNTER
401B  20 E9                 JR NZ,SHIFT     ;IF NOT DONE, SHIFT AGAIN
401D  18 E1                 JR RUN          ;ELSE RUN AGAIN
```

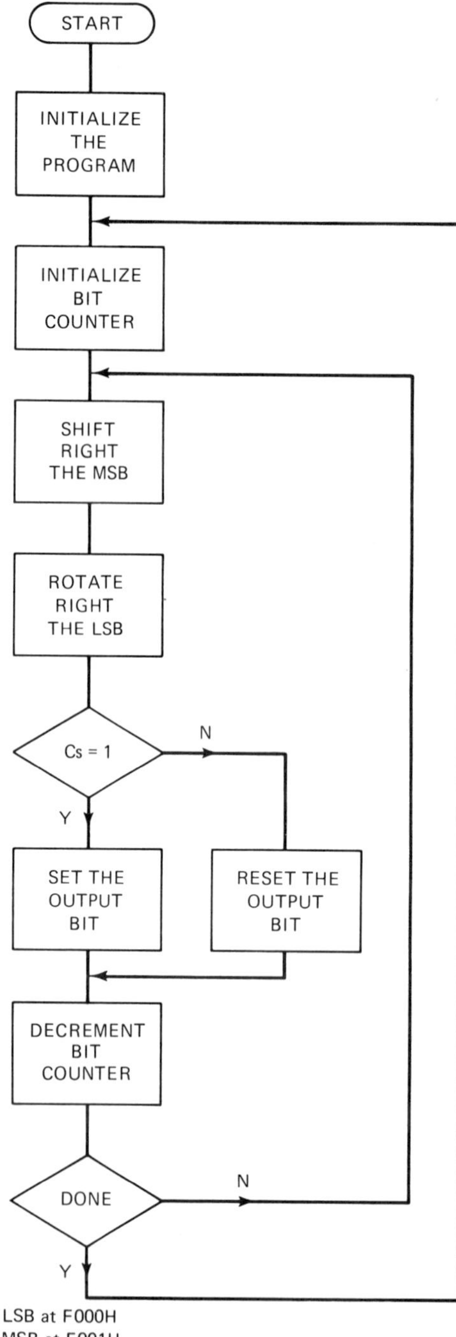

Figure 15-9 Flowchart for the task in Example 15-7.

and to the output. There are 16 bits, rather than 8, to be shifted out in this example. Earlier examples of this type shifted 8-bit data.

The sequence of instructions beginning at label SHIFT does the actual 16-bit shifting operation. SRL (IX+01H) shifts the MSB of the data one place to the right, and RL (IX+00H) picks up the Cs bit from the previous shift and shoves it into the B7 position of the LSB. Everything else in the LSB is shifted one place to the right, with the original B0 going to the Cs flag bit position.

If that bit in the Cs flag position happens to be a 0, the program does a jump to the instruction labeled OUT1. Otherwise, the B0 position of the output address (F002H) is reset to zero by the instruction, RES 0,(IX+02).

Whether the output bit is set or reset, the instructions beginning at label NEXT decrement the bit counter. If it is not decremented to zero, it means that more bits have to be shifted out of the system, and control loops back to SHIFT again. But if the bit counter is decremented to zero, the shifting is done, and the system loops back to RUN to start the operation all over again.

Exercises for Section 15-2

1. Verbally describe the nature of the following Z-80 instructions:
   (a) SLA L   (b) SRA (HL)   (c) SRL D
   (d) RLC (IX+*indx*)   (e) RRC L   (f) RR (HL)
2. What is the operational difference between RLA and RL A? RRA and RR A? RLCA and RLC A? RRCA and RRC A?
3. Cite the Z-80 mnemonic and object code for the following kinds of operations.
   (a) Left shift the content of the D register.
   (b) Right shift the content of the A register.
   (c) Do a left circular rotate with the content of the C register.
   (d) Rotate left through carry the content of the memory address pointed by the HL register pair.

15-3 SHIFT AND ROTATE INSTRUCTIONS FOR THE 6800

The family of shift and rotate instructions for the 6800 device includes:

Shift left

Logical shift right

Arithmetic shift right

Rotate left through carry

Rotate right through carry

All that is missing with respect to the Z-80's full family of such instructions are the circular rotate instructions. You will see that it isn't difficult to simulate the behavior of those instructions, however.

TABLE 15-4   SHIFT INSTRUCTIONS FOR THE 6800

Source code	Object code	Notes
ASLA	48	Shift left
ASLB	58	(see Fig. 15-1)
ASL *addr*	78 *byte byte*	
ASL *indx*,X	68 *byte*	
LSRA	44	
LSRB	54	Logical shift right
LSR *addr*	74 *byte byte*	(see Fig. 15-1)
LSR *indx*,X	64 *byte*	
ASRA	47	
ASRB	57	Arithmetic shift right
ASR *addr*	77 *byte byte*	(see Fig. 15-2)
ASR *indx*,X	67 *byte*	

Shift Instructions and Operations

Table 15-4 shows the three sets of shift instructions available to the 6800 system. As far as the shift-left instructions are concerned, their literal meanings are:

ASLA	Shift left the content of the A accumulator.
ASLB	Shift left the content of the B accumulator
ASL *addr*	Shift left the content of a byte located at the 16-bit address, *addr*
ASL *indx*,X ASL *indx*,X	Shift left the byte located at an effective address found by summing the current content of the X register with the index term, *indx*. As usual for the 6800, the index term is an unsigned 8-bit value.

The instructions for logical shift right and arithmetic shift right have that same set of addressing modes, but of course the opcodes are slightly different.

EXAMPLE 15-8

Rewrite the task in Example 15-3 to conform to 6800 standards. In short, fetch an unsigned 8-bit value from address $F000, multiply it by 5, and check to see whether or not the result is less than the original value. If so, repeat the procedure from the beginning; otherwise, send the result to address $F001.

The suggested listing in Program 15-8 carries out the task using indexed addressing. The first instruction sets up the base address, $F000, in the 16-bit IX register, and the second instruction fetches the input byte from address $F000. The third instruction—STAA $FF,X—saves the byte at address $F0FF for future reference.

The sequence of two ASLA instructions effectively multiply the original byte by 4 in the A accumulator. The ADD instruction—ADDA $FF,X—

```
7000 CE FF 00    START   LDX  #$F000   INITIALIZE PORT POINTER
7003 A6 00       FETCH   LDAA $00,X    FETCH THE INPUT BYTE
7005 A7 FF               STAA $FF,X    SAVE IN $F0FF
7007 48                  ASLA          DOUBLE THE VALUE IN A
7008 48                  ASLA          DOUBLE THE VALUE IN A
7009 AB FF               ADDA $FF,X    ADD ORIGINAL VALUE
700B A1 FF               CMPA $FF,X    COMPARE WITH ORIGINAL
700D 27 02               BEQ  OPUT     IF EQUAL, OUTPUT IT
700F 25 F2               BCS  FETCH    IF LESS, FETCH AGAIN
7011 A7 01       OPUT    STAA $01,X    OUTPUT THE RESULT
7013 20 EE               BRA  FETCH    AND FETCH AGAIN
```

sums the original byte with the content of the A accumulator to yield a multiply-by-5 result.

The result is compared with the original byte by the instruction CMPA $FF,X; and the subsequent branch instructions take action based on the result. If the result is greater than or equal to the original value, the instruction at label OPUT is executed, sending the result from the A accumulator to address $F001. Otherwise, operations jump back to FETCH.

Using indexed addressing, as opposed to absolute addressing, shortens the program by a significant amount.

EXAMPLE 15-9

Write and assemble a 6800 program that does the following:

1. Fetch a data byte from address $F00 to the A accumulator.
2. Left shift the bits, one at a time, sending the resulting Cs status of B0 of address $F001.
3. When all 8 bits have been sent out in this fashion, loop back to step 1.

Use the flowchart in Fig. 15-5 as a guide, and begin the listing at program address $6100.

This is the same task specified for the Z-80 system in Example 15-1. The similarities between the two listings, Program 15-1 and Program 15-9, are hardly obvious, however. The differences between the two listings has little to do with the nature of the shifting operations. Rather, the differences come about because the 6800 does not have instructions for setting or resetting a selected bit within a particular byte of data.

The program begins by initializing the stack pointer and setting up the base address for the IX register. Later in the program, the stack is used as a place for saving the current shifted byte while the same accumulator is used for the output bit manipulations.

The two instructions under label FETCH fetch the data byte to be shifted from address $F000 and initialize the bit counter, accumulator B, to $08.

```
6100 8E FF FF   START    LDS  #$FFFF    SET STACK AT $FFFF
6103 CE FF 00            LDX  #$F000    SET ADDRESS POINTER INDEX
6106 A6 00      FETCH    LDAA $00,X     FETCH THE BYTE AT $F000
6108 C6 08               LDAB #$08      INITIALIZE BIT COUNTER
610A 48         SHIFT    ASLA           SHIFT LEFT
610B 24 09               BCC ZEROUT     IF CARRY IS ZERO, JUMP
610D 36                  PSHA           ELSE SAVE BYTE ON STACK
610E 86 01               LDAA #$01      READY SET BIT
6110 AA 01               ORAA $01,X     OR WITH OUTPUT
6112 A7 01               STAA $01,X     OUTPUT THE NEW BYTE
6114 20 07               BRA NEXT       AND JUMP TO NEXT
6116 36         ZEROUT   PSHA           SAVE BYTE ON STACK
6117 86 FE               LDAA #$FE      READY RESET BIT
6119 A4 01               ANDA $01,X     AND WITH OUTPUT
611B A7 01               STAA $01,X     OUTPUT THE NEW BYTE
611D 5A         NEXT     DECB           DECREMENT BIT COUNTER
611E 27 E6               BEQ FETCH      IF DONE, FETCH A NEW BYTE
6120 32                  PULA           ELSE GET BYTE FROM STACK
6121 20 E7               BRA SHIFT      AND JUMP TO SHIFT AGAIN
```

The actual left shift takes place at label SHIFT. That is the heart of the program, but it is also the simplest part of it.

Once the shift is done, BCC ZEROUT branches instructions to label ZEROUT if the bit shifted to the Cs flag is a logic 0. Otherwise, the program executes a series of instructions aimed at setting B0 of address $F001 to logic 1. In that series of instructions, PSHA pushes the current shift byte to the top of the stack. That clears the way for doing some bit manipulations in the A accumulator:

LDAA #$01	Load a logic 1 to B0 of accumulator A
ORAA $01,X	Get the output byte into accumulator A, and set its B0 position to logic 1
STAA $01,X	Output the byte to address $F001
BRA NEXT	Branch to label NEXT

The sequence of instructions under ZEROUT effectively reset B0 at the output. Notice that the shifted byte is saved on the stack before the bit resetting sequence takes place.

Whether the output bit is set or reset, the program eventually comes to the sequence of operations under label NEXT. At that point, DECB decrements the bit counter. If it has been decremented to zero, the bit shifting operation is done, and operations branch back to FETCH. Otherwise, the shifted byte is retrieved from the top of the stack—PULA—and operations branch back to SHIFT to do another left-shift operation.

Rotate Through Carry Instructions

Table 15-5 shows the 6800's family of rotate instructions. They all perform the operations diagrammed in Fig. 15-4, and they use the same addressing modes described for the shift instructions.

TABLE 15-5 ROTATE THROUGH CARRY INSTRUCTIONS FOR THE 6800

Source code	Object code	Notes
ROLA	49	
ROLB	59	Rotate left through carry
ROL *addr*	79 *byte byte*	(see Fig. 15-4)
ROL *indx*,X	69 *byte*	
RORA	46	
RORB	56	Rotate right through carry
ROR *addr*	76 *byte byte*	(see Fig. 15-4)
ROR *indx*,X	66 *byte*	

There are no circular rotate instructions, but it is possible to simulate that sort of rotation with the help of the rotate through carry instructions. The general idea is to do a left or right rotate through carry, and then force the resulting carry bit into one end of the register. See the flowcharts in Fig. 15-10.

Using Fig. 15-10a as a guide, a left circular rotate can be done this way:

```
49                  ROLA        ROTATE LEFT THROUGH CARRY
25 04               BCS SB0     IF CARRY IS SET, SET BIT 0
84 FE               ANDA #$FE   ELSE RESET BIT 0
20 02               BRA DONE    AND JUMP TO DONE
8A 01       SB0     ORAA #$01   SET BIT 0
            DONE
```

The first instruction does a left rotate through carry. The most-significant bit in accumulator A is rotated to the Cs bit (as required for a circular

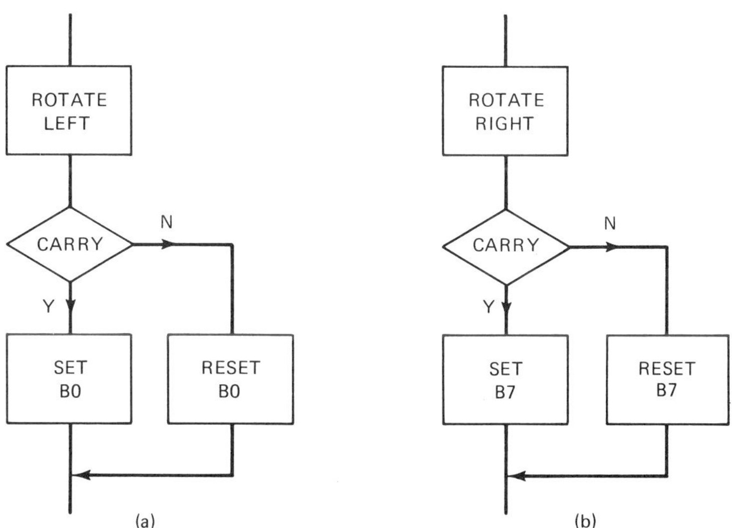

Figure 15-10 Flowcharts for simulating circular rotates with the 6800's rotate through carry instructions.

left rotate), but the least-significant bit position, B0, is set to an undetermined state. The trick is to set it equal to the current Cs bit status. That is the purpose of the remaining instructions in the listing.

Here is how to simulate the right circular rotate that is flowcharted in Fig. 15-10b:

```
46                  RORA        ROTATE RIGHT THROUGH CARRY
25 04               BCS SB7     IF CARRY IS SET, SET BIT 7
84 7F               ANDA #$7F   ELSE SET BIT 7
20 02               BRA DONE    AND JUMP TO DONE
8A 80      SB7      ORAA #$80
           DONE
```

In that case, bit 7 is set or reset according to the status of the Cs flag following the right rotate through carry.

When a program calls for executing a series of such simulated circular rotates, they can be written as subroutines and called as they are needed.

15-4 SHIFT AND ROTATE INSTRUCTIONS FOR THE 6502

The shift and rotate instructions available for the 6502 microprocessor are:

Shift left

Shift right

Rotate left through carry

Rotate right through carry

See Tables 15-6 and 15-7.

There are no instructions for arithmetic shift-right and circular rotates. As shown shortly, however, those operations can be built from the available shift and rotate instructions.

The addressing modes for the 6502's shift and rotate instructions follow those of the 6800 system. It is possible to shift and rotate the content of the

TABLE 15-6   SHIFT INSTRUCTIONS FOR THE 6502

Source code	Object code	Notes
ASL A	0A	
ASL $addr_0$	06 *byte*	Shift left
ASL *addr*	0E *byte byte*	(see Fig. 15-1)
ASL $addr_0$,X	16 *byte*	
ASL *addr*,X	1E *byte byte*	
LSR A	4A	
LSR $addr_0$	46 *byte*	Shift right
LSR *addr*	4E *byte byte*	(see Fig. 15-1)
LSR $addr_0$,X	56 *byte*	
LSR *addr*,X	5E *byte byte*	

TABLE 15-7 ROTATE THROUGH CARRY INSTRUCTIONS
FOR THE 6502

Source code	Object code	Notes
ROL A	2A	
ROL $addr_0$	26 *byte*	Rotate left through carry
ROL *addr*	2E *byte byte*	(see Fig. 15-4)
ROL $addr_0$,X	36 *byte*	
ROL *addr*,X	3E *byte byte*	
ROR A	6A	
ROR $addr_0$	66 *byte byte*	Rotate right through carry
ROR $addr_0$,X	76 *byte*	(see Fig. 15-4)
ROR *addr*,X	7E *byte byte*	

accumulator, a byte residing in zero-page memory, a byte in absolute memory, and bytes whose address is found by indexing the zero-page or absolute memory.

Combining the available shift and rotate instructions makes it possible to do double-register shifts. Doing a double-register left shift, for instance, is a matter of applying this sequence;

```
06 2A   ASL $2A   SHIFT LSB
26 2B   ROL $2B   ROTATE MSB
```

In that particular example, the bytes to be shifted are in zero-page memory locations $2A and $2B. The first instruction—a left shift—shifts the LSB byte one bit position to the left. Its original bit 7 goes to the Cs flag bit. Then the ROL instruction rotates the MSB, shoving the original bit 7 from the LSB into the low-order bit position.

Doing a double-register right shift is a matter of shifting the MSB to the right, and then rotating the LSB to the right.

The next example shows how to simulate an arithmetic right shift. The routine begins by testing the B7 position of the byte to be shifted. If it is a zero, the Cs bit is reset to zero; if it is a 1, the Cs bit is set to 1. A rotate right through carry completes the operation. B7 remains unchanged, and a copy of it is effectively shifted to the B6 position. The remaining bytes effectively shift one location to the right.

```
        LDA #$80
        BIT $2A     TEST B7 OF BYTE AT $2A
        BEQ CB0     IF ZERO, RESET CARRY BIT
        SEC         ELSE SET THE CARRY BIT
        JMP ROT     AND JUMP TO ROTATE
CB0     CLC         CLEAR THE CARRY BIT
ROT     ROR $2A     AND ROTATE THE BYTE AT $2A
```

Circular rotates can be simulated by the same procedures flowcharted in Fig. 15-10 for the 6800 system.

Table 15-8 completely summarizes the rotate instructions for the 8080A/8085 system. The only choices are circular rotates and rotates through carry. The shift instructions ought to be quite conspicuous by their absence. But as you might imagine, the necessary shift instructions can be simulated from those available here.

Suppose that you are using an 8080A/8085 system and want to do a shift-left operation of the sort illustrated in Fig. 15-1. The general procedure is to clear the carry flag, and then to a circular rotate left:

```
ANA A   ;CLEAR THE CARRY FLAG
RLC     ;ROTATE LEFT CIRCULAR
```

A shift right can be done this way:

```
ANA A   ;CLEAR THE CARRY FLAG
RRC     ;ROTATE RIGHT CIRCULAR
```

Can you justify the use of the ANA A instruction as one that clears the carry flag bit?

Arithmetic right shifts can be done this way:

```
         ADI  0H    ;TEST SIGN BIT
         JM CSET    ;IF SET, JUMP TO CSET
         ANA A      ;ELSE CLEAR THE CARRY FLAG
         JMP  ROT   ;AND JUMP TO ROTATE
CSET STC            ;SET THE CARRY FLAG
ROT  RRC            ;ROTATE RIGHT CIRCULAR
```

Those procedures might seem a bit peculiar at first, but one has to bear in mind that the 8080A/8085 has no formal bit testing operations nor any for resetting the Cs bit position. The first instruction, then, is aimed at testing the B7 position of the byte in the accumulator. The idea is to sum the current content of that register with zero—the value in the register will not change,

TABLE 15-8 ROTATE INSTRUCTIONS FOR THE
8080A/8085

Source code	Object code	Notes
RLC	07	Rotate left circular
RRC	0F	Rotate right circular (see Fig. 15-3)
RAL	17	Rotate left through carry
RAR	1F	Rotate right through carry (see Fig. 15-4)

but the sign flag bit will respond accordingly. What does the sign flag represent after any sort of arithmetic operation? It takes on the value of the B7 position in the result. So the sign bit in the flag register is adjusted according to the current value of the B7 position, and the conditional jump instruction, JM CSET, will drive the program to label if the sign bit is a 1—a status representing a negative value.

The ANA A instruction, when it is required, is a trick used by 8080A/ 8085 programmers to reset, or clear, the Cs bit. You should recall that any logic operation will automatically reset the Cs flag; and ANA A is one such logic operation that does not affect the value in the accumulator at the time.

16

Input and Output Instructions

All the examples cited so far in this book have used memory-mapped input and output functions. That is, the input and output devices have been connected as virtual memory locations. They are hardwired to the address bus in such a way that an output device is treated as a section of memory having some data written into it. The input devices are treated as though they are a section of memory that is providing data to the data bus.

That, in short, is the essence of memory-mapped I/O.

There is an alternative, however: *I/O-mapped I/O*; and there are families of special instructions to support it. (Memory-mapped procedures do not require any special instructions.)

I/O-mapped I/O operations need not make any direct reference to memory addresses. These input and output ports work independent of the memory.

Only the Z-80 and 8080A/8085 devices feature special input and output instructions for this sort of mapping. The 6502 and 6800 have no alternatives to memory-mapped I/O operations.

16-1 8080A/8085 I/O INSTRUCTIONS

Table 16-1 shows the I/O instructions for the 8080A/8085 system. Yes, there are only two of them, but you will see that they are quite adequate for the task assigned to them.

Both are 2-byte instructions: an opcode followed by a port number. The *port* designation is a 1-byte number between 00H and FFH. There are 256 of them, each effectively addressing a different I/O port.

Source code	Object code
IN *port*	DB *byte*
OUT *port*	D3 *byte*

In a manner of speaking, the port designation works something like the zero-page addressing for the 6502 and 6800 devices. The main difference is that the I/O ports are quite separate from any 16-bit memory addresses and locations.

The microprocessor engineer can wire decoding devices to any or all of the 256 available I/O port locations. The programmer, having a knowledge of which port numbers are connected to working I/O devices, can then specify IN *port* and OUT *port* instructions as necessary. If, for example, the system is wired with working I/O ports at port numbers 00H through 09H, the programmer has the ability to write or read a byte of data to any one of them.

The IN or OUT instruction itself specifies the port to be used at any given time. IN 01H, for instance, fetches a byte of data from port 01H. An instruction such as OUT 08H, on the other hand, will output a byte of data to port 08H.

Thus a byte of data can be stored to a port number or picked up from it. Here is the next critical question: What is the source of the data byte when using an OUT *port* instruction, and where does the data byte go when using an IN *port* instruction?

As far as the 8080A/8085 system is concerned, the central register in any IN or OUT instruction is the A register in the microprocessor. An OUT 03H instruction will thus send the current content of the A register to the device wired at output port 03H. By the same token, an IN 2AH instruction will fetch a byte of data from a device at port 2AH and load it to the A register in the microprocessor.

Consider this instruction sequence:

```
DB 02   IN 02H    ;FETCH A BYTE FROM PORT 2
D3 03   OUT 03H   ;LOAD THAT BYTE TO PORT 3
```

The first instruction fetches the data byte at some sort of input device connected to port 2, and loads it to the microprocessor's A register. The second instruction takes the byte out of the A register and stores it to the output device at port 3.

These are actually data transfer instructions. Thus the content of port 2 in the preceding example is not affected by the IN 02H instruction; and the content of the accumulator (A register) is not affected when its byte is stored to port 3 by the OUT 03H instruction.

1. What is the essential difference between the 8080A/8085's IN 2AH instruction and the 6502's LDA $2A instruction?

2. What is the essential difference between the 8080A/8085's IN 2AH instruction and its STA 002AH instruction?

3. Write and assemble an 8080A/8085 program that does the following:

   1. Fetch a data byte from port 01H.

   2. If the byte is greater than zero, output the byte to port 02H; return to step 1 in either case.

16-2 Z-80 I/O INSTRUCTIONS

Table 16-2 summarizes the Z-80's basic I/O port instructions. (More are introduced in Chapter 17.) There are more instructions here than are offered by the 8080A/8085 system, but the general ideas are the same in both cases.

Two instructions are, for all practical purposes, identical to the 8080A/8085 versions: IN A,(*port*) and OUT (*port*),A. The first loads register A with the content of a specified, 1-byte *port* number, and the second stores the content of register A to the specified *port*.

The remaining instructions use the content of the C register to point to an input or output port, then they transfer a byte of data between that port and a specified register. So an instruction such as IN L,(C) loads the L

TABLE 16-2 I/O INSTRUCTIONS FOR
THE Z-80

Source code	Object code
IN A,(C)	ED 78
IN B,(C)	ED 40
IN C,(C)	ED 48
IN D,(C)	ED 50
IN E,(C)	ED 58
IN H,(C)	ED 60
IN L,(C)	ED 68
IN A,(*port*)	DB *byte*
OUT (C),A	ED 79
OUT (C),B	ED 41
OUT (C),C	ED 49
OUT (C),D	ED 51
OUT (C),E	ED 59
OUT (C),H	ED 61
OUT (C),L	ED 69
OUT (*port*),A	D3 *byte*

register with the content of an input port that is pointed by the content of the C register. The following sequence loads the L register with the content of port 4EH:

```
LD C,4EH   ;SET PORT POINTER
IN  L,(C)   ;FETCH INPUT BYTE TO L
```

Using the same line of thinking, the instruction OUT (C),E will store the content of the E register to an output device found by noting the content of the C register.

EXAMPLE 16-1

Write and assemble a Z-80 program that does the following:

1. Continuously *poll* (scan) input ports 0 through 24 decimal.

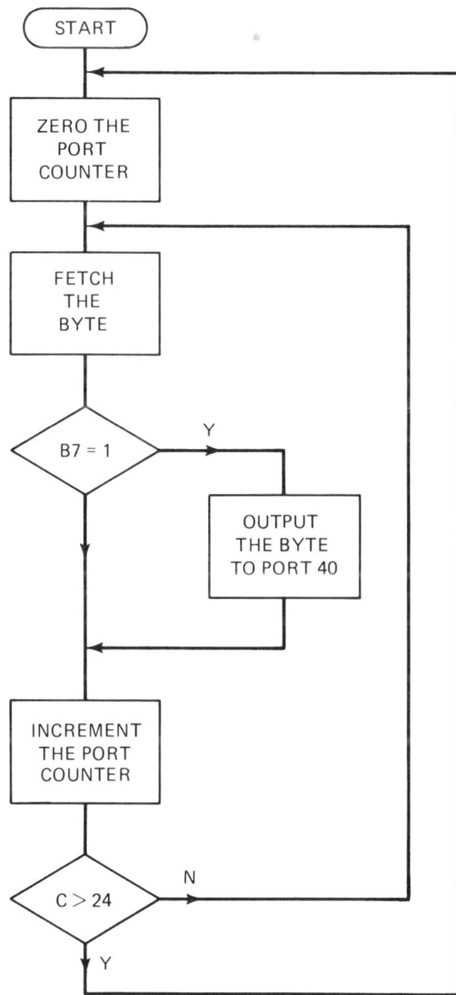

Figure 16-1   Flowchart for the task in Example 16-1.

```
1000  0E  00   START   LD  C,00H      ;ZERO THE PORT COUNTER
1002  ED  78   FETCH   IN  A,(C)      ;FETCH THE BYTE
1004  CB  7F           BIT  7,A       ;TEST BIT 7
1006  28  02           JR  Z,NEXT     ;IF ZERO, SKIP THE OUTPUT
1008  D3  28           OUT (28H),A    ;OUTPUT TO PORT 40
100A  0C     NEXT      INC  C         ;INCREMENT THE PORT COUNTER
100B  79               LD  A,C        ;TRANSFER COUNT TO A
100C  FE  18           CP  18H        ;COUNT AT 24?
100E  30  F2           JR  NC,FETCH   ;IF NOT, FETCH AGAIN
1010  18  EE           JR  START      ;ELSE START ALL OVER
```

2. If bit 7 of the port being queried is a logic 1, output the byte to port 40; otherwise, continue the scanning operation.

Begin the listing at program address 1000H, and use the flowchart in Fig. 16-1 as a guide.

The flowchart follows the specified task rather closely. The first operation initializes the port counter, register C, to zero. Then the program fetches the byte from that port and tests the bit 7 position. If it is a logic 1, the byte is directed to the output port; but in either case, operations resume by incrementing the port counter and testing its value for the endpoint of the polling operation—for port 40, or 28 hexadecimal. If the polling has not yet completed one cycle, the value in the C register is less than or equal to 24 (decimal) and operations loop back to fetch the new byte. When the port counter increments past 24, operations loop back to the beginning. There, the polling operation is begun from zero again.

See the suggested listing in Program 16-1.

Exercises for Section 16-2

1. Cite the literal meaning of the following instructions.
   (A) IN A,(*port*)   (B) OUT (*port*),A   (C) IN A,(C)   (D) OUT (C),A
2. Suggest how the program in Example 16-1 might be implemented on the 8080A/8085. Comment on the usefulness of the Z-80's additional I/O instructions.

17

Memory Block Operations

A *memory block* is generally defined as a group of data bytes residing in successive address locations in memory. A good many types of computing and system control applications require special treatment of memory blocks:

Memory block transfers: transferring the entire content of a section of memory from one place to another in memory.

Memory block exchanges: swapping the content of one block of memory with the content of another.

Memory block outputs: systematically running through a block of memory, sending the data bytes, one at a time, to an external output device.

Memory block inputs: systematically loading data from an external input device to successive address locations in memory.

Memory block searches: systematically searching a block of memory for certain well-defined data bytes.

There are two special programming requirements that are common to all of these memory block operations: specifying the starting address of the memory block, or blocks, involved, and specifying some means for terminating the operation. The first requirement is generally easy to meet—a programmer should certainly know the starting address of the memory block involved. The second requirement, knowing when and how to terminate the operation, can vary from one kind of application to another.

A memory block operation can be terminated when the system finds an endpoint address, when a specified number of bytes have been transferred or searched, or when a certain byte comes out of the memory block.

The Z-80 system will be used as the model for introducing these memory block operations in more detail. The reason for selecting the Z-80 for this particular role is a rather straightforward one: it is the only one that features special memory block instructions. So after seeing how the Z-80 system executes memory block operations, the remainder of the chapter shows you how to implement the same ideas with the other microprocessors.

17-1 MEMORY BLOCK INSTRUCTIONS AND OPERATIONS FOR THE Z-80

The Z-80 instructions introduced in this section are tailormade for doing memory block operations. They are among the few microprocessor instructions that involve more than one register at a time. Fortunately, the processes used by these complex instructions can be clearly defined and transferred, almost directly, to other microprocessors.

Memory Block Transfer Instructions

Table 17-1 lists the Z-80 instructions that transfer data from one memory location to another.

In all instances, the operations begin by transferring a byte of data that is addressed by the HL register pair to an address indicated by the DE register pair. See the first blocks in the flowcharts in Fig. 17-1.

Equivalent instructions for that sort of data transfer would have this form:

```
LD A,(HL)  ;FETCH THE BYTE AT ADDRESS HL
LD (DE),A  ;STORE THAT BYTE TO ADDRESS DE
```

The equivalent instructions fetch the byte to be transferred to register A from an address contained in the HL register pair. The second instruction then transfers that same byte from register A to an address contained in the DE register pair. The transfers for the memory block instructions do not pass the byte through the A register, however. In essence, the transfer is a direct one—at least none of the working registers serves as an intermediate register.

The HL register pair always points to the source of data—the source block. The DE register pair always points to the destination block address.

Figure 17-1a shows that the LDD instruction follows the data transfer with a series of double-register decrements. The HL, DE, and BC register pairs

TABLE 17-1 BLOCK TRANSFER INSTRUCTIONS FOR THE Z-80

Source code	Object code	Notes
LDD	ED A8	See Fig. 17-1a
LDI	ED A0	See Fig. 17-1b
LDDR	ED B8	See Fig. 17-1c
LDJR	ED B0	See Fig. 17-1d

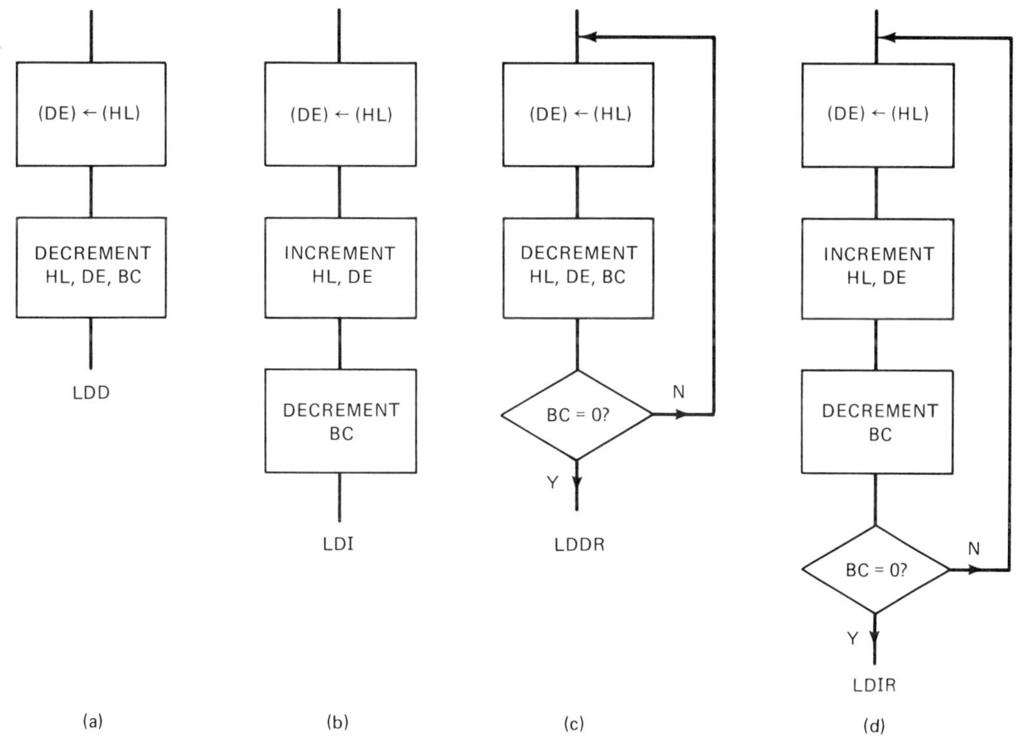

Figure 17-1　Flowcharts for the Z-80's block transfer instructions.

are all decremented by one count. The LDI instruction (Fig. 17-1b), on the other hand, follows the initial data transfer with instructions that increment the HL and DE register pairs, but decrements the BC register pair.

Using the A register as a transfer register, an equivalent set of instructions for the single LDD instruction looks like this:

```
LD  A,(HL)
LD  (DE),A
DEC HL
DEC DE
DEC BC
```

The equivalent instructions for LDI are

```
LD  A,(HL)
LD  (DE),A
INC   HL
INC   DE
DEC  BC
```

The LDDR and LDIR instructions do the same sort of job as far as the HL, DE, and BC register pairs are concerned, but they carry the operation one step further. Following the decrement of the BC registers, these instructions test the content of the BC register pair for zero. If the result is not zero, the instruction is repeated; otherwise, it comes to an end.

Equivalent instructions for the LDDR instruction can look like this:

```
XFER    LD  A,(HL)
        LD  (DE),A
        DEC HL
        DEC DE
        DEC BC
        LD  A,C
        OR  B
        JR  NZ,XFER
```

and the equivalent LDIR instruction like this:

```
XFER    LD  A,(HL)
        LD  (DE),A
        INC HL
        INC DE
        DEC BC
        LD  A,C
        OR  B
        JR  NZ,XFER
```

These equivalent sets of instructions are shown only for illustrative purposes, the actual memory block transfer instructions differ inasmuch as the A register never sees the data byte being transferred. Instructions introduced later will bring the transferred byte to the A register, but these do not.

So the HL register pair point to the source of data, and the DE register pair point to the destination of that data. In two cases, the instructions decrement these register pairs, and in the two other cases, those registers are incremented. Thus the data transfer can take place from a high memory address to a low memory address (the decrementing cases), or it can take place quite systematically from a low memory address to a higher one (the incrementing cases).

The BC register pair is always decremented. Through all of these memory block instructions, the BC register pair plays the role of a byte counter. As the data transfers take place, the BC register pair keeps track of the number of bytes remaining to be transferred.

EXAMPLE 17-1

Write and assemble a Z-80 program that transfers 127 (decimal) bytes of data from a block of memory beginning at 4000H to a block beginning at 3C00H. Use the LDIR instruction so that the data is transferred into successively higher address locations. Begin the listing at program address 1000H.

The first three instructions initialize the whole operation (see Program 17-1). The HL register pair is set to the starting address of the source block—

```
1000 21 00 40   LD HL,4000H   ;POINT TO START OF SOURCE BLOCK
1003 11 00 3C   LD DE,3C00H   ;POINT TO START OF DEST. BLOCK
1006 01 7F 00   LD BC,007FH   ;LOAD NUMBER OF BYTES TO BC
1009 ED B0      LDIR          ;DO THE TRANSFER
```

the block of data to be transferred. The DE register pair is set to the starting address of the block to receive the data, and the BC register pair is set with the number of bytes to be transferred (the hexadecimal version of 127 bytes is 00FEH).

That example is written so that the transferred byte comes from and goes to successively higher address locations. Using the LDDR instruction would do the same transfer, but at successively lower address locations.

The block transfer program in Example 17-1 is deceptively simple. The principle is good, but practical applications often call for a more complicated set of preparations than the example suggests. Consider, for instance, that three register pairs are occupied by these block transfer instructions. Those same registers might be holding valuable programming data prior to the execution of the block transfer; and that means that it is often necessary to save the original content of those registers, set up and carry out the transfer, and then restore the registers to their original status.

There are two ways to go about saving the contents of the HL, DE, and BC registers prior to doing a block transfer operation. First, the registers can be saved in the alternate register section of the Z-80. That means that the block transfer operations should be preceded by an EXX instruction. With the registers thus safely tucked away in the alternate registers, the transfer scheme can be initialized and executed. And when the transfer is done, a second EXX instruction will restore the affected registers to their original states.

A second, if somewhat more cumbersome technique for preserving the original registers is to place them onto the stack before setting up and executing the transfer. When the block transfer is done, the original register data can be POPped from the stack to the appropriate register pairs.

Memory Block Exchanges

The memory block transfer operations just described copy the content of the source block into the destination block. The original data in the destination block is lost; and sometimes that is not a desirable consequence of the operation.

A memory block exchange literally swaps the contents of two separate memory blocks, leaving the data unchanged by the whole thing. There are two different approaches to block exchanges; one is conceptually simple, but it uses an additional block of memory that is equal in size to either of the blocks being exchanged. The second approach uses no additional data memory, but it takes a bit of study to see how it works.

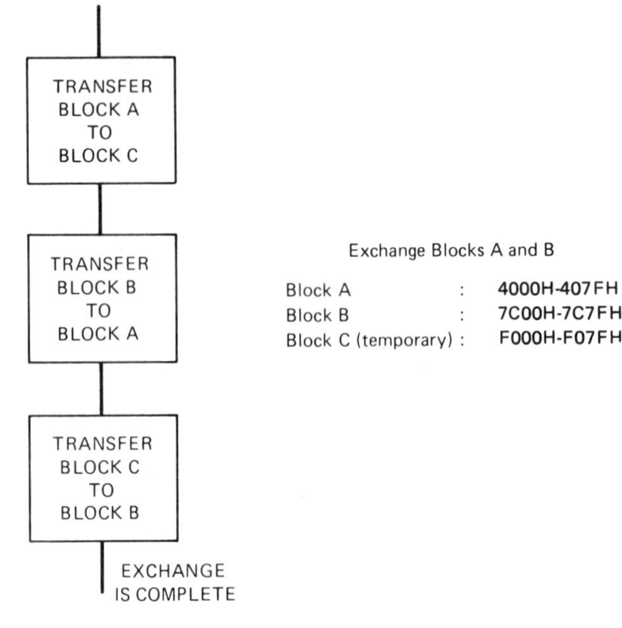


```
1000   21  00  40     LD HL, 4000H      ;POINT TO START OF BLOCK A
1003   11  00  F0     LD DE, 0F000H     ;POINT TO START OF BLOCK C
1006   01  80  00     LD BC, 0080H      ;SET FOR 128-BYTE TRANSFER
1009   ED  B0         LDIR              ;TRANSFER BLOCK A TO BLOCK C
100B   21  00  7C     LD HL, 7C00H      ;POINT TO START OF BLOCK B
100E   11  00  40     LD DE, 4000H      ;POINT TO START OF BLOCK A
1011   01  80  00     LD, BC 0080H      ;SET FOR 128-BYTE TRANSFER
1014   ED  B0         LDIR              ;TRANSFER BLOCK B TO BLOCK A
1016   21  00  F0     LD, HL, 0F000H    ;POINT TO START OF BLOCK C
1019   11  00  7C     LD DE, 7C00H      ;POINT TO START OF BLOCK B
101C   01  80  00     LD BC,0080H       ;SET FOR 128-BYTE TRANSFER
101F   ED  B0         LDIR              ;TRANSFER BLOCK C TO BLOCK B
```

Figure 17-2 Flowchart and a listing for doing block exchange operations with the Z-80.

The simpler approach is illustrated in Fig. 17-2. The general idea is to set aside a third memory block that serves as a temporary storage place for one of the blocks to be exchanged. In this example, Block A is first transferred to the temporary block, Block C. That will preserve the data from Block A while the second phase of the job is taking place—transferring the content of Block B to Block A. Once that transfer is done, the content of Block C can be transferred to Block B, thereby completing the exchange.

The technique calls for doing three block transfers in succession. As described earlier, the HL register pair is initialized to the starting address of the source block, the DE register pair is set up for the starting address of the destination block, and the BC pair is initialized to the number of bytes to be transferred (128 bytes, in this case).

The second technique for exchanging two memory blocks is illustrated

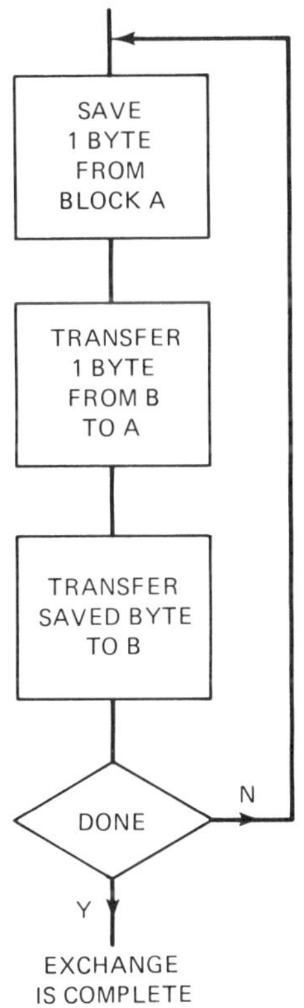


```
1000   21  00  7C   START   LD HL, 7C00H      ;POINT TO START OF BLOCK B
1003   11  00  40           LD DE, 4000H      ;POINT TO START OF BLOCK A
1006   01  80  00           LD BC, 0080H      ;SET NUMBER OF BYTES
1009   1A           XFER    LD A, (DE)        ;SAVE BLOCK A BYTE
100A   ED  A0               LDI               ;TRANSFER B TO A
100C   2B                   DEC HL            ;GET OLD BLOCK B ADDRESS
100D   77                   LD (HL), A        ;XFER SAVED BYTE TO B
100E   23                   INC HL            ;RESTORE NEW BLOCK B ADDRESS
100F   79                   LD A, C           ;FETCH LSB OF BYTE COUNT
1010   B0                   OR B              ;OR WITH MSB
1011   20  F6               JR NZ, XFER       ;IF NOT DONE, XFER ANOTHER BYTE
```

Figure 17-3 Flowchart and listing for doing a more memory-conservative block exchange with the Z-80.

in Fig. 17-3. The first three instructions in the program set things up for a block transfer from Block B to Block A. Before the transfer instruction, LDI, is executed, however, a single byte from the destination register, Block A, is saved in the accumulator. Later in the program, that byte will be transferred to the appropriate address in the source block.

In the meantime, the system executes the LDI instruction. That instruction transfers a byte from Block B to Block A, increments the HL and DE registers, and decrements the BC register pair. That is doing just a one-way transfer, though. The transfer from Block A to Block B has not been done.

The transfer from Block A to Block B is carried out by the instruction sequence:

```
DEC HL
LD (HL),A
INC HL
```

The first of those three instructions decrement the Block B address pointer back to its previous point. The byte originally saved in the accumulator is then loaded to that Block B address; finally, the INC HL instruction restores the Block B pointer back to where it should be for the next transfer from Block B to Block A.

The LDI instruction used in this listing has no provisions for automatically sensing the end of the operation. Thus it is necessary to test the contents of the BC register pair for a zero. That is the purpose of the sequence

```
LD  A,C
OR  B
JR  NZ,XFER
```

The first instruction gets the LSB of the byte counter to the accumulator, and the second instruction logically ORs it with the MSB of the counter. If the result is not zero, the conditional jump instruction loops operations back to XFER. The transfer continues until the jump instruction is no longer satisfied. At that time, all 128 bits have been exchanged.

Memory Block Inputs and Outputs

The idea behind a memory block input is to load a sequence of data bytes from a single source to successive address locations in memory. The block output does the same sort of thing, but the other way around—outputting a sequence of data bytes from a block to a single destination address.

These input and output operations can be compared with memory block transfers where either the source or destination has a single address.

Suppose that it is necessary to "dump" a block of memory to an output device that is memory mapped to address F001H. The block begins at address 4000H and runs upward for 1024 bytes. Since the operation has some similarities to a block transfer operation, the job could be done this way:

```
         LD HL,4000H   ;POINT TO START OF BLOCK
         LD DE,F001H   ;POINT TO OUTPUT
         LD BC,0400H   ;SET NUMBER OF BYTES (1024 DECIMAL)
OPUT     LDI           ;TRANSFER A BYTE FROM (HL) TO (DE)
         LD A,C        ;LSB OF BYTE COUNT TO ACCUMULATOR
         OR B          ;LOGIC OR WITH MSB
         JR Z,DONE     ;IF ZERO, JUMP TO DONE
         DEC DE        ;ELSE POINT TO OUTPUT
         JR OPUT       ;AND OUTPUT THE NEXT BYTE
DONE     JR DONE       ;LOOP TO SELF
```

Since the LDI instruction increments the output pointer as well as the block source pointer, it is necessary to decrement the output pointer—the DE register pair—back to its original content after each LDI instruction is executed. That way, the block pointer advances as it should, but the output pointer remains at F001H each time a new output operation is done.

That might be a trick of sorts, but it does the memory "dump" operation quite nicely.

An alternative technique does away with the block transfer instruction altogether:

```
        LD  HL,4000H   ;POINT TO START OF MEMORY BLOCK
        LD  DE,F001H   ;POINT TO OUTPUT ADDRESS
        LD  BC,0400H   ;SET NUMBER OF BYTES TO BE TRANSFERRED
OPUT    LD  A,(HL)     ;FETCH THE BYTE FROM MEMORY
        LD  (DE),A     ;OUTPUT THE BYTE
        INC HL         ;INCREMENT MEMORY POINTER
        DEC BC         ;DECREMENT BYTE COUNTER
        LD  A,C        ;GET LSB OF COUNTER TO ACCUMULATOR
        OR  B          ;OR WITH MSB
        JR  NZ,OPUT    ;IF NOT DONE, OUTPUT THE NEXT BYTE
DONE    JR  DONE       ;ELSE LOOP TO SELF
```

The choice of techniques is more a matter of personal style than anything else. Both transfer a data block to an output address.

Bytes can be loaded from a single data source and to a block of memory by a similar set of instructions. Consider this:

```
        LD  HL,F001H   ;POINT TO INPUT
        LD  DE,4000H   ;POINT TO START OF MEMORY BLOCK
        LD  BC,0400H   ;SET NUMBER OF BYTES TO BE LOADED
INPUT   LDI            ;TRANSFER A BYTE FROM INPUT TO BLOCK
        LD  A,C        ;GET LSB OF BYTE COUNT
        OR  B          ;OR IT WITH MSB
        JR  Z,DONE     ;IF ZERO, IT IS DONE
        DEC HL         ;ELSE POINT TO INPUT
        JR  INPUT      ;AND INPUT THE NEXT BYTE
DONE    JR  DONE       ;LOOP TO SELF
```

In this case, it is the input address pointer—the HL register pair—that is decremented back to the original value prior to repeating the LDI instruction. Overall, the HL pair will remain pointing at the single source address, F001H; but the DE pair will increment with each data transfer operation, effectively placing each new byte into a higher address location in memory.

This example, like the earlier ones, transfers 1024 (decimal) bytes.

The same task can be accomplished without using any of the Z-80's block transfer instructions:

```
        LD  HL,F001H   ;POINT TO INPUT
        LD  DE,4000H   ;POINT TO START OF MEMORY BLOCK
        LD  BC,0400H   ;SET NUMBER OF BYTES TO BE LOADED
INPUT   LD  A,(HL)     ;FETCH THE INPUT BYTE
        LD  (DE),A     ;LOAD THE BYTE TO MEMORY
```

```
            INC  DE          ;POINT TO NEXT MEMORY ADDRESS
            LD   A,C         ;GET LSB OF BYTE COUNTER
            OR   B           ;OR WITH MSB
            JR   NZ,INPUT    ;IF NOT DONE, INPUT THE NEXT BYTE
DONE        JR   DONE        ;ELSE LOOP TO SELF
```

TABLE 17-2 MEMORY BLOCK INPUT AND OUTPUT INSTRUCTIONS FOR THE Z-80

Source code	Object code	Notes
IND	ED AA	
INI	ED A2	Input from port (C)
INDR	ED BA	to memory block
INIR	ED B2	
OUTD	ED AB	
OUTI	ED A3	Output from memory
OTDR	ED BB	block to port (C)
OTIR	ED B3	

But what if the data to be loaded to a block of memory come from an input port that is not memory mapped? Or what if the data is to be transferred, one byte at a time, from a memory block to an output port that is not memory mapped? The preceding examples all assumed memory-mapped I/O ports.

Table 17-2 shows the Z-80's block transfer instructions that deal with I/O-mapped I/O ports—ports introduced in Chapter 16.

The instructions function much the same way as the memory block transfers in Table 17-1. The differences are that the 1-byte source or destination remains fixed—fixed at a port address contained in the C register. In essence, the input instructions do an operation that can be characterized as (HL)←(C); the byte at the port indicated by the C register is transferred to a memory address contained in the HL register pair. The output versions of the instructions transfer the data the other way around, (C)→(HL); the data byte at the address pointed by the HL register pair is transferred to an output port specified by the C register.

The B register is the byte counter for these instructions. It is always decremented with each execution; but unlike the byte counter for the transfer instructions, this single-byte counter can handle no more than a sequence of 256 bytes in a single run.

The following events take place whenever these memory block I/O instructions are executed:

IND   transfer a byte from input port (C) to memory address (HL); decrement the HL pair and the B register.

INI   transfer a byte from input port (C) to memory address (HL); increment the HL pair, decrement the B register.

INDR   transfer a byte from input port (C) to memory address (HL); decrement the HL pair and the B register; repeat until B is zero.

INIR   transfer a byte from input port (C) to memory address (HL); increment the HL pair, decrement the B register; repeat until B is zero.

OUTD   transfer a byte from memory address (HL) to output port (C); decrement the HL pair and the B register.

OUTI   transfer a byte from memory address (HL) to output port (C); increment the HL pair, decrement the B register.

OTDR   transfer a byte from memory address (HL) to output port (C); decrement the HL pair and the B register; repeat until B is zero.

OTIR   transfer a byte from memory address (HL) to output port (C); increment the HL pair, decrement the B register; repeat until B is zero.

Suppose that the task is to load 128 bytes of data from input port 25 decimal to a memory block that begins at address 4000H. If the block is to be loaded with successively lower addresses, the sequence of instructions looks like this:

```
LD HL,4000H   ;POINT TO BEGINNING OF MEMORY BLOCK
LD C,19H      ;POINT TO INPUT PORT 25 DECIMAL
LD B,80H      ;SET FOR LOADING 128 BYTES
INDR          ;LOAD THE MEMORY
```

The first instruction initializes the address pointer—the HL register pair—to the beginning of the memory block. The second instruction points to the input port, and the third one sets the byte counter for loading 128 bytes of data to the memory. The INDR instruction takes care of everything else.

If it were not for the Z-80's memory block I/O instructions, the instruction sequence for this task would look something like this:

```
     LD HL,4000H   ;POINT TO BEGINNING OF MEMORY BLOCK
     LD C,19H      ;POINT TO INPUT PORT 25
     LD B,80H      ;SET FOR LOADING 128 BYTES
IPUT IN A,(C)      ;FETCH THE BYTE
     LD (HL),A     ;LOAD THE BYTE TO MEMORY
     DEC HL        ;POINT TO NEXT MEMORY LOCATION
     DEC B         ;DECREMENT BYTE COUNTER
     JR NZ IPUT    ;IF NOT DONE, INPUT AGAIN
```

The output instructions follow the same general format as the input versions. Such instructions are commonly used for outputting a block of data to an external device such as a CRT terminal, line printer, or magnetic data storage medium (tape or disk).

Memory Block Search Instructions

Searching a block of data memory for certain data bytes is a powerful tool for control and computing applications. Generally, the data to be searched is included in a data *table*, and the objective is to search the data, one byte at a time, until a certain byte is found.

TABLE 17-3 MEMORY BLOCK
COMPARE INSTRUCTIONS FOR
THE Z-80

Source code	Object code
CPD	ED A9
CPI	ED A1
CPDR	ED B9
CPIR	ED B1

Table 17-3 represents the Z-80's instructions for doing data searches through a block of memory.

Actually, they are compare instructions. The data byte residing at an address indicated by the HL pair is compared with the current content of the accumulator. The HL register pair is the memory pointer and the BC register pair is the byte counter. Upon executing the instructions, the following events take place:

CPD   Compare the byte from (HL) with register A, and adjust the flags accordingly; decrement the HL and BC register pairs.

CPI   Compare the byte from (HL) with register A, and adjust the flags accordingly; increment the HL pair and decrement the BC pair.

CPDR   Compare the byte from (HL) with the current content of the A register; decrement the HL pair and BC pair; repeat until (HL) and A are the same or BC is zero.

CPIR   Compare the byte from (HL) with the current content of the A register; increment the HL pair, decrement the BC pair; repeat until (HL) is the same as A or BC is zero.

Setting up one of these block searches is a matter of loading the starting point of the memory block to the HL register pair, setting the number of successive locations to be checked into the BC pair, and loading the byte to be found into the accumulator. After that, the block compare instruction can be executed.

Suppose that you wish to search a block of data memory between 4000H and 40FFH for data 2AH. The instruction sequence looks like this:

```
LD HL,4000H   ;SET STARTING ADDRESS FOR THE SEARCH
LD BC,0100H   ;SET NUMBER OF BYTES TO BE SEARCHED
LD A,2AH      ;SET BYTE BEING SEARCHED
CPIR          ;SEARCH
```

The program comes to a conclusion under one of two circumstances: either a 2AH is found in the memory block, or BC is decremented all the way to zero. In the first case, the byte is found. In the second case, it was not found anywhere in the memory block.

Without the help of the block compare instruction, the listing would have to take a form resembling this one:

```
        LD  HL,400H     ;SET STARTING ADDRESS FOR THE SEARCH
        LD  BC,0100H    ;SET NUMBER OF BYTES TO BE SEARCHED
COMPR   LD  A,(HL)      ;FETCH THE BYTE
        CP  2AH         ;COMPARE WITH 2AH
        JP  Z,DONE      ;IF SAME, JUMP TO DONE
        INC HL          ;ELSE INCREMENT ADDRESS POINTER
        DEC BC          ;DECREMENT BYTE COUNTER
        LD  A,C         ;LSB OF BYTE COUNT TO A
        OR  B           ;OR WITH MSB
        JR  NZ,COMPR    ;IF NOT END, COMPARE AGAIN
DONE    JR  DONE        ;LOOP TO SELF
```

Exercises for Section 17-1

1. Which of the following Z-80 block instructions work through some memory block addresses in ascending order? descending order?
(a) LDD	(b) LDI	(c) LDDR	(d) OUTD
(e) INIR	(f) CPD	(g) CPI	(h) CPIR

2. Which of the following Z-80 block instructions loop automatically until certain criteria are met?
(a) LDD	(b) LDIR	(c) INI	(d) INIR
(e) OUTI	(f) OTIR	(g) CPDR	(h) CPI

3. What is the role of the HL register pair for the following instructions?
(a) LDD	(b) LDDR	(c) OUTD	(d) CPIR

4. What is the role of the C register for the IND and OUTD instructions? for the LDD and LDDR instructions?

17-2 MEMORY BLOCK OPERATIONS FOR THE 8080A/8085

The 8080A/8086 has no special memory block instructions, but the principles behind the Z-80's block instructions can be applied directly to the 8080A/8085.

Memory Block Transfers

Figure 17-4 illustrates a block transfer operation. In this case the source block begins at address 4000H and runs upward through 2048 consecutive address locations. The destination block begins at 7C00H and runs upward as well.

Before the transfer can begin, those transfer parameters have to be initialized. The starting address of the source block is loaded to the HL register pair, the starting address of the destination block goes to the DE register pair, and the number of bytes to be transferred goes into the BC register pair. Perhaps the choice of registers is arbitrary, but this particular format follows the Z-80 plan.

The first transfer step is to load the accumulator with a byte from the source block. That is done with the MOV A,M instruction in the program listing. The next instruction, STAX D, transfers the byte to the current destination block address—one indicated by the content of the DE register pair.

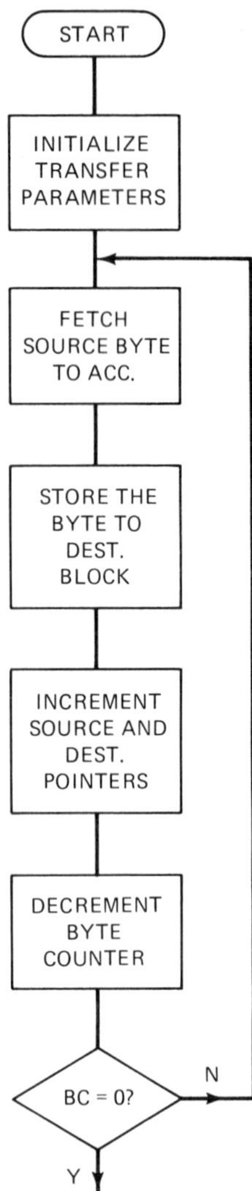

Source block   :   4000H↑
Destination block :   7C00H↑
Number of bytes :   2048D

```
1000   21   00   40              LXI H, 4000H      ;POINT TO START OF SOURCE BLOCK
1003   11   00   7C              LXI D, 7C00H      ;POINT TO START OF DEST. BLOCK
1006   01   00   08              LXI B, 0800H      ;SET NUMBER OF BYTES
1009   7E              XFER      MOV A, M          ;FETCH BYTE FROM SOURCE BLOCK
100A   12                        STAX D            ;TRANSFER IT TO DEST. BLOCK
100B   23                        INX H             ;INCREMENT SOURCE POINTER
100C   13                        INX D             ;INCREMENT DEST. POINTER
100D   0B                        DCX B             ;DECREMENT BYTE COUNTER
100E   79                        MOV A, C          ;GET LSB OF BYTE COUNT
100F   B0                        ORA B             ;OR WITH MSB
1010   C2   09   10              JNZ XFER          ;IF NOT ZERO, TRANSFER AGAIN
```

Figure 17-4   Flowchart and listing for doing a block transfer with the
8080A/8085.

The transfer of one byte is completed at that point in the program, and the remaining instructions increment the source and block pointers, decrement the byte counter (content of the BC register pair), and check the byte counter for zero. If it has not yet counted down to zero, the transfer operation is repeated with the new source and destination addresses. Otherwise, the program comes to an end.

The routine differs from the shorter Z-80 version in two important respects. First, the byte to be transferred must be passed through the A register; and second, the BC register pair must be checked for zero by ORing the LSB and MSB of the current count. (Recall that the DCX BC instruction does not affect the Z flag.)

Memory Block Exchanges

Memory block transfers for the 8080A/8085 can be set up to follow the Z-80's versions. Here, however, both bytes have to pass through the A register, and that means that one of the bytes has to be saved elsewhere in data memory while the other is moving through that register—all the other internal working registers are occupied with other tasks.

The following example carries out an extensive block exchange, using the stack as a temporary storage place for one of the bytes being transferred.

EXAMPLE 17-2

Two blocks of data have the following parameters:

Block A begins at address 4000H and runs upward through 2048 bytes.

Block B begins at address 7C00H and runs upward through 2048 bytes.

Write and assemble an 8080A/8085 routine that exchanges the content of the two blocks. Initialize the stack pointer at FFFFH and begin the listing at program address 1000H. See the flowchart in Fig. 17-5.

The flowchart shows the operation beginning by setting up the transfer parameters: establishing the starting addresses for the two blocks, and setting up the number of bytes to be transferred. Immediately after the initialization routine is done, the system fetches a byte from the current Block A address and pushes it onto the stack. That Block A byte will remain on the stack for a short time.

Then a byte is fetched from the current Block B address and immediately transferred to the current Block A address. Those two operations complete the first half of the exchange—transferring the byte from Block B to Block A.

After that is one, the original byte from Block A is fetched from the stack to the accumulator. From there it is transferred to the current Block B address. And that completes the exchange of one set of bytes between the two blocks.

All that remains is to increment the two block addresses, decrement the byte counter, and check to see whether or not all bytes have been exchanged. If not, the whole process is repeated.

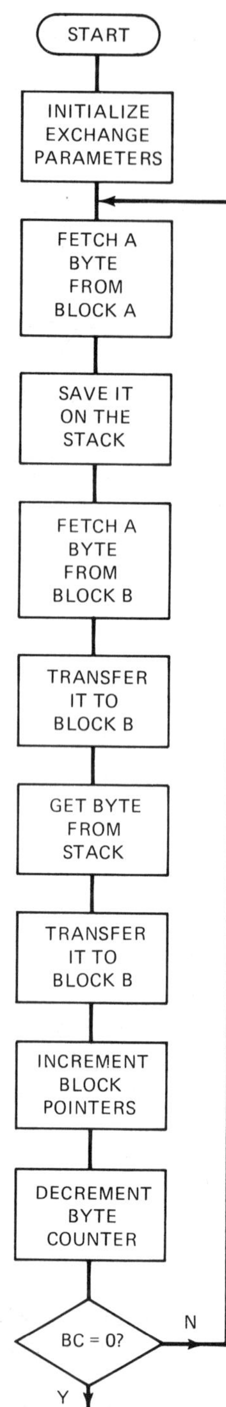

Figure 17-5   Flowchart for the 8080A/8085 block exchange in Example 17-2.

PROGRAM 17-2 8080A/8085 BLOCK EXCHANGE LISTING FOR EXAMPLE 17-2

```
1000  31 FF FF          LXI   SP,0FFFFH  ;SET STACK AT FFFFH
1003  21 00 40          LXI   H,4000H    ;POINT TO START OF BLOCK A
1006  11 00 7C          LXI   D,7C00H    ;POINT TO START OF BLOCK B
1009  01 00 08          LXI   B,0800H    ;SET NUMBER OF BYTES TO EXCHANGE
100C  7E          XFER  MOV   A,M        ;FETCH BYTE FROM BLOCK A
100D  F5                PUSH  PSW        ;SAVE IT ON THE STACK
100E  1A                LDAX  D          ;FETCH BYTE FROM BLOCK B
100F  77                MOV   M,A        ;TRANSFER IT TO BLOCK A
1010  F1                POP   PSW        ;GET BLOCK-A BYTE FROM STACK
1011  12                STAX  D          ;AND TRANSFER IT TO BLOCK B
                        ;END OF BYTE EXCHANGE
1012  23                INX   H          ;INCREMENT BLOCK A POINTER
1013  13                INX   D          ;INCREMENT BLOCK B POINTER
1014  0B                DCX   B          ;DECREMENT BYTE COUNTER
1015  79                MOV   A,C        ;GET LSB OF BYTE COUNT
1016  B0                ORA   B          ;OR WITH MSB
1017  C2 0C 10          JNZ   XFER       ;IF NOT DONE, TRANSFER ANOTHER SET
                                         :OF BYTES
```

The listing for this program is shown in Program 17-2. It follows the flowchart rather closely.

Following the Z80 exchange format, the HL pair carries the Block A addresses, the DE pair carries the Block B addresses, and the BC register pair is used as the byte counter. Notice how they are initialized in the opening program instructions. Since the stack is used as a temporary storage place for the byte being transferred from Block A to Block B, the initialization routine also includes an instruction for setting the stack—setting it at FFFFH in this case.

**Loading and Dumping Memory Blocks
to Memory-Mapped I/Os**

Figure 17-6 illustrates an 8080A/8085 routine for loading a block of memory from a fixed, memory-mapped input port. The routine accepts 2048 (decimal) bytes from input address 7C00H and loads them to a block of memory beginning at 4000H. The loading takes place in ascending order—from 4000H, upward.

The HL register pair, as usual, points to the current block address, the DE register pair points to the input address, and the BC register pair serves as the byte counter.

After initializing those transfer parameters, the routine fetches a byte from the input address (LDAX D) and immediately transfers it to the current block address (MOV M,A). Then the block address is incremented, and the byte counter is decremented. The final instructions in the listing test the BC register pair—the byte counter—for a countdown to zero. If the byte counter has not yet reached zero, operations loop back up to the line carrying label XFER. From there, another byte is transferred from the fixed input address, 7C00H, to the new block address.

Figure 17-7 shows how a block of memory can be dumped to a fixed

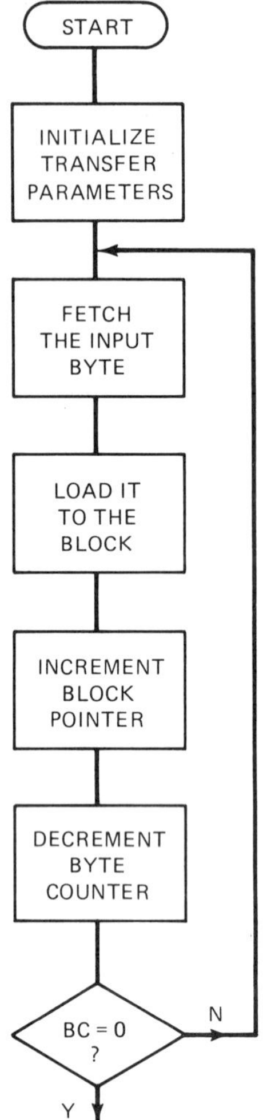

Memory block   :   4000H↑
Memory-mapped input address :   7C00H
Number of bytes   :   2048D

```
1000   21   00   40            LXI H, 4000H    ;POINT TO START OF BLOCK
1003   11   00   7C            LXI D, 7C00H    ;POINT TO INPUT ADDRESS
1006   01   00   08            LXI B, 0800     ;SET NUMBER OF BYTES
1009   1A              XFER    LDAX D          ;FETCH BYTE FROM INPUT
100A   77                      MOV M, A        ;LOAD IT TO BLOCK
100B   23                      INX H           ;INCREMENT BLOCK POINTER
100C   0B                      DCX B           ;DECREMENT BYTE COUNTER
100D   79                      MOV A, C        ;GET LSB OF BYTE COUNT
100E   B0                      ORA B           ;OR WITH MSB
100F   C2   09   10            JNZ XFER        ;IF NOT DONE, TRANSFER ANOTHER BYTE
```

Figure 17-6   Flowchart and listing for doing a block load from a
memory-mapped input—8080A/8085 version.

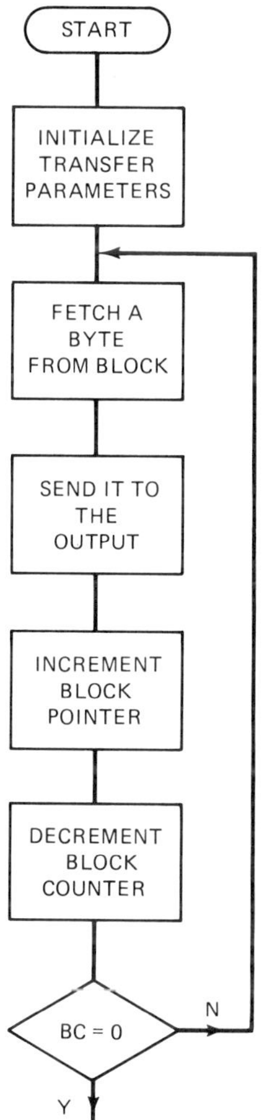

Memory block   :   4000H↑
Memory-mapped output :   7C00H
Number of bytes   :   2048D

```
1000   21   00   40            LXI H, 4000H    ;POINT TO START OF BLOCK
1003   11   00   7C            LXI D, 7C00H    ;POINT TO OUTPUT ADDRESS
1006   01   00   08            LXI B, 0800H    ;SET NUMBER OF BYTES TO TRANSFER
1009   7E              XFER    MOV A, M        ;FETCH BYTE FROM BLOCK
100A   12                      STAX D          ;SEND IT TO THE OUTPUT
100B   23                      INX H           ;INCREMENT BLOCK POINTER
100C   0B                      DCX B           ;DECREMENT THE BYTE COUNTER
100D   79                      MOV A, C        ;GET LSB OF BYTE COUNT
100E   B0                      ORA B           ;OR WITH MSB
100F   C2   09   10            JNZ XFER        ;IF NOT DONE, TRANSFER ANOTHER BYTE
```

Figure 17-7   Flowchart and 8080A/8085 listing for dumping a block of memory to a memory-mapped output.

output address. The initialization routine is identical to the loading operation described in connection with Fig. 17-6. In this case, however, a byte is
transferred from the current block address to the memory-mapped output
address by the sequence

```
MOV  A,M
STAX  D
```

The remaining instructions increment the block address and test the byte
counter for zero.

Loading and Dumping Memory Blocks to I/O-Mapped I/Os

The procedures for loading a block of memory from a designated input port,
or dumping a block of memory to a given output port, follow the precedent
already described in connection with the Z-80 device. The only differences, in
principle, of special note are that the byte to be transferred in either direction
must pass through the accumulator, and the port number must be specified
directly in the program (indirect reference to the port number via the C register cannot be done with the 8080A/8085's IN and OUT instructions).

Rather than simply rewriting the routines to match the function of the
Z-80 versions already described in this chapter, this is a good place to introduce the notion of *handshaking* operations.

Microprocessor programs run much faster than most kinds of external
devices that receive or supply memory block data. When outputting a block
of memory to a port connected to a line printer, for instance, the data must
not be delivered to the printer any faster than it can accept and print the information. As you might imagine, a mechanical printing operation runs much
slower than a memory dumping routine of the type described in previous
examples.

The problem of feeding blocks of data to a slow-acting output device
can be solved by a handshaking process. That is a process whereby the output instrument is equipped with circuitry that generates a "ready" signal
whenever it is able to accept the next byte of data from the microprocessor
system.

The following example assumes that a block of memory data is to be
dumped to a slow-acting output device that is equipped with the "ready"
signal feature.

EXAMPLE 17-3

A system has the following specifications:

1. A block of 2048 bytes of data beginning at address 4000H

2. A data output port at port 1

3. A handshaking input port at port 2

4. An output device that generates a logic 1 in the B0 position at port 2 whenever it can accept the next byte of data

Write and assemble an 8080A/8085 program that will dump the memory block to the output device. Begin the listing at program address 7000H, and use the flowchart in Fig. 17-8 as a guide.

The transfer parameters to be initialized at the beginning of the routine are only the starting address of the memory block and the number of bytes to be dumped to the output port.

After setting up those parameters, the flowchart shows the microprocessor picking up a data byte from the handshaking input port. If the output device is not ready, the program simply loops back up to a point where it checks the "ready" bit again.

The moment the output device is ready to receive a byte of data from the memory block, that byte is fetched from the block and transferred to the output port. Then the block address pointer is incremented and the byte counter is decremented. If the entire block of data has been transferred to the output device, the routine comes to an end. But if there are more bytes to be transferred, the system loops back to the place where it begins testing the handshaking bit again—waiting in that loop until the output device is ready to receive the next byte of data.

This is an example of asynchronous outputting of data. The pace of the entire operation is fixed by the operating speed of the output device. The output device can pause as long as necessary without upsetting the timing of the operation.

The suggested listing in Program 17-3 shows the handshaking operation beginning at the instruction labeled BIT. IN 02H fetches the handshaking input byte from I/O port 2, and ANI 01H isolates B0 in that byte. B0 from port 2 is set to a logic 1 whenever the output device is ready for a new byte of data—the output device itself generates that bit.

As long as the input handshaking bit is at logic 0, the JZ BIT operation is satisfied, and the program continues looping between there and the BIT instruction. When the output device is ready for the next byte of data, it sets B0 at port 2 to logic 1, and the microprocessor responds by doing the

PROGRAM 17-3 8080A/8085 MEMORY DUMP LISTING FOR EXAMPLE 17-3

```
7000  21  00  40        LXI   H,4000H  ;POINT TO BEGINNING OF BLOCK
7003  01  00  08        LXI   B,0800H  ;SET NUMBER OF BYTES
7006  DB  02      BIT   IN  02H        ;FETCH OUTPUT HANDSHAKE BYTE
7008  E6  01            ANI  01H       ;CHECK B0—IS THE OUTPUT READY?
700A  CA  06  70        JZ  BIT         ;IF ZERO, FETCH AGAIN
700D  7E               MOV  A,M        ;ELSE FETCH BYTE FROM BLOCK
700E  D3  01            OUT  01H       ;OUTPUT IT TO PORT 1
7010  23               INX  H          ;INCREMENT BLOCK POINTER
7011  0B               DCX  B          ;DECREMENT BYTE COUNTER
7012  79               MOV  A,C        ;GET LSB OF BYTE COUNT
7013  B0               ORA  B          ;OR WITH MSB
7014  C2  06  70        JNZ  BIT        ;IF NOT DONE, OUTPUT ANOTHER BYTE
```

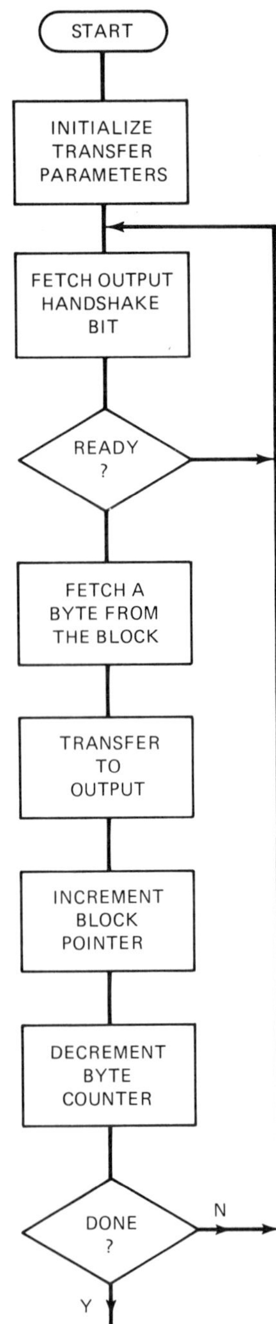

Figure 17-8 Flowchart for the 8080A/8085 block dumping routine, with port handshaking, in Example 17-3.

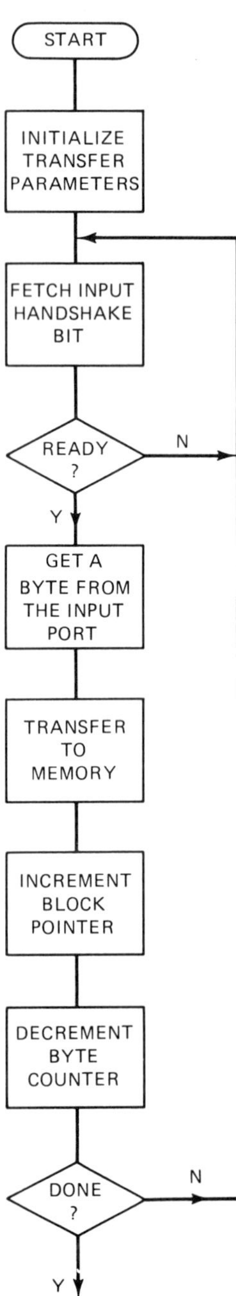

Figure 17-9 Flowchart for the 8080A/8085 block load routine in Example 17-4.

PROGRAM 17-4 8080A/8085 MEMORY BLOCK LOADING ROUTINE FOR
EXAMPLE 17-4

```
7000  21  00  40       LXI   H,4000H  ;POINT TO BEGINNING OF BLOCK
7003  01  00  08       LXI   B,0800H  ;SET NUMBER OF BYTES
7006  DB  02      BIT  IN 02H         ;FETCH INPUT HANDSHAKE BYTE
7008  E6  02           ANI   02H      ;IS INPUT READY?
700A  CA  06  70       JZ BIT         ;IF NOT, FETCH AGAIN
700D  DB  01           IN 01H         ;ELSE FETCH THE INPUT BYTE
700F  77               MOV M,A        ;STORE BYTE TO BLOCK
7010  23               INX   H        ;INCREMENT BLOCK POINTER
7011  0B               DCX   B        ;DECREMENT BYTE COUNTER
7012  79               MOV A,C        ;GET LSB OF BYTE COUNT
7013  B0               ORA   B        ;OR WITH MSB
7014  C2  06  70       JNZ   BIT      ;IF NOT DONE, INPUT ANOTHER BYTE
```

output routine. In this example the byte from the current block address is
sent to output port 1, which, presumably, is connected to the output device.

The next example illustrates both the matter of loading a block of data
from an I/O-mapped input device and input handshaking.

EXAMPLE 17-4

Write and assemble an 8080A/8085 routine that loads a block of memory from an
input device at port 1. Load 2048 memory locations, running upward from 4000H,
and do not accept a new byte until the input device is ready to deliver it—a logic-1
level at B1 of port 2. Begin the listing at address 7000H, and use the flowchart in
Fig. 17-9 as a guide.

The flowchart and suggested program listing in Program 17-4 are quite
similar to the memory dumping routine in Example 17-3. Here, however, the
microprocessor system will not accept a new byte until B1 of the data from
port 2 is at a logic-1 level.

Memory Block Searches

Figure 17-10 illustrates a basic block search operation for the 8080A/8085
system. In this particular case, the block begins at address 4000H and runs
upward through 2048 bytes. The data byte being searched is 2AH. The general idea is to search the block, one byte at a time, until either of two things
happen: the byte, 2AH, is found, or the entire block is searched.

The HL pair serves as the block address pointer, so it is initialized at
4000H at the beginning of the routine. The BC register pair is the byte counter,
and it is initialized at 0800H (2048 decimal). The byte being searched, 2AH,
is loaded into the D register.

The actual search operation begins at the line labeled FECH. At that
point, a byte of data is fetched from the current memory block address, and
then it is compared with the byte residing in the D register—the search byte.
If there is a match, the JZ DONE instruction branches operations to the
DONE instruction. Otherwise, the block address is incremented and the byte
counter is decremented. If the byte counter is decremented to zero, the sys-

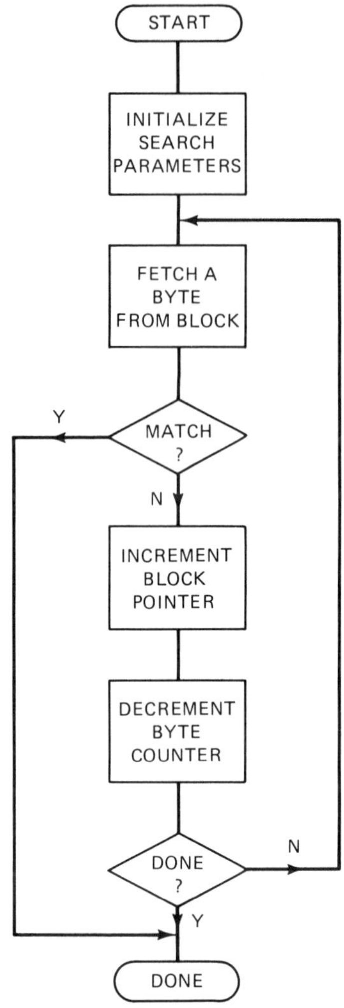


```
1000   21  00  40           LXI H, 4000H    ;SET BEGINNING OF MEMORY BLOCK
1003   01  00  08           LXI B, 0800H    ;SET NUMBER OF BYTES IN BLOCK
1006   16  2A               MVI D, 2AH      ;SET COMPARE BYTE
1008   7E            FECH    MOV A, M        ;FETCH A BYTE F ROM THE BLOCK
1009   BA                   CMP D           ;COMPARE
100A   CA  14  10           JZ DONE         ;IF SAME, JUJP TO DONE
100D   23                   INX H           ;ELSE INCREMENT BLOCK POINTER
100E   0B                   DCX B           ;DECREMENT BYTE COUNTER
100F   79                   MOV A, C        ;GET LSB OF BYTE COUNT
1010   B0                   ORA B           ;OR WITH MSB
1011   C2  08  10           JNZ FETCH       ;IF NOT DONE, LOOK AT THE NEXT BYTE
1014   C3  10  10    DONE    JMP DONE        ;LOOP TO SELF
```

Figure 17-10   Flowchart and listing for an 8080A/8085 block search routine.

tem executes the DONE instruction—the same one that is executed if, and when, the search byte is found.

But as long as the search byte is not found and the byte counter has not yet counted down to zero, the program continues looping in such a way that it checks each successive byte in the memory block.

The following example extends the matter of block searching to a more practical sort of application. In this case the program searches a block of memory for a certain byte; and whenever that byte is found, the current block address is loaded to another memory block. The scheme searches for *all* search bytes, and does not come to a conclusion whenever the first one is found.

EXAMPLE 17-5

Write and assemble an 8080A/8085 program that does the following:

1. Search a block of memory that begins at 4000H and runs upward 2048 address locations.

2. If the content of the current address is 2AH, save that address in successive block locations beginning at address 7C00H.

3. Continue the search-and-load operation until the entire block has been searched.

Begin the listing at program address 7000H, and use the flowchart in Fig. 17-11 as a guide.

The routine deals with two different blocks of memory. The block to be searched, the source book is initialized at 4000H in the HL register pair. The block that is to be loaded with addresses holding byte 2AH is initialized at 7C00H in the DE register pair. That will be the destination block as far as the address transfer operations are concerned.

The byte counter is started at 0800H in the BC register pair.

See the listing in Program 17-5.

PROGRAM 17-5   8080A/8085 BLOCK SEARCH LISTING FOR EXAMPLE 17-5

```
7000 21 00 40          LXI  H,4000H   ;POINT TO START OF SOURCE BLOCK
7003 11 00 7C          LXI  D,7C00H   ;POINT TO START OF DEST. BLOCK
7006 01 00 08          LXI  B,0800H   ;NUMBER OF BYTES TO SEARCH
7009 7E          FETC  MOV  A,M       ;FETCH BYTE FROM SOURCE BLOCK
700A FE 2A             CPI  2AH       ;COMPARE
700B C2 14 70          JNZ  NEXT      ;IF NO MATCH, JUMP TO NEXT
700E 7D                MOV  A,L       ;GET LSB OF SOURCE ADDRESS
700F 12                STAX D         ;STORE TO DEST. BLOCK
7010 13                INX  D         ;INCREMENT DEST. BLOCK POINTER
7011 7C                MOV  A,H       ;GET MSB OF SOURCE ADDRESS
7012 12                STAX D         ;STORE TO DEST. BLOCK
7013 13                INX  D         ;INCREMENT DEST. BLOCK POINTER
7014 23          NEXT  INX  H         ;INCREMENT SOURCE BLOCK POINTER
7015 0B                DCX  B         ;DECREMENT BYTE COUNTER
7016 79                MOV  A,C       ;GET LSB OF BYTE COUNT
7017 B0                ORA  B         ;OR WITH MSB
7018 CS 09 70          JNZ  FETC      ;IF NOT DONE, FETCH NEXT BYTE
701B C3 1B 70    DONE  JMP  DONE      ;LOOP TO SELF
```

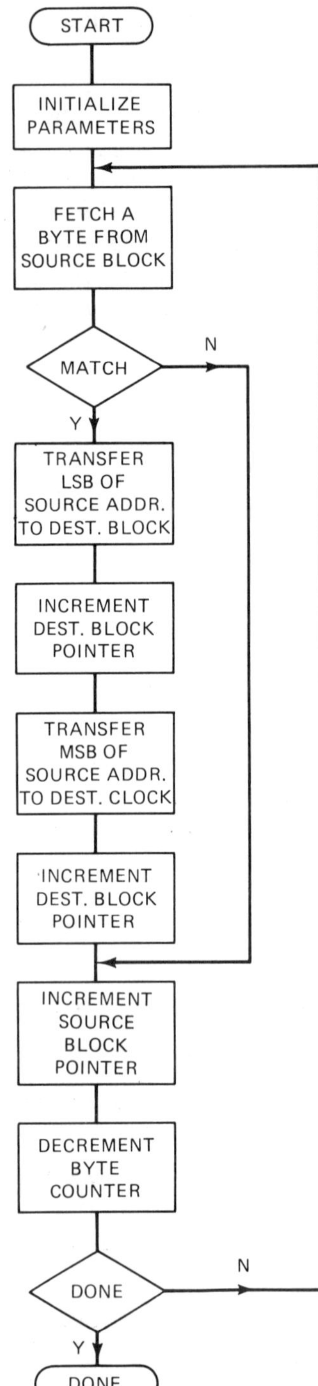

Figure 17-11 Flowchart for the 8080A/8085 block search routine in Example 17-5.

The first step in the matching process is to fetch a byte from the current source block address location. The listing shows that byte being compared with 2AH, the search byte, in the instruction CPI 2AH. If there is no match, the listing calls for branching down to the instruction at label NEXT. The NEXT sequence increments the source block pointer, decrements the byte counter, and tests the byte counter to see whether or not the entire block has been searched. If so, operations come to a conclusion; otherwise, the program loops back up to FETC, where the next byte in the source block is tested.

Whenever a match is found, the program executes a series of instructions:

```
MOV  A,L
STAX  D
INX   D
MOV  A,H
STAX  D
INX   D
```

The first of those instructions loads the LSB of the current source address to the accumulator, and the next instruction stores it to the current desti-nation block address. It is the LSB of the source address itself (and not the data at the location) that is loaded to the destination block.

The destination block pointer, the DE register pair, is then incremented. Then the MSB of the current source address is loaded to the destination block.

As a result of running those six instructions, the current 2-byte source address is loaded to successive address locations in the destination byte. The INX D instruction at the conclusion of that sequence gets the destination register ready for the next source address that happens to hold data 2AH.

Exercises for Section 17-2

1. Suppose that a block transfer routine is just part of a larger program that uses the working registers for other critical applications. What would be the simplest procedure for saving the data in those registers while they are being used for the transfer routine?

2. What is the primary purpose for handshaking operations?

3. Programs, themselves, are often treated as blocks of data to be saved on magnetic tape or disk. Which of the following kinds of block operations would be appropriate for that program-storing task?
   (a) Block-to-block transfer   (b) Loading a block from an input port
   (c) Dumping a block to an input port (d) Block search

17-3 MEMORY BLOCK OPERATIONS
FOR THE 6502

Block operations for the 8080A/8085 and Z-80 take advantage of the gener-ous number of internal registers that are available to them. The 6502, by comparison, has a considerable shortage of such registers; as a result, its block operations must keep track of block addresses and byte counts in external memory locations.

The 6502's unique post-indexed addressing mode is well suited for memory block operations. Recall that post-indexed instructions pick up a 2-byte address from two successive locations in zero-page memory. Then the current content of the Y register is summed with that base address to make up an effective address elsewhere in memory. See Section 9-4 if you think a review of the topic is in order.

Using post-indexed addressing, the approach to block operations is somewhat different from that used by the Z-80 and 8080A/8085 systems. One of those differences, as far as the programmer is concerned, is the need to establish some well-defined address locations in zero-page memory—address locations that point to the beginning of blocks and serve as byte counters. In essence, the idea is to substitute zero-page memory locations for the register pairs that are used by the two previously described microprocessor systems.

Block Transfer Operations

The matter of passing a data byte from a source block to a destination block is generally handled by moving the byte through the A register. Only the Z-80, with its special block instructions, can do without that feature.

Perhaps the best way to approach the procedure for doing block transfers with the 6502 system is with a specific example.

EXAMPLE 17-6

Write a 6502 program routine that transfers 255 bytes of data from a source block that begins at address $4000 to a destination block that begins at address $7C00. Transfer the data in ascending address order, and begin the listing at program address $1000.

See the suggested procedure in Program 17-6.

PROGRAM 17-6 6502 BLOCK TRANSFER LISTING FOR EXAMPLE 17-6

```
1000  A9 00        LDA  #$00
1002  85 10        STA  $10       LSB OF SOURCE POINTER TO $10
1004  A9 40        LDA  #$40
1006  85 11        STA  $11       MSB OF SOURCE POINTER TO $11
1008  A9 00        LDA  #$00
100A  85 12        STA  $12       LSB OF DEST. POINTER TO $12
100C  A9 7C        LDA  #$7C
100E  85 13        STA  $13       MSB OF DEST. POINTER TO $13
1010  A9 FF        LDA  #$FF
1012  85 14        STA  $14       NUMBER OF BYTES TO $14
1014  A0 00        LDY  #$00      ZERO THE BYTE COUNTER
                   ;INITIALIZATION DONE
1016  B1 10   XFER LDA  ($10),Y   FETCH SOURCE BLOCK BYTE
1018  91 12        STA  ($12),Y   TRANSFER TO DEST. BLOCK
101A  C8           INY            INCREMENT BYTE POINTER
101B  C4 14        CPY  $14       COMPARE WITH NO. OF BYTES
101D  D0 F7        BNE  XFER      IF NOT DONE, TRANSFER ANOTHER BYTE
```

Since the relevant addresses and byte count are to be in zero-page memory, the routine calls for a relatively lengthy set of initialization steps.

The first two instructions load the LSB of the beginning of the source address to zero-page address $10. The next two instructions then load the MSB of that block address to zero-page address $11. Considered together, those first four instructions load $4000 into zero-page address locations $10 and $11, with the LSB being in the lower address location.

The next four instructions load the starting address of the destination block, $7C00, to zero-page memory addresses $12 and $13; again, the address is loaded with its LSB into the lower zero-page address.

Finally, the number of bytes to be transferred, $FF, is loaded to zero-page address $14, and the Y index register is initialized to zero.

That entire opening sequence does nothing more than initialize the system for doing the block transfer operations. The transfer operations themselves occupy only a handful of instructions. Beginning at label XFER, the program fetches the current source block byte via a post-indexed loading operation. If the Y index register is at zero—the case when the program is just starting—the effective address is found by summing the address pointed by $10 and summing it with zero. What address can be found at $10? The starting address of the source block. So when Y is equal to zero, the post-indexed loading instruction fetches the data byte from $4000—the starting address of the source block.

The next instruction—STA ($12),Y—refers to the destination address, storing the content of the accumulator to that place in memory. What is in the accumulator at that moment? The data byte from the current source block.

Thus the instruction sequence

```
LDA  ($10),Y
STA  ($12),Y
```

does the actual byte-transfer operation.

Having taken care of the transfer, the next instruction increments the value in the Y index register. The base addresses at $10 and $12 remain unchanged; it is the index term that increments in order to point to the next-higher set of block addresses.

So instruction INY sets up matters for doing a byte transfer at the next-higher address location. But before the next transfer can take place, the program must see whether or not all the bytes have been transferred.

Recall that the number of bytes to be transferred is saved in zero-page memory location $14. The instruction CPY $14 compares the current value in the Y index register with that value. If they are not equal, it means that the transfer job is not done, and operations loop back up to XFER.

In summary, zero-page memory locations $10 and $11 are set up to point to the starting address of the source block. In a similar fashion, zero-page addresses $12 and $13 are set to the starting address of the destination

block. The content of neither of these locations changes through the execution of the routine—locations $10 and $11 still point to the starting address
of the source block, and the $12 and $13 locations always point to the start
of the destination block.

It is the Y index register that increments after each data transfer takes
place. The overall effect is that the scheme works with successively higher
data address locations. The idea would not work at all without having access
to the 6502's post-indexed addressing mode.

Just as the initial addresses never change, neither does the number-of-
bytes register—zero-page address $14. The Y index register actually serves
two purposes; it is both an index term and a byte counter.

Block Exchanges

Block exchanges with the 6502 follow the same general pattern already
described for the Z-80 and 8080A/8085. And as far as the details of the
matter are concerned, the format is similar to the block transfer scheme
just described for the 6502.

EXAMPLE 17-7

Write and assemble a 6502 program for doing a block exchange that has the following parameters:

> Block A start address: $4000
>
> Block B start address: $7000
>
> Number of bytes to transfer: 255
>
> Exchange in ascending order.

Referring to the listing in Program 17-7, the initialization part of the
program:

1. Loads the LSB of Block A's starting address to zero-page address $10
2. Loads the MSB of Block A's starting address to zero-page address $11
3. Loads the LSB of Block B's starting address to zero-page address $12
4. Loads the MSB of Block B's starting address to zero-page address $13
5. Loads the number of bytes to be exchanged to zero-page address $14
6. Zeros the index/byte counter

This matter of loading relevant addresses and other important program
parameters into zero-page memory locations is quite typical of opening
routines for the 6502 system.

The actual exchange operation begins by loading the current content of
Block A to the accumulator, then transferring it to the X register. The X
register in this particular example serves as the temporary storage place for
one of the bytes being exchanged. The stack could be used instead, but this
example assumes the X register is available.

PROGRAM 17-7 6502 BLOCK EXCHANGE LISTING
FOR EXAMPLE 17-7

```
1000  A9  00              LDA  #$00
1002  85  10              STA  $10        LSB OF BLOCK A START ADDR. TO $10
1004  A9  40              LDA  #$40
1006  85  11              STA  $11        MSB OF BLOCK A START ADDR. TO $11
1008  A9  00              LDA  #$00
100A  85  12              STA  $12        LSB OF BLOCK B START ADDR. TO $12
100C  A9  7C              LDA  #$7C
100E  85  13              STA  $13        MSB OF BLOCK B START ADDR. TO $13
1010  A9  FF              LDA  #$FF
1012  85  14              STA  $14        NUMBER OF BYTES TO $14
1014  A0  00              LDY  #$00       ZERO THE BYTE COUNTER
                  INITIALIZATION IS DONE
1016  B1  10      XFER    LDA  ($10),Y    FETCH BLOCK A BYTE
1018  AA                  TAX             SAVE IN X
1019  B1  12              LDA  ($12),Y    FETCH BLOCK B BYTE
101B  91  10              STA  ($10),Y    TRANSFER TO BLOCK A
101D  8A                  TXA             GET SAVED BLOCK A BYTE
101E  91  12              STA  ($12),Y    TRANSFER TO BLOCK B
                  ONE-BYTE EXCHANGE IS DONE
1021  C8                  INY             INCREMENT BYTE COUNTER
1022  C4  14              CPY  $14        COMPARE WITH NO. OF BYTES
1024  D0  F1              BNE  XFER       IF NOT DONE, TRANSFER AGAIN
```

The next instruction—LDA ($12),Y—fetches the current byte from Block B, and the instruction following that one transfers the byte to Block A. That completes half the exchange operation.

TXA transfers the original byte from Block A to the accumulator, and STA ($12),Y loads it to the current Block B location. That completes the exchange.

The remainder of the program increments the byte counter and index, compares it with the number of bytes to be exchanged, and then branches back to XFER if the job is not done.

**Loading or Dumping a Memory Block
to a Single Address**

After studying the block loading and dumping operations for the Z-80 and 8080A/8085 systems, and after seeing how memory block operations are generally executed on the 6502, you should have little trouble working out routines for the 6502's versions of memory loading and dumping operations.

The general idea is to set up the starting address of the memory block somewhere in zero-page memory and load the number of bytes to be transferred. When loading a block of memory from an input address, the Y register both counts the bytes and indexes the block addresses. The source address does not change.

Dumping a block of memory to a fixed output address works just the other way around. The Y register is still the key to running the routine.

Handshaking, or at least some form of "ready" signaling, must be incorporated into such routines whenever the input or output device operates more slowly than the microprocessor does.

Block Searches

The following example illustrates a simple form of block search for the 6502 system.

EXAMPLE 17-8

Write and assemble a 6502 program that searches a block of memory for data byte $2A. The block begins at address $4000 and runs upward through 255 bytes.

The program sets up the starting address of the block in zero-page addresses $10 and $11 (see Program 17-8). The number of bytes to be searched goes into address $12, and the byte being searched goes to address $13. Once the routine is initialized in this fashion, using post-indexed addressing makes matters rather simple from there on.

First, the current block byte is fetched to the accumulator, then it is compared with the search byte. If there is a good match, the program loops to DONE. Otherwise, the index register/byte counter is incremented and tested for the end of the search. If the content of that index register is equal to the number of bytes to be searched, the program comes to a conclusion; otherwise, it searches the next block address.

Exercises for Section 17-3

1. Describe the function of post-indexed addressing instructions.
2. Suppose that a certain block routine requires use of the A, X, and Y registers. Those registers, however, contain important data for other program operations. What is the most effective way to save those data while the registers are being used for the block operations?
3. It appears that the 6502 requires some rather extensive programming that is devoted only to initializing a block routine. The same procedures for the Z-80 and 8080A/8085 seem to be simpler. Why is there such a difference?

PROGRAM 17-8 6502 BLOCK SEARCH LISTING
FOR EXAMPLE 17-8

```
1000  A9 00            LDA  #$00
1002  85 10            STA  $10       LSB OF START ADDRESS TO $10
1004  A9 40            LDA  #$40
1006  85 11            STA  $11       MSB OF START ADDRESS TO $11
1008  A9 FF            LDA  #$FF
100A  85 12            STA  $12       NUMBER OF BYTES TO $12
100C  A9 2A            LDA  #$2A
100E  85 13            STA  $13       BIT TO FIND TO $13
1010  A0 00            LDY  #$00      ZERO BYTE COUNTER
                  ;END OF INITIALIZATION
1012  B1 10     FETCH  LDA  ($10),Y   FETCH BLOCK BYTE
1014  C5 13            CMP  $13       IS IT THE ONE?
1016  F0 05            BEQ  DONE      IF SO, JUMP TO DONE
1018  C8               INY            ELSE INCREMENT BYTE COUNTER
1019  C4 12            CPY  $12       IS IT DONE?
101B  D0 F5            BNE  FETCH     IF NOT, FETCH NEXT BYTE
101D  4C 1D 10  DONE   JMP  DONE      LOOP TO SELF
```

The 6800 has no special block instructions and it does not have any instructions that take advantage of post-indexed addressing. So even though the general principles of the block operations are much the same as those of the other devices described in this chapter, the approach to programming them with the 6800 has to be somewhat different.

The 6800's lone indexing mode must be used for its block operations, but it has to be applied in a somewhat less than ideal way.

Block Transfers

Figure 17-12 shows a block diagram for a 6800 routine that transfers a block of data from one place in memory to another. Compare it with the "standard" block transfer flowchart in Fig. 17-4. The differences are wholly dictated by the nature of the 6800's indexed addressing mode.

The routine begins by initializing the transfer parameters: starting addresses of the source and destination blocks, and the number of bytes to be transferred. Immediately after that, the system fetches the byte from the source block. To that point, the flowchart is similar to all the other block transfer flowcharts. But the next step is to increment the source block address. In all previous examples, the block address is not incremented until the transfer is completed.

In the 6800 routine, the byte is transferred to the destination block after the source block address is incremented. The destination address is incremented after the transfer is done.

Finally, the byte counter is decremented and tested for zero. If that register has not been counted down to zero, the program loops back up to the point where it fetches the next byte from the source block. Otherwise, the routine comes to a conclusion.

EXAMPLE 17-9

Write and assemble a 6800 block transfer routine where:

1. The source block begins at address $4000.
2. The destination block begins at address $7C00.
3. There are 255 bytes to be transferred in ascending order.

The rationale behind the initialization phase of the suggested listing in Program 17-9 is identical to the 6502 block schemes described in Section 17-3. The fact that the 6800 has a 16-bit X register simplifies the programming task, however.

The first two instructions in the listing effectively load the starting address of the source block, $4000, into zero-page memory addresses $10 and $11. The 6800 always loads the MSB first; so contrary to the same operation

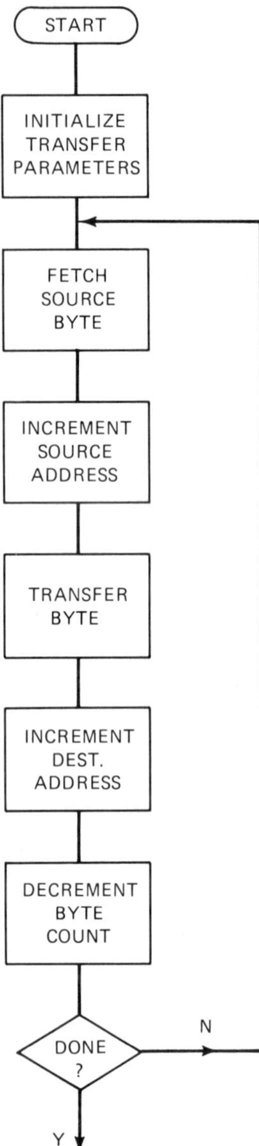

Figure 17-12 Flowchart for the 6800 block transfer routine in Example 17-9.

for the 6502, it turns out that the MSB of the souce starting address goes to zero-page address $10 and the LSB goes to $11.

The next two instructions use the X register to load the starting address of the destination block to zero-page addresses $12 and $13.

The initialization routine concludes by loading the 1-byte number-of-bytes parameter to zero-page address $14.

The instruction at label XFER simply loads the X register with the content of zero-page memory addresses $10 and $11. That is the current source

PROGRAM 17-9 6800 BLOCK TRANSFER LISTING
FOR EXAMPLE 17-9

```
1000 CE 40 00              LDX  #$4000   SOURCE BLOCK START ADDRESS
1003 DF 10                 STX  $10      TO $10,$11
1005 CE 7C 00              LDX  #$7C00   DEST. BLOCK START ADDRESS
1008 DF 12                 STX  $12      TO $12,$13
100A 86 FF                 LDAA #$FF     NUMBER OF BYTES
100C 97 14                 STAA $14      TO $14
                END OF INITIALIZATION ROUTINE
100E DE 10        XFER     LDX  $10      FETCH SOURCE ADDRESS
1010 A6 00                 LDAA 0,X      FETCH SOURCE BYTE TO A
1012 08                    INX           INCREMENT SOURCE ADDRESS
1013 DF 10                 STX  $10      SAVE IT
1015 EF 12                 LDX  $12      FETCH DEST. ADDRESS
1017 A7 00                 STAA 0,X      TRANSFER THE BYTE
1019 08                    INX           INCREMENT DEST. ADDRESS
101A DF 12                 STX  $12      SAVE IT
                END OF TRANSFER/INCREMENT ROUTINE
101C 7A 00 14              DEC  $0014    DECREMENT BYTE COUNTER
101F 26 ED                 BNE  XFER     IF NOT DONE,TRANSFER AGAIN
```

block address. The next instruction—LDAA O,X—loads the A accumulator with the byte at the current source block address. Referring to the flowchart, those two instructions satisfy the operation FETCH SOURCE BYTE.

After that, the INX instruction increments the content of the X register, and the instruction after that—STX $10—saves the new value at zero-page addresses $10 and $11. Taken together, those two instructions are responsible for incrementing the source block address and saving it in its place in zero-page memory. Unlike the 6502 block schemes, the block address that is kept in zero-page memory *does* increment as the routine progresses.

The byte being transferred is now in accumulator A. LDX $12 fetches the current source block address to the X register, and STAA O,X transfers the byte of data to that destination address.

The transfer phase concludes by incrementing the destination block address and storing it in its place in zero-page memory.

The routine then decrements the content of absolute memory address $0014. That, you should recall, is the zero-page location of the number representing the number of bytes to be transferred. If that number is decremented to zero, all bytes have been transferred; otherwise, the routine loops back up to XFER, where another byte-transfer sequence begins.

Microprocessor technology, and electronics in general, is noted for having to make trade-offs between mutually exclusive conditions. Comparing block routines for the 6502 and 6800 illustrate the point. The matter of initializing a block operation for the 6800 is made simpler by its ability to use a 16-bit X register. The limited indexing power of that register, however, makes it comparatively cumbersome through the actual exchange portion of the programs. The 6502 listings show long initialization routines, but short exchange routines. The 6800 has rather short initialization routines, but longer exchange listings. Certainly, a microprocessor engineer should not make hasty judgments when it comes to selecting a microprocessor for a new project.

Memory Block Exchanges

The fact that the 6800 has two separate, but functionally identical accumulators, makes its block exchange routines run rather smoothly. The flowchart for a block exchange in Fig. 17-13 shows the data byte from Block A going to accumulator A, and the byte from Block B going to accumulator B. Once that situation is set up, all that remains is to store the byte in accumulator A to the destination address and store the byte in accumulator B to the source address.

In the meantime, the source and destination addresses are incremented as described for the simple block transfer routine.

EXAMPLE 17-10

Write and assemble a block exchange routine for the 6800 microprocessor. Initialize the source block at $4000 and the destination block at $7C00. Exchange 255 bytes in ascending order.

Compare the listing in Program 17-10 with the flowchart.

Memory Block Dumps and Loads

The general principles of block operations do not change from one kind of microprocessor device to another. Once a programmer understands the general principles, writing the actual routines is a matter of adapting those principles to the characteristics of the system at hand.

```
PROGRAM 17-10  6800 BLOCK EXCHANGE LISTING
FOR EXAMPLE 17-10

1000  CE 40 00            LDX  #$4000   BLOCK A START ADDRESS
1003  DF 10               STX  $10      TO $10,$11
1005  CE 7C 00            LDX  #$7C00   BLOCK B START ADDRESS
1008  DF 12               STX  $12      TO $12,$13
100A  86 FF               LDAA #$FF     NUMBER OF BYTES
100C  97 14               STAA $14      TO $14
                END OF INITIALIZATION ROUTINE
100E  DE 10        XCH    LDX  $10      FETCH BLOCK A ADDRESS
1010  A6 00               LDAA O,X      BLOCK A BYTE TO ACC. A
1012  DE 12               LDX  $12      FETCH BLOCK B ADDRESS
1014  E6 00               LDAB O,X      BLOCK B BYTE TO ACC. B
1016  A7 00               STAA O,X      XFER BLOCK A BYTE TO BLOCK B
1018  08                  INX           INCREMENT BLOCK B ADDRESS
1019  DF 12               STX  $12      SAVE IT
101B  DE 10               LDX  $10      FETCH BLOCK A ADDRESS
101D  E7 00               STAB O,X      XFER BLOCK B BYTE TO BLOCK A
101F  08                  INX           INCREMENT BLOCK A ADDRESS
1020  DF 10               STX  $10      SAVE IT
                END OF EXCHANGE/INCREMENT ROUTINE
1022  7A 00 14            DEC  $0014    DECREMENT BYTE COUNTER
1025  26 E7               BNE  XCH      IF NOT DONE, EXCHANGE AGAIN
```

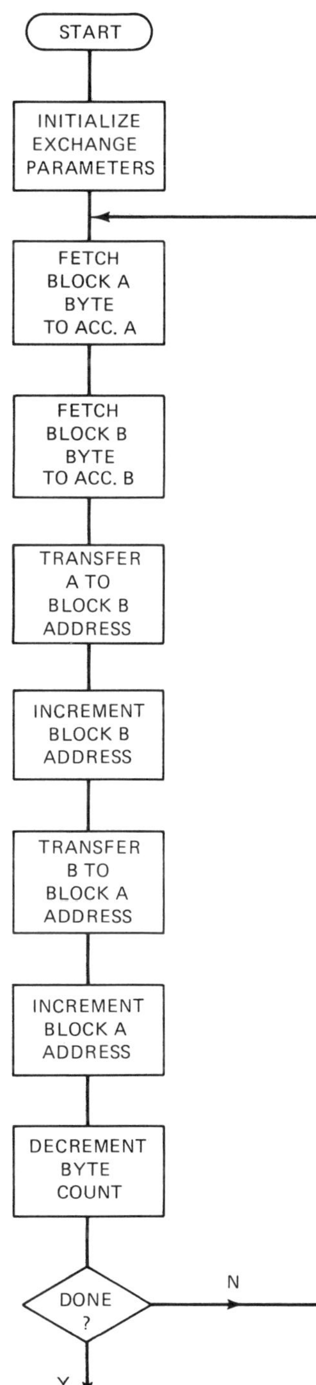

Figure 17-13 Flowchart for the 6800 block exchange routine in Example 17-10.

The next example illustrates a routine that dumps a block of memory to a fixed, memory-mapped output device. Using a handshaking signal to control the rate of transfer of data, the overall principle is the same one applied to the 8080A/8085 system in Example 17-3. The instructions are merely adapted to the 6800 system.

EXAMPLE 17-11

Write and assemble a 6800 routine for doing a block transfer to a fixed, memory-mapped address. Use the following parameters:

Starting address for the source block: $4000

Output address: $7C00

Handshaking bit: B0 at input port $7C01

Number of bytes to transfer: 2048

Aside from illustrating a block dump to a slow-acting output device, the listing in Program 17-11 suggests a technique for doing block operations on a number of bytes that exceeds 255. In this case, the routine dumps 2048 bytes to the output port, and that number is initialized to zero-page addresses $12 and $13. See the initialization instruction sequence:

```
LDX  L$0800
STX  $12
```

After each transfer to the output device, the following series of instructions decrement that 16-bit byte counter and test its content for a countdown to zero:

```
LDX  $12
DEX
BEQ  DONE
STX  $12
BRA  BIT
```

The first instruction in that sequence pulls the current byte count to the 16-bit X register. There it is decremented by the DEX instruction. The conditional branch instruction brings the entire routine to a conclusion if the content of the X register is decremented to zero. Otherwise, STX $12 saves the new byte count at its assigned location in zero-page memory. The branch-always instruction then loops the operations back to BIT.

Block Searches

A block search for the 6800 fetches the current byte from the block, compares it with the search byte, and takes the appropriate action. See Program 17-12.

The block to be searched begins at address $4000, and the routine

PROGRAM 17-11 6800 BLOCK DUMP LISTING
FOR EXAMPLE 17-11

```
1000 CE 40 00          LDX  #$4000   BLOCK START ADDRESS
1003 DF 10             STX  $10      TO $10,$11
1005 CE 08 00          LDX  #$0800   NUMBER OF BYTES
1008 DF 12             STX  $12      TO $12,$13
                 END OF INITIALIZATION ROUTINE
100A B6 7C 01  BIT     LDAA $7C01    FETCH HANDSHAKE BYTE
100D 84 01             ANDA $01      ISOLATE B0
100F 26 F9             BNE  BIT      IT NOT SET, FETCH AGAIN
                 END OF HANDSHAKE SENSING ROUTINE
1011 DE 10             LDX  $10      FETCH BLOCK ADDRESS
1013 A6 00             LDAA O,X      FETCH BLOCK BYTE
1015 B7 7C 00          STAA $7C00    OUTPUT IT
1018 08               INX           INCREMENT BLOCK ADDRESS
1019 DF 10             STX  $10      SAVE IT
                 END OF TRANSFER/INCREMENT ROUTINE
101B DE 12             LDX  $12      FETCH BYTE COUNT
101D 09               DEX           DECREMENT IT
101E 27 02             BEQ  DONE     IF ZERO, JUMP TO DONE
1020 DF 12             STX  $12      ELSE SAVE NEW BYTE COUNT
1022 20 E6             BRA  BIT      AND OUTPUT ANOTHER BYTE
1024 20 FE     DONE    BRA  DONE     LOOP TO SELF
```


PROGRAM 17-12 6800 BLOCK SEARCH LISTING

```
1000 CE 40 00          LDX  #$4000   BLOCK START ADDRESS
1003 DF 10             STX  $10      TO $10,$11
1005 CE 08 00          LDX  #$0800   NUMBER OF BYTES
1008 DF 12             STX  $12      TO $12,$13
100A 86 2A             LDAA #$2A     SEARCH BYTE
100C 97 14             STAA $14      TO $14
                 END OF INITIALIZATION ROUTINE
100E DE 10     FETC    LDX  $10      FETCH BLOCK ADDRESS
1010 A6 00             LDAA O,X      FETCH BLOCK BYTE
1012 91 14             CMPA $14      COMPARE WITH SEARCH BYTE
1014 27 08             BEQ  DONE     IF SAME, JUMP TO DONE
1016 08               INX           INCREMENT BLOCK ADDRESS
1017 DF 10             STX  $10      SAVE IT
                 END OF COMPARE ROUTINE FOR ONE BYTE
1019 DE 12             LDX  $12      FETCH BYTE COUNT
101B 09               DEX           DECREMENT BYTE COUNT
101C 26 F0             BNE  FETC     IF NOT DONE, FETCH AGAIN
101E 20 FE     DONE    BRA  DONE     LOOP TO SELF
```

searches 2048 bytes for data $2A. The routine comes to a conclusion if the
byte is found or the program decrements the 2-byte counter to zero.

Exercises for Section 17-4

1. Describe how the 6800's index instruction works.

2. Suggest an approach to doing block operations without using the 6800's indexed
   instructions.

18

BCD Arithmetic Instructions

Virtually all the examples of microprocessor arithmetic operations presented so far in this book have used full 8- or 16-bit binary numbers. Using such a format, unsigned 8-bit values have a decimal working range from 0 through 255, and the 16-bit unsigned values can be anywhere between 0 and 65,535.

A lot of simpler calculation routines can be executed more effectively using BCD (binary-coded decimal)numbers, however. This is especially true when a major portion of a routine is devoted to input and output operations that use decimal characters.

Suppose you are working with a microprocessor system that is to accept strings of decimal integer values from a keyboard—numbers represented by numeric characters 0 through 9. That would be a human-oriented input scheme. Further, suppose that the output device is a display mechanism that shows strings of decimal integers. Such a display might be a row of seven-segment LED display devices.

Now, here is the problem: How is a string of decimal characters such as 1234 to be accepted by the microprocessor? How is the result of some computing operations, perhaps a number such as 5467, to be processed before it can be presented to the decimal-oriented output device?

The programmer has two options. First, the string of decimal numbers from the input can be transformed into a strictly binary format. The decimal number 1234, for instance, can be transformed into the binary form 0000010011010010, or hexadecimal 04D2. After that, the microprocessor can treat it as a full 16-bit binary value. The result of the operation can then be transformed back into a decimal format before it is presented to the decimal-oriented display system.

The second option is to keep the values in a decimal format throughout the entire computing process. A decimal input such as 1234 is treated as four separate BCD values. And when the BCD computations are completed, the "answer" will be in a decimal form that is ready to be sent to the decimal-oriented output.

The idea of tranforming a series of BCD characters into a multibyte binary number has the distinct disadvantage of being a very cumbersome task in its own right. Similarly, transforming a multibyte binary result into a BCD format is an awkward and time-consuming process. Its only redeeming value is that the computations taking place between the input and output operations are relatively simple.

The matter of keeping the values in a BCD format throughout the entire operation has the advantage of being relatively simple at the input and output ends of the task. The computation techniques for BCD numbers can be cumbersome if the computations are fairly extensive. But if the required computations are relatively simple, such as summing two strings of BCD numbers, the idea of staying with a BCD format from beginning to end is an appealing one.

Referring to one of the opening comments in this chapter, then, the notion of keeping strings of numerical values in a BCD format justifies itself under those conditions where the computations are relatively simple. The procedures for transforming BCD numbers to full binary and then transforming the result of some simple computations back into a BCD format can use up more memory and valuable programming time than the computations themselves.

It would be unwise for anyone to suggest that one technique is better than the other under all circumstances. It is a matter of judgment—a matter of considering all the elements of the programming situation at hand. The purpose of this chapter is to illustrate some BCD computing techniques and introduce a small handful of instructions that are devoted exclusively to BCD arithmetic operations. When such techniques and instructions should be used, if at all, is a matter of personal judgment and programming style.

18-1 BCD REGISTER PACKING

A BCD number occupies no more than 4 bits. The largest possible BCD number is 1001, or decimal 9. Any 4-bit binary number larger than 1001 is not a valid BCD number.

Since any BCD number can be represented by a 4-bit binary number, it is possible to pack two different BCD values into a single 8-bit register. Whenever this is done, the numbers are said to be using a *packed BCD* format. Two 4-bit binary numbers are packed into a single 8-bit register.

Someone with a sense of humor decided to call a 4-bit binary number a *nybble*. A nybble, then, is half a byte. Interestingly enough, that nomenclature is now being accepted throughout the microprocessor business.

Thus two BCD characters can be packed into a single microprocessor register. The most-significant of the two BCD digits, and the least-significant nybble is the least significant of the two numerals. Decimal 75, for example, can be packed as 0111 followed by 0101, or 01110101. The hexadecimal form of that two-digit decimal number is 75H.

The largest valid packed BCD number is 99 decimal or 99H. Clearly, BCD packing does not take advantage of the full numbering capacity of an 8-bit binary register. An 8-bit binary number can be as large as 255 decimal, or FF hexadecimal.

Unfortunately, a microprocessor does not recognize packed BCD numbers as such. The packed BCD number 75, or 75H, is interpreted by the microprocessor as 117 decimal. So in order to work with packed BCD values, each microprocessor must have an instruction that tells it whether or not an 8-bit value is a straight binary number or a packed BCD number. And that is the purpose of the microprocessors' *decimal adjust* instruction.

Exercises for Section 18-1

1. Which of the following binary nybbles represent valid BCD numbers?
   (a) 0010   (b) 1000   (c) 1100   (d) 0111
2. What BCD value is represented by the following hexadecimal bytes? If the value is invalid, list it as such.
   (a) 09H   (b) 05H   (c) 0AH   (d) 00H
3. What two-digit BCD value is represented by the following 8-bit binary numbers? If the value is invalid, list it as such.
   (a) 10011000   (b) 01111000   (c) 10100000   (d) 01100110
4. What is the hexadecimal, packed BCD form for the following decimal numbers?
   (a) 78   (b) 12   (c) 00   (d) 5

18-2 DECIMAL-ADJUST OPERATIONS

Suppose that a microprocessor is to sum two BCD numbers, 8 and 3. The correct solution is, of course, 11 decimal. The microprocessor, however, does not arrive at that solution directly.

As far as the microprocessor is concerned, the problem is one of summing 08H and 03H. In a binary form, the operation looks like this:

```
00001000    BCD 8
00000011    BCD 3
00001011    binary sum
```

The microprocessor does not recognize the two numbers as BCD numbers. So when the summation is done, it provides hexadecimal 0B as an "answer." That solution is *not* a valid representation of a BCD value. The proper, packed BCD solution should be 11H.

Whenever a BCD addition turns up an invalid BCD number as an answer, it can be corrected—adjusted to a BCD form—by adding 6 to the sum. In the preceding example, summing the result with a 6 looks like this:

          00001011   binary sum
          00000110   decimal-adjust factor, 6
          00010001

The final solution, after making the necessary decimal adjustment, is
11H. That is a packed BCD representation of the sum of BCD numbers 8 and
3.

Decimal adjustments are often required for subtraction operations as
well. Consider 12H minus 7H:

          00010010   BCD 12
          00000111   BCD 7
          00001011   binary difference (see Table 7-5)

The binary difference is invalid because the lower-order nybble is a number
larger than 9. The necessary decimal adjustment is minus 6:

          00001011   binary difference
          00000110   minus decimal-adjust factor, 6
          00000101   BCD solution

Indeed, the BCD solution, after making the necessary decimal adjustment, is
05H.

The decimal adjustment must be used only when working with numbers
in a packed BCD format. Applying the adjustment to arithmetic operations
for full binary numbers yields some strange and misleading results.

There is a second condition that calls for applying the decimal adjustment factor of 6. Consider the situation where BCD 39 is summed with BCD
48:

          00111001   BCD 39
          01001000   BCD 48
          10000001   binary sum

In that example, neither nybble exceeds 9, but the solution is clearly "incorrect." It looks like BCD 81, but that certainly is not the sum of 39 and 48.

When summing those numbers, however, notice that there is a carry of
1 between the two nybbles. There is, in other words, a carry of 1 between
the bit-3 and bit-4 positions in that particular binary sum. That is the second
condition that calls for making a decimal adjustment of 6—plus 6 in this
case.

          10000001   binary sum
          00000110   decimal-adjust factor, 6
          10000111   packed BCD solution

Now the final solution, in a packed BCD format, is correct. It is BCD 87,
which is indeed the sum of BCD 39 and 48.

Subtraction operations, when using Table 7-5 as a guide, often show a
carry of 1 between the third and fourth bit positions. Even if neither nybble
in the binary difference is greater than 9, the carry of 1 between those two

bit positions signals the need for subtracting a decimal adjust factor of 6 from the answer. That will adjust the solution to a true, packed BCD form.

But how does the microprocessor know when there is a carry of 1 between the bit-3 and bit-4 positions? That is the purpose of the Ac flag bit.

The Ac flag bit, sometimes called the *half-carry* bit, is set to a logic 1 whenever an arithmetic instruction causes a carry of 1 between bits 3 and 4. When the decimal adjust scheme is used, having the Ac bit set to 1 forces the system to make the plus or minus 6 decimal adjustment.

Exercises for Section 18-2

1. Under what two conditions are the decimal-adjust factors used in conjunction with BCD arithmetic operations?
2. Which of the following addition and subtraction operations call for making a decimal adjustment? Why?

(a) 20H	(b) 58H	(c) 29H	(d) 39H	(e) 42H
+35H	+23H	+18H	-12H	-25H

18-3 DECIMAL-ADJUST INSTRUCTIONS

The Z-80, 8080A/8085, and 6800 microprocessors have a special decimal-adjust instruction, DAA. That mnemonic is the same for all three instruction sets. The 1-byte opcode is 27 for the Z-80 and 8080A/8085, and it is 19 for the 6800.

The DAA (*decimal accumulator adjust*) instruction is inserted into the program immediately following an addition or subtraction operation applied to packed BCD numbers. The instruction takes care of everything: It decides whether or not the decimal adjustment is needed, and it applies it as required by the nature of the operation.

Suppose a pair of packed BCD numbers appear in the B register and accumulator of a Z-80 system. They are to be summed and adjusted, if necessary, to get a packed BCD result. The instruction sequence looks like this:

```
80   ADD  A,B
27   DAA
```

That's all there is to it.

As far the 6800 is concerned, the decimal-adjust can take place only on numbers in accumulator A. The B accumulator is not affected by the DAA instruction.

The number to be adjusted must be in the accumulator, or A register, for the Z-80 and 8080A/8085 systems.

Decimal arithmetic is handled a bit differently for the 6502 system. Instead of following each BCD addition or subtraction operation with a special

DAA instruction, a special decimal bit in the 6502's flag register is set to logic 1 whenever BCD operations are to be performed. Once the flag is set, the microprocessor assumes that all arithmetic operations performed thereafter are to be carried out in a BCD format. The decimal adjust then goes into effect without having to specify it each time it is needed.

The decimal-mode setting instruction for the 6502 is

```
F8   SED
```

Once that instruction is executed, all arithmetic operations will run in a BCD format.

Getting out of the BCD mode is a matter of executing a decimal-mode clearing instruction:

```
D8   CLD
```

After executing that instruction, further addition and subtraction operations will be run as full binary arithmetic operations.

EXAMPLE 18-1

Assume that packed BCD numbers reside in the C, D, and E registers. Write a Z-80 program that does the following:

1. Do a BCD sum on the content of C and D registers.
2. Output the BCD result to memory-mapped port F000H.
3. Sum the previous result with the content of the E register.
4. Output the BCD result to memory-mapped port F001H.
5. Loop back to step 1.

Begin the listing at program address 7000H.
Repeat the program for the 8080A/8085.

In both listings in Program 18-1, the first step is to get the content of the C register into the accumulator. That is the only place that addition and DAA operations can take place. The next step is to add the content of the C register to the packed BCD number in the accumulator. Then the DAA instruction is applied. It might not affect the result; but on the other hand, it might. So it is always inserted after a BCD arithmetic instruction.

After making that first decimal adjustment, the current content of the accumulator is sent out to address F000H. Then the current content of the accumulator, already suitably adjusted for a BCD format, is summed with the packed BCD number in the E register.

The DAA instruction is executed again, and the guaranteed BCD result is set to address F001H.

Z-80 Version

```
7000 79         START   LD  A,C        ;GET BCD NUMBER FROM C
7001 82                 ADD A,D        ;SUM WITH NUMBER FROM D
7002 27                 DAA            ;DECIMAL ADJUST
7003 32 00 F0           LD  (F000H),A  ;OUTPUT RESULT TO F000H
7006 8B                 ADC A,E        ;SUM WITH BCD NUMBER FROM E
7007 27                 DAA            ;DECIMAL ADJUST
7008 32 00 F1           LD  (F001H),A  ;OUTPUT RESULT TO F0001H
700B 18 F3              JR  START      ;AND START ALL OVER
```

8080A/8085 Version

```
7000 79         START   MOV A,C        ;GET BCD NUMBER FROM C
7001 82                 ADD D          ;SUM WITH NUMBER FROM D
7002 27                 DAA            ;DECIMAL ADJUST
7003 32 00 F0           STA F000H      ;OUTPUT RESULT TO F000H
7006 8B                 ADC E          ;SUM WITH BCD NUMBER FROM E
7007 27                 DAA            ;DECIMAL ADJUST
7008 32 00 F1           STA F001H      ;OUTPUT RESULT TO F001H
700B C3 00 F0           JMP START      ;AND START ALL OVER
```

EXAMPLE 18-2

Assume that packed BCD numbers reside in zero-page memory locations $2A, $2B, and $2C. Write a 6800 program that does the following:

1. Sum the BCD content of $2A and $2B.
2. Output the BCD result to memory-mapped port F$000.
3. Sum the previous result with the content of $2C.
4. Output the BCD result to port $F001.
5. Loop back to step 1.

Begin the program listing at address $700.

The only real difference between the 6800 listing of Program 18-2 and the listings in Program 18-1 is the need for using external memory locations for holding the BCD numbers to be summed in the accumulator. As in the case of the Z-80 and 8080A/8085 listings, it is necessary to follow each BCD-oriented arithmetic step with a DAA instruction.

PROGRAM 18-2   6800 LISTING FOR EXAMPLE 18-2

```
7000 96 2A      START   LDAA $2A      GET BCD NUMBER FROM $2A
7002 9B 2B               ADDA $2B      SUM WITH BCD FROM $2B
7004 19                  DAA           DECIMAL ADJUST
7005 B7 F0 00            STAA $F000    OUTPUT TO $F000
7008 99 2C               ADCA $2C      SUM WITH BCD FROM $2C
700A 19                  DAA           DECIMAL ADJUST
700B B7 F0 01            STAA $F001    OUTPUT TO $F001
700E 20 F0               BRA START     AND START ALL OVER
```

```
7000 F8                  SED              SET DECIMAL MODE
7001 A5 2A      START    LDA $2A          GET BCD NUMBER FROM $2A
7003 18                  CLC              CLEAR CARRY FLAG
7004 65 2B               ADC $2B          SUM WITH BCD FROM $2B
7006 8D 00 F0            STA $F000        OUTPUT TO $F000
7009 65 2C               ADC $2C          SUM WITH BCD FROM $2C
700B 8D 01 F0            STA $F001        OUTPUT TO $F001
700E 4C 01 70            JMP START        AND START ALL OVER
```

EXAMPLE 18-3

Rewrite the task in Example 18-2 to take advantage of the 6502's decimal-set mode of operation. See the listing in Program 18-3.

Notice in the 6502 listing that the decimal mode is set as the first instruction. Thereafter, there is no need to be concerned about making decimal adjustments—the decimal-adjust mode assumes that such adjustments are often required after every arithmetic operation.

Incidentally, it is always a good idea to insert a CED instruction early in any 6502 program that will not be using BCD arithmetic. Why is this so?

19

Restart and Interrupt Routines

All the microprocessors described in this book include some provisions for interrupting the ongoing program and calling another one. An interrupt of this sort is not caused by some instruction that had been inserted into the program at an earlier time. Rather, an interrupt is initiated by an electrical signal that is applied directly to a special interrupt terminal on the microprocessor device itself.

During the normal course of executing program instructions, the microprocessor concludes each one by checking the 1-or-0 status of its interrupt terminals. Generally speaking, the interrupt terminals have a logic-1 level applied to them when no interrupt is to take place. So when the microprocessor checks the interrupt terminals at the end of each program instruction, it is really looking for a sudden change in the interrupt signal level—normally a change from logic 1 to zero.

When such an interrupt signal occurs, the microprocessor can break out of the normal routine it is running at the moment and call another subroutine that is especially written to deal with the situation that initiated the interrupt signal in the first place.

Suppose, for instance, that the microprocessor is being used in an application where a failure of the commercial utility power system can cause some terrible problems. At best, such a power failure could wipe out all the programming and data stored in RAM space; at worst, such a power failure might cause a microprocessor control system to shut down some very critical industrial devices.

The system could be set up in such a way that a utility power failure initiates an interrupt subroutine. That subroutine could be written in such a way that it operates a solid-state switch that removes the system from the utility power lines and connects it to a set of rechargable batteries. The system could then carry out its most critical operations, using the batteries as a power source. When utility power is finally restored, the system could return to its normal operations, leaving that special subroutine until it is needed again.

Interrupt routines need not be used exclusively for emergency applications. In fact, some programmers like to apply interrupts on a regular basis. As an example, a microprocessor system used in an industrial control application might be capable of running its tasks without any human intervention. There are times, however, when a operator will want to interrupt the ongoing routine and enter some special data. In that case the keys on a control keyboard can be connected to an interrupt terminal on the microprocessor; so when the operator strikes a certain key, the system breaks out of its normal routine and begins accepting new information from the keyboard. The keyboard input routine, in this case, is written as a special interrupt subroutine, and it can remain in force until the operator strikes a key that signals the end of the routine and returns normal control to the system.

Interrupts, you see, can take place at any time. That is why they are not written into the normal programs. If interrupts were written into the normal programs, the system could be interrupted only when it was looking at that particular instruction.

19-1 INTERRUPT SEQUENCES

An interrupt is, in essence, a call instruction. Whenever the microprocessor senses an interrupt signal, it automatically calls an interrupt subroutine at some well-defined address in program memory. One of the first responses to an interrupt, then, is to save the content of the program counter on the stack. Doing that, the system knows where to resume normal program execution when the interrupt routine is concluded. Viewing interrupts as a calling operation, it should be clear that the interrupt subroutine itself should conclude with a return instruction—an instruction that signals the end of the routine, pops the previously saved program address back into the program counter, and generally gets things running normally again.

In some instances, initiating an interrupt sequence pushes the contents of all the working registers onto the stack. When the interrupt sequence is done, those registers are restored to their _.iginal states. Normal programming thus resumes as though no interrupt took place at all.

In other instances, the programmmer has to write the interrupt subroutine in such a way that it is responsible for pushing the contents of all the working registers onto the stack, and then restoring the contents just before returning to the program sequence that had been interrupted.

Microprocessors have at least two interrupt terminals on them. One is for maskable interrupt routines and the other is for nonmaskable interrupts. A *maskable interrupt* is one that can be at least temporarily disabled by a normal program instruction. There are sequences of operations that ought not be interrupted as a matter of course; then there are less critical sequences that can be interrupted without causing more harm than good.

The programmer can designate blocks of program instructions that must not be interrupted under normal circumstances by beginning those blocks with a special *disable interrupt* instruction. Those blocks can then end with an *enable interrupt* instruction that allows maskable interrupts to occur anytime thereafter. Instructions residing between a disable and a subsequent enable instruction cannot be interrupted by a maskable interrupt signal. If such a signal occurs during the execution of the disabled sequence, the actual interruption will take place only after the system executes the corresponding enable instruction.

Nonmaskable interrupts, on the other hand, cannot be disabled by any software instruction. Whenever the nonmaskable interrupt terminal on the microprocessor is energized, the ongoing program—even one initiated by a maskable interrupt—is interrupted.

A nonmaskable interrupt is said to have *priority* over any maskable interrupt situation.

So interrupts are always initiated by electrical signals applied to the microprocessor; and if the maskable interrupt is enabled or a nonmaskable interrupt situation occurs, the system saves the current program address on the stack (and perhaps the contents of all the working registers as well), and goes immediately to the beginning of a special interrupt subroutine. the question at this point is: How does the system know where the interrupt subroutine begins?

There are several different answers to that question. It depends on the particular microprocessor being used. In fact, most of the work regarding system interrupt routines concerns the matter of specifying the starting address of the interrupt subroutine. Since there is a significant variation in the procedure for specifying the starting address of interrupt subroutines, those procedures will be described in the light of the microprocessor devices that use them.

Before looking at the interrupt characteristics of some specific microprocessors, one further interrupt feature ought to be introduced. Every microprocessor described in this book has a program instruction that stops all program execution until an interrupt occurs. These halt, or wait, instructions are inserted at the desired place in the normal program routine. When the system encounters that instruction, everything comes to a halt and the microprocessor is effectively isolated from the bus system until an interrupt signal occurs. That is a programming option that many programmers use for purposes that are not normally associated with the emergency character of interrupts.

The 6502 and 6800 have similar interrupt features. They both have maskable and nonmaskable interrupt terminals on them, identical enabling and disabling mnemonics, the same sort of return instructions, and some instructions for halting operations until an interrupt occurs. Compare the instructions in Tables 19-1 and 19-2.

Nonmaskable Interrupts

Whenever a nonmaskable interrupt signal occurs, the 6502 device immediately saves the current content of the PC and flag registers on the stack. The 6800 saves the contents of all the working registers, including both accumulators, on the stack.

After that, both systems automatically disable the maskable interrupt feature. The idea is to prevent any maskable interrupt signal from interrupting a higher-priority nonmaskable routine that is running at the moment.

Finally, the systems fetch starting addresses for the nonmaskable interrupt subroutine from two successive address locations in memory. Those two locations must be devoted exclusively to that application if, indeed, the nonmaskable interrupt feature is used at all.

As far as the 6502 system is concerned, the starting address of the non-

TABLE 19-1 INTERRUPT-RELATED INSTRUCTIONS
FOR THE 6502

Source code	Object code	Notes
CLI	58	Enable interrupt
SEI	78	Disable interrupt
RTI	40	Return from interrupt
BRK	00	Break (forced interrupt)

TABLE 19-2 INTERRUPT-RELATED INSTRUCTIONS
FOR THE 6800

Source code	Object code	Notes
CLI	0E	Enable interrupt
SEI	0F	Disable interrupt
RTI	3B	Return from interrupt
WAI	3E	Wait for interrupt
SWI	3F	Forced interrupt

maskable subroutine is stored at $FFFA and $FFFB, with the LSB of the address being at $FFFA. Now, those addresses hold the starting address of the subroutine—they do not represent the beginning of the subroutine itself.

The nonmaskable interrupt subroutine can be placed anywhere in the memory system. Suppose that you want to start it at address $4C00. In order to use the routine with the 6502 system, you must also place $00 (the LSB of the starting address) into location $FFFA and $4C into address location $FFFB. When a nonmaskable interrupt occurs, then, the system will look at $FFFA and $FFFB to pick up the starting address for the interrupt subroutine—$4C00 in this particular example.

The 6800 responds in the same fashion, but picks up the starting address of the interrupt subroutine from addresses $FFFC and $FFFD. In keeping with the reverse order of bytes used by the 6800 system, the MSB of the starting address is saved at $FFFC and its LSB is at $FFFD.

The starting address of the nonmaskable interrupt subroutine is thus found in an indirect fashion. It is stored in a pair of memory locations dedicated to that purpose.

In both instances, Tables 19-1 and 19-2 show that an interrupt subroutine ends with an RTI (return from interrupt) instruction. It does the same job as the RTS instruction, but applies specifically to interrupt subroutines, rather than to ordinary program subroutines.

When returning in this way from a nonmaskable interrupt subroutine, the 6502 system immediately restores the original content of the flag register and program counter. Those registers, you recall, are pushed onto the stack by the nonmaskable interrupt signal. The 6800 system responds to its RTI instruction by pushing the content of all working registers, including the PC and F register, into their original places in the microprocessor.

So the 6800 saves the content of all the registers on the stack upon initiating an interrupt subroutine, and it replaces them from the stack at the conclusion of that subroutine. But what if you are using a 6502 system and you want to save the content of the A, X, and Y registers as well as the PC and F registers? In that case, the interrupt subroutine should begin this way:

```
PHA    SAVE ACCUMULATOR ON STACK
TXA    TRANSFER X TO A
PHA    SAVE X ON STACK
TYA    TRANSFER Y TO A
PHA    SAVE Y ON STACK
```

The desired interrupt sequence can begin after that.

When it is time to return to normal program operations, this sequence restores the contents of the A, X, and Y registers *before* the return is executed:

```
PLA    GET Y FROM THE STACK
TAY    TRANSFER TO Y
PLA    GET X FROM THE STACK
TAX    TRANSFER TO X
```

The 6502 will automatically restore the contents of the PC and F register upon executing the RTI instruction.

Maskable Interrupts

The instructions that are unique to maskable interrupts are CLI and SEI. The 6502 and 6800 use the same mnemonics in this case, but the opcodes are different.

CLI enables the maskable interrupt feature, making it possible to interrupt an ongoing routine via the maskable interrupt terminal on the microprocessor device. SEI, on the other hand, is a program instruction that is used for overriding any maskable signal.

When the maskable interrupt is enabled and such an interrupt occurs, the sequence of operations is virtually identical to those found for nonmaskable interrupt routines. The only significant difference is the memory locations holding the starting address of the interrupt subroutine.

When beginning a maskable interrupt routine, the 6502 looks to addresses $FFFE and $FFFF for the starting address of the interrupt subroutine. (Recall that nonmaskable subroutines are started at addresses stored in memory at $FFFA and $FFFB.)

As far as the 6800 system is concerned, the starting address of a maskable interrupt subroutine is saved at $FFF8 and $FFF9.

A maskable interrupt subroutine should conclude with the RTI instruction. That being the case, normal programming will resume from the point where it was interrupted.

WAIT and Forced Interrupt Instructions

A *forced interrupt* instruction mimics the action of a hardware interrupt signal. Included in the normal program sequence, a forced interrupt instruction initiates a subroutine that has a starting address located at two well-defined locations in memory.

The forced interrupt instruction for the 6502 is the 1-byte instruction, BRK, or "break." Upon executing that instruction, the system calls a subroutine having a starting address that is stored in memory locations $FFFE and $FFFF. Indeed, they are the same locations used for saving the starting address of a maskable interrupt subroutine. Unless the content of those two memory locations is altered during the course of the program operations, a software BRK instruction and a hardware maskable interrupt will call the same subroutine.

The 6800 uses the instruction SWI as its forced interrupt instruction. When that instruction is executed, the system begins at an address designated at memory locations $FFFA and $FFFB. The instruction simulates the activity of a hardware maskable interrupt, but it picks up the starting address of the subroutine from different memory locations. (The 6800 picks up its starting address for a maskable interrupt subroutine from $FFF8 and $FFF9.)

Forced interrupts are frequently used as 1-byte subroutine calling operations. The usual JSR subroutine-calling instructions are 3-byte instructions; and if you have a certain subroutine that has to be called many times during the normal course of operations, it is possible to save a lot of program memory space by using the forced interrupt feature instead.

The 6800 has an additional interrupt-related instruction, WAI. This instruction brings all program operations to a halt and, in effect, disengages the microprocessor from its bus connections. The only way out of a *wait* situation is by doing a hardware interrupt or, in the most extreme case, switching power to the system off and on again.

The 6502 and 6800 both have a third hardware terminal labeled RESET. When this terminal is enabled by setting it to a logic-0 level, the program counter is automatically set to a value found in two successive address locations. The reset operation forces the system to abandon any ongoing activity and go immediately to an address found in those particular locations. For the 6502, the reset addresses $FFFC and $FFFD. The 6800 goes to an address pointed by the content of locations $FFFE and $FFFF.

Table 19-3 summarizes the locations of the subroutine pointers for the 6502 and 6800.

Exercises for Section 19-2

1. What is the essential difference between a maskable and a nonmaskable interrupt operation? Which will take priority in the event both occur at the same time?

2. Which registers are saved on the stack whenever an interrupt routine is initiated on the 6502 system? the 6800 system?

3. How does the SEI instruction affect subsequent maskable interrupt signals? nonmaskable signals?

4. How is it possible to do away with the effects of a disable interrupt instruction?

TABLE 19-3 SOURCES OF INDIRECTLY ADDRESSED INTERRUPT SUBROUTINES

Function	Source of start address
6502	
Maskable interrupt, and BRK	$FFFE, $FFFF
Hardware RESET	$FFFC, $FFFD
Nonmaskable interrupt	$FFFA, $FFFB
6800	
Hardware RESET	$FFFE, $FFFF
Nonmaskable interrupt	$FFFC, $FFFD
Forced interrupt	$FFFA, $FFFB
Maskable interrupt	$FFF8, $FFF9

5. What is the essential difference between a forced interrupt instruction and a hardware interrupt?

6. The text cites two ways to "escape" the 6800's WAI condition. There is a third way implied by a later statement. What is that technique?

7. What effect does the RTI statement have on an interrupt routine? Where is it generally located in the system programming?

19-3 RESTART AND INTERRUPT INSTRUCTIONS FOR THE 8080A/8085

The interrupt-related instructions for the 8080A/8085 perform the same general functions as those for the 6502 and 6800. The mechanisms for handling those functions are quite different in many respects, however.

Restart Instructions

Table 19-4 shows a set of eight instructions having the general mnemonic form RST n, where n is an integer between 0 and 7. These are program instructions that work in a fashion closely related to the forced interrupts of the 6502 and 6800 systems.

Upon encountering these instructions in a normal program, the system immediately calls a subroutine beginning at the absolute addresses shown in the table. Suppose that an RST 2 is written into a program. That 1-byte instruction saves the current content of the PC register on the stack and goes to address 0010H. Unlike the forced-interrupt instructions for the 6502 and 6800, these restart instructions use absolute, rather than indirect, addressing. Doing a RST 2 will force operations to resume at address 0010H.

There are eight different starting locations available, and each is called by a separate restart instruction. A close look at those addresses shows that there are only 8 bytes of memory available between each starting address. The implication is that the subroutines contained within those available spaces have to be incredibly short. Speaking realistically, there is not much that can be done within an 8-byte subroutine.

So the restart instructions force the system to call a well-defined set of

TABLE 19-4 RESTART INSTRUCTIONS FOR THE 8080A/8085

Source code	Object code	Notes
RST 0	C7	"Call" 0000H
RST 1	CF	"Call" 0008H
RST 2	D7	"Call" 0010H
RST 3	DF	"Call" 0018H
RST 4	E7	"Call" 0020H
RST 5	EF	"Call" 0028H
RST 6	F7	"Call" 0030H
RST 7	FF	"Call" 0038H

addresses. In order to make some good use of those instructions, the restart addresses generally contain nothing more than a few instructions that do an unconditional jump to some other address location in memory.

Suppose, then, that you want to write a fairly extensive subroutine that begins at address 4C00H. You can, of course, accomplish the task by writing a CALL 4C00H instruction into the program. Alternatively, you could call that subroutine with an RST 2 instruction, provided that you wrote this sequence beginning at address 0010H:

```
CALL 4C00H
RET
```

That is a 4-byte instruction sequence that fits nicely between the RST 2 and RST 3 starting addresses.

But what is the point of using the RST 2 instead of CALL 4C00H in the main program? For one thing, the restart instruction has just one byte in it. If that subroutine has to be called many times during the course of a program, using the 1-byte version can save a substantial amount of program memory.

The family of restart instructions are used for simple subroutine-calling operations. But they also play a vital role in interrupt operations.

Nonmaskable Interrupts

The programming procedures for the 8080A and 8085 differ a great deal with respect to nonmaskable interrupts. In fact, the 8080A has no nonmaskable interrupt feature. The nonmaskable interrupt on the 8085 is a hardware terminal labeled TRAP.

Whenever the TRAP terminal is activated (to initiate a nonmaskable interrupt subroutine), the current content of the PC register is popped onto the stack. That program address is saved so that the system can resume from that same place after the interrupt subroutine has been executed. None of the other registers are saved on the stack. If that is necessary, the interrupt subroutine must begin with a series of push instructions to do that job.

After saving the PC register on the stack, the TRAP interrupt immediately begins program execution from address 0024H. Generally, a programmer will insert a call instruction at that address, thus making it possible to bring out an interrupt subroutine from anywhere in program memory.

A noninterruptable subroutine can conclude with the usual RET instruction—one that will return operations from that routine.

Maskable Interrupts

The 8080A and 8085 both have a standard maskable interrupt input terminal. The instructions common to both microprocessors are EI (enable interrupts) and DI (disable interrupts). See Table 19-5.

Source code	Object code	Notes
EI	FB	Enable interrupts
DI	F3	Disable interrupts
SIM	30	Set interruptable mask (8085 only)
RIM	20	Reset interruptable mask (8085 only)
HLT	76	Wait for interrupt or reset

The SIM and RIM instructions are relevant to maskable interrupt operations, but they are unique to the 8085 device. They are described later in this section.

Whenever the maskable interrupt system is enabled and an interrupt signal appears at the microprocessor device, the system automatically saves the current content of the program counter. After that, it does something quite different from the 6502 and 6800: It looks to the data bus for a 1-byte instruction—an instruction telling the system what it is supposed to do next.

The 1-byte instruction on the data bus will be one of the eight restart instructions. Remember that those instructions amount to a 1-byte call instruction, telling the system to call an address location listed in Table 19-4. So, in effect, a maskable interrupt routine begins by asking: Which restart instruction do you want to use? The answer to that question must take the form of a 1-byte object code on the data bus: C7, CF, D7, DF, and so on. That 1-byte code must be one of the eight opcodes for the restart instructions.

But how does that byte get onto the data bus? That is a good question, and its answer represents what many believe is the most awkward feature of the 8080A/8085 system. The restart opcode is placed onto the data bus in a purely hardware fashion. External hardware, in the form of pullup resistors or active digital devices, provides the patterns of 1's and 0's that represent the restart opcode.

So when an interrupt sequence begins, the current PC status is saved on the stack, the entire external memory system is disabled, and the microprocessor looks to the data bus for a hardware-generated restart code. Once that restart code is picked up, the interrupt routine begins execution from that restart address.

A normal RET instruction at the conclusion of the interrupt subroutine returns the system to the program location where the interrupt originally occurred.

The SIM and RIM instructions set and reset three separate, priority-organized interrupts on the 8085 device. Three additional interrupt terminals, labeled RST 5.5, RST 6.5, and RST 7.5, can initiate an interrupt sequence. When a SIM instruction enables those interrupts and an activating signal oc-

curs at one of those terminals, the system responds by saving the current PC
on the stack and going to one of three address locations:

To 002CH for a RST 5.5

To 0034H for a RST 6.5

To 003CH for a RST 7.5

Those special memory locations are generally loaded with call instructions
that initiate subroutines elsewhere in memory.

An interrupt signal at terminal RST 7.5 takes priority over any other
except a nonmaskable interrrupt. RST 6.5, on the other hand, takes priority
over an RST 5.5 and the normal maskable interrupt scheme. RST 5.5 takes
priority only over the normal maskable interrupts.

Besides being arranged in order of priority, these special 8085 hardware
interrupts have the advantage of not requiring external devices for specifying
the starting addresses of their subroutines.

The HLT instruction, common to both the 8080A and 8085 works just
like the 6800's WAI instruction—it saves the current content of the PC register on the stack, effectively disengages the microprocessor from the memory
system, and waits for an interrupt signal to occur.

Exercises for Section 19-3

1. Cite an application of the RST instructions when they are considered in a purely software format. How are they applied as part of an interrupt sequence?
2. How do the EI and DI instructions affect the interrupt schemes for both the 8080A
   and 8085?
3. Cite at least two differences between the 8085's maskable, priority interrupts and the
   normal maskable interrupts.
4. How do the SIM and RIM instructions affect the interrupt scheme for the 8085?

19-4 RESTARTS AND INTERRUPTS FOR THE Z-80

The Z-80 system offers several options as far as formatting interrupts is concerned. It is like the 8080A/8085 system in many respects, and we will describe those similarities first.

Restart Instructions

Table 19-6 summarizes the Z-80's restart instructions. They follow the same
general pattern as those of the 8080A/8085 system. Only the mnemonics are
different. The mnemonics for the Z-80 indicate the actual target address. Executing an RST 28H, for example, sends program operations immediately to
address 0028H.

When executing one of the RST instructions from a main program, the
system automatically saves the content of the PC register (the return address)

TABLE 19-6 RESTART
INSTRUCTIONS FOR THE Z-80

Source code	Object code
RST 00H	C7
RST 08H	CF
RST 10H	D7
RST 18H	DF
RST 20H	E7
RST 28H	EF
RST 30H	F7
RST 38H	FF

on the stack and jumps to the address indicated by the source code listing. A return instruction at the end of the subroutine will bring the execution sequence back to the instruction that immediately follows the RST.

Used in the main body of a program, these instructions offer a 1-byte call option.

Nonmaskable Interrupts

The Z-80 microprocessor device has a special terminal dedicated to sensing a nonmaskable interrupt condition. When that terminal is activated, the system completes the instruction currently being executed, saves the content of the PC register on the stack, and calls address 0066H. Another jump or call instruction inserted at that address will initiate a subroutine that is relevant to the interrupt condition that has taken place.

The nonmaskable interrupt subroutine should conclude with the special return instruction RETN. See Table 19-7.

Maskable Interrupts

The Z-80 system offers three options with regard to maskable interrupts. The mode to be used is selected by the programmer by writing in the desired IM instruction. Those instructions set up maskable interrupt modes 0, 1, or 2.

The *mode 0* interrupt follows the principles already outlined for normal interrupts in the 8080A/8085 system. With IM 0 in effect, an interrupt disengages the memory system and forces the microprocessor to look for a 1-byte instruction on the data bus. That 1-byte instruction is, of course, one of the eight RST instructions summarized in Table 19-6.

The system will jump to that address and begin executing the interrupt subroutine from that point. These subroutines should conclude with the RETI return instruction.

The *mode 1* interrupt is much simpler to implement because it requires no external hardware. Whenever it is used, program operations begin at address 0038H. Its only disadvantage compared to the mode 0 option is that it

TABLE 19-7 INTERRUPT-RELATED INSTRUCTIONS FOR THE Z-80

Source code	Object code	Notes
EI	FB	Enable maskable interrupts
DI	F3	Disable maskable interrupts
RETI	ED 4D	Return from interrupt
RETN	ED 45	Return from nonmaskable interrupt
IM 0	ED 46	Set interrupt mode 0
IM 1	ED 56	Set interrupt mode 1
IM 2	ED 5E	Set interrupt mode 2
HALT	76	Wait for interrupt or reset
LD I,A	ED 47	Transfer register A to I (interrupt) register
LD A,I	ED 57	Transfer I register to A register

offers just one subroutine starting address (as opposed to eight of them for mode 0).

The *mode 2* interrupt is truly unique to the Z-80 system. It is an instruction that uses the device's interrupt register, I. When IM 2 is in force and an interrupt occurs, the following things happen:

1. Other maskable interrupts are disabled.
2. The current content of the PC register is saved on the stack.
3. The MSB of an indirect address is taken from the I register.
4. The LSB of an indirect address is taken from a hardware-generated byte on the data bus.
5. The content of the indirect address points to the start of a mode 2 interrupt subroutine.

Suppose that you have used the following program sequence to load 2AH into the I register:

```
LD A,2AH
LD I,A
IM 2
```

The final instruction in that sequence tells the system to respond to a maskable interrupt in a mode 2 fashion. The content of the interrupt register is set to 2AH by the first two instructions.

Further suppose that the system includes some hardware that will place a binary pattern representing FFH onto the data bus whenever a mode 2 interrupt is initiated.

When that interrupt is initiated, then, the system will put together a 2-byte address 2AFFH. The MSB comes from the I register and the FF comes from the hardware connected to the data bus.

Now, the system does not begin executing an interrupt subroutine at address 2AFFH. Rather, it picks up a starting address from 2AFFH and 2B00H. The addressing, in other words, is indirect. Recall that the 6502 and 6800 both used this form of indirect addressing for their maskable interrupt operations. The Z-80 system is a great deal more flexible, however, since it can pull the starting address from two successive memory locations situated in memory.

Exercises for Section 19-4

1. Where should the RETN instruction be used?
2. Describe the essential features of the IM 0, IM 1, and IM 2 interrupt modes.

Appendices

n	2^n
0	1
1	2
2	4
3	8
4	16
5	32
6	64
7	128
8	256
9	512
10	1 024
11	2 048
12	4 096
13	8 192
14	16 384
15	32 768

APPENDIX B:
HEXADECIMAL/DECIMAL CONVERSION AID

MSB						LSB	
Hex.	Dec.	Hex.	Dec.	Hex.	Dec.	Hex.	Dec.
0	0	0	0	0	0	0	0
1	4 096	1	256	1	16	1	1
2	8 192	2	512	2	32	2	2
3	12 288	3	768	3	48	3	3
4	16 384	4	1 024	4	64	4	4
5	20 480	5	1 280	5	80	5	5
6	24 576	6	1 536	6	96	6	6
7	28 672	7	1 792	7	112	7	7
8	32 768	8	2 048	8	128	8	8
9	36 864	9	2 304	9	144	9	9
A	40 960	A	2 560	A	160	A	10
B	45 056	B	2 816	B	176	B	11
C	49 152	C	3 072	C	192	C	12
D	53 248	D	3 328	D	208	D	13
E	54 344	E	3 584	E	224	E	14
F	61 440	F	3 840	F	240	F	15

APPENDIX C:
Z-80 INSTRUCTION SET

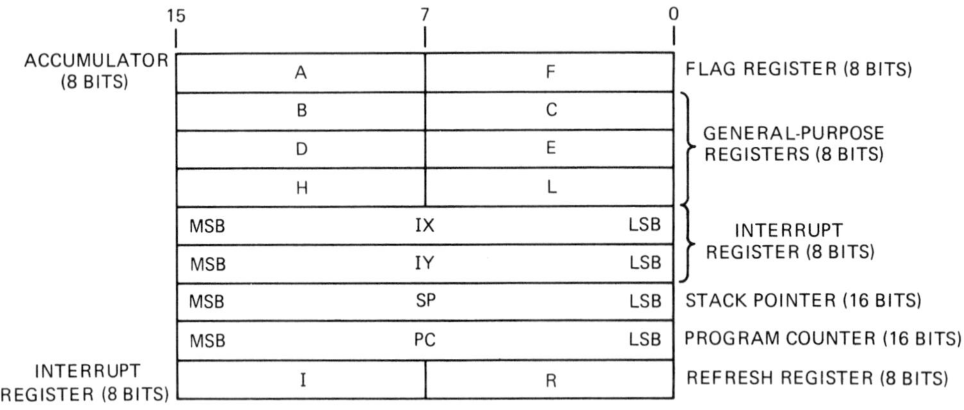

Figure C-1

ADC A,A	8F		
ADC A,B	88		
ADC A,C	89		
ADC A,D	8A		
ADC A,E	8B		
ADC A,H	8C		Add accumulator with carry
ADC A,L	8D		
ADC A,(HL)	8E		
ADC A,(IX+*indx*)	DD 8E *byte*		
ADC A,(IY+*indx*)	FD 8E *byte*		
ADC A,*data*	CE *byte*		

ADC HL,BC	ED 4A	
ADC HL,DE	ED 5A	Add with carry (16-bit)
ADC HL,HL	ED 6A	
ADC HL,SP	ED 7A	
ADD A,A	87	
ADD A,B	80	
ADD A,C	81	
ADD A,D	82	
ADD A,E	83	
ADD A,H	84	Add
ADD A,L	85	
ADD A,(HL)	86	
ADD A,(IX+*indx*)	DD 86 *byte*	
ADD A,(IY+*indx*)	FD 86 *byte*	
ADD A,*data*	C6 *byte*	
ADD HL,BC	09	
ADD HL,DE	19	
ADD HL,HL	29	
ADD HL,SP	39	
ADD IX,BC	DD 09	
ADD IX,DE	DD 19	Add (16-bit)
ADD IX,IX	DD 29	
ADD IX,SP	DD 39	
ADD IY,BC	FD 09	
ADD IY,DE	FD 19	
ADD IY,IY	FD 29	
ADD IY,SP	FD 39	
AND A	A7	
AND B	A0	
AND C	A1	
AND D	A2	
AND E	A3	
AND H	A4	Logical AND
AND L	A5	
AND (HL)	A6	
AND (IX+*indx*)	DD A6 *byte*	
AND (IY+*indx*)	FD A6 *byte*	
AND *data*	E6 *byte*	
BIT 0,A	CB 47	
BIT 0,B	CB 40	
BIT 0,C	CB 41	
BIT 0,D	CB 42	
BIT 0,E	CB 43	
BIT 0,H	CB 44	Bit 0 test
BIT 0,L	CB 45	
BIT 0,(HL)	CB 46	
BIT 0,(IX+*indx*)	DD CB *byte* 46	
BIT 0,(IY+*indx*)	FD CB *byte* 46	
BIT 1,A	CB 4F	
BIT 1,B	CB 48	
BIT 1,C	CB 49	
BIT 1,D	CB 4A	
BIT 1,E	CB 4B	
BIT 1,H	CB 4C	Bit 1 test
BIT 1,L	CB 4D	
BIT 1,(HL)	CB 4E	
BIT 1,(IX+*indx*)	DD CB *byte* 4E	
BIT 1,(IY+*indx*)	FD CB *byte* 4E	

BIT 2,A   CB 57
BIT 2,B   CB 50
BIT 2,C   CB 51
BIT 2,D   CB 52
BIT 2,E   CB 53   Bit 2 test
BIT 2,H   CB 54
BIT 2,L   CB 55
BIT 2,(HL)   CB 56
BIT 2,(IX+*indx*)   DD CB *byte* 56
BIT 2,(IY+*indx*)   FD CB *byte* 56

BIT 3,A   CB 5F
BIT 3,B   CB 58
BIT 3,C   CB 59
BIT 3,D   CB 5A
BIT 3,E   CB 5B   Bit 3 test
BIT 3,H   CB 5C
BIT 3,L   CB 5D
BIT 3,(HL)   CB 5E
BIT 3,(IX+*indx*)   DD CB *byte* 5E
BIT 3,(IY+*indx*)   FD CB *byte* 5E

BIT 4,A   CB 67
BIT 4,B   CB 60
BIT 4,C   CB 61
BIT 4,D   CB 62
BIT 4,E   CB 63   Bit 4 test
BIT 4,H   CB 64
BIT 4,L   CB 65
BIT 4,(HL)   CB 66
BIT 4,(IX+*indx*)   DD CB *byte* 66
BIT 4,(IY+*indx*)   FD CB *byte* 66

BIT 5,A   CB 6F
BIT 5,B   CB 68
BIT 5,C   CB 69
BIT 5,D   CB 6A
BIT 5,E   CB 6B   Bit 5 test
BIT 5,H   CB 6C
BIT 5,L   CB 6D
BIT 5,(HL)   CB 6E
BIT 5,(IX+*indx*)   DD CB *byte* 6E
BIT 5,(IY+*indx*)   FD CB *byte* 6E

BIT 6,A   CB 77
BIT 6,B   CB 70
BIT 6,C   CB 71
BIT 6,D   CB 72
BIT 6,E   CB 73   Bit 6 test
BIT 6,H   CB 74
BIT 6,L   CB 75
BIT 6,(HL)   CB 76
BIT 6,(IX+*indx*)   DD CB *byte* 76
BIT 6,(IY+*indx*)   FD CB *byte* 76

BIT 7,A   CB 7F
BIT 7,B   CB 78
BIT 7,C   CB 79
BIT 7,D   CB 7A
BIT 7,E   CB 7B   Bit 7 test

Mnemonic	Object Code	Description
BIT 7,H	CB 7C	
BIT 7,L	CB 7D	
BIT 7,(HL)	CB 7E	
BIT 7,(IX+*indx*)	DD CB *byte* 7E	
BIT 7,(IY+*indx*)	FD CB *byte* 7E	
CALL *addr*	CD *byte byte*	
CALL NZ,*addr*	C4 *byte byte*	
CALL Z,*addr*	CC *byte byte*	
CALL NC,*addr*	D4 *byte byte*	
CALL C,*addr*	DC *byte byte*	Call subroutine
CALL PE,*addr*	EC *byte byte*	
CALL PO,*addr*	E4 *byte byte*	
CALL P,*addr*	F4 *byte byte*	
CALL M,*addr*	FC *byte byte*	
CP A	BF	
CP B	B8	
CP C	B9	
CP D	BA	
CP E	BB	
CP H	BC	Compare
CP L	BD	
CP *data*	FE *byte*	
CP (HL)	BE	
CP (IX+*indx*)	DD BE *byte*	
CP (IY+*indx*)	FD BE *byte*	
CFF	3F	Complement the carry flag
CPD	ED A9	Compare decrementing memory
CPDR	ED 89	Search decrementing memory
CPI	ED A1	Compare incrementing memory
CPIR	ED B1	Search incrementing memory
CPL	2F	1's-complement the accumulator
DAA	27	Decimal adjust
DEC A	3D	
DEC B	05	
DEC C	0D	
DEC D	15	
DEC E	1D	
DEC H	25	
DEC L	2D	
DEC BC	0B	
DEC DE	1B	Decrement
DEC HL	2B	
DEC IX	DD 2B	
DEC IY	FD 2B	
DEC SP	3B	
DEC (HL)	35	
DEC (IX+*indx*)	DD 35 *byte*	
DEC (IY+*indx*)	FD 35 *byte*	
DJNZ *disp*	10 2E	Decrement B and jump if zero

EI	FB	Enable interrupts
EX (SP),HL	E3	
EX (SP),IX	DD E3	
EX (SP),IY	FD E3	
EX AF,AF'	08	Exchange
EX DE,HL	EB	
EXX	D9	
HALT	76	Halt
IM 0	ED 46	
IM 1	ED 56	Set interrupt mode
IM 2	ED 5E	
IN A,(C)	ED 78	
IN B,(C)	ED 40	
IN C,(C)	ED 48	
IN D,(C)	ED 50	
IN E,(C)	ED 58	Input
IN H,(C)	ED 60	
IN L,(C)	ED 68	
IN A,(*data*)	DB *byte*	
INC A	3C	
INC B	04	
INC C	0C	
INC D	14	
INC E	1C	
INC H	24	
INC L	2C	
INC BC	03	
INC DE	13	
INC HL	23	Increment
INC IX	DD 23	
INC IY	FD 23	
INC (HL)	34	
INC (IX+*indx*)	DD 34 *byte*	
INC (IY+*indx*)	FD 34 *byte*	
INC SP	33	
IND	ED AA	Decrementing block load from INPUT port
INI	ED A2	Incrementing block load from INPUT port
INDR	ED BA	Decrementing block transfer
INIR	ED B2	Incrementing block transfer
JP *addr*	C3 *byte byte*	
JP NZ,*addr*	C2 *byte byte*	
JP Z,*addr*	CA *byte byte*	
JP NC,*addr*	D2 *byte byte*	
JP C,*addr*	DA *byte byte*	Jump direct
JP PE,*addr*	EA *byte byte*	
JP PO,*addr*	E2 *byte byte*	
JP P,*addr*	F2 *byte byte*	
JP M,*addr*	FA *byte byte*	
JP (HL)	E9	
JP (IX)	DD E9	Jump indirect
JP (IY)	FD E9	

JR *disp*	18 *byte*	
JR NZ,*disp*	20 *byte*	
JR Z,*disp*	28 *byte*	Jump relative
JR NC,*disp*	30 *byte*	
JR C,*disp*	38 *byte*	
LD A,A	7F	
LD A,B	78	
LD A,C	79	
LD A,D	7A	
LD A,E	7B	
LD A,H	7C	
LD A,L	7D	
LD A,(HL)	7E	
LD A,(IX+*indx*)	DD 7E *byte*	Load to register A
LD A,(IY+*indx*)	FD 7E *byte*	
LD A,(*addr*)	3A *byte byte*	
LD A,(BC)	0A	
LD A,(DE)	1A	
LD A,I	ED 57	
LD A,R	ED 5F	
LD A,*data*	3E *byte*	
LD B,A	47	
LD B,B	40	
LD B,C	41	
LD B,D	42	
LD B,E	43	
LD B,H	44	Load to register B
LD B,L	45	
LD B,(HL)	46	
LD B,(IX+*indx*)	DD 46 *byte*	
LD B,(IY+*indx*)	FD 46 *byte*	
LD B,*data*	06 *byte*	
LD C,A	4F	
LD C,B	48	
LD C,C	49	
LD C,D	4A	
LD C,E	4B	
LD C,H	4C	Load to register C
LD C,L	4D	
LD C,(HL)	4E	
LD C,(IX+*indx*)	DD 4E *byte*	
LD C,(IY+*indx*)	FD 4E *byte*	
LD C,*data*	0E *byte*	
LD D,A	57	
LD D,B	50	
LD D,C	51	
LD D,D	52	
LD D,E	53	
LD D,H	54	Load to register D
LD D,L	55	
LD D,(HL)	56	
LD D,(IX+*indx*)	DD 56 *byte*	
LD D,(IY+*indx*)	FD 56 *byte*	
LD D,*data*	16 *byte*	

LD E,A	5F	
LD E,B	58	
LD E,C	59	
LD E,D	5A	
LD E,E	5B	
LD E,H	5C	Load to register E
LD E,L	5D	
LD E,(HL)	5E	
LD E,(IX+*indx*)	DD 5E *byte*	
LD E,(IY+*indx*)	FD 5E *byte*	
LD E,*data*	1E *byte*	
LD H,A	67	
LD H,B	60	
LD H,C	61	
LD H,D	62	
LD H,E	63	
LD H,H	64	Load to register H
LD H,L	65	
LD H,(HL)	66	
LD H,(IX+*indx*)	DD 66 *byte*	
LD H,(IY+*indx*)	FD 66 *byte*	
LD H,*data*	26 *byte*	
LD L,A	6F	
LD L,B	68	
LD L,C	69	
LD L,D	6A	
LD L,E	6B	
LD L,H	6C	Load to register L
LD L,L	6D	
LD L,(HL)	6E	
LD L,(IX+*indx*)	DD 6E *byte*	
LD L,(IY+*indx*)	FD 6E *byte*	
LD L,*data*	2E *byte*	
LD BC,*data data*	01 *byte byte*	
LD BC,(*addr*)	ED 4B *byte byte*	
LD DE,*data data*	11 *byte byte*	
LD DE,(*addr*)	ED 5B *byte byte*	
LD HL,*data data*	21 *byte byte*	
LD HL,(*addr*)	2A *byte byte*	
LD SP,HL	F9	Load to 16-bit register
LD SP,IX	DD F9	or register pair
LD SP,IY	FD F9	
LD SP,*data data*	31 *byte byte*	
LD SP,(*addr*)	ED 7B *byte byte*	
LD IX,*data data*	DD 21 *byte byte*	
LD IX,(*addr*)	DD 2A *byte byte*	
LD IY,*data data*	FD 21 *byte byte*	
LD IY,(*addr*)	DD 2A *byte byte*	
LD (BC),A	02	
LD (DE),A	12	
LD (HL),A	77	
LD (HL),B	70	
LD (HL),C	71	Load to memory
LD (HL),D	72	(indirect register pair)
LD (HL),E	73	
LD (HL),H	74	
LD (HL),L	75	
LD (HL),*data*	36 *byte*	

LD (IX+*indx*),A	DD 77 *byte*	
LD (IY+*indx*),A	FD 77 *byte*	
LD (IX+*indx*),B	DD 70 *byte*	
LD (IY+*indx*),B	FD 70 *byte*	
LD (IX+*indx*),C	DD 71 *byte*	
LD (IY+*indx*),C	FD 71 *byte*	
LD (IX+*indx*),D	DD 72 *byte*	
LD (IY+*indx*),D	FD 72 *byte*	Load to memory
LD (IX+*indx*),E	DD 73 *byte*	(indirect, indexed)
LD (IY+*indx*),E	FD 73 *byte*	
LD (IX+*indx*),H	DD 74 *byte*	
LD (IY+*indx*),H	FD 74 *byte*	
LD (IX+*indx*),L	DD 75 *byte*	
LD (IY+*indx*),L	FD 75 *byte*	
LD (IX+*indx*),*data*	DD 36 *byte byte*	
LD (IY+*indx*),*data*	FD 36 *byte byte*	
LD (*addr*),A	32 *byte byte*	
LD (*addr*),BC	ED 43 *byte byte*	
LD (*addr*),DE	ED 53 *byte byte*	
LD (*addr*),HL	22 *byte byte*	Load to specified address
LD (*addr*),IX	DD 22 *byte byte*	
LD (*addr*),IY	FD 22 *byte byte*	
LD (*addr*),SP	ED 73 *byte byte*	
LD I,A	ED 47	Load A to I
LD R,A	ED 4F	Load A to R
LDD	ED A8	Decrementing block transfer
LDDR	ED B8	Auto-decrementing block transfer
LDI	ED A0	Incrementing block transfer
LDIR	ED B0	Auto-incrementing block transfer
NEG	ED 44	2's-complement the accumulator
NOP	00	No operation
OR A	B7	
OR B	B0	
OR C	B1	
OR D	B2	
OR E	B3	
OR H	B4	Logical OR
OR L	B5	
OR (HL)	B6	
OR (IX+*indx*)	DD B6 *byte*	
OR (IY+*indx*)	FD B6 *byte*	
OR *data*	F6 *byte*	
OTDR	ED BB	Auto-decrementing block load to OUTPUT port (C)
OTIR	ED B3	Auto-incrementing block load to OUTPUT port (C)
OUTD	ED AB	Decrementing block load to OUTPUT port (C)

OUTI	ED A3	Incrementing block load to OUTPUT port (C)
OUT (C),A	ED 79	
OUT (C),B	ED 41	
OUT (C),C	ED 49	
OUT (C),D	ED 51	Output
OUT (C),E	ED 59	
OUT (C),H	ED 61	
OUT (C),L	ED 69	
OUT (*data*),A	D3 *byte*	
POP AF	F1	
POP BC	C1	
POP DE	D1	Load from top of stack
POP HL	E1	
POP IX	DD E1	
POP IY	FD E1	
PUSH AF	F5	
PUSH BC	C5	
PUSH DE	D5	Load to top of stack
PUSH HL	E5	
PUSH IX	DD E5	
PUSH IY	FD E5	
RES 0,A	CB 87	
RES 0,B	CB 80	
RES 0,C	CB 81	
RES 0,D	CB 82	
RES 0,E	CB 83	Reset bit 0
RES 0,H	CB 84	
RES 0,L	CB 85	
RES 0,(HL)	CB 86	
RES 0,(IX+*indx*)	DD CB *byte* 86	
RES 0,(IY+*indx*)	FD CB *byte* 86	
RES 1,A	CB 8F	
RES 1,B	CB 88	
RES 1,C	CB 89	
RES 1,D	CB 8A	
RES 1,E	CB 8B	Reset bit 1
RES 1,H	CB 8C	
RES 1,L	CB 8D	
RES 1,(HL)	CB 8E	
RES 1,(IX+*indx*)	DD CB *byte* 8E	
RES 1,(IY+*indx*)	FD CB *byte* 8E	
RES 2,A	CB 97	
RES 2,B	CB 90	
RES 2,C	CB 91	
RES 2,D	CB 92	
RES 2,E	CB 93	Reset bit 2
RES 2,H	CB 94	
RES 2,L	CB 95	
RES 2,(HL)	CB 96	
RES 2,(IX+*indx*)	DD CB *byte* 96	
RES 2,(IY+*indx*)	FD CB *byte* 96	

RES 3,A   CB 9F
RES 3,B   CB 98
RES 3,C   CB 99
RES 3,D   CB 9A
RES 3,E   CB 9B   Reset bit 3
RES 3,H   CB 9C
RES 3,L   CB 9D
RES 3,(HL)   CB 9E
RES 3,(IX+*indx*)   DD CB *byte* 9E
RES 3,(IY+*indx*)   FD CB *byte* 9E

RES 4,A   CB A7
RES 4,B   CB A0
RES 4,C   CB A1
RES 4,D   CB A2
RES 4,E   CB A3   Reset bit 4
RES 4,H   CB A4
RES 4,L   CB A5
RES 4,(HL)   CB A6
RES 4,(IX+*indx*)   DD CB *byte* A6
RES 4,(IY+*indx*)   FD CB *byte* A6

RES 5,A   CB AF
RES 5,B   CB A8
RES 5,C   CB A9
RES 5,D   CB AA
RES 5,E   CB AB   Reset bit 5
RES 5,H   CB AC
RES 5,L   CB AD
RES 5,(HL)   CB AE
RES 5,(IX+*indx*)   DD CB *byte* AE
RES 5,(IY+*indx*)   FD CB *byte* AE

RES 6,A   CB B7
RES 6,B   CB B0
RES 6,C   CB B1
RES 6,D   CB B2
RES 6,E   CB B3   Reset bit 6
RES 6,H   CB B4
RES 6,L   CB B5
RES 6,(HL)   CB B6
RES 6,(IX+*indx*)   DD CB *byte* B6
RES 6,(IY+*indx*)   FD CB *byte* B6

RES 7,A   CB BF
RES 7,B   CB B8
RES 7,C   CB B9
RES 7,D   CB BA
RES 7,E   CB BB   Reset bit 7
RES 7,H   CB BC
RES 7,L   CB BD
RES 7,(HL)   CB BE
RES 7,(IX+*indx*)   DD CB *byte* BE
RES 7,(IY+*indx*)   FD CB *byte* BE

RET	C9	
RET NZ	C0	
RET Z	C8	
RET NC	D0	
RET C	D8	Return from subroutine
RET PE	E8	
RET PO	E0	
RET P	F0	
RET M	F8	
RETI	ED 4D	Return from interrupt
RETN	ED 45	Return from nonmaskable interrupt
RLA	17	
RL A	CB 17	
RL B	CB 10	
RL C	CB 11	
RL D	CB 12	
RL E	CB 13	Rotate left through carry
RL H	CB 14	
RL L	CB 15	
RL (HL)	CB 16	
RL (IX+*indx*)	DD CB *byte* 16	
RL (IY+*indx*)	FD CB *byte* 16	
RLCA	07	
RLC A	CB 07	
RLC B	CB 00	
RLC C	CB 01	
RLC D	CB 02	
RLC E	CB 03	Rotate left circular
RLC H	CB 04	
RLC L	CB 05	
RLC (HL)	CB 06	
RLC (IX+*indx*)	DD CB *byte* 06	
RLC (IY+*indx*)	FD CB *byte* 06	
RLD	ED 6F	Decimal rotate left
RRA	1F	
RR A	CB 1F	
RR B	CB 18	
RR C	CB 19	
RR D	CB 1A	
RR E	CB 1B	Rotate right through carry
RR H	CB 1C	
RR L	CB 1D	
RR (HL)	CB 1E	
RR (IX+*indx*)	DD CB *byte* 1E	
RR (IY+*indx*)	FD CB *byte* 1E	

RRCA	0F	
RRC A	CB 0F	
RRC B	CB 08	
RRC C	CB 09	
RRC D	CB 0A	
RRC E	CB 0B	Rotate right circular
RRC H	CB 0C	
RRC L	CB 0D	
RRC (HL)	CB 0E	
RRC (IX+*indx*)	DD CB *byte* 0E	
RRC (IY+*indx*)	FD CB *byte* 0E	
RRD	ED 67	Decimal rotate right
RST 00H	C7	
RST 08H	CF	
RST 10H	D7	
RST 18H	DF	Restart
RST 20H	E7	
RST 28H	EF	
RST 30H	F7	
RST 38H	FF	
SBC A,A	9F	
SBC A,B	98	
SBC A,C	99	
SBC A,D	9A	
SBC A,E	9B	Subtract with carry
SBC A,H	9C	(borrow)
SBC A,L	9D	
SBC A,(HL)	9E	
SBC A,(IX+*indx*)	DD 9E *byte*	
SBC A,(IY+*indx*)	FD 9E *byte*	
SBC A,*data*	DE *byte*	
SBC HL,BC	ED 42	Subtract 16-bits with carry
SBC HL,DE	ED 52	(borrow)
SBC HL,HL	ED 62	
SBC HL,SP	ED 72	
SCF	37	Set carry status
SET 0,A	CB C7	
SET 0,B	CB C0	
SET 0,C	CB C1	
SET 0,D	CB C2	
SET 0,E	CB C3	Set bit 0
SET 0,H	CB C4	
SET 0,L	CB C5	
SET 0,(HL)	CB C6	
SET 0,(IX+*indx*)	DD CB *byte* C6	
SET 0,(IY+*indx*)	FD CB *byte* C6	

SET 1,A	CB CF	
SET 1,B	CB C8	
SET 1,C	CB C9	
SET 1,D	CB CA	
SET 1,E	CB CB	Set bit 1
SET 1,H	CB CC	
SET 1,L	CB CD	
SET 1,(HL)	CB CE	
SET 1,(IX+*indx*)	DD CB *byte* CE	
SET 1,(IY+*indx*)	FD CB *byte* CE	

SET 2,A	CB D7	
SET 2,B	CB D0	
SET 2,C	CB D1	
SET 2,D	CB D2	
SET 2,E	CB D3	Set bit 2
SET 2,H	CB D4	
SET 2,L	CB D5	
SET 2,(HL)	CB D6	
SET 2,(IX+*indx*)	DD CB *byte* D6	
SET 2,(IY+*indx*)	FD CB *byte* D6	

SET 3,A	CB DF	
SET 3,B	CB D8	
SET 3,C	CB D9	
SET 3,D	CB DA	
SET 3,E	CB DB	Set bit 3
SET 3,H	CB DC	
SET 3,L	CB DD	
SET 3,(HL)	CB DE	
SET 3,(IX+*indx*)	DD CB *byte* DE	
SET 3,(IY+*indx*)	FD DB *byte* DE	

SET 4,A	CB E7	
SET 4,B	CB E0	
SET 4,C	CB E1	
SET 4,D	CB E2	
SET 4,E	CB E3	Set bit 4
SET 4,H	CB E4	
SET 4,L	CB E5	
SET 4,(HL)	CB E6	
SET 4,(IX+*indx*)	DD CB *byte* E6	
SET 4,(IY+*indx*)	FD CB *byte* E6	

SET 5,A	CB EF	
SET 5,B	CB E8	
SET 5,C	CB E9	
SET 5,D	CB EA	
SET 5,E	CB EB	Set bit 5
SET 5,H	CB EC	
SET 5,L	CB ED	
SET 5,(HL)	CB EE	
SET 5,(IX+*indx*)	DD CB *byte* EE	
SET 5,(IY+*indx*)	FD CB *byte* EE	

SET 6,A   CB F7
SET 6,B   CB F0
SET 6,C   CB F1
SET 6,D   CB F2
SET 6,E   CB F3   Set bit 6
SET 6,H   CB F4
SET 6,L   CB F5
SET 6,(HL)   CB F6
SET 6,(IX+*indx*)   DD CB *byte* F6
SET 6,(IY+*indx*)   FD CB *byte* F6

SET 7,A   CB FF
SET 7,B   CB F8
SET 7,C   CB F9
SET 7,D   CB FA
SET 7,E   CB FB   Set bit 7
SET 7,H   CB FC
SET 7,L   CB FD
SET 7,(HL)   CB FE
SET 7,(IX+*indx*)   DD CB *byte* FE
SET 7,(IY+*indx*)   FD CB *byte* FE

SLA A   CB 27
SLA B   CB 20
SLA C   CB 21
SLA D   CB 22
SLA E   CB 23
SLA H   CB 24   Shift left
SLA L   CB 25
SAL (HL)   CB 26
SLA (IX+*indx*)   DD CB *byte* 26
SLA (IY+*indx*)   FD CB *byte* 26

SRA A   CB 2F
SRA B   CB 28
SRA C   CB 29
SRA D   CB 2A
SRA E   CB 2B   Arithmetic shift right
SRA H   CB 2C
SRA L   CB 2D
SRA (HL)   CB 2E
SRA (IX+*indx*)   DD CB *byte* 2E
SRA (IY+*indx*)   FD CB *byte* 2E

SRL A   CB 3F
SRL B   CB 38
SRL C   CB 39
SRL D   CB 3A
SRL E   CB 3B   Logical shift right
SRL H   CB 3C
SRL L   CB 3D
SRL (HL)   CB 3E
SRL (IX+*indx*)   DD CB *byte* 3E
SRL (IY+*indx*)   FD CB *byte* 3E

SUB A	97	
SUB B	90	
SUB C	91	
SUB D	92	
SUB E	93	
SUB H	94	Subtract
SUB L	95	
SUB (HL)	96	
SUB (IX+*indx*)	DD 96 *byte*	
SUB (IY+*indx*)	FD 96 *byte*	
SUB *data*	D6 *byte*	
XOR A	AF	
XOR B	A8	
XOR C	A9	
XOR D	AA	
XOR E	AB	
XOR H	AC	Logical EXCLUSIVE-OR
XOR L	AD	
XOR (HL)	AE	
XOR (IX+*indx*)	DD AE *byte*	
XOR (IY+*indx*)	FD AE *byte*	
XOR *data*	EE *byte*	

APPENDIX D:
8080A/8085 Instruction Set

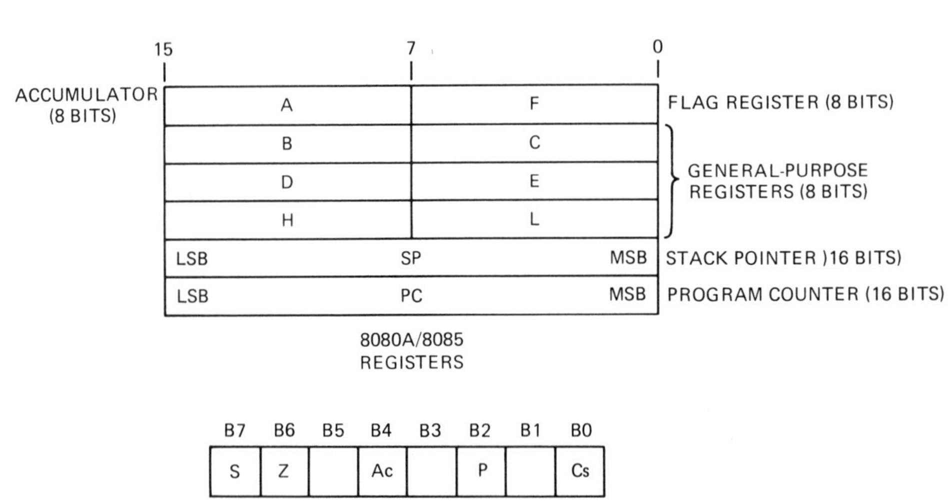

Figure D-1

ACI *data*	CE *byte*	
ADC A	8F	
ADC B	88	
ADC C	89	
ADC D	8A	Add with carry
ADC E	8B	
ADC H	8C	
ADC L	8D	
ADC M	8E	
ADD A	87	
ADD B	80	
ADD C	81	
ADD D	82	
ADD E	83	Add
ADD H	84	
ADD L	85	
ADD M	86	
ADI *data*	C6 *byte*	
ANA A	A7	
ANA B	A0	
ANA C	A1	
ANA D	A2	
ANA E	A3	Logical AND
ANA H	A4	
ANA L	A5	
ANA M	A6	
ANI *data*	E6 *byte*	
CALL *addr*	CD *byte byte*	
CNZ *addr*	C4 *byte byte*	
CZ *addr*	CC *byte byte*	
CNC *addr*	D4 *byte byte*	
CC *addr*	DC *byte byte*	Call (subroutine)
CPO *addr*	E4 *byte byte*	
CPE *addr*	EC *byte byte*	
CP *addr*	F4 *byte byte*	
CM *addr*	FC *byte byte*	
CMA	2F	Complement the accumulator
CMC	3F	Complement the Cs status
CMP A	BF	
CMP B	B8	
CMP C	B9	
CMP D	BA	
CMP E	BB	Compare
CMP H	BC	
CMP L	BD	
CMP M	BE	
CPI *data*	FE *byte*	
DAA	27	Decimal adjust
DAD B	09	
DAD D	19	Double-register add
DAD H	29	
DAD SP	39	

DCR A	3D	
DCR B	05	
DCR C	0D	
DCR D	15	Decrement
DCR E	1D	
DCR H	25	
DCR L	2D	
DCR M	35	
DCX B	0B	
DCX D	1B	Double-register decrement
DCX H	2B	
DCX SP	3B	
DI	F3	Disable interrupts
EI	FB	Enable interrupts
HLT	76	Halt
IN *data*	DB *byte*	Input
INR A	3C	
INR B	04	
INR C	0C	
INR D	14	
INR E	1C	Increment
INR H	24	
INR L	2C	
INR M	34	
INX B	03	
INX D	13	Double-register increment
INX H	23	
INX SP	33	
JMP *addr*	C3 *byte byte*	
JNZ *addr*	C2 *byte byte*	
JZ *addr*	CA *byte byte*	
JNC *addr*	D2 *byte byte*	
JC *addr*	DA *byte byte*	Jump
JPE *addr*	EA *byte byte*	
JPO *addr*	E2 *byte byte*	
JP *addr*	F2 *byte byte*	
JM *addr*	FA *byte byte*	
LDA *addr*	3A *byte byte*	Load accumulator direct
LDAX B	0A	Load accumulator indirect
LDAX D	1A	
LHLD *addr*	2A *byte byte*	Load HL pair direct
LXI B, *data data*	01 *byte byte*	
LXI D, *data adta*	11 *byte byte*	Load immediate double register
LXI H, *data data*	21 *byte byte*	
LXI SP, *data data*	31 *byte byte*	

MOV A,A	7F	
MOV A,B	78	
MOV A,C	79	
MOV A,D	7A	Transfer to A register
MOV A,E	7B	
MOV A,H	7C	
MOV A,L	7D	
MOV A,M	7E	
MOV B,A	47	
MOV B,B	40	
MOV B,C	41	
MOV B,D	42	Transfer to B register
MOV B,E	43	
MOV B,H	44	
MOB B,L	45	
MOV B,M	46	
MOV C,A	4F	
MOV C,B	48	
MOV C,C	49	
MOV C,D	4A	Transfer to C register
MOV C,E	4B	
MOV C,H	4C	
MOV C,L	4D	
MOV C,M	4E	
MOV D,A	57	
MOV D,B	50	
MOV D,C	51	
MOV D,D	52	Transfer to D register
MOV D,E	53	
MOV D,H	54	
MOV D,L	55	
MOV D,M	56	
MOV E,A	5F	
MOV E,B	58	
MOV E,C	59	
MOV E,D	5A	Transfer to E register
MOV E,E	5B	
MOV E,H	5C	
MOV E,L	5D	
MOV E,M	5E	
MOV H,A	67	
MOV H,B	60	
MOV H,C	61	
MOV H,D	62	Transfer to H register
MOV H,E	63	
MOV H,H	64	
MOV H,L	65	
MOV H,M	66	
MOV L,A	6F	
MOV L,B	68	
MOV L,C	69	
MOV L,D	6A	Transfer to L register
MOV L,E	6B	
MOV L,H	6C	
MOV L,L	6D	
MOV L,M	6E	

MOV M,A	77	
MOV M,B	70	
MOV M,C	71	
MOV M,D	72	Transfer to M
MOV M,E	73	(pointed by the HL pair)
MOV M,H	74	
MOV M,L	75	
MVI A,*data*	3E *byte*	
MVI B,*data*	06 *byte*	
MVI C,*data*	0E *byte*	
MVI D,*data*	16 *byte*	
MVI E,*data*	1E *byte*	Move immediate to register
MVI H,*data*	26 *byte*	
MVI L,*data*	2E *byte*	
MVI M,*data*	36 *byte*	
NOP	00	No operation
ORA A	B7	
ORA B	B0	
ORA C	B1	
ORA D	B2	
ORA E	B3	Logical OR
ORA H	B4	
ORA L	B5	
ORA M	B6	
ORI *data*	F6 *byte*	
OUT *data*	D3 *byte*	Output
PCHL	E9	Transfer HL to PC
POP B	C1	
POP D	D1	Load from stack
POP H	E1	
POP PSW	F1	
PUSH B	C5	
PUSH D	D5	Store to stack
PUSH H	E5	
PUSH PSW	F5	
RAL	17	Rotate through carry
RAR	1F	
RET	C9	
RNZ	C0	
RZ	C8	
RNC	D0	
RC	D8	Return (from subroutine)
RPO	E0	
RPE	E8	
RP	F0	
RM	F8	
RIM	20	Reset interrupt mask (8085 only)
RLC	07	Rotate circular
RRC	0F	

RST 0	C7	
RST 1	CF	
RST 2	D7	
RST 3	DF	Restart
RST 4	E7	
RST 5	EF	
RST 6	F7	
RST 7	FF	
SBB A	9F	
SBB B	98	
SBB C	99	
SBB D	9A	
SBB E	9B	Subtract with borrow
SBB H	9C	
SBB L	9D	
SBB M	9E	
SBI *data*	DE *byte*	
SHLD *addr*	22 *byte byte*	Store HL direct
SIM	30	Set interrupt mask (8085 only)
SPHL	F9	HL to SP
STA *addr*	32 *byte byte*	Store accumulator direct
STAX B	02	Store accumulator indirect
STAX D	12	
STC	37	Set Cs
SUB A	97	
SUB B	90	
SUB C	91	
SUB D	92	
SUB E	93	Subtract
SUB H	94	
SUB L	95	
SUB M	96	
SUI *data*	D6 *byte*	
XCHG	EB	Exchange DE, HL
XRA A	AF	
XRA B	A8	
XRA C	A9	
XRA D	AA	
XRA E	AB	Logical EXCLUSIVE-OR
XRA H	AC	
XRA L	AD	
XRA M	AE	
XRI *data*	EE *byte*	
XTHL	E3	Exchange top of stack, HL

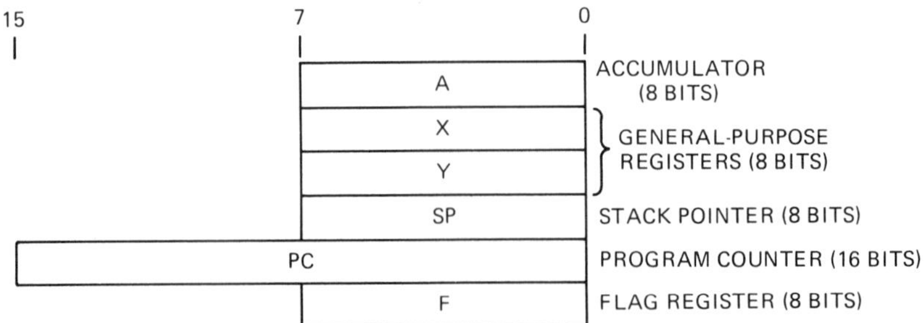

Figure E-1

ADC #*data*	69 *byte*		
ADC *addr*$_0$	65 *byte*		
ADC *addr*	6D *byte byte*		
ADC *addr*$_0$,X	75 *byte*		
ADC *addr*,X	7D *byte byte*		Add with carry
ADC *addr*,Y	79 *byte byte*		
ADC (*data*,X)	61 *byte*		
ADC (*data*),Y	71 *byte*		
AND #*data*	29 *byte*		
AND *addr*$_0$	25 *byte*		
AND *addr*	2D *byte byte*		
AND *addr*$_0$,X	35 *byte*		
AND *addr*,X	3D *byte byte*		Logical AND
AND *addr*,Y	39 *byte byte*		
AND (*data*,X)	21 *byte*		
AND (*data*),Y	31 *byte*		

ASL	A	0A			
ASL	*addr*$_0$	06	*byte*		
ASL	*addr*	0E	*byte*	*byte*	Shift left
ASL	*addr*$_0$,X	16	*byte*		
ASL	*addr*,X	1E	*byte*	*byte*	
BCC	*disp*	90	*byte*		
BCS	*disp*	B0	*byte*		
BEQ	*disp*	F0	*byte*		
BMI	*disp*	30	*byte*		
BNE	*disp*	D0	*byte*		Branch
BPL	*disp*	10	*byte*		
BVC	*disp*	50	*byte*		
BVS	*disp*	70	*byte*		
BIT	*addr*$_0$	24	*byte*		
BIT	*addr*	2C	*byte*	*byte*	Bit test
BRK		00			Break
CLC		18			Clear Cs status
CLD		D8			Clear decimal status
CLI		58			Clear interrupt status
CLV		B8			Clear overflow status
CMP	#*data*	C9	*byte*		
CMP	*addr*$_0$	C5	*byte*		
CMP	*addr*	CD	*byte*	*byte*	
CMP	*addr*$_0$,X	D5	*byte*		
CMP	*addr*,X	DD	*byte*	*byte*	Compare accumulator
CMP	*addr*,Y	D9	*byte*	*byte*	
CMP	(*data*,X)	C1	*byte*		
CMP	(*data*),Y	D1	*byte*		
CPX	#*data*	E0	*byte*		
CPX	*addr*$_0$	E4	*byte*		Compare register X
CPX	*addr*	EC	*byte*	*byte*	
CPY	#*data*	C0	*byte*		
CPY	*addr*$_0$	C4	*byte*		Compare register Y
CPY	*addr*	CC	*byte*	*byte*	
DEC	*addr*$_0$	C6	*byte*		
DEC	*addr*	CE	*byte*	*byte*	
DEC	*addr*$_0$,X	D6	*byte*		
DEC	*addr*,X	DE	*byte*	*byte*	Decrement
DEX		CA			
DEY		88			
EOR	#*data*	49	*byte*		
EOR	*addr*$_0$	45	*byte*		
EOR	*addr*	4D	*byte*	*byte*	
EOR	*addr*$_0$,X	55	*byte*		
EOR	*addr*,X	5D	*byte*	*byte*	Logical EXCLUSIVE-OR
EOR	*addr*,Y	59	*byte*	*byte*	
EOR	(*data*,X)	41	*byte*		
EOR	(*data*),Y	51	*byte*		

INC $addr_0$	E6 *byte*	
INC *addr*	EE *byte byte*	
INC $addr_0$,X	F6 *byte*	
INC *addr*,X	FE *byte byte*	Increment
INX	E8	
INY	C8	
JMP *addr*	4C *byte byte*	
JMP (*addr*)	6C *byte byte*	Jump
JSR *addr*	20 *byte byte*	
LDA #*data*	A9 *byte*	
LDA $addr_0$	A5 *byte*	
LDA *addr*	AD *byte byte*	
LDA $addr_0$,X	B5 *byte*	
LDA *addr*,X	BD *byte byte*	Load accumulator
LDA *addr*,Y	B9 *byte byte*	
LDA (*data*,X)	A1 *byte*	
LDA (*data*),Y	B1 *byte*	
LDX #*data*	A2 *byte*	
LDX $addr_0$	A6 *byte*	
LDX *addr*	AE *byte byte*	Load X register
LDX $addr_0$,Y	B6 *byte*	
LDX *addr*,Y	BE *byte byte*	
LDY #*data*	A0 *byte*	
LDY $addr_0$	A4 *byte*	
LDY *addr*	AC *byte byte*	Load Y register
LDY $addr_0$,X	B4 *byte*	
LDY *addr*,X	BC *byte byte*	
LSR A	4A	
LSR $addr_0$	46 *byte*	
LSR *addr*	4E *byte byte*	Left Shift
LSR $addr_0$,X	56 *byte*	
LSR *addr*,X	5E *byte byte*	
NOP	EA	No operation
ORA #*data*	09 *byte*	
ORA $addr_0$	05 *byte*	
ORA *addr*	0D *byte byte*	
ORA $addr_0$,X	15 *byte*	
ORA *addr*,X	1D *byte byte*	Logical OR
ORA *addr*,Y	19 *byte byte*	
ORA (*data*,X)	01 *byte*	
ORA (*data*),Y	11 *byte*	
PHA	48	Push accumulator to stack
PHP	08	Push flag register to stack
PLA	68	Load stack to accumulator
PLP	28	Load stack to flag register
ROL A	2A	
ROL $addr_0$	26 *byte*	Rotate left through
ROL *addr*	2E *byte byte*	carry
ROL $addr_0$,X	36 *byte*	
ROL *addr*,X	3E *byte byte*	

ROR A	6A		
ROR *addr*$_0$	66 *byte*		Rotate right through
ROR *addr*	6E *byte byte*		carry
ROR *addr*$_0$,X	76 *byte*		
ROR *addr*,X	7E *byte byte*		
RTI	40		Return from interrupt
RTS	60		Return from subroutine
SBC #*data*	E9 *byte*		
SBC *addr*$_0$	E5 *byte*		
SBC *addr*	ED *byte byte*		
SBC *addr*$_0$,X	F5 *byte*		Subtract with carry
SBC *addr*,X	FD *byte byte*		(borrow)
SBC *addr*,Y	F9 *byte byte*		
SBC (*data*,X)	E1 *byte*		
SBC (*data*),Y	F1 *byte*		
SEC	38		Set Cs flag
SED	F8		Set decimal status
SEI	78		Set interrupt status
STA *addr*$_0$	85 *byte*		
STA *addr*	8D *byte byte*		
STA *addr*$_0$,X	95 *byte*		
STA *addr*,X	9D *byte byte*		Store accumulator
STA *addr*,Y	99 *byte byte*		
STA (*data*,X)	81 *byte*		
STA (*data*),Y	91 *byte*		
STX *addr*$_0$	86 *byte*		
STX *addr*	8E *byte byte*		Store X register
STX *addr*$_0$,Y	96 *byte*		
STY *addr*$_0$	84 *byte*		
STY *addr*	8C *byte byte*		
STY *addr*$_0$,X	94 *byte*		
TAX	AA		Transfer A to X
TAY	A8		Transfer A to Y
TSX	BA		Transfer SP to X
TXA	8A		Transfer X to A
TXS	9A		Transfer X to SP
TYA	98		Transfer Y to A

6800 INSTRUCTION SET

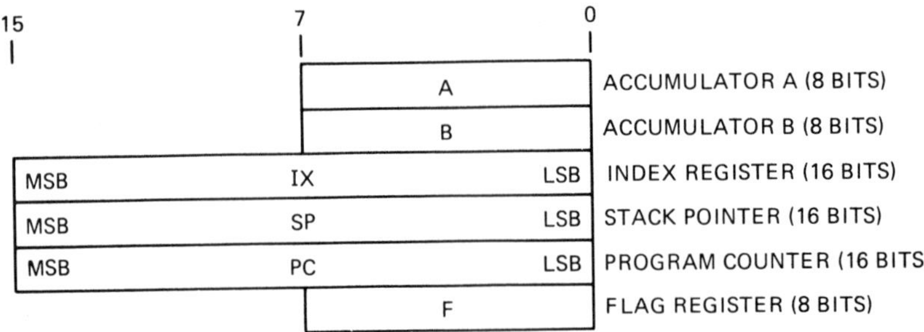

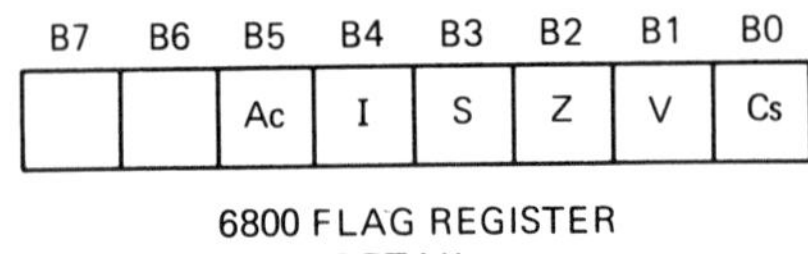

Ac, auxiliary carry bit
I, interrupt-status bit
S, sign bit
Z, zero-status bit
V, overflow-status bit
Cs, carry-status bit

Figure F-1

ABA		1B		Add accumulators A and B
ADCA	#*data*	89	*byte*	
ADCA	*addr*$_0$	99	*byte*	
ADCA	*addr*	B9	*byte byte*	
ADCA	*indx*,X	A9	*byte*	Add with carry
ADCB	#*data*	C9	*byte*	
ADCB	*addr*$_0$	D9	*byte*	
ADCB	*addr*	F9	*byte byte*	
ADCB	*indx*,X	E9	*byte*	
ADDA	#*data*	8B	*byte*	
ADDA	*addr*$_0$	9B	*byte*	
ADDA	*addr*	BB	*byte byte*	
ADDA	*indx*,X	AB	*byte*	Add
ADDB	#*data*	CB	*byte*	
ADDB	*addr*$_0$	DB	*byte*	
ADDB	*addr*	FB	*byte byte*	
ADDB	*indx*,X	EB	*byte*	

ANDA #*data*	84 *byte*			
ANDA *addr*$_0$	94 *byte*			
ANDA *addr*	B4 *byte* *byte*			
ANDA *indx*,X	A4 *byte*		Logical AND	
ANDB #*data*	C4 *byte*			
ANDB *addr*$_0$	D4 *byte*			
ANDB *addr*	F4 *byte* *byte*			
ANDB *indx*,X	E4 *byte*			
ASL *addr*	78			
ASL *indx*,X	68		Shift left	
ASLA	48			
ASLB	58			
ASR *addr*	77			
ASR *indx*,X	67		Arithmetic shift right	
ASRA	47			
ASRB	57			
BCC *disp*	24 *byte*			
BCS *disp*	25 *byte*			
BEQ *disp*	27 *byte*			
BGE *disp*	2C *byte*			
BGT *disp*	3E *byte*			
BHI *disp*	22 *byte*			
BLE *disp*	2F *byte*			
BLS *disp*	23 *byte*		Branch	
BLT *disp*	2D *byte*			
BMI *disp*	2B *byte*			
BNE *disp*	26 *byte*			
BPL *disp*	2A *byte*			
BRA *disp*	20 *byte*			
BSR *disp*	8D *byte*			
BVC *disp*	28 *byte*			
BVS *disp*	29 *byte*			
BITA #*data*	85 *byte*			
BITA *addr*$_0$	95 *byte*			
BITA *addr*	B5 *byte* *byte*			
BITA *indx*,X	A5 *byte*		Bit test	
BITB #*data*	C5 *byte*			
BITB *addr*$_0$	D5 *byte*			
BITB *addr*	F5 *byte* *byte*			
BITB *indx*,X	E5 *byte*			
CBA	11		Compare accumulators A and B	
CLC	0C		Clear carry status	
CLI	0E		Clear interrupt mask	
CLR *indx*,X	6F *byte*			
CLR *addr*	7F *byte* *byte*		Clear to zero	
CLRA	4F			
CLRB	5F			
CLV	0A		Clear overflow status	

CMPA	#*data*	81	*byte*	
CMPA	*addr*$_0$	91	*byte*	
CMPA	*addr*	B1	*byte*	*byte*
CMPA	*indx*,X	A1	*byte*	
CMPB	#*data*	C1	*byte*	
CMPB	*addr*$_0$	D1	*byte*	
CMPB	*addr*	F1	*byte*	*byte*
CMPB	*indx*,X	E1	*byte*	
CPX	#*data data*	8C	*byte*	*byte*
CPX	*addr*$_0$	9C	*byte*	
CPX	*addr*	BC	*byte*	*byte*
CPX	*indx*,X	AC	*byte*	

Compare

COM	*addr*	73	*byte*	*byte*
COM	*indx*,X	63	*byte*	
COMA		43		
COMB		53		

1's complement

DAA	19

Decimal adjust

DEC	*addr*	7A	*byte*	*byte*
DEC	*indx*,X	6A	*byte*	
DECA		4A		
DECB		5A		
DES		34		
DEX		09		

Decrement

EORA	#*data*	88	*byte*	
EORA	*addr*$_0$	98	*byte*	
EORA	*addr*	B8	*byte*	*byte*
EORA	*indx*,X	A8	*byte*	
EORB	#*data*	C8	*byte*	
EORB	*addr*$_0$	D8	*byte*	
EORB	*addr*	F8	*byte*	*byte*
EORB	*indx*,X	E8	*byte*	

Logical EXCLUSIVE-OR

INC	*addr*	7C	*byte*	*byte*
INC	*indx*,X	6C	*byte*	
INCA		4C		
INCB		5C		
INS		31		
INX		08		

Increment

JMP	*addr*	7E	*byte*	*byte*
JMP	*indx*,X	6E	*byte*	

Jump

JSR	*addr*	BD	*byte*	*byte*
JSR	*indx*,X	AD	*byte*	

Jump (call subroutine)

LDAA	#*data*	86	*byte*	
LDAA	*addr*$_0$	96	*byte*	
LDAA	*addr*	B6	*byte*	*byte*
LDAA	*indx*,X	A6	*byte*	
LDAB	#*data*	C6	*byte*	
LDAB	*addr*$_0$	D6	*byte*	
LDAB	*addr*	F6	*byte*	*byte*
LDAB	*indx*,X	E6	*byte*	

Load accumulators

LDS #*data data*	8E *byte byte*		
LDS *addr*$_0$	9E *byte*		
LDS *addr*	BE *byte byte*		
LDS *indx*,X	AE *byte*	Load 16-bit registers	
LDX #*data data*	CE *byte byte*		
LDX *addr*$_0$	DE *byte*		
LDX *addr*	FE *byte byte*		
LDX *indx*,X	EE *byte*		

LSR *addr*	74 *byte byte*		
LSR *indx*,X	64 *byte*	Logical shift right	
LSRA	44		
LSRB	54		

NEG *addr*	70 *byte byte*		
NEG *indx*,X	60 *byte*	2's complement	
NEGA	40		
NEGB	50		

NOP	01	No operation

ORAA #*data*	8A *byte*		
ORAA *addr*$_0$	9A *byte*		
ORAA *addr*	BA *byte byte*		
ORAA *indx*,X	AA *byte*	Logical OR	
ORAB #*data*	CA *byte*		
ORAB *addr*$_0$	DA *byte*		
ORAB *addr*	FA *byte byte*		
ORAB *indx*,X	EA *byte*		

PSHA	36	Load accumulators to stack
PSHB	37	

PULA	32	Load accumulators from stack
PULB	33	

ROL *addr*	79 *byte byte*		
ROL *indx*,X	69 *byte*	Rotate left through carry	
ROLA	49		
ROLB	59		

ROR *addr*	76 *byte byte*		
ROR *indx*,X	66 *byte*	Rotate right through carry	
RORA	46		
RORB	56		

RTI	3B	Return from interrupt

RTS	39	Return from subroutine

SBA	10	Subtract accumulator B from A

SBCA #*data*	82 *byte*		
SBCA *addr*$_0$	92 *byte*		
SBCA *addr*	B2 *byte byte*		
SBCA *indx*,X	A2 *byte*	Subtract with carry	
SBCB #*data*	C2 *byte*	(borrow)	
SBCB *addr*$_0$	D2 *byte*		
SBCB *addr*	F2 *byte byte*		
SBCB *indx*,X	E2 *byte*		

SEC	0D		Set carry status
SEI	0F		Set interrupt mask
SEV	0B		Set overflow status
STAA *addr*$_0$	97 *byte*		
STAA *addr*	B7 *byte byte*		
STAA *indx*,X	A7 *byte*		Store accumulators
STAB *addr*$_0$	D7 *byte*		
STAB *addr*	F7 *byte byte*		
STAB *indx*,X	E7 *byte*		
STS *addr*$_0$	9F *byte*		
STS *addr*	BF *byte byte*		
STS *indx*,X	AF *byte*		Store 16-bit registers
STX *addr*$_0$	DF *byte*		
STX *addr*	FF *byte byte*		
STX *indx*,X	EF *byte*		
SUBA *#data*	80 *byte*		
SUBA *addr*$_0$	90 *byte*		
SUBA *addr*	B0 *byte byte*		
SUBA *indx*,X	A0 *byte*		
SUBB *#data*	C0 *byte*		Subtract
SUBB *addr*$_0$	D0 *byte*		
SUBB *addr*	F0 *byte byte*		
SUBB *indx*,X	E0 *byte*		
SWI	3F		Software interrupt
TAB	16		Transfer A to B
TAP	06		Transfer A to flag register
TBA	17		Transfer B to A
TPA	07		Transfer flag to A
TSX	30		Transfer SP to IX
TXS	35		Transfer IX to SP
TST *addr*	7D *byte byte*		
TST *indx*,X	6D *byte*		Bit test
TSTA	4D		
TSTB	5D		
WAI	3E		Wait for interrupt

Answers to Exercises

Section 2-1

3. (a) Output   (b) Input   (c) Input   (d) Output
    (e) Input   (f) Output   (g) Output   (h) Output

Section 2-2

1. A *bus* is a group of hardware terminals or wires that serve a common function.
2. A *bidirectional bus* is capable of carrying information in two different directions (but only one direction at any given moment).
3. The LSB is 0; the MSB is 1. (The binary version of hexadecimal 7F is 01111111.)
4. Address bus
5. Data bus
6. Control bus

Section 2-4

1. 8
2. 2
3. 1

Chapter 3

3. 3873 bytes
4. 49FB hexadecimal

Section 4-1

1. A, B, C, D, E, H, and L

2. B and C, D and E, H and L

3. SP, IX and IY

4. A register (accumulator)

5. LD D,2AH   or   LD DE,2A1FH
   LD E,1FH

6.
```
1000  3E 1F   LD  A,1FH   ;1FH TO REGISTER A
1002  06 2E   LD  B,2EH   ;2EH TO REGISTER B
1004  0E 3D   LD  C,3DH   ;3DH TO REGISTER C
1006  16 4C   LD  D,4CH   ;4CH TO REGISTER D
1008  1E 5B   LD  E,5BH   ;5BH TO REGISTER E
100A  26 6A   LD  H,6AH   ;6AH TO REGISTER H
100C  2E 79   LD  L,79H   ;79H TO REGISTER L
```

7.
```
1000  01 3D 2E   LD  BC,2E3DH   ;2EH TO REGISTER B, AND
                                ;3DH TO REGISTER C
1003  11 5B 4C   LD  DE,4C5BH   ;4CH TO REGISTER D, AND
                                ;5BH TO REGISTER E
1006  21 79 6A   LD  HL,6A79H   ;6AH TO REGISTER H, AND
                                ;79H TO REGISTER L
```

Section 4-2

1. A, B, C, D, E, H, and L

2. B and C, D and E, H and L

3. A register, or accumulator

4. SP

5.
```
1000  3E 1F   MVI  A,1FH   ;1FH TO REGISTER A
1002  06 2E   MVI  B,2EH   ;2EH TO REGISTER B
1004  0E 3D   MVI  C,3DH   ;3DH TO REGISTER C
1006  16 4C   MVI  D,4CH   ;4CH TO REGISTER D
1008  1E 5B   MVI  E,5BH   ;5BH TO REGISTER E
100A  26 6A   MVI  H,6AH   ;6AH TO REGISTER H
100C  2E 79   MVI  L,79H   ;79H TO REGISTER L
```

6.
```
1000  01 3D 2E   LXI  B,2E3DH   ;2EH TO REGISTER B, AND
                                ;3DH TO REGISTER C
1003  11 5B 4C   LXI  D,4C5BH   ;4CH TO REGISTER D, AND
                                ;5BH TO REGISTER E
1006  21 79 6A   LXI  H,6A79H   ;6AH TO REGISTER H, AND
                                ;79H TO REGISTER L
```

Section 4-3

1. There are no 16-bit registers that can be affected by a load immediate instruction.

2.
```
1000  A9 1F   LDA  #$1F   $1F TO REGISTER A
1002  A2 2E   LDX  #$2E   $2E TO REGISTER X
1004  A0 3D   LDY  #$3D   $3D TO REGISTER Y
```

3. Pound-sign symbol (#) preceding the data

4. Dollar-sign symbol ($) preceding a hexadecimal number

Section 4-4

1. A and B

2. IX and SP

3.
```
1000 86 01      LDAA  #$01     $01 TO THE A REGISTER
1002 C6 2F      LDAB  #$2F     $2F TO THE B REGISTER
1004 CE 1F 2E   LDX  #$1F2E    $1F2E TO THE IX REGISTER
1007 8E FF 00   LDS  #$FF00    $FF00 TO THE SP REGISTER
```

4. The byte following the opcode goes to the MSB portion of the register, and the second byte following the opcode goes to the LSB position. Other processors load the LSB part of the register first.

Section 5-1

1. (a) 79 LD A,C   (b) 4F LD C,A   (c) 65 LD H,L   (d) 5B LD E,E

2. (a) Load the content of L to E, 5D.
   (b) Load the content of A to C, 4F.
   (c) Load the content of C to A, 79.
   (d) Load the content of A to A, 7F.
   (e) Load the HL register pair to the SP register, F9.

3. There are many different, yet correct, ways to handle this programming situation. Here are two of them:

```
0A00 01 FF FF   LD BC,FFFFH   ;FFH TO B AND FFH TO C
0A03 78         LD A,B        ;FFH TO A
0A04 50         LD D,B        ;FFH TO D
0A05 60         LD H,B        ;FFH TO H
0A06 6C         LD L,H        ;FFH TO L
0A07 5A         LD E,D        ;FFH TO E
```

That first approach uses a 16-bit load immediate to fill registers B and C with F's in one instruction. Such a "trick" is possible in this particular case, and programmers become increasingly conscious of using such "tricks" to shorten programs. Alternatively,

```
0A00 3E FF   LD A,FFH   ;FFH TO A
0A02 47      LD B,A     ;FFH TO B
0A03 4F      LD C,A     ;FFH TO C
0A04 57      LD D,A     ;FFH TO D
0A05 5F      LD E,A     ;FFH TO E
0A06 67      LD H,A     ;FFH TO H
0A07 6F      LD L,A     ;FFH TO L
```

Chosing to use an 8-bit load immediate in this case, the scheme must use six register transfers to load the registers with FF's.

4.
```
0A00 3E FF      LD A,FFH       ;FFH TO A
0A02 01 FF FF   LD BC,FFFFH    ;FFH TO B AND FFH TO C
0A05 11 FF FF   LD DE,FFFFH    ;FFH TO D AND FFH TO E
0A08 21 FF FF   LD HL,FFFFH    ;FFH TO H AND FFH TO L
```

This program requires 10 bytes of program memory. By contrast, the same overall job is completed in Problem 3 with just 7 bytes of program memory. Given the choice of using multiple load immediate operations or register transfers to do the same job, the register transfer approach will generally use up less program memory space.

```
5. 0A00 3E 21      LD  A,21H      ;21H TO A
   0A02 01 FF 34   LD  BC,34FFH   ;34FFH TO BC PAIR
                                  ;BEGIN THE EXCHANGE
   0A05 57         LD  D,A        ;SAVE A IN D
   0A06 78         LD  A,B        ;ORIGINAL B TO A
   0A07 41         LD  B,D        ;ORIGINAL A TO B
                                  ;EXCHANGE IS DONE
   0A08 51         LD  D,C        ;LOAD C TO D


6. 0A00 01 00 3C   LD  BC,3C00H   ;3C00H TO BC PAIR
   0A03 61         LD  H,C        ;LOAD C TO H
   0A04 68         LD  L,B        ;LOAD B TO L
   0A05 3E FF      LD  A,0FFH     ;LOAD A WITH FFH
   0A07 5F         LD  E,A        ;LOAD A WITH FFH
```

A=FFH, B=3CH, C=00H, D=undefined, E=FFH, H=00H, L=3CH

Section 5-2

1. (a) MOV H,E   63
   (b) MOV B,B   40
   (c) MOV D,C   51
   (d) SPHL   F9

2. (a) Load the content of register L to register H,   65.
   (b) Load the content of register A to register E,   5F.
   (c) Load the content of register E to register A,   7B.
   (d) Exchange the DE and HL register pairs,   EB.

```
3. 4A00 4C   MOV C,H   ;SAVE H IN C
   4A01 62   MOV H,D   ;LOAD D TO H
   4A02 51   MOV D,C   ;LOAD C TO D
                       ;THE H-D EXCHANGE IS DONE
   4A03 4D   MOV C,L   ;SAVE L IN C
   4A04 6B   MOV L,E   ;LOAD E TO L
   4A05 59   MOV E,C   ;LOAD C TO E
                       ;THE L-E EXCHANGE IS DONE


4. 7000 01 00 3C   LXI  B,3C00H   ;MOVE IMMEDIATE 3C00H TO
                                  ;THE BC REGISTER PAIR
   7003 61         MOV  H,C       ;TRANSFER C TO H
   7004 68         MOV  L,B       ;TRANSFER B TO L
   7005 3E FF      MVI  A,FFH     ;LOAD IMMEDIATE FFH TO A
   7007 5F         MOV  E,A       ;TRANSFER A TO E
```

A=FFH, B=3CH, C=00H, D=undefined, E=FFH, H=00H, L=3CH

Section 5-3

1. (a) TXA   (b) TAX   (c) TYA   (d) TAY
   (e) TYA   (f) TXA   (g) TSX   (h) TAX
       TAX   TAY   TXA   TXS

(i) TSX	(j) TXS	(k) TSX	(l) TYA
		TXA	TAX
		TAY	TXS
2. (a) LDA	(b) LDX	(c) LDY	(d) LDX
			TXS

```
3. 0C00 A9 FF   LDA #$FF   $FF TO A
   0C02 AA      TAX        $FF TO X FROM A
   0C03 9A      TXS        $FF TO SP FROM X
   0C04 A8      TAY        $FF TO Y FROM A


4. 0C00 A2 00   LDX #$00   $00 TO X IMMEDIATE
   0C02 9A      TXS        $00 TO SP FROM X
   0C03 A0 0C   LDY #$0C   $0C TO Y IMMEDIATE
   0C05 98      TYA        $0C TO A FROM Y
```

A=$0C, X=$00, Y=$0C, SP=$100

Section 5-4

1. (a) 17 TBA	(b) 16 TAB	(c) 07 TPA	(d) 06 TAP
(e) 07 TPA	(f) 17 TBA	(g) 30 TSX	(h) 35 TXS
16 TAB	06 TAP		

```
2. 0A00 86 FF      LDAA #$FF      $FF TO A IMMEDIATE
   0A02 16         TAB            $FF TO B FROM A
   0A03 06         TAP            $FF TO F FROM A
   0A04 CE FF FF   LDX #$FFFF     $FFFF TO IX IMMEDIATE
   0A07 35         TXS            $FFFF TO SP FROM IX
```


Section 6-2

1. (a) 3A 34 12	(b) 32 01 04	(c) 2A 25 16
(d) 22 5A 25	(e) ED 7B FF 00	(f) ED 73 00 F0
2. (a) LD (00FFH),A	(b) LD A,(3412H)	(c) LD HL,(9A00H)
(d) LD SP,(7F11H)	(e) LD BC,(2301H)	

3. LD BC,2000H is a load immediate operation that loads the B register with 20 and the C register with 00 from the program. LD BC,(2000H), on the other hand, is a memory-to-register transfer that uses direct memory addressing; the content of data memory address 2000H goes to the C register, and the content of address 2001H goes to the B register.

4. (a) B=20H	(b) C=00H	(c) D=00H	(d) E=3AH
(e) H=3AH	(f) L=FFH	(g) (4000H)=FFH	(h) (4001H)=3AH
(i) (4002H)=00H	(j) (4003H)=20H	(k) IX=3AFFH	(l) IY=2000H

```
5. 7000 01 00 20      LD BC,2000H     ;2000H IMMEDIATE TO BC PAIR
   7003 21 FF 3A      LD HL,3AFFH     ;3AFFH IMMEDIATE TO HL PAIR
   7006 22 00 40      LD (4000H),HL   ;HL TO ADDRESS 4000H
   7009 ED 43 02 40   LD (4002H),BC   ;BC TO ADDRESS 4002H
   700D DD 2A 00 40   LD IX,(4000H)   ;CONTENT OF 4000H TO IX
   7011 FD 2A 02 40   LD IY,(4002H)   ;CONTENT OF 4002H TO IY
   7015 ED 5B 01 40   LD DE,(4001H)   ;CONTENT OF 4001H TO DE PAIR
```

6.
```
4C00  DD 22 00 10   LD  (1000H),IX  ;SAVE IX AT 1000H
4C04  FD 22 02 10   LD  (1002H),IY  ;SAVE IY AT 1002H
4C08  DD 2A 02 10   LD  IX,(1002H)  ;LOAD ORIGINAL IY TO IX
4C0C  FD 2A 00 10   LD  IY,(1000H)  ;LOAD ORIGINAL IX TO IY
```

Section 6-3

1. LXI H,4000H is a load immediate instruction—the value 4000H is loaded to the HL register pair from the program instruction itself. LHLD 4000H is a memory-to-register transfer instruction—the data resident at address 4000H are loaded to the L register, and the data at address 4001H are loaded to the H register.

2. (a) LDA 3C00H   (b) STA 421FH   (c) LHLD 3C00H
MOV B,H
MOV C,L

  (d) MOV H,B   (e) LHLD 3C00H   (f) XCHG
MOV L,C   XCHG   SHLD 4100H
SHLD 4100H

  (g) LHLD 3C00H   (h) SHLD 4100H   (i) LHLD 3C00H
SPHL

3. (a) A=2AH   (b) D=00H   (c) E=FFH
  (d) H=2AH   (e) L=20H   (f) (4000H)=FFH
  (g) (4001H)=00H   (h) (4002H)=20H   (i) 4003H=2AH

4.
```
7000  3E 20        MVI  A,20H    ;LOAD IMMEDIATE 20H TO A
7002  11 00 20     LXI  D,2000H  ;LOAD IMMEDIATE 2000H TO
                                 ;THE DE REGISTER PAIR
7005  21 FF 3A     LXI  H,3AFFH  ;LOAD IMMEDIATE 3AFFH TO
                                 ;THE HL REGISTER PAIR
7008  22 00 40     SHLD 4000H    ;HL PAIR TO 4000H
700B  EB           XCHG          ;ORIGINAL DE TO HL
700C  22 01 40     SHLD 4001H    ;ORIGINAL DE TO 4001H
700F  32 03 40     STA  4003H    ;A REGISTER TO 4003H
7012  2A 00 40     LHLD 4000H    ;CONTENT OF 4000H TO HL
7015  EB           XCHG          ;HL TO DE
7016  2A 02 40     LHLD 4002H    ;CONTENT OF 4002H TO HL
```

Section 6-4

1. (a) AD 00 4C   (b) 85 4C   (c) 86 2A   (d) 8C 00 33   (e) A4 2A

2.
```
7000  85 CD   STA  $CD   SAVE A AT $CD
7002  84 CE   STY  $CE   SAVE Y AT $CE
7004  A5 CE   LDA  $CE   LOAD A WITH ORIGINAL Y
7006  A4 CD   LDY  $CD   LOAD Y WITH ORIGINAL A
```

4. (a) A=$FF   (b) X=$FF   (c) Y=$4A
  (d) ($0025)=$4A   (e) ($0026)=$FF   (f) ($4FFF)=$3E

5.
```
2000  A9 4A      LDA#$4A    $4A IMMEDIATE TO A
2002  A2 FF      LDX#$FF    $FF IMMEDIATE TO X
2004  A0 3E      LDY#$3E    $3E IMMEDIATE TO Y
2006  85 25      STA  $25   $4A TO ADDRESS $25
2008  86 26      STX  $26   $FF TO ADDRESS $26
200A  8C FF 4F   STY  $4FFF $3E TO ADDRESS $4FFF
200D  A5 26      LDA  $26   $FF TO A FROM $26
200F  A4 25      LDY  $25   $4A TO Y FROM $25
```

Section 6-5

1. B6 4C 00 2. D7 4C 3. 9F 2A 4. FF 33 00 5. D6 2A

Section 7-1

1. (a) 00000011	(b) 0001000	(c) 11110000	(d) 00000000
2. (a) 00001111	(b) 11111111	(c) 11110001	(d) 11111110
3. (a) 00001100	(b) 11101111	(c) 00000001	(d) 11111110
4. (a) 00010010 Cs=0	(b) 00001111 Cs=1	(c) 11100001 Cs=1	(d) 11111110 Cs=0
5. (a) 00010010 Cs=0	(b) 00001111 Cs=1	(c) 11100001 Cs=1	(d) 11111110 Cs=0
6. (a) 00010011 Cs=0	(b) 00010000 Cs=1	(c) 11100010 Cs=1	(d) 11111111 Cs=0
7. (a) 00000100 Cs=0	(b) 00010101 Cs=0	(c) 00000001 Cs=0	(d) 11111110 Cs=1
8. (a) 00000011 Cs=0	(b) 00010100 Cs=0	(c) 00000000 Cs=0	(d) 11111101 Cs=1

Section 7-2

1. (a) E6 81 AND 81H	(b) E6 F0 AND F0H	(c) E6 18 AND 18H
(d) F6 81 OR 81H	(e) F6 F0 OR F0H	(f) F6 18 OR 18H
(g) 37 SCF	(h) E6 03 AND 03H	(i) EE 81 XOR 81H
(j) EE 0F XOR 0FH	(k) EE 18 XOR 18H	(l) 3F CCF
2. (a) A=0AH Cs=0 Z=0	(b) A=0AH Cs=0 Z=1	(c) A=0AH Cs=1 Z=0
(d) A=0FH Cs=0 Z=0	(e) A=14H Cs=0 Z=0	(f) A=19H Cs=0 Z=0
(g) A=05H Cs=0 Z=0	(h) A=00H Cs=0 Z=1	(i) A=FBH Cs=1 Z=0

3. A=86H, Cs=0, Z=0

```
4. 4C00  3E 27  LD   A,27H   ;27H IMMEDIATE TO A
   4C02  C6 11  ADD  A,11H   ;38H IN A
   4C04  EE FF  XOR  FFH     ;C7H IN A
   4C06  D6 11  SUB  11H     ;A6H IN A
   4C08  E6 0F  AND  0FH     ;06H IN A
   4C0A  F6 80  OR   80H     ;86H IN A

5. 1000  3E 64  LD   A,100D  ;100 TO A
   1002  D6 14  SUB  20D     ;SUBTRACT 20
   1004  C6 05  ADD  A,05    ;ADD 5
   1006  C6 32  ADD  A,50D   ;ADD 50
```

Section 7-4

1. (a) 29 81   AND #$81   (b) 29 F0   AND #$F0
   (c) 29 18   AND #$18   (d) 29 01   AND #$01
   (e) 09 18   ORA #$18   (f) 18   CLC
   (g) 38   SEC   (h) 49 81   EOR #$81

2. (a) $A=\$0A$ (b) $A=\$0A$ (c) $A=\$0A$
   $Cs=1$ $Cs=1$ $Cs=0$
   $Z=0$ $Z=0$ $Z=0$
   (d) $A=\$0F$ (e) $A=\$14$ (f) $A=\$19$
   $Cs=0$ $Cs=0$ $Cs=0$
   $Z=0$ $Z=0$ $Z=0$
   (g) $A=\$05$ (h) $A=\$00$ (i) $A=\$FB$
   $Cs=1$ $Cs=1$ $Cs=0$
   $Z=0$ $Z=1$ $Z=0$

3. A $86, $Cs=1$, $Z=0$

4.
```
1C00  A9 27    LDA  #$27    $27 IMMEDIATE TO A
1C02  18       CLC          CLEAR CS TO 0
1C03  69 11    ADC  #$11    ADD $11
1C05  49 FF    EOR  #$FF    COMPLEMENT THE REGISTER
1C07  38       SEC          SET CS TO 1
1C08  E9 11    SBC  #$11    SUBTRACT $11
1C0A  29 0F    AND  #$0F    AND WITH $0F
1C0C  09 80    ORA  #$80    OR WITH $80
```

Section 7-5

1. (a) 84 81   ANDA #$81   (b) C4 F0   ANDB #$F0
   (c) 84 18   ANDA #$18   (d) 0C   CLC
   (e) 8A 81   ORAA #$81   (f) CA F0   ORAB #$F0
   (g) 0D   SEC   (h) 88 03   EORA #$03
   (i) C8 0F   EORB #$0F

2. (a) $A=\$0A$ (b) $A=\$0A$ (c) $A=\$0A$
   $Z=0$ $Z=1$ $Z=0$
   $Cs=0$ $Cs=0$ $Cs=1$
   (d) $A=\$0F$ (e) $A=\$14$ (f) $A=\$19$
   $Z=0$ $Z=0$ $Z=0$
   $Cs=0$ $Cs=0$ $Cs=0$
   (g) $A=\$05$ (h) $A=\$00$ (i) $A=\$FB$
   $Z=0$ $Z=1$ $Z=0$
   $Cs=0$ $Cs=0$ $Cs=1$

3. $B=\$83$, $Z=0$, $Cs=0$

4.
```
1C00  C6 27    LDAB  #$27    $27 IMMEDIATE TO B
1C02  CB 11    ADDB  #$11    AND IMMEDIATE WITH $11
1C04  C8 FF    EORB  #$FF    COMPLEMENT THE B ACCUMULATOR
1C06  C0 11    SUBB  #$11    SUBTRACT IMMEDIATE 11 FROM B
1C08  C4 0F    ANDB  #$0F    ISOLATE 4 LOWER-ORDER BITS OF B
1C0A  CA 80    ORAB  #$80    SETS BITS 4 AND 7 TO 1
```

Section 8-2

2. (a) A0   (b) E6 1A   (c) B1   (d) F6 1A
   (e) AD   (f) EE 1A   (g) B9   (h) FE 1A

3. (a) A=01H   (b) A=05H   (c) A=04H
       B=01H   B=01H   B=01H
       Z=0   Z=0   Z=0
       Cs=0   Cs=0   Cs=0
   (d) A=05H   (e) A=06H   (f) A=04H
       B=01H   B=01H   B=01H
       Z=0   Z=0   Z=0
       Cs=0   Cs=0   Cs=0

Section 8-3

1. (a) A=00H   (b) A=2BH   (c) A=2BH
       B=01H   B=01H   B=01H
       Z=1   Z=0   Z=0
       Cs=0   Cs=0   Cs=0
   (d) A=2AH   (e) A=2AH   (f) A=00H
       Z=0   Z=0   Z=1
       Cs=0   Cs=0   Cs=0
   (g) A=2AH   (h) A=2AH   (i) A=2AH
       B=01H   B=2AH   B=2CH
       Z=0   Z=1   Z=0
       Cs=0   Cs=0   Cs=1
   (j) A=2AH   (k) A=2BH   (l) A=2BH
       Z=1   B=01H   B=01H
       Cs=0   Z=0   Z=0
                 Cs=0   Cs=0
   (m) A=2CH   (n) A=29H   (o) A=00H
       B=01H   B=01H   B=2AH
       Z=0   Z=0   Z=1
       Cs=0   Cs=0   Cs=0
   (p) A=FEH   (q) A=28H   (r) A=FFH
       B=2CH   B=01H   B=2AH
       Z=0   Z=0   Z=0
       Cs=1   Cs=0   Cs=1
   (s) A=FDH   (t) A=2BH   (u) A=29H
       B=2CH   Z=0   Z=0
       Z=0   Cs=0   Cs=0
       Cs=1

Section 8-4

1. (a) A=$2A   (b) A=$2A   (c) A=$2A
       Z=0   Z=1   Z=0
       Cs=1   Cs=1   Cs=0

(d) A=$2A
    Z=1
    Cs=1
(e) A=$2B
    Z=0
    Cs=0
(f) A=$2B
    Z=0
    Cs=0
(g) A=$2C
    Z=0
    Cs=0
(h) A=$28
    Z=0
    Cs=1
(i) A=$29
    Z=0
    Cs=1

3. None of the instructions affect the status of the Cs flag bit. It will thus retain whatever status it held prior to executing those instructions—and that status cannot be determined from the information supplied in the exercise.

Section 8-5

1. The Cs bit responds to logic instructions as it does for the 6502—the Cs bit is unaffected.

2. The Cs bit responds to arithmetic instructions as it does for the Z-80 and 8080A/8085.

3. The INC and DEC instructions do not affect any internal register. They affect only the byte contained in the location addressed by the instruction.

Section 9-2

1. (a) Load to A the byte from memory addressed by the HL pair.
   (b) Load the byte in register B to an address indicated by the BC register pair.
   (c) Load immediate the *data* byte to the address indicated by the HL register pair.
   (d) Logically AND the content of the A register with a byte from memory addressed by the HL register pair.
   (g) Decrement the byte located at an address indicated by the HL register pair.
   (h) Load the accumulator with the byte found at an address determined by the sum of the content of the IY register and an index term, *indx*.
   (i) Load the content of the B register to an address determined by summing the content of the IX register with an index term.
   (j) Load *data* immediate to an address determined by summing the content of the IX register an the index term.

2. IX and IY registers

3. 00H through FFH; −128 through +127

4. (a) 3C2CH (b) 3C00H (c) 3C81H (d) 3C02H (e) 3B82H (f) 3C01H

5. (a) 36 3E (b) DD 36 15 3E (c) FD 36 15 3E

Section 9-3

1. IX register

2. $00 through $FF; 0 through 255

3. (a) $3C2C (b) $3D00 (c) $3C81 (d) $3C02 (e) $3C82 (f) $3D01

4. (a) STS $02,X (b) AF 02 (c) $02 in $3402
                                                              $35 in $3403

Section 9-4

1. Effective address is $45; A contains $4F.
2. Effective address is $4F05; A contains $0D.
3. Effective address is $2A02; A contains $0A.
4. Effective address is $6106; A contains $0E.
5. Effective address is $4F05; A contains $0D.

Section 10-1

2. (a) Z is set to logic 1 when any arithmetic or logic operation yields a result of zero.
   Z is cleared to 0 when any arithmetic or logic operation yields a nonzero result.
   (b) Cs is set to logic 1 when any arithmetic operation causes a wraparound condition to occur in the accumulator.
   Cs is cleared to logic 0 by any logic operation and by any arithmetic operation that does not cause a wraparound to occur.
   Cs is also set to logic 1 by the execution of the STC instruction, and it is complemented by the CMC instruction.
   (c) S is set to 1 by any arithmetic or logic operation that yields a 1 in the most-significant bit position of the A register.
   S is cleared to 0 by any arithmetic or logic operation that yields a 0 in the most-significant bit position of the A register.
   (d) P is set to 1 by any arithmetic or logic operation that produces a number having even parity.
   P is cleared to 0 by any arithmetic or logic operation that yields a number having odd parity.
3. (a) Flag conditions are not relevant to an unconditional jump instruction.
   (b) Cs=0   (c) Z=1   (d) S=0   (e) P=1   (f) S=1
4. The instruction loops to itself.

Section 10-2

2. An overflow occurs only for item B. A wraparound occurs for items C, E, and F.
4. (a) 2002H   (b) 2010H   (c) 1FFFH   (d) 1FEDH
5. (a) 05H   (b) 25H   (c) FCH   (d) E7H
6. JR FEH calls for doing a relative absolute jump by − 2 program addresses. The effect is that the instruction loops to itself.

Section 10-3

2.
```
3100 A2 00      LDX  #$00    ZERO THE COUNTER
3102 E0 3B      CPX  #$3B    IS IT 59 DECIMAL?
3104 F0 FA      BEQ  $FA     IF SO, START OVER
3106 E8         INX          ELSE INCREMENT COUNT
3107 4C 02 31   JMP  $3102   AND COMPARE AGAIN
```

Section 10-4

2. $452A

3. (a) $402A   (b) $3FFE   (c) $3F80   (d) $3F7F

4. 6800 version—7E 3A 2E;   6502 version—4C 2E 3A

5.
```
4F        CLRA        ZERO THE COUNT
81 3B     CMPA #$3B   IS IT 59 DECIMAL?
27 FB     BEQ $FB     IF SO, START OVER
4C        INCA        ELSE INCREMENT COUNT
20 F9     BRA $F9     AND COMPARE AGAIN
```

Section 11-1

1. (a) 13H, 29H   (b) 10H, 29H   (c) 1H, 9H
   (d) 0H, 10H   (e) F0H, FDH   (f) Not possible

Section 12-1

1. The byte from register B goes to address 2FFFH; the byte from register C goes to ad-
   address 2FFFEH.

```
POP BC
POP IX
POP AF
```

Section 12-2

2.
```
2000 31 00 40   LXI SP,4000H   ;INITIALIZE STACK AT 4000H
2003 C5         PUSH B         ;BC PAIR TO STACK
2004 D5         PUSH D         ;DE PAIR TO STACK
2005 C1         POP B          ;ORIGINAL DE TO BC FROM STACK
2006 D1         POP D          ;ORIGINAL BC TO DE FROM STACK
```

Section 12-3

1. Z-80—0000H through FFFH; 8080A/8085—0000H through FFFFH; 6502—$0100 through $01FF

2.
```
7000 A2 4F      LDX #$4F    LOAD $4F TO X
7002 9A         TXS         INITIALIZE STACK AT $4F
7003 08         PHP         F REGISTER TO TOP OF STACK
7004 68         PLA         ORIGINAL F TO A FROM STACK
7005 8D 00 20   STA $2000   OUTPUT ORIGINAL F TO $2000
```

Section 12-4

1. The 6502 and 6800 transfer data between registers and the stack. The Z-80 and
   the stack. The Z-80 and 8080A/8085 transfer 16-bit data.

2.
```
3C00 8E 40 00   LDS #$4000   SET STACK AT ADDRESS $4000
3C03 36         PSHA         LOAD A TO TOP OF STACK
3C04 37         PSHB         LOAD B TO TOP OF STACK
3C05 32         PULA         LOAD A WITH ORIGINAL B FROM STACK
3C06 33         PULB         LOAD B WITH ORIGINAL A FROM STACK
```

Section 13-2

```
1. 7000  31  00  F0   MAIN    LXI  SP,F000H   ;INITIALIZE THE STACK
   7003  21  00  40   START   LXI  H,4000H    ;POINT TO OUTPUT 4000H
   7006  CD  1E  70           CALL OPUT       ;CALL OUTPUT ROUTINE
   7009  21  20  40           LXI  H,4020H    ;POINT TO OUTPUT 4020H
   700C  CD  1E  70           CALL OPUT       ;CALL OUTPUT ROUTINE
   700F  21  40  40           LXI  H,4040H    ;POINT TO OUTPUT 4040H
   7012  CD  1E  70           CALL OPUT       ;CALL OUTPUT ROUTINE
   7015  21  80  40           LXI  H,4080H    ;POINT TO OUTPUT 4080H
   7018  CD  1E  70           CALL OPUT       ;CALL OUTPUT ROUTINE
   701B  C3  03  70           JMP  START      ;AND START ALL OVER
                      ;BEGINNING OF COUNT WITH DELAY SUBROUTINE
   701E  AF           OPUT    XRA  A          ;ZERO THE ACCUMULATOR
   701F  77           SEND    MOV  M,A        ;OUTPUT THE COUNT
   7020  3C                   INR  A          ;INCREMENT THE COUNT
   7021  FE  0A               CPI  0AH        ;IS IT 10?
   7023  C8                   RZ              ;IF SO, RETURN TO MAINLINE
   7024  CD  2A  70           CALL TDLY       ;ELSE CALL TIME DELAY ROUTINE
   7027  C3  1F  20           JMP  SEND       ;AND SEND AGAIN
                      ;BEGINNING OF TIME DELAY ROUTINE
   702A  01  FF  FF   TDLY    LXI  B,0FFFFH   ;INITIALIZE DELAY AT FFFFH
   702D  79           CPR     MOV  A,C        ;LSB OF TIME TO A
   702E  B0                   ORA  B          ;OR WITH MSB OF TIME
   702F  C8                   RZ              ;IF ZERO, RETURN
   7030  0B                   DCX  B          ;ELSE DECREMENT TIME
   7031  C3  2D  70           JMP  CPR        ;AND CHECK AGAIN
```

Section 13-3

```
2. 7000  A2  F0               LDX  #$FF
   7002  9A                   TXS             SET THE STACK POINTER
   7003  A0  00       START   LDY  #$00       POINTER INDEX TO $00
   7005  20  20  70           JSR  DOIT       DO COUNTING ROUTINE
   7008  A0  20               LDY  #$20       POINTER INDEX TO $20
   700A  20  20  70           JSR  DOIT       DO COUNTING ROUTINE
   700D  A0  40               LDY  #$40       POINTER INDEX TO $40
   700F  20  20  70           JSR  DOIT       DO COUNTING ROUTINE
   7012  A0  80               LDY  #$80       POINTER INDEX TO $80
   7014  20  20  70           JSR  DOIT       DO COUNTING ROUTINE
   7017  4C  03  70           JMP  START      AND START ALL OVER

   7020  A2  00       DOIT    LDX  #$00       ZERO THE X REGISTER
   7022  96  00  40   SEND    STX  $4000,Y    OUTPUT THE COUNT
   7025  E8                   INX             INCREMENT THE COUNT
   7026  E0  0A               CPX  #$0A       IS IT 10?
   7028  D0  F8               BNE  SEND       IF NOT, SEND AGAIN
   702A  60                   RTS             ELSE RETURN TO MAINLINE
```

Section 14-1

3. (a) 01H (b) 02H (c) 04H (d) 08H (e) 10H (f) 20H (g) 40H
   (h) 80H

4. (a) 01H (b) 06H (c) 70H (d) 18H (e) 80H (f) C0H (g) 87H

5. (a) FDH (b) F5H (c) 8FH (d) 7EH (e) F0H

START
FETCH INPUT BYTE
SAVE IT
TEST BIT 3
B3 = 1
N
Y
TEST BIT 7
B7 = 1
Y
N
SET B0, B1
RESET B0, B1
RESET B3, B4
SET B5, B6
OUTPUT THE NEW BYTE

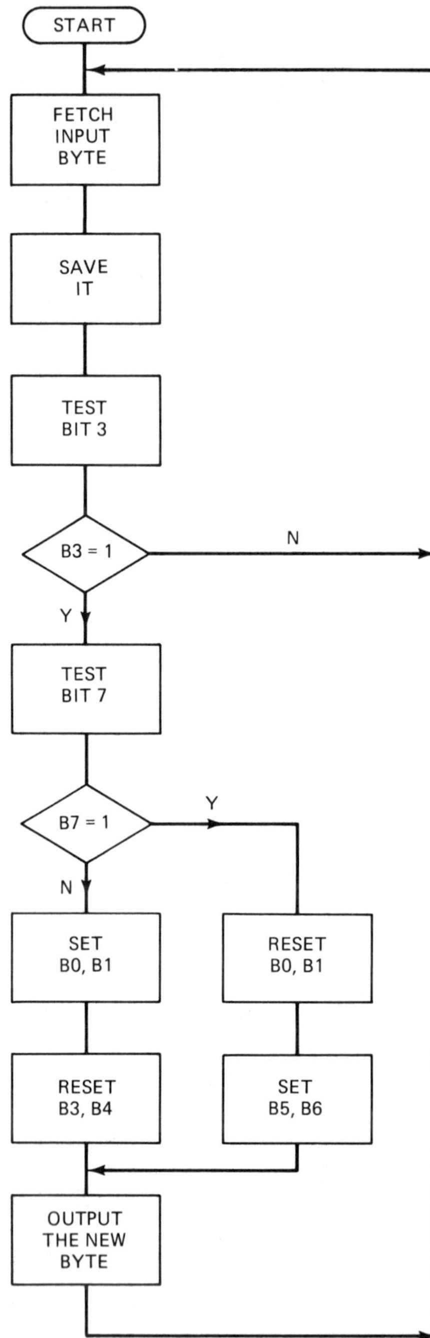

Figure A14-1

6. 7000 3A 00 70   FETCH   LDA F000H   ;FETCH THE INPUT BYTE
   7003 47   MOV B,A   ;SAVE IT IN B
   7004 E6 08   ANI 08H   ;TEST B3
   7006 CA 00 70   JZ   FETCH   ;IF RESET, FETCH AGAIN
   7009 78   MOV A,B   ;GET ORIGINAL BYTE FROM B
   700A E6 80   ANI 80H   ;TEST B7
   700C CA 17 70   JZ   STP6   ;IF RESET, DO STEP 6
   700F 78   MOV A,B   ;GET ORIGINAL BYTE FROM B
   7010 E6 FC   ANI 0FCH   ;RESET B0 AND B1
   7012 F6 60   ORI 06H   ;SET B5 AND B6
   7014 C3 1C 70   JMP OPUT   ;AND JUMP TO OUTPUT TASK
   7017 78   STP6   MOV A,B   ;GET ORIGINAL BYTE FROM B
   7018 F6 03   ORI 03H   ;SET B0 AND B1
   701A E6 E7   ANI 0E7H   ;RESET B3 AND B4
   701C 32 01 F0 OPUT   STA F001H   ;OUTPUT THE ALTERED BYTE
   701F C3 00 70   JMP FETCH   ;AND JUMP TO FETCH AGAIN

Section 14-2

1. 1000 A9 08   START   LDA #$08   SETUP B3 TEST
   1002 24 F0   TEST   BIT $F0   TEST B3 AT ADDRESS $F0
   1004 D0 FC   BNE TEST   IF B3 1, TEST AGAIN
   1006 A9 80   LDA #$80   SETUP B7 TEST
   1008 24 F0   BIT $F0   TEST B7 AT ADDRESS $F0
   100A F0 08   BEQ F1OUT   IF B7 0, JUMP TO F1 OUTPUT

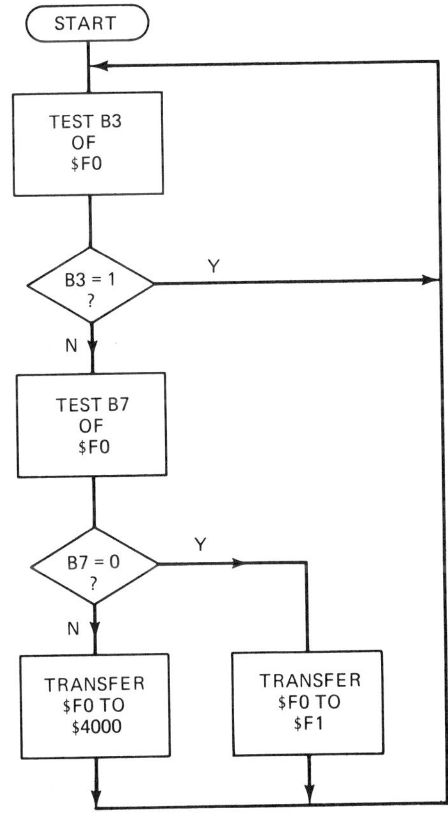

Figure A14-2

```
100C  A5 FO            LDA $FO       ELSE FETCH BYTE FROM $FO
100E  8D 00 40         STA $4000     AND LOAD TO ADDRESS $4000
1011  4C 00 10         JMP START     JUMP TO START
1014  A5 FO     F1OUT  LDA $FO       FETCH BYTE FROM $FO
1016  85 F1            STA $F1       LOAD TO ADDRESS $F1
1018  4C 00 10         JMP START     AND START ALL OVER
```

2. (a) $F0,   (c) $11   and   (d) $F7

3. To address $4000: (a) $80
   To address $F1:   (b) $71, (c) $47, (d) $77, and (e) $11

Section 14-3

1. (a) B2   (b) B7   (c) B1   (d) B4

2.
```
7000  96 FO     START  LDAA $FO      DATA BYTE TO ACCUMULATOR A
7002  85 01            BITA #$01     TEST B0
7004  27 FA            BEQ START     IF ZERO, START AGAIN
7006  85 02            BITA #$02     TEST B1
7008  26 05            BNE STEPF     IF SET, JUMP TO STEP F
700A  84 BF            ANDA #$BF     ELSE RESET B6
700C  20 04            BRA OPUT      AND JUMP TO OUTPUT PHASE
700E  8A 40     STEPF  ORAA #$40     SET B6
7010  84 DF            ANDA #$DF     RESET B5
7012  8A 80     OPUT   ORAA #$80     SET B7
7014  97 10            STAA $10      OUTPUT THE RESULT
7016  20 E8            BRA START     AND BEGIN ALL OVER
```

Section 14-4

1. (a) 46H   (b) 56H   (c) 46H   (d) 46H   (e) 46H   (f) 46H

2. (a) 1   (b) 1   (c) 0   (d) 1   (e) 1

3.
```
7000  21 00 FO  START  LD HL,F000H   ;SET PORT POINTER
7003  CB 5E     TEST   BIT 3,(HL)    ;TEST B3
7005  28 FC            JR Z,TEST     ;IF RESET, TEST AGAIN
7007  CB 7E            BIT 7,(HL)    ;ELSE TEST B7
7009  28 0A            JR Z,STEPE    ;IF RESET, JUMP TO STEP E
700B  CB 86            RES 0,(HL)    ;RESET B0
700D  CB 8E            RES 1,(HL)    ;RESET B1
700F  CB EE            SET 5,(HL)    ;SET B5
7011  CB F6            SET 6,(HL)    ;SET B6
7013  18 08            JR OPUT       ;AND JUMP TO OUTPUT PHASE
7015  CB C6     STEPE  SET 0,(HL)    ;SET B0
7017  CB CE            SET 1,(HL)    ;SET B1
7019  CB 9E            RES 3,(HL)    ;RESET B3
701B  CB A6            RES 4,(HL)    ;RESET B4
701D  7E        OPUT   LD A,(HL)     ;FETCH THE INPUT BYTE
701E  32 01 FO         LD (F001H),A  ;OUTPUT IT TO F001H
7021  18 DD            JR TEST       ;AND START TEST AGAIN
```

Section 17-1

1. Ascending order: (b), (e), (g), (h); descending order: (a), (c), (d), (f)
2. (b), (d), (f), (g)
3. Source block address pointer
4. IND and OUTD: port pointer; LDD and LDDR: LSB of byte counter

Section 18-1

1. a, b, and d

2. (a) 9	(b) 5	(c) Invalid	(d) 0
3. (a) 98	(b) 78	(c) Invalid	(d) 66
4. (a) 78H	(b) 12H	(c) 00H	(d) 05H

Section 18-2

2. (b) Lower nybble is larger than 9.
   (c) Carry of 1 between B3 and B4.
   (e) Lower nybble is larger than 9, and a carry of 1 from the B3 to B4 positions.

Index